5th November 2023
the 134th anniversary
of the shooting of
Colonel Falkner
on the Square,
Ripley, Miss.

To Collene,
with all best wishes!

Jack Elliott

D1523460

TO THE RAMPARTS OF INFINITY

Figure 0.1 Colonel W. C. Falkner, portrait, made at Mora Studios, 707 Broadway, New York. Date unknown. This image possibly served as the model for the portrait engraving of Falkner in his 1884 *Rapid Ramblings in Europe* (fig. 12.6). An original copy is in the Center for Faulkner Studies at Southeast Missouri State University. There is only one other known photograph of Falkner (fig. 14.1).

To the
RAMPARTS
of INFINITY

❖━━◆━━━━◆━━❖

COLONEL W. C. FALKNER
and the
RIPLEY RAILROAD

JACK D. ELLIOTT JR.

University Press of Mississippi / Jackson

The University Press of Mississippi is the scholarly publishing agency of
the Mississippi Institutions of Higher Learning: Alcorn State University,
Delta State University, Jackson State University, Mississippi State University,
Mississippi University for Women, Mississippi Valley State University,
University of Mississippi, and University of Southern Mississippi.

www.upress.state.ms.us

The University Press of Mississippi is a member
of the Association of University Presses.

Library of Congress Cataloging-in-Publication Data available
Library of Congress Control Number 2022022512
Hardback: 978-1-4968-4187-2
Epub Single: 978-1-4968-4188-9
Epub Institutional: 978-1-4968-4189-6
PDF Single: 978-1-4968-4190-2
PDF Institutional: 978-1-4968-4191-9

British Library Cataloging-in-Publication Data available

*To Tommy Covington, who for decades worked at preserving the
records of his beloved Ripley and Tippah County, in the hope
that this work might shed some light on his community.*

*To Melinda Marsalis, the organizer of Ripley's annual
Faulkner Heritage Festival, in the hope that this work will
in a small way be seen as a vindication of her efforts.*

*To my wife, Kathy, who throughout the research and
writing endured and even occasionally prevailed.*

"People at Ripley talk of him as if he were still alive, up in the hills some place, and might come in at any time. It's a strange thing; there are lots of people who knew him well, and yet no two of them remember him alike or describe him the same way. . . . There's nothing left in the old place, the house is gone . . . , nothing left of his work but a statue. But he rode through the country like a living force."
—WILLIAM FAULKNER, 1938

Contents

Acknowledgments

Isaac Newton famously stated that he had accomplished what he had because he had stood on the shoulders of giants. This reflects the truism that everything that we think, say, write, and otherwise create doesn't come full blown from our heads but is largely a reworking of the productions of our predecessors. So, it has been with me.

Tommy Covington, who for decades served as the director of the Ripley Public Library and worked to build up a collection of material on Colonel Falkner. In particular, his collection of historical photographs has been of the utmost value for my research and for the resulting book. Tommy was born in the heart of rural Tippah County, birthed by Dr. Charlie Murry, the great-uncle of William Faulkner, while, as legend has it, a panther screamed outside the farmhouse door.

Melinda Marsalis, who for years served as the organizer and promoter of Ripley's Faulkner Heritage Festival and who was always ready to provide assistance and moral support. My attendance at the annual festivals triggered the inspiration to write this book, which might be seen as a byproduct of the event. Also, Melinda's husband, Chris Marsalis—who has described himself as "the man who's married to the mayor's wife"—was always ready to assist. He also spearheaded the creation of an online tour guide to Colonel Falkner's Ripley.

Melissa McCoy-Bell, a native of Walnut, Mississippi, located on Falkner's railroad and a genealogist and local historian, who first invited me to attend the Faulkner Heritage Festival in 2010. She later introduced me to a section of the Library of Congress's website, Chronicling America, which provided access to a world of old newspapers.

Elizabeth Reid Behm, director of Ripley's Main Street office and a leading promoter of all things W. C. Falkner. Elizabeth's daughter is named Holland in honor of Falkner's first wife, while in 2005 her grandmother Frances Reid placed a marker for Holland Falkner in Ripley Cemetery.

The Tippah County Historical and Genealogical Society, which financed the restoration of old photos.

Sidney W. Bondurant, MD, a friend who has for decades served as my go-to Civil War expert and who pitched in and wrote the first draft of the section on the Battle of First Manassas.

Staff at the Ripley Public Library.

I spent an enormous amount of time in the Tippah County Chancery Clerk's Office and came to know the staff as friends. Even today on visits to Ripley, I'll drop by to say hello.

Rodney McBryde, former chancery clerk.

Mike Long, current chancery clerk.

Sara Baker.

Kim Estes.

There were also other chancery clerk's offices where I worked: Lafayette County in Oxford, Pontotoc County in Pontotoc, and Union County in New Albany.

Staff who were always generous with their time and charity at the Bryan Public Library, West Point, Mississippi, which I often resorted to for research on ancestry.com: Tanna Taylor, Priscilla Ivy, Valerie Hargrove, Jayme Evans, and Virginia Ellis.

Staff at the *Southern Sentinel*, especially Hank Wiesner, former editor, who graciously allowed me to spend weeks perusing back issues.

Tippah County Archives, Felecia Caples.

Staff in the Tennessee Room of the Jackson–Madison County Library, Jackson, Tennessee, with special thanks to Evelyn Keele, who went out of her way to help me track down and obtain a copy of the one known surviving issue of the newspaper *Uncle Sam* from the Tennessee State Library and Archives in Nashville.

Staff at the East Texas Research Center, Stephen F. Austin University, Nacogdoches, Texas.

Jennifer Ford, head, and her staff in Special Collections, J. D. Williams Library, University of Mississippi.

Tom Murry, attorney and grandson of Dr. Charlie Murry, with whom I went in search of the Murry homestead and cemetery in McNairy County, Tennessee.

My high school English teachers Lucille Deas Armstrong and Nita King Keys Wyman, for encouraging my earliest interest in Falkner, Faulkner, and Yoknapatawpha.

Seth Berner, Seth Berner Books, Portland, Maine, rare bookdealer specializing in William Faulkner.

Lovejoy Boteler for suggestions regarding publication.

The late Edmond A. Boudreaux Jr., friend and Gulf Coast historian extraordinaire.

Richard Cawthon, Shreveport, Louisiana.

John Cofield, Oxford, of the Cofield family of photographers.

Harold Cross, native of Falkner, Mississippi.

Meg Faulkner DuChaine, Oxford, Mississippi.

Bert and Sharon Falkner, West Point, Mississippi.

J. M. "Rusty" Faulkner Jr., Jackson, Mississippi.

Marcus Gray, St. Andrews, Scotland.

Robert W. Hamblin, former director of the Center for Faulkner Studies at Southeast Missouri State University.

Gwyn Price Lawson, McKinney, Texas.

Bobby Mays, Ripley, Mississippi.

Bob McGee, Pontotoc, Mississippi.

Genette Carpenter McKinney, Chalybeate, Mississippi, who took me to and identified the grave or graves of the Adcock family.

Jill Smith, director, Union County Heritage Museum, New Albany, Mississippi.

Tim Smith, University of Tennessee at Martin.

Carl Rollyson, Baruch College, City University of New York.

Christopher Rieger, current director of the Center for Faulkner Studies at Southeast Missouri State University.

Phillip Knecht, attorney and local historian, Holly Springs, Mississippi.

Rufus A. Ward of West Point and Columbus, recovering lawyer (his term, not mine) and local historian.

Stephen Slimp, University of West Alabama.

Joseph Alley of the Helena Museum, Helena, Arkansas.

My friends—owners, employees, and patrons—at Pheba's Diner, Pheba, Mississippi, where I took my lunches and relaxed in rural splendor.

The University Press of Mississippi, notably Mary Heath and Norman Ware.

My family, who tolerated me.

Finally, for all of those who in some way assisted me but whose names have slipped my mind, I thank them with all due apologies for my failure of memory.

TO THE RAMPARTS OF INFINITY

Introduction

❖━◦━━◦━◦❖

*As usual, old man Falls had brought John Sartoris into the room
with him, . . . fetching, like an odor, like the clean dusty smell of his
faded overalls, the spirit of the dead man into that room where the
dead man's son sat and where the two of them, pauper and banker,
would sit for a half an hour in the company of him who had passed
beyond death and then returned.*[1]

And with an image of the past retrieved through memory and story, so begins
Sartoris, the first novel in William Faulkner's Yoknapatawpha mythos, a collection of stories set in fictional Yoknapatawpha County, Mississippi, and its
county seat, Jefferson. The memory of Colonel John Sartoris looms large over
the landscape of Yoknapatawpha County, where he vicariously stands as a
statue atop a monumental pedestal in the Jefferson cemetery and from there
surveys all that surrounds. A similar monument stands beside the grave of
Sartoris's prototype and the great-grandfather of William Faulkner, Colonel
William C. Falkner, in the cemetery in Ripley, Mississippi. The likeness
between the two—men and monuments—is not coincidental but reflects a
deep connection by which the colonel who once walked the streets of Ripley
was transformed into a mythical figure.

In his own time, Colonel Falkner was a celebrity due in part to his military service to the Confederate States of America. Consequently, most knew
him as Colonel W. C. Falkner,[2] or simply Colonel Falkner, a title first used
in 1858, while his intimates knew him as Bill.[3] Years after his death, his son,
J. W. T. Falkner, who had no military background, took on the honorific title
of "Colonel." The family began to refer to the father as the Old Colonel to
distinguish him from his son, who then became the Young Colonel. Falkner's
celebrity was also seen as derived from his being a self-made man, a Horatio
Alger–like figure who had pulled himself up from poverty to affluence and

accomplishments, including several endeavors in the literary field. However, by the end of his life he was primarily renowned for building a railroad from Middleton, Tennessee, to Pontotoc, Mississippi, a road that brought the advantages of the rail system to rural areas along with the vision of a route that would span the continent from Chicago to the Gulf of Mexico. Days after he was fatally shot on Ripley Square in 1889 by a former business associate, R. J. Thurmond, the masonic lodge published a tribute proclaiming that the railroad was "the crowning glory of his life" and that the people were "largely indebted [to him] for the railroad facilities they now enjoy."[4]

Decades later, Falkner returned to the public eye—clandestinely at first— as an inspiration for the Yoknapatawpha stories serving as the prototype for Colonel John Sartoris, who was also a prominent railroad developer, and later as a historical figure in his own right. The younger Faulkner summarized the achievements and influence of his ancestor, describing him succinctly— although not with total accuracy:

> My great-grandfather, whose name I bear, was a considerable figure in his time
> and provincial milieu. He was a prototype of John Sartoris: raised, organized, paid
> the expenses of and commanded the 2nd Mississippi Infantry, 1861–2, etc. Was
> part of Stonewall Jackson's left at 1st Manassas.... He built the first railroad in our
> county, wrote a few books, made [the] grand European tour of his time, died in a
> duel and the county raised a marble effigy which stands in Tippah County.[5]

I first became aware of Colonel Falkner in 1973 when I simultaneously developed an interest in the local history of my home area in northeastern Mississippi and in the Yoknapatawpha stories of William Faulkner. The two interests had more similarity than one might suspect, suggesting as they did that the seeming inertness of place and historical fact actually represented a surface beneath which lay hidden depths.

The history of my home county, where various branches of my family have resided since the 1830s, bears marked similarities to Yoknapatawpha County, with almost identical historical and geographic frameworks. The two areas were both part of the Chickasaw Cession lands of northern Mississippi that were ceded to the United States by the 1832 Pontotoc Treaty, following which my family as well as the Falkner family settled there. Besides their similar settings, the stories had characters, events, and places with which I was familiar.

Local history almost invariably has a personal dimension—a personal connection to place—and builds on the intuition that something happened in particular places. For me, this began during my childhood with the finding of artifacts in our garden at home—ceramic shards, cut nails, and broken glass—which led to asking my father about their origin. In reply, he sketched out a simple history: my family had been there for over a century; there was once a log house where my home was located, and this was in the midst of what had been a town named Palo Alto. By the twentieth century the town had become extinct, and by my childhood it was only a memory. Having heard this rudimentary story, I saw the familiar landscape around my home in a different light.

Conscious experience is structured by two complementary modes: the temporal and the spatial, the verbal and the visual, the logical and the holistic. Narrative modes of expression such as this book by their very nature are oriented to the former member of this pair. This does not abrogate the importance of the spatial/visual, which is an ever-present component of experience that lurks behind that narrative. Lived experience always has a spatial dimension and context, much of which is the landscape. In narrative, the landscape is only implicit and often unmentioned. However, in local history, the landscape element often comes into focus by serving as a catalyst for narrative through evoking wonder and a sense of mystery that demand explanations, however inadequate they might be. Although books by their very nature are oriented to the verbal, spatial images can be evoked either verbally or through the use of pictorial images as I have attempted to do.

The histories of places are recalled through a complex process of memory, story, and symbols, with the web of associations between people, events, and places forming a microcosm that frames a person's existence in time and space. In doing so it focuses on the history of small localities—communities, villages, towns, urban neighborhoods, and counties—and the people who resided therein, most of whom would not be considered of notable significance. It incorporates elements of the landscape—homes, stores, farms, post offices, roads, farms, and streams, in other words the everyday material fabric of life—and the range of people who lived there—farmers, merchants, professionals, sharecroppers, and mill workers—whose family trees with their complex linkages and associations tied them to the larger process of history and to the rise and fall of communities. Composed of texts, photos, and maps, the published local history constitutes a symbolism of words and images that quietly hints that there is more to places—indeed to all reality—than meets the eye.

The local historian, like all people, doesn't observe from a detached Cartesian perspective seeing reality laid out in clarity and ready to be reduced to narrative with himself or herself as the teller of the tale. Instead, he or she is usually if unconsciously an actor in the tale connected by the diaphanous strands of memory and family tree to the people and places. The local historian is in the midst of the *Lebenswelt*, or "lifeworld," the subjectively experienced world that is not only the everyday world of objects but also the experience of the same in which the objects are filtered through the conscious mind with its memories and associations. The lifeworld recalls us to an awareness of the way that we experience world in all of its complexity, to become aware of often subliminal aspects of our experience. We confront, for example, an old house or the site of an abandoned settlement and immediately perceive the physical parameters, size, and layout and other details. Although many local historians may not realize it, the investigation of local history affords the insight that the familiar and commonplace are but a surface that partially conceals and reveals something more, where the interplay of visual image, memory, and story are like moving shadows on the wall of a cave indicating a source of light beyond.

Our memories of previous visits along with the knowledge that people once lived there and that events transpired there raise deeper questions. By way of illustration, Niels Bohr, a founder of quantum physics, visited Kronborg Castle in Denmark, once the home of the historical Prince Hamlet, and reflected:

> Isn't it strange how this castle changes as soon as one imagines that Hamlet lived here? As scientists, we believe that a castle consists only of stones and admire the way the architect puts them together. The stone, the green roof with its patina, the wood carvings in the church, constitute the whole castle. None of this should be changed by the fact that Hamlet lived here, and yet it is changed completely. Suddenly the walls and the ramparts speak a different language. The courtyard becomes an entire world, a dark corner reminds us of the darkness in the human soul, we hear Hamlet's "To be or not to be." . . . [E]veryone knows the questions Shakespeare had him ask, the human depths he was made to reveal. . . . And once we know that, Kronberg [*sic*] becomes quite a different castle for us.[6]

While the castle is in part an empirical object, Bohr observed that in light of the play *Hamlet* it is changed. But what is changed? Certainly not the physical castle. Here we must consider that the castle is a part within a much larger whole of the lifeworld. The objective image of the castle is only part of the experience. Behind the image lie the remembered historical associations: Who built it? When was it built? Who was associated with it? Then there are associations with Shakespeare's play, which raise broader, more philosophical associations in "the human depths he was made to reveal." All contribute to a symbolic potency emerging from a web of associations onto endless horizons eventually pointing to the mystery of being itself as classically evoked by the question: Why is there something rather than nothing?

The intuitions associated with this symbolic potency are inchoate and often difficult to verbalize, relating as they do to the deepest aspects of being. The philosopher Paul Ricœur pointed to this when he rhetorically asked:

> Is it simply a residual phenomenon, or an existential protest arising out of the depths of our being, that sends us in search of privileged places, be they our birthplace, the scene of our first love, or the theater of some important historical occurrence—a battle, a revolution, the execution ground of patriots? We return to such places because *there* a more than everyday reality erupted and because the memory attached to what took place there preserves us from being simply errant vagrants in the world.[7]

The Yoknapatawpha stories aren't mere retellings of historical episodes; they point beyond themselves to larger contexts, as ceramic shards suggest the forms of vessels no longer extant. In Faulkner's novel *The Town*, the greater whole is glimpsed by his character lawyer Gavin Stevens in a panoramic view of Yoknapatawpha from a ridgetop where, looking back, he views his world beneath him:

> There is a ridge; you drive on beyond Seminary Hill and in time you come upon it: a mild unhurried farm road presently mounting to cross the ridge and on to join the main highway leading from Jefferson to the world. And now, looking back and down, you see all Yoknapatawpha in the dying last of day beneath you. . . .
>
> And you stand suzerain and solitary above the whole sum of your life . . . the cradle of your nativity and of the men and women who made you, the records and chronicle of your native land proffered for our perusal in ring by concentric ring like the ripples on living water above the dreamless slumber of your past; you to preside unanguished and immune above this miniature of man's passions and hopes and disasters.[8]

Yoknapatawpha is the "sum of [his] life," implying a personal linkage to history and place while also being a "miniature of man's passions and hopes and disasters"—with the implication that it was a microcosm of the universal conditions of human existence. This insight lay behind Faulkner's oft-quoted lines that his "own little postage stamp of native soil was worth writing about" and that through it he had created a "cosmos of [his] own."⁹ The associated stories were designed to represent, as he noted in his Nobel Prize acceptance speech, "the old verities and truths of the heart, the universal truths lacking which any story is ephemeral and doomed."¹⁰ In his own locale, in the multidimensionality of his lifeworld, he intuited the symbolic potential that revealed those verities, and here is where I saw the connection between Yoknapatawpha and my experience of local history.

Local history and the Yoknapatawpha stories emerge from the symbolic potency of history and place. The Yoknapatawpha stories constitute a local history modeled on the places that Faulkner knew including Lafayette and Tippah Counties and would constitute a "cosmos," or perhaps more appropriately a microcosmos, a miniature reflection of the cosmos in its intricacy, all undergirded by the ineffable Mystery that draws us on and that can only be inadequately symbolized as God. The symbolic potency of history and place are an integral part of human experience with its need and ability to organize images into cognitive maps and stories that constitute an analog of the cosmos that is about the world while simultaneously being part of it.

In 1974, the year after my interest in local history and Yoknapatawpha began, I first ventured into the lifeworld that Faulkner had known and wrote about when I attended the first Faulkner and Yoknapatawpha Conference at the University of Mississippi. At the age of twenty, I was without a doubt one of the youngest attendees. The towns visited were certainly not unfamiliar, but at that time I began to see them with different eyes. Field trips took conferees to sites in and around Oxford, while on another day we traveled to Ripley, the home of Colonel Falkner, a town with a population of a few thousand, in many ways still evocative of the town that he had known. While most of the business had moved away from the square and onto nearby State Highway 15, the courthouse still maintained its dominant position. There, I walked in the places where Falkner had lived including the site of his last home and of Renfrow's Café on the courthouse square, where he had supposedly been shot.

However, the most vivid image in my memory was the Falkner monument in Ripley Cemetery adjacent to the railroad that he had constructed. The monument consists of a granite pedestal surmounted by a marble statue of the colonel with a total elevation of about nineteen feet that dominates the cemetery and is visible from a considerable distance. In *Sartoris*, the younger Faulkner describes the counterpart statue of Colonel Sartoris in the cemetery of the counterpart town, Jefferson, Yoknapatawpha County:

Figure I.1. Renfrow's Café, 1942, as photographed by Andrew Brown III. Constructed in 1937, it burned in 2012. This building was once erroneously pointed out as the site of R. J. Thurmond's office and of the shooting of Colonel Falkner. It was actually the site of Thurmond's son, C. M. Thurmond's law office. Courtesy of Tommy Covington.

> [He] stood on a stone pedestal, in his frock coat and bareheaded, one leg slightly advanced and one hand resting lightly on the stone pylon beside him. His head was lifted a little in that gesture of haughty pride which repeated itself generation after generation with a fateful fidelity, his back to the world and his carven eyes gazing out across the valley where his railroad ran and the blue, changeless hills beyond, and beyond that, the ramparts of infinity itself.[11]

In my memory, "a more than everyday reality erupted" at the monument. As part of the lifeworld, symbols attain their power through their history and multivalent associations. The power of the monument arises in part through recalling the man who was a legend in his time and place and also by serving as a linchpin where the history and geography of Tippah County interfaced with the history and geography of Yoknapatawpha and thereby with the world of the imagination. We intuit a sense of the boundlessness of vision that Falkner/Sartoris represent, looking ever outward to "the ramparts of infinity," which says much about his vision for the railroad as we will see but also about the orientation of human existence toward the Transcendent.

My own rebirth of interest in Colonel Falkner was linked to my experience or reexperience of the places and stories related to his life on the occasion of my attending Ripley's Faulkner Heritage Festival on November 6, 2010, the 121st anniversary of his death. This event was formerly held annually to

Figure I.2. Falkner monument, more than stone, an evocation. Photograph by Jack D. Elliott Jr.

coincide with the anniversary of the murder of Colonel Falkner. I drove up to Ripley early that Saturday morning, where I met for the first time Melinda Marsalis, the indefatigable organizer and driving force behind the festival, and also Melissa McCoy-Bell, who had invited me to attend and who owns several websites devoted to Tippah County history and genealogy. Not present at the event—being out of town at the time—was Tommy Covington, the retired director of the Ripley Public Library, who for decades worked to assemble a collection of Falkner-related materials, documents, and photographs. In 1974, he had been on the committee that welcomed the touring conferees to Ripley and later became of great assistance in my work in Ripley. The festival consisted of presentations on the history of Falkner and Ripley, following which there was a tour of Falkner-related sites led by the late Bruce Smith, a Ripley native. I saw again sights remembered from my 1974 visit including Renfrow's Café and Falkner's funerary monument, and others by then long forgotten. The monument, I later recognized, was for me the equivalent of Bohr's Kronborg Castle, multivalent and questioning. Following the festival, those places through memory deepened my fascination with the man whose statue surveyed Ripley and the railroad and the hills beyond.

During the weeks and months that followed, I was drawn frequently back to Ripley, where I began a rather desultory scheme of research intended to identify places associated with Falkner, which led me to delve into "the bottomless labyrinths of chancery,"[12] that repository of records of property ownership that sheds light on where buildings were located and where events had occurred, thereby acquiring fresh insights into Falkner's life and world. For example, Renfrow's Café had been presented for decades as the place of his shooting. However, as it turned out, it was not that at all; the identification was a mistake, with the real site being a half block to the south.[13] This discovery led me to confront an aspect of the man who had become legend, namely the number of stories that surrounded him, many of questionable reliability. In 1956, Maud Morrow Brown of Oxford noted that "even while he lived," he was "the subject of amazing and contradictory stories. After his death these stories multiplied into such fantastic and exaggerated legends that today it is often impossible to divide the true from the false."[14] The tales were perpetuated and augmented by short, poorly researched historical pieces that repeated rather than critically examined them. Furthermore, even the more thorough research began to appear inadequate.

This brought forcibly to mind the fact that Falkner's life had been inadequately researched. Subsequently, my initial research focus became considerably less desultory as I set my sights on producing a new biography, eventually devoting considerable time to perusing Tippah County deed books, nineteenth-century newspapers, and many other sources. During the course of my work I visited old buildings associated with him, walked through the woods of Bearman Creek Valley in search of the site where A. J. McCannon murdered the Adcock family in 1845, and stood precariously twelve feet off the ground on a ladder propped against the Falkner monument to determine its elevation.

The archival sources are varied. Newspapers have served to flesh out in some detail Falkner's railroad activities and the McCannon affair. The Ripley newspapers—primarily the *Ripley Advertiser* and the *Southern Sentinel*—are available primarily in bound volumes or on microfilm, and I took considerable time perusing them a page at a time. However, in recent years hundreds of newspapers have been digitized and placed online where they can be read and searched, thereby providing access to many important regional newspapers such as those from Jackson, Mississippi; Memphis, Tennessee; and New Orleans, Louisiana. There is also a considerable quantity of correspondence and newspaper material concerning Falkner and the Civil War. I have used several archives, including Joseph Blotner's source material in the L. D. Brodsky Collection at Southeast Missouri State University and the Special Collections at the University of Mississippi. However, Falkner's personal papers are largely lost. With his public connections and legal and business operations, he must have accumulated a quantity of correspondence, ledgers, business papers, family communications, photographs, and so on. One would also expect numerous photos, but only a few survive. These include only two known photos of Falkner and none of his two wives. There are no photos of his son Henry, and there are also none of the railroad during his lifetime or even the Ripley depot. Why so little has survived, I do not know. Certainly, much was lost in 1864 when Falkner's Ripley home was burned by Federal troops; records from the subsequent decades could have survived, but apparently they did not.

The loss of these documents of course results in deficiencies in coverage of his life. This is most notable in areas pertaining to personal interactions with family, friends, and associates. For example, there is little documentation of his relationships with either of his two wives or his children. However, insights into his personal character can be gathered from the published account of his grand tour of Europe in 1883, *Rapid Ramblings in Europe* (1884).

As my work progressed, I assessed the secondary sources on Falkner, which had grown considerably since his great-grandson received the Nobel Prize in Literature in 1950. Of these publications there was one biography per se, while others presented biographical sketches in works devoted to different subjects.

For example, much of importance on Falkner appeared in a history of Tippah County by Andrew Brown III, while Joseph Blotner, Joel Williamson, and others presented Falkner's life as introductory to their biographies of his great-grandson. In dealing with the older Falkner, these works were far from exhaustive in their use of the source materials, and from this derives much of my justification for producing the work at hand.

I began to realize that many of these sources also possessed a distinctly negative tone as an overreaction to the legends about Falkner. In fact, this material came in part to constitute a counterlegend. If the primary legend presented Falkner as a magnanimous leader who built the Ripley Railroad, the counterlegend downgraded his importance as a railroad builder while depicting him during his later years as having a pathological personality that virtually drove him to his fatal confrontation with R. J. Thurmond. These elements became so pervasive in the literature that it is necessary to address them before proceeding further.

While the legendry about Falkner distorted his image, sometimes for the better, sometimes for the worse, the person primarily responsible for introducing the counterlegend to the historical material was Andrew Brown III (1896–1964),[15] a native of Ripley and a relative by blood or by law of many of the main families in Ripley. He was a great-nephew of Mrs. R. J. Thurmond and Mrs. John Y. Murry Sr., the latter being the step-great-grandmother of William Faulkner (although he was not a relative of the aforementioned Maud Brown). Brown worked for years as a geologist with the Mississippi Geological Survey and the US Geological Survey while also having a strong interest in the history of Tippah County. His articles on the subject appeared in the *Southern Sentinel* as early as the 1930s.[16] In the late 1950s or early 1960s, he wrote *History of Tippah County, Mississippi: The First Century*, in which Falkner appeared as a major figure.[17] His familiarity with the people who had known the colonel along with his critical perspective provided much-needed depth to the treatment of Falkner. His long connection to Tippah County and its history meant that he was an obvious contact for anyone delving into this subject.

While Brown was writing his county history, Donald P. Duclos (1932–1988) was researching a doctoral dissertation on Falkner and corresponded regularly with Brown. Duclos's primary interest lay in Falkner's connection to the literary works of his great-grandson, William Faulkner. In 1959, he traveled to Ripley to dig through county records and old newspapers among other documents. He also interviewed members of the Falkner family in Oxford and Memphis, including Falkner's last living child, Bama Falkner McLean. His dissertation entitled "Son of Sorrow: The Life, Works, and Influence of

Colonel William C. Falkner" was completed in 1961 and served as a source
for Blotner's 1974 biography of William Faulkner,[18] which in turn served as a
major source for subsequent biographies of Faulkner that used the life story
of the colonel as an introduction. Despite its impact, "Son of Sorrow" wasn't
published until 1998, ten years after Duclos's death.[19]

Another source of note is *The Falkner Feuds* (1964), a pamphlet devoted to
a rambling look at the Falkner-Thurmond incident written by Thomas Felix
Hickerson (1882–1968), a cousin of R. J. Thurmond's and correspondent of
Andrew Brown's. Hickerson wrote in his preface that "the motive here is to vin-
dicate Thurmond," which gives the reader an idea where his sympathies lay.[20]
Whether Brown and Hickerson knew one another personally is not known.
However, they certainly corresponded and doubtless influenced one another.

One component of the Falkner counterlegend is the claim that Falkner's
role in the construction of the railroad was inconsequential. Instead of being
a pivotal character in the effort, he was merely one person in a communal
effort. As Brown wrote to Hickerson: "I am disgusted with the often repeated
falsehood that Falkner *built the railroad*, the inference being that it was his
idea, his money, etc."[21] In his *History of Tippah County*, Brown wrote:

> The fact that 36 men incorporated the Ripley Railroad should set at rest for all
> time the legend, which has been published and republished so many times that
> it has become accepted widely as a fact, that the railroad was the brainchild of
> Colonel Falkner, and that he alone built the little line. Actually, the railroad was
> a community undertaking, in which Falkner took a leading part, but far from
> the only part.[22]

The stories to which Brown alluded—such as the claim that Falkner invented
the railroad himself or built it himself—are obviously naïve and therefore easily
serve as straw men in attempts to downplay Falkner's importance. As will be
discussed below, the claim that Falkner invented the idea of the Ripley Railroad
tells us nothing, because such an idea was so commonplace as to be of no consequence. Ultimately, what mattered was who could bring the idea to fruition,
and where many had failed, Falkner succeeded. The railroad's construction can
indeed be described as a community effort in that many people were involved;
however, to state this reveals no insight: few such projects are without a communal dimension. However, it was Falkner who brought the social, political,
and financial elements together and made it happen.[23]

The second component of the counterlegend claims that instead of being
a model citizen, Falkner's personality became increasingly pathological

in his later years, inevitably leading to his destruction. Brown, Duclos, and Hickerson all described him as a megalomaniac, which they suggested was evidenced in part by the large addition to his house, as though the desire to have a large home is evidence of mental pathology.[24] For Brown, Falkner had gained fame and recognition through a railroad project in which he was only a minor player and gained subsequent fame through his novels. Toward the end, "Falkner was going down hill mentally and physically during the last three or four years of his life. He became more and more truculent and was widely feared. In his attacks on Thurmond he was the aggressor, but Thurmond never tried to dodge him."[25] Hickerson would similarly write, clearly influenced by Brown, that Falkner had been "a fairly law-abiding, progressive, and public spirited citizen (with occasional indications of megalomania)"; then, in the final years of his life, "his disposition appeared to become more and more overbearing and intolerable."[26] Brown also summed up Falkner's last years in dark terms, claiming that he "was practically unbearable and begged for trouble, and Thurmond was one of the few who dared stand up to him."[27] In sum, according to Brown and Hickerson, Falkner had become a dangerous person. However, as will be seen, such claims were to a large degree exaggerated and were substantially motivated by family animosity toward Falkner.

Elsewhere, Brown further elaborated on Falkner's last years:

> It may be that Colonel Falkner simply lived too long. He was not numbered among those fortunate ones who make their exits from the stage of life at the height of their powers, mourned the more because their ends seemed so untimely. Rather it was his fate to pass over the crest and continue his way amid the deepening shadows of the downhill road.[28]

To claim that Falkner was past "the height of [his] powers" and on "the downhill road" is both unjustified and erroneous. Brown's maternal uncle, L. P. "Pink" Smith, the editor at the time of Ripley's *Southern Sentinel*, observed that upon Falkner's April 1889 entry into the political arena he had "reached the top round," and his subsequent success would only take him higher. If anything, as was generally recognized by his contemporaries, Falkner was at the pinnacle of achievement on the November evening with expectations of more to come when he was shot down.

In 1964 and shortly before his death, Brown wrote to Hickerson regarding *The Falkner Feuds* with a candid admission: "I am somewhat handicapped in judging it because, as you well know, I am so close to it that it is difficult at times to see the woods for the trees, and also I am very strongly on the

Thurmond side in the Falkner-Thurmond business, just as you are."[29] As already noted, Hickerson wrote *The Falkner Feuds* "to vindicate Thurmond." Indeed, Brown and Hickerson were prejudiced against Falkner probably in part because they had grown up within the extended family of Thurmond and in effect had absorbed a negative element of Falkner's legend, one disseminated by those who bore a grudge against him. So, contrary to the Falkner legend as one that magnified his good traits, there were also counterelements that depicted him in a negative light. Those who were not involved in Thurmond's family network—by far the majority—certainly saw Falkner differently.

In 1993, years after the deaths of Brown, Duclos, and Hickerson, Joel Williamson published his *William Faulkner and Southern History*, which followed his predecessors' interpretation. While not using the word "megalomania," Williamson was not far off in claiming that Falkner was "an egoist—a person who believes that the world revolves around himself and works for the ends he desires." Although Falkner could, as we shall see, be described as very self-confident, this was not the egoism that Williamson claimed resulted in a "capacity for alienating himself" from his community by his "independence" and "willfulness" with fateful results: "In 1889 . . . he played the role his character dictated one time too many, and the jury seemed to say that he got what he deserved. . . . Very few people in Tippah County would have killed Falkner as Thurmond did, but once it was done by him, many could approve the action."[30] Considering Falkner's acts of charity, his ability to mingle and laugh with fellow travelers, his friendship with many, and the affection of the hundreds who voted for him and attended his funeral, Williamson was out of line with the evidence.

In sum, all four men—Brown, Duclos, Hickerson, and Williamson—depicted Falkner's feud with Thurmond as more than an idiosyncratic personal dispute. Instead, they claimed that there was a deeper flaw, a pathology, identified variously as megalomania, egoism, and an increasing alienation from family and community; this dark force drove him into an inevitable showdown with Thurmond.

The evidence for such a scenario is weak and the conclusion little more than a strained surmise that was bolstered by repetition. On the other hand, the evidence presented here will demonstrate that Falkner was not considered unbearable by the overwhelming majority of the people who knew him. While he did enjoy being in the limelight, he was well liked by most and even idolized by many such as editor and later state legislator Pink Smith. He wouldn't have been seen as unbearable except to R. J. Thurmond and a few others. Unfortunately, the two men let their personal conflict become all-consuming, bringing with it tragic results. The historians cited failed to see the feud in terms of a conflict over differing visions for the railroad, over whether it would continue as a spur-line railroad and a safe investment or whether it would grow into a transcontinental trunk line albeit at considerable financial risk. Thurmond followed the former vision, while Falkner the latter.

Although the impulse to stain Falkner with the image of violence came in part from stories told by Thurmond's family and supporters, his own great-grandson also encouraged this image. Although the younger Faulkner had been strongly influenced by his namesake, his knowledge of the history of his ancestor was not impressive. While on one hand he emphasized the heroic qualities of the colonel, on the other he seems to have absorbed elements of the negative legend from the Thurmonds describing him as an "overbearing man" filled with "arrogance," "hard to get along with," and having "no humor." Faulkner went on to say that because his great-grandfather "had killed two or three men," he supposed that "when you've killed men something happens inside you—something happens to your character."[31] Of course, the two (not three) killings were ruled as being in self-defense and seemingly provoked by a family that was determined to destroy him. For the rest of Falkner's life there were no other killings or acts of violence.

William Faulkner carried these dark overtones over into his depiction of Colonel John Sartoris, who killed several men with no justification—two of whom were involved in registering freedmen to vote—all seemingly to emphasize the author's notion that his great-grandfather was humorless, arrogant, and prone to violence. As will be seen, there is little justification for any of this. For example, instead of being humorless, Colonel Falkner had an irrepressible sense of humor, which was probably more likely the cause of his death than any supposed tendency toward violence.

Having examined and disposed of theories involving psychological pathologies, I will examine Falkner's life without this monkey on my back. The work that follows will hopefully provide fresh insights while never completely capturing the subject's personality, a goal comparable to catching a will-o'-the-wisp in a jar.

The purpose of this work is to inquire into the image of a man long dead, an image partly frozen into that of a marble statue. As in much of local history, the memory of a place draws us to delve into the matrix of interconnected symbols, whether stories or documents or associated places. Like Old Man Falls, we shall retell the primary stories and others and perhaps in the process provide a defensible reconstruction of the life of Colonel Falkner using comprehensive research. As I alluded, there is a personal dimension at the root of this life, a sense of wonder inspired by the evocative nature of place and its manifestation in story. Although spatial experiences don't translate well into the verbal, I've tried to maintain an awareness of the spatial throughout.

My introductory remarks on the nature of local history are intended to accentuate a dimension of life that is ever present but often neglected, life in its context in the cultural landscape with all that implies regarding human existence in time—time as remembered, time as experienced as the eternal now, and time as anticipated.

Places, buildings, and gravestones serve to recall that we passed this way and in the memory to inspire others to the same transcendental horizons.

This work was born out of a sense of wonder through the experience of history and place and of the process of imagination that it stimulates. It examines the life of Colonel Falkner with the most complete documentation available while trying to identify as many places associated with him as possible. The spatial focus is brought to the fore in the appendix, "A Field Guide to Colonel Falkner's Ripley," which provides the reader with information about the cultural landscape—as known by Falkner—and its spatial organization.

His life took place at many sites, American and foreign, urban and rural, ranging from farmsteads to P. T. Barnum's American Museum and Shakespeare's birthplace. However, the place where he resided from 1842 through 1889, where he raised his family, and where he established his base of operations was Ripley. I cannot visit Ripley today without imagining him on the sidewalks conversing with his numerous friends and acquaintances.

Falkner's later years were dominated not by the goal of merely building a railroad to Ripley—that goal was accomplished in 1872—but by transforming the little spur line into a transcontinental railroad. Ironically, this seemingly quixotic goal led to his untimely death and subsequently to the transformation of his life into legend, a legend that became the foundation of his great-grandson's Yoknapatawpha mythos.

Hopefully this book will constitute a symbology, a collection of verbal and visual symbols—which through memory and imagination are painted onto the landscape of Ripley, Mississippi, where it will be seen as constituting more than a collection of material objects but a multidimensional lifeworld.

As we recover the images both visual and verbal, they may initially seem static, frozen glimpses of the past. Yet, reflection tells us that in our common appropriation of them we can be pulled into a dynamic of wonder that is the birthplace of creativity, much as Falkner was led to see the railroad as not merely a local carrier but as leading to infinite horizons, to the ramparts of infinity.

Chapter 1

❖━◈━◇━━◇━◈━❖

Settling the Land
Cumberland Gap and Beyond

Speaking at the 1893 meeting of the American Historical Association, the historian Frederick Jackson Turner famously remarked: "Stand at Cumberland Gap and watch the procession of civilization, marching single file—the buffalo following the trail to the salt springs, the Indian, the fur-trader and hunter, the cattle-raiser, the pioneer farmer—and the frontier has passed by."[1] This panoramic image evokes the process through which people and regions transitioned from wilderness to civilization, involving millions of westward-bound Americans including Falkner and his family during the late eighteenth and nineteenth centuries. His life, which spanned the period from 1825 to 1889, was played out against the backdrop of this process, the westward advance of the frontier of settlement through which new communities were formed and linked to a hierarchy of evolving towns and cities. Falkner's early years witnessed the movement of settlement from Tennessee to Missouri, yet the part of the frontier most relevant to his life was the opening and settling of the 1832 Chickasaw Cession lands, which were primarily in northern Mississippi. This block of land was merely one in a patchwork of Indian cession lands through which land west of the Appalachians was transferred piecemeal from tribes to the federal government then to individual landowners, thereby implementing the westward advance of settlement and in the process transforming the land from sparsely populated wilderness to farms and newly founded towns.

This process occurred simultaneously with another, with each affecting the other. This other process was the explosion of technological innovations emerging from the Industrial Revolution, which facilitated the interconnectedness of these settlements through improved communications and transportation to coastal cities and to the entire world. For example, Falkner's life saw the development of the railroad, telegraph, lightbulb, telephone, and internal

combustion engine. Of notable importance to Falkner was the beginning and
development of the railroad network. When he was born on July 6, 1825, there
were no public carrier railroads in existence. However, in September of that
year, the Stockton and Darlington Railway opened in England, the first public
steam-powered railway in the world. The following year saw the establishment of the Baltimore and Ohio Railroad, America's first public railroad, with
its first section opening for service in 1830. The coming of the railroad would
dramatically transform North America, as it expedited the movement of passengers and freight and linked the continental interior to the coastal cities
and thereby to the world.

Falkner's parents, William Falkner (or William Forkner, as we shall see)[2]
and Caroline Word,[3] were married on or shortly after June 1, 1816, the day they
filed for a license in Surry County, North Carolina, a county that primarily
lies in the Piedmont just east of the Blue Ridge Mountains. Caroline's father,
Thomas Adams Word I, served as bondsman.[4] Both families, Falkners and
Words, had been in the county for several decades and even longer in the
Cis-Appalachian South between the Atlantic and the Appalachian Mountains,
where English settlement had been confined for two centuries.

The name "Falkner" derives from "Falconer," which over time metasta-
sized into a number of variants including Falkner, Farkner, Faukner, Faulkner,
Fockner, Forkner, and Fortner, in a complex interplay between vernacular
phonetics and spelling. In the case of the family line under consideration, the
spelling gravitated to "Forkner" by the eighteenth century in North Carolina.
The earliest known representative of the family was a William Falconer (or
however it was spelled), a draper in England, during the seventeenth century.
His son, John Sr., and family sailed to the New World in 1665 and settled in
Kent County, Maryland. A descendant, William Forkner Sr., moved to Rowan
County, North Carolina, by the late 1760s. In 1771, Surry County was formed
from Rowan and probably included the area that the Forkners lived in.[5] About
1780, a William Forkner, probably the son of William Sr., received a grant of
three hundred acres on Forkner Creek in Surry County. Obviously named for
the family, the creek lay in northern Surry, flowing into the Ararat River at the
town of Mount Airy. Today, the name is spelled Faulkner Creek.[6]

Genealogical sketches for such an early time period are often based on
fragmentary evidence accompanied by shaky leaps of inference. Regardless,
the general outline appears to be correct. Furthermore, it appears that the
preferred spelling of the family name for most of this time period was
"Forkner," meaning that when Colonel Falkner's father was born around 1795
he was named William Forkner.[7] While his connection to the family tree is

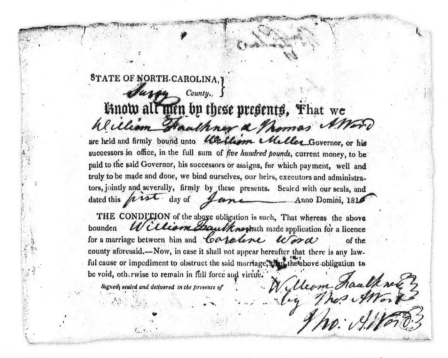

Figure 1.1. Falkner-Word marriage bond. Ancestry.com, "North Carolina, U.S., Index to Marriage Bonds, 1741–1868."

certain, the specific branch through which he was connected is not so certain, although Franklin Moak has credibly suggested that William's father was Joseph Forkner, his grandfather was William Forkner Jr., and his great-grandfather was William Forkner Sr.[8]

We might ask if the family's name was spelled Forkner, how did it become Falkner? In the 1820 census for Surry County, William is listed under the surname "Farkner," obviously a phonetic rendering. However, four years earlier he had married, and in his 1816 marriage record his name is spelled "Faulkner," which includes a signature following an *X*, reading in full: "*X* William Faulkner by Thos. A Word." This indicates that his future father-in-law signed for him and that consequently William was probably illiterate and therefore presumably had no preferred spelling. It also indicates that Word had injected his idea for the correct spelling of a surname that he must surely have known was commonly spelled Forkner. About the same time, on October 11, 1816, Thomas A. Word's son James Word was bonded to marry "Nancy Forkner," certainly a relative if not a sister of William. However, in his family memoir James refers to Nancy as a "Faulkner," and in a letter written years later referred to his nephew as "Bill Faulkner."[9] Thus the Words seemed to have preferred the Faulkner spelling, perhaps thinking that contrary to local use, this was the "correct" spelling. Of course, with William being illiterate, the matter was probably moot. His wife, Caroline, may have insisted on the Faulkner, or perhaps Falkner, spelling as opposed to Forkner. Her son and the subject of this work, W. C. Falkner, clearly settled upon Falkner, as it was spelled in the earliest known listing of his name in his 1845 pamphlet on the McCannon murders.[10]

The lineage of Caroline Word is clearer than that of her husband. Her great-grandfather Charles Word Sr. was born in Virginia in 1710 and died there in 1792. His son, Charles Jr. (b. 1740, New Kent County, VA; d. October 7, 1780, SC), was married circa 1768 to Elizabeth Adams (b. 1753, VA; d. 1834, GA) and settled in Surry County, North Carolina; their children included Thomas Adams Word I and William Word. After enlisting in the Continental Army during the American Revolution, Charles Jr. was killed at the Battle of King's Mountain, South Carolina, in October 1780. Afterward, his widow was remarried, to Richard Hooper. One of Charles Jr's brothers, Cuthbert Word, also fought during the revolution and died in 1780 aboard the prison ship the HMS *Jersey*. Cuthbert was an old name in the Word family, one that appeared regularly over the generations.[11]

Thomas A. Word I was born on December 10, 1768, in Surry County and was married there in 1792 to Justiania Dickinson (March 4, 1776–February 20, 1865, Ripley, MS); they raised a family there. In a time and place when most men were involved in agriculture, Thomas pursued different professions. Following the path of George Washington and Thomas Jefferson, he was a surveyor and was involved from as early as 1794 through as late as 1820 in Surry County in that capacity. Many surveys were for land that he purchased from the state of North Carolina.[12] He was also involved in politics, serving as the Surry County sheriff about 1798, and was apparently an attorney, making him the first of a long line of lawyers in the Word-Falkner family.[13] In the 1820s he and several family members left Surry County and settled in Habersham County, Georgia, located in the Blue Ridge region adjacent to South Carolina.[14] The move to Georgia was apparently associated with Thomas's writing and publishing a book in 1828 entitled *A Topographical Analysis of the State of Georgia for the Year 1828 to Be Continued Annually*.[15] He died there soon after in 1831 at the age of sixty-two,[16] and there his youngest child, Justiania (b. 1815), met and married J. W. (John Wesley) Thompson (b. 1809, Haywood County, NC) on July 24, 1834.[17] The couple would play a major role in the history of Ripley and their nephew, W. C. Falkner. However, three weeks after their marriage, Thompson was arrested and incarcerated in the Habersham County jail in Clarkesville on a charge of stabbing one Calvin J. Hanks to death. Also charged were Thompson's brother-in-law Cuthbert Word and two others listed as accomplices. Regarding the circumstances behind the slaying, we know nothing. When the case was brought to trial in October, Thompson and the others were acquitted.[18] He and Justiania soon left Georgia for Mississippi.

The newly married William and Caroline Forkner continued to reside in Surry County for a few years and by 1820 had two children. Like most on the frontier, William was a farmer and sought to cultivate as many fertile acres as possible.[19] By 1825, the family had followed the path blazed decades before by Daniel Boone, James Harrod, and James Robertson, crossing the Blue Ridge into the basin of the Tennessee River, where they settled in Knox County, Tennessee. There, on July 6, their son William—at least their fourth child—was born. His given name came from his father, while his middle name was possibly Cuthbert after his mother's brother Cuthbert Word and other Cuthbert Words that preceded.[20] By 1840, the Falkners had leapfrogged across Tennessee perhaps following the Tennessee and Ohio Rivers to the Mississippi River and were living in Saline Township, Ste. Genevieve County, Missouri, where the family continued to farm. With his father a farmer with no indication of having much land or slaves, the young William probably knew only a hardscrabble life as the family attempted to produce enough for their own subsistence while also attempting to produce a small surplus for sale.[21]

Meanwhile, the Words began to settle in Mississippi. The first were the family of William Word (1772–1826), the brother of Thomas A. Word I. William Word was born in Surry County, North Carolina, and married Elizabeth Bryson, also of Surry County. They and their children moved first to Carroll County, Georgia, and in 1820–1821 settled in Mississippi near the east bank of the Tombigbee River. This area had been ceded by the Chickasaws and Choctaws in 1816, with the Mississippi portion being organized in 1821 as Monroe County.[22] At this time, the land on the west bank of the Tombigbee was still Indian Territory. The county court of Monroe County met in William's home on October 1, 1821, and continued to meet there for the next year or more, with the site being designated as the first county seat, Hamilton.[23] Word was appointed as the first jailer, with the first public building, a log jail, being constructed late in 1821, while a courthouse was authorized the following year.[24]

At this time, the land across the Tombigbee River to the west of Monroe County was still Indian Territory, the last remnants of the domains of the Chickasaw and Choctaw Nations. Since 1797, the two nations had maintained political connections to the United States via agencies, with each overseen by an agent who was appointed by the president. These two blocks of land constituted about one-third of Mississippi along with smaller portions of Alabama and Tennessee. This block of Indian Territory vanished as a result of the Dancing Rabbit Creek Treaty with the Choctaws in 1830 and the Pontotoc Treaty with the Chickasaws in 1832. In the latter treaty, the Chickasaws ceded land that extended from the west bank of the Tombigbee near the Words to the east bank of the Mississippi River and almost to Memphis and agreed to move west of the Mississippi River. In part because of its humid, subtropical climate the land was in demand primarily for cotton production. Like so much of the South, the cession lands were of variable fertility with the most fertile being the Black Prairie in the east and the loess uplands and alluvial Yazoo bottomlands to the west. For the land to be sold, it had first to be surveyed into a grid system made up of six-square-mile townships each subdivided into one-square-mile sections. The survey work was coordinated by Surveyor General John Bell at the Pontotoc Land Office, which was established in 1833 as a collection of three identical log structures with one serving as Bell's office and the other two serving as the offices of the registrar and the receiver, all presidential appointees. To expedite communication with the outside world, Pontotoc Post Office was established in October 1833. Within a short time, surveying parties were in the field each headed by a deputy surveyor operating under contract to the surveyor general.[25] One of the first was Thomas Adams Word II, the son of William Word, who began working in March 1834 as a deputy surveyor laying out the interior section lines of townships.[26] His interest in surveying may have come from his uncle, T. A. Word I. Given the proximity of his home, it was only natural that young Word was lured to the Chickasaw Cession lands to work.

As the surveys were proceeding, Chickasaw agent Benjamin Reynolds began working with the Chickasaws to locate their allotments. The Chickasaw Agency at that time was located in northwestern Alabama near the Tennessee River, a considerable distance from the land office and from the center of Chickasaw activity. Consequently, Reynolds was compelled to base his operations at Pontotoc beginning in early fall 1834.[27] Within a few months, it became necessary to establish a branch office of the Chickasaw Agency at Pontotoc. Thus by 1835 Pontotoc had become a cluster of federal offices—land offices, a post office, and a branch office of the Chickasaw Agency.[28]

During the summer and fall of 1834 and long before the actual assigning of allotments of land to individual Chickasaws and the selling of the

remainder, land speculators began to operate through middlemen who provided money or store accounts to Chickasaws in exchange for title bonds
obligating them to convey title to their lands once they obtained them.[29] As
Chickasaw allotments were located and assigned to their claimants, an influx
of land buyers and Chickasaws with land to sell converged on Pontotoc
along with grog shops to supply liquor to the crowds assembled. Some of
the new arrivals had interests beyond merely buying and selling land and
liquor. By the summer of 1835 a church and academy were established, the
New York and Mississippi Land Company and other land companies began
to establish permanent offices, and others provided services in the form of
food and accommodations.

With the allocation of allotments to the Chickasaws in full swing, public
land sales began. Announced well in advance, the first sale began on January
4, 1836, and extended through January 31 with 960,023 acres offered to the
highest bidders.[30] The second sale ran from September 5 through November
20, 1836, with 2,601,130 acres offered for sale, more than twice that offered in
January. On November 23, the young Edward Fontaine arrived for the first
time in Pontotoc and described the scene:

> Pontotoc is a flourishing embryo town in the centre of the Chickasaw Nation;
> it is located in a fine salubrious region. . . . The first house was built here in June
> 1835; now there are 40 Stores and near 2000 inhabitants. Its present prosperity is
> entirely ephemeral. The extensive mercantile establishments and expensive tav
> erns are supported almost exclusively by the crowd of speculators and adventur
> ers who attend the land sales, and the Indians who have sold their reservations
> and received their value. Hundreds of these are now in the streets. Many drunk
> and most of them wasting their money as fast as they can. It is amusing to see
> their displays of finery. The dress are all of the most fanciful kinds—of every
> variety of cut and colour. Some of them are ridiculously gaudy, while others
> are rich and tasty—giving the wearer a martial and splendid appearance. As
> soon as the land sales are over and the money of these [Indians] is expended
> the glory of Pontotock [*sic*] will fade, and its wild novelty vanish—and it will
> appear but as the other respectable inland towns of our country. At present it
> resembles a Methodist Camp ground. Its buildings are a collection of rude ill
> constructed huts, with the exception of a few neat little framed painted dwell
> ings. These are tenanted by a collection of people from every State, and from
> many foreign countries. In this collection is centered perhaps more shrewdness
> and intelligence than can be found in any other congregation of the same size.[31]

These were the "Flush Times" of Mississippi when millions of acres were made available for sale, credit was cheap, and fantasies were peddled as the wave of the future. Joseph G. Baldwin, who lived through this era, recalled:

> Marvellous accounts had gone forth of the fertility of its virgin lands; and the productions of the soil were commanding a price remunerating to slave labor as it had never been remunerated before. Emigrants came flocking in from all quarters of the Union, especially from the slaveholding States. The new country seemed to be a reservoir, and every road leading to it a vagrant stream of enterprise and adventure. Money, or what passed for money, was the only cheap thing to be had. Every cross-road and every avocation presented an opening,—through which a fortune was seen by the adventurer in near perspective. . . .
>
> Under this stimulating process prices rose like smoke. Lots in obscure villages were held at city prices; lands, bought at the minimum cost of government, were sold at from thirty to forty dollars per acre, and considered dirt cheap at that.[32]

Colonel T. J. (Thomas Jefferson, "Jeff") Word, the son of Thomas A. Word I, brother of Caroline Word Falkner, and first cousin of Thomas A. Word II, had arrived in Pontotoc by July 1835. Jeff Word was an attorney and a former politician, having served one term representing Surry County in the North Carolina House of Commons, 1832–1833.[33] His arrival at Pontotoc was probably due in part to contacts with family members already in Mississippi. With land and money changing hands, there were plentiful opportunities for a man with his skills. In part he invested in real estate and acquired eleven patents for land in four counties in the cession. All but one of these were acquired in partnerships, most with John Word Hooper, apparently his cousin. Jeff's brother James Word arrived in Pontotoc and also began investing in land. He received sixty-seven patents primarily in Tishomingo County for a total of 10,245 acres, which placed him in the class of large land speculators—individuals and companies—with the largest purchasing over 77,000 acres.[34] By August 1835, Jeff Word had become a member of the board of trustees for a newly founded Pontotoc Academy, which may have been the lure to bring his brother-in-law J. W. Thompson to Pontotoc by December 1835, where he initially taught school.[35] About 1840, Jeff married Mary Elizabeth Jackson, a native of Ireland, whose brother Alexander Melvourne Jackson would later play a large role in Ripley.

Following the establishment of Pontotoc County, Jeff Word was admitted to the county bar on November 7, 1836, while the following day Thompson was

Figure 1.2. T. J. Word. Photograph courtesy of Tommy Covington.

admitted.[36] Both continued their involvement in political and civic activities. An early political opponent, Reuben Davis of Monroe County, later recalled that Jeff

> was a remarkably fine-looking man, and his manner was polished and agreeable. Added to this, he had a fine, humorous way of telling anecdotes, and could play well upon the violin.
>
> He was a good lawyer and a most agreeable stump-speaker. If I also add that he was a courteous and honorable gentleman, I do him no more than justice.
>
> Many of my friends thought that the extensive acquaintance and many popular accomplishments of Mr. Word made him too formidable to encounter with any hope of success, and seriously advised me to withdraw.[37]

Word and Davis faced each other in the 1837 election for circuit court judge, and Davis won in the summer primary elections.[38] However, Word was not out of the political arena. In October he was selected as a Whig candidate to run alongside Sergeant S. Prentiss for Congress. The two won in the November election and departed for Washington, DC, in December. However, after completing their term, neither ran for reelection.

As Jeff Word flourished, other family members arrived. Around 1837, Charles Word Humphreys Sr. (b. ca. 1800, SC; d. September 3, 1865, near Ripley, MS) settled in Tippah County.[39] He was the son of David Humphreys and Martha Word Humphreys, with Martha being the daughter of Charles Word Jr. and sister of Thomas Adams Word I. He married his first cousin, Elizabeth Adams Word (b. ca. 1802, NC; d. ca. 1870–1880), the daughter of Thomas Adams Word I and the sister of Jeff Word, Caroline Word Falkner, and Justiania Word Thompson.

The migration continued. About 1818, another William Word (b. 1771, Laurens District, SC; d. 1851, AL) and his wife, Janette Fairbairn, settled in Limestone County, Alabama. This William was the son of another Thomas Word (1743–1838), who was the brother of Charles Word Jr., who was killed at the Battle of King's Mountain. William was also the first cousin once removed of T. J. "Jeff" Word. William and his family became established in Limestone County. However, in the late 1830s his sons began to trickle into Monroe County, Mississippi, where they settled in the prairies west of the Tombigbee. Around 1839, son Samuel Word (b. 1799, Laurens District, SC; d. 1878, Monroe County, MS) moved there[40] and was followed soon after by his brothers, Thomas and Alexander.[41]

Taken together, the migrations of Words to Mississippi illustrate a complex process of family-based immigration through which early immigrants provided the information, encouragement, and financial support for other family members who followed after. In lieu of having documentation of the communications between family members, we can only interpolate the existence and nature of these letters. During this process, no Falkners or Forkners were involved unless they were related to the Words.

To provide local government for the newly ceded lands in northern Mississippi, the state legislature established a patchwork quilt of new counties. In December 1833, counties were created for the Choctaw Cession lands, and on February 9, 1836, they were created to cover the Chickasaw Cession lands. The county as a unit of local government has had a long and complex history in North America. In 1634 the Virginia House of Burgesses by order of King Charles I created the first eight "shires," which were soon renamed "counties," both terms derived from local governments in England. Over the centuries under various colonial and state governments, the county units were defined and redefined, evolving in the process. The various manifestations of county governments were defined by colonial governments and later by state constitutions. By the 1830s, the county had become a political template that could be duplicated endlessly, superimposed upon tracts previously without local

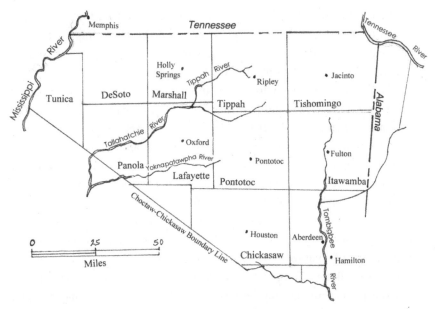

Figure 1.3. Map of the 1832 Chickasaw Cession lands in Mississippi and Alabama with a selection of towns. Although most of the land is divided into nine Mississippi counties that were
established in 1836, portions around the edge are often included in counties that overlap the
cession boundaries, which includes land that lies in Alabama.

government to serve as the basis for new political and social orders, all centered on the county seat and its courthouse. The Mississippi counties created
in the 1830s were organized according to specifications provided by the 1832
state constitution. Once established in legislation, they became real political
entities by filling the offices prescribed. Elections were organized to select
officials who would carry out the requisite duties along with selecting a centrally located site for a county seat. From the beginning, county governments
were associated with buildings that housed the officials and concomitantly
acquired the symbolic aura of the social order. With the passage of time, government buildings began to be housed in large buildings referred to as courthouses, which included not only the courtrooms themselves but also offices
for county officials. As new counties were organized, county seat towns were
surveyed, with each having a centrally located block, or square, on which the
courthouse would be constructed.[42]

On February 14, 1836, five days after the Chickasaw Cession counties were
established, another bill passed appointing commissioners for each county to
organize the first elections for the respective county Boards of Police. These
newly elected officials constituted the basis of each county's government

(comparable to the supervisors of today). Once in office, they held new elections to select the other county officials while also selecting a site for a county seat town with its courthouse square. The new counties and county seats included Pontotoc County and the town of Pontotoc, surveyed adjacent to the land office grounds; Chickasaw and Houston; Lafayette and Oxford; Tishomingo and Jacinto; and Tippah and Ripley, all named after national images and Indian-named streams. The process of settlement entailed not only physical modification of the landscape as farms and towns were created but also the creation of a collective perceptual geography of the lifeworld in which places were established and named, creating political entities and communities, most having the character of Faulkner's Frenchman's Bend in terms of being "definite yet without boundaries,"[43] having emerged through physical processes of construction while being bounded by no more than the collective agreement of what more or less defines the space.

William Faulkner's Yoknapatawpha County and its seat of Jefferson followed the pattern of naming counties and county seats. Yoknapatawpha derived from the name of the Yoknapatawpha River, which has its headwaters in western Pontotoc County and flows west to its confluence with the Tallahatchie River. The name was later corrupted into "Yocona," or "Yokney" as it's often pronounced.[44] Jefferson, as will be seen, was apparently named for President Thomas Jefferson.

Tippah County, where W. C. Falkner spent most of his life, is located on the northern periphery of the Chickasaw Cession and was named after one of its largest streams, the Tippah River, a tributary of the Tallahatchie River. The Tippah River was once believed to be named after the wife of a Chickasaw chief named Pontotoc. However, no such persons are known to have existed. Instead, the word "Tippah" apparently means in Chickasaw "to eat one another."[45]

Although Tippah County was settled primarily by farmers, it did not have the most fertile soil in the Chickasaw Cession lands. Furthermore, it was a considerable distance from navigable streams, with the closest being the upper reaches of the Tallahatchie and Tombigbee Rivers, which meant that merchants and farmers had to haul goods and cotton for miles between river landings and their homes.

The three commissioners appointed for Tippah County included Jeff Word.[46] They converged on the rectangular parcel of earth defined as Tippah and organized an election. By March 23, 1836, they had certified returns electing members of the Tippah County Board of Police,[47] who then held a second election on April 25, 1836, for the remaining officials.[48]

The Board of Police selected a centrally located site, purchased the land, and engaged a surveyor to lay out the streets, blocks, and lots. On June 15, the board advertised: "Valuable Lots . . . in the Town of Ripley will be offered for sale at public auction on the 1st Monday and days following in September next." While praising the prospects of the surrounding land for agricultural and mechanical development, the advertisement went on to note that the town "is laid out with a spacious, handsome public square, [while] elegant business lots surround the same"[49] Thus, by June 15, the site for the county seat had been selected and named with a survey in the works; the first sale of lots was announced for September 5. The name chosen—Ripley—probably came from General Eleazar Wheelock Ripley (1782–1839), a hero of the War of 1812 and congressman from Louisiana at the time the town was established. As lots were sold, residential and business houses were built. The first construction was of logs, taking advantage of the abundance of timber that had to be cleared. This was superseded by frame construction using milled lumber. Indeed, except for a few brick buildings, most of the buildings around the square were of frame construction throughout the nineteenth century. It wasn't until the late nineteenth and early twentieth centuries that brick construction spread and began to dominate.

Early settler Charles Peter Miller later recalled that he and his family arrived in Ripley on July 24, 1836, "before there was any town." The lots had been surveyed but none sold. He soon built a cabin, probably of logs, and organized the beginnings of a Methodist congregation.[50] He also opened a tavern or hotel, known as the Ripley Inn, the original part of which was made of logs.[51] His family played a prominent role in Ripley over the decades.[52]

J. W. Thompson moved from Pontotoc to Ripley about the first of January, 1837, where he opened a law office and was later remembered as the first lawyer in town.[53] He built a large house off the northeast corner of the square (see the appendix). Although he and his wife never had any children, they took in several. One of these was the orphan William W. Bailey, whose father, Edmund I. Bailey, had been the county's first probate clerk and a friend of Thompson's.[54] They would later take in W. C. Falkner, and even later Falkner's son, J. W. T. Falkner. All three eventually became attorneys. After practicing law for several years, Thompson was elected district attorney in 1843, a position he held until 1857, when he was elected to the state legislature.[55]

Reuben Davis later recalled standing for the defense in court cases against Thompson:

He conducted his prosecutions with great skill and vigor, and many a hard and long contest I had with him. . . . His keen eyes never overlooked a blunder in the defence, and I had to be wary indeed to escape him, especially as he had always the concluding arguments. I look back even from this distance of time with some complacency upon the fact that he never succeeded in hanging one of my men, though it is but justice to say that he pressed me hard.[56]

Soon after Ripley was established, a twenty-four-foot-square temporary courthouse was constructed of logs off the northeast corner of the square, to be followed in 1838 by a permanent fifty-foot-square, two-story brick building built on the square by Peter Garland.[57] The courthouse in part housed the courtroom on the upper floor, where justice was meted out. It also housed offices for those who administered the county government and to keep records of land sales, marriages, and property ownership. The five members of the Board of Police also met here on a regular basis.

On May 9, 1837, the town was chartered by the Mississippi legislature.[58] That same year, the Mississippi Union Bank was also chartered to consist of the "mother bank" in Jackson with branch banks in seven districts around the state. District 3 in northeastern Mississippi was initially to be served by a branch bank in Aberdeen; however, the following year its location was moved to Ripley, a change with implications for this narrative. A brick building was soon constructed by Peter Garland on the northeastern corner of the square across the street from J. W. Thompson's law office. The bank charter designated Jeff Word as one of the local representatives to oversee the sale of bank stock, but with the passage of time he played a more active role as an attorney for the bank.[59] The bank would play a pivotal albeit brief role in the life of W. C. Falkner.

Towns and their rural hinterlands grew symbiotically. The economy was agricultural. The farms through their sale of cash crops, in this case primarily cotton, provided the base that brought money into the economy, and the ability to produce cotton and therefore money was directly linked to soil fertility. Towns were agricultural service centers that provided goods and services for the surrounding farms. As the sale of cotton rose, the ability of farmers to support the merchants and service providers rose, as did the quality and availability of goods and services. The most successful towns were those that had the greatest trade, and the volume of trade was related not only to variations in soil fertility and cotton production but to factors encouraging farmers to travel distances to trade at a point. Towns on navigable rivers possessed advantages—in part explaining the success of Memphis on the Mississippi River and Aberdeen and Columbus on the Tombigbee. A county seat served to a degree as a magnet for trade, but no county seat in the Chickasaw Cession reached the thousand mark in population without the benefit of a navigable river, or later a railroad, except for Holly Springs, which was endowed with a highly fertile hinterland.

Ripley was neither on nor near a navigable river. Nor did it have an especially fertile hinterland, although its soils were not unproductive. However, it did have the advantage of being a county seat. The cluster of buildings around the courthouse represented a pattern replicated throughout the Chickasaw Cession counties and beyond, the physical manifestation of a new social order.

The same pattern that provided the geographic backdrop for both Colonel Falkner and Colonel Sartoris was described years later by Falkner's great-grandson:

> [A] Square, the courthouse in its grove the center; quadrangular around it, the stores, two-storey, the offices of the lawyers and doctors and dentists, the lodge-rooms and auditoriums, above them; school and church and tavern and bank and jail each in its ordered place; the four broad diverging avenues straight as plumb-lines in the four directions, becoming the network of roads and by-roads until the whole county would be covered with it.[60]

It has been insightfully observed that "the struggle to build new communities" has been "the primal experience" of the Americas, a transforming experience fundamental to the self-understanding of American societies.[61] Land was cleared, farms were established, and trade centers agglomerated as a new social system emerged around a hierarchy of towns and hamlets. The story of community foundations is a key dimension of the consciousness of the inhabitants in terms of their own self-identification and in the work of local historians.

The younger Faulkner's Yoknapatawpha stories present parallels to the settlement of the Chickasaw Cession, although not always with attention to historical accuracy. The stories hearken back to the foundation of the county and even to preceding times when the Chickasaws still remained and were the dominant social element. Faulkner's primary mythos of the founding of Yoknapatawpha County focuses on Jefferson and is found in his *Requiem for a Nun* (1951). Most county seats in the Chickasaw Cession were established at unoccupied sites chosen for centrality in the respective county, the presence of transportation routes, the availability of water, and good drainage, such as Ripley. However, a few counties already had nascent settlements that were close enough to the county's center to be chosen as the seat of government, namely Holly Springs, Oxford, and Pontotoc. Jefferson followed this pattern, although it otherwise demonstrates only the most cursory similarity to anything else on the frontier.

For example, the town of Jefferson began in the late 1790s as the site of the Chickasaw Agency, run by a Dr. Samuel Habersham, who was agent for decades, an unprecedented time in the history of Indian affairs bureaucracy. The site was initially known as "Habersham's" or simply "Habersham" long before it came to be known as Jefferson.[62] Faulkner demonstrates little familiarity with operations of the Chickasaw Agency, which during most of this time (late 1790s–1826) was located near the site of present-day Houlka, Mississippi. The settlement was eventually named Jefferson, purportedly to honor a mail rider on the Natchez Trace, Thomas Jefferson Pettigrew, by using his middle name![63] However, considering the unlikelihood of using a middle name for such an honor considering that few would even perceive the connection, one suspects that this was a joke by Faulkner, the greater probability being that the town was actually named after the most likely honoree, President Thomas Jefferson. A courthouse was constructed to store the record book—as a shed-room addition to a jail, all constructed without reference to or benefit of the county offices that provided for the recording and maintenance of records.

Despite the errors and deviations from known history, the story of the origins of Jefferson and Yoknapatawpha calls to mind a function of origin stories, that is to provide a tale that places its subject within the greater context of existence. Here, Faulkner provided a beginning for the Yoknapatawpha mythos, which like the story of the opening of the Chickasaw Cession served as an origin myth that placed the events and localities into a larger context, pointing to a mythic dimension latent in much local history.

After the land was opened for sale and settlement, the population of Tippah County rapidly grew. By 1838 it had reached 5,080, with 3,823 white (75 percent) and 1,257 enslaved Black (25 percent). By 1840, the population had more than doubled, reaching 10,434. By 1850 it had almost doubled again, reaching 20,741, after which the growth rate began to level off, reaching 22,550 in 1860 (16,206 white [72 percent] and 6,344 Black [28 percent]). Ripley developed a population of a few hundred, which by 1860 reached 683.[64]

As land and towns were developed, attention turned to the promise of the new transportation technology, the railroad. With little experience of their use and construction cost, promoters nevertheless chartered railroads with abandon, while supporters freely subscribed capital that they may or may not have actually possessed. In his study of the building of an antebellum Southern railroad, Thomas D. Clark evocatively describes the environment of railroad promotions:

Southerners were romantic dreamers first and experience made of them practical builders afterwards. Nothing pleased them more than a grand flourish at the beginning of their projects. While their northern brothers were earnestly working toward the improvement of their communities, they were spending time in making long-winded speeches and impossible prophecies.[65]

Promotions that linked nascent towns to projected railroads were numerous. For example, in 1836 the newly founded seat of Chickasaw County, Houston, advertised lots with the promise that the town was located "within a few miles of the route surveyed for the Nashville and New-Orleans Rail-Road."[66] The following year the legislature chartered the Pontotoc, Oxford, and Delta Railroad Company, which planned to build a road from Pontotoc west through Oxford and Panola to the town of Delta on the Mississippi River. Promoters included Jeff Word of Pontotoc and Charles G. Butler of Oxford. Butler's granddaughter Maud Butler would years later marry Word's great-great-nephew, Murry Falkner, and their first-born son was William Faulkner.[67] Other railroads chartered in northern Mississippi at the time included the Aberdeen and Pontotoc Railroad and Banking Company (1836), the Tallahatchie Railroad Company (1836), the Grenada Railroad Company (1837), the Hernando Railroad and Banking Company (1837), and the Paulding and Pontotoc Railroad Company (1838).[68]

The fate of the Aberdeen and Pontotoc Railroad and Banking Company suggests the fate of many. Linked to the company that had founded the town of Aberdeen, it was chartered to build a railroad from the Tombigbee River at Aberdeen to Pontotoc, with the project intended to promote the sale of lots in the town.[69] W. B. Wilkes, who was living in the area at the time, recalled how the project played out:

> On the morning before the [Aberdeen] lot sales, on 15th of January, 1836, [Robert] Gordon [the founder of Aberdeen] subscribed $40,000 to the Railroad company; others subscribed liberally; the talk was the Road would be running in 2 years.
>
> It was flush times, anyway and the price of lots, under the spur went up beyond all bounds. Now came the beauty of those flush subscriptions. Gordon, and others, after the sale, refused to close up their subscriptions; they were worth no more than blank paper, but they had accomplished the purpose in view—the sales footed up $115,000.00 for the first lots sold. . . .
>
> To comply with the charter, it was required that work on the Railroad should commence by a specified date. Dr. Anderson (then living in Aberdeen) was the

President of the Railroad company. Before the specified date, he and about a dozen others, took a spade and a bottle of champagne, went to where the depot had been located, on the banks of the river. . . . Dr. Anderson stuck the spade in the ground and turned the spade full of dirt, then drank the bottle of champagne, returned to town and reported work had been commenced on the Aberdeen and Pontotoc Railroad. That secured the continuance of the bank charter. But that spade full was the first and last work done on that railroad.[70]

This railroad and the others all came to naught; not a mile was constructed, implying that it was easier to imagine a railroad than to build one.

Chapter 2

◆━━◇━━━◇━━◆

Arrival in Mississippi

In the early 1840s, Ripley was little more than a collection of newly built houses and stores of modest construction on a rudimentary system of unpaved, ungraveled streets clustered around a brick monolith, the courthouse. At this time yet another member of the Word clan, W. C. Falkner, was drawn to the Chickasaw Cession lands in Mississippi. Until that time, he had still been living with his family in Saline Township, Ste. Genevieve County, Missouri, where they are listed in the 1840 census. The family apparently was not flourishing economically, so for a young man coming of age the prospects in Mississippi must have looked good, with so many Word relatives to possibly assist him, including a former congressman.[1] His year of arrival in the state is not clear—it appears that he first arrived in Pontotoc—although his 1842 arrival in Ripley after leaving Pontotoc is fairly certain.[2] The story of his arrival in Mississippi became the primary element in a Horatio Alger–like rags-to-riches story, which became embellished with questionable motifs.

In 1859, an article appeared in *Quid Nunc*, a newspaper in Grand Junction, Tennessee, that presented a biographical sketch of Falkner's life. Little about the author or his sources is known, and the story is filled with errors and few facts. However, it represents a significant development in the mythologizing of his origins. According to this account, at the age of seventeen and following his father's death, Falkner was determined to "better his fortune" and left his home, which is erroneously reported to be in Blount County, Tennessee, and traveled by steamboat to Memphis, ultimately bound for Pontotoc and his uncle T. J. "Jeff" Word. Upon arriving in Memphis, he began walking:

> [Covering] twenty-five miles the first day, (his money having entirely given out,) he stopped and cut a cord of wood for an old gentleman, living on the road side, who paid him in provisions, ready cooked. Thus supplied with "rations" for

37

the "campaign" into Mississippi, he pursued his journey, and when night came, kindled a fire by a log, ate his own bread and meat, which he had earned by the sweat of his brow, and slept upon the ground. Arriving at Tippah river, he found his provisions growing scarce, and was compelled to sell his coat to the ferry-man for one dollar and a passage across the river.

In due time, . . . our young friend arrived at Pontotoc, where to his great mortification, he found that his uncle, Col. Word, had removed to Ripley. The very next day, however, he set out for that place, which he reached the same day, barefooted, without a coat, but with thirty cents "in clean cash" in his pocket.

It is an honest and worthy boast of Gen. Falkner,[3] that during his journey . . . he never received a single cent of money or a morsel of food as a charitable donation, but faithfully worked on the steamboats and by the roadside for all that he got.[4]

The article termed this "the darkest period of his life," following which upon settling in Ripley and relying upon his own industry he would set out on a course of success.

Almost three decades later, Falkner told a variant account of his arrival in Mississippi. In spring 1886 he was riding high astride the world. Having built a railroad that connected Ripley with the outside world, he had begun an extension intended to carry the railroad southward to New Albany, Pontotoc, and points beyond. With the intent of raising funds, he visited the town of Pontotoc, where local expectations were running high.

While staying at the Roberson House Hotel, Falkner responded to enthusiastic supporters with an address that—with his penchant for the theatrical and the melodramatic—was "as touching as [it was] beautiful." He recalled his humble origins in his first arrival in Pontotoc nearly a half century before when he came by foot from Memphis to meet his uncle T. J. Word, then a resident of Pontotoc. Upon arrival, he discovered that his uncle had left the previous day for Aberdeen. "He was a poor, sick, ragged, barefoot, penniless boy. His cup of sorrow was filled to the brim." He sat down on the steps of a hotel and "wept bitterly, as though his heart would break." A little girl found him in this state and, empathizing with his plight, obtained money to pay for a room in the hotel until his uncle returned. Falkner never forgot the little girl, marrying her in Pontotoc years later, clearly alluding to his second and then current wife, the former Elizabeth "Lizzie" Houston Vance. As Falkner finished the story, he "became so affected that utterances failed him, and he had to pause until his emotion subsided."[5]

Although true in part, the story was embellished for rhetorical purposes. Falkner was no stranger to the use of embellishment to captivate his audience. For example, it's certain that neither of his future wives were involved—neither resided in the state at the time—so the claim that the little girl would become his future wife was probably added for melodramatic effect. Nevertheless, indications are that Falkner arrived in Pontotoc to link up with his uncle T. J. Word in 1840–1842, which is to say between his departure from Missouri and his arrival in Ripley. It is probable that he descended the Mississippi River from Missouri to Memphis via steamboat and from there walked to Pontotoc, although it is possible that, despite the tales to the contrary, he traveled on one of the stagecoaches that crisscrossed the area.

Upon arriving in Pontotoc, he wasn't entering an area with only one relative. He was arriving at the epicenter of Word family settlement. Not only was there Jeff Word, but within the distance of a county or two, there were two other Word uncles—James and Cuthbert—along with two aunts—Justiania Word Thompson and Elizabeth Word Humphreys—to say nothing of several Word cousins. By the end of the 1850s, the Word clan would be supplemented by the arrival in Ripley of Falkner's mother, Caroline, and two children; and grandmother, Justiania Dickinson Word.

Soon after Falkner arrived in Pontotoc to reside with his uncle, Jeff Word left Pontotoc and moved to Ripley, a move that was associated with his involvement with the Mississippi Union Bank. As noted, there was a branch office in Ripley, and throughout 1841 and 1842 there was correspondence between Word and Samuel Craig, the cashier in Ripley, and between Word and John Davis, an agent for the bank. Much of this concerned problems that the bank was facing, and eventually Davis and Craig gave possession of the bank to Word, which required that he move to Ripley. He and his family moved between July 15 and September 8, 1842, and almost certainly brought young Falkner with them, with the dates corresponding well with the 1842 date suggested above.[6] The Words established a home across Siddell Street from the Thompsons.[7] However, soon after arriving in Ripley, the Mississippi Union Bank collapsed, but by that time he had other lines of income, partly involving a law partnership with his brother-in-law J. W. Thompson.[8] During the summer of 1843, Word was called away from Ripley when the US Board of Choctaw Commissioners appointed him as their agent to collect testimonies and examine county records pertaining to land claims by Choctaw Indians. Leaving his young wife and infant children behind in Ripley, he worked for the next few months in remnant Choctaw settlements with names such as

Hopahka and the Yazoo Old Village and in newly established courthouses in the Choctaw Cession counties.[9]

The arrival of Word and Falkner in Ripley closely coincided with the founding of the *Ripley Advertiser* in October 1842 by John F. Ford.[10] Founded as a Whig newspaper, it eventually shifted its allegiance to the Democratic Party and continued to be published through 1896. Ford and his son and successor, Richard F. Ford, were friends and supporters of Falkner over the decades. Word's brother-in-law, Alexander M. Jackson, an attorney, and his law partner, Nathaniel S. Price, served in 1845 as editors of the newspaper while Ford continued as its proprietor.

After arriving in Ripley, Falkner found himself associated with another prominent kinsman, his uncle J. W. Thompson, who in 1842 was elected district attorney and would later serve as legislator and circuit judge. The mytholo-gized accounts of Falkner's early years claimed that he arrived in Ripley "a poor penniless boy."[11] He may well have been penniless upon arrival in Mississippi, but he was not without the resources that family connections provided.

Falkner perhaps initially resided with his uncle Jeff Word, but by 1845 he was living with the Thompsons.[12] While it is not known why Falkner moved from the household of one family member to that of another, a contributing factor must have been convenience. Jeff Word and his wife had small chil-dren, while the Thompsons were childless and prone to taking in and raising children. Furthermore, Jeff Word soon left Ripley. About the first of January, 1846, he moved to the larger town of Holly Springs, where he established a law partnership with H. W. Walter,[13] and in December 1856 he moved to Palestine, Texas, where he spent the rest of his life.[14]

With his attorney uncles as his primary connections, it is not surprising that Falkner became an attorney. Exactly when he was admitted to the bar is not known. But given the fact that two of his uncles were attorneys, as was Jeff Word's brother-in-law Alexander M. Jackson, he was almost certainly exposed to the practice of law immediately after his arrival in Mississippi. He eventu-ally read law probably under both of his uncles and by 1850 was admitted to the bar[15] and listed in partnership with Thompson under the name Thompson & Falkner, a partnership that remained through 1858, when Thompson was elected circuit judge and had to withdraw from legal practice.[16] Other mem-bers of the Ripley legal community in 1851 were Alexander M. Jackson & Nathaniel S. Price, Orlando Davis, Thomas C. Hindman Jr., William J. Maclin, Daniel B. Wright, and H. F. Morrison & James Keenan.[17]

Of Falkner's formal education, little is known. While his family could not afford much, he nevertheless had some formal training. In his 1884 travelogue

Rapid Ramblings in Europe, he alluded to studying as a schoolboy classical texts such as the works of Cicero and Julius Caesar.[18] His early exposure to books bore fruit in his fertile mind.[19] An analysis of quotations and literary references in his 1881 novel *The White Rose of Memphis* indicates an interest in and familiarity with primarily Shakespeare, the Bible, and Sir Walter Scott. Other than these he also was familiar with Byron, Cervantes, Defoe, Dickens, Homer, Milton, Swift, and Twain, among others. In sum, he "liked literature and made an important place for it in a busy and turbulent life in a way that his counterparts in our days could hardly imagine, much less practice."[20] Although this analysis was of a work written in 1880–1881, it is indicative of interests that began decades earlier.[21] Falkner's interests in literature and history, as we shall see, would also become manifest in *Rapid Ramblings in Europe*.

Although, as has been pointed out, Falkner did not belong to a particular Christian denomination, he certainly regarded himself as a Christian. This is indicated in part by his support of various local churches and also by comments in *Rapid Ramblings* in which he frequently alludes to biblical events while referring to Jesus as the Savior and the Christ. This allegiance is also manifest in *White Rose*.

Falkner was also a member of the Masonic Lodge. Ripley Lodge no. 47 of the Free and Accepted Masons was given a dispensation in 1840 and chartered in 1841, a year before Falkner's arrival. He was certainly a lodge member by 1847 and may have joined a year or so earlier.[22] Membership in the Masonic Lodge did not require adherence to any particular religious sect, although it did require a belief in God, and much of Masonic teaching and ritual centers on God the Great Architect of the universe along with the construction and symbology of the Solomonic Temple in Jerusalem. The Ripley Lodge was housed from about 1850 in the second story of the Ripley Methodist Church, and there it continued meeting until 1864 when the church was burned down along with much of the town.[23]

Chapter 3

◈━━◇━━◈

Things That Go Bump in the Night
The McCannon Affair

When the sun goes down and light vanishes into the dark, the clear and familiar become ambiguous and strange. Night brings the cover of darkness behind which evil acts unseen. This is also the realm of the imagination where the numinous and fearful both repel and attract. This fascination at the center of the imagination founds our interest in the macabre, ghost stories, murder mysteries, and film noir. It was closely connected to Falkner's first appearance in history.

Soon after his arrival in Ripley, a crime occurred in Tippah County that shocked and enraged the public, and the story appeared in newspapers around the country. In the vortex of the fascination circling this event, Falkner at the age of twenty delved into it, writing and publishing an account of the crime as seen through the eyes of the perpetrator.

In early June 1845, a family departed from Pontotoc in a wagon filled with household furniture bound for an unknown destination to the north. The party consisted of Beverly A. Adcock,[1] his wife Paralee Paradise Adcock, his mother Sarah Adcock, two children (a boy and a girl),[2] and two slave boys, Cook, aged eleven, and Abram, or Abe, aged ten.[3] After passing through Ripley, the family followed the road northward on the east side of Muddy Creek toward Pocahontas and Jackson, Tennessee. About eight miles north of Ripley, they stayed overnight with an "Isaac Friar,"[4] and while there met a peddler named Andrew Jackson McCannon of Columbus, Mississippi. McCannon was described as "a middle sized man" with "blue eyes." "Rather badly dressed," he was "dull in conversation" and had "the appearance of dissipation."[5] The following day the Adcocks continued northward, while McCannon in his horse-drawn carriage tagged along.

On the evening of Sunday, June 8, the family camped about a mile south of the Tennessee state line on the south side of Bearman Creek. That night the moon was a thin crescent in the west that set early, plunging the night into almost complete darkness. After dining, the Adcocks went to bed to prepare for another hard day of travel. When McCannon judged them to be asleep, he drew out his axe and crept up on the sleeping couple. Standing over them, he could hear them breathing before he began swinging the axe, dispatching them with a few chops to their torsos and necks. He then proceeded to dispatch those who remained:

> By this time the old lady . . . was awakened, he therefore commenced the attack on her, a fight ensued, and the noise made by them aroused the little negroes who say that the old lady, though covered with blood, defended herself with frightful and desperate ferocity. The inhuman monster, however, succeeded.[6]

He then approached the two small white children, who were probably awake and crying with no one to console them, and expeditiously cut their throats while sparing the lives of the Black boys, undoubtedly because they had monetary value. However, he let them know that they would suffer a similar fate if they divulged what they had witnessed. One can only imagine their trauma and terror. McCannon collected the Adcocks' money, valuables, slaves, and two horses. Leaving his carriage and the Adcock wagon, he departed hurriedly northward on horseback to put as many miles behind him as possible.[7] He crossed Bearman Creek and soon after the state line of Tennessee and headed north toward Jackson, Tennessee. Behind him, the vacated campsite was littered with blood and gore.

The next day, Monday the ninth, came with its June heat accelerating the decay. Passersby never noticed the vacated campsite off to the side of the road. In those days, hogs were allowed to range freely, finding sustenance in the woods. Hogs are omnivorous; they eat plants along with small animals such as snakes as well as the carrion from larger animals. A herd of ranging hogs wandered onto the scene of carnage. The remains of the Adcocks were discovered on Tuesday morning. Body parts were scattered over the site. The bodies of two of the victims were considerably eaten. The *Ripley Advertiser* provided a graphic description of the carnage:

> [T]heir throats [were] cut and their bodies most inhumanly mangled.—The body of Mr. Adcock was split open diagonally from the breast bone; and his

wife by his side was also much mangled. The head of the old lady was nearly cleft in two. She was on her knees, reclining on the body of her son-in-law. The body of the youngest child was nearly eaten up by the hogs.[8]

The people who first arrived at the scene looked about for clues to the identities of the murderer and his victims. After rummaging through the family's possessions, they found a Bible. Inside, they found the name Beverly Adcock of Pontotoc.[9]

Considerable excitement and horror ensued as news of the discovery spread throughout the neighborhood. Newspapers would almost shriek their indignation: "Can it be possible that a sane man can be so unutterably guilty and depraved as to murder five innocent, fellow beings, in their silent midnight sleep, and two of them babes or children, and all for a few dollars?"[10] For those surveying the scene of the crime, it was readily apparent that customary funeral practices were neither practical nor possible. Consequently, all the body parts that could be located were collected and probably placed into one or two coffins. A hole was excavated at the site and the remains placed within. A prayer was said and the hole backfilled.[11] The shocked attendees pieced together as best as they could what had happened, and who the culprit was and where he had gone, and then organized a posse to follow in pursuit. In the midst of this activity, the northbound stagecoach arrived, having passed through Pontotoc and Ripley bound for Jackson, Tennessee, and Nashville. The driver and passengers were all briefed on the crime, then the stage continued on its way. That evening, McCannon passed through Jackson.

The following morning, Wednesday the eleventh, the stagecoach arrived in Jackson with news of the crime. Some bystanders recalled seeing a white man with two little Black boys who had wasted no time in exiting town on the road toward Nashville. About this time the posse from Tippah County arrived, but their horses were too exhausted to continue the pursuit.[12] However, others took their place with about "six or eight gentlemen" of Jackson following in pursuit. At Spring Creek about sixteen miles northeast of Jackson they came upon a crowd, and in its midst was the stagecoach that had passed by the scene of the murder the day before. The passengers along with men from Spring Creek had apprehended McCannon with the two boys. Blood was found on his knife and pants. One of the boys stated that he had frequently attempted to wash the blood off but to no avail.

With McCannon captured, the posse escorted him back to Jackson, where they were met by an outraged crowd of two to three hundred people. The local press reported that the crowd was so "incensed at this savage butchery, that it was seriously thought by some, he would be dealt with without the ordinary process of law." Nevertheless, the forces of law and order won out over the mob, and McCannon was placed in jail for the night.[13]

On Friday, June 13, McCannon was turned over to a group from Tippah County who escorted him the seventy miles back to Ripley.[14] Because the crime had taken place in Tippah, he would be tried in that county's circuit court. One of his escorts was almost certainly the young W. C. Falkner, who was introduced by *Ripley Advertiser* editor John F. Ford as "a young man than whom, for unexceptionable morals, integrity of character and a high sense of honor, no young man in this community stands higher." Ford elaborated that Falkner, "at the hour of midnight, mounted his horse and rode twenty miles, as one of the Sheriff's posse, to aid in bringing McCannon under the control of the civil authorities."[15] The party arrived back in Ripley on Saturday evening, but "owing to the popular excitement" a mob surrounded the guards and briefly took McCannon from them, preventing them from jailing him until Monday evening.[16] During this tension, as Ford recalled, Falkner "stood in the front ranks when cocked guns were presented to resist the execution of that officer's process."[17] After the guards reclaimed McCannon, he was carried to a place safe from the mob and remained there for two days before being transferred to the county jail, where he remained until his trial.

The trial began on Friday, October 3, presided over by Nathaniel S. Price, who had only recently been appointed circuit judge.[18] Price was formerly a member of the Tippah County bar and had coedited the *Ripley Advertiser* for a few months in 1845. The prosecutor was almost certainly J. W. Thompson, the district attorney at the time.

Yesterday [October 3], for which day the case was set, McCannon was placed at the bar for trial. . . . Twelve or fifteen witnesses appeared on the part of the State, none on the part of the prisoner. Counsel on both sides acquitted themselves with great ability. But the counsel for the defendant exerted themselves in vain; the evidence was too strong to be successfully resisted.—The jury retired about half past seven o'clock, P.M., and returned after being absent about ten minutes, with a verdict of "Guilty." This morning [October 4] at nine o'clock sentence of death was passed upon him by the court, accompanied by appropriate remarks. The first of November is the day set for his execution. He received the sentence with the same composed hardihood he evinced throughout the progress of the trial.[19]

McCannon was incarcerated in the Tippah County jail from June 16 until November 1. During this time, he became the subject of a morbid curiosity on the part of the public. From this arose a demand that resulted in the first publication by young W. C. Falkner, a pamphlet fully entitled *The Life and Confessions of Andrew Jackson McCannon, Tried and Sentenced for the Murder of the Adcock Family, and Executed at Ripley, Miss., November 1st, 1845, Detailed by Himself, While in Prison, under the Sentence of Death*. This was a more or less firsthand account of McCannon's life and his final crime.[20] The publication of death-row confessions was not uncommon.[21] The editor of the *Ripley Advertiser* provided background to the confession and its publication. When McCannon returned to Ripley under guard in June and had been wrested from his guards, he apparently promised his captors that "if they would allow him time, he would prepare and leave them a narrative of his life, including all the circumstances of the murder."[22] This promise whetted the appetites of the curious already enthralled by the horror of the murder. According to Ford, "hundreds of individuals . . . visited the criminal and conversed with him in prison, learned his story and told it abroad, in detached portions, to hundreds of others—a means of dissemination best adapted to exaggerate than diminish those parts reflecting upon individuals."[23]

The editor continued:

> The conversations subsequently had with him, whilst he was in prison, by various individuals, and related abroad by them, but increased the desire manifested on all sides to see a full report of his confessions. There was a general wish to have M'Cannon's story, true or false; and that too just as he himself told it. After his condemnation, therefore, the publication of his narrative was urged not only by citizens of this, but of the adjoining counties, and its execution suggested to different individuals.[24]

Aware of this demand, "Mr. Falkner procured a copy of the narrative, as given by M'Cannon himself, and had it published. In so doing, he but responded to the call made by the public."[25] This implies that the narrative was initially composed by McCannon himself, then given to Falkner; however, this was not the case. It was indeed written by Falkner but in the first person as though told by McCannon. This is evidenced in part by a passage from the pamphlet indicating that the text was "as given by M'Cannon."[26] A paragraph from the pamphlet as copied into a newspaper article illustrates the first-person perspective. Besides being the only known surviving passage from the publication, it is the earliest known example of Falkner's writing:

I then returned to Tuscumbia, where my family had remained, and then got into a rather expensive difficulty. A man named Henry Williams was indebted to me $132[.]oo, balance on some horses and a wagon I had sold to him. He took the Bankrupt act, and then laughed at me, saying he had paid me in full by his oath. I told the gentleman I wished him to keep away from me; but he showed no such disposition. I armed myself with a cow-hide, met him in the street, and administered it well. And although he struck me first, with a stick, which I took from him, I had to pay $125[.]oo for my evening's amusement.[27]

Alfred C. Matthews, editor of Tuscumbia, Alabama's, newspaper, the *Franklin Democrat*, thought that the pamphlet wasn't actually written by McCannon, because it was "*embellished* in a style and language of which M'Cannon was incapable."[28] The editor of the *Ripley Advertiser* took exception to the use of "embellished," which implied that the "substance of the narrative" had been altered. He elaborated:

We presume every man who has read the pamphlet was aware, whilst he was perusing it, that it did not, in all instances, pretend to give the *exact words* which M'Cannon uttered, nor to adhere to the *precise form of language* in which that individual's story fell from his lips. . . . Such minute exactness is not adhered to in giving a second-handed version of any transaction. It is not even strictly carried out in taking down an individual's *testimony*, in which case, of all others, it is most important to get as near as possible the deponent's exact words. All that is necessary in preparing an ordinary narration of incidents detailed by another person is to express distinctly what the party says, using his own words or such as will meet that condition. This done, the narrative becomes, to all intents and purposes, as much the narrator's own as though it had been taken down in his precise language.[29]

The narrative provided McCannon's own account of the murder and also sketched out his background including his arrival at the Muscle Shoals area of Alabama in 1839 and soon after his marriage to Peggy Ann Gibson of Courtland, Alabama.[30] Afterward, he moved to Tuscumbia, where he opened a cake and beer shop, which his wife operated while he worked as a day laborer.[31]

Years later, M. C. Gallaway, the longtime newspaper editor and publisher and friend of Falkner's, told a story about how Falkner's pamphlet came to be published. Although the version we have has several errors,[32] details of the pamphlet's publication do coincide with the history of publishing in Memphis in 1845:

> Col. Matt C. Gallaway tells an interesting story of how Col. W. C. Falkner got his start in life. . . . Two weeks before the time fixed for the hanging young Falkner entered the jail and extorted a confession from the doomed man. He wrote it out and hurried to Memphis on horseback for the purpose of having it printed in pamphlet form. He showed the manuscript to Col. [Henry L.] Guion,[33] business manager of the Evening Enquirer,[34] and father of H. L. Guion [1852–1899]. He told Guion he did not have a dollar, and asked him if he could print the matter on credit immediately. Guion read it and saw the story was thrillingly interesting and agreed to give credit for the $200 charged for the printing. Three thousand copies were printed [and] in order to carry the pamphlets to Jacinto [*sic*; should be Ripley] a one-horse cart was hired. Falkner reached home late the night before the execution.[35]

November 1, 1845—the day set for McCannon's execution—was on a Saturday, the day of the week that found the most people in town. However, given the occasion, there was a far larger crowd than normal, estimated at four thousand. The square took on the character of a combination camp meeting and carnival, a theater of the macabre replete with a sermon, prayers, and a freak show. It was an opportune time for Falkner to offer his pamphlet for sale, and this he did, circulating through the crowd selling them for one dollar a copy, no small sum in those days when $2.50 could purchase a year's subscription to the *Ripley Advertiser*.

At about 10:45, McCannon was brought out of the jail accompanied by Sheriff Samuel N. Pryor, guards, and a Reverend Roden, who was present at McCannon's request. There was relatively little preparation. A scaffold would have afforded a drop that would have mercifully broken the criminal's neck. However, none was constructed. Instead, a cart was placed under a tree—one of the few remnants of the forest primeval allowed to survive for purposes of shade on the courthouse grounds—and a rope was dangled from a limb. This afforded no drop; the prisoner would indeed "swing" as the cart was driven from beneath him, leaving him dangling until he died by strangulation.

In the meantime, the cart served as a podium for a spectacle that played out over the next two hours and more. The editor of the *Advertiser*, A. M. Jackson at the time, recorded the event: "Upon mounting the cart, holy services were commenced by singing an appropriate hymn; after which the Reverend gentleman offered up a fervent and affecting prayer in behalf of the doomed man." Another hymn was sung, then Reverend Roden delivered an "impressive discourse" upon Jeremiah 22–23, a text especially selected by McCannon. Roden concluded his sermon with another prayer, then announced that McCannon wished to speak to the crowd:

> He did so at some length, but rather disconnectedly. We cannot give even an abstract of his remarks. He expressed himself ready to meet his end, even in so shameful and ignominious a manner; protested his innocence of the crime for which he was to die; exhorted those assembled to embrace religion and meet him in heaven; and concluded by wishing them farewell and invoking upon them the blessings of God. A few moments were given him, at his request, for prayer. He prayed aloud, and prayed in an appropriate and very affecting style. He evinced much emotion during the service. Many of the crowd were much moved. After rising from his knees, he made a few more remarks, and, on his conclusion, the Sheriff proceeded to adjust the rope.[36]

Whereas McCannon had apparently provided a detailed confession of his crime to Falkner, when he faced retribution for his crime, he vigorously protested his innocence. The protests must have seemed hollow to the onlookers who had invested a dollar—a not inconsequential sum at the time—to purchase and read a copy of the killer's confession. At about 1:30, the cart was driven out from under him, leaving him dangling a few feet above the ground struggling to breathe. After four or five minutes, his legs then his body moved convulsively, and it was over. The *Advertiser* concluded: "Thus died Andrew J. McCannon, convicted of one of the grossest murders upon the records of any country."[37]

The McCannon affair provides a first glimpse of Falkner's innovativeness and sense of the flamboyant along with his ability to turn unorthodox situations into lucrative ones. The affair was a financial boon for him. According to Gallaway's recollection, he sold about 2,300 copies at $1 apiece, after which he returned to Memphis to pay Guion the $200 owed him. If this is correct, Falkner cleared $2,100.[38] Several months later the pamphlet was still offered for sale by the Southern Literary Emporium, a Memphis bookstore.[39]

Following the execution, McCannon's body was possibly displayed for a time to titillate the curious and later buried, probably in an out-of-the-way corner of Ripley Cemetery.[40] However, at some unknown time possibly before burial, the head was removed. It was not uncommon to publicly display skeletal material from executed criminals who had some notoriety.[41] By 1888, McCannon's skull was in the possession of phrenologist William

Windsor, who lectured to large crowds on phrenology and popular topics such as "How to Become Rich" and "How to be Healthy and Handsome." Windsor's public presentations were accompanied by his collection of skulls, which he used to illustrate the behavioral characteristics that were evidenced in their configuration.

Speaking to a reporter for the *Los Angeles Tribune*, Windsor held McCannon's skull up and announced: "This is the skull of Andrew J. McCannon, executed in Mississippi, more than forty years ago, for the murder of the Adcock family." He compared the skull to the head of a murderer named Fritz Anschlag then on death row in Los Angeles, stating emphatically that the McCannon skull exemplified "a case of moral idiocy more pronounced than Anschlag's."[42] A few years later, Windsor observed that the McCannon skull was the most valuable in his collection. He considered it worth $300, although people, so he claimed, had offered him as much as $800 for it.[43] Why he did not accept the $800, he did not say.

Chapter 4

❖⸺◇⸺◇⸺❖

Mexico
Going to See the Elephant

As the McCannon affair was running its course, international events were developing that would briefly thrust young Falkner onto an international stage, providing his first look at the outside world. In 1845, as the Republic of Texas was moving toward becoming another state in the United States, it brought with it a dispute over the boundary with Mexico. For Texas the boundary was the Rio Grande, while for Mexico it was the Nueces River, which lay farther to the north leaving a strip of contested land between the rivers known as the "Nueces Strip."

In anticipation of the annexation of Texas, President James K. Polk ordered General Zachary Taylor to move US troops into Texas. After these troops were moved into the disputed Nueces Strip, they were confronted by Mexican forces under General Mariano Arista at the Battles of Palo Alto (May 8, 1846) and Resaca de la Palma (May 9, 1846), with Arista withdrawing. On May 13, the US Congress approved a declaration of war against Mexico. On May 17, after crossing the Rio Grande, Taylor occupied the town of Matamoros, which Arista had abandoned the night before.

As news of these events spread, men clamored to volunteer, to drop their family life and profession and head to places they had never dreamed of before. Few anticipated that their experience would be far different and far more ambiguous than their expectations. On Thursday, May 14, a meeting was held in Ripley to organize a volunteer company to join Taylor "in the event a requisition should be made" upon the state governor; meeting attendees had no knowledge of the declaration of war.[1] Two weeks later, a volunteer company of seventy-seven had been organized with officers who included A. M. Jackson, lawyer and one-time editor (age twenty-two) as captain; W. C. Falkner (age twenty) as first lieutenant; and T. C. Hindman Jr. (age eighteen),

51

son of a prominent planter, as second lieutenant. Hindman's older brother, Robert H. Hindman (age twenty-four), later became second sergeant. The Hindmans were members of a prominent planting family that lived two miles east of Ripley. After purchasing land, the family arrived in 1842 and built an imposing two-story house.[2] The men were regarded as "brave, fearless, high-strung . . . aggressive in the extreme, and rather inclined to be reckless."[3] They would figure large in Falkner's life over the next few years and not always for the good.

Falkner's election to the second-highest rank is testimony of his popularity among his peers. Of course, there was very little military experience among the new volunteers except for a few having possibly belonged to a local militia. The company was named the "Tippah Guards," while a second company was in the process of being formed under the command of Falkner's uncle, J. W. Thompson, as captain.[4] Jackson soon marched his company to a field six miles west of Ripley, where they established a camp and drilling ground. For about two weeks "they drilled by day, posting and relieving guard and pickets by night, and played soldier"[5] while remaining "ready to march at a moment's warning, into the service of the United States."[6]

On May 29, 1846, President Polk called for states to furnish infantry regiments for the war effort; Mississippi was to supply one regiment. In response, Mississippi governor Albert G. Brown issued a proclamation on June 1 for ten companies to assemble at Vicksburg and form the regiment.[7] On Friday, June 5, news of the proclamation was received in Ripley. However, editor J. F. Ford reported that Vicksburg was already crowded with volunteers and that it was "impossible for a company from this distance to Vicksburg, to be marched into service before the whole requisition shall be filled up by companies nearer the place of rendezvous."[8] Two weeks later Ford noted that, as predicted, "there is now a violent struggle among the different volunteer companies of our State to get into the Regiment to be raised. Twenty-five Companies have tendered themselves; and of course, the call limiting the Companies required to ten has bitterly disappointed a large number."[9] The following week he reported that the ten companies were all filled, which left many out.[10] The "Pontotoc Rovers," for example, traveled the entire distance from Pontotoc to Vicksburg via Memphis only to be rejected and return home.[11] Fearing the worst, the Tippah Guards never attempted the long trek. Meanwhile, they returned to daily life and waited for another requisition of troops.

The ten companies selected were organized into the First Mississippi Rifles led by Colonel Jefferson Davis, a West Point graduate who resigned his seat in Congress to serve. The regiment would receive considerable fame as they accompanied General Taylor at the Battles of Monterrey (September 21–24, 1846) and Buena Vista (February 22–23, 1847).

In November, President Polk issued another call for volunteers and authorized Governor Brown to raise another regiment. The Tippah Guards emerged from dormancy with its members reenlisting in early December. The captain and lieutenants would remain the same as first elected, that is Jackson as captain and Falkner and Hindman as lieutenants. The number of troops in the company had increased from 77 to 111, which probably included the initial members along with members from the second company that was being organized under J. W. Thompson. Falkner relatives were well represented. Captain Jackson's sister, Mary, was married to Falkner's uncle Jeff Word, while Jeff's brother Cuthbert was enlisted along with a cousin, David W. Humphreys. The volunteers had to wait a month before being ordered to report in Vicksburg. They then marched to Memphis arriving on January 1, embarked on a steamer the same evening, and disembarked the next day. All incoming companies were moved to Camp McClung three miles north of town to organize the regiment that became the Second Mississippi Rifles; the Tippah Guards became Company E. Elections were held on the eighth, and Reuben Davis of Aberdeen, an attorney and politician with no previous military experience, was elected colonel. He regretted his selection almost from the start.[12]

At Camp McClung, the unseasonably warm weather took a change for the worse; bitter cold and rain set in followed by sickness in the form of influenza, pneumonia, and rheumatism.[13] It was an omen of things to come. Sickness would constantly plague the Tippah Guards and other troops. During the Mexican War, ten times as many troops died of disease as were killed in action.

The companies were placed on river steamers for transfer to New Orleans, where volunteers from several states were converging. At least two members of the regiment died while on the river.[14] The Tippah Guards arrived on January 17 to await ships to transfer them to Mexico and camped below the city on "the Battleground" at Chalmette, the site of the 1815 Battle of New Orleans. Conditions were again miserable due to inclement weather. As many as seven a day in the regiment died while camped there. Initially, even the sick and dying were prevented from being housed in regular structures. Boredom, resentment, and lack of discipline led to incidents of violence between volunteers and local citizens. The approximately eight hundred troops of the Mississippi regiment were eventually crowded onto three ships. The Tippah Guards and three other companies boarded the *Henry Pratt*, which departed on January 30. After descending the Mississippi, the ships passed into the Gulf bound for Mexico. Over the next few weeks illness continued, and burials at sea were common, including that of Stephen Jones of the Tippah Guards. Food was poor and the men were packed below deck, so tempers ran high. At breakfast on February 17, Lieutenant Hindman smashed his plate over a steward's head, an action that exemplified the Hindmans' notorious aggressiveness.[15]

Falkner later recalled, not without hyperbole, an unfortunate incident during stormy weather:

> While crossing the Gulf of Mexico . . . I saw a man instantly killed by a cask of water that was dashed against him. It first made a charge on the pantry, crushing the thin blank walls like an eggshell and demolishing everything in its way. A brave sailor attempted to capture it, when it threw him against the railing and then, by a sudden lurch of the ship, it was dashed against him with tremendous force, killing him on the spot. A perfect stampede then ensued, and a dozen men were detailed, who finally captured it.[16]

Along the way sealed orders that had been presented to Colonel Reuben Davis were read, revealing that their destination was the island of Lobos, the staging ground for General Winfield Scott's campaign. Heretofore, the war's major conflicts had been led by General Zachary Taylor in northeastern Mexico, but a new strategy was being initiated. Scott would strike at the heart of Mexico. First, he would capture the port city of Veracruz, then advance inland toward the capital, Mexico City. The possibility of involvement in such a campaign must have provided a sense of mission to the dispirited volunteers.

On February 18, their ships arrived at Lobos, and two days later the Tippah Guards were allowed to go ashore after being aboard ship for three weeks. The following day General Scott arrived, and new orders were presented to the regiment. Their destination had been changed. They were to be deployed back to the north to the mouth of the Rio Grande to join General Taylor. However, Taylor was on the verge of fighting and winning the Battle of Buena Vista on February 22–23, and the battle would be long over by the time the Second Mississippi arrived. The future of the war would lie with Scott. Soon after the Mississippians departed, Scott deployed his armada down the coast to Veracruz, where on March 9 he launched an amphibious invasion of ten thousand troops and began a siege that lasted until the city's surrender on the twenty-ninth. Afterward, he marched on Mexico City, which he occupied on September 14.

On the morning of the twenty-fourth, the Mississippi troops were shipped back to the north. Dr. Thomas N. Love, regimental surgeon, noted that the men were "all discouraged—They had no hopes of ever getting in a fight— some were delighted with the idea of going on to Monterey [*sic*], that if we did have to be stationed that was of course the best place."[17] By early March they reached the Rio Grande and were transported upstream to Matamoros.

Upon reaching Matamoros, the regiment had its first occurrence of small-pox, a disease that would plague them for weeks.[18] There also on March 14, Falkner's uncle Cuthbert Word was discharged from duty under a Surgeon's Certificate of Disability and transported back to New Orleans via military convoy. On the way home from New Orleans, he died near Baton Rouge.[19]

The Second Mississippi Regiment continued its trek inland from Matamoros and eventually arrived at Monterrey on April 6, more than three months after the Tippah Guards had departed from Ripley. The regiment marched into the city along a major thoroughfare lined with ancient flat-roofed buildings to the central plaza. Founded in 1596, Monterrey was the oldest and most exotic city—more so than New Orleans—that Falkner and his fellow troops had ever seen. He surely observed, as did Dr. Love, that "hundreds of ladies, and some very handsome too, were looking through their grated windows at us."[20]

From the plaza they marched northward and out of the city to the military camps, passing as they did under the infamous Black Fort around which much of the Battle of Monterrey had played out half a year before. As they marched through the camp of General Taylor, who had just returned from Buena Vista, the general stood watching them wearing a "ragged checked shirt" and "more ordinarily dressed than any one among them." Few in the regiment recognized him. The following year he would be elected president of the United States. The regiment was assigned a camp about a half mile from the general's, a place blessed with a nearby spring and numerous oak and walnut trees to provide welcome shade from the sun.[21] They would call the place "Walnut Springs,"[22] and from there they carried on daily life while patrolling the area.

While at Walnut Springs, Falkner heard the story of the young Mexican woman Doña María de Jesús Dosamantes, who during the battle for Monterrey had appeared before the Mexican general in chief donned in a captain's uniform and ready to fight. The general ordered her "to ride the whole line so that all the corps that make up this army would see her, and . . . show the respect due to her."[23] Even the American press called her a "second Joan of Arc," reporting that as she "paraded before the troops, [she] greatly excited and augmented their courage . . . [and she] led the charge of lancers which proved fatal to some of our command. . . . There's an example of hero-ism worthy of the days of old!"[24] Falkner was impressed by the erotic image. He later incorporated a young Mexican woman fighting in military garb into his two 1851 published works: *The Siege of Monterey*, with Isabel who dressed in uniform and fought against the Americans at Monterrey, and *The Spanish Heroine*, with Ellen Aakenzas doing the same.

Despite the merits of their campsite, disease was still rampant among the troops. On April 10, Dr. Love wrote a medical discharge for Joseph Goodman for an unspecified disease and noted that "the news of his discharge ran like wild fire through the camp, and in less than two hours, some home-sick fellows, who had seen enough of the army life, and felt enough of its bitter sufferings," presented themselves with exaggerated symptoms in hopes of also receiving discharges. On the twelfth, Love reported that the regimental commander, Colonel Reuben Davis, had procured a sixty-day furlough and gone home on "private business": "He has gained rapidly upon the affections of his regiment since we have been in camp. But now, to leave us so suddenly will do him injury[;] it will be discouraging to others and it will have an injurious influence."[25] He would return, briefly, in the summer but soon resigned on account of his health.[26]

Company commander Captain Jackson was also having problems. On March 10, he contracted diarrhea complicated by jaundice and nephritis.[27] By April 14 he had become so incapacitated that the command of the company devolved upon his increasingly restless first lieutenant, Falkner, who was suffering from the malaise that would continue to impede his careers in the military—that is, boredom and the inability of his restless mind to cope with the monotony of camp life replete with regimentation, disease, and lack of prospect. That day Falkner rode out of camp bound for a village known as Aguas Calientes about four miles away, a place described as a "very common resort" for regimental officers.[28] One does not know why officers were attracted to the place but suspects that women and alcohol were involved. Although there were no more active Mexican troops in the area, there was always the possibility of being attacked by irregulars, Mexicans resentful of the American presence. A few days earlier, one soldier, James Carson, allowed himself to be separated from the body of troops; he was caught and his throat was cut. The culprits were later captured and shot by a firing squad.[29]

Falkner had a similar encounter on the way to Aguas Calientes; about two miles from camp, he was fired upon by three Mexicans, wounding him and killing his horse. With his mount down he drew his pistol and Bowie knife,[30] preparing to defend himself, but his assailants fled. Early that afternoon Falkner was carried back to camp by troops who had found him. He had been shot in the left foot and left hand. One bullet had passed between the first and second metatarsals, smashing the second. The other struck the first phalanges

of three fingers. After reaching camp, an armed party was sent out to investigate.[31] They found Falkner's dead horse—nothing on it had been touched—but
the attackers had fled. Dr. Love had to amputate parts of two fingers, which
Falkner "bore with more nerve than any one I ever saw." This was one of the
few casualties suffered by the regiment from enemy fire. The speculation was
that the attack was motivated by revenge against the Americans.[32] On April 18,
Dr. Love certified that Falkner was unfit for his duties because of his wounds
and "will *not* be able to resume them in less than three months."[33] Five days
later, Dr. Love also discharged Sergeant Robert H. Hindman permanently on
the basis of disability.[34] However, neither Falkner nor Hindman could leave
immediately because of the smallpox outbreak.

As noted, the disease first appeared in the Second Mississippi at Matamoros.
Undiagnosed, it was carried along as the regiment marched deeper into
Mexico, infecting other regiments along the way. By late April there were
sixty-nine cases, earning the Second the name "the Infected Regiment." On the
twenty-fourth, General Taylor ordered that the regiment place a line of sentries around its camp to prevent anyone from leaving or entering. Regiments
camped nearby were to do likewise, thereby cutting off communication and
interaction between themselves and the Infected Regiment.[35]

On May 1, following urgings from his fellow officers, Captain Jackson asked
for and received a sixty-day leave of absence because of his ongoing medical
condition.[36] By this time, the quarantine on the Second Regiment had apparently been lifted. On May 2, Company G from Jefferson County left camp for
Camargo to the northeast to escort a wagon train. With them went Falkner,
Jackson, Robert Hindman, and other officers and troops who had been discharged or disabled.[37] Following a long journey, Falkner reached Ripley by
June. Soon after, he was examined by Dr. James B. Ellis,[38] a Ripley physician
who attested that "he will not be able to perform active military duty before
the middle of October or first of November. He is yet unable to put his foot
to the ground & small fragments of bone are passing out occasionally. His
general health is very good."[39]

Falkner's mind was on other matters, though. He began seeing the orphan
Holland R. Pearce, who had recently moved to Ripley with her siblings,[40] the
five children of Joseph Pearce Sr. and his wife Elizabeth Harrison Pearce.[41]
About 1831, the Pearces moved to the 1818 cession lands in western Tennessee
and settled in Weakley County, where Elizabeth died in 1835.[42] After Joseph
died in 1846 or earlier,[43] the children became dependents of their cousin
Simon R. Spight,[44] a prominent businessman of Ripley who became their legal

guardian and brought them to his home in Ripley, a two-story house that served as a hotel. It was located on Commerce Street, a block north of the J. W. Thompson home, where Falkner resided.[45] By the time of his departure for Mexico, Falkner was engaged to Holland.[46]

He departed Ripley on August 16 accompanied by T. C. Hindman Sr. and Hindman's son and former sergeant Robert H. Hindman. Although the latter two were not in or were no longer in the military, they traveled with him the entire route. The reason for their making such a long and arduous trip is not known, but it may have concerned obtaining the release of son and brother Second Lieutenant T. C. Hindman Jr., who spent August under arrest in a military jail for unknown charges.[47]

Decades later, Falkner recalled an incident that occurred while in passage on the Rio Grande, which at first seemed like an unfolding tragedy that subsequently took on a comedic twist:

One day I was travelling up the Rio Grande on a small steamboat. All of a sudden the cry of "Man overboard!" came ringing through the cabin. The passengers all rushed out to see the show. A tall, slim man was struggling and floundering about in the water. The captain and the pilot were convulsed with laughter, and made no effort to save the man's life.

"It is a burning shame," cried half a dozen ladies, "to let the poor man drown like a dog!"

My blood boiled with indignation at the inhuman conduct of the officers.

At length a couple of Texas desperadoes approached the captain with cocked revolvers, and said,—

"If you let that man drown we will blow off the top of your head and toss you into the river."

The captain seemed at once to realize the situation. Stepping close to the outer edge of the deck, he cried in a loud voice,—

"Stand up! stand up on your feet!"

The man obeyed instructions, when, lo and behold! The water did not come so high as his hips.

I think it was the most ludicrous exhibition I ever beheld. The man was about to drown in water only three feet deep. I believe he would have been drowned, if let alone.

A loud shout of laughter rose from all the passengers, except the two desperadoes, who now wanted to shoot the unfortunate victim who had caused them to make fools of themselves.[48]

By the time Falkner and the Hindmans arrived, the regiment's encampment had been moved to the higher elevations of Buena Vista, where life continued much as it had outside Monterrey.[49]

Following his leave of absence, Captain Jackson had already returned to the regiment on July 3. He noted that Falkner arrived in camp on September 20, with the Hindmans coming a day or two later. Jackson alluded to certain "slanders or libels current against me at Ripley." Falkner denied any involvement with these, and he and Jackson resolved to remain friends. However, the Hindmans were a different story. For unstated reasons possibly connected with the younger Hindman's arrest, Jackson viewed them as threats:

> Being advised, as indeed I know, that their purposes were anything but friendly to me I looked out for difficulties. Both however, approached me in a friendly manner, but they did not and do not deceive me. I think the old Gentleman is afraid to commence the attack as so far he has made no demonstrations. Many of my company were much irritated by the rumors afloat as to his designs, and would have kicked him out of camp, had I said the word. Whether he will attempt anything is more than I can say, but if he does I do not think he can effect much.[50]

Upon his return to camp, Falkner applied to Dr. Love in regard to resigning his commission for medical reasons. Love reported that Falkner's foot wound made him lame possibly for life while his fingers were subject to considerable pain. He concluded by saying that Falkner's wounds made resignation justifiable, and subsequently he was given a medical discharge on October 6.[51] Two years later, T. C. Hindman Sr. claimed that the real reason for Falkner's resignation was his desire to return to Ripley and marry Holland.[52] However, this must be seen in light of the animosity that he developed toward the younger man. Additionally, Hindman claimed that after Falkner was discharged, but still in Mexico, he had seen him at "a Fandango, [where] in my presence, [he] danced a considerable time, without any apparent inconvenience." Hindman also recalled that in January 1850 following a snow in Ripley, he had seen Falkner "engaged for several hours in breaking wild horses to run in a sleigh. The day was cold, he wore no gloves, and [despite his wounds] seem'd to use both hands equally well; there not being the slightest appearance of soarness or swelling neither did I hear him complain of any sensitiveness from the effects of the weather."[53] There is irony in Hindman's constant complaints that Falkner was not as ill as he claimed to be in that his own son-in-law,

Dr. James B. Ellis, was the physician who had excused Falkner from service for several months on account of his wounds. About October 10, Falkner and the Hindmans departed for Ripley.[54]

The signing of the Treaty of Guadalupe Hidalgo on February 2, 1848, brought not only peace but also the Mexican territories of California and New Mexico into US possession and started the American troops on their long journey home. The First Mississippi Rifles returned to considerable fanfare as "arguably the most famous volunteer regiment" of the war as a result of their victories under Jefferson Davis.[55] However, the Second was barely noticed when it arrived in Vicksburg to be mustered out of service. While the First lost fifty-four killed in action and four who died from wounds, the Second lost none in battle, because it had seen no battles. However, the Second did lose 186 from disease, which exceeded the First's combined casualties from disease (sixty-three) and battle (fifty-eight).[56]

Falkner's first experience of war involved little actual battle but was instead dominated by the grind of everyday marching and camp life, and the ensuing boredom, all accompanied by the ever-present specter of death by disease. This provided little incentive to stay on once an excuse for a medical discharge presented itself. However, the sights and memories of rugged landscapes, the talk of battles never witnessed, and the image of Doña Dosamantes resplendent in martial garb, stayed with him.

His experience in Mexico displays the beginning of a pattern that was evidenced in his later military exploits. Upon initially joining, his personality—charismatic and innovative—took him to the top, entering as he did as a first lieutenant and second in command of his company. However, when confronted with the actual exigencies of war—the days and weeks of boredom and disease—his enthusiasm wilted and he looked for other means to occupy his time, such as adventures to Aguas Calientes. It was as if his dynamic, protean mind could not conform to the structures that threatened to suffocate him. How much better, he thought, it would be back in Ripley with the young woman who awaited him.

Back in Ripley probably in November, Falkner married his beloved Holland, most likely in the Spight home.[57] One of their first concerns was the division of her father's estate among the five children. In late 1847, Holland and Bill along with her sister Mary and husband D. L. Killgore petitioned the Tippah County Probate Court for a division of the estate, which included twenty-eight slaves; the court appointed commissioners, who met on December 27, 1847, and divided the estate into five parts, with Holland's share to include seven slaves valued at $2,450, whose names were Charles, Washington, Phillis, John,

Joe, Susan, and Caesar. The latter was deaf and blind and therefore a liability rather than an asset—unable to work, he would have to be taken care of—so he was given a value of negative $200 in calculating the shares of the estate.[58]

On September 2, 1848, Holland gave birth to their only child, John Wesley Thompson Falkner, named for his uncle. Falkner soon purchased or built a home for his wife and son located on the west side of Main Street south of the Methodist Church. The house would remain his home until its burning during the Civil War.[59]

Chapter 5

◇━◇━◇━◇

The Hindman Feud

To support his little family, Falkner continued his law practice and other activities. In May 1849, his world would almost be destroyed. He would lose his wife and be plunged into a dispute with the Hindman family—people not to be trifled with—and be tried twice for murder.

As discussed earlier, the Hindman family resided a short distance east of Ripley and in the 1840s and 1850s played a major role in the small town. Falkner was intimately associated with the father, T. C. Hindman Sr., and the two sons, Robert H. and T. C. Jr., during the Mexican War. On May 8, relations between Falkner and the Hindmans took a turn for the worse when the older son, Robert, attempted to shoot Falkner. The incident arose at a meeting of the Sons of Temperance, an exclusive organization devoted to opposing the consumption and sale of alcohol.[1] Falkner already belonged, and Hindman wanted to join. "Temperance" originally referred to one of the cardinal virtues and pertained to moderation in thought and action. By the early nineteenth century, it had come to refer primarily to moderation, and indeed total abstinence, from the consumption of alcohol. Matters might have turned out better if moderation in thought and action had remained a viable ideal.

The most detailed and reliable account appeared in 1881 in an article by Falkner's law partner, C. J. Frederick, who was born on June 11, 1849, a month after the killing, implying that his long, detailed account was essentially dictated to him by Falkner. The Sons of Temperance required that prospective members gain the approval of all others before being admitted. Falkner spoke in favor of Hindman's acceptance, but "malicious" persons reported to Hindman that Falkner had opposed his admission.[2] Of course, the Hindmans were not known for temperate behavior:

Hindman (Now Booker) House 1936

Figure 5.1. Hindman home, 1842, burned in January 1936. Photograph by Andrew Brown, 1936. Courtesy of Tommy Covington.

When Hindman was informed that Falkner had made a speech against him he flew into a passion and publicly declared that he would kill him, and calling Falkner to where he was, demanded in an angry tone to know why he had opposed his admission. Falkner denied having done so. Hindman replied. "You are a d—d liar," at the same time drawing from his right-hand pants pocket a small revolver and attempting to shoot. Falkner seized Hindman's wrist with both hands and tried to take the pistol away from him. A scuffle ensued for possession of the pistol. Hindman, being a very strong man, managed to throw Falkner back against a house and extricated his wrist from Falkner's grasp, when he presented the pistol within two feet of the colonel's breast and pulled the trigger, but the weapon failed to fire. Hindman then cocked the pistol and again attempted to shoot, but the pistol again failed to fire. Falkner then drew his knife, and as Hindman made the third attempt to shoot him, he stabbed Hindman, inflicting a wound from the effects of which Hindman died immediately.[3]

Falkner turned himself in to the law and was presumably incarcerated in the Tippah County jail to await trial, which soon came up at the next term of court.[4] It is not known whether he was allowed out on bail. The charge of murder prevents the accused from obtaining bail, although it's likely that Falkner faced a lesser charge given the nature of the incident. In the meantime Falkner's wife, Holland, who may have already been sick, died on or about

Figure 5.2. Not known for temperate behavior, the Hindman brothers, T. C. Jr. (on the left) and Robert, late 1840s, courtesy of the Helena Museum of Phillips County, Arkansas, Hindman Family Collection.

May 31.[5] She was presumably buried in Ripley Cemetery in an unmarked grave.[6] For the time being, Falkner apparently retained their infant son.[7]

When Falkner's case came into court, he was tried under Judge Hugh R. Miller. The attorney for the defense was P. T. Scruggs of Holly Springs, while the prosecution was led by N. S. Price of Ripley, filling in for the district attorney, J. W. Thompson, who undoubtedly had to recuse himself because the defendant was his nephew.[8] Price was assisted by young Tom Hindman, the brother of the deceased, who had read law following his return from Mexico and had just been admitted to the bar. He made "his maiden speech against the defendant on the trial, which, though very eloquent, was pregnant with bitter denunciation." However, the evidence was "short, conclusive, and totally free from contradictions, making out a clear case of self-defense." After the case was brought to a conclusion, the jury was sent out to reach a verdict. Because of the nature of the evidence, there was little debate. Within minutes they returned with a verdict: not guilty.[9]

Falkner was free, but the Hindmans would not forget, nor did Price. They buried Robert in the family lot next to their home two miles east of Ripley. His name was carved on a headstone beneath which the inscription read: "Killed at Ripley Miss. by Wm. C. Falkner May 8, 1849."[10]

ROBERT HOLT,
eldest son of
Thomas C. & Sarah
HINDMAN.
BORN
June 20, 1822,
Killed at Ripley Miss.
by Wm.C.Falkner
May 8, 1849
AGED
26 yrs. 10 mo. 18 d.

Figure 5.3. Headstone of Robert H. Hindman, Hindman Cemetery, Ripley, Mississippi. Courtesy of Tommy Covington.

Later the same year Falkner applied for and was granted a pension of $220 per year as a wounded officer based in part on a certificate dated September 5, 1849, from Drs. William McRea and Benjamin Jones of Ripley, who indicated that they had examined him and found him

> entirely incapacitated from following any occupation requiring the use of his hand. And we are informed and believe it to be true from their appearance, that both his foot and hand are exceedingly sensitive to the effects of cold, inflaming, swelling, and becoming very tender upon the least exposure. Upon the whole, we consider said Falkner not only incapacitated from military duty from the effects of said wounds; in his hand and foot. But in our opinion he is totally disabled thereby from obtaining subsistence from manuel [*sic*] labor.[11]

The symptoms may have been exaggerated.

Soon after, attorney Price, who had prosecuted Falkner, found out about the pension and notified T. C. Hindman Sr., who was furious and saw this as an opportunity for revenge against the man who had been acquitted for killing his son. He began a letter-writing campaign to Congressman Jacob Thompson and to the US secretary of the interior objecting to the pension, noting that "Judge Price and probably others may write you confidential letters in relation to this matter." His letters were devoted in part to attacking the credibility of the descriptions of Falkner's physical condition, claiming that he "now and for a long time back, walks, runs, jumps, and dances, with as much activity and apparent ease, as any young man in our country, and uses his hands, with no apparent inconvenience whatever—I see him frequently and have not been able to discover any halt or lameness in his walk." Not content with addressing Falkner's physical condition, Hindman also attacked his military record in Mexico, in particular the event in which he had been wounded, claiming that he had violated orders in riding to Aguas Calientes and had provoked the attack by "some indecent and improper advances upon a Mexican female," this despite the fact that isolated Americans were subject to attack by guerrillas. Hindman further explained that others who might have complained were "deterred by the known character of Falkner for violence. His Bowie knife & pistols are constantly about his person."[12] Accusing Falkner of having a "character" for violence seems disingenuous, considering the Hindmans' penchant for violence and that Robert had apparently initiated the attack that resulted in his own death. Furthermore, Hindman didn't mention questionable behavior on the part of his sons in Mexico, such as Robert's having obtained a medical discharge months before Falkner or T. C. Jr.'s having spent a month in military jail while in Mexico.

W. E. Rogers of Ripley, who had served with Falkner in Mexico, came to his defense stating that Falkner was "in the discharge of his duty" when wounded and went further to state that Hindman was motivated "by a desire of revenge & hatred he bears said Falkner, & not for any benefit he may be to the governm't."[13]

The correspondence was but one manifestation of the smoldering resentment. The animosity came to a boil on Friday, February 28, 1851, when Falkner shot Erasmus Morris, a twenty-four-year-old tailor who had become involved as a friend of the Hindmans. What provoked the fight is unknown. All that is known is that while in John Henderson's Grocery on the north side of the square, Falkner shot Morris in the left side of the face, killing him almost instantaneously. After being jailed, Falkner was released the following day on $5,000 bond with his uncle J. W. Thompson being one of the bondsmen.[14] The next week on Friday, March 7, the grand jury met and considered the case, filing an indictment against Falkner on a charge of murder.[15] Prospective jurors were summoned, and on Wednesday, March 12, a jury of twelve was selected including Joshua G. Frederick, the father of the infant C. J. Frederick who would years later serve as Falkner's law partner.[16] Falkner later recalled that an unnamed "Mr. P." "electioneered with the *venire* [jury] after they were summoned to try me."[17] That is, he was jury tampering.

The trial was held the following day, and despite possible jury tampering, the jury found him not guilty.[18] The Hindmans were furious. Could they not stop this man?

According to Falkner's friend, editor M. C. Gallaway, T. C. Hindman Jr. tried to end his family's problem. Immediately after Falkner's acquittal, Hindman

attempted to shoot him across the table at a hotel, but accidently dropped his pistol on the floor, when it fired, sending a bullet through the ceiling just above Falkner's head. Falkner instantly presented a revolver at Hindman, and instead of shooting him down, as many a man would have done, he merely required Hindman to let his pistol remain where it was, telling him that he did not want to shed any more blood, and he was determined not to do it when he could avoid it without giving up his own life.[19]

During the last days of March, Falkner left home probably traveling to Memphis, where he caught a steamboat bound for the Ohio River. Presumably before this he had turned over his toddler son John to the Thompsons to raise. Upon hearing of Falkner's departure, T. C. Hindman Sr. immediately wrote to the secretary of the interior in Washington to explain that Falkner had just departed for New York City and Washington with the intent of having his pension reinstated.[20]

It is unlikely that he made it to New York, but he probably visited Washington. Another objective of his trip was the city of Cincinnati for the purpose of publishing two small books that he had written, one a narrative poem and the other a short novel, entitled, respectively *The Siege of Monterey: A Poem* and *The Spanish Heroine: A Tale of War and Love, Scenes Laid in Mexico*. Both were concerned with the Mexican War and certainly grew out of his experience in Mexico. Most of the texts had probably been written before his departure, although he did write the opening canto of the former book while in Cincinnati residing at the Dennison House, a landmark hotel at the corner of Main and Fifth Streets. He wrote in a jocular manner in doggerel verse with rhyming couplets:

I write this in the city of Cincinnati,
Among the upper-tens and *literati*;
At the Dennison House, room No. twenty,

They give me eggs and onions plenty,
They use me right and feed me well,
And I'm always there at the ringing of the bell,
I'm now in my room, in the fourth story,
About as near as I often get to glory.[21]

The light-hearted manner of writing was characteristic of Falkner and will be seen repeatedly in the years to come. It almost certainly reflects something about his personality.

He enjoyed visiting the Olympic Theatre in Cincinnati, which featured a variety of entertainment including plays and other performances. On this occasion he witnessed a Mrs. Saunders, apparently an exotic dancer, and he recalled it in his *Siege of Monterey*:

You have heard of Mrs. Saunders, I suppose,
To see her play a crowd always goes,
If you haven't seen her, it don't matter,
I went last night to get a peep at her,
I entered the saloon at precisely seven,
Instead of seeing the lady I saw her heaven. . . .
I saw,—sure enough, it don't matter what,
I paid my money and begrudge it not;
At any rate I saw the heavenly sight,
And I intend to see it again to-night,
For such sights my money is freely spent,
I saw something new every time I went.[22]

In these rather unmemorable rhymes Falkner shows a bit of his personality, always jesting in his observations. This tone will appear in later writings, including his travelogue, *Rapid Ramblings in Europe* (1884).

Before he left home, he had acquired a new lady friend, Elizabeth "Lizzie" Houston Vance, as an indirect result of the opening of the Ripley Female Academy in 1850. Mary Jane Vance Buchanan and her husband Isaac Buchanan arrived in town at about that time, with Mary Jane scheduled to take over the principalship of the school. Tagging along with them was her eighteen-year-old sister Lizzie.[23] Falkner presumably met Lizzie soon after she moved to Ripley, and they were soon in love. In Cincinnati, Mrs. Saunders's provocative dance inspired thoughts of his beloved Lizzie. She was often on his mind as he makes clear:

I am in love clear up to the nose,

And want to marry so bad I'm nearly froze;

When I lay down at night my thoughts are busy

With the phantom of my angelic Lizzie.[24]

As noted, although Falkner had little formal schooling, his familiarity with literature was broad. *The Siege of Monterey* attests to this. The poem has two narrative threads: (1) the story of the American attack on and conquest of Monterrey, raised to epic status; and (2) the love story of the Mexicans Bibo and Isabel. Donald Duclos notes that Falkner was clearly influenced by Byron, particularly *Don Juan* and *Childe Harold's Pilgrimage* and especially by "Byron's references to the Maid of Saragoza." The "Maid" was Agustina de Aragón (1786–1857), the "Spanish Joan of Arc" who helped defend Spain against the incursion of Napoleonic troops during the Peninsular War. However, it will be remembered that Falkner had had a much closer experience of a similar figure in the story of María de Jesús Dosamantes, who had fought at Monterrey. Robert Cantwell saw a Homeric influence in *Siege*, describing it as "a most remarkable work in which Zach Taylor, Jeff Davis, . . . and others appear as Homeric heroes. It is written in what Hawthorne in another connection called a dog-trot rhythm and is in all probability the strangest poetical composition in the language."[25]

Falkner also wrote a preface to *Siege* that had little to do with the work, but instead was a reflection upon the troubles he had passed through with the Hindmans. He expressed remorse for the deaths of Robert Hindman and Erasmus Morris, "whose lives were as dear to them as mine is to me." He continued to meditate upon the situation that he faced with his enemies, "who are anything but few," and in melodramatic tones noted: "I have been persecuted, and hunted down like a savage wild beast, and at every corner, instead of meeting friendship sweet, I find deadly foes, ready to take advantage when they find me unarmed." He also wrote of a "Mr. P.," who was "going around the streets trying to turn public feeling against me, and taking every undue advantage of my situation that he could."[26] He did not identify Mr. P., although the man was almost certainly N. S. Price, who had prosecuted Falkner and continued to fraternize closely with T. C. Hindman Sr. in opposition to Falkner. According to Andrew Brown, Price had a "fiery temper, and stories are told of his clashes with opposing counsel, which were memorable even for a period when courtroom tactics were of no-holds-barred variety."[27]

Falkner recalled that soon after his acquittal at the Hindman trial he was riding through the country when he was "overtaken by night and a tremendous storm." He sought shelter at the nearest house, which was inhabited by a widow and several children. The woman offered him shelter, but when he told her his name, her demeanor changed.

"Leave my house this instant, you black-hearted murderer," stormed the old lady at the top of her voice. "My house is no place to shelter murderers." She commanded her son to saddle my horse, and threatened to set the dogs on me if I did not leave instantly. "What," said she, "You, that unfeeling demon, who took Mr. H[indman] to dine with you, then took him out and assassinated him—you expect to find shelter under my roof? No, I had rather give shelter to Satan himself."[28]

Trying to assuage her fear, he asked her who had provided her information. She replied: "A very respectable gentleman, Mr. P. of Ripley." Falkner replied that he had a statement by Hugh R. Miller, the judge who had occupied the bench during his trial, and if she would permit, he would read it aloud. She did so, and he read it while she listened attentively. Upon completion, she was so moved that she "begged to be forgiven for the treatment" she had leveled against Falkner. He then explained to the reader that his reason for relating the incident was to exemplify how Mr. P. was trying to damage his character.[29]

The two books were published in Cincinnati probably at Falkner's own expense. It is unlikely that a publisher would have considered the two manuscripts without an outside investment. *The Spanish Heroine* was published first. The title page indicates that it was published by I. Hart & Co. of 41 Columbia Street, Cincinnati. On the copy apparently used to register the volume there is an inscription: "Deposited May 1, 1851/Wm Miner clk.," and on the copyright page is printed: "Entered, according to Act of Congress, in the year 1851, by W. C. FALKNER, In the Clerk's Office of the district Court for the district of Ohio." *The Siege of Monterey* has an identical printed statement, while on the title page there is an inscription stating that it was "Deposited May 16, 1851," fifteen days after *The Spanish Heroine*. The title page indicates that the volume was published not by I. Hart but "BY THE AUTHOR" in Cincinnati, although Hart probably was the printer. This completed his two volumes, and he was on his way home with several boxes of books. We know virtually nothing about number of copies printed or their sales. However, nothing suggests that the two works were a success. Falkner didn't return to literary pursuits for years.

Clearly fuming, on May 17 T. C. Hindman Sr. drafted another letter to the secretary of the interior informing him that Falkner had returned to Ripley a few days before. He did not know if Falkner had been to Washington, but

"since his return he has boasted of having had his pension allowance reinstated for the term of six months."[30] It was infuriating to have Falkner return
with his pension restored along with boxes of newly published books, all
guaranteed to make Falkner a local attraction.

Once back in Ripley, Falkner began to set his affairs in order. His small
son had probably been kept by the Thompsons, who would effectively adopt
the boy. He also had to work matters out with Lizzie, who agreed to marry
him. On October 14, he and his friend, attorney William J. Maclin,[31] rode to
Pontotoc and signed a $200 bond on the condition that a marriage be "shortly
intended to be solemnized between W. C. Falkner and Elizabeth H. Vance."
The fact that this had to be done in Pontotoc County rather than Ripley and
Tippah County suggests that Lizzie might have moved to Pontotoc. It's probable that her sister and brother-in-law, who were teachers, had moved to
Pontotoc County for teaching positions, taking Lizzie with them.[32] All would
soon be back in Ripley, though.

William Maclin soon became a principal in the death of the man who
may well have been Falkner's nemesis, "Mr. P." In early 1854, Price was the
attorney for a plaintiff who brought charges against Maclin with the judgments being against the defendant. On Thursday morning, April 13, Price was
at his desk in his office located on the south side of the square.[33] He heard a
voice and looked up to see Maclin standing in his doorway. Price immediately
ordered him to leave and moved to the door to force him out into the street,
then closed the door behind him. Outside, Maclin began cursing Price, who
retaliated, grabbing a hickory stick, stepping outside, and ordering Maclin to
leave. Maclin threw a brickbat, which struck Price in the side, causing him to
advance and strike Maclin, who then drew a revolver and shot Price in the
abdomen. The two fell together with Maclin striking at Price's head with his
pistol. By this time bystanders had separated them. Price struggled to his feet
and staggered a few doors away to a doctor's office, but the doctor was not
there. He returned to his office, where he took to a bed. He dictated a will and
died the following day.[34]

It is unlikely that Falkner was involved in Price's death. There was probably
already animosity between Price and Maclin as there was between Price and
Falkner, and the friction over the lawsuit was just enough to trigger violence.
Whatever the deeper roots of the violence were, the result was the same: an
implacable foe of Falkner was gone.

After their marriage the couple resided in Falkner's home on Main
Street, and Falkner resumed his practice of law in partnership with his
uncle, J. W. Thompson.

Falkner had also invested in new means of income: he purchased houses for rent—according to the 1850 census, he owned $4,000 in real estate—and by 1853 had opened a store on the square with E. B. Word, probably his cousin in a partnership termed Falkner & Word. An agent of R. G. Dun and Company, a credit reference agency, noted that Falkner had "some means" which included "3 improved houses & lots in Town to rent out" and slaves inherited from his first wife (according to the 1850 census, he owned five slaves). Rent on each house was about $5,000 per annum. On the other hand, his partner Word had no property but was "honest & faithful." By the beginning of 1854 the firm had dissolved, with Word continuing the business alone although without capital.[35]

In 1854 Falkner purchased two adjacent brick store buildings on the north side of the square, a structure that came to be known as "Falkner's brick building." The following year he went into partnership with L. C. Norvell, who had been in business on the square for two years, and the two probably moved their business into one of Falkner's brick stores.[36] This business didn't last long, being dissolved by the beginning of 1856. On January 3, Simon Spight, who among other things had a business on the square, advertised that he had bought out "the entire Stock of Goods of Mesrs. Norvell & Falkner" and was offering them for sale "at his old stand," while the brick store building was soon occupied by the firm Cross, Veal, and Company.[37] The R. G. Dun agent reported in December 1856 that Falkner "has gone into the practice of law," as if he hadn't already been in it.[38] In late 1858 Falkner became an agent for R. G. Dun. His duties required that he keep the company "fully posted on mer[chants] in any part of North Miss. as he is well acquainted with nearly all of them."[39]

Being released from store responsibilities allowed Falkner to take on yet another profession, editor for *Uncle Sam*, a Ripley newspaper dedicated to support of the American, or "Know-Nothing," Party. The name "Uncle Sam" or simply "Sam" became a nickname for the party.

Falkner ran for the legislature in 1855 under the banner of the American Party against the Democratic candidate, who happened to be his uncle, J. W. Thompson. The competition between the two was not without intrafamily stress. Thompson won. Falkner would be more successful in 1858 when he ran for and was elected brigadier general in the Mississippi Militia.

The same election saw another young man running for the office of circuit clerk and winning. His name was R. J. Thurmond (1829–1907), and over the following years the lives of Thurmond and Falkner would increasingly interact. Thurmond was four years younger than Falkner, having been born in

Wilkes County, North Carolina. By 1840 his family had moved to Hardeman County, Tennessee, north of and adjacent to Tippah, and by 1850 he was residing in Ripley with his sister and brother-in-law, Daniel and Sarah Hunt. In 1854, he married Margaret Mariah Miller (1836–1900), one of the daughters of the early settler Charles P. Miller.

On August 11, 1855, *Uncle Sam* published its first issue. Editor H. H. Powers chose the motto "Americans SHALL rule America!," placed prominently in each issue. Part of Powers's salutatory read:[40] "We shall advocate the principles of the American party as set forth in the Platform of the National Convention, not careing [*sic*] who the opposers of those principles may be, where they may be found, by what names they may call themselves, or what may be their number." By the spring of 1856 Falkner had become editor. The publishers were Nash and Block, while the office was located above the O. F. Philbrick Store on the northwest corner of the square.[41] In the one surviving issue, the paper advertised that "Original Tales will appear on the first page written expressly b[y UN]CLE SAM," referring undoubtedly to Falkner as the author. With only one copy surviving, we have no idea about the nature of these tales.[42]

The coming of *Uncle Sam* meant that there were two newspapers in Ripley, with the other being the well-established *Ripley Advertiser*, which had begun publication as a Whig paper but by the 1850s was oriented to the Democratic Party. While only one issue of *Uncle Sam* survives, many copies of the *Advertiser* are extant, and these often allude—usually unfavorably—to the politics of its competitor.

In this environment, Falkner entered the political fray as a Know-Nothing candidate for the state legislature. Running as the Democratic candidate for the same position was his uncle and law partner, J. W. Thompson. Although the Know-Nothings were a new party, they gained a quick foothold throughout much of the country. In Tippah County, all offices up for election in 1855 had Know-Nothing candidates running against Democrats. All did well in the election in November, although, except for one position on the five-man Board of Police, the Democratic candidates all received majorities of the votes. J. W. Thompson defeated his nephew, 1,560 votes to 1,163.[43]

The next year, 1856, was a presidential election year. The American Party held its national convention in February in Philadelphia with Millard Fillmore, a former president and former Whig, receiving the nomination.[44] In April and May, Falkner was in New York, Philadelphia, Baltimore, and Washington, DC,[45] from whence he wrote letters for *Uncle Sam* under the pseudonym "Uncle Sam." Some appear in the one known surviving copy of the newspaper. Although with only one issue surviving there is little context

for his trip—we have no idea why he was there—the letters provide a fasci-
nating insight into Falkner's personality, one seldom seen in his business and
military correspondence. He refers several times to his unnamed traveling
companion, whom he calls "the Arkansaw Traveler," a name borrowed from
a popular musical piece for fiddle.[46] Although Falkner's letters were intended
for the readership of a politically oriented newspaper, there is relatively little
politics in them except for oblique references to notable political figures. The
tone is light and jocular and often self-deprecating, foreshadowing the narrative of his later travelogue *Rapid Ramblings in Europe*.

While in New York City, he stayed at the five-story Astor House Hotel
on Broadway. Built in the 1830s by businessman John Jacob Astor, it was for
decades one of the most famous and prestigious hotels in the country. From
there, he ventured out to see the sights. On one occasion he and the "Arkansaw
Traveler" visited P. T. Barnum's renowned American Museum on Broadway, a
combination museum, theater, zoo, and freak show. At the time of the visit,
the museum was advertising evening presentations of the play *Uncle Tom's
Cabin* along with the notification that "the largest woman and the smallest
one alive are now here" and that Mademoiselle Eloise would enter the lion's
den—two times daily.[47]

Falkner's description was written in his jocular manner with an experimental narrative style consisting of short, choppy sentences and sentence fragments
probably intended to convey the cacophony of images and sounds encountered:

> Enter Uncle Sam and Arkansaw Traveler. The Lion curls his tail and roars hid-
> eously—Zebra brays—Ourang Outang bleats—Monkeys scream—Bear growls
> dolefully—Tiger bawls—Egyptian mummies stink and grin[48]—Arkansaw Trav-
> eler looks wild, and rolls the white of his eye—large audience in attendance—
> tremendous squeeze at the door—Arkansaw traveler walled in by forty Dutch
> fat gals, who all endeavored to get through the door at once. Arkansaw becomes
> alarmed for his safety—cries for help—dutch fat gals heed him not.[49]

Falkner also attended the production of *Uncle Tom's Cabin*. The novel
by Harriet Beecher Stowe on which it was based had appeared in 1852 and
quickly became one of the best-selling books of the nineteenth century.
Depicting as it did the practice of slavery in the South in a melodramatic,
moving, and condemnatory fashion, it had a large impact in promoting opposition to slavery. The play was produced and acted in by George Howard, who
had originally adapted the novel for the stage. His daughter, eight-year-old
Cordelia Howard, starred as Little Eva, one of the principal characters, whose

death moved all who saw the play. The Arkansaw Traveler cursed "without intermission" throughout. Falkner observed that the "institutions of the South" were "outrageously distorted" and "vilified by fools who know nothing of our institutions."[50]

On April 24, Falkner saw James Buchanan of Pennsylvania, the former ambassador to the United Kingdom, who had just emerged as a principal contender for the Democratic presidential nomination. According to Falkner, Buchanan was "exhibited" to the public at New York City Hall at noon "pretty much after the same fashion that a Jockey would show a blooded horse." The number of people coming to see him was enormous, resulting in "a tremendous squeeze at the door by the crowd desirous of getting a peep." At 9:30 that evening Falkner gathered amid another crowd outside the Everett House Hotel on Union Square, where Buchanan was staying. They had a long wait. At 10:30 Buchanan appeared on a balcony above them. Falkner recalled that he "was called on from all sides to give his views on Kansas and Slavery, but he went on as though he never heard the questions. His game is mum till after the Cincinnati Convention."[51] In early June the Democratic National Convention was held in Cincinnati, and Buchanan was selected as the nominee for president. He was elected in November.

On the night of April 29,[52] Falkner also visited a meeting of the fledgling Republican Party that was held at the Broadway Tabernacle.[53] The large sanctuary was crowded with orators and a "very enthusiastic" audience, and the meeting was called to order by Edwin D. Morgan, chairman of the Republican National Committee.[54] Together they agreed that "there should be no more compromises with slaveholders, that the day had come for the North to strike for liberty."[55] Falkner published a few observations:

If you ever saw [the Shakespearean actor] Ned Forrest[56] playing Richard the third, and saw his countenance portray the passions of an enraged murderer, you can guess how [Edwin D.] Morgan looked while he was cursing the institutions of the South, and abusing Mr. [Millard] Fillmore for signing the fugitive slave law. You know my temper is high, but I made out with a tight squeeze to control it. My pulse beat at the rate of about *two forty*, while I inwardly cursed the whole concern. Negroes and Irish Democrats and Dutch, were the component parts of the whole audience, except myself and friend the Arkansaw Traveler, who cursed loudly, when a free negro arose and said that he had always been a Democrat, and that he thought that it was anti-Democratic to oppress the poor colored race. Many speeches were made, and every one took occasion to denounce Mr. Fillmore as the blood-hound who hunted down the poor slave.[57]

He also visited the New York City Halls of Justice and Detention Center, an imposing masonry structure that occupied an entire block in lower Manhattan. Built in 1838 in the Egyptian Revival architectural style, it could easily be described as attractive. However, such was its reputation that it was nicknamed "the Tombs." Falkner observed:

> [W]ell does it deserve that name—it resembles one vast Sepulcher, and in one sense, it is a grave where the hopes of many a fond parent are buried beneath the cold clods of dishonor and misery. Nearly every cell was occupied by some bloated faced worshiper of *Bachus*, whose birth place might be found on foreign soil; not one fifth of the inmates were native born citizens. The Toombs is an edifice built of solid stone of a bright gray color, the walls appear as one piece without a seam, four tall pillars project from each corner; the roof is flat, while an iron fence surrounds the spot. Upon the whole it presents a lonely and desolate appearance.[58]

After being in the city for several days during which he had ample time to observe the social conditions, he remarked with some dissatisfaction:

> Well, I have seen the Elephant, and now steal a moment to drop you a line about matters and things in general. I have arrived at the conclusion that New York is a considerable place, I have visited all places worthy of note and am pretty well posted up on regard to city matters. My heart is sick and tired of the place—I have witnessed more misery and wretched degradation among the poor class here in five days, than I ever [witness]ed in the whole course of m[y life]. . . . [A]ll this misery is nought compared with the loathsome dens inhabited by at least twenty thousand helpless starving creatures of New York, cooped up in filthy cellars, like hogs in a pen—they drag out a miserable existence of crime and prostitution. At every corner may be seen some emaciated specimen of starving humanity.[59]

Subsequently, accompanied by the Arkansaw Traveler, Falkner traveled to Philadelphia, where he described his hotel accommodations in his usual comical style:

> And here am I as sound as a dollar, but not half so current; safely bunked in a room No. 119, at Girard Hotel.[60] My room is something less, but not much under a mile above ground; in fact, I occupy what learned people call an elevated position, but d—n such elevation—it is rather too laborious for a lame

man to climb forty flights of stairs[61] to go to bed, but by starting immediately after an early supper, I made out to reach my room at a late hour last night.[62]

While there Falkner visited Girard College[63] and planned to visit the Fairmount Water Works, and see again the famous actor Edwin Forrest play Richard III, demonstrating his love of Shakespeare. Overall, he preferred Philadelphia to New York: "I like the appearance of Philadelphia much better than New York, the streets are cleaner, the buildings more neat, and there is not half the beggars here, that there are in New York, though God knows there is enough here for all practical purposes."[64]

Soon after, Falkner departed Philadelphia for Washington, where he arrived on May 6 and checked into the National Hotel.[65] While in the capital he apparently visited Mount Vernon and saw the key to the Bastille that Lafayette had sent to George Washington in 1790.[66] By mid-May he had returned to Ripley to continue editing *Uncle Sam* while maintaining his law practice. However, the American Party was beginning to develop interests contrary to Southern interests. In July the *Ripley Advertiser* carried an article from the *Richmond Enquirer* entitled "Rapid Decline of Know-Nothingism in the South," which noted that in Georgia sixty-three American Party members had publicly repudiated the party because of positions it had taken inimical to Southern interests.[67] Shortly after while at the Democratic Ratification meeting in Ripley Falkner announced that he too was changing parties for the very same reasons. In the words of the *Ripley Advertiser*, he

> formally announced his separation from, and determination to act no longer with the American Party. He told us how he got out of the Know Nothing Party, not like Clinton got out of the Democratic wagon, by jumping out; but that he was standing firmly on the 12th Section of the American Platform when it was suddenly pulled from under him and he fell flat, when he got up he was standing on something as firm as the Rock of Gibraltar; he looked around and found it was the Democratic Platform.
>
> That he was in favor of the Kansas Nebraska Act, repealing the Missouri Compromise, that Fillmore and the American Party were now opposed to it, and therefore he could not go with them. He announced his position in a bold, manly manner, and declared his intention to vote for Buchanan and Breckinridge in November next.[68]

With Falkner having returned to the Democratic Party, *Uncle Sam* probably ceased publication. At any rate, there are no further references to it anywhere. The Democratic candidates, Buchanan and his running mate John C. Breckinridge, won in November. The American Party soon disintegrated, with antislavery factions aligning with the Republican Party and proslavery factions aligning with the Democrats.

At the local level of politics and a few years earlier, T. C. Hindman Jr. was elected in 1853 to represent Tippah County in the Mississippi legislature. In 1854, following the legislature's adjournment, he moved to Helena, Arkansas, on the bank of the Mississippi River, where he joined a law partnership. Increasingly active in Democratic politics, he barely escaped involvement in several duels. By 1855 he was actively involved in opposing the American Party in Arkansas, a party that he linked to abolitionism. A focus of his venom was local politician W. D. Rice, whom he regarded as a Know Nothing. The tension between the two came to a head on the streets of Helena on the afternoon of May 24, 1856. Rice and associates confronted Hindman and his friend, Patrick Cleburne. After the first shot was fired, it became a shooting war that left Hindman and Cleburne seriously wounded while Rice's nephew, Dr. James T. Marriott, lay dead. After Hindman and Cleburne were exonerated by a grand jury, the two traveled to Ripley to recuperate at the Hindman home.[69] Shortly after they returned to Helena, T. C. Hindman Sr. was killed on July 18 in an accident involving a cotton gin on his farm near Ripley.[70] He was buried in the family cemetery near his son Robert. With his death passed the third of Falkner's antagonists.

The feud between Falkner and Hindman subsided, no doubt due in part to the distance between the two with approximately a hundred miles separating Ripley from Helena. It was later recalled that the conflict was revived in early 1857 for unknown reasons with "redoubled bitterness by General Hindman and his friends, which kept our town in a constant fever of excitement. Finally, Falkner, in order to prevent his friends from becoming seriously involved, being convinced that a fight would be forced on him, in which many others would be likely to get killed," agreed to meet Hindman. The details were worked out via correspondence between the two men, and a time and place were agreed upon.[71]

They were to meet across the river from Memphis. The bluff city had become a magnet for duelists, some of whom traveled considerable distances to face their opponents there. Much of the lure of Memphis was that duelists could cross the river into a quiet part of Arkansas, conduct the duel, then cross back into Tennessee before Arkansas law enforcement became aware of the illegal activity. The meeting was set for 6:00 a.m., April 1, 1857, on the Arkansas side of the river, four hundred yards from the riverbank opposite the foot of Jefferson Street in Memphis. Each was to be armed with only two revolvers.[72] Varying numbers were usually invited to these affairs. In 1870, a small steamboat, the *Cheek*, was hired to carry parties across the river to witness George R. Phelan and James Brizzolara attempt to kill each other. For the Falkner-Hindman engagement, there would be few attendants: no seconds, no surgeons, no entourage of friends and supporters. Only one person was to accompany them, a friend to both, M. C. Gallaway, then editor of the *Sunny South* in Aberdeen, Mississippi,[73] who was recognized as an authority on the code of dueling. He advocated "dueling in the interest of peace," claiming ironically that "it saves human life." He argued that duels are "more decent than street rencounters and not so fatal—that it makes the man physically weak, the equal of the muscular bully—and says that men punctilious in observing the code, seldom give or receive insults." Nevertheless, Gallaway was also known to have successfully reconciled some duelists.[74]

Shortly after the parties arrived in Memphis the day before the appointed date, Gallaway began working to stop the coming duel, a task that he successfully accomplished, although we don't know the details behind his intervention. He later recalled that

it has ever been a source of gratification to him [Gallaway] to know that he did not only prevent the fight, but that he succeeded in making two bosom friends out of two deadly enemies. We have often heard General Hindman since that time speak of Colonel Falkner in the highest terms of praise. He said that through all of those troubles, Colonel Falkner's conduct was that of a brave, honorable man, who only fought in self-defense. When General Hindman was bitterly assailed by political enemies in Arkansas, Colonel Falkner espoused the general's cause, got up a barbecue at Ripley, Mississippi, and invited Hindman to speak, and had resolutions passed indorsing him. Hindman was triumphantly elected to congress and until his death was a staunch friend to Colonel Falkner. The colonel has resided at his present home for forty years, during which time he has never been involved in any feuds, quarrels, or difficulties, except the unfortunate affair with Hindman and Morris.[75]

In effect, Gallaway's effort at mediation finally brought to a close the long-running Falkner-Hindman feud. Decades later in appreciation of his role in averting the duel, Falkner dedicated his novel *The White Rose of Memphis* to Gallaway, recalling as he did the feud with the Hindmans: "In days long since past, when dark, angry clouds of misfortune lowered over me and dangers clustered thick around me—a time when friends of mine were few, though much needed and greatly desired—it was my good fortune to find in your generous heart those noble sentiments of true friendship that have proved of inestimable value to me."[76]

Hindman became a major general in the Confederate Army during the Civil War. In this capacity he provided a recommendation, albeit a lukewarm one, for Falkner's unsuccessful bid for advancement to a generalship. Following the war, on the night of September 27, 1868, Hindman was at home with his wife and children when shots fired through the window hit him in the jaw and neck. He died the following morning just before sunrise. His last words were purportedly, "I forgive everybody, and hope they will forgive me." His killer was neither caught nor identified.

In assessing Falkner's role in the feud with the Hindmans, although we might wish for more detailed evidence, overall his role seems to have been defensive. Whereas the Hindmans are documented as engaging in conflicts with people other than Falkner, Falkner was involved in only one conflict, namely with the Hindmans. And his role from the first was largely defensive. He had been first attacked by Robert Hindman and in defending himself had prevailed, to the consternation of the Hindmans and their friends.

Despite Falkner's being relatively guiltless, the affair generated enough rumors to unjustifiably distort his image into one of violence, so years later the great-grandson, as previously noted, would say that "when you've killed men something happens inside you—something happens to your character." The implication was clear—that the earlier Falkner had found it easier to kill. However, there is no evidence of this.

Chapter 6

◆──◇──◇──◇──◆

Building Railroads

A decade after Falkner's death, the story was told that as a young man, he was sitting on the square in Ripley watching freight wagons arriving, when the idea dawned on him that a railroad should be constructed to expedite the shipment of freight.[1] Although the story is almost certainly apocryphal, there's no reason to believe that he didn't imagine building a railroad, but he certainly wouldn't have been the first. There were probably few in Ripley who didn't envision building a railroad to connect their town to the outside world.

Years after the proliferation of imaginary railroads across northern Mississippi in the mid-1830s, the situation hadn't improved much. Indeed, very little railroad mileage had been constructed in the South. On October 23–26, 1849, a railroad convention was held in Memphis that brought together railroad promoters and visionaries and encouraged fertile imaginations. The participants were from eleven states ranging from Texas to New York. Attending from Ripley were attorney Orlando Davis, businessman S. R. Spight, and a twenty-four-year-old Bill Falkner, who would have his first sustained exposure, if not to actual railroads, then to talk of railroads. At the convention exuberant, if not naïve, boosterism dwelt on ambitious plans to build transcontinental railroads. Demonstrating more critical discernment than was typical for such coverage, one newspaper reporter described the affair a "humbug convention."[2] Nevertheless, in eight years the first railroad connection between the Atlantic and the Mississippi would open in Memphis, and twenty years later the first transcontinental railroad would be completed, demonstrating that humbug can have results.

The first railroads were designed to connect port cities on oceans and rivers with their hinterlands. These cities were staging grounds for construction in part because their waterway connections provided the means for importing the components for building and operating the railroads. However, there was another consideration—building a railroad required considerable capital, and large cities were far more capable of raising it than smaller cities and towns. Consequently, the best hope for small towns was to be located on the route of a major trunk line, thereby taking advantage of the capital investments primarily of outsiders. If bypassed by a trunk line, a town's only option was to connect to it through a spur line. Ripley found itself in this predicament and having to raise the requisite capital.

During the late 1840s and 1850s, three trunk lines were constructed, all projected sufficiently close to Ripley to raise the hope that the small town might be included on one of the routes. First, the Mobile and Ohio Railroad (M&O) was constructed from Mobile to a point on the Mississippi River near the mouth of the Ohio. Its closest approach to Ripley was Booneville to the east. The second road, the Mississippi Central, linked southward with railroads leading to New Orleans and northward to the M&O at Jackson, Tennessee. Its closest approach to Ripley was Holly Springs to the west. However, the railroad that initially offered the best hope for Ripley was the Memphis and Charleston (M&C), a road designed to connect Memphis with Stevenson, Tennessee, where it would connect to other roads that linked to Charleston, South Carolina, on the Atlantic.

While the M&C was in the planning stage, one of its proposed routes was surveyed through Holly Springs, Ripley, and Jacinto, Mississippi, and it remained a viable option through 1850. However, on January 15, 1851, the railroad's board finalized a route that lay to the north of the hoped-for route.[3] In response, delegates from Marshall, Pontotoc, Tippah, and Tishomingo Counties met in Ripley on March 3 to consider their options, although in reality there was little they could do.[4] On November 1, 1851, construction began on the western end of the railroad at Memphis building east,[5] and about the same time construction began in the east at Stephenson, Alabama, building west with the two sections to connect midway.

In August 1855 construction reached its nearest approach to Ripley at Middleton, Tennessee, twenty-five miles to the north; the following month the rails reached Pocahontas, a few miles east of Middleton,[6] where rail laying halted until resuming in May 1856.[7] On March 27, 1857, the eastern and western sections united near Iuka, Mississippi, completing the M&C and making it the first rail connection between the Mississippi River and the Atlantic.[8]

This event was comparable to the opening of the Erie Canal, which connected the Atlantic with the Great Lakes, an event celebrated with New York governor DeWitt Clinton pouring a jar of Atlantic water into Lake Erie. In like fashion a festival was held in Memphis on May 1–2 with parades, bands,

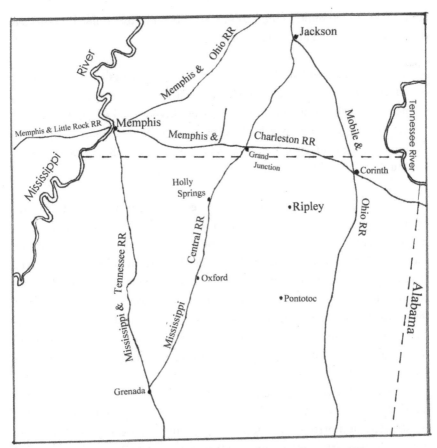

Figure 6.1. Map of railroads in northern Mississippi and western Tennessee, 1861.

and marching military organizations, attended by thousands. In preparation for the event, firemen of the Phoenix Fire Company of Charleston, South Carolina, filled a fire engine with Atlantic water and transported it by rail to Memphis. To symbolize the "Mingling of the Waters" on the morning of the second, they spewed the entire tank in a great arc into the river to the delight of the crowd.[9] This dramatized the occasion, which was made all the more auspicious by the fact that only a few years before there were virtually no tracks in the area. The importance was certainly not lost on Falkner and all of Ripley, who found themselves tantalizingly close to this major railroad.

Once the hope of being included on the M&C route was dashed, the citizens of Ripley began to look to their only option—building a spur line connecting the town to a nearby trunk line.[10] In 1857, in hopes of linking to this new national highway, citizens of Ripley and Tippah County made several sporadic efforts to build a connection.[11] A contributor to a Bolivar, Tennessee, newspaper described how this process began:

> [T]he movers get up "called meetings," in which many things are said *pro* and *con*. Then they get up a line of barbecues, at which the people are addressed by speakers who know as good as nothing about *how* to build a railroad. These orators, with great zeal, go on to show the people what great benefits they will reap from the road when built. The excitement runs high. Books are opened [and] . . . [t]he citizens on or near the "air line" subscribe.[12]

The first effort to bring rails to Ripley resulted in the passage of a law on January 31, 1857, incorporating the Ripley Railroad Company and authorizing it to connect Ripley with any one of the three nearby trunk lines—the M&C, the M&O, or the Mississippi Central. The corporation's stock was fixed at $400,000 with the par value set at $25. After $200,000 was subscribed, officers and directors were to be elected and construction started.[13] On April 6, 1857, a meeting of the company's incorporators was held in Ripley. The act of incorporation was accepted, and commissioners were appointed to begin receiving subscriptions for capital stock in the company.[14] Apparently, little was accomplished.

A year and a half later, on December 2, 1858, another legislative act increased the capital stock to $1,500,000 and, although nothing had been constructed, authorized the continuation of the railroad south from Ripley through New Albany to Pontotoc and then to the M&O Railroad, presumably somewhere in Chickasaw County.[15] In sum, the modified route was apparently to begin in the north on the M&C at or near Middleton, Tennessee, and connect to the M&O in the south.

In November 1859 the legislature authorized the Tippah County Board of Police to invest county funds in railroad stock if they thought proper.[16] On the tenth, a meeting of the railroad incorporators was held in the courthouse in Ripley. In attendance were W. C. Falkner (at that time a general in the state militia), his uncle J. W. Thompson, and S. R. Spight, along with other prominent citizens: Dr. John Y. Murry, C. P. Miller, W. R. Cole, Orlando Davis, and L. S. Holcombe. The participants approved and adopted all actions and proceedings of the meeting of the original incorporators held on April 6, 1857, thereby implying that little had been done over the past two and a half years. Chairman C. P. Miller appointed fifteen commissioners to "open new books and solicit subscriptions to stock." Falkner was among the fifteen. J. W. Thompson moved that five men be appointed "to canvass the county and solicit subscriptions to stock," with Falkner being one of the five. This was his initiation into raising funds for railroad construction, a skill that he honed over the next few years. The company also established the second and fourth Mondays of each month as the regular meeting times for the incorporators and commissioners.[17] They apparently intended to make up for lost time.

Meetings were held into the next year. However, there were difficulties. A correspondent of the *Ripley Advertiser* noted that the area had experienced several hopes over the years, then observed that "there are a number of discouraging circumstances in connection with the present effort to build a road." Apparently, many were indeed becoming discouraged. "There is no use in talking about giving it up, neither because some are lukewarm and others frozen, nor because we have made efforts before and failed. It requires no very small amount of money to build railroads; and because the people have not subscribed money enough in a few months to build it, is no sensible reason for abandoning so great a work." The writer then proceeded to lay out the economic advantages of a town having a railroad.[18] While few would have disagreed, nevertheless the financial problem remained. With this and the oncoming war, the effort to build a railroad connection for Ripley faded away for the time.

Falkner's role in the railroad was increasing as the decade came to an end. He was also a practicing attorney and had edited a newspaper, operated a store, and run for political office. In 1850 he owned $4,000 in real estate and five slaves, and by 1860 his worth had increased to $10,000 in real estate with a personal estate of $40,200, which included six slaves, all listed as mulattos: a man aged twenty-one, a woman twenty-seven, two boys aged eight and one, and two girls aged six and four. Falkner had purchased the woman, who was named Emeline, from a Benjamin E. W. Harris on October 1, 1859. She was pregnant at the time and already had two daughters, the above-mentioned girls, Delia aged about six and Helen about four.[19] Soon after, Emeline gave birth to a son, whom she named Arthur. Emeline was born in Virginia as was her owner, Harris, who brought her to Tennessee and then to Ripley and was apparently the father of the three children.[20] After Falkner purchased these people, they subsequently took the name Falkner, as was common practice.[21]

In the mid-1860s, Emeline gave birth to another daughter, named Frances "Fannie" Forrest Falkner. Her descendants claim that Falkner was her father, which is entirely possible. However, there is insufficient evidence for extrapolating further. The date of Fannie's birth in 1866 suggests that there was an ongoing liaison between her mother and Falkner.[22]

During the late 1850s there was one last immigration of Words/Falkners into Tippah County. These consisted of family members from Ste. Genevieve County, Missouri, and included W. C. Falkner's mother, Caroline Word Falkner; Caroline's mother, Justiania Word; and two of Caroline's younger children, James Word Falkner and Francis/Frances Falkner. In 1860 Justiania Word, by then eighty-four years old, was residing with her daughter and namesake Justiania Thompson. J. W. Falkner was in a separate residence yet close to the Thompsons, perhaps on their property. Caroline Falkner resided with her son and his family on South Main Street, as did Francis/Frances.

J. W. Falkner, who was in his mid-twenties, entered law school at the University of Mississippi and graduated in 1860, and would need a position to fill.[23] W. C. Falkner, meanwhile, had for years been in a legal partnership with his uncle under the name Thompson & Falkner. However, after J. W. Thompson was elected to a circuit judgeship, he had to give up his legal practice, so Falkner had to practice alone under the name W. C. Falkner, Attorney at Law, in the "Office formerly occupied by John W. Thompson."[24] After younger brother James graduated, he joined Bill in a new partnership, Falkner & Falkner, Attorneys at Law.[25]

In September 1858, Falkner announced his candidacy for the office of brigadier general of the First Brigade of the Fifth Division of the Mississippi Militia. The state militia at the time was directed by five major generals (each commanding a division), while ten brigadiers each headed half a division or a brigade. The brigade that Falkner aspired to command consisted of Marshall, Tippah, and Tishomingo Counties, that is, the northeastern corner of the state. In announcing his candidacy, he used for the first time the title "colonel," probably to increase his public gravitas.[26] After all, who would have voted for a mere lieutenant or captain for the vaunted position of brigadier general? "Colonel" certainly sounded better. Of course, any title had its limitations, given that they were so liberally used that there was a concomitant inflation in the associated prestige. A newspaper humorously observed: "Almost every man you meet in Mississippi has some military title. . . . The convenience of the thing will be in the fact that you can address every man as Colonel or Major, without making any mistake."[27] Falkner was elected and for more than two years was known as "General Falkner." He never forgot the title.[28]

Soon after his election, a newspaper article previously alluded to appeared and was widely reprinted that focused on Falkner as a "self-made man." Although filled with errors, the article examined in some detail his trip on foot from Memphis by way of Pontotoc to Ripley, and proclaimed: "It is an honest and worthy boast of Gen. Falkner, that during his journey . . . he never received a single cent of money or a morsel of food as a charitable donation, but faithfully worked on the steamboats and by the roadside for all that he got." His studying for the bar was examined along with his time in Mexico, embellished with adventures, some of which may never have occurred.

> By honest industry and close attention to business he has accumulated some property, and is, we hear, in a fair way to become as rich as he cares to be. For many years past he has taken both pride and pleasure in contributing largely to the support of his aged mother, and in maintaining and educating his younger brothers and sisters—all of whom reside with him.

The writer then concluded: "Of him more truly than of almost any man we know, may it be affirmed that he is the architect of his own fortunes." This image would persist for the rest of his life and beyond.[29]

With the 1860 presidential elections coming, General Falkner would soon be put to the test along with the entire country. The political environment had become rife with sectional division primarily associated with the extension of slavery into the territories to the west. The election held on Tuesday, November 6, resulted in the victory of Abraham Lincoln, the Republican nominee, regarded as strongly opposed to the extension of slavery to the west. Within days, political developments began that eventually led to the secession of Southern states.

Chapter 7

❖━◦━━◦━❖

And History Shall Never Forget You
The War, Part 1[1]

At dawn on April 12, 1861, South Carolina militia in Charleston fired on the Federal garrison at Fort Sumter in Charleston Harbor. Although this is widely regarded as the beginning of the Civil War, its origins had been long coming. The war provided the means for Falkner's second involvement in military life, which had actually begun three years earlier with his election as brigadier general of the state militia. By the late 1850s, the United States was drifting toward a dissolution as Southern states were talking increasingly of secession. In Mississippi, this was perceived as foreordained. In order to prepare for this inevitability, the Mississippi legislature in 1858 appropriated $275,000 to update the state's deteriorated militia shortly before Falkner's election to a brigadier generalship. Following John Brown's raid on Harper's Ferry, Virginia, in December 1859, Mississippi appropriated another $150,000 "for the purchase of arms, in order to prepare her to resist effectually such a fanatical raid, should an attempt be made to perpetuate such an act within her borders." It also created a Volunteer Military Board to coordinate the new companies. Soon after the monies were made available, military organizations began to spring up throughout the state.[2]

The O'Connor Rifles were organized in Ripley, a company formed under the area's brigadier general, Falkner.[3] The company was named, strangely enough, after a New York attorney, John Charles O'Conor, who despite the geography of his residence was a staunch supporter of the right of any state to secede if pressed too far by the federal government.[4]

In late 1860, a second company, described as "a company of minute men," was organized under W. T. Stricklin, captain, and J. W. Falkner, first lieutenant, but it seems to have been in a state of flux.[5] The following month, W. C. Falkner reported to Governor John J. Pettus: "I have just completely organized

88

a company of cavalry; and we have most of our uniforms already prepared."[6] However, this company apparently metamorphosed into an infantry company, known as the Magnolia Rifles (or Magnolia Guards).

Following the election of Abraham Lincoln on November 6, 1860, several Southern states moved toward secession and independence. The first, South Carolina, voted for secession on December 20, 1860, while a Mississippi secession convention met at the state capitol on January 7, 1861, and on the ninth voted to secede, making it the second state to do so. Afterward, the convention remained in session to conduct other business and on the twenty-third formed a state army—known as the Army of Mississippi—replacing the old militia. The army was to be headed by a major general who would oversee four brigadier generals. Having just resigned as US senator from Mississippi, Jefferson Davis was nominated to run for the major general position against Earl Van Dorn and Reuben Davis. Jefferson Davis was overwhelmingly elected with eighty-eight votes, each of his opponents having only one. The brigadier generals were then elected through several ballots with nominees including Falkner. The four chosen were J. L. Alcorn, Charles Clark, C. H. Mott, and Earl Van Dorn. Each was in charge of a brigade consisting of two regimental districts. Mott, from Holly Springs, headed the Fourth Brigade, which covered much of northern Mississippi.[7] There was a constant turnover in these personnel as they quickly advanced to higher positions in the government and military of the Confederate States of America. For example, after being chosen as major general of the Army of Mississippi, Davis was soon selected to be the president of the Confederacy.[8]

By mid-April, ten companies were organized as the second regiment of Mott's brigade of Mississippi state troops, who would later be redesignated as the Second Mississippi Infantry. The ten included two from Ripley, the O'Conner Rifles and the Magnolia Rifles, with the latter commanded by Falkner as captain. An election was held at the parade ground in Ripley on April 1 for regimental officers. Only fifty-eight votes were cast, suggesting that only a small percentage of the regiment was present. Falkner was elected as colonel with all fifty-eight votes, B. B. Boone of Tishomingo County as lieutenant colonel, and David Humphreys, Falkner's cousin, as major. Soon after, Falkner reported to Governor Pettus in Jackson.[9] While there, he ordered military buttons for about eighty uniforms for the Magnolia Rifles from General William Barksdale, quartermaster general for the state.[10] For most of the new soldiers, their only semblance of military apparel was their buttons.

After the Confederate government issued a call for troops in April, the companies from northern Mississippi intended for Mott's regiment of state troops were instead transferred to the Confederate Army. By the end of the month they were ordered to be deployed to Virginia, which had voted in the convention on the seventeenth to join the Confederacy. Troops were required there as a deterrent to invasion by the United States. This became even more imperative after May 8, when the Confederate Congress voted to make Richmond the capital of the Confederacy. The two companies—the O'Connor Rifles and the Magnolia Rifles—had already been redesignated as, respectively, Company B and Company F of the Second Mississippi Infantry Regiment. Captain John H. Buchanan headed the O'Connor Rifles, while the Magnolia Rifles were under former brigadier general, then captain, then colonel, and now captain once again W. C. Falkner.

On the early morning of April 30, the two companies assembled on the square in Ripley for a ceremony in preparation for their departure for Virginia. Similar ceremonies were being held in hundreds of towns throughout the Confederacy. Mrs. C. A. Green presented the O'Connor Rifles with "a beautiful silk flag," while Mrs. W. R. Cole presented a similar one to the Magnolia Rifles. Excitement was in the air at the anticipation of adventure, even though the men realized that many might never see Ripley again. As families and friends looked on, the new troops marched northward out of town bound for Saulsbury, Tennessee, twenty-eight miles away on the M&C Railroad, where they were to catch a train. Falkner apparently brought with him a male slave to serve as his personal cook and valet.[11] While Falkner led the troops, his brother James remained behind, presumably to keep the law partnership Falkner & Falkner in operation. James may also have been concerned about leaving his new wife, Helen Hancock Falkner, whom he had just married on February 26, 1861, in Shelby County, Tennessee. Following behind the troops were ox wagons carrying baggage and tents. They reached Saulsbury the following morning and at 1:00 in the afternoon boarded an M&C train and arrived at Corinth, thirty-three miles away. At the intersection of two major trunk lines, the M&C and M&O Railroads, Corinth was ideally situated to become a trading hub. Within five years it was transformed from undeveloped land into a town of over a thousand. With the outbreak of war, it acquired new significance as a strategic military site, first serving as a staging ground for new units to assemble and organize before being shipped out. At Corinth the Second Mississippi set up camp among about 1,500 other troops already assembled. That night some were assigned guard duty. Clearly not used to military discipline, they objected on the ground that "they did not enlist to do guard duty but to fight the Yankeys." Nevertheless, despite such lackluster tasks, "all was fun & frolick."[12]

On May 3, the Second Mississippi was organized (again) after having initially been organized as part of the state's Army of Mississippi. It consisted of three Tippah County companies, three from Tishomingo, three from Pontotoc, and one from Itawamba. The same three officers were again elected: Falkner as colonel, B. B. Boone as lieutenant colonel, and David Humphreys as major. Other positions were apparently filled by Falkner's appointment: J. J. Guyton as quartermaster sergeant, Dr. John Y. Murry as surgeon,[13] and Lawson Hovis as adjutant. Interestingly, all three were from Tippah County, and the last two were from Ripley. William L. Davis replaced Falkner as company captain.[14] The Eleventh Mississippi Infantry Regiment was also organized in Corinth. Both this regiment and the Second remained together for most of the war.

Soon after, the troops were loaded onto a train and departed for Virginia following the five-foot gauges leading to Chattanooga, then through the Valley and Ridge Region to Knoxville and into western Virginia. On May 7, upon arriving in Greenville, Tennessee, a stronghold of abolitionism, they saw the first US flag on their route. However, there were "many Southern flags" in evidence. Their next stop was Jonesborough, Tennessee, where US senator, former Tennessee governor, and future US president Andrew Johnson was scheduled to speak that day. However, Johnson, a Union sympathizer, was not in favor that day; "the people would not let him [speak]. Secession seems to prevail here & is on the increase." Instead, Falkner "was called on for a speech," indicating that he had some degree of fame outside Mississippi. The speech no doubt addressed the dominant political sentiments and goals of the newly organized regiments and "called forth much applause & cheering" from the crowd.

The following day the troops entered Virginia at Bristol, and later the train stopped at Wytheville, where Falkner made another speech. Early the following morning, Falkner and others made speeches to the assembled citizenry at Liberty (now Bedford), Virginia, and later that day the regiment arrived at their camp, Camp Walker, near Lynchburg, where the following day the regiment was mustered into the Confederate Army by a Major Clay, who seemed "to be a fine officer & of good deportment." They remained there until May 20, when they were transferred by rail to Harper's Ferry, Virginia, on the banks of the Potomac River, the northern boundary of the state and the Confederacy.[15]

All the regiments camped at Harper's Ferry were inspected by Lieutenant Colonel George Deas, inspector general of the Confederate Army. Although some such as those from Virginia were well armed, the two from Mississippi were not. They had with them "their tents and camp equipage," while their arms were "chiefly of the old flint-lock musket altered into percussion. As usual with troops of this description, they all want rifles. They were informed that, for the present, they must rest content with such arms as it was in the power of the Government to give them."[16]

Deas noted that, as one might expect from companies with little institutional support, resources were not abundant. However, matters in the Second Mississippi were especially dire:

> [U]nder Colonel Falkner, almost every necessary is wanting. They seem to have come away from home without making proper preparations in this respect, and, indeed, it would seem that they expected to receive on their arrival in Virginia all the appointments of a soldier. Fortunately, the approach of warm weather will obviate the necessity of a full supply of clothing for these men; otherwise they could not enter upon a campaign in their present condition.[17]

Of the two Mississippi regiments, the Eleventh was deemed "very superior to the other (the Second), under Colonel Falkner. The latter is badly clothed and very careless in this appointment. The officers are entirely without military knowledge of any description, and the men have a slovenly and unsoldier-like appearance."[18] If the negative description was accurate, it was soon to change.

Soon after, Howard Falconer of the *Oxford Intelligencer* of Oxford, Mississippi, arrived early one morning to visit the Oxford companies of the Eleventh Mississippi and was misdirected to the camp of the Second. Despite the early hour, the regiment was already on parade.[19] Falkner was intent on training his troops to march with choreographic precision and to organize a band that could accompany it with music, thereby turning the regiment into a source of pride by indulging in his love of theatrics. Reverend T. D. Witherspoon, the regimental chaplain, later recalled:

> Col. Falkner, the commander of the regiment, prided himself very much on the splendid appearance of his men on dress parade. He was fond of exercising them in all the various movements of the line, and especially in one which, insofar as my observation went, was peculiar to himself. This was what the boys of the regiment will recall as the "spiral movement."
>
> The regiment was formed in columns of fours—and moved right in front, the head of the column describing the circumference of a circle, just large enough to allow the head and rear of the column to overlap each other a little. The head of the column at the point of overlapping was deflected a little to the left so as to come alongside the rear of the column, and thus moving forward,

keeping just within light touch of the moving column on the right, the whole regiment was "wound up" like the mainspring of a watch or the coil of a serpent, until the head of the column reached the center and the whole command stood completely coiled around.

When the time to "unwind" came, the order was given to "about face," the column moved left in front, reversing the movement until the coil was unwound. The regiment moved off on a straight line again. This was the movement usually executed by him [Falkner] when he wished to address his men and to bring them all within easy hearing.

Another of his fancies was to have the regimental band, which he had organized and drilled with great care, to sound on Sabbath morning, at the hour of reveille, either Old Hundred or some other glorious sacred tune. Well do I remember the impression made upon my mind and heart, in the gray dawn of a clear and frosty morning, by hearing from our regimental band, in subdued and mellowed tones, the strain of "Safely through another week, God has brought us on our way."

This band was always employed at the hour of public service to march in front of the regiment and with sacred music lead the way to the appointed place of worship.

You can therefore understand and appreciate the scene of my service in camp. In an open field at some little distance from the quarters of the men, a rude stand for a Bible had been erected, and a rough stand prepared behind it for the chaplain. A few camp-stools for "field and staff" were placed around; the rest of the space was left entirely open unprovided with seats.

Having repaired to the spot and taken my place at the stand, I was kept waiting but a few minutes when Col. Falkner appeared on foot at the head of his regiment; the officers and men under arms, and in full parade dress. The band marched a few steps in front, playing Old Hundred. Behind came the solid tramp of nearly a thousand men, their bayonets flashing in the sunlight. They formed a circle about me, the band meanwhile suspending its music, and taking its place immediately in front of the stand. Round and round goes the serpent-like coil—nearer and nearer the head approaches. The ground fairly quakes with their concerted tread. My head begins to swim and all nature seems to have joined in the whirl of the forest of bayonets around me. I grasp the bookstand in front of me—shut my eyes—not in a spirit of devotion, but with the hope of relief. At last comes the welcome shout, "Column, halt!" "Order arms!" "In place—rest!" I opened my eyes timidly upon the great sea of faces. The Colonel touches his hat to me with a military salute and says: "You may proceed, sir."[20]

Such an extravaganza allowed Falkner to display his sense of the theatrical, which would manifest itself in grand ceremonies and in the theater. To create such extravaganzas required coordinating movement and music, which was not accomplished without considerable effort. Although his troops could take pride in this, many probably regretted the loss of more lackadaisical hours that were sacrificed. Indeed, Reverend Witherspoon recalled: "I need hardly say that this Sabbath holiday parade did not continue long. The men soon wearied of it and it gave such stiffness and formality to all our services that I prevailed on the Colonel to dispense with it."[21] On June 27, Falkner reported that his regiment could "perform all battalion maneuvers at quick or double-quick time."[22] A month later, a war correspondent reported that Falkner was "one of the most distinguished volunteer officers now at this seat of war." He "has his regiment in the most perfect drill, and though exceedingly strict with his men, is universally popular."[23]

As the regiments were integrated into larger units in the evolving Confederate Army, the two major units initially formed were the Army of the Potomac and the Army of the Shenandoah. The two would later be merged and the following year renamed the Army of Northern Virginia, commanded by Robert E. Lee. The Army of the Shenandoah, commanded by Brigadier General Joseph E. Johnston, received its name from its strategic position guarding the Shenandoah Valley from penetration by Union troops. It was formed in mid-June from five brigades: the First Brigade commanded by Brigadier General Thomas J. Jackson; the Second by Colonel Francis S. Bartow; the Third by Brigadier General Barnard E. Bee; the Fourth by Colonel Arnold Elzey; and the Fifth by Brigadier General E. Kirby Smith. The Third Brigade consisted of the Second and Eleventh Mississippi Regiments. When on June 17 Bee was appointed to head the Third Brigade, he was in Charleston, South Carolina, and until his arrival Falkner served as commanding officer. Sergeant Augustus L. P. Vairin of the Second Mississippi recorded erroneously that Falkner had been "promoted to Brigadier General." Two days later Bee arrived in the camp of the Third Brigade, and Vairin, still thinking that Falkner had been promoted, noted: "Gen. Falkner resigned his brigadiership & is succeeded by Gen. Bee." The latter according to Vairin was "a fine looking officer & very highly spoken of." No one could know that his command would last only a month. The Second Mississippi along with the associated troops of the Army of the Shenandoah remained for several months in the vicinity of Harper's Ferry and Winchester, Virginia, both in the Shenandoah Valley.[24]

The other division of the Confederate Army in the area, the Army of the Potomac, was commanded by Brigadier General P. G. T. Beauregard, who had

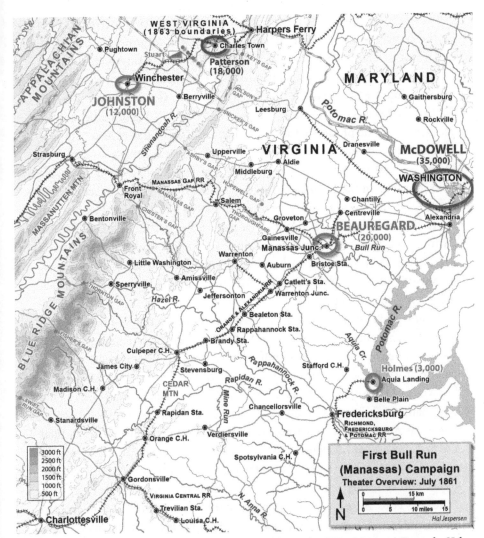

Figure 7.1. Strategic situation in northern Virginia prior to the Battle of First Manassas. Drawn by Hal Jespersen in Adobe Illustrator CC from Wikimedia Commons.

led the Confederate forces that fired on Fort Sumter in April. This army was strategically placed between Richmond and Washington, DC, at Manassas Junction, where the Orange and Alexandria Railroad intersected the Manassas Gap Railroad about thirty miles west of Washington.[25] The Orange and Alexandria linked to the Virginia Central Railroad, with the two providing a rail connection between Richmond and Washington. Beauregard placed his troops with their backs to the railroad junction and their faces toward a stream called Bull Run, which would serve as a barrier to impede the onslaught of a Federal attack.

Federal forces under the field command of General Irvin McDowell were on the south bank of the Potomac River interposed to protect Washington, DC, from Confederate forces. McDowell was under strong pressure from President Lincoln to advance against the Confederates and capture Richmond, although both McDowell and his superior officer, General Winfield Scott, felt that McDowell's forces were "too green" to launch a major battle. But the pressure from the president and others high in the Federal government prevailed, and Scott ordered McDowell to begin his attack. The plan was to have Major General Robert Patterson of the Union Department of Pennsylvania hold Johnston in the Shenandoah Valley while McDowell advanced against Beauregard. This was put into play when on July 16 McDowell and his army of thirty-five thousand departed Washington on course to attack the Confederate Army at Manassas Junction and remove the major impediment between themselves and Richmond. Earlier the same day, Mrs. Rose Greenhow, a spy in Washington, sent a message by courier to Beauregard informing him that the Federal advance had started.

Beauregard began preparing a defensive position on the west bank of Bull Run, concentrating his troops around Mitchell's Ford, where the topography favored a Federal approach. Within days the first major engagement of the Civil War would be fought there for control of the railroad junction, a battle known in the South as the Battle of First Manassas and in the North as the First Battle of Bull Run. On July 18, the first of McDowell's army began arriving at the village of Centreville east of Bull Run. General Daniel Tyler headed the first division of McDowell's force to arrive at the creek. There, he miscalculated the Confederate strength on the other side of the creek. Disregarding orders, he sent one regiment against Blackburn's Ford and three against Mitchell's Ford. As they advanced, the pine thickets around Bull Run erupted with Confederate fire, smoke, and Minié balls. Quickly realizing his mistake, Tyler pulled his men back and retreated to Centreville.[26]

On July 18, both General Beauregard and Confederate Adjutant General Samuel Cooper telegraphed General Johnston that Beauregard had been attacked at Bull Run and that Johnston's army was urgently needed. At the time, Johnston and his twelve thousand troops were in Winchester, Virginia, where they also faced a vastly superior force in the form of Major General Patterson's eighteen thousand troops. However, while leaving two brigades in defensive positions to keep General Patterson occupied, Johnston was able to slip most of his troops out of Winchester. The troops began departing about noon in a column headed by Jackson's First Brigade. The column stretched for miles across the Shenandoah Valley before ascending through the Blue

Ridge at Ashby's Gap. After camping the night, Jackson's men reached Piedmont Station on the Manassas Gap Railroad at 9:00 in the morning of the nineteenth and boarded the first train bound for Manassas Junction. Given the number of troops, several trips by train were required. Generals Johnston and Bee and portions of Bee's Third Brigade, including the Second Mississippi, boarded the train on the morning of the twentieth. After three months of drilling and other ignominious duties, Falkner's Mississippians were finally on their way to fight Yankees. They had little comprehension as to what war would really be like. Upon arriving at Manassas Junction, they set up camp near Mitchell's Ford.[27]

Tyler's ill-advised attack was of value to McDowell, demonstrating as it did that the Confederate forces were heavily concentrated in the vicinity of Blackburn's and Mitchell's Ford. Rather than venture another frontal assault against such a force, he began looking at routes to carry his main force around the Confederate left. The plan that he settled on would have two of his generals march their troops to Sudley Ford on Bull Run, a few miles north of the Confederate left. After crossing, they would attack the Confederates flank, while General Tyler would divert their attention farther to the south at Stone Bridge on Bull Run.

At about 6:00 a.m., Sunday the twenty-first, fighting began with a Federal feint toward Blackburn's Ford near the Confederate center. This was to provide a diversion while thousands of Union troops were moved to flank the Confederate left. Although Beauregard still felt that the main Federal attack would be against his center, he had received reports of Federal activity on his left, so he ordered Bee's brigade including Falkner's Second Mississippi and Bartow's brigade to the left to bolster Colonel Nathan G. Evans, commander of the Seventh Brigade of the Army of the Potomac, stationed at Stone Bridge. It was a fortuitous move that probably saved the day for the Confederates. Evans had been watching the Federals forming up against him, but after some skirmishing and artillery fire it appeared that they were not going to advance in force against him. He was correct. About this time one of his sentries reported Federal movement around Sudley Ford to the north, while soon after he received a message that warned: "Look to your left, you are turned."

As General Bee and his brigade including Falkner marched the six hot miles to the Confederate left, "going all the time in quick and double quick time,"[28] Colonel Evans moved most of his troops even farther to the left onto Matthews Hill to face two divisions of Federal troops. As the Federal vanguard began to move up the slope, Evans opened fire on them.[29] Realizing that he ran the risk of being overwhelmed, Evans soon requested that Bee

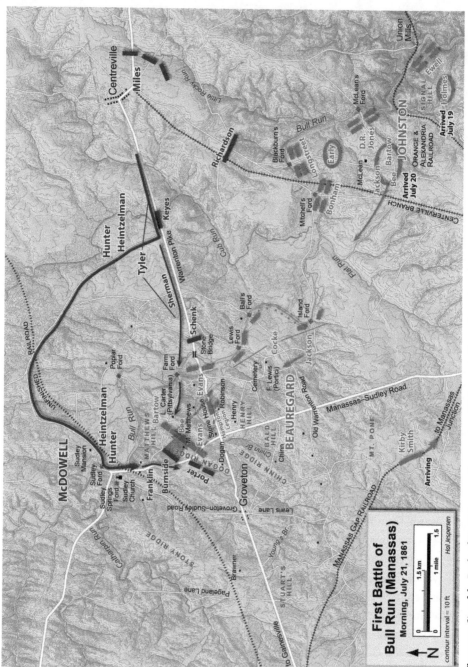

Figure 7.2. Site of the Battle of First Manassas, the morning of July 21, 1861. Drawn by Hal Jespersen in Adobe Illustrator CC from Wikimedia Commons.

bring his troops into the action. Falkner and his Second Mississippi Infantry were about to see their first combat. Bee placed them on Evans's right, where they soon found themselves facing Federal troops only a hundred yards away.[30] As the men prepared for battle, Falkner addressed them: "Now boys remember your homes, your wives and children and sweet hearts and give 'em hell." Captain W. L. Davis, who had replaced Falkner as the commander of Company E, recalled that "every man walked into the fight determined to win or die."[31] During the fighting Falkner ordered three companies of the Second Mississippi to attack a Yankee battery while he stayed with the remaining companies on Matthews Hill. Davis recorded that the regiment

> charged on and took four pieces of cannon supposed to be a portion of Sherman's old battery. . . . My Company suffered severely in the charge upon the battery. . . . [Two lieutenants] of my company fell dead just in front of and within thirty paces of the battery, four of my privates and one Sergeant fell mortally wounded just at the cannon's mouth. . . . Among the wounded was our gallant Colonel [Falkner], a fragment of a bomb struck him on the left cheek and knocked him off his horse; his horse was killed but he got another and remained on the field until the close of the action.[32]

After an hour it was clear that the increasing number of Federals would outflank the Confederates on both sides, and General Bee ordered a retreat to the south onto nearby Henry Hill.[33] As Bee's routed brigade retreated, McDowell gathered some of his senior officers on the newly won Matthews Hill and, standing up in his stirrups, proclaimed: "Victory! Victory! The day is ours!" As events soon proved, his proclamation was premature.[34]

Much like Matthews Hill, Henry Hill was a low, rolling hillock largely covered in crops and pasture, typical of much of the surrounding terrain. It was named for the Henry family, who owned it and resided there. Dr. Isaac Henry (1771–1829), one-time surgeon on the USS *Constitution*, had died many years before but was survived by his wife, Judith Carter Henry (ca. 1776–1861), a great-granddaughter of Robert King Carter of Virginia. By 1861 Judith was an eighty-five-year-old invalid. On the twenty-first, she remained at home, perhaps hoping that the battle would pass her by. However, it soon became evident that that wouldn't happen, as Henry Hill became the center of the fight. While Mrs. Henry huddled inside, an artillery shell penetrated the wall and ripped her foot off, causing her to quickly bleed to death.

As the Confederates were surrounded on three sides, the retreat to Henry Hill was not orderly; they had to run for their lives. Falkner and the other surviving officers of Bee's brigade tried to rally the troops, but it seemed impossible to keep them in line. At this point, though, Beauregard and Johnston were arriving on the hill with fresh Confederate troops. Colonel Wade Hampton and his South Carolina Legion were among the first, followed by General Thomas J. Jackson and his Virginia brigade.

Upon arriving at Henry Hill, Beauregard found that "Bee's troops, after giving way, were fleeing in disorder. . . . We found the commanders resolutely stemming the further flight of the routed forces, but vainly endeavoring to restore order, and our own efforts were as futile. Every segment of line we succeeded in forming was again dissolved while another was being formed; more than two thousand men were shouting each some suggestion to his neighbor, their voices mingling with the noise of the shells hurtling through the trees overhead, and all word of command drowned in the confusion and uproar."[35] Meanwhile Falkner managed to get his regiment somewhat reorganized on the far slopes of the hill, and Beauregard ordered him to the far left of the line.[36]

Colonel William F. Smith, commanding a battalion of the Forty-Eighth Virginia Volunteers, recalled:

> Shortly after this bloody strife began, looking to my left, I saw a heavy mass of the enemy advancing. . . . [I] resolved to stand my ground, cost what it might, when, to my great relief, the Sixth North Carolina, Colonel Fisher, and the Second Mississippi, Colonel Falkner, came up from the direction of the Lewis house, and formed in much confusion on my left, relieving me, however, in a great degree from my perilous position. I had three times stopped these regiments as previously described, and now they came up so opportunely to my relief that it almost seemed to be an act of Providence.[37]

From a grove of trees, Colonel J. E. B. Stuart's First Virginia Cavalry covered Beauregard's left flank. When they received word that the Federals were flanking the Confederate left, Stuart ordered a charge that stopped the advance. About this time, the Second Mississippi Infantry and others moved into their assigned position on Smith's left to form the extreme left of the Confederate infantry line. Stuart recalled being reinforced by "Colonel Falkner's regiment . . . whose gallantry came under my own observation."[38] The Federals were moving up the slopes of Henry Hill, primarily against the position of Stonewall Jackson's Virginia brigade. One full Federal battery consisting of six ten-pound Parrott rifles commanded by Captain James Ricketts and part of Captain Charles Griffin's battery advanced ahead of the infantry up Henry

Hill. McDowell's plan was to pound the Confederate line with artillery and then sweep over it with infantry.[39]

It then turned into a slugfest. Private Abner South, Company F, Second Mississippi, recalled that "bumbs shells, and mortars [were] buzing and flying in evey direction all over the field and when faling bursting and spreading destruction all around."[40] Troops on both sides were firing away at each other. Beauregard recalled: "The enemy suffered particularly from the musketry on our left, now further reenforced by the Second Mississippi—the troops in this quarter confronting each other at very short range."[41] Both Confederates and Federals surged over Henry Hill trying to force their enemy to retreat or be annihilated. Men and animals died that day, and legends were made. As he rallied his troops, Bee caught sight of General Jackson astride his mount urging his men to stand fast and shouted: "Look, men, there is Jackson standing like a stone wall! Let us determine to die here, and we will conquer! Follow me!" Soon after, Bee was mortally wounded and died the following day. However, "stone wall" lived on as a nickname for Stonewall Jackson and his Stonewall Brigade, and the name swept through the Confederate Army and down through history.[42]

As the lines ebbed and flowed, the artillery pieces of Griffin and Ricketts were captured and recaptured. As reported at the time, Falkner was "ever in the van[guard] of the battle . . . had two horses killed under him. When the second horse fell under him, he was thrown violently against a stump, and for some moments lay senseless. Recovering, he again mounted and went forward to engage the foe." Beauregard watched as Falkner with his Mexican War hat and black plume led in charge after charge, provoking the general to shout enthusiastically, "Go ahead, you hero with the black plume; *history shall never forget you!*" This enthusiastic admonition was immediately recorded by the press.[43]

Falkner's friend M. C. Gallaway presented his version of events twenty years later, which, although probably embellished by time, nevertheless corresponds to known events. He began by alluding to the capture of Ricketts's battery:

This occurred late in the evening on that memorable day, when the left flank of our army was being pressed back by a fresh division of Federal reserves, Ricketts's battery was pouring grape and canister at short range into the Confederate ranks, mowing them down like wheat, and fate seemed on the eve of deciding the day against the south. The battle-field was thickly strewn with the dead and wounded. General Bee was killed, and Colonel Falkner was the only field-officer of the brigade who was not killed or disabled. General Johnston, who had been engaged at another part of the field, now came galloping up to the

spot to where his presence was so much needed. The general instantly compre-
hended the critical situation, and said to Colonel Falkner: "That battery must
be silenced immediately at all hazards, and, Colonel Falkner, I shall depend on
you to do it." "If I do not succeed, general," the colonel replied, "you will please
have my dead body sent home to Mrs. Falkner." Within three minutes afterward
Colonel Falkner was quietly seated on one of the captured guns, superintending
the collection of the gallant dead and wounded of his command.[44]

The batteries changed hands at least three times, as did the Henry house
itself. At the end of the day there was little left of the house. The third and
final charge by the Confederates settled the day. More Confederate troops
had come up from Manassas Junction and the far right of their lines to bolster the exhausted fighters on Henry Hill. McDowell had more troops than
Beauregard, but he had fed his units in piecemeal, and they had been bloodied
and demoralized. General Bee's replacement, General William H. C. Whiting,
reported: "The Second Mississippi, in particular, seven companies strong,
charged with other troops and captured Ricketts's Battery."[45]

Following this third capture of Ricketts's guns, the Federal troops all
seemed to decide that they had tried hard enough to settle the issue of the
day and it was time for them to head back to Washington. And they did just
that, throwing away equipment and personal belongings, crowding the roads,
and ignoring all orders to stop and stand fast, and so they returned to the
Potomac. The exhausted Confederates made a feeble effort to pursue with
little result, but for the time there was no further effort to destroy the Federal
forces or capture Washington.[46]

Abner South recalled the aftermath of the battle:

In the evening toward night our boys walked over the field to see what havoc
had been done. They saw the most awful sights. some cry for water. Our
waggons and men were gathering up our dead and wounded bringing them
into the junction about 5 miles from the field. it rained all the rest of day, but
our dead and wounded came in . . . with prisoners from one to fifty. As fast as
our guard house became full we sent them off to Richmond this was going on
for days, we buried all of our boys at the junction.

Wednesday [July 24] We were close to where the enemy were unburied and
they became so offensive that we had to move. We left and went about 2 miles
on Bull Run after the first rains maggots came down the creek from the field of
battle by millions and we had to leave there and come to this place some 8 miles
off on the orange & Alexandria Rail Road. We have a fine camping ground and

are doing very well. We have a good many sick but none very dangerous. We do not know how long we will stay here.[47]

On July 30, Buchanan's Company B erected a stone on Henry Hill to mark the spot where General Bee had been mortally wounded.[48] The total casualties for the Federals were 2,708, and 1,982 for the Confederates. The reported casualties of the Second Mississippi Infantry for the Battle of First Manassas were: 25 killed, 82 wounded, 1 missing.[49] Commanding General Johnston listed Falkner among the officers that deserved distinction.[50]

While this was Falkner's second war, it was actually the first battle in which he participated, but he acquitted himself well, even gaining a nickname, "the knight of the black plume," a name too cumbersome to ever become as commonplace as "Stonewall." Although Falkner would participate in many other military engagements, this was the only battle of such magnitude. Its memory would play large in his life.

For the remainder of 1861 and into the winter of 1862, the Second Mississippi experienced no more combat. After it became clear that the Yankees would not be coming south toward Richmond anytime soon and that it would not be practical for the Rebels to go north to Washington, the regiment did not return to the Shenandoah but were stationed in various camps such as Camp Fisher near the Potomac south of Manassas Junction, where one diarist recorded that "there was a gay round of feasting and entertainments."[51] But it was not all fun and games. The regiment moved on to winter quarters on the Potomac River and resumed drilling and training.

On September 5, Lizzie Falkner, who was several months pregnant when her husband left home, gave birth to a girl. After being notified by mail, Falkner replied, expressing his wish that the baby should be named Elizabeth after her mother and Manassas in honor of the great battle. She was named Elizabeth Manassah Falkner but called "Lizzie" after her mother. However, little Lizzie didn't live out the month, dying on the last of September. She was followed four days later by her two-year-old brother Vance—Thomas Vance Falkner. The two were buried in Ripley Cemetery, the little girl having never been seen by her father. Before he could be notified of the deaths, Falkner had sent for his family, entrusting their care into the hands of J. J. Guyton, who would years later be an executor of Falkner's estate. Guyton departed for Ripley on September 29 and arrived several days later. The family, including the mother and her two living children, Henry (age eight) and Willett "Willie" Medora (age five), departed from Ripley for the Shenandoah Valley. On October 13, Falkner left the regimental camp to pick up his family, probably at the nearest railhead. In preparation for their arrival, he rented a house, and not knowing that they were dead had a small cot and crib prepared for Vance and Lizzie. Upon his family's arrival, he immediately noticed that the smallest children were not with them. Willie later recalled that "the impression made upon her by her father's grief as he ordered the cot and the crib to be removed, will never be forgotten." For the next three months the Falkners had a semblance of home life—military style. They remained through Christmas and into the new year, departing on January 13, 1862.[52]

However, the enlistment of men would soon come to an end, and the Confederate Army system subsequently allowed a regiment that reenlisted for the duration of the war to elect new officers. This naturally led to "politics" in the regiments so that officers who bestowed furloughs on their men and did other favors hoped to be looked on favorably when the officer elections were held. Falkner himself recognized this as not being (as the present-day military puts it) "conducive to good order and discipline." He expressed these feelings in a January 3, 1862, letter to Confederate adjutant general Samuel Cooper, saying: "The President is well aware of the fact that an officer who manages to make them effective is not likely to stand much chance for re-election." He also expressed the need for reenlistments. The one-year enlistment period for his troops would end within a few months, and he pointed out the need to have them reenlist, without which the regiment would be decimated. The men had been away from home for a considerable period, and if furloughs were granted, they might be encouraged to reenlist.[53]

In February, several men of the Second Mississippi including Falkner were given furloughs to return home and assist in enlisting new recruits. On February 10, they departed on foot for Bristoe Station on the Orange and Alexandria Railroad, a few miles from Manassas Junction. From there they followed a slow and tedious path catching trains whenever available back through Richmond, Lynchburg, Knoxville, Chattanooga, and Huntsville, arriving late on the eighteenth at Saulsbury, Tennessee. After spending the night, they walked the remaining distance to Ripley, arriving at 4:00 in the afternoon. The following day, the twentieth, Captain Buchanan noted in his diary that there was "some Excitment about the Fort Donalson [sic]," alluding to the attack on and capture of Confederate Fort Donelson on the Cumberland River in Tennessee shortly after the capture of Confederate Fort Henry on the Tennessee River. The invasion of Tennessee by Union flotillas would soon lead to a Federal base established on the outskirts of Ripley.[54]

After arriving and enjoying being back home, Falkner and other volunteers who were trickling in made some effort to recruit new troops. On

March 3, Falkner's younger brother J. W. Falkner signed up, thereby effectively placing in abeyance for the foreseeable future the law partnership of
Falkner & Falkner. On the twenty-sixth, an organizational meeting of the
new company eventually called the Liberty Guards Rifles was held in the
Tippah County courthouse.[55] Meanwhile, it was apparent that Falkner was
lobbying for advancement to brigadier general through seeking and acquiring support from various prominent people. Locally, D. B. Wright of Ripley
wrote to President Jefferson Davis to report: "I have just finished an extensive canvass in the northern portions of the State for the purpose of raising
troops for the war and the desire general if not universal to serve under Col.
Falkner as Brigadier Genl." Wright noted: "I know him to be honest capable
energetic and faithful in all respects well qualified and that there is no man
in Miss. under whom Mississippians would prefer to serve."[56] Falkner felt
entitled to the rank of brigadier, given that he had served for two years in the
state militia under the title and later commanded his brigade for two days
prior to the arrival of General Bee.

On March 20, the men from the Second Mississippi—both on furlough
and newly enlisted—had to say their goodbyes and depart for Virginia.
The day was clearing following rain, and they walked to Saulsbury where
after some difficulty they were able to catch a train for Corinth on the
twenty-first, arriving there at 3:00, and there they remained for the time
with the chances of getting transportation out rather difficult.[57] When
Falkner arrived, Corinth was filling up with Confederate generals and their
troops sent to resist the Federal troops who at the time were ascending the
Tennessee River with their sights on the town where two railroads crossed.
As the troops arrived, they began creating defensive earthworks and rifle
pits around the town's perimeter. While waiting to leave town, Falkner didn't
dawdle. He was canvassing for support for his bid for a brigadiership and
was able to find several generals with whom he was acquainted willing to
commend him. These were Generals James R. Chalmers, Charles Clark, and
Falkner's erstwhile enemy Thomas C. Hindman. Within two weeks all three
would be engaged at the great Battle of Shiloh about twenty miles northeast
of Corinth. Chalmers indicated his pleasure in recommending Falkner, noting that he knew him to be "a bold and gallant man" and believed him to be
"a competent military officer"; however, he indicated that he hadn't served
with Falkner, so he stated that he could only "speak from his general reputation." In his recommendation, Hindman spoke favorably of him, character-
izing him as "brave, energetic, and temperate, and I consider him otherwise
well qualified for this position."[58]

On the twenty-third, they were finally able to get rail transportation eastward; however, progress was very slow. On the twenty-sixth, they spent the night in Chattanooga, and the next day Captain Buchanan recorded that "the Col gone on I in command." Evidently Falkner, having access to a faster mode of transportation, had gone ahead, leaving Buchanan in charge.[59]

While passing through Richmond, Falkner sought out J. W. Clapp, an attorney from Holly Springs serving in the Confederate Congress, whom he presented with the letters of recommendation from Generals Chalmers, Clark, and Hindman solicited in Corinth along with recommendations from General Johnston and Major Whiting. Clapp passed these on to President Davis with a note stating: "I have known Col. Falkner for a number of years, and known him favorably, and he entered the service under favorable auspices, but as to the manner in which he has since performed his duties and his claim to promotion you are, of course, the best judge and will act as your sense of duty may dictate."[60]

On April 4, Buchanan and the other members of the Second Mississippi arrived back in regimental camp, which had been removed to a site three miles west of Fredericksburg, Virginia. It is not known whether Falkner arrived with them, but he probably returned about the same time. On the sixth, the newly formed company from Tippah was officially mustered into the regiment as Company L. On the morning of the eighth, the regiment struck their tents and departed, marching the next few days deep into the Virginia Peninsula between the James River to the south and the York River to the north, an area containing sites seminal in Virginian and American history, specifically Jamestown, Williamsburg, and Yorktown. They were ordered there by General Johnston to reinforce Confederate troops under attack at Yorktown. This was the beginning of the Peninsula Campaign in which Union Major General George B. McClellan began a large-scale offensive sending 120,000 troops to land at the end of the peninsula from whence they were to march inland and capture Richmond. However, they soon encountered their first stumbling block in the Warwick Line, a Confederate defensive position organized by General John B. Magruder near Yorktown. Although the Confederate forces were only one-fourth that of the Federals, McClellan did not attack and instead laid siege beginning on April 4. In response, Confederate reinforcements were sent in. On the eighteenth, the Second Mississippi marched through Williamsburg and camped that evening near Yorktown amid the remnants of George Washington's camps. There they remained for some time. Captain Buchanan reported that as they arrived cannons were fired until sunset and resumed the following day. At Yorktown, the Second Mississippi was on the battlefront again, although a relatively lackadaisical one.[61]

The brigade was soon confronted with the need to reelect officers. Officers had enlisted for only one year, and that term was now up, requiring the units to elect new officers. Falkner looked on this with apprehension because he knew that many of the men resented his emphasis on discipline. The process began on April 21, a gloomy and rainy day. After balloting for several officers, the voting began for colonel, with Falkner being opposed by Captain John M. Stone of Company K and Captain Hugh R. Miller of Company G, with Falkner coming in just behind Stone and Miller trailing further behind. Then, because of the late hour and the hard rain, voting ended to resume the following morning, at which time Miller withdrew from the balloting. Several candidates—including Falkner and Stone—gave speeches to the assembled troops, with Falkner presumably explaining his need to maintain discipline. When the votes were in, Stone had won over Falkner, but not by a large majority. This was indeed a humiliating defeat for someone who had once been a brigadier general and aspired for the office again. Falkner attributed his defeat to "a combination of demagogues," which was somewhat hyperbolic given that he had not lost by many votes, while it should be expected that any field officer could easily lose political support as the result of the exigencies of day-to-day life, which is the reason that officers are not normally elected. It was actually fairly common for officers to lose their positions at reelection time. Most simply went home, but a few joined the ranks as privates and stayed on to fight. Falkner didn't have to think long to make his decision. Already disappointed by his lack of promotion despite his success at Manassas, his options were to either retire or face interminable days of grinding marching and camping as a mere foot soldier. Rather than face such ennui, he decided to return to Mississippi and try something else.

Vairin noted: "Much dissatisfaction [was] manifested by Col. F.'s friends." David Humphreys, Falkner's cousin, was elected lieutenant colonel and was ordered "to command the regt. until protests of election questions are settled."[62] Humphreys would die a year later in Pickett's Charge at Gettysburg. On the twenty-second, General Whiting, commanding the Second Mississippi Brigade, issued the following order:

> To the great regret of the Brig. General commanding, a regret expressed also by his superiors Maj. Gen. [E. Kirby] Smith and Gen. [J. E.] Johnston, Colonel Falkner in consequence of the vote of his regiment in the election just held, retires from the command.

The services of this distinguished officer of Mississippi, from Harper's Ferry to Winchester, Manassas, the 21st of July, Evansport to Yorktown, merit the approval of his countrymen and the reward of his government. Faithful, careful, diligent and strict, he has combined and displayed in his career all the qualities which make a colonel of first class. The Brig. General is happy to be able to say, that while he has commanded the brigade, Col. Falkner's regiment has been brought by the constant care of that officer, to a high state of discipline and efficiency.[63]

The following day, possibly at Falkner's instigation, Whiting wrote a letter to the Confederate secretary of war, George W. Randolph (the grandson of Thomas Jefferson), in regard to Falkner:

Colonel Falkner is one of the best officers in this army. His entire devotion to his regiment, its condition, efficiency and discipline due to him, his extraordinary exertions to recruit it, the skillful manner in which he has commanded it all entitle him to the gratitude of the men, and especially the consideration of the Government. But he has been defeated by demagogues and affords another illustration of the crying evils that the election system in our army has wrought, and is producing. . . .

I forward an order published in the withdrawal of Col. Falkner who will in the impending engagement give me the advantage of his services on my staff. I most earnestly recommend Colonel Falkner to the consideration of the President, once more expressing my regret that he who led the 2nd so well on the day of Manassas, should be so untowardly debarred from its command at present.[64]

General Johnston also wrote a letter to Randolph in regard to Falkner, whom he testified "has served with me in command of that admirable regiment [the Second Mississippi] for the last eleven months. Its discipline and instruction during all that time prove his zeal and capacity—as his courage was proved on the field of Manassas. I regret very much to lose him. If he can be replaced in the army in a position adequate to his merit, be assured that it will be fortunate for the service as well as the efficiency of the troops he may command."[65]

On the twenty-third, the dispute having been settled, Stone took command as colonel. Vairin noted on the twenty-fifth that "[a]ll the old non-re-elected company & regimental officers relieved from duty . . . start for Richmond this morning by order of the Secretary of War." In early May, following a month of defending the Warwick Line, the Confederates retreated to Williamsburg, where they made another stand. Their stand at Yorktown presented a major impediment to McClellan's strategy for the Peninsula Campaign. In the end the Confederates successfully resisted his advance on Richmond.[66] On his way home, Falkner passed through Richmond, where on April 29 he received $1,400 in back pay.[67] He realized that if he was to have further military involvement, he would have to start from scratch.

Chapter 8

◆━◇━━◇━◆

Belt of Desolation
The War, Part 2

Upon returning to Ripley in early May, Falkner found a changed military situation that would bring the war to northern Mississippi and Ripley, where it would hover. While he was stationed in Virginia, there had been little action other than the major battle at Manassas Junction. Now the Union Army was practically at his own backdoor. Following their victory at the Battle of Shiloh (April 6–7, 1862), Federal troops had marched overland to the railroad center at Corinth. After almost a month of siege, the Confederate forces withdrew southward, allowing the Federals to occupy the town on May 30 and establish a major military base with up to twenty-five thousand troops protected by outlying bases, while the Confederate forces were restationed fifty miles to the south in and around Tupelo. This left a "no-man's land" between Corinth and Tupelo. On June 7, Memphis was occupied by Federal troops, effectively giving the Union a corridor of control along the M&C Railroad from Memphis to Corinth and just to the north of Tippah County. As Federal control over northern Mississippi and western Tennessee grew, Confederate military control in the area withered, leaving a corridor across those regions where Union forces were able to intrude to enact arbitrary retribution. By the end of 1862, reports of both armies began to refer to this corridor "in north Mississippi in general and to Tippah County in particular as 'the belt of desolation,' an area in which nearly everything that an army needed to live had been destroyed. The four horsemen of the Apocalypse—War, Famine, Disease, and Death— rode roughshod over the land."[1]

On July 22, Major General Braxton Bragg, who commanded the Confederate forces at Tupelo, moved the majority of the troops out on their way toward underdefended Chattanooga. This left only Major General Sterling Price commanding two divisions with about fifteen thousand troops at Tupelo.[2]

Although Ripley wasn't permanently occupied by Federal troops, it was sufficiently close to the Federal base at Corinth to be subject to frequent incursions by troops protecting Union supply lines and capturing troublemakers.

After returning home, Falkner attempted to reestablish himself in the Confederate Army. On May 16 at Ripley, he wrote a letter to President Jefferson Davis noting that there were several new regiments in Mississippi that could be formed into a new brigade and placed under "some efficient officer." He also observed that he would be "very pleased to be remembered by your excellency in the creation of new Generals of Brigade provided you should consider me worthy of . . . confidence."[3] On June 8, the State of Mississippi offered him an appointment as commandant of the camp of instruction, where he would be in charge of the enrollment and training of conscripts. However, the position would only be accompanied by a commission as major.[4] Falkner wasn't impressed.

Falkner was also certainly aware that on April 21, shortly before he returned home, the Confederate Congress passed the Partisan Ranger Act, which was intended to stimulate recruitment of irregulars into the Confederate Army with an emphasis on guerrilla warfare. Such recruits were particularly needed for areas where there was little protection afforded by the regular army. Northern Mississippi was such an area following the Federal occupation of Corinth, Memphis, and much of western Tennessee. Providing for the organization of "bands of partisan rangers" would have a major impact on the next year of Falkner's life.[5] Partisan rangers were effective as irregular cavalry that could operate as guerrilla forces often behind enemy lines. An advantage to being a member of such a force was that at times when there was no activity the troops could return home and effectively melt back into the civilian population. Although Falkner had no experience with this type of military activity, he immediately recognized an opportunity to act in an effective manner. He would take advantage of the new legislation by creating his own military unit that would operate in the shadows against the nearby Federal presence. Probably in June he began organizing, not a company, but an entire regiment of partisan rangers. By July he had 115 recruits and more coming in daily. By his account, the troops were "armed and equipped . . . by captures from the enemy," while they captured their "transportation" (presumably their horses), too.[6] This was the only such unit recruited in Mississippi as a regiment, when most regiments were formed of companies that were each recruited independently.[7]

Apparently, the military leadership in Corinth was aware of his activities. On June 27, Ripley first saw Union troops when the Second Michigan Cavalry arrived at sunset and remained all night. An objective may have been in part to capture Falkner and stymie his recruiting efforts. W. T. Stricklin reported that he and Falkner were able to escape from the town but "were closely pursued and the country scoured by [the Union troops] for miles around." When the cavalry left the following morning, they "took all the corn, fodder and meat they wanted."[8] With this, Ripley knew that the war had arrived.

Falkner's recruiting continued. By the end of July, he had almost six hundred men. Most of the recruits were from Tippah and neighboring counties, and Falkner already knew many. With him as colonel, his lieutenant colonel was Lawson B. Hovis of Ripley (Hovis had been Falkner's adjutant in the Second Mississippi), and his major was William L. Davis, who the previous year had replaced Falkner as captain of Company E of the Second Mississippi. Davis had obviously not reenlisted at the end of his one-year term and returned with Falkner to Mississippi. Upon signing up for the partisan rangers, he was initially chosen as captain of Company A before being promoted to major. W. W. Bailey was adjutant. It will be recalled that Bailey was orphaned and adopted by the J. W. Thompsons, in whose home he and Falkner lived as youths. The position of surgeon was filled by Dr. W. D. Carter of Ripley, whose son, Dr. N. G. Carter, would later marry Falkner's daughter Willie.

The Federals were aware of this growing threat and attempted to nip it in the bud. On July 28, two regiments of Union cavalry—the Seventh Kansas and the Second Iowa—suddenly appeared in Ripley, swarming into town with the Seventh Kansas continuing westward to the farm of Dr. James B. Ellis, where they had information that "600 rebel soldiers [were] encamped." By the time they arrived, the Confederates had eluded them and fled toward Salem. The Federal troops did capture Falkner's uncle, Judge J. W. Thompson, whom they were ordered to arrest for unknown reasons. The intention of the raid may have been in part to crush Falkner's new regiment at its inception. He apparently intended to muster his companies in on the very day that the raid occurred, thereby delaying this rite of passage to full membership in the army.

Despite their setback, on August 1, Falkner assembled his new recruits at Orizaba, about six miles south of Ripley, where they were mustered into the Confederate service as the First Mississippi Partisan Rangers.[9] The regiment was organized under the authority of General Price, then based at Tupelo, which later caused Falkner problems with bureaucrats who did not recognize Price's authority in the matter.[10]

Early on August 5, Falkner wrote to the adjutant general, Colonel Thomas Snead, for instructions on procedural matters, such as: what was he supposed to do with (1) prisoners of war, (2) those caught selling cotton to the enemy, and (3) Union sympathizers in the area? The first two groups were to be turned over to headquarters. As for the latter, if they were not suspected of providing aid and comfort to the enemy, they were to be dealt with in a kind manner. However, if they were suspected of aiding the enemy, they were to be arrested and placed under guard.[11]

By August Ripley had already been subject to two invasions by Federal troops—June 27–28 and July 28—and more were to come. Someone in Ripley writing under the nom de plume "Bertrand," possibly Falkner himself, complained that the formerly quiet town was now subject to considerable trouble: "In their two visits the enemy's jayhawkers spread devastation among our defenseless people; but in those two raids, also, the dragon's teeth were sown from which has sprung a host of resolute avengers, who have already begun the work of retribution." On August 24, Falkner with a portion of the partisan rangers and a small detachment of cavalry under Colonel Echols for a total of about three hundred men left Ripley and moved to the Corinth area endeavoring to draw out a force to pursue them. Near Corinth, they came upon and captured seven Union soldiers who were "regaling themselves with melons, peaches, apples, etc., on a farm just within their lines." Afterward they moved toward Rienzi, a small town on the M&O Railroad twelve miles south of Corinth, in hopes of encountering "some of our jayhawking visitors." Rienzi was one of several outlying sites that were garrisoned to protect the massive concentration of troops at Corinth. In mid-August 1862, the Fifth Division of General William Rosecrans's Army of the Mississippi, about 2,500 troops, was stationed in Rienzi, a formidable force when compared to the partisan rangers. Unable to find any "jayhawkers," Falkner determined to "announce the debut of his battalion by taking the picket post" outside Rienzi. On the morning of the twenty-sixth, three battalions of Union cavalry departed Rienzi to scout to the south. Falkner probably knew this and believed that the town was in consequence largely vacated of Federal troops, which was not the case; there was still a substantial number, far greater than the number commanded by Falkner.[12]

Falkner divided his command of about three hundred into two parties to attack from the front and flank. It was about 2:00 in the afternoon. Colonel Philip Sheridan, commanding at Rienzi, recalled: "The day was excessively hot, one of those sultry debilitating days that had caused the suspending of all military exercises; and as most of the men were lounging or sleeping in their tents, we were literally caught napping." The company of pickets was surprised and overwhelmed. Several were killed or captured, while the balance fled panic-stricken eastward where the main body of troops lay. Hearing the shots and shouts woke them from their naps, and they grabbed their rifles and cartridge belts and formed lines waiting. The fleeing Federals were followed by the enthusiastic Southerners, who suddenly realized that they had come face-to-face with a force many times the size of theirs. At that point they pursued a retrograde movement—and retreated hastily.[13]

Colonel Edward Hatch was directed to pursue with two battalions of his Second Iowa Cavalry along with Colonel Albert Lee and two battalions of his Seventh Kansas Cavalry, the Jayhawkers; both groups were involved in the July 28 raid on Ripley. About five miles to the west they came upon Falkner's forces formed into a battle line at Newland's Store and Antioch Church to resist the coming onslaught.[14] However, the Confederates were soon overwhelmed by superior numbers and forced to flee, "scattering in every direction" and leaving the road "strewn with shot-guns, hats, coats, blankets, dead horses, &c." Colonel Sheridan reported that "Colonel Falkner, commanding this rebel force, was so hard pushed that he separated from his command on one of the little by-paths and made his escape. He left us his hat, however, as did nearly the whole of his command." The rangers were pursued to five miles outside Ripley, at which point with the sun setting and their horses exhausted the Union forces gave up the chase to return to camp. They collected two hundred shotguns, twenty horses, and a large number of pistols, besides eleven prisoners.[15]

Following the skirmish at Rienzi, Presbyterian minister Samuel Agnew reported a rumor that Falkner had been killed and "his command cut to pieces." However, he subsequently amended his account by reporting that the colonel had been seen (presumably alive) in Ripley.[16]

Despite the Union victory at Rienzi, an inevitability given their superior numbers, the partisan rangers were nevertheless a real problem. Although it was unlikely that they could win in a confrontation with regular troops, they could make life difficult for the Federals by destroying property and tying them down. Writing about Falkner and the incident at Rienzi, General Gordon Granger complained that "there must be some definite and fixed policy on our part to combat and break up this most infernal guerrilla system of theirs; it is bound soon to waste our entire army away and for no equivalent." He went on to suggest a Draconian scheme in which they would "push every man, woman, and child before us or put every man to death found in our lines," a plan that was fortunately never carried out.[17]

A few days later, "Bertram" provided an assessment of Falkner's new military venture that was clearly designed to boost Falkner's military prestige:

> The moral effect of such raids as these upon the enemy is very great. Col. Falkner has proved himself an accomplished infantry officer at the head of the 2d Mississippi regiment, in Virginia, and he has even now given convincing

evidence of possessing in a high degree that dexterous boldness and peculiar combination of qualities requisite in a cavalry leader; he has the unbounded confidence of his men and officers, and all who know him. Three weeks since he went into camp with *five* men; his command now numbers eight hundred, and recruits continue to flock to him every day.[18]

On August 30, General Henry Little was given command of one of Price's two divisions, and simultaneously Falkner's rangers were placed under Little with orders to report to him.[19] Soon after, the entire command under Price was preparing to move. On September 1, Price received a dispatch from his commander, General Bragg, ordering him to watch General Rosecrans's army and prevent it from joining that of General Don Carlos Buell. While Rosecrans was in Corinth, it was thought that he would move eastward to cross the Tennessee River to join Buell. On the sixth or shortly after, Price's forces began to move north and northeast toward Iuka on the M&C Railroad, where it was thought that Rosecrans might be.[20] Rosecrans wrote that it was reported that Falkner and his troops served as Price's bodyguard. Whether or not this was true is unknown.[21] The first of the long column arrived in the town on the morning of the fourteenth; they saw many burned farmhouses and found that the town had been abandoned by Northern forces, who in their hurry to escape had left behind thousands of dollars in commissary and quartermaster stores, much to the delight of the Southerners.[22]

On the morning of the nineteenth, a courier reached Price in Iuka informing him that on the eleventh President Jefferson Davis had placed General Earl Van Dorn in command of both armies in Mississippi and that Van Dorn had ordered Price to evacuate Iuka and move to Baldwyn, where his army would be combined with Van Dorn's. Price issued orders and prepared to depart the following morning.[23] However, before his orders could be carried out, the situation began to deteriorate.

General Ulysses S. Grant, commanding the forces in Corinth, planned to smash Price before he could leave Iuka and unite with Van Dorn. He planned for Major General Edward O. C. Ord to attack Iuka from the northwest while Rosecrans attacked from the southwest.[24] Among Rosecrans's forces, Colonel Hatch's Second Iowa Cavalry shielded the right flank of the southern approach. About noon and well before the beginning of the conflict, Hatch encountered Falkner's rangers at Paden's Mill[25] on Mackey's Creek about fifteen miles south of Iuka, where they were either scouting or guarding Price's flank. Hatch had previously encountered Falkner at Rienzi in August, and Falkner reported the incident:

I was attacked at Peyton's [Paden's] Mill on yesterday at noon by the enemy, supposed to be about 1,000 strong. They were deployed in the woods as skirmishers and poured a destructive fire upon us and a little confusion ensued, but we formed a line and returned the fire. A brisk fire was kept up on both sides for a half hour, [and] when I ordered a charge, enemy had fled and reformed on the other side of the creek. The enemy had a decided natural advantage of us.[26]

The rangers' casualties were five killed and ten wounded. Falkner, who could only guess the enemy's casualties, noted that the rangers "killed and wounded a goodly number."[27]

That afternoon at about 4:00, as Rosecrans moved toward Iuka from the southwest, Price attacked. Although the Confederates fought hard, they were eventually overwhelmed by the Federals' superior numbers. The following morning the Confederates evacuated to the south along Fulton Road accompanied by Falkner's rangers providing a cavalry screen to cover the retreat.[28]

As September came to a close, Confederate forces under Generals Van Dorn and Price were preparing for a massive assault to reclaim Union-held Corinth. Having been placed in command of all Confederate troops in Mississippi, Van Dorn transported his one division from Jackson northward and by the eighteenth, the day before the Battle of Iuka, was in Holly Springs planning a rendezvous with Price for a march on Corinth. On the twenty-third, Price suggested that they meet at Ripley, a location likely suggested by Falkner.[29] The generals and their troops met in the town on September 28, and there they were said to have dined with Falkner, who probably played host to them.[30] Soon after they left Ripley, Price reported the strength of troops in his command as 14,363. "Falkner's cavalry" was listed in the tabulation with the number only "approximated" as 500, with the difference in specificity being the difference between regular troops and irregular troops.[31]

As their part of the attack on Corinth, the partisan rangers were apparently assigned the task of destroying the M&O rails north of Corinth to prevent the movement of troops into the area. A detachment of about one hundred men appeared on the railroad near Ramer's Crossing, Tennessee, a few miles north of Corinth, and began tearing up the track and cutting the adjacent telegraph wire. They were eventually seen by Federal troops, who intervened, causing them to flee. A boy who lived nearby identified the marauders as Falkner's rangers. By the following morning, the broken rails were replaced and the telegraph wire repaired.[32] However, other sections of track weren't so lucky. Considerable damage was reported on the M&O north of Corinth, while three bridges were reportedly burned. Rail traffic into Corinth from the north was stopped. This had presumably been accomplished by Falkner and his rangers.[33]

The battle to retake Corinth began on the morning of October 3 and lasted through the following day. The partisan rangers were not equipped to fight in regular battle situations and probably played no major role. The Confederates were unable to take the town. Following the battle and thousands of casualties, they hobbled back to Holly Springs, passing through Ripley on the seventh and eighth. Falkner was rumored to have been killed, but again the rumors were greatly exaggerated.[34] Following behind, Federal troops under Rosecrans entered Ripley on the night of the eighth. They were not in a good humor. Attorney Orlando Davis recalled what happened:

> Col. Lee of the 7th Kansas [Jayhawkers] mustered his regiment in front of Spight's Hotel, called the roll and then dismissed them, saying, "Boys, do as you please." Sacked Spight's hotel, taking spoons, knives and forks, blankets, quilts, bacon, flour, salt, corn, fodder, potatoes, cabbage, etc. Took 28 negroes. Broke the safe of A. Brown & Co., took $2000 worth of goods and $700 in money. On this visit of the Federals every possible indignity and outrage was committed on the citizens, including robbery, burglary, arson, theft and even rape. Houses were pillaged and robbed of every article of wearing apparel and bedding. Men were robbed of their money by robbers with pistols at their breasts; women were robbed in the same way. Corn, fodder, meat, horses, mules, stolen without limit.[35]

General Rosecrans was in Ripley for at least one night and chose the Falkner home on South Main Street as his headquarters and residence. At a meeting of the national Democratic Party in 1884 attended by both Rosecrans and Falkner, the two were affable, even jocular toward one another. They recalled that while in Falkner's home, Rosecrans "protected the family and the property as well as the town of Ripley generally with scrupulous care."[36] Of course, the comments were made years afterward and in an attempt to be conciliatory. The claim that Ripley property was protected differs markedly from contemporary accounts, which speak of destruction and looting.

Also recalled in 1884 was interaction involving Lizzie Falkner, who occupied her home when Rosecrans was there:

> Mrs. Falkner desired to send a letter to her husband, who then commanded a regiment in the opposing forces, a few miles distant. Permission was granted. General Rosecrans also wrote a letter and sent it along under the flag of truce. He said: "Your wife and children are safe, and will be protected while I am here.

I send you a basket of champagne; do not get drunk on it or I will capture you."
The Colonel was not captured, so it is presumed that he gave the champagne to
the boys by the spoonful, or shipped it to the rear for future reference.[37]

On October 24, Falkner's guerrilla activities continued outside Corinth.
He and the partisan rangers "made a successful dash upon the Federals in
the vicinity of Bone Yard, capturing seven Yankees, fourteen wagons loaded
with cotton, and driving the enemy back to their stronghold, in the neighborhood of Corinth."[38]

The Union command attempted once again to rid themselves of Falkner
and his motley band. Having heard that the partisan rangers were meeting
in Andrew Brown Sr.'s store in Ripley on November 19, Colonel A. L. Lee and
his command of 1,024 Union cavalry left Grand Junction and before dawn
the following day surrounded the town, moving in at daybreak. The inhabitants soon awoke to find Ripley occupied. The Federals were able to capture
Lieutenant Colonel Hovis as well as several officers and enlisted men for a
total of about sixty. However, Falkner and about one hundred others managed to evade the cavalry and flee in the direction of Holly Springs. Despite
sending cavalry out in all directions, the Federals weren't able to capture
Falkner, although they did catch a few of his regiment. Colonel Lee wrote triumphantly if not with false hope: "I consider Colonel Falkner's regiment now
broken beyond any hope of reorganization, and a great source of petty annoy-
ance to our forces entirely removed." After looting Ripley of foodstuffs, horses,
and mules, the cavalrymen departed on the morning of the twenty-first.[39]

Although Falkner had operated for months almost in the enemy's backyard and had managed to avoid capture, he would soon run up against a
bureaucratic problem outside his control. The partisan ranger project, which
had been created in April, was becoming problematic. To maintain a steady
supply of recruits for the Confederate military, the states were conscripting
men for service. However, some were avoiding regular service by enlisting as
members of various partisan ranger outfits, which in many cases allowed for
a rather lackadaisical military involvement. This does not seem to have been
the case of the First Mississippi Partisan Rangers.

Conscription for the Confederate military had been a bone of contention
between the Confederate government and Mississippi governor John J. Pettus,
who wanted men available for service in the state forces for home defense.

On October 10, John C. Pemberton was elevated to lieutenant general and
placed in charge of all Confederate troops in Mississippi and eastern Louisiana.
On the twenty-eighth, he issued an order that all men of conscription age

who had joined partisan ranger units after July 31 did so in violation of law and therefore were to be conscripted into the regular army. Falkner's regiment had been mustered in on August 1, one day after the cutoff date, making almost everyone subject to conscription.[40] This was an unfortunate technicality made all the worse because the official creation of Falkner's regiment was delayed by the Federal attack on Ripley on July 28. The day after Pemberton issued his order, M. R. Clark, assistant adjutant general for Mississippi, wrote to G. W. Randolph, secretary of war, apprising him that there were partisan ranger units composed entirely of conscripts and asking for an order to take conscripts from all those units. Three days later he published an order for all commanders of partisan ranger units raised in Mississippi to furnish him with a copy of their authority for raising their units.[41]

According to General James R. Chalmers, Falkner's regiment had been organized under authority from Major General Sterling Price. However, the conscript officers would not for whatever reason recognize Price's authority in this matter, thereby deeming Falkner's enterprise illegitimate. Then, "some time in November," the Conscription Bureau attempted to conscript the regiment's members; they "disbanded and the men fled in every direction."[42]

Once again without a regiment, Falkner presumably returned home. He had demonstrated considerable initiative in forming the rangers, and they had performed well, then they were shut down due to circumstances beyond his control. He wrote: "Does it look right that an officer who has been tried and found faithful should be turned out of service at such a time as this?"[43] He understandably felt that the system had let him down.

In January, Falkner departed Ripley for Mobile, Alabama, traveling on the M&O Railroad, which terminated there. After boarding probably at or near Tupelo, he disembarked fifty miles to the south at the town of West Point, where he remained for an undetermined time while indicating that he would be back there upon his return from Mobile.[44] He did not indicate why he was spending time in West Point; however, we can offer a probable explanation—his wife Lizzie's sister Sarah, who had married A. L. Brame, resided in West Point.[45] It is probable that part of Falkner's trip involved placing his family with other family members out of harm's way in an area far from the incursions of Federal troops. West Point, located about a hundred miles south of Corinth, was seldom subject to such depredations. Falkner implied this scenario when he wrote: "All of my property has been taken by the enemy, and my family driven from home."[46]

Following the dissolution of his regiment, Falkner began working to rebuild it. Through his congressman, J. W. Clapp, he obtained the authority from the secretary of war to reorganize it. He also gained a similar authorization from Governor Pettus.[47] Indeed, Pettus and General Pemberton came to an agreement in which the northern tier-and-a-half of counties including Tippah and the northern half of Pontotoc County would be placed outside the range for conscription into Confederate service, which essentially made them available for state service such as with Falkner's rangers.[48] Whereas in 1862 his headquarters was in or near Orizaba, a few miles south of Ripley, his headquarters was now in or near Pontotoc, about forty miles south of Ripley, a location much less susceptible to Union raids.[49]

In early February he reported: "I am now authorized to raise or organize the same Regt. by enlisting conscripts within, or near the enemy's lines. I am employed now in that business, and with fair prospects of success."[50] An unnamed correspondent in a Memphis newspaper reported encountering Falkner "in the city," apparently referring to Memphis, although it is not known what he was doing in the occupied city. Falkner informed him that he had "received authority to recr[uit] his old regiment of partisan rangers, together with as many new recruits as are disposed to join his force, for the protection and defense of the two northern tiers of counties in this State. His old regiment is already partially reorganized, and in camp in Pontotoc county. If the people of the northern counties will rally to his standard as they should, he will be enabled to put a stop to the depredations of the enemy in that section of the State."[51] On March 13, Falkner reported to Jacob Thompson: "I shall soon have my Regiment completely organized. Men are rapidly rallying to me. I have now got arms through the lines of the enemy, sufficient to arm all the men, who are with me. . . . I am now forming new companies and making a complete re-organization"[52] However, in reassembling his regiment, many members had in the meantime joined other units, so his unit never regained its original size and strength.[53]

General Pemberton soon placed Brigadier General Chalmers in command of a district composed of the northern ten counties in Mississippi, constituting that no-man's land in which control was so problematic. Falkner with his reorganizing regiment was placed under Chalmers.[54]

The perils of proximity to the Union line reappeared with a vengeance. On March 23, the Seventh Illinois Cavalry rode into Ripley coming from LaGrange, Tennessee. During their stay of about twenty-four hours, for reasons unknown they torched the business houses on the north side of the square, which included the only three brick commercial buildings in town, the old Mississippi Union Bank and Falkner's two store buildings. Orlando Davis reported:

They fired my office in two places, but one of their officers put it out. They threw my law books out into the street in a heavy rain and broke every sash in my windows. Also broke up my furniture, burnt up my papers, etc. They broke up all the furniture in the stores and broke all the window glasses in the square. They took Jim Whitten's family away in my wagon, stole my mule and harness, corn and fodder.[55]

Samuel Agnew wasn't present but recorded what he had been told:

The strange spectacle was seen of Yankees going about sticking fire under houses while other Yankees were exerting themselves to extinguish the flames. It is thought in Ripley that the house burners had too much liquor. The officer is said to be angry and declared that if he can find out who started the fire, he will punish him severely.[56]

Whether or not anyone was punished for this atrocity, the damage was done. A significant part of Ripley's commercial infrastructure had been destroyed. However, the war was only halfway over.

On July 4, 1863, Lieutenant General Pemberton surrendered the city of Vicksburg to Union forces following a month-and-a-half-long siege. This allowed Union forces to move unimpeded along the entire length of the river while also providing a base near the center of Mississippi. Confederate hopes were becoming increasingly clouded.

From his base at Pontotoc, Falkner addressed a letter on the twentieth to Brigadier General Chalmers requesting permission to detach his regiment from Chalmers's brigade in order to operate more independently, explaining that since the fall of Vicksburg, it was "evident that a huge portion of our State will be overrun by Yankees, and our best plan is to fight in the 'Guerilla' style." He went on to write: "I do not complain of my Government at the bad treatment I have received, but I do think I am entitled to a better position than to command one hundred and fifty men." He predicted optimistically that he could soon raise his troop numbers to one thousand if his request were granted.[57] We don't have Chalmers's reply, but it is doubtful that he honored the request.

Falkner was feeling as if his avenues for promotion were closing. On August 29, he wrote to Captain L. J. Gaines, acting assistant adjutant general, tendering his resignation as colonel of the partisan rangers to take effect two days later on the thirty-first. Attached to the letter was a statement by his regiment's surgeon, Dr. Carter, stating that he had found Falkner "unable to perform military duty in consequence of general debility, internal haemorrahoids, and indigestion, the effects of which this officer has suffered from for the last four months."⁵⁸

However, the following day Falkner wrote to Chalmers stating that after submitting his resignation, his officers had expressed their unwillingness to part with him as their commander and had asked him to withdraw his resignation and to ask instead for sixty days of sick leave. Apparently, Chalmers had already "cheerfully approved" Falkner's suggestion, and Falkner was therefore withdrawing his resignation.⁵⁹

Falkner was probably at home in Ripley while on sick leave. However, on September 30, Rev. Agnew noted that Falkner was "in camp and made a speech this morning. He is a candidate for Congress."⁶⁰ Nothing more is known about this possible attempt at politics.

However, little changed over the next two months of sick leave, and when his leave was up, he sent in another resignation effective October 31—seventeen years to the day after his resignation in Mexico. The stated reason was for "*protracted ill health*." Chalmers endorsed the resignation, giving no indication that he would be missed: "Respectfully forwarded and recommended. Col Falkner has not been in command of his regt. since 14th last May."⁶¹

It appears that with his chances for advancement circumscribed to little more than a seemingly futile, monotonous drudgery, Falkner had given up on thoughts of a military career. His once large regiment had been abolished and scattered as the result of seeming bureaucratic ineptitude. When he was permitted to reassemble it, he couldn't rebuild it to the same strength because many members had rejoined other units in the meantime. As in his previous military ventures, he had demonstrated initiative but couldn't cope with the long-term exigencies of bureaucracies. So, he departed.

With Falkner's retirement, Chalmers consolidated the First Mississippi Partisan Rangers with the Eighteenth Mississippi Partisan Rangers and appointed L. B. Hovis, formerly Falkner's adjutant in the Second Mississippi Infantry and lieutenant colonel in the First Mississippi Partisan Rangers, to command the consolidated regiment.⁶² Falkner himself effectively disappeared from the historical record for the remainder of the Civil War. However, he emerged from the Civil War, not financially destitute, but with sufficient resources to quickly recover. Brown notes that for the period from late 1863 through early 1865, it was "generally accepted" that Falkner and R. J. Thurmond "had worked together and built up their fortunes 'running the blockade' into [Federally controlled] Memphis late in the war."⁶³

The economy of northern Mississippi, like in most of America during the nineteenth century, was based upon commerce, usually an agricultural base in which farmers sold their produce for manufactured goods and other commodities. For Tippah County, the primary trade entrepôt was Memphis. After the Federal conquest of Memphis in the summer of 1862, Tippah was cut off from its major trade center by a blockade of military lines across which trade was forbidden by the Federals, who wanted to starve the Southerners of needed supplies, and by the South, which wanted to starve the Union of cotton. However, when there is a need for supplies, there will usually be some form of trade whether legal or not.

An illegal trade began to develop following the conquest of Memphis, as described in January 1863:

> [T]here are hundreds of wagons going from this county of Tippah to Memphis, laden with cotton, which they exchange for goods and greenbacks, introducing the latter into the country, depreciating our currency, buying up greenbacks in order to trade with the Yankees, giving two dollars in Confederate money for one in greenbacks. Every man who goes to Memphis is compelled to take the oath of allegiance to Lincoln's government. The legislative or the military authorities should put a stop to such proceedings at once or it will soon be the case that a bushel of Confederate money will not buy a pound of meat or a peck of meal.[64]

Despite the writer's opposition to the trade, people regardless needed to make a living. As the war dragged on, the blockade runners who were initially condemned began to be regarded as heroes. In this setting, Falkner and Thurmond may have prospered while being highly regarded for their efforts. At any rate, Falkner came out of the war surprisingly financially sound, ready to purchase land and engage in varied financial and philanthropic activities, so blockade running seems a possible explanation for his financial well-being. However, it must be pointed out that there is no documentation for this surmise.

In early 1863, Ripley remained in a vulnerable position in the "belt of desolation":

> Every now and then the Yankees make a heroic raid in this place—a gallant descent upon the women and children, and conscripts—and rob them of money, bed-clothes, wearing apparel, etc., levying contributions upon the larders and pantrys of the frightened people hereabout. Mules, horses, negroes, hogs, cattle, geese, chickens and *pies* seem to be the grand perfection of all their endeavors.[65]

During the summer of 1864 two Federal incursions passed through Ripley with each affecting the Falkners to varying degrees. Military attention focused on General William Sherman's campaigns in Georgia. The irrepressible Confederate general Nathan Bedford Forrest played havoc with Sherman's railroad supply line in Tennessee. To tie Forrest down, two Federal thrusts were planned into northern Mississippi to keep him occupied.

The first of these was in June 1864, when Major General Samuel D. Sturgis was ordered to move out of Memphis and take control of northern Mississippi from Forrest. He departed with over eight thousand troops with the intention of taking the M&O Railroad near Tupelo. On the way, his force passed through Ripley, and there Colonel DeWitt C. Thomas, commanding the Ninety-Third Indiana Infantry, encountered Lizzie Falkner, someone he "took to be a very intelligent person." Upon asking her where Forrest was, she replied "in a laughing manner" that "Forrest had gone away from there with two divisions to re-enforce Johnston, but had returned again and that we would have plenty to do in a few days. I asked her if she knew of the number of men that Forrest had, and she said he had some 28,000." Of course, Forrest's entire cavalry force consisted of only 3,500 troops, less than half of Sturgis's force. Thomas reported to Sturgis what Mrs. Falkner had said, and they both got a good laugh. Neither treated her seriously.[66]

On the morning of June 10, Forrest's cavalry unexpectedly struck Sturgis near the southeast corner of Tippah County at Brice's Crossroads. The battle turned into a chaotic rout with Sturgis's forces wildly retreating back toward Memphis and safety. They passed through Ripley in retreat on the following day. Orlando Davis described what happened: "Saturday, June 11, at 4 A.M. Gen. Sturgis' army reached Ripley on their retreat from Brice's Crossroads. They were the worst demoralized set ever seen in these parts. They rested here until after breakfast."[67]

That morning, Colonel Thomas saw Mrs. Falkner again. "She had breakfast prepared, and she called me in, and I took breakfast with her. She wanted to know if I did not find her words very nearly correct." Thomas didn't report his reply.[68]

Davis continued:

[A]t 7 A.M. [the Federals] were attacked by Forrest's pursuing cavalry and the fight raged in and around the town for two hours. The Yanks were again defeated and left, scattering in every direction through the woods. They abandoned a portion of their Artillery train in the northwest part of town, in Miller's field, to-wit 1 cannon, 3 caissons, 2 ambulances. Over 200 dead Yankees killed in the fight buried here, besides about 100 wounded were left behind. Every wagon, ambulance and cannon was captured, 21 in all.[69]

The second diversionary campaign was in July when Union major general A. J. Smith, commanding the Sixteenth Army Corps consisting of thirteen thousand infantry and three thousand cavalry, advanced out of LaGrange, Tennessee, on July 5. On the seventh, a small Confederate force briefly stood against the vanguard of this enormous army at Whitten Branch about three miles west of Ripley.

The following day, the eighth, thousands of Union troops passed through Ripley on their way to New Albany and Pontotoc. Although many of their reports mentioned passing through the small town, none mentioned the devastation that the thousands of troops wrought there. Orlando Davis was not so reticent, recording:

> At 7 A.M. the Federal army under Gen. A. J. Smith commenced arriving on the LaGrange road, and were until 3 P.M. passing through Ripley. The scenes of this visitation were the most terrible we have ever experienced in Ripley. The Yankees were infuriated because of their former defeat here and came swearing vengeance on the town. Thirty-five stores, dwellings and churches, including the courthouse were burned. The south side of the square was fired by the cavalry in the morning, the rest by negroes in the evening. Mrs. Prince's, Col. Falkner's and Mrs. Ford's dwellings were burned. The courthouse, Cumberland Presbyterian Church, the Methodist Church and the Female Academy shared the same fate.[70]

Not all of the Federal troops were so malicious. Davis noted: "My own dwelling was saved by the exertions of a guard left by Col. McMillen."[71]

The Falkners' home was gone. Whether the family was there at the time of the burning is unknown. Regardless, they had no place to stay, so another would have to be acquired after the war. Where they resided in the meantime is unknown.

As a result of its proximity to the Union lines and Union marauding forces, Ripley was devastated by the war. In early 1863, a visitor to the town observed:

> I am told that Ripley was once a beautiful, flourishing village, with churches, and Sabbath schools, and quiet homes, and happy citizens, where all the social and domestic virtues were in full fruition; alas, as I hobbled around I gazed upon ruin and desolation. Empty storehouses, deserted homes, broken

furniture, and all the lonely insignia of war, told that the Federal army—the Plymouth Rock Puritans, the philanthropic emalgamationists [*sic*]—had bivouacked here, in this garden of Eden, and left it a barren wilderness— a "deserted village"—poverty, doubt, and sorrow, and dread, and alarm, sit brooding on almost every face you meet.[72]

If one adds to this image the effect of an additional two and a half years of war and two major burnings, one can possibly imagine the condition and appearance of Ripley when the war ground to a close in April 1865.

Two decades after the war's end, Falkner reflected back and described his military career in self-deprecating terms, often exaggerated for humorous effect:

> My title of "colonel" was honestly obtained by four long years of bloody war, through which I gallantly fought by proxy. I won a famous reputation as a first-class life-preserver. My regiment was always full of men, because they were not afraid of getting hurt while under my command. It was safer than staying at home. It was said that I killed more enemies than any colonel in the service. In a single engagement I destroyed a hundred men and twice as many horses. They ran themselves to death trying to catch me.[73]

He clearly didn't hold a romanticized memory of his role in the war, although at First Manassas he had certainly given a good showing, and consequently he looked back on that battle with a degree of pride.

Chapter 9

Reconstruction and Rebuilding

The Civil War devastated the South. Of over seventy-eight thousand Mississippians who went to war, twenty-seven thousand, one-third, never returned, and many who did return were disabled. Cities and towns such as Ripley had been leveled as the result of burnings and bombardments. Assets had been lost and the capital invested in slaves was gone. The freed slaves were without their former means of sustenance and had to look for alternative means of income. The 1865 crop was poor. The first few years following the war were called Reconstruction, a time in which the North politically domi- nated the South. The first two years were governed by a lenient plan devised by Abraham Lincoln and implemented by his successor, Andrew Johnson. However, because the Mississippi legislature didn't cooperate with the goals of Congress, the latter body imposed its own less lenient plan, one that imposed political restrictions on Southern whites while extending suffrage to former slaves.[1] Much of Reconstruction in the South was devoted to rebuilding the infrastructure that had been destroyed. The railroads constructed before the war were significantly damaged by Union troops, and they had to be repaired before service could resume. For the time there was little interest in building the railroad to Ripley. Other problems were far more pressing.

In 1865 Kate Sperry Hunt, the newly married wife of Dr. E. N. Hunt of Ripley, came to Ripley for the first time after being married in Virginia. The Hunts arrived first at Memphis on board the steamboat *City of Cairo* and soon after left for Ripley on the M&C Railroad. Kate noted that they were accompanied by Colonel and Mrs. Falkner and their two children, Henry and Willie, who had been in the city shopping. This is one of the first known postbellum mentions of Falkner. The two families rode the railroad to Saulsbury, "passing through a country utterly desolated by the war." Upon disembarking they found that Saulsbury was "almost entirely destroyed and there is nothing to be seen but chimney stacks and where the principal part of the town stood is now occupied by old Yankee fortifications." The Hunts and Falkners eventually caught a ride to Ripley in "an old army ambulance with two lazy mules and a driver."[2]

Upon arriving in Ripley, Kate recorded her first impression of the town that was to be her home: "[T]he town is almost entirely burned up—two churches, the Court House and every public business in the place—it's a scene of desolation."[3] She didn't exaggerate. The area around Ripley's square was completely destroyed. The courthouse and the commercial buildings were gone, burned down, only a few remnants of the few brick commercial buildings standing. Homes and churches had been burned.

The resumption of civilian life for Falkner and many others meant rebuilding—rebuilding the infrastructure of the town and surrounding farms along with the economic, political, and social life. Former Confederate military including Falkner were required to take an oath of allegiance to the United States. Like so many other former Confederate political and military leaders, he demonstrated a strong allegiance to the United States and to the Democratic Party for the remainder of his life.

The town was gradually rebuilt. Much of the construction focused on the square, the business heart of the town. All the new stores—with the exception of W. R. Cole's new brick store—were of frame construction and so remained vulnerable to fires. For the rest of his life, Falkner would know a square surrounded by frame stores and offices, with one brick store on the west side.

One of the first businesses rebuilt was Dr. John Y. Murry's two-story commercial building, with the lower floor serving as a drugstore and medical office while the upper story served as the Masonic Lodge to which Falkner and many others belonged. Murry played a leading role in the lodge as he did in the Methodist Church. His second wife was the daughter of the old founder of the Methodist Church in Ripley, Charles P. Miller, who also had daughters married to Ripley businessmen Andrew Brown Jr. and R. J. Thurmond. In 1869, Murry's family became allied with the Falkners when his daughter Sallie married Falkner's son John. The following year their first son, Murry Cuthbert Falkner, was born.[4]

Falkner also needed a new home for his growing family—his home of many years had burned in 1864 along with much of Ripley. However, regarding his family from Missouri, his mother and grandmother had apparently died during the previous few years. His sibling Francis or Frances had either died or moved off. Only his brother James and his family remained. In 1865, Bill purchased from R. J. Thurmond a block on Main Street one block north

Baby Roy　　　　　　　　*Effie*

Figure 9.1. Engraving of Bama "Baby Roy" Falkner and Effie Falkner from *Rapid Ramblings in Europe.*

of the square and built his new home there; the yard with its collection of out-buildings surrounding the house encompassed the entire block. Initially only one story, it would be greatly expanded in 1884, becoming a local landmark.[5] He and his family would make a new start a few blocks north of his former home. Here, the last two children would be born: Stephanie Dean "Effie" in 1868 and Alabama Leroy "Bama" in 1874. The home was frequently the setting for social gatherings.[6]

Constructing the new courthouse would take a few more years, given its size and the associated construction costs. Little was done for several years. In the meantime, the County Board of Police met wherever they could find an available space.[7] Finally, on January 13, 1869, commissioners were appointed to let a contract for rebuilding the courthouse, and two months later a contract was awarded to builders George Vaughn and Francis "Frank" Pledge. The specifications stated that the new courthouse essentially should duplicate the 1838 courthouse with a few additions. The structure was to be built on the same foundations as the old courthouse, presumably reusing as much of the remaining brick structure as possible, which would have certainly meant that the old basement was incorporated. It was to be rebuilt "according to the plan of the one that was burned . . . of the same size same height same shape, same number of rooms all to be of the same kind of material and finished in the same style of the one that was burned." The only difference was that there were to be porticos on the east and west sides, with four monumental brick columns supporting each. Also added were two two-story wings, one on the north and the other on the south.[8] On March 17, another group of commissioners consisting of Falkner along with A. L. P. Vairin and James B. Taylor were appointed to oversee the construction and see that the specifications were adhered to and the construction materials up to standard.[9]

Actual construction probably didn't begin for several months, but finally by early July 1870 contractor Frank Pledge had completed the Tippah County courthouse for $25,000 and was already at work on the Lee County courthouse in Tupelo.[10] After having carefully monitored the construction, Falkner and Vairin filed a report in March 1871 to the effect that the work was satisfactory and that the contractor should be paid all remaining sums due him.[11] Falkner was soon after engaged to serve as attorney and agent for Tippah County to collect "all the money due and owing from Union County."[12] Union County had just been created in 1870 in part from a portion of southern Tippah, and evidently certain taxes were still due from that portion to Tippah.

Of Falkner's immediate family, his mother Caroline and her mother Justiania Dickinson Word died during the war, and his sibling Frances/Francis disappeared from the record.[13] Of W. C. Falkner's siblings, only J. W. Falkner was in Ripley after the war at a time when his brother was having to rebuild among other things his law practice. When the circuit court resumed session in January 1866, the first five cases on the docket listed "Thompson & Falkner" as representing the plaintiffs, and they appeared regularly for years to come, as did "W C. Falkner."[14] The partnership between the two appears to have split up. By the late 1860s, Falkner was a member of the partnership Falkner & Falkner, which presumably included his brother J. W. Falkner.[15] By 1872, Falkner was in the partnership Falkner & Mitchell, which included James W. Mitchell, who had just been admitted to the bar.[16] About 1876 he went into partnership with C. J. Frederick, who had just graduated from the Cumberland University Law School, as Falkner & Frederick, and the two apparently remained in partnership until 1887 when the younger man moved to Fort Smith, Arkansas.[17]

After the war, J. W. Thompson soon partnered with his stepson W. W. Bailey, who had in 1864 married Thompson's niece, Ruth Sellers, the daughter of his sister Jane. After the war, Bailey studied law with his stepfather, was admitted to the bar, and soon after went into partnership with him in the firm Thompson & Bailey, which had ended by 1870, at which time Bailey was living with his family in rural Tippah working as a farmer.[18] Thompson's other step-son, J. W. T. Falkner, after graduating from the University of Mississippi Law School in 1869, went into partnership with him as Thompson & Falkner, which lasted until the former's death in 1873.[19] J. W. T. Falkner later joined the firm Falkner & Frederick.[20]

In addition to his law practice, Falkner also opened a dry goods store before the beginning of 1867. The agent for R. G. Dun and Company gave him a positive assessment. The store had $6,000–$7,000 worth of stock, while Falkner was estimated to be worth $10,000–$15,000 and owned $4,000–$5,000 in real estate with "no liens on his property." He was of "good character, fine bus[iness] habits and attends to bus[iness]. [He] pays punctually and is never sued on mercantile [account]. . . . He is worthy of credit to any amount he would ask for. He is remarkable for punctuality and is not in the habit of asking for credit."[21]

In 1875 Falkner turned over the operation of his general store in Ripley to his son Henry in the hope that, given the right start, he might come to operate a viable business.[22] But Falkner probably knew that it would prove to be a futile effort. What little we know of Henry suggests that he was a problem, a young man without a higher compass.

Falkner also began investing in farmland. On January 11, 1868, he purchased 560 acres on Ishatubby Creek from his uncle J. W. Thompson for $2,000[23] and later that year bought another contiguous 40 acres also on Ishatubby.[24] Much of this was prime farmland in the bottomlands of Ishatubby, which could be supplemented by farming on the ridgetops. This land was the first building block of an enormous landholding that Falkner called Ishatubby Farm, also known simply as the Falkner farm. In 1881, his law partner, C. J. Frederick, wrote that Falkner "runs a farm near this place [Ripley], cultivating 1200 acres, and successfully manages over a hundred tenants; runs a grist-mill, cotton-gin, saw-mill, . . . [and] a dozen small farms."[25]

By the time he sold the farm in 1886, it consisted of 2,005 acres and included bottomlands associated not only with Ishatubby Creek but also with North Tippah Creek and its tributaries Bowling Branch and Medlock Branch. The farm was occupied by former Black slaves, who by then were tenant farmers. Falkner had a superintendent on the farm who looked after matters, possibly making certain that the farmers were working regularly and supervising the allocation of resources such as mules and seed. One superintendent, R. H.

Brown, died of pneumonia on January 18, 1881.[26] Another was Ira South,[27] who either preceded or succeeded Brown. A note from Falkner to South concerned maintaining and using a steam-powered cotton gin and press:

> When it rains so you cant work out, fix the press complete. Have the lint room cleaned out, and clear out the Gin house. Drive the hoops on all of those barrels, and put them in the water. Put Mart [?] Stanford to work, and make him work like hell. Take those barrels off of the top of the Gin house, and get them so they will hold water. You may hire hands to help you at 60 cts per day. Fix the Gin Belt, and the press belt, and make every thing ready for gining. Tell Elbert Smith, that I am out of corn, and he must bring me some immediately. Send pattern for key to the press. Any thing you need send for it. Get hands to tear down the old engine house so we can put it up over the new engine. Move things ahead as fast as you can.[28]

This illustrates Falkner's concerns with the minutia of operating the gin and press and with the overall productivity of the work he was paying for. He also referred to the working and care of mules: "See that my mules are fed and watered, and when they are not at work, let them be kept in the pasture."[29] Falkner's mules were presumably for the use of the tenant farmers on his place. Although there is much that we do not know about the operation of Ishatubby Farm, it was probably experimental in the transition from slave labor to free labor, looking for workable means of production that was beneficial to all. Most of the freemen owned neither land nor mules nor any other capital for production. Falkner brought land with residences and capital to the operation while hiring a resident supervisor to coordinate. For the use of these, the resident farmers paid either rent or a share of what they produced in the fall.

In 1874, Falkner's store was characterized as a general store rather than a dry goods store as it had been formerly, "mostly run for the benefit of his employees on his plantation." That is to say, he was in the furnishing business, furnishing the tenant farmers with needed goods throughout the year, to be paid when their cotton crops were harvested. The R. G. Dun agent reported that Falkner owned $50,000 worth of real estate, showing a notable increase over the $15,000 of real estate recorded by the 1870 census. Overall, he was worth over $100,000 above liabilities, while maintaining a good law practice.[30]

When he wasn't at home, Falkner was often in Memphis, and if he or his family members visited Memphis they invariably stayed at the Peabody Hotel.[31] The Memphis papers carried daily lists of prominent visitors to the

Figure 9.2. The Peabody Hotel, Memphis, circa 1870–1880.

main hotels. In May 1870, the *Memphis Daily Appeal* reported: "Col. W. C. Falkner, Ripley, Miss. [is] in the city and stopping at the Peabody Hotel."[32] This is the earliest known notice of Falkner's staying at the Peabody. Similar notices would appear for the next twenty years of the Falkners "stopping at the Peabody." Five stories tall, the original Peabody Hotel, named after financier and philanthropist George Peabody (1795–1869), was constructed in 1868 by attorney and railroad promoter R. C. Brinkley (1816–1878) on a commercial block formerly known as the Brinkley Block at the northwest corner of Main Street and Monroe Avenue. It was opened for business in December 1868. Soon it became a landmark, its name synonymous with that of the city. A later version of the Peabody, replete with a flowing fountain in the lobby filled with ducks, continues to gather fame. Native Mississippian David Cohn knew the hotel as a place of elegance where the well-heeled met: "The Peabody is the

Paris Ritz, the Cairo Shepheard's, the London Savoy of this section. If you stand near its fountain in the middle of the lobby, where ducks waddle and turtles drowse, ultimately you will see everybody who is anybody in the Delta and many who are on the make."[33]

Shortly after the war ended, Falkner assisted in rebuilding the Ripley Female Academy, which had been burned during the war.[34] It was rechristened Stonewall College by Falkner, evidently in honor of General T. J. "Stonewall" Jackson, whose nickname was a legacy of Manassas, a battle that loomed large in Falkner's memory and as a part of his reputation.[35] Part of his assistance in rebuilding the school was through composing a play to be performed as a fundraiser. Entitled *The Lost Diamond*, the play also involved a link to Manassas.[36] The protagonist of the melodrama is George Clifton, "a poor, but worthy young man who by his labor supports his mother and her three little children," who is in love with Rosalind Raymond, the daughter of a wealthy widow. During a visit by Clifton to Rosalind's home, a valuable diamond belonging to Mrs. Raymond is stolen, and Clifton is falsely accused by John Gaylor, "a rejected suitor of Rosalind's." Sometime later amid "thrilling scenes on the bloody field" at Manassas, Clifton, serving as a Confederate soldier, engages in a sword fight with Federal soldiers and wins. One of the latter is revealed to be John Gaylor, who before he dies confesses to have stolen the diamond. With Clifton vindicated, the play ends with a "grand tableaux by the troup in gorgeous costumes and military uniform." The play was said to have created "a sensation" at the opening of Stonewall College, where it played three nights to a "crowded house" and was even performed later in South Carolina.[37]

In addition, John Ford, the editor of the *Ripley Advertiser*, was ebullient over the expeditious construction, which reflected the "highest credit" on Falkner. Through this, Falkner "endeared himself to the community in which he lives, and all public-spirited men will accord to him the high praise which his energy and liberality deserve."[38] This activity was the beginning of a career of public fundraising and public relations work. As will be seen, he later resurrected *The Lost Diamond* as a fundraiser twice in 1883. When the yellow fever was raging in nearby Memphis and Holly Springs in 1878, Falkner and others donated foodstuffs to supply the impacted areas.[39] During the 1880s he loaned Gus Cowan, a young African American man, money to help subsidize his education at Rust College in Holly Springs.[40] Falkner's philanthropy was not one of sending vast sums to fund institutions; he was not that well heeled. Instead, he responded to local needs with cash and with his own services. Such an ability to interact and respond to a wide range of people would serve him well when he emerged as the leader of the movement to build a railroad to Ripley in 1869.

If, as has been indicated, Falkner wasn't the first to dream of a spur-line railroad, he was the first to actually build it. While efforts to build a railroad before the war had failed, under Falkner things would be different. He had the ability to project often extravagant visions while being able to actualize them. Furthermore, he had the audacity to radically transform the railroad from something that many had envisioned into something that few could have envisioned.

Chapter 10

✧━◈━◦━━◦━◈━✧

The Railroad to Ripley

Near the end of the summer of 1869 a project was initiated, probably by Falkner and certainly headed by him, to build a railroad connecting New Albany and Ripley with the M&C Railroad, to be known as the Middleton, Ripley, and New Albany Railroad. On August 21 he was slated to speak at the Tippah County courthouse on "railroad subjects" no doubt to promote the project and raise funds.[1] A meeting was later held in early September at Orizaba in the southern part of the county. The *Ripley Advertiser* reported that there was no opposition there while "everybody [was] willing to subscribe, and stock [was] taken freely."[2] A few days later, on September 21, a meeting was held in New Albany (then in Pontotoc County) to raise support for building a railroad "from the most favorable point on the Memphis and Charleston Railroad, via Ripley, Miss., to New Albany." The project was bolstered by the plans of another proposed railroad, the Memphis and Selma, which was intended to pass through New Albany, placing the town in an advantageous location. If this scheme panned out, the Ripley road would have a rail connection at both ends.[3] The well-attended meeting was held "under one of nature's pavilions, a clump of sturdy oaks," where the crowd listened to Falkner and other speakers appealing to "the good sense of the audience." When the books were opened, almost the entire audience including Blacks subscribed for shares of stock, bringing the total to $80,000.[4]

However, above and beyond using merely local sources of capital, Falkner realized that outside sources were needed and consequently began to focus on government programs and outside corporate interests, eventually courting investors in the center of finance, New York City. This shift greatly aided Falkner's subsequent successes. At that particular time, a key area that would benefit was clearly Memphis. This was enunciated by the editor of the *Memphis Daily Appeal*, who noted that the Ripley railroad would bring ten to fifteen thousand additional bales of cotton to the river city.[5] On October 30, Falkner spoke to the Memphis Chamber of Commerce outlining the trade advantages that would accrue to the river city with the construction of the "Ripley, Middleton, and New Albany Railroad" while calling for financial support from the city's merchants. The grading was already provided for, and he claimed—perhaps overoptimistically—that "the cost cannot but be moderate." All that was needed was $50,000. The chamber resolved to support the effort and stated its intention to appoint a committee to put the matter before the citizenry of Shelby County. However, the committee would not be appointed until the next Board of Trade meeting.[6]

Soon after, Falkner met with the directors of the M&C Railroad in Memphis. By his account they committed to providing several key components to construction, presumably in exchange for some form of control over the road. Their contributions would include iron rails, free transportation for construction materials, use of a construction train, and a depot building at the northern terminus in Middleton. On the other side, Tippah and Pontotoc Counties would have to raise the money to grade the route. He thought that only $35,000 would be needed, this above what had already been raised. Furthermore, he optimistically predicted that Memphis would provide $50,000 to $100,000 in aid. He thought it best to initially build the road only as far south as Ripley and extend it south to New Albany at a later date. He presented a cost estimate from the chief engineer of the M&C to build to Ripley, which did not include the cost of the rails:

25 miles grading, at $3,000 per mile $75,000
60,000 cross-ties, at 50 cents each $18,000
Laying 25 miles track, $400 per mile. $10,000
Total. . . . .$103,000[7]

On Wednesday, December 15, a meeting of the stockholders of the railroad was held in Ripley during which seven directors were elected, including Falkner. The newly constituted Board of Directors then voted Falkner in as its president. A newspaper article noted that his election was "a compliment he well deserved, as being the originator of the enterprise, and for his untiring efforts in its behalf from its first inception up to the present time." The board was to meet again on the first Monday in February when the organization would be completed.[8]

In the meantime, undoubtedly at the instigation of the directors, the Tippah County Board of Police met on January 4 and ordered that a county-wide election be held on January 18 to determine whether or not the county should purchase eight thousand shares of capital stock in the railroad for $200,000. It was stipulated that only $120,000 would be applied to construction between Middleton and Ripley, while $80,000 would be applied to construction from Ripley south to New Albany to reassure the southern part of the county that its money would not be expended getting the railroad to Ripley. The route between Ripley and New Albany was not to deviate more than half of a mile from an air line route between the two, which would have located it a considerable distance east of the route that was eventually constructed. Furthermore, it was specified that two depots were to be located between Ripley and New Albany with one at Orizaba.[9] The election was held on the appointed day. While the people were apparently supportive of railroad construction, they were not willing to pay for it. The measure lost on a vote of 566 for and 879 against.[10]

Certainly, the failure to gain the county's support for $200,000 was a problem. The support of locals, while fervent and well intended (after all, why would they not support the railroad?), probably manifested in pledges made on credit rather than with hard cash, and without the latter the former is useless. Unable to muster the needed capital, Ripley must have experienced déjà vu.

In the meantime, another railroad project emerged that was intended to be not just a mere spur line, but a major trunk line that would pass through Ripley. Chartered on July 8, 1870, it was named the Ship Island, Mississippi City, and Paducah Railroad Company (SI, MC & P).[11] Although a Ripley citizen, W. R. Cole, was among the incorporators, the group was not Ripley based but included promoters from throughout the region. Most notable was W. H. Hardy, an attorney from Meridian, Mississippi, who would be involved years later in railroad activity. The SI, MC & P was actually the resurrection of a much earlier project called the Gulf and Ship Island, a railroad envisioned to connect the Mississippi Gulf Coast with the Ohio River. The southern terminus was to be Mississippi City, a coastal town and the county seat of Harrison County.[12] Previous railroad construction had terminated at cities with natural harbors such as Memphis, Mobile, and New Orleans. However, this project intended to build a port city where there was none and avoid shipping through a non-Mississippi city. The plan entailed using the deepwater harbor at Ship Island with a possible trestle connection to Mississippi City. From there, the railroad would run inland between the two railroad corridors that crossed Mississippi south to north. This project had initially been attempted before the war, with charters for the Gulf and Ship Island Railroad dating to 1850 and 1856. The SI, MC & P was to follow the same route as the G&SI and pass through Ripley before continuing north to the Ohio River. Falkner knew that the construction of this road through Ripley would obviate the need for his spur line. However, like many other railroad projects, the SI, MC & P came to naught. After the charter was enacted, there were only a few meetings followed by nothing. Not one shovel of dirt was moved; not one rail was laid.[13] The project simply died. This meant that the spur line to Ripley was still needed, and Falkner was free to continue.

Despite his failure to receive county financial support, Falkner was resilient. While the loss of local funding was a devastating blow to the prospects of building the railroad, events of the following year provided a new ground for optimism. One was the prospect of receiving state subsidies and the other was a plan to build a railroad of narrower gauge, and therefore considerably cheaper, than planned. In the meantime, although the SI, MC & P was dead, the idea that it stood for, of building a regional trunk line, would remain in his mind.

By the spring of 1871 Falkner was ready for another campaign. On May 13, the Mississippi legislature passed an act incorporating the Ripley Railroad Company for the purpose of building and operating a railroad to connect Ripley with one out of several trunk lines, either the Memphis and Charleston Railroad, the Mobile and Ohio Railroad, the Mississippi Central Railroad, or the proposed Selma, Marion, and Memphis Railroad.[14] The creation of the company was likely influenced by legislation that was passed on the same day as the railroad's charter, entitled "An Act to Encourage Internal Improvements in the State of Mississippi." Intended to promote railroad construction in the state, it offered a $4,000 per mile subsidy to any railroad company that constructed twenty-five miles of road by September 1, 1872, provided that the road was constructed "in first-class manner, with iron rails of not less than fifty-six (56) pounds weight per yard, [and] twenty-five miles of its projected line within the State." There was no specification precluding the construction of a narrow-gauge railroad, probably because such were almost unheard of when the legislation was drafted. The law also authorized the creation of a state board of railroad commissioners who would examine and report on any railway that wanted to take advantage of the offer of subsidy.[15]

For a railroad that never had adequate funds, this was an irresistible temptation. Twenty-five miles had to be constructed, and it was twenty-five miles from the M&C to Ripley. However, the first four miles were in Tennessee, and the legislation required that at least twenty-five miles be constructed in Mississippi, not in some other state. The state grant—if it could be obtained—would bring in upwards of $80,000, no small sum at that time.

What Falkner may not have understood was that the promise of a subsidy was not a definite promise. Following the war, the state was not overflowing with cash, and only a little could be given to any concern, no matter how meritorious. Furthermore, the new constitution of 1868 had seemingly forbidden such activities. The law offering the subsidy was drafted to encourage railroad development, and to get around the constitutional problem, its drafters worded it in a manner that might evade the problem. However, that was not a certainty. And so, matters rested until the law was put to the test by the first company to attempt to claim the subsidy.[16]

After advertising for four weeks in the *Ripley Advertiser*, the railroad's incorporators held an organizational meeting in the Tippah County courthouse on September 18, 1871. The first order of business was to sign an agreement indicating their acceptance of the charter of incorporation passed by the legislature in May. Afterward, directors were elected with Falkner's name being at the head of the list. Then officers were elected who in turn unanimously elected Falkner president, H. W. Stricklin treasurer, and R. J. Thurmond secretary. Additionally, the capital stock of the company was set at $500,000 with shares at $25 each. Agents were appointed with authority to open subscriptions for stock, indicating that the campaign was on to acquire commitments of resources.[17]

By the next meeting on November 9, also in Ripley, the directors were well on their way to locating the route of the railroad. The charter provided the option of building from Ripley to any of four railroad connections: the Memphis and Charleston to the north, the Mobile and Ohio to the east, the Mississippi Central to the west, and the Selma, Marion, and Memphis, a railroad that had not yet been constructed. By the November meeting they had determined to build north to the Memphis and Charleston via what they termed "the Muddy Route," so named because it followed the alluvial plain of Muddy Creek, which began a few miles north of Ripley and extended northward to the Hatchie River intersecting the M&C about three miles east of Middleton, Tennessee.[18] The logic behind this is clear. By following the relatively level valley, the builders would minimize expenditures in terms of earthmoving, and earthmoving was the most variable cost in railroad construction.

At the same meeting a variant of this route was proffered to the citizens of Middleton. If they subscribed $10,000, then the northern terminus would be located in their town. This required that the railroad leave the plain of the Muddy and build across the uplands leading to Middleton. The point of departure would be a short distance south of present-day Walnut, Mississippi. While this variation was somewhat costlier, it was certainly reasoned that terminating the railroad at a town, albeit a small town, would provide much of the personnel and infrastructure (such as hotels, residences, and cafés) needed to service the trains and passengers while providing the potential for more subscribers to the project than would likely be found at the M&C's crossing of the Muddy. If they did not subscribe the desired amount, then the railroad would be built on "the cheapest and most practicable route," presumably to follow the Muddy route the entire distance to the M&C connection.

The occasion for determining whether Middleton was willing to invest was a "grand railroad barbecue" held on Friday, December 8. Falkner arrived in Middleton at the M&C depot to meet a crowd estimated at 1,500, a sizeable turnout for a town with a population of only 150 according to the 1870 census. At 11:00 a.m., Falkner and the crowd were escorted by the Middleton brass band amid a medley of rousing tunes to a grove on the north side of town where a speaker's stand had been erected. The master of ceremonies, Major G. W. Wilson, introduced Falkner, who then addressed the crowd in a speech that lasted an hour and a half; he seldom spoke briefly. The crowd was so impressed that when the ledger was opened, the requisite $10,000 was promptly subscribed, and Middleton had secured the railroad. With the purpose of the gathering fulfilled, they sat down to dinner on the grounds to contemplate the future of the railroad from Middleton to Ripley.[19] The amount subscribed in Middleton would constitute about one-sixth of the estimated $60,000 subscribed locally.[20]

An even more important decision was made about the same time, one that would have a dramatic impact upon cutting costs and thereby completing the road. At the November 9 meeting, the board ordered that President Falkner should "proceed without delay to employ a first-class engineer" and begin with the survey of the route. The choice of engineer would revolutionize the development, promotion, and completion of the railroad.[21] Whether Falkner had anyone in mind at the time is not known. Regardless, two weeks later the *Memphis Appeal* announced that the railroad had secured the services of Frederick de Funiak, who was already engaged in surveying a route from Ripley to the M&C, and that the road would be put under contract on the first of January.[22]

De Funiak brought an element of the exotic to the project, and the exotic certainly appealed to Falkner. Born on August 15, 1839, in either Trieste or Rome, the son of a colonel in the employ of the Papal States, de Funiak attended the military academy in Vienna, from which he graduated in 1857 as a lieutenant of engineers. Afterward in Egypt he served as an assistant engineer in the construction of the railroad connecting Alexandria to Cairo. In

1862 he emigrated to the Confederate States of America, where he served as captain of engineers in the army. In 1871 a consortium of railroads sent him to Europe as their joint agent, in part to investigate the burgeoning narrow-gauge railway system.[23] Through exposure to the narrow-gauge movement in Europe, his trip was apparently pivotal in determining the nature of the Ripley Railroad's construction. The announcement of his selection for the railroad also noted that he had just returned from Europe, where he had inspected several narrow-gauge railroads. He pronounced them to be "perfectly successful and everywhere approved" and that they "subserve all the purposes of the broad-guage [sic] roads."[24] The revolutionary aspect of this news was that the gauge of the Ripley Railroad would be narrow at three feet, rather than the standard five-foot gauge that dominated southern railroading, and that this would be the first narrow gauge "completed in this portion of the South."[25]

Several months later, Falkner recalled that his interest in building a narrow-gauge railroad was piqued by a pamphlet just published in August 1871 entitled *The Narrow Gauge Railway* by Colonel Edward Hulbert, who would become America's leading advocate of the narrow-gauge movement. Falkner does not say whether he read the pamphlet before engaging de Funiak or if de Funiak had introduced the pamphlet to him—probably the latter. At any rate, this was a vanguard publication for a nascent movement in railroading—the narrow gauge—and it transformed the course of the Ripley Railroad.[26]

Until this time virtually all of the railroads in North America were built according to gauges much wider than three feet. What is now known as "standard gauge," 4′ 8½″, dominated much of the British Empire and the northern part of the United States, while most of the South used a 5′ gauge. However, by the 1860s questions began to arise—first in the United Kingdom—about the suitability of broader gauges in areas with low populations and modest resources. One of the first attempts to push for narrow gauges was Robert F. Fairlie, a Scottish engineer, who presented a widely publicized paper on September 19, 1870, entitled "On the Gauge for the Railways of the Future." By 1871 the movement had spread to the United States, and in February of that year the American Major Alfred F. Sears published a pamphlet, *On Small Gauge Railroads*, advocating a gauge of 2′ 6″ in its first edition and 3′ in the second edition. In July, James P. Low also argued for a 3′ gauge, and in August the aforementioned Edward Hulbert published his work. As claimed in the movement's publications, narrow-gauge roads reduced costs significantly while resulting in a higher ratio of cargo weight to car weight.[27] With such works to rely upon along with the testimony of de Funiak, Falkner was soon sold on the idea, stating that by his calculation a narrow-gauge road would only cost about $10,000 per mile as opposed to about $26,000 for a broad gauge.[28] These figures must have been compelling to Falkner given the difficulty raising funds in the Ripley area. On top of that, he could hope that the state would be forthcoming with its promise of $4,000 per mile if completed on time.

As Falkner had done two years earlier, he worked out an agreement in which the M&C Railroad would heavily subsidize the construction. On December 18, 1871, a contract was signed between the M&C Railroad and the Ripley Railroad. According to this agreement, the Ripley company was to build a rail connection to the M&C and establish a roadbed including the earthwork, crossties, bridges, trestles, and culverts. The M&C would furnish the iron rails—with the rails not exceeding thirty-six pounds per yard (a very light rail)—and other metal components, along with one locomotive costing no more than $7,000, one passenger coach, three boxcars, and three flatcars, all suited for a narrow-gauge railroad. To secure payment for these materials, the Ripley Railroad was to issue the M&C its first mortgage bonds, bearing a 10 percent rate of interest, with no other bonds being issued. The purpose of this was to convey a lien on the railroad. It was also agreed that the Ripley Railroad would not build any farther south than Ripley. The contract would not be ratified until the April 22, 1872, meeting of the Ripley Railroad Company.[29]

The construction of the railroad occurred in three phases with each overlapping in time. First there was the survey, then the earthwork, and finally the laying of the crossties and rails. The survey phase provided the basic parameters for construction. It determined the specific alignments and grades and consequently the quantity of dirt to be moved. The survey began almost immediately after de Funiak was selected to head up the work, because the newspaper article that announced his selection on November 24, 1871, also noted that he "is now engaged in locating the road."[30] This was about two weeks before it was determined that Middleton would be the northern terminus. A few weeks later, the route had been established and the landowners identified, permitting the signing of a deed on December 25 in which all owners deeded their required portion of a one-hundred-foot-wide strip to the railroad company.[31] In March 1872, de Funiak accepted the position of engineer and superintendent of the road department of the Louisville division of the Louisville and Nashville Railroad and left the Ripley Railroad.[32] However, by this time he had established the basic construction parameters, and other engineers were hired to carry out the plan while supervising ongoing work. His successor was Niles Meriwether, who had been chief engineer

for the M&C since 1868 and was apparently on loan to oversee the construction of the Ripley road.[33] After the road's completion, Meriwether was succeeded by Captain A. W. Glouster in September when the Ripley Railroad
began employing its own chief engineer.[34]

The earthmoving phase probably began on March 1, 1872, with a groundbreaking ceremony at Middleton in which Falkner "threw the first dirt."[35] For
those who had struggled for so long—enduring failure after failure—moving
the first dirt was deeply satisfying, the first physical manifestation of construction culminating years of aspirations and dashed hopes. Falkner had come
into his own. His military career demonstrated the difficulty of his restless,
protean mind to adapt in the long term to regimented, bureaucratic environments. But now with the railroad, he was at his best using often unorthodox
procedures to accumulate capital and political support.

However, most would have been content to carry the project to its completion, as he was well on his way to doing, then relax while riding the rails
between Ripley and Middleton. But this was not to be. Just as construction was
finally beginning, the project was transformed in a fashion that would change
its scope while also changing the direction of Falkner's life, leading indirectly
to his death. The railroad was initially conceived as a twenty-five-mile-long
spur line, a project easy enough to imagine but not easy to accomplish.

However, this was all changed by legislation passed on March 16 and 18
only two weeks after the groundbreaking that changed the company from the
Ripley Railroad Company to the Ship Island, Ripley, and Kentucky Railroad
Company (SIR&K), effectively re-envisioning the project from a short spur
line into a major trunk line that would not stop at Ripley but continue southward to Mississippi City on the Gulf of Mexico.[36] The northern terminus was
not specified but was reported to be either Paducah, Kentucky, or a point
on the Ohio River opposite Cairo, Illinois.[37] The difference was of little consequence because for the foreseeable future all efforts would be devoted to
building south from Middleton to Ripley, then to the Gulf. The idea for the
project was obviously based on the defunct SI, MC & P project that had been
chartered and died in 1870.

Who suggested and promoted the idea is not recorded, but no one other
than Falkner had the vision to take on such a task. In fact, he made several
trips to Jackson to promote the bill before the legislature.[38] He probably
received solid support from the other board members and stockholders, but it
is unlikely that any were as committed to this vision as he was. Most probably
liked the idea but didn't think that it was realizable, perhaps dismissing the
idea as a personal affectation of Falkner's. Attempting such a project after all

seemed quixotic. It had begun as a project with broad-based support across the state and had failed. Now Falkner had turned it into a project based out of Ripley. What chances of success did it likely have? Little, most would have said. In the long term, Falkner would face opposition when he attempted to implement the plan, notably from another colleague, R. J. Thurmond. Nevertheless, the vision inspired Falkner for the rest of his life. Regardless of the change of the railroad's name to the Ship Island, Ripley, and Kentucky, it continued to be known informally as the Ripley Railroad for years to come.

During construction, much of the earthwork was apparently accomplished by local labor from supporters of the road. Falkner later recalled how this work was accomplished, not without hyperbole and exaggerated sentimentality:

> The road was built by a combination of *"labor & capital"* gotten up among the people at each end, and along the line of the Road. I had at one time as many as fifteen hundred private citizens working on the road. I have seen the Sheriff of our County, and all his deputies, in company with the Circuit & Chancery Clerks, all at work togeather [sic] on our road. I have seen many Preachers engaged at work on the road. There was a universal combination here among all classes, both black and white, to aid in building the road. The Ladies subscribed liberally to aid in building the road. Large Basket dinners, were given by the ladies frequently, in order to get crowds togeather [sic] to hear rail road speeches. I have seen widow Ladies, take the last side of Bacon, from her Smoke House, to feed the laborers on this road.[39]

Furthermore, as noted, not all local supporters were white. According a newspaper account: "[T]he colored people of Tippah county subscribed about $20,000, which amount was paid by labor on the road." The writer went on to note that this "speaks volumes for the enterprising spirit displayed by the colored men, who sometimes worked at night to pay up their subscriptions."[40]

These accounts were not the entire story, though. They were clearly intended to depict railroad construction as the product of the determination of a community that would accomplish its end no matter how Herculean the effort required. However, it is unlikely that the ad hoc efforts of farmers, civil servants, and preachers could have built twenty-five miles of roadbed no matter how many widow ladies supplied them with smoked bacon. Much of the work was probably provided by crews of paid workmen who could be relied on for continuous labor. In addition, all workers—paid and volunteer—had to work under the supervision of engineers to ensure that the resulting grades and alignments met the project specifications.

With the earthwork in progress, other matters had to be arranged. On April 22, at a meeting in the courthouse, the contract made on December 18 with the M&C was ratified. This did not take into account that on March 5, the M&C had been taken over by the Southern Railway Security Company (SRSC) because of its growing debts.[41] The SRSC was a holding company organized in Pennsylvania in 1871 to secure control of southern railroads.[42] Furthermore, Falkner was authorized to execute the mortgage and bonds as specified by the contract and to issue $7,000 of bonds for every mile of road with the bonds being secured by a mortgage with the M&C, which was by then in the hands of the SRSC.[43]

Additionally, the stockholders were clearly pleased with the progress made on the railroad. For them, there was one man responsible for the railroad's success; a resolution was passed recognizing that Falkner "has by his energy, perseverance, and liberality succeeded in placing said railroad on a foundation which insures its completion at an early day." Furthermore, the stockholders indicated that they were "desirous of expressing to him our gratitude for his zeal and invaluable services in behalf of said enterprise," and in consequence they resolved that the first locomotive on the railroad would be named the *Col. W. C. Falkner*, while the first station north of Ripley would be called "Falkner."[44] This was the only station on the line to be named after a railroad executive, suggesting that they didn't name stations lightly.

The following day, April 23, the railroad board began to look into acquiring land in Ripley for a depot site.[45] The depot was constructed by the end of August, using funds loaned to the railroad by Falkner.[46] More importantly, with the contract signed, Falkner had the authorization to arrange the final stage: constructing trestles and laying ties and rails. On April 27, he passed through Memphis en route to New York City, "where he goes to superintend the shipment of the iron and rolling stock for his road."[47] While in Memphis he apparently contracted with the partnership of Gilmer & Rather[48] to lay the track. On the twenty-ninth, the firm began advertising for one hundred laborers to work on the railroad, with applications to be made at the M&C depot in Middleton.[49]

On May 4, while in New York, Falkner signed a contract with the SRSC that was essentially the same as that signed and ratified with the M&C Railroad. This was due to the SRSC's having taken over the M&C. In the new document, the SRSC agreed to provide the Ripley Railroad Company with the following:

[S]even hundred tons of iron rails of thirty-five pounds weight, and spikes and fastenings sufficient to lay said rails, and also all necessary switch iron, also one locomotive and tender and three flat cars suitable for a narrow gauge; and on or before the first day of July, 1872, . . . seven hundred tons of iron rails of thirty-five pounds weight, and the spikes and fastenings necessary to lay the same, and also all the iron necessary for switches, also three flat, two box, and one first class passenger cars. . . .

All to be delivered to Middleton by June 1.[50]

The debt owed the SRSC bore 10 percent interest, and as security the Ripley Railroad gave it $215,000 in mortgage bonds dated June 3, 1872, and bearing an interest rate of 7 percent with the first payment coming due the first of January.[51]

On May 24, the *Memphis Daily Appeal* reported that Falkner had just returned from New York and, having accomplished his mission, was staying at the Peabody Hotel. It was further reported that "[t]wenty-one carloads of iron have arrived at Middleton, and as soon as the locomotives, expected every day, arrive, track-laying will be begun."[52] The rails arrived via the port of New Orleans, where they were loaded onto flatcars—eight tons per car— then shipped northward on the Mississippi Central to Grand Junction on the M&C, then east to Middleton, where the rails were transferred to narrow-gauge flatcars to be transferred to construction sites. It was noted that the much smaller narrow-gauge cars each carried eight tons, the same as the broad-gauge cars.[53]

The railroad's stockholders met at the courthouse on June 3 and ratified the contract that Falkner had worked out with the M&C Railroad, the SRSC, and the United States Security Company for the purpose of obtaining iron rails, rolling stock, and other equipment. They also resolved that Falkner, in recognition of a $500 contribution, would be granted a first-class passenger ticket for himself and his family members valid for fifty years.[54] That day, the railroad issued $250,000 in bonds that were purchased by the United States Security Company.[55]

Tracklaying was initiated with ceremony at Middleton on June 7. Falkner, standing in front of a crowd, addressed them in a speech that was "short but appropriate." He then took a sledgehammer and raised it over his head to drive the first spike. A witness later recalled with humor that Falkner "took a tremendous swing . . . and—missed the spike clean." For someone inexperienced with driving spikes, this was not an unexpected result. In his usual self-deprecating manner, Falkner probably laughed—and carried on. The reporter for the *Memphis Daily Appeal* noted that the crowd cheered him for having "justly earned . . . the title of the most rapid railway builder in the South."[56] As soon as the rails were laid, a work train could be used to transport equipment

Figure 10.1. G&C depot at Middleton, Tennessee, 1905, shortly after the tracks were converted to standard gauge. From the GM&O Historical Society archives.

from Middleton south and men from work camps to their places of work. However, rail laying was slow in getting started. Ties had to be laid and ballasted, and there was the weather to contend with.

In the meantime, Falkner had other business to attend to in St. Louis, where a long-heralded narrow-gauge convention began on June 19 at the Southern Hotel bringing together promoters and builders of narrow-gauge roads to share ideas and plan for the future. The convention was called by Colonel Edward Hulbert, the pioneer narrow-gauge promoter, who planned for it to be held at an emerging transportation hub.[57] It was to include several prominent leaders in the narrow-gauge industry including Frederick de Funiak, employed at the time by the Ripley Railroad. He was reported to have "seen most of the narrow-gauge railroads in Europe, and his views will command and deserve great consideration."[58] However, by June he had changed jobs and did not attend. On the other hand, Falkner attended. Within less than a year he had become a leader in the narrow-gauge movement. On the second day of the convention he was appointed to a newly formed central committee to head the movement.[59] He spoke to the meeting on his railroad effort, noting that he had projected a broad-gauge road to cost $26,000 per mile while, as he had discovered, a narrow gauge would only cost $10,000 per mile. At the time, he reported, there were two and a half miles of track in operation, while the entire project would be built from the Gulf of Mexico to the Ohio River. He also noted that some broad-gauge railroad men were deriding the narrow-gauges as "Dolly Varden roads,"[60] taking the name from a frilly style of women's dress popular at the time.[61] The style was in turn named after the character in Charles Dickens's *Barnaby Rudge* (1841). An "irreverent" reporter at the St. Louis meeting first applied the name to narrow-gauge railroads alluding to the promoters' "habit of giving free play to the fancy" through extravagant claims for saving money.[62] Falkner took the name in stride and later responded, alluding to Dickens's character Dolly Varden rather than the dress fad: "The broad-gauge fellows call ours the Dolly Varden road, by way of poking fun at us; but I do not care; because so far as my information extends, Miss Dolly Varden was a very respectable young lady any way; and I wish them to know that ours is a very respectable railroad, too."[63]

A major thrust of the convention was to work toward building a narrow-gauge trunk line from the east coast to St. Louis that would link the various narrow-gauge railroads then under construction—a few miles here and a few miles there—into a vast network that would compete with the existing network of broad-gauge roads.[64] Although the promoters could not anticipate it, a movement to standardize gauges at 4' 8½" would emerge and doom the narrow-gauge effort.

Construction proceeded smoothly until July, at which time "the rains descended and the floods came," with approximately sixteen successive days of rain forcing construction to slow to a grind. "Some of the contractors thought the prospect hopeless. The President [Falkner] called on them and inquired if any contractor had fears of failing? If so, to speak it out, and give up the contract; that the Road could and should be completed in due time; that if there was any faltering he could find men and contractors to go through. This gave a new impetus to the work, and it was pressed on."[65]

To complicate matters, the railroad's resident engineer, Major H. W. Lockett, was killed in a knife fight at Middleton on July 16 by Robert McKnight, reportedly a former freight conductor on the Mississippi Central Railroad.[66] A newspaper account described the affair:

McKnight, for some trivial cause, at the breakfast table where both were boarding, remarked that Lockett had insulted him, and he intended to see if he had any resentment about him. After this McKnight met Lockett on the street and after a few words passed both parties began striking at each other with knives. Locket was cut twice, the second stab penetrating the heart. He died in ten minutes. McKnight was also cut. His wound being a slight one on the shoulder. He was arrested and tried before a committing court and was required to give bail in the sum of $3000, failing to do which, he was brought to this place [Bolivar, Tennessee, the county seat of Hardeman County] and put in jail and will have to answer before our Circuit Court upon a charge of murder in the second degree.[67]

When McKnight was finally brought to trial in November on a charge of first-degree murder, the jury found him not guilty.[68] Although no details of the trial are known, he was probably acquitted on grounds of self-defense.

With the bad weather, only six miles of track had been laid by early August—just barely getting it into Mississippi—leaving nineteen more to go. However, with the deadline in sight and with everything else working toward completion, the nineteen miles of iron were laid between August 8 and August 27, with the last spike driven on that day.[69] However, the rails were apparently laid to Ripley by the twenty-fourth, three days before the last spike was driven, because it was reported that the train reached town on that day.[70] The three days from the twenty-fourth through the twenty-seventh may have been used in constructing sidings and the Y to turn the train at Ripley along with other finishing touches. At any rate, the railroad was completed five days before September 1, the deadline for receiving the state subsidy. The southern extent of the tracks in Ripley ended just north of the Stonewall College property and remained there for fourteen years.[71]

Falkner claimed that the cost of building the road was "exactly" $13,000 per mile, "including all the equipments."[72] Another source elaborated on this, stating that the construction costs were about $6,000 per mile while the iron and equipment of rolling stock was about $6,500 per mile, making for a total of about $12,500 per mile, with the former constructed by the Ripley Railroad Company and the latter supplied by the Southern Railway Security Company.[73] Figuring from $12,500 to $13,000 per mile indicates that the overall cost would have been about $312,500–$325,000, and the state subsidy would only pay about one-fourth of this.

The *Memphis Daily Appeal* was effusive over Falkner's achievement:

> The happiest man in all these States is Colonel W. C. Falkner, of Ripley, Mississippi, whose narrow-gauge road will be completed to-day. He thus secures the State aid required to insure the completion of the road to the Gulf coast, and thus the construction of a commercial emporium within the limits of Mississippi. Falkner will ever be deemed a great public benefactor, because he has shown how the greatest possible good may be done with the narrowest possible resources. It is easier now for him to build two hundred than it was to finish and equip the thirty miles of completed road.[74]

While Falkner's success was in part due to his vision and persistence, it was also due to his ability to work with, as noted, "the narrowest possible resources." In other words, he was adept at cutting corners to save time and

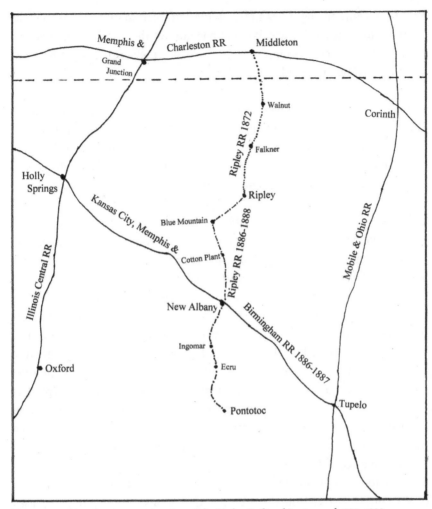

Figure 10.2. Map showing construction of the Ripley Railroad in 1872 and 1886–1888.

money. Grading was minimized by curving around hills, a practice primarily used at the southern and northern ends of the track, where the land was hillier; the intermediate section lying along the bottomlands of Muddy Creek was more level and hence easier to grade without accommodations for changes in elevation. In lieu of crushed rock, cinders were used for ballasting the crossties.[75] In May 1873, an inspector, L. D. Myers, reported that the road was built "imperfectly" and with "too much haste in order to get the State subsidy." The crossties were "too small and too short, the embankments were too narrow, and the excavations did not have sufficient slope to their sides."[76] Additionally, W. J. Ross, superintendent of the M&C, reported in the same month: "We find the light ties sink into the soft earth so much . . . as to make the track too uneven for use. We will have to put them closer together and make some other changes in the track."[77] Despite the construction problems, Myers proclaimed the road a "success":

> The passenger coach ran with great smoothness, ease and comfort. The cars carried twice their weight in freight, whilst cars on the broad gauge roads only carried pound for pound. The train, if it should happen to run off, could be put on with little difficulty, and no danger. . . . Take it all in all, it was, with all its imperfections, a satisfactory example of what narrow gauge roads could do.[78]

Nevertheless, the subsidy legislation had required, as noted, that a railroad be constructed "in first-class manner, with iron rails of not less than fifty-six (56) pounds weight per yard, [and] twenty-five miles of its projected line within the State." The road fell short in all categories. Instead of fifty-six-pound iron rails, thirty-five-pound rails had been used; and while the road was twenty-five miles long, only about twenty miles were in Mississippi, the rest being in Tennessee. In sum, the Ripley Railroad met only one criterion: it had been completed by the deadline. In the end, none of this seemed to pose a problem, presumably because Falkner had managed to have the rules modified. To his advantage was the fact that his was the only railroad to even remotely qualify for the subsidy. Those in the state government eager to encourage rail development were obviously willing to overlook deviation from the specifications if the program could be shown to have borne fruit.

The projected completion date was August 29, a day marked not so much by the actual completion of work, which had occurred a few days earlier, as by the fanfare surrounding the occasion. Invitations were sent to dignitaries, while newspapers carried general invitations to all "friends of the company." At 9:00 on the designated morning, two trains left Middleton consisting of the company's two locomotives pulling a total of nineteen flatcars, covered against the sun and the possibility of rain, with an estimated seven hundred passengers aboard. Among them was the state engineer, Captain Thomas C. Hardee, and other state railroad commissioners who were there for the festivities and to examine the road and determine whether or not its construction fully complied with the Subsidy Act. They found no problems despite its apparent lack of compliance with the specifications from the law. Serving as host for the occasion, Falkner "treated his guests in a princely manner, being ever on the alert to see that their wants were properly attended to." Moving along at twenty miles per hour, the party stopped to pick up additional passengers at a series of impromptu designated stops such as Gatlin's, Moore's, Hopkins's, Buchanan's, and Luker's. For the most part these weren't established stations; in fact, there weren't any regular stations at the time except possibly for Falkner Station, which had recently been named by the company after its president.[79]

The group arrived at the new depot in Ripley at about 11:30, where they were met by the Committee of Reception consisting of W. R. Cole, L. Robbins, and Falkner's son, J. W. T. Falkner, only recently out of University of Mississippi Law School. They conducted the crowd about a quarter of a mile to a large grove of oaks, which "formed a grateful and pleasing shelter from the scorching rays of the noontide sun." Total attendance was estimated at seven to ten thousand. Tables and chairs had been set up in the grove for dinner along with a stand for the speakers and a band. As the master of ceremonies, Falkner welcomed the crowd[80] with what the *Memphis Daily Appeal* called "the most eloquent speech ever made" on railroads.[81] If anything, he was a master of eloquence, that beau ideal of southern oratory, the artistry of which could draw a crowd into a vision of how the world might be. He then introduced the guest speakers, the first of whom was Captain Hardee, who was, as noted, state engineer and member of the State Railroad Commission. Hardee congratulated the people in general and Falkner in specific on the completion of the railroad and noted that Mississippi was making a good investment in extending aid to the project. The second speaker was State Senator H. C. Carter of Vicksburg, another railroad commissioner, who spoke on his role in passing the State Subsidy Act, which he called "Colonel Falkner's bill" (presumably because Falkner was the only one able to avail himself of it), and noted that "he was proud he could go back to Jackson and relate with what gentlemanly courtesy a colored man had been treated in Northern Mississippi." He concluded with several flattering remarks about Falkner and his ability to complete the railroad. The speaker was interrupted several times by cheers from the crowd. After the speeches, dinner was served under the shade of the trees while music was provided by the LaGrange cornet band from LaGrange, Tennessee. That night, a ball was held in the courthouse as the grand finale of "one of the most memorable days in the history of Tippah county."[82]

However, before the ball began, Falkner left for Jackson accompanied by Hardee to secure the subsidy warrants that the railroad was entitled to. Hardee was to present his observations on the condition of the road. After riding the rails to Middleton, then Memphis, they stayed overnight at the Peabody Hotel and arrived the following day, Friday, September 30, in Jackson, enthusiastic about the remuneration that would presumably be forthcoming. However, he first needed to obtain the governor's approval before the warrants could be issued.[83]

In order to stress his urgency, he regaled everyone with tales of the peril that Ripley faced, that there was a camp of one hundred to two hundred laborers in town, mostly Irishmen, who if not promptly paid would likely under the influence of liquor descend like an avenging angel upon the hapless town and burn it to the ground. In order to avert such an eventuality, Falkner had been feeding the workers during the last days of construction at his own expense, using money borrowed from a Memphis bank. However, he had borrowed to his limit and as a last resort to pacify their fears "would read the Subsidy Act to them and make speeches, in order to induce them to keep at work." So, it was imperative that he acquire the warrants to alleviate the growing resentment. Fearful of the repercussions, he was "absolutely afraid to go home," or so he claimed.[84]

However, Falkner learned that the governor was not in town. He and Hardee then went to the office of the attorney general, Joshua S. Morris, where they inquired as to whether the governor could be reached by telegraph to obtain his approval. Morris replied that it would be best to wait for the governor's return.[85]

By Monday, September 2, Governor Ridgely C. Powers had returned. After Falkner and Hardee presented their case to him, he approved the requisition, which authorized the state auditor, Henry Musgrove, to issue the warrants. Then they encountered the first sign of trouble. Upon presenting the written authorization to the auditor, he "stated that the Attorney General desired the matter referred to him, and he could not issue the warrants until his opinion was obtained. Attorney General Morris stated that he had grave doubts about the constitutionality of the Subsidy Act and preferred that it should be adjudicated by the courts." For someone urgently needing funding—funding that was expected—Falkner "could not have been more astonished by a clap of thunder in a clear sky."[86]

Facing this new problem, Hardee, who was much wiser to state politics, advised Falkner that money would get the warrants released from the auditor. Upon later being asked whether such payments would constitute bribery, Hardee skirted the question but did indicate that he had suggested that money might overcome political hurdles.[87] Realizing the dire predicament he faced and the need for an expeditious resolution, Falkner immediately approached an old friend, Charles A. Brougher, a former member of the Tippah County bar and by that time a law partner of Attorney General Morris with his office in Jackson. Years earlier, both Brougher and Falkner had been members of the Sons of Temperance when Brougher accused Falkner of drinking cider in his presence, charges that were subsequently dropped. Seemingly by 1873 they had let bygones be bygones; Falkner informed Brougher of his problem and asked for his assistance, promising him $2,000 in subsidy warrants in return for "favorable opinions." Brougher agreed to help on the ground that his old friend had "succeeded in building his road upon the faith of receiving Subsidy from the State."[88] Falkner also promised $1,000 in warrants to Judge Josiah A. P. Campbell and $3,125 to Hardee to disburse as he saw fit.[89]

On Wednesday, September 4, Attorney General Morris advised Musgrove to issue the warrants,[90] valued at $81,968.20.[91] At $4,000 per mile, this figure covers approximately 20.5 miles, presumably the mileage within the state. Altogether, 124 warrants were issued according to sums specified by Falkner[92] with values ranging from $68.20 to as high as $2,500.[93] Releasing the warrants provided considerable relief to Falkner, given the debts he owed. After receiving them, on the fifth he left warrants or currency as payment for Brougher, Campbell, and Hardee to cover the sums promised them providing the warrants were released.[94] He soon left Jackson and returned to Ripley, where he began to pay salaries and other debts.[95] On October 10, he reported to the railroad directors that he had sold (and apparently dispersed to contractors and laborers) all but $4,300 of the warrants, with the balance paid into the company treasury.[96]

All seemed to be going well until some of the warrants were presented to the state treasurer for redemption. On October 2, Attorney General Morris, claiming that the subsidy bill was unconstitutional, instructed the state treasurer, W. H. Vasser, not to pay the warrants.[97] However, by that time Falkner had few if any warrants left.

The governor was indignant at the manner in which Falkner and his railroad had been treated. This had resulted in many of the warrants passing into "the hands of poor men who had received them for services in the construction of the railroad, and nearly all of them were in the hands of parties who had received them in good faith." Stating that the good faith of the state was at stake, the governor purchased them and immediately wrote to Falkner to notify him and the holders of any warrants that "full current rates would be paid them for all warrants."[98]

In March 1873, "a large portion" of the warrants were reported by the state treasurer to be in the vaults in his office.[99] Three years later, some were still on deposit in the State Treasury, where they were intended to remain.[100]

In the end, Falkner had succeeded where others had failed and found himself as president of a twenty-five-mile railroad that connected his hometown to the outside world. In doing this, he proved to be a master at generating enthusiasm and coordinating interests ranging from local citizenry and the M&C Railroad to the Mississippi state government, as well as building the railroad as part of the new narrow-gauge movement, which served to cut costs. During construction, the narrow-gauge movement was rapidly gaining new supporters. As hundreds of miles of new track were laid, leaders envisioned a nationwide system of interconnected tracks. However, that was not to be. By 1880, new construction was slowing in part due to the realization that some of the heralded advantages of narrow gauges were not all they were promised to be. Furthermore, at the same time the country's railroads were moving toward a standardization of gauges, which would facilitate movement of freight across the country and between different carriers. The gauge that became "standard gauge" was the 4' 8½" measure used in the North and in the United Kingdom. This meant that the narrow gauges—products of an outmoded dream—would have to be standardized along with the rest or continue to be mere local carriers with little prospect for future development. Falkner had ridden the wave of the narrow gauges and had brought a new road into being. However, it was not in him to simply rest on his laurels; he had after all envisioned that his short-line road would become a transnational road. To do that, he would have to keep his eyes open for new opportunities to come his way.

Prior to the building of the Ripley Railroad, the primary corridor leading northward from Ripley was the old Ripley-Pocahontas Road that had been part of the old stagecoach route leading from Pontotoc to Jackson, Tennessee. The Adcock family had followed this route during their fateful journey in 1845. While this route lay in the uplands east of Muddy Creek bottom, the construction of the railroad shifted the primary corridor to the west of Muddy Creek and created a line of villages and towns that during the twentieth century State Highway 15 would follow.

By the end of 1872, the Ripley Railroad began transforming the transportation network and the settlement landscape in northern Tippah County. Passengers passed over terrain that had taken hours to traverse, and cargoes were shipped in to stores from distant market centers, while agricultural production was shipped out with little concern for muddy roads. At the end of the year it was estimated that seven to eight thousand bales of cotton had been shipped out via Middleton.[101]

The building of the railroad required the development and acquisition of both fixed stock and rolling stock, with the former consisting of infrastructure that was "fixed" to the land such as tracks, depots, water tanks, signals, and signage while the latter consisted of moving property, primarily locomotives and various cars that moved on the tracks. Because Ripley was the center of operations, most construction occurred there. As already noted, a depot was constructed just south of Jefferson Street prior to the opening of the road. Additionally, a water tower was erected two blocks north of the depot, while a car barn was located a block to the south of the depot near the terminus of the rails. Railroad shops were built to the west of the tracks on Block 25, which was, as noted, one of the blocks acquired in conjunction with the establishment of the road. Railroad cars were constructed there.[102]

Within the first few months of operation, the Ripley Railroad constructed two depots between Ripley and Middleton, for a total of four.[103] The first—constructed by late September—was Falkner Station, about nine miles north of Ripley, which the company had named after Colonel Falkner.[104] A post office was soon established,[105] and a town was surveyed.[106] The town of Falkner was incorporated on April 2, 1874.[107]

The second depot was initially called Hopkins, and following a later name change the site developed into the town of Walnut. For a few months in 1872, two sites competed for the depot with a permanent one settled on by November 4 when the railroad directors ordered that "the depot be located at Mitchell's on condition that 2 acres for depot is donated," and this site became Hopkins.[108] Hopkins Post Office was established on November 8, 1872, and the following month a town plat was surveyed.[109] Hopkins became Walnut in 1876[110] and under that name was incorporated as a town on May 1, 1912.[111]

Soon after, a third depot/town, Tiplersville (sometimes referred to as Tiplers) was established with a post office authorized on April 17, 1873, with William M. Burns as postmaster.[112] Although never incorporated, it did grow into a substantial village.

The fourth depot/station, Brownfield, was established several years after the first three. Initially known as Gatlin's Switch, the name was changed to Brownfield[113] while a post office was established on May 17, 1900[114] and a depot about that time. Like Tiplersville, Brownfield developed into a village but was never incorporated.

Upon beginning service in 1872, the company initiated a schedule operating a "regular train" that followed a timetable consisting of a daily round trip over the railroad's full twenty-five miles. A train required four men to operate: an engineer, a fireman, a brakeman, and a conductor. Maintaining the roadbed over its twenty-five-mile length required five or six hands.[115] The train left Ripley every morning and headed north to Middleton, where passengers, freight, and mail were deposited to connect with the M&C, and then the train

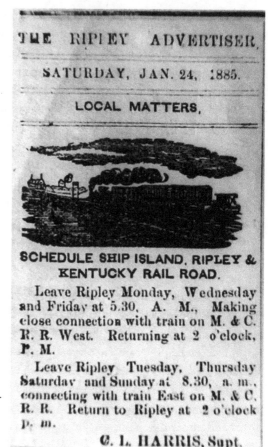

Figure 10.3. Typical railroad schedule featuring the route from Ripley to Middleton, 1872–1886. From the *Ripley Advertiser*, January 24, 1885.

returned to Ripley.[116] This daily train was a "mixed train" in that it mixed both passenger and freight service together.[117] The locomotives and cars not operating as part of the regular train service were "specials," trains that were used for special purposes, passenger or freight.[118]

At the end of the day, the locomotive had to be turned around in preparation for the next day's trip. In lieu of a turntable or roundhouse at Ripley, a Y configuration of rails was constructed on the north side of town.[119] Here, a locomotive could be run onto one branch of the Y, then backed down the other branch and thereby turned around. Presumably a similar facility was at the northern end at Middleton.

The railroad's first rolling stock was to be supplied by the SRSC according to contract with the Ripley Railroad and consisted of one locomotive and tender, one first-class passenger coach, two boxcars, and three flatcars.[120] These were delivered about the time that the track began to be laid.

Figure 10.4. Locomotive #3, the *Colonel W. C. Falkner*, nicknamed *Tanglefoot*, one of the first two locomotives acquired in 1872, being used in railroad maintenance near Pontotoc in 1898. From the GM&O Historical Society archives.

This equipment was initially used for transporting men, ties, and rails to construction sites. However, by the time the railroad was completed three months later, the inventory of rolling stock had risen to two locomotives, one passenger coach, eight boxcars, and twenty-eight flatcars.[121] The increase to two locomotives permitted the operation of regular train service while also allowing for a special train for various purposes including maintenance, passenger service, and freight. Two months later the inventory had grown by an additional baggage car, express car, and post office car, while the passenger cars had increased from the one luxury, first-class car to include two less luxurious second-class cars. The operation of a post office car implies that the railroad contracted with the US Post Office to carry and sort mail that had been brought into Middleton on the M&C and then shipped southward to the post offices along the railroad. The number of flatcars had decreased from twenty-eight to twelve.[122]

Both of the locomotives were constructed by the firm Dawson and Bailey of Connellsville, Pennsylvania. The larger of the two was the freight locomotive numbered #3 and named the *Colonel W. C. Falkner*, as specified by the railroad stockholders. It weighed fifteen tons, had six three-foot driving wheels, and cost $7,800. The smaller weighed twelve tons, had four three-foot driving wheels, and was numbered #1. It was initially named the *Ripley* but was soon renamed the *Hardy W. Stricklin* in honor of the company's treasurer, who had just died. It cost $7,000.[123] The two locomotive were soon nicknamed, respectively, *Tanglefoot* and *Dolly*, with the latter presumably referring to Dolly Varden, whose name had become associated with narrow-gauge railroads.[124] However, within a few years the name "Dolly Varden" in reference to the railroad was soon forgotten, and in its place the populace began referring to it as the "Doodlebug line."

The first-class passenger car was named the *Effie D. Falkner* after the colonel's daughter. It was described as "very neatly upholstered and . . . arranged with double seats on one side and single seats on the opposite and is calculated to transport passengers with as much comfort as anyone can desire." The seats were covered in red velvet, while the interior woodwork was of polished black walnut. All three of the passenger cars were described as thirty-six feet long, seven feet two inches high from floor to ceiling, and about seven feet wide. Each would comfortably seat about thirty passengers. All were constructed by Jackson and Sharpe of Wilmington, Delaware.[125] Both flatcars and boxcars were constructed by Billmeyer and Small of York, Pennsylvania. The flatcars could carry sixty barrels of flour, or fourteen to sixteen bales of cotton. The average speed of the train was fifteen miles per hour, although it could do up to twenty-five.[126] In years to come, the Ripley Railroad would begin constructing its own cars in its shop in Ripley.

The result of constructing the twenty-five miles of railroad was a transformation of the landscape of Tippah County. Where once people were required to ride horses or walk, they now had steam-powered trains providing both passenger and freight service. Depots had been built and new towns founded. The main route between Ripley and Middleton had been shifted. But the connection to the outside world was still one way, with Ripley at the end of the route. For Falkner, there should be more.

Chapter 11

◈━○━━○━◈

The Railroad Plods Along

On January 1, 1874, Falkner's oldest daughter, Willie, was married in a ceremony that underscored his new position as president of a railroad. The ceremony was held at 3:00 in the afternoon in the Ripley Presbyterian Church on North Union Street, where Lizzie was a member.[1] The groom was Dr. N. G. Carter of Ripley, the son of Dr. W. D. Carter, who had served as surgeon in the partisan rangers. Reverend W. C. Johnston of Memphis presided over the ceremony with a "very large congregation" looking on. "All the railroad men were on hand ready to do all in their power to afford pleasure to the accomplished daughter of the president." A special train waited for the couple and their party outside the church. The engineer had "gaily dressed" the engine for the occasion. When all had boarded, the train pulled out accompanied by "the sweet strains of music mingled with the cheerful voices of hundreds of young and lovely maidens, and gallant gentlemen, who accompanied the happy couple as far as Middleton." By the time the train reached the northern terminus, it was night or almost night, and they checked into Leliard's Hotel for a night of festivities and dancing overseen by the railroad's superintendent, B. P. Robson. The following day, the Carters departed on the M&C for Memphis, where they checked into the Peabody.[2]

However, not all was well with Falkner's family. In 1873, William Henry Falkner was enrolled in Washington and Lee University, a colonial-era college located in Lexington, Virginia, in the Shenandoah Valley. He was listed in the school of law and also under moral philosophy, and the intent was probably for him to follow the Word tradition and become a lawyer.[3] The school's president had been former Confederate general Robert E. Lee, from the end of the war until Lee's death in 1870. Henry probably remembered the Shenandoah Valley, when as a child he was taken to visit his father in his winter camp there.

Figure 11.1. Willett
"Willie" Medora Falkner
Carter. Courtesy of
Tommy Covington.

On Saturday night, October 4, 1873, Henry was involved in a brawl with a
fellow student, Philip Dandridge of West Virginia, at the Blue Hotel on Main
Street in Lexington where the two boarded. The circumstances behind this
rencounter provide one of the few glimpses available into Henry's personality.

The incident originated the previous night when Henry was reported to
have been drinking heavily. One account described him as "pretty far gone—
staggering." He was in this condition when he encountered Dandridge—
nicknamed "Judge"—and called out to him, "Judge, come here!" Seeing that
Falkner had been drinking, Dandridge ignored him. In response, Henry
called out: "Judge, if you don't come here, you are a d—n son of a b—h." Then
Dandridge turned to knock him down but was stopped by friends. Later, the
town marshal encountered Falkner and found that he "was so drunk he didn't
know what he was doing. Afterwards he was sitting in Anderson's door vomit-
ing; couldn't walk without being supported."[4]

The next day Dandridge, feeling insulted, boasted that "he would whip Falkner if he did not apologize." That evening a number of students including Dandridge and Falkner were standing on the back porch of the Blue Hotel. Dandridge demanded an apology, and Falkner replied: "If I don't, what then?" Dandridge then hit him, and the two began fighting until the former was knocked off the porch. After regaining his feet, Dandridge advanced and struck Falkner, while Falkner almost simultaneously struck Dandridge's belly. The latter "retreated a few steps . . . held his hand at his right side and said he was stabbed." Falkner was discovered to have a pocketknife in his hand, and was arrested and placed in jail.[5]

Dr. John A. Graham was immediately called in and found Dandridge in bed with substantial blood on his clothes and the bed linens. Graham's initial impression was that the young man was dying, but a closer examination revealed that no internal organs were damaged and that the wound was not life threatening. Indeed, within a few weeks Dandridge had recovered. On October 14, Henry was brought before the mayor's court in a session that lasted several hours. The defense attorney asked for bail, and it was denied by the major. Dandridge asked for leniency toward Henry, who was held over for trial at the February term of court.[6] The outcome of the case is unknown, but it can be guessed that the sentence was light. Henry was back in Ripley by February 1874, the same month as his trial.[7]

Back at home with nothing to show for his enrollment in the university except a criminal record, Henry again became active in the Sons of Temperance in the summer months. By February 1875, he was the marshal of the organization and in June, the treasurer.[8] Later that year his father attempted to involve him in business, including, as mentioned earlier, the mercantile trade. An R. G. Dun agent noted in October 1875 that Bill Falkner had turned the operation of his store over to Henry. Although this involved giving his son a small stock of goods, Bill hadn't much confidence in him and refused "to become respons[ible] for anything he owes or does." The agent described Henry as a "young single man dissipated but so far has paid up promptly" and said that he had no real estate or "means outside this business." A few days later he observed that Henry was "very intemperate has no stdg [standing] here pecuniarily morally socially or politically." Such a person was not likely to stay in business for long. At the end of May 1876, the agent tersely observed that Henry was "out of bus[iness]." There's no indication that his father stepped in to resume operation of the store.[9]

What Henry did over the next few years is largely unknown. However, he apparently died violently on January 5, 1878, at the hands of James A. Plummer of Ripley. Unfortunately, the major sources for his death are oral and are thereby subject to question. One account comes from John W. T. Faulkner Jr. of Oxford as recorded by Donald Duclos. According to this account, Henry began making advances on Nannie Plummer, the newly married (November 29, 1876) wife of James. Details of the relationship between Henry and Nannie are unknown, but Plummer apparently caught Henry with his wife and shot and killed him.[10] Another somewhat variant account comes from the same Falkner as recorded by Judge W. H. Anderson of Ripley, according to which Plummer

> had done some mighty strong talking about how sorry Henry was, and how sorry the Colonel was for letting Henry behave like he did. Henry went into Mr. Plummer's place of business, told Mr. Plummer that he had heard what he had been saying, that he didn't care what was said about him, but resented what he had said about his father, and was going to "whip hell out of him." Mr. Plummer told him not to come any further, drew a small pistol which shot one time. Henry told him that since he was crippled (Mr. Plummer had a club foot) and since he had that little gun that he guessed that made them about even, and advanced to do what he had gone in there to do, when Mr. Plummer shot and killed him.[11]

However, until better sources are forthcoming, the facts surrounding Henry's death will remain unclear. He had certainly been a letdown to his parents. Regardless, they were devastated to see their son dead at the age of twenty-four. Henry was buried in Ripley Cemetery under a large cenotaph with the stone on top inscribed with only one word, "Henry." Falkner was often lax in marking the graves of his family and the ones that were marked were usually small, but the size of Henry's monument stands out in contrast. His little sister Bama was only three, almost four, when he died. A lifetime later she recalled her only image of him: "He was tall and handsome and everything a gentleman should be. I remember, though I was just a little girl then, looking up to him as the handsomest young man I'd ever seen."[12]

Following the Civil War and martial law during early Reconstruction, the Republican Party played an ever larger role in state government, supported to a large degree by the freed Blacks who were now able to vote. Falkner assumed a prominent role in the Democratic Party during the last years of Reconstruction when the Democrats were making a play for control of the state government. At a meeting of the Democratic Convention of Tippah County on December 18, 1874, he was selected as a delegate to attend the state convention to be held in Vicksburg on January 8, 1875.[13] That year he signed up to run for the state Senate.

On July 15, a large rally was organized by the Democrats at the town of Falkner. An estimated two to three thousand were brought in by special trains on the Ripley Railroad. The crowd gathered in a grove west of town where a barbecue had been prepared for them. The primary speaker was Congressman and former Confederate colonel L. Q. C. Lamar, who spoke for over three hours in the midday heat haranguing against the Republican Party and Governor and former Union general Adelbert Ames, whom he blamed for the deterioration of race relations.

A Memphis reporter recorded: "The grove was literally packed in close proximity to the speaker's stand, and the approaches to it thronged with buggies, wagons, horses and mules, forcibly reminding one of the barbecues of old times." Lamar was the first to speak, starting at eleven.[14] Later, after everyone had eaten, Falkner came onto the stand and delivered a "powerful address in his usual eloquent style" on matters concerning the Republican legislature:

> [Falkner] paid his respects to the legislature of the State, and held them up to the scorn and contempt of all honest men. He presented his claims to the position in a forcible manner, and stated that as far as he was individually concerned, he did not care for the office, but believed that at this time he could be of service to the people of the district, and pledged himself to do all in his power to put down Radicalism and advance the interests of his constituents. Colonel Falkner was listened to with marked attention, and he left the impression on his hearers that to elect him to the State senate was to put "the right man in the right place."[15]

Later, delegates to the state and national conventions were announced, with W. C. Falkner among the former and J. W. T. Falkner among the latter.[16] A few months later, the elder Falkner—for reasons unknown—withdrew from the race for Senate.[17] The election in November would have revolutionary implications. The Democrats through coordination were able to have a strong turnout at the polls, while Republican voters, largely Blacks, were intimidated into not voting. The Democrats swept the elections and took control of the legislature. Republican Lieutenant Governor Alexander K. Davis, an African American, was impeached and removed from office. Governor Ames, realizing that his situation was hopeless, resigned. He was replaced as acting governor by the president pro tempore of the Senate, John M. Stone, Falkner's former compatriot in the Second Mississippi who had replaced him as colonel by a slim margin.

As Reconstruction ended in 1876, the Mississippi Democrats focused on electing one of their party for president, the first one since before the war.

The nominee of choice was Samuel J. Tilden, the governor of New York, who launched a strong campaign throughout the country. Tilden had gained the reputation of a reformer during his term as governor, while the Republicans under President Ulysses S. Grant had suffered a number of scandals. Tilden's running mate was Thomas A. Hendricks, serving then as governor of Indiana.

On June 3, the Conservative Democracy of Tippah County convened in Ripley. Falkner was elected chairman and W. W. Bailey secretary. In addressing the convention, Falkner explained

> the object of its meeting with great force and effect, convincing his fellow citizens how important it was to be up and doing, and at all times for the party to be ready for the struggle to maintain that reform and good government, the era of which is just dawning upon us, and that it might be ever kept alive and that the action of the party in maintaining honest rule would certainly prove a blessing to every individual, irrespective of his race.[18]

Soon after, Falkner was selected to serve as an elector from Mississippi's District 2, pledged to support the Democrat Tilden in the presidential race in which Rutherford B. Hayes of Ohio was the Republican candidate. To build support for Tilden, Falkner campaigned throughout his district on behalf of the Tilden ticket. For example, in September a Tilden and Hendricks Club was organized in Ripley. The organizational meeting was addressed in "eloquent and appropriate speeches" by Falkner as elector for the district and by Thomas Spight, their legislative representative.[19] Within a few weeks similar clubs were organized in other towns and communities in Tippah including Blue Mountain, Dumas, Falkner, Orizaba, and Ruckersville.[20] Others were being organized all over the state.

As the general election in November neared, a massive rally of Democrats was held in Ripley on Saturday, October 21, that was characterized by theatrics of the kind that Falkner liked to stage. A procession was formed at the fairgrounds and then, led by the "Rienzi silver band," wound its way through the town's streets,

> amid the booming of cannon, the shouts of the multitude, the waving of ladies' kerchiefs and the sweet strains of martial music. . . . The company of colored men, uniformed with red shirts and mounted on white steeds, presented the grandest sight of the day. . . . One hundred shots were fired while the procession was moving. The roar of cannon, the shouts of men, and the glad greeting of ladies, all combined to make it one of the grandest scenes ever witnessed by the writer.[21]

The procession ended at the courthouse square, where everyone assembled to hear Falkner speak for two hours. "The colonel made one of his best efforts on this occasion and was frequently greeted with loud and prolonged applause."[22] Another correspondent noted that "our zealous and warm hearted old soldier, Col. W. C. Falkner, led out in a speech of about two hours length, and was listened to with uncommon interest. . . . I must say that there never was a more efficient and earnest worker than our able and gallant friend Col. Falkner."[23]

The election was held on November 7 with a resounding Democratic victory that selected the eight electors to attend the state electoral college, which met on December 6 in Jackson. All eight electors including Falkner were present in the Senate chamber of the Capitol building at 11:00 a.m. Their work was predetermined and uneventful. The first ballot was for president and the unanimous vote was for Tilden. A second ballot was held for vice president, and again the results were unanimous, for Hendricks. Howard Falconer of Marshall County, not a member of the Electoral College, was then selected as messenger to deliver the ballots to the president of the US Senate, after which the meeting adjourned.[24]

However, the remaining part of the electoral process wasn't conducted so easily. There were disputes regarding the electors from certain states, and the process dragged on into the new year before finally being resolved. In the end, Tilden carried the country with a significant majority but a minority of the electors. Republican Rutherford B. Hayes became the next president. Falkner and others would have to wait before a Democrat would reclaim the office.

But in the meantime, financial problems of the railroad claimed Falkner's attention. As if the subsidy warrant matter wasn't enough, there were other serious financial problems to contend with. In October 1872, Falkner notified all who owed the company money that they must settle by November 10 or be sued. The reason for this was that the company was having difficulty paying its employees.[25] Soon after, its treasury was empty and couldn't cover salaries for December, so Falkner loaned the company $600 to cover salaries for the month.[26] Of course, if employees couldn't be paid, then the interest on the mortgage bonds owed the SRSC and due the first of January would certainly pose a problem.

The railroad was leased to the SRSC, which soon undertook renovations to compensate for deficiencies resulting from cutting corners during initial construction. For example, the five-foot crossties originally used were replaced with seven-foot ties.[27]

Under the trusteeship of the SRSC, many things continued as before. The directors continued to function, with Falkner staying on as president. In fact, he would retain the presidency for the rest of his life; such was his prestige within the company. The only major change was that the company was placed under the supervision of Benedict P. Robson, an Englishman formerly employed by the M&C, as general business manager or general superintendent, a position that he held until about 1878.[28] Despite the fact that he had been sent to Ripley as an agent for an outside entity, he was nevertheless well liked. R. J. Shannon recalled that Robson was "a most energetic and able man . . . [who] acted as superintendent, conductor, and agent-at-all stations from Middleton to Ripley."[29] He was also known for his acts of kindness, such as bringing a small pine tree from Ripley to a Middleton church to serve as a Christmas tree.[30]

Near the end of his first year, Robson received an unexpected recognition. On Thursday, December 18, 1873, a crowd gathered in front of the Tippah County courthouse to hear Falkner speak on a railroad matter. Falkner stepped up onto the portico and began speaking in a feigned stern manner as though a rebuke was coming, when in fact it was an award for meritorious service:

> Gentlemen—I, as the president of the Ripley railroad company, have felt it to be my duty to guard its interests, and at all times keep a vigilant eye on the employees. While doing this, I have discovered that Major Robson, the superintendent, has been gambling largely. He has played a deep and successful game. . . . It has always been the case that honesty, energy and industry would win the hearts of business men; and that kindness and courtesy would win the affections of the people. Major Robson has played the game to perfection, and has succeeded in winning the hearts of this community.[31]

At this time, Falkner pulled an expensive watch from his pocket and presented it to Robson. It was inscribed inside its case: "Presented to B. P. Robson, general manager of Ripley railroad, by Colonel Falkner, president of the company, and the merchants of Ripley, for his efficiency as a railroad manager." Major Robson replied: "Gentlemen, while managing the Ripley railroad I have endeavored to discharge my whole duty; and no language is strong enough to convey an idea of the gratification which I feel at this generous manifestation of approval from the people here. I feel grateful to this community for the kindness they have bestowed upon me while laboring among them." The reporter noted the "immense quantity of business" transacted in Ripley as the result of the railroad. It reminded him of the port of Memphis in years past "when hundreds of wagons, loaded with cotton, were to be seen crowding the streets. About two hundred bales of cotton were being traded daily while the railroad was doing a good business with freight."[32]

After almost two years, in October 1874 the trusteeship of the railroad was obtained by R. T. Wilson,[33] a New York investor with a southern background. Born in Georgia, he was a merchant there and in Tennessee. During the war he had worked for the commissary department of the Confederacy and was eventually appointed by Jefferson Davis as commissary general. Following the war, he moved to New York City to become a financier and was soon wealthy, residing on Fifth Avenue in the home formerly occupied by Boss Tweed. A daughter married Cornelius Vanderbilt III, the grandson of the railroad magnate, while a son married an Astor. Wilson was involved in purchasing several railroads that were consolidated into the East Tennessee, Virginia and Georgia Railroad (ETV&G), of which he soon became president. Soon after, the ETV&G acquired the M&C and Wilson became president. With the Ripley Railroad having problems and with its being closely linked to the M&C, it is not surprising that it was finally taken over by Wilson. At a November 1875 meeting of the railroad's board of directors, he was reported to be "in full possession of and . . . running the said company's road." It was also noted that he was

> hereby authorized and empowered to give orders, or draw drafts, or receive in person and receipt for any money which may now be due or which may hereafter become due (until further instructions) to the said company for carrying the mail or for other government services, and his receipt therefor shall be a full and complete ban against any and all further demands of this company for the same.[34]

Despite this, Wilson probably saw little of the Ripley Railroad. He was, after all, based in New York City, from where he oversaw railroads covering hundreds of miles, with the Ripley road only a small concern. He did come to Memphis for annual meetings of the M&C stockholders in 1875 and 1876.[35] It is conceivable that he stopped at Middleton on the way to Memphis and even rode the twenty-five miles to Ripley, although there's no evidence for it.

For several years, there was little financial ability to extend the road. In 1874, Falkner observed that because "money matters, remain, so depressed as they are now, it is impossible to build our road further south." However, as soon "as financial confidence is restored," he expected to resume construction.[36] The first attempt at continuing construction southward occurred in the summer of 1876, when the *Ripley Advertiser* reported that the survey of the route from Ripley to New Albany was underway, and that one hundred penitentiary inmates had been secured to grade it and that their arrival was imminent.[37] At a July 3 meeting of the railroad's directors, resolutions were passed to empower President Falkner to make arrangements for the extension of the road to New Albany and Pontotoc, while Major Wright, the company's engineer, was ordered to begin surveying the route.[38] A few days later, about one hundred convicts were at work grading "an extension of 15 miles from Ripley."[39] The use of convict labor had been authorized by the state legislature the previous year, and on June 9, 1876, the state leased the penitentiary to Jones S. Hamilton and John L. Hebron, who would operate it and lease inmates to serve as laborers for private concerns.[40] The lease date coincided closely with the arrival of the inmates in Ripley, suggesting that a deal had been worked out with Hamilton and Hebron. Convict labor would play a major role in constructing the railroad extension during the 1880s.[41]

Construction was revived the following spring when Union County, south of and adjacent to Tippah County, voted for a special tax to aid in extending the road to its county seat, New Albany.[42] A few weeks later, Superintendent Robson reported that construction would begin about the first of June with the road expected to reach New Albany by November 1.[43] In August it was reported that thirty thousand shovels and picks had been shipped to Ripley for construction work to be done by "contractor Hamilton," evidently referring to Jones S. Hamilton of Hamilton and Hebron, who were leasing the penitentiary.[44] The fact that there was a contractor and that tools were being imported suggests that something was being done. However, little is known about it.

In October 1877, the Ripley Railroad was reclaimed by local interests involving two new key players, C. E. Hines[45] and C. L. Harris.[46] A Memphis newspaper reported that "the Ripley railroad has been purchased by Colonel W. C. Falkner, Mr. R. J. Thurmond and Messrs. Hines and Harris, jointly—that each of the parties mentioned own[s] a third interest in the road. Major B. P. Robson has sold out his interest in the road, but still holds his position as superintendent."[47] According to another account, the men paid "one hundred thousand dollars cash for the entire franchise."[48]

Hines and Harris were able to buy into the railroad as a result of their successful sawmill operation. Along with their families, they would play major roles in decades to come, not only as owners but also as operators. Hines and Harris were business partners as well as brothers-in-law; Hines had married Cornelia Elizabeth Harris. By 1870, the two were operating a sawmill in Ripley, and in 1874 they purchased two city blocks (25 and 34) adjacent to the railroad on which a large sawmill was constructed.[49] Along with buying into the railroad, Hines and Harris sold two-thirds interest in the two blocks to Falkner and Thurmond including the sawmill, along with a second sawmill located about two miles north of town. This gave all of the owners a one-third interest in the sawmills.[50] The mills were operated in concert with the railroad and were a notable addition to the railroad's infrastructure.[51] The railroad shop would be constructed on Block 25.

About 1881, the Hines family constructed a two-story hotel known initially as the Hines House located across the railroad from the depot.[52] Shortly after, in 1882, son Lee Hines, who became prominent with the Ripley Railroad, constructed a two-story home on the west side of the hotel.[53]

Although it was reported that Robson would retain his job, by 1879 he had been replaced by C. L. Harris as general superintendent.[54] Whether he was forced out to make a position for a new owner is not known. Regardless, Harris would serve in this position for over two decades. Soon after the purchase of the railroad, on February 11, 1878, R. T. Wilson, who had been the trustee under the deed of trust, was replaced by R. J. Thurmond as trustee, one of the new owners, making the railroad once again independent of outside interests.[55]

With the railroad under new ownership and with the legislature back in session in 1878, Falkner was again in a position to fulfill his vision of a transcontinental railroad, and an effort was soon launched to extend the road southward to the Gulf. In early February, a bill was introduced into the Mississippi House of Representatives by M. A. Metts of Winston County, through which the railroad was intended to pass. On February 5, Falkner addressed the state Senate, where the bill was sponsored by Senator H. W. Foote, who represented Kemper, Noxubee, and Neshoba Counties, with the latter intended to be another beneficiary of the road's extension.[56] Authorized on the twenty-eighth of that month, the bill provided support for the Ripley Railroad's extension southward to Mississippi City on the coast and northward to St. Louis. Funding would come from state-owned lands, which the railroad could obtain for two cents on the acre and then resell for revenue with a provision being that construction had to be commenced within six months of the passage of this act. The railroad was also given the right to contract with the lessees of the penitentiary (which was still under Jones S. Hamilton, now operating under the firm name of J. S. Hamilton and Company) for "as many hands as can be advantageously employed upon said road."[57] A few days later, a supplementary act authorized the construction of a branch from a point on the (projected) main line in Union or Pontotoc County running northwesterly through Ashland, county seat of Benton County, to Grand Junction, Tennessee, on the M&C.[58] This bill seems a fanciful embellishment in which a twenty-five-mile railroad, in projecting itself into a three-hundred-plus-mile trunk line, was throwing in as an afterthought a fifty-plus-mile shortcut to Memphis.

The *Public Ledger* of Memphis was enthusiastic about the plan, reporting in mid-March that "Gen. Faulkner [*sic*], of Ripley, president of the road, is in the city to-day to make arrangements looking to an early commencement of work. He is confident that the entire line of over 325 miles can be built in less than three years. This would give Memphis a direct route to the gulf."[59] A few days later, Robson was also in Memphis attempting to drum up $7,000 in subscriptions.[60] However, their efforts and optimism came to naught.

On July 12, a railroad meeting was held in Ripley attended in part by Falkner, Jones Hamilton, and M. A. Metts, the legislator from Winston County. Metts painted a more somber picture of the railroad's prospects:

> We found on our arrival [at the Ripley meeting], that the part of the road completed from Middleton, Tenn., to Ripley, Miss., 24 miles, had issued bonds to the amount of $250,000, which were secured by a mortgage on the road. . . . This mortgage is held by [Colonel W. C. Falkner] and three other gentlemen. We also found that there were judgments against the road to the amt. of several thousand dollars, while there is forty to fifty thousand dollars of stock insecured [*sic*]. Col. Hamilton proposed that if Col. Falkner would cancel the mortgage, satisfy the judgments, and consent to reorganization of the company, as had been agreed upon, . . . the holders of the present mortgage should be paid in bonds on the new company, to the full value of the road now built, and . . . he, Hamilton, would place on the road all the convicts not under contract, and others that might be sent him in the future. This proposition Col. Falkner refused to accept, but said that he would reduce his bonds to $150,000, but would not cancel the mortgage. Hamilton feeling that he could not invest in an enterprise wherein his interest would be subject to an existing mortgage, refused to accept this proposition.
>
> From this it would seem that the Ripley road itself is insolvent, and that Col. Falkner is in a very poor condition to undertake such an enterprise. A narrow guage [*sic*] road of 24 miles, that has 40 or 50,000 dol[lars] of unsecured stock and is encumbered with unsatisfied judgments, and a mortgage to very nearly its full value, is a failure, and will most likely have to be sold to satisfy its creditors. At all events no advantage can be taken of the grant by the State, as the act requires that the land shall be selected within six months from the approval of the bill, and the time will expire on the 28th, of next month.[61]

Metts concluded: "Messrs. Falkner and Hamilton could not agree as to the construction of the road"; thus it "has turned out a complete failure."[62] The bill's authorization was to expire on August 28, and that day came and went. Next year, Ripley's *Southern Sentinel* lamented: "We thought when the last Legislature passed the bill to aid in its construction that a great work had been accomplished and we felt proud of the part we bore in it, but were deeply mortified when we found that not a shovel full of dirt was thrown, as a result of the determined effort of those members of the Legislature of '78. . . . Where the fault was it is not, now, necessary to discuss; we know it was a complete failure."[63]

Near the end of the year, the railroad suffered its worst accident when one of the owners, C. E. Hines, was killed. As noted, Hines and Harris, besides being part owners of the road, were also employees with Hines serving as engineer. On November 19, 1878, Hines was running between Ripley and Falkner and approaching a trestle when he encountered an animal, probably a mule or cow. Given their small size, narrow-gauge locomotives ran a strong risk of being derailed by collisions that may have posed less problem to larger engines. The impact caused the locomotive to derail, run off the trestle, and flip over, rupturing its pipes and spewing massive amounts of steam that scalded Hines to death.[64]

The following year, M. A. Metts expressed his concern regarding building a railroad through the center of the state to the coast. Acknowledging the importance of the project to the state's economy, he stated that the SIR&K shouldn't carry this out. Instead, an "altogether new company" should be chartered for the purpose, having all the rights and privileges granted to the SIR&K Railroad in 1878.[65] Metts had clearly lost faith in the road's ability to accomplish its goals.

The situation was indeed bleak. Falkner wrote: "It has been with the greatest difficulty that we have been able to keep the road in running order and we are hopelessly insolvent." There had been no net earnings over the past year. The major problem was that "[t]he road is too short to do any good . . . with but little business today."[66] Expansion would be the only way to overcome the problem, yet where would the financing come from? Falkner faced a seemingly insurmountable obstacle.

The opening of the 1880 state legislature brought a fresh attempt to continue the road southward. On the night of January 28, Falkner addressed the legislature on the subject of extending his railroad to the Gulf using convict labor. There was reported to be "considerable enthusiasm" for the project, and prospects were thought to be favorable.[67] Various plans were considered to additionally support the construction. One involved using local interests to construct the earthwork, following which the railroad would pay for the track.[68] A month later, Congressman H. D. Money introduced a bill into the US House of Representatives calling for the donation of federal lands to subsidize the construction.[69] Things appeared to be going well; Falkner was "completing his arrangements for doing the work" and had engaged the service of Colonel E. D. Frost to supervise construction.[70] The *Memphis Daily Appeal* reported that a contract had been signed to begin construction.[71]

Despite the rosy projections, Falkner had his reservations. Following his trip to Jackson, he reported to the editor of the *Clarion* on how quickly his hopes had been dashed. He had a bill introduced into the Senate to amend the railroad's charter, following which it was altered without his authorization in a manner detrimental to acquiring further investment. As he noted, "if a joint Select Committee had been appointed by the Legislature with instructions to invent a scheme to prevent the construction of the road to the Gulf, that committee could not have invented a more complete and successful plan to prevent the building of the road than was invented by the Senate."[72] The 1880 campaign soon faded from the news without anything being accomplished. Falkner's dreams of a transcontinental road would be placed on hold for a time. One thing clearly evident was that the fulfillment of his vision would not be easy, but perhaps an opportunity would turn up.

Chapter 12

◈══◦══◦══◦══◈

Novelist and World Traveler

For the next few years, Falkner attempted little in terms of further railroad construction—no opportunities were forthcoming—and he was left to manage his various business affairs and pursue his literary interests, which had periodically emerged over the decades. These years were dominated by a series of projects into which he could pour his seemingly boundless energy. The first of these grew out of a disaster in Ripley.

On the night of April 7, 1880, the office of the *Ripley Advertiser*, located on the southeast corner of the square, burned along with several other nearby buildings. All of the equipment was destroyed and publication ceased for a time.[1] When publication resumed in June, the newspaper began carrying weekly installments of a novel written by Falkner entitled *The White Rose of Memphis*.[2] Falkner apparently loaned funds to the editor, Richard F. "Dick" Ford, to rebuild while supplying him with the newly written chapters in order to boost circulation.[3] When Falkner began the writing is not known. His law partner at the time, C. J. Frederick, noted that his writing was conducted in the midst of a hectic schedule:

> The greatest mystery to me is that Colonel Falkner could find time to compose such a charming novel as the *White Rose*, and at the same time keep up and manage more business than any other man in this community. He is the president of the Ripley Railroad company, and has been for ten years; he runs a farm near this place, cultivating 1200 acres, and successfully manages over a hundred tenants; runs a grist-mill, cotton-gin, saw-mill, a law office, a dozen small farms, helps to build churches, schoolhouses, and leads in all public enterprises in this county.[4]

When did he write? Andrew Brown observed in this regard:

> He was a fluent and methodical worker; he did his writing at night, in a brick
> outhouse to his home, and set apart a certain period each night for the work.
> One of his daughters said years later that he would go to this office immediately
> after supper, write until 9 o'clock and then return to the house.[5]

The White Rose of Memphis is a story within a story. The primary framing
narrative is that of a voyage from Memphis to New Orleans aboard a river
steamer named *The White Rose of Memphis*. Prior to the boat's departure, a
masquerade ball[6] is held with the passengers in disguise wearing costumes
based on historical or literary personages, such as Don Quixote, the Duke of
Wellington, Henry of Navarre, Ivanhoe, Mary, Queen of Scots, the Queen of
Sheba, and others. Acting in disguise proves to be so popular that the passengers decide to remain so for the entirety of the trip, and most of the novel.

The passengers decide that Mary Queen of Scots would reign as "the grand
sovereign" while amusement would be provided by telling stories. The first
and—as it turns out only—storyteller is Ingomar, the barbarian chieftain,
whose story dominates the novel from beginning to end. Ingomar is derived
from Maria Lovell's translation of a German play, which she entitled *Ingomar,
the Barbarian*.[7] Ingomar and Queen Mary, or rather their real-life counterparts, prove to be the central characters in the novel.

Ingomar begins telling his life story, soon "unmasking" himself in that it
becomes apparent that his real name is Edward Demar, a medical doctor who
was born in Nashville to a once prosperous merchant. He was orphaned early
along with his two step-siblings, Harry and Charlotte "Lottie" Wallingford.
With almost no financial resources, the three children were forced to under-
take the arduous two-hundred-mile journey from Nashville to Memphis
to reside with an uncle. Along the way they suffered from lack of food, the
elements, a rattlesnake bite, and the persecution of a bully, Ben Bowles.
Additionally, Harry saved the life of a young girl of wealthy parentage named
Viola Bramlett who had also become an orphan.

After the passage of a few years, all four orphans were near adulthood,
and romance was developing between Edward and Lottie on one hand and
Harry and Viola on the other. However, darkness again surrounded them
when Viola was accused of murdering her small brother with strychnine
and was imprisoned to await trial for murder. False accusations of criminal
behavior were a favorite theme for Falkner. Recall *The Lost Diamond* and
the accusation that George Clifton had stolen the "lost diamond." Although

Viola's friends knew that she was not a person inclined to murder, the evidence accumulated during the investigation was uniformly against her, causing all to doubt her innocence except Lottie, who delved deep into the case while remaining secretive about her discoveries. In a climactic courtroom scene, Lottie's adoptive father, Nathaniel Rockland, an attorney, defended Viola while Lottie by his side was allowed to question witnesses. Through her superior investigation she proved that Ben Bowles had framed Viola in order to acquire her inheritance; years before, Bowles had tormented the orphans. Bowles was able to make his escape and fled the courthouse and Memphis. At one point, Lottie could well be speaking for Falkner when she observed: "I used to be simple enough to think that courts were the very fountains of justice, where the weak and helpless could procure redress for wrongs inflicted on them by the strong and powerful, but the scales of ignorance have lately been removed from my eyes."[8]

As the novel comes to an end, Ingomar's story merges with events onboard the *White Rose*, with his characters revealed as masked personae aboard the boat. Besides Edward Demar as Ingomar, Queen Mary proves to be Lottie, now married to Edward. Harry Wallingford is Henry of Navarre, and a mysterious woman in a black domino robe is Viola. But most importantly, Napoleon proves to be the archvillain Ben Bowles. After shooting and wounding Viola, he leaps from the boat to make his escape. Hot in pursuit, Harry also leaps into the Mississippi and catches Bowles, and after being stabbed by Bowles, kills him. The book concludes a few years later with Harry and Viola married and living next door to Edward and Lottie.

Like most works of melodrama, *The White Rose of Memphis* relies heavily on coincidence, mistaken identities, and sentimentality. However, although wordy by modern standards, it can still enthrall the reader. Many characters are Dickensian with eccentric behavior and speech, and odd names such as the gossips Jemima Tadpoddle and Jerusha Clattermouth.

In an examination of the numerous literary sources alluded to or quoted in *White Rose*, Calvin S. Brown remarks on Falkner's hurried schedule, which had also been noted by C. J. Frederick: "Clearly, he had no time to hunt up literary allusions or check quotations, even if he had been inclined to do so. Thus, we can be confident that the extensive literary material in the novel is material that Falkner knew well enough to be able to use it impromptu and casually." This contention is supported by the manner in which the quotations he uses often slightly vary from the originals, indicating that he is quoting from memory.[9] This is a testimony to Falkner's intellectual abilities, achieved with little formal schooling.

Throughout the novel there are allusions to and quotations from literary and historical works, some of the former represented by the masked personae assumed by the passengers on the steamboat. Calvin Brown compiled these into a three-page table, with the sheer number suggesting Falkner's familiarity with a broad range of literature. Of these, the largest number comes from the works of William Shakespeare, with thirty-eight personae and references to fourteen plays with which he showed considerable familiarity. We have already seen Falkner referring in 1856 to seeing a presentation of *Richard III*. Indeed, one of his characters seems to speak for him when she states: "Shakespeare is my poet."[10] The second most prominent source is the Bible, with twenty-six references, and third is Walter Scott, with twelve references. Beyond this, there are numerous references to Byron, Cervantes, Dickens, Homer, Milton, and others.

The serialized novel met with considerable popularity locally. The editor of the *Ashland Register* in the neighboring town of Ashland complained that because of the serial's popularity he could hardly keep a copy of the *Ripley Advertiser* around his office long enough to finish each installment. He furthermore indicated his hope that "the Colonel will put his admirable story in book form, [so] that all who desire may get a chance to read it."[11] He was not the only one to think that. In early 1881, the publisher D. Appleton and Company of New York City indicated interest in publishing the novel.[12] On April 24, Falkner left for New York to oversee the publication and a few weeks later notified Ripley that there had been a change of plans. Instead of Appleton, *White Rose* would be published by G. W. Carleton and Company, also of New York.[13] Shortly before Falkner's return on June 10, Memphis's *Public Ledger* announced that the handsomely bound novel had been released and was for sale at Mansford's on Main Street, priced at $1.50 a copy.[14] The book was dedicated to Falkner's old friend M. C. Gallaway, who was by then editor of the *Memphis Daily Appeal*. The lengthy dedication recalled bleaker times and the near duel between Falkner and T. C. Hindman Jr. in which Gallaway had intervened:

> In days long since past, when dark, angry clouds of misfortune lowered over me and dangers clustered thick around me—a time when friends of mine were few, though much needed and greatly desired—it was my good fortune to find in your generous heart those noble sentiments of true friendship that have proved of inestimable value to me.[15]

Within a month, the first printing of eight thousand copies sold out and a second was in the works.[16] By the end of the year there were reportedly twelve thousand copies in print, and ten thousand had been sold.[17] The novel would remain in print for years and was by far Falkner's greatest literary success.[18] In response to his success, the *Memphis Daily Appeal* provided a description of the new celebrity, who

> has become quite a hero since the publication of his novel, *The White Rose of Memphis*. His book has reflected credit upon him, and it is hoped will be the means of inaugurating a boom in the literature of the South equal to that we are now enjoying in all that concerns our material interests. . . . There is much curiosity to see and know Colonel Faulkner, who has suddenly become prominent in literary circles.[19]

On July 6, Falkner and his family left Ripley to spend several weeks of relaxation at Bailey Springs, Lauderdale County, Alabama. This was the first known occasion of their visiting the mineral spa, and it would not be their last. Bailey Springs was typical of the mineral spring spas that developed during the nineteenth century as vacation resorts.[20] It was located nine miles northeast of Florence, Alabama, from where it could be reached by a stagecoach that served the resort.[21]

Bailey Springs was established in the 1840s. Like at most such spas, the springwaters purportedly had curative properties. In 1881, the proprietors claimed that "[c]ases of dropsy, scrofula, dyspepsia, debility, and diseases of the Kidneys, bladder, and skin that have defied the doctors and resisted all other medical springs, are getting well there every week."[22] Five springs were located under an open-sided roof, 150 by 60 feet, where guests could exercise and bathe. Despite the promises of curative properties, few guests at the springs were actually ill; most came seeking simply a pleasurable experience, which they would find at a site whose "crowning beauty" was its "rugged and picturesque location, convenient and yet retired."[23] The resort lay in an Arcadian setting amid scattered shade trees and a cluster of buildings that included a two-story hotel, dining facilities, a ballroom, a bowling alley, and a bar. Much of the pleasure of staying there came from interactions with other visitors.

About two hundred people were staying there when the Falkners arrived, and a new guest and old friend soon arrived, Mrs. M. C. Gallaway of Memphis. When she appeared for breakfast on the day of her wedding anniversary, she found her table decorated with flowers, mounds of fruits, and a sumptuous basket put together by Effie Falkner. Mrs. Gallaway was presented with a copy of *The White Rose*, which had been dedicated to her husband and inscribed: "Colonel W. C. and Mrs. L. H. Falkner have the honor to present this book to

Figure 12.1. Bailey Springs Hotel. Courtesy of Tommy Covington.

Mrs. Fanny B. Gallaway on the thirty-ninth anniversary of her marriage with Colonel M. C. Gallaway, with sincere wishes for a long continuation of unalloyed happiness."[24]

Despite the lures of relaxation and entertainment, Falkner had things to do. In early August he returned to Ripley, then on to Memphis before returning to the Springs. The object of the trip is unknown.[25]

A few weeks later, on August 17, the Springs featured a "Grand Dress and Masquerade Ball," reminiscent of *The White Rose of Memphis*. One young lady played Marie Antoinette, another Cinderella, and another Cupid. Thirteen-year-old Effie Falkner played the Gypsy Queen, a character in the opera *The Bohemian Girl* (1843). In reporting the event, M. C. Gallaway described the players, including Effie's "queenly form, dark, liquid eyes and raven hair, and the ease, grace and dignity with which she deported herself. . . . She was dressed in black silk velvet skirt, trimmed with Spanish lace."[26] However, all good things must come to an end; people came and went. As Gallaway observed: "The crowd at these Springs, like the Mississippi river, is constantly coming and going. The same vehicle that conveys the departing visitors returns with a new accession." Soon after the masquerade ball, the Falkners took the departing stagecoach to the railhead and from there home to Ripley.[27]

Bolstered by the success of *The White Rose*, Falkner was soon at work on another novel. On May 2, 1882, the *Memphis Daily Appeal* noted that he was in Memphis at the Peabody Hotel having "just completed another novel" entitled *The Little Brick Church*. The reporter, probably M. C. Gallaway, went on to note: "The unprecedented sale and great popularity of *The White Rose of Memphis* will induce the public to look for Colonel Falkner's new book with great eagerness. He is the first Southern author who has made literary pursuits pay, and it is hoped this will be a stimulus to the dormant literary talent of the South."[28]

On May 6, Falkner departed for Philadelphia to work with his new publisher, J. B. Lippincott and Company, in preparing *The Little Brick Church* for publication.[29] By June 13, he was back in Memphis with the news that the novel would be in bookstores by the end of the month.[30] By early July, Memphis bookstores were offering it for sale.[31]

The book was "elegantly and substantially bound" in green with gold-stamped lettering and was "well printed on strong paper."[32] A portrait of its tragic heroine, Lady Olivia, appeared on the frontispiece. *The Little Brick Church* was shorter than *White Rose* with 429 pages compared to the latter's 531. There were notable similarities between the two. Both began on a steamboat, both involved two intertwined narratives, both involved sentimental love stories between foster siblings, and both had a primary character who was falsely accused and tried for murder. *The Little Brick Church* begins with the main narrator, an unnamed attorney, deciding to take a trip up the Hudson River:

> Early in the month of May, 1850, I was employed by one of the banks of Cincinnati to visit the city of New York, for the purpose of securing a doubtful claim which the bank held against a failing merchant of that place. The compensation that I was to receive for my services was, by the terms of the contract, made to depend upon the success of the enterprise. It was agreed that if I succeeded in securing or collecting the debt, I should have the privilege of visiting all the Northern cities at the expense of the bank, in addition to the usual fees charged by attorneys in such cases. With such a strong incentive to urge me on, it may well be imagined that I did not "allow the grass to grow under my feet" while engaged in the business. Madame Fortune showered upon me her most gracious smiles from the moment I left Cincinnati until the final conclusion of the negotiations. I was indescribably happy to be able, at the close of the first week after my arrival in the city, to inform my employers by telegraphy that their debt had been collected. The money I sent by express, except a liberal share I had reserved to pay expenses while engaged in my sight-seeing peregrinations. My mind was filled with an ardent desire to view the romantic scenery that lines both banks of the Hudson river. I had, in my youthful days, read many glowing descriptions of the majestic mountains and lofty hills that rear their craggy crests high above the banks of that charming river.
>
> It was on the morning of the 25th of May, 1850, that I found myself seated on the boiler-deck of a magnificent steamboat that was advertised to start at ten o'clock. A motley crowd of people thronged the wharf, jostling each other in their heedless movements. Carriages, buggies, omnibuses, drays, and express-wagons rattled over the rocky road, while steam-whistles and yelling drivers filled the air with a deafening noise.[33]

Although it cannot be documented, one wonders if this passage may have been autobiographical. Both Falkner and the narrator were attorneys, and Falkner visited New York on several occasions when he could have traveled on the Hudson.

Upon boarding the steamboat, the narrator encounters an elderly man, Braddock Barnard, who is two months short of being one hundred years old and who invites the narrator to spend a few days with him at his home farther upstream overlooking the Hudson. Once there, Barnard begins telling a story that transpired in his youth both before and during the American Revolution. The interlacing of Barnard's narrative of the 1700s with the narrator's framing tale of 1850 makes Barnard's story the equivalent of Ingomar's tale in *White Rose*.

The main characters in Barnard's story are his neighbors Olivia Delroy and Oscar Falkland, with Olivia having been adopted and raised by Oscar's parents. Although raised as siblings, they gradually fall in love as they grow to adulthood, a relationship reminiscent of the love between Edward Demar and Lottie Wallingford in *White Rose*. Falsely accused of murder, Oscar is brought to trial and eventually acquitted, recalling the trial of Viola Bramlett in *White Rose*. Before they can marry, Olivia is killed after falling through the ice on a creek, and soon after Oscar collapses on her body and dies of a "broken heart." They are buried together in a single coffin in the cemetery of the titular "little brick church" on the Hudson. At the end of the story and back in the 1850s, the narrator is summoned to Barnard's funeral and burial in the cemetery beside the brick church.

The reviews were generally favorable. A writer for the Memphis *Public Ledger* noted that the book possessed a style that was "very attractive, realistic and terse" and was "creditable to the pen of the gifted author and to the literature of the day." The reviewer predicted that it would "no doubt have a general circulation."[34] The *Memphis Appeal* predicted that there would be "an eager demand" for the book. Additionally, it was noted that "[t]he book is not, however, an apologist for slavery, or an approver of its existence or principles; much the contrary, it simply exposes, with bitter irony, the inconsistency of the Easterners upon the question now, thank God, put out of the way forever."[35]

Not all were impressed. In a review entitled "Can Anything Good Come Out of Nazareth?," an anonymous contributor to the *Daily Memphis Avalanche* wrote: "Since the days of Munchausen, perhaps, there has never been compressed into one innocent looking volume such a number of remarkable incidents. . . . All storied epics, all Homeric odes, all

Shakespearean lore, all dime novel wisdom fades into insignificance before the incidents we have here recorded."[36]

There is no evidence that *The Little Brick Church* was reprinted by Lippincott. However, in 1895, the publishers of *White Rose*, G. W. Dillingham and Company, released a revised and shortened edition of the novel, retitled *Lady Olivia*.[37]

Following the release of *The Little Brick Church* in July, Falkner and his wife and daughters departed for Bon Aqua Springs in Hickman County, Tennessee, and Bailey Springs, where they spent almost a month.[38]

With the emergence of Falkner as a literary celebrity, it is not surprising that his play, *The Lost Diamond*, would be resurrected in part as one of his philanthropic efforts, and probably in part for the sheer joy of producing the play. The effort was triggered by the formation of a musical group, the Ripley Cornet Band, in late 1882. The members of the band were young men largely unable to afford the cost of uniforms. Upon hearing of their plight, Falkner stepped in and offered to purchase the uniforms, suggesting that they could pay him back with the proceeds from a presentation of *The Lost Diamond*. The band members readily agreed, and the uniforms of Confederate gray were soon ordered.[39]

In January 1883, the *Southern Sentinel* reported: "There is a rumor afloat that our Amateur Dramatic Company will reproduce the popular Drama 'The Lost Diamond' by W. C. Falkner. This thrilling drama was presented here some fifteen years ago and met with good success. We think its reproduction will meet a like result."[40]

Falkner pitched in with enthusiasm to direct the play and was certainly in his element, coordinating a theater production of his own composition. Walter L. Smith, one of the lead actors, recalled: "He drilled us through every rehearsal personally and made quite [a] few changes after rehearsals started. Each was given his part, with the cues, but no one had a complete copy."[41] The maligned hero of the play, George Clifton, was played by R. O. Prewitt, principal of the Ripley Institute, the male high school,[42] while the lead female role and Clifton's love interest, Rosalind Raymond, was played by fifteen-year-old Effie Falkner.[43] In the process of producing the play, Falkner decided that the lead Black character, Pompey Smash, required a love interest, so impromptu he created one named Jamima Jumper with an entirely new scene for her, which expanded the play from eight scenes to nine.[44] A shipment soon arrived from New York consisting of "handsome uniforms, and gorgeous costumes," which would be used in the play and as uniforms for the band.[45]

The play was scheduled for presentation in Ripley's new city hall, which occupied the second floor of a double-wide, frame commercial building located in the center of the south side of the square. The second floor apparently accommodated an auditorium that would soon become known as the Ripley Opera House.[46] In practice, "opera houses" in small-town America saw little opera; instead, they were the stages for the variety of acts—plays, skits, comedy routines, and musical performances—that constituted vaudeville.

The play would be presented on Wednesday, March 7, with the proceeds to help defray the expense of the band uniforms while paying the music teacher for the band.[47] On that night, the crowd lined up for access to the opera house and filled the auditorium. The actors played out their roles—both tragic and comic.[48] The play was not without excitement, as it included a "battle scene [in which] the hero and villain fought on the stage with swords, [and] guns were fired on the other side of the square, with anvils representing musketry, and artillery, which they said made it very realistic."[49] One attendee reported: "It was my pleasure to attend at City Hall, last Wednesday night a thrilling drama, 'The Lost Diamond.' . . . To say that the play was a grand and brilliant success and reflecting honor upon the Col., is but a just tribute to his talent and genius. . . . [It] added another plume in the Colonel's cap."[50] The *Memphis Daily Appeal* reported:

> The people of Ripley, and Tippah county . . . are all agog over Col. W. C. Falkner's new play, the *Lost Diamond*, recently performed at the Ripley Operahouse. The crowd was large, delighted, enthusiastic, and the proceeds, appropriated to charitable purposes, far surpassed all expectations. Col. Falkner is a wonderful man. Vivid and romantic as is his imagination, he surpassed himself in preparing the *Lost Diamond*.[51]

The leader of the Ripley Cornet Band wrote in gratitude for everyone's support for the play, including that of "Col. W. C. Falkner and his excellent Lady."[52] The success of *The Lost Diamond* was such that it was presented again that winter, on the night of December 27, again in the opera house, with the proceeds going to the Ripley Presbyterian Church to help them build a new parsonage. An announcement stated: "Three splendid bands of music will parade the streets on Thursday evening in wagons at the same time. A complete representation of the great battle of Manassas will appear on the stage by soldiers in full uniform.—Artillery, musketry and sword fighting thrillingly represented."[53] As before, a large audience was present. Most of the cast remained the same, except that R. O. Prewitt wasn't available to play the lead, George Clifton, so Pink Smith had to fill in.[54] As in the previous presentation, Effie Falkner played the leading lady, Rosalind Raymond, while

Figure 12.2. Pink Smith, editor of the *Southern Sentinel*, in costume as the hero George Clifton in Falkner's play *The Lost Diamond*. On the set in the opera house, Ripley, Mississippi, December 1883. Courtesy of Tommy Covington.

in this presentation both of her sisters also had roles. Willie Carter played Fannie Carroll, the southern lady who was in love with Union general D. W. Rosemond, a role formerly played by Mollie Harris, daughter of C. L. Harris of the Ripley Railroad. Little nine-year-old Bama Falkner played Medora Clifton, the sister of hero George Clifton. During the intermissions, the audience was entertained by bands along with a recitation by Bama Falkner. In all, over $150 was raised and the performance declared a success.[55]

Early in April, Falkner was sick and bedridden. On Monday, April 9, he left town via train bound for New Orleans and "other points on the Gulf Coast for the benefit of his health." He apparently traveled alone. He returned to Ripley on May 1, with his health much improved; reports stated that he had spent time on "the Mississippi Gulf Coast, and at Pensacola, Cedar Keys and other points in Florida."[56]

A stuffed alligator once stood erect in the hallway just inside the door of Falkner's home in Ripley. Standing in an anthropomorphic position, it once held a large seashell in which visitors could leave their calling cards. The figure was apparently produced by a tourist-related industry along the Gulf Coast that manufactured stuffed alligators in various positions for sale to visitors. This particular stuffed alligator was probably purchased by Falkner during his travels along the coast.[57]

Upon his return from the coast, it was also reported that he and Effie would soon leave for a tour of Europe.[58] Falkner had been corresponding for two years with several friends in regard to organizing a group who would travel to Europe together. Ten signed on, but apart from Effie, only two others went through with the trip. They were schoolteachers from Texas, Mary Bell and Mattie Stevenson; we are not told how Falkner connected with them, but he apparently didn't know them beforehand.[59] Considering that they would be gone for months, preparation for the trip was soon underway, with Falkner taking time for certain duties such as handing out diplomas at the graduation ceremony for Stonewall College held at the opera house on May 11.[60]

On May 23, 1883, Falkner and Effie left Ripley by rail bound for New York, where they would board the steamer *City of Berlin*, which was scheduled to depart on June 2 for Europe. L. P. "Pink" Smith had become the editor of the *Sentinel* in April. After having submitted the manuscript of *The White Rose of Memphis* to the *Ripley Advertiser* for serialization in 1881, Falkner thought that he would do the same for the newer paper. Smith noted that "[the] Colonel has promised to write an occasional letter to the Sentinel and our readers may expect something interesting from his pen."[61] The resulting texts, which would be turned into Falkner's next book, provide some of the best available insights into Falkner's personality.

After some stops along the way, the Falkners arrived in New York City in time for their June 2 departure only to find that the *City of Berlin* was days behind schedule. A flaw had been found in its crankshaft and repairs had to be made. Consequently, the ship didn't arrive until June 4, with its new departure time set for 6:00 a.m. on June 7. When Falkner discovered that they would have five days to wait, he tried to book passage on another ship but was unsuccessful. Consequently, he and Effie checked into the Grand Central Hotel on Broadway to wait. This prominent hotel had gained notoriety as the site of the 1872 shooting and killing of the financier James Fisk. They were then free to explore the city, a place that Falkner was not unfamiliar with, having visited the New York Stock Exchange, Central Park, the Zoological Garden, Trinity Church, and the Halls of Justice and Detention Center or the "Tombs," which he had first visited in 1856.[62]

Falkner loved to stroll in Central Park, where the scenery reminded him of Paradise. The park also provided a panorama on the breadth of the human condition, including the less than paradisiacal:

> It is here where the over-worked mechanic and the pale-faced factory-girl may be seen on Sunday evenings sitting on a bench enjoying the fresh air, vainly dreaming of better days that will never come. It is here where the lovesick maiden, sitting in some obscure shady bower, listens to the sweet whisper of

her lover's renewed pledges of unending devotion. Here it is that we see the millionaire seated in his gilded carriage dashing by the penniless beggar. This is the place where the ruined speculator usually comes to cool his fevered brain and to compose his shattered nerves. It is here where the painted Jezebel plots and plans for the disposal of her fast-failing charms. This is the field where the brokers, bankers, bulls and bears congregate to talk over the last week's battle, while they discuss the plan of the next campaign. Here is the stage on which New York society struts to show its feathers, and to flaunt its finery in the face of its envious enemies.[63]

The *City of Berlin* was a state-of-the-art ocean liner owned by the Inman Line, one of the three largest British passenger lines. Ocean liners developed during the mid-nineteenth century as the result of technological developments such as the steam engine and the use of steel hulls; they were part of the same transportation revolution that produced railroads. Emerging from their development was the establishment of regular shipping routes connecting ports on either side of the Atlantic. The development of ocean liners facilitated the development of European tours for inhabitants of the Americas. Constructed in 1874, the *City of Berlin* plied a route from Liverpool to New York via Queenstown (now Cobh), Ireland. Although it was steam powered, it had three masts on which sails could be hoisted if needed. The ship was 520 feet long by 44 feet beam. It could transport about 1,770 passengers—170 first class, 100 second class, and 1,500 steerage—with a crew of 150. In 1875 the ship won the Blue Riband prize as the fastest liner on the Atlantic and in 1879 was the first steamer to be outfitted with internal electric lights. She traversed her route from Liverpool to New York in about eight days.[64]

On the afternoon of the sixth, as their departure approached, Falkner, Effie, Mary Bell, and Mattie Stevenson left their hotel and were soon at the long wooden warehouse of the Inman Line at Pier 41 on the Hudson River in lower Manhattan, where they boarded the *City of Berlin* as it waited for departure in twelve hours.[65] The following morning, the remaining passengers began boarding while visitors were required to depart. The gangplanks were raised, and the ship began to ease into the river.

The great city was bathed in a sea of golden rays from the rising sun as the ship began to glide over the water. Hundreds of tearful eyes were intently gazing at the crowd of friends and relatives who with white handkerchiefs waved adieu from the wharf. Solemn silence prevailed among the multitude of passengers who covered the deck, watching the receding shore as it rapidly faded from view.

Then we were on the bosom of the broad blue ocean. What a grand prospect! Such an exhilarating breeze! Such an expansive view!

"Oh, my! Ain't it delightful?" exclaimed Miss Bell.

"Delicious! Exquisite!" cried Effie.

"Wonderful! Magnificent!" said Miss Stevenson.

"I'm half starved," muttered Effie. "I do wish breakfast was ready."[66]

While at breakfast, seasickness began to strike. Person after person was forced to abandon their meal to seek solace on the deck. Falkner soon followed:

An awful epidemic was prevailing when I arrived on top; the passengers were getting down to their work handsomely. I joined the band as soon as I could reach the railing. I was performing my part of the task admirably, when a man offered me his sympathy. I then and there determined to kill him, but neglected to do it, on account of the important business which constantly demanded my attention.[67]

His sickness continued for several days.

At the end of the third day my stomach and I made friends, buried the hatchet, and smoked the pipe of peace together. . . . I felt like a new man. . . . I was a boy again, with a disposition to prance and race about the deck with children. . . . Who would not endure three days of misery for such exquisite delight as one experiences after recovering from a spell of sea-sickness?[68]

On the fourteenth the ship stopped briefly at Queenstown, Ireland, to deliver mail. While there, Falkner dispatched a letter to his wife with the mail going ashore. He reported that all were well and that the voyage had been "pleasant." He apparently didn't mention the bouts with seasickness.[69]

Late on the fifteenth, the ship anchored on the Mersey River in Liverpool, one of England's preeminent port cities, and with a cold, drizzling rain falling began unloading passengers onto smaller boats for delivery to shore. Upon reaching the docks, the passengers were directed into the customshouse for processing. Falkner and his party stood in some confusion until they heard a voice calling, "Is Colonel Falkner in this crowd?" Falkner replied in a "meek voice": "Here is a melancholy wreck—a feeble representation of Colonel Falkner." It was their courier, or guide, Alfred Schmitsuebel, an Italian (probably Tyrolian judging by his name) who resided with his family in London. He was "well educated and speaks all the languages of the countries through which we expect to travel." Besides guiding the group, he was also in charge of all matters concerning baggage and tickets. Schmitsuebel expeditiously saw their baggage through customs and onto a carriage in which the party was soon en route to the Compton House hotel.[70]

As he had promised editor Pink Smith, Falkner began writing lengthy accounts of his travels, which he then mailed home for publication. Following departure from New York, he began keeping a diary. His first contributions consisted of little more than a transcript of day-to-day entries. As he got into the swing of writing, his contributions became longer and began to include vignettes of scenes and events he had witnessed, often written with obvious exaggerations for the sake of humor. The installments appeared weekly and continued long after his return home. Afterward, they were revised into the published volume *Rapid Ramblings in Europe*. Falkner's travel narrative provided extremely valuable insights into his personality and his personal relations with others. When these were published in book form, the earlier chapters differed markedly from the texts as originally submitted to and published in the *Southern Sentinel*, so much had he revised his texts, while the later chapters were almost verbatim as initially published.

In the first installment, probably mailed from Queenstown, Falkner noted the difficulties he faced while writing at sea, not without exaggeration: "This letter was written under difficulties. The table on which it was written had the advantage of me, it was fastened to the floor and I was not. When the Ship would stand on her beam end, I and the table would part. The floor and myself became intimately acquainted, and often embraced each other affectionately."[71]

In another passage from the newspaper but not in the book, he briefly mentioned his writing and the need to correct his manuscripts: "Most of my letters are written while traveling, as we are very seldom idle. Sometimes I write in a railway coach, sometimes in a boat and sometimes on a bench in a park. Therefore you must pardon errors, and I shall expect you to correct the manuscript before publishing."[72] While *The White Rose of Memphis* and *The Little Brown Church* were often stilted with unrealistic dialog as common in novels of the time, in his new travel narrative he reverted to a more natural tone, the one seen in his 1856 New York letters, characterized by a strong sense of humor at all that he observed.

European tourism had its origins during the seventeenth century with the Grand Tour in which young, wealthy European men crossed the continent to view classical and Renaissance remains in Italy. This evolved into a broader, more accessible form of tourism with the construction of the European railroad system during the mid-nineteenth century, which

Figure 12.3. Warwick Castle, circa 1879, by William Pitt, from the Framed Works of Art collection at the National Library of Wales.

expedited the passage of people throughout the continent. Falkner's tour took full advantage of the new rail system.

After sightseeing in Liverpool, Falkner and his party traveled inland by rail bound for London and then the continent. Along the way, their first stops were at Chester and Warwick Castle, followed by Stratford-upon-Avon. Falkner devoted several pages to Warwick Castle and its history.

Having deposited our baggage at the Warwick Arms and ordered lunch to be served at twelve o'clock, we bent our course toward the renowned castle of

Warwick, which occupies an elevated position on the crest of a lofty eminence overlooking the town. . . .

The castle, though nearly nine hundred years old, is yet in an excellent state of preservation, and will no doubt withstand the storm of nine centuries more, if properly cared for. It is well worth a visit to England to see this famous old castle, where the great king-maker [Richard Neville, Sixteenth Earl of Warwick (1428–1471)] resided over four hundred years ago.[73]

The castle impressed Falkner so much that he later named his home in Ripley "Warwick Place."

From Warwick, Falkner and company took a "delightful carriage-ride" to Stratford-upon-Avon, the town where his beloved William Shakespeare was born. Falkner indicated his respect for the bard:

Charming, cosey little Stratford! Thy fame as the birthplace of the Bard of Avon is co-extensive with the limits of civilization. Who does not envy England, in whose bosom sleeps the body of William Shakespeare? Who does not envy Stratford for the glory she claims as his birthplace?[74]

While visiting the birthplace of Shakespeare, Falkner observed: "On one of the window panes of Shakespeare's house may be seen the name of Walter Scott. It was written by Sir Walter with a diamond ring while on a visit to the place."[75] Later he rewrote the incident, embellishing it in the process and exemplifying how he proceeded from a dry observation to a more entertaining retelling:

On one of the panes of glass in a front window appears the name of Sir Walter Scott, which was written by himself with a diamond ring. I proposed to give the superintendent a shilling to let me write my name under that of Sir Walter, which offer she promptly accepted. But when I was ready to begin writing, I found that I had neglected to bring my diamond ring with me, and it did not require much conversation to convince me that the same misfortune prevailed among my travelling-companions. The next time I go there I will not leave my diamond ring.[76]

The visit to Stratford reverberated with Falkner, with scenes from Shakespeare's plays coming to mind. In describing Holy Trinity Church, where the bard is buried, he wrote (while probably back in Ripley) of a vision in which phantasms from the plays appeared before him quoting from Shakespeare:

Seating myself near the poet's tomb, I leaned back against the pulpit, fell asleep, and in my dream conversed with him, thus,—

"Come, thou grand master of song, thou king of poets, rise from the marble jaws of thy prison-house, and I'll speak to thee though hell itself should gape and bid me hold my peace. . . ." [the second clause is from *Hamlet*, act 1, scene 2]

At this instant the marble slab that covered the poet's bones began to tremble, while from the earth came a mysterious sound like the rumblings of distant thunder. The walls of the old church shook and the wind shrieked among the trees.

As soon as silence again prevailed I covered my face with my handkerchief and endeavored to convert myself into a spiritual medium, in order that I might have a conversation with the dead poet. My fancy at once began to perform wondrous work. It flew two or three centuries toward the rear, and investigated things that existed in those days. A hunchback demon came limping before me, crying,—

"A horse, a horse! My kingdom for a horse!" [*Richard III*, act 5, scene 4]

Next a tall, athletic negro came tearing along, pulling the wool out of his head, and yelling as he passed me,—

"Blood, Iago, blood!" [*Othello*, act 3, scene 3][77]

As Falkner watched in amazement, other characters appear in sequence: the ghost of Hamlet's father, Falstaff, Lady Macbeth, Cleopatra, and Juliet.

Next came to the stage a sad-faced young man with pale, hollow cheeks, tangled hair, torn and disordered garments, speaking in a deep bass voice. When he came very close to me, he suddenly stopped, faced toward me, and said,—

"Be thou a spirit of health, or goblin damned?

Bring with thee airs from heaven, or blast from hell?

Thou comest in such a questionable shape

That I will speak to thee." [*Hamlet*, act 1, scene 4]

"Avaunt, crazy fool!" I exclaimed; "you are mistaken in your man."

He seemed to be greatly offended as he straightened himself proudly up and moved on.

Another female phantom with soft, dreamy eyes and tricky, smiling face now stole in on tiptoe, as if she was trying to pass unseen; but when she drew near me, she thrust a little twig into my left ear, when, with a sudden exclamation, I sprang to my feet, while heavy drops of cold perspiration stood thick on my brow.

"It is impolite to snore in presence of ladies," said Miss Bell. "And then it is time for us to go; they are all waiting for you outside."[78]

The group then moved on to Anne Hathaway's home just outside Stratford. In the next few days they visited Kenilworth Castle, the spa town of Leamington, Coventry, and Oxford before arriving in London on the nineteenth, where Falkner remarked: "Nobody manifested a particle of surprise at our arrival in London, though we had neglected to notify the citizens of our contemplated visit. The people hurried past us, attending to their own business, just as they did before we invaded the city."[79] Falkner's group would not stay long; they would return later. The following day they toured the National Gallery, the Palace of Westminster, Westminster Abbey, and the Tower of London.[80]

On the morning of June 21, Falkner and his party departed London for the continent. They crossed the English Channel near Dover and arrived in Paris at 5:00 p.m., where they were put in a hotel for the night. They would not stay long there—indeed they would spend several days in Paris on their return journey—and departed the following morning, arriving at night at the spa town of Aix-les-Bains. Along the way Falkner, Effie, and the Misses Bell and Stevenson all found the landscape to be unsurpassed in beauty. He noted:

> I sat at the coach window, gazing with straining eyes at the apparently moving panorama, intoxicated with delight. I have heard and read much about the beauties of Southern France, and was therefore prepared to expect something grand, but it is more charming than I had imagined.[81]

He also had accolades for their courier, Alfred Schmitsuebel:

> We were quite fortunate in the selection of our courier, for he has proved himself worthy of the highest praise. He is never out of place when wanted; is energetic, sensible, and efficient; speaks French, Italian, Swiss, German, and Spanish elegantly. Were it not for his unpronounceable, unspellable, jaw-breaking name, we could get along with him very well; but I fear the ladies have seriously injured their health by trying to pronounce it.[82]

The following morning, the twenty-third, the party departed Aix-les-Bains and after passing through the Mont Cenis Tunnel into Italy arrived in Genoa late at night on June 23.[83] The following day while touring the city they met a party of six Americans—Judge and Mrs. S. O. Thacher and their daughters, Mollie and Nellie, Walter M. "Dick" Dickson, and J. M. Chittenden—accompanied by their courier, Charley Shurg.[84] Mrs. S. Greenough had previously joined Falkner's party in Paris, with the combined group numbering eleven. The two groups found each other so convivial that they decided to merge into one, thereby providing more camaraderie. Falkner observed:

> I am delighted with the new addition of numbers to our party, because it makes one feel more comfortable to be among our own countrymen. . . . Dick's humorous wit and Chittenden's dry satire, seasoned with Charley's ludicrous broken English, never failed to evoke a hearty laugh from every member of the party. Indeed, take it all in all, I am happy in the belief that we have made a profitable treaty in uniting the two parties.
>
> The dignified judge . . . diligently discharges the duties of the office of moderator. His decisions usually settle all disputes arising out of the civil branch of service, while all questions connected with the military department are submitted to me. I have been unanimously elected commander-in-chief of Uncle Sam's brigade,—the new name given to our united forces.[85]

The only unpleasant aspect of this union of forces was the need to lay off one of the couriers. Each was quite popular with his respective group. However, the majority of Uncle Sam's brigade knew Charley Shurg and consequently favored him, while fewer knew Alfred Schmitsuebel. So the latter was terminated with well wishes and was fortunately able to acquire a position with a party bound for Palestine.[86] Thus Charley became the "adjutant" for the brigade, performing "the duties of commissary, quartermaster, transportation-agent, and interpreter. We do not, by any means, require or expect him to perform menial service. We furnish funds, and he superintends their disbursement. Thus completely organized, we mean to invade the entire continent."[87]

The tour predictably required considerable walking. While in Genoa, Falkner commented on Effie's quick adaptation to the physical requirements:

> Effie endures the fatigue of travel better than I do. In fact she has learned the art of traveling perfectly—can walk four miles at a stretch. She has discarded high-heeled boots, and wears commonsense, flat-heeled shoes. She carries her own valise, and has become quite self-reliant and independent.[88]

Although he was thoroughly enjoying seeing the landscapes and sights of Europe, Falkner also clearly missed home and his family. He spoke of sleeping in Genoa and "dreaming of the loved ones at home."[89] He also remarked: "In all my wanderings I have seen no place I love so well as I do dear old Ripley, and dear old Tippah. Truly *there is no place like home.*"[90]

Falkner had apparently notified his family and friends of locations where they could address letters for him to receive upon arrival. When his party arrived in Rome on June 27,[91] he found letters waiting, one from his daughter Bama, who signed herself as "Roy," a nickname derived from her middle name, "Leroy":

Dear Papa,
    Do pray hurry home. Mamma is crying her eyes out about you and Effie, and I am so very lonesome without you. Everything looks so sad since you went away. I have thought and thought about you, until I have thought you clear out of my mind, and I can't, to save my life, think how you used to look. Old Duke is fat and sleek, but he has become quite lazy since you left. Mamma and I are well; my big doll got its nose broken clear off. Hoping these few lines will find you enjoying the same blessing, I am your affectionate baby, "Roy."[92]

He was so touched by the letter from the "little brown-haired lass of nine (the pet of the household)" that he published the letter on the dedication page of *Rapid Ramblings in Europe*, dedicating the book to her with the note that he didn't think "she meant to express a wish that the letter would find my nose broken."[93]

While in Rome, Uncle Sam's brigade visited all the main sites—Saint Peter's, the Forum, the Pantheon, and the Colosseum—and also a Capuchin monastery, which resulted in an unusual incident in the monastery crypt where deceased Capuchins were interred, often in mummified condition hanging on walls. Afterward, Falkner told a story about his being mistaken for a mummy that recalled his Mexican War misadventure in which portions of three fingers were shot off:

After satisfying myself with the curiosities of the monastery, I leaned my body against the wall and fell into a thoughtful revery, which, for the time being, lifted my mind out of the present and carried it back to the epoch when Nero was emperor. My left hand, on which remains only one whole finger (the other three having been overtaken by a bullet one day while I was hunting a safe place), was hanging down by my side. All of a sudden, a pretty little blue-eyed girl seized my only whole finger and tried to break it off, to carry home as a relic, having mistaken me for a mummy. At first, I paid no attention to her; indeed, my mind was on distant objects that had existed twenty centuries ago.
    "La! mamma! this is a brand-new mummy," exclaimed the little lady, as she made a vigorous effort to twist my finger off.

Oh! Mamma..that mummy is alive.
I saw its head move

Figure 12.4. "Mamma, that mummy is alive! I saw its head move." Falkner is mistaken for a mummy in the crypt of the Capuchin Convent, Rome. Courtesy of Tommy Covington.

I now for the first time turned my head and looked down at the young relic-hunter, when she instantly fled.

"Oh, mamma," she cried, "that mummy is alive; I saw its head move."

The whole crowd, who had been intently watching the operation, now burst into loud laughter.[94]

Falkner subsequently made several tongue-in-cheek comments about his having been mistaken for an "Egyptian mummy" on several occasions.[95]

After five days of "diligently groveling among the catacombs, churches and crumbling ruins of Rome," they left on the morning of July 2 and arrived in Naples the same day. After touring the city, Pompeii, and the Isle of Capri, they visited Mount Vesuvius on the fifth, "bent on a thorough invasion of her sulphuric precincts."[96] Falkner recorded:

We ventured beyond the danger line, and I am now convinced that we triumphantly acted the fool. A shower of hot lava was thrown several hundred feet in the air, and when it came down some of it fell in the midst of the brigade. You may be sure that a hasty retreat was made, regardless of order. In fact it was a stampede, your correspondent leading the retreat. A game of marbles could have been played on your correspondent's coat tail.[97]

A few days later he retold the story in an embellished form:

> Our party [Uncle Sam's brigade] has organized a school, called the "Meritorious
> Prize Gift Society." Its object is the promotion of science and the encourage-
> ment of social enjoyment. When anyone performs a meritorious act, or invents
> a brand new idea, he is awarded the post of honor at the head of the class, which
> he holds until turned down by another. I held this exalted position until the
> little girl at Rome took me for an Egyptian mummy, and attempted to break
> off one of my fingers as a relic.—The class unanimously ordered me to go foot.
> Mrs. Greenough, an estimable lady from New York, was then promoted to the
> office from which I had been ousted.—But while on top of Vesuvius, she lost
> her place as head of the class. When the Volcano threw a thousand red hot slugs
> of lava high in the air, which came hissing down in the very midst of the bri-
> gade, every one except Mrs. Greenough fled rapidly from the spot. She bravely
> stood her ground, but it was proven by her own confession that she hoisted her
> umbrella for the purpose of warding off the falling lava. This confession settled
> the case against her, consequently she was ordered to go foot. The gallant and
> rapid manner in which I led the retreat, secured for me my former post at the
> head of the class. A good general should always be in the van on a retreat, and
> in the rear when advancing, personal safety being the first and main object to
> be looked after by sensible commanders, "one of whom I am known to be."[98]

After departing from Naples on July 6, Uncle Sam's brigade returned northward through Rome and Florence, arriving on July 10 in Venice. The following
day after viewing the Bridge of Sighs and Saint Mark's Cathedral, they visited
a lace factory, where Falkner intended to purchase a gift for his wife.

> I had often heard the ladies talking of the cheap laces they expect to purchase
> at Venice. I had made up my mind to buy a quantity to carry as a present to the
> lady who pours coffee for me at home. I wish it to be distinctly understood that
> I am a better judge of good coffee than I am of Venice lace. It is well known
> that when I undertake an enterprise I go it strong. I never do things by halves. I
> would not insult Mrs. F. with an insignificant present,—she should have bushels
> of lace. This was the prevailing idea that found lodgment in my brain as we
> entered the lace-factory.[99]

Upon entering the salesroom, the women of the party, who had spoken of
the cheapness of the lace, began to make their selections "sparingly." Falkner,
having not noticed, determined to purchase a large quantity for his wife. As

he recalled: "When I . . . in an imperious tone ordered the entire contents of one of the drawers to be sent to my hotel, I supposed that lace was as cheap as Kentucky bagging." Upon being presented a bill for $1,800, he was dumfounded and had to resort to haggling, eventually being charged a smaller price by reducing the size of his purchase to only $30 worth of lace. He made a note to himself: "Don't listen to ladies when they are discussing cheap laces." He later made a reflection upon his tendency to exaggerate for the sake of humor: "I hope the reader will be able to separate my jokes from facts; I mean no reflections upon the ladies. When I joke, I mean it; when I strike hard-pan, I dig for facts."[100]

That night after Uncle Sam's brigade traveled along the Grand Canal Falkner noted that "nothing is more charmingly beautiful than Venice by moonlight," concluding that it "beats a Fourth-of-July barbecue." Upon stopping at the Rialto Bridge, he recalled its mention in Shakespeare's *Merchant of Venice* as the place where "merchants do congregate."[101]

On July 13, the brigade departed Venice for Verona and from then worked their way into the Alps and Switzerland, after which they passed through Lyon, France, arriving in Paris on August 7. Over the next few days, they visited the city's primary attractions including Versailles, the Tuileries Garden, the Hôtel des Invalides, and Père Lachaise Cemetery. A few days into their stay they visited the Champs-Élysées, or the Elysian Fields, named after the paradisiacal land of the dead. They began their tour of the avenue at its western end by ascending the massive Arc de Triomphe. From an elevation of over 160 feet, they gazed down the broad avenue upon

> a scene of picturesque enchantment surpassing anything in the power of language to describe. . . . Innumerable little shady parks, filled with cosey seats, may be seen on both sides of this gay road, where, in good weather, thousands of men, women, and children assemble to enjoy the lovely scenery. Open-air concerts, legerdemain shows, Punch and Judy exhibitions, and a dozen other different amusements, such as please and amuse children, are continually in operation here.[102]

However, for Falkner, the idyllic scene called to mind another side of life:

> It is the illusions of travel that charm the tourist. Everything wears a holiday appearance, everybody seems to be happy, everything looks delightful. The traveller very seldom sees the dark side of a picture. He sees not the thousands of miserable creatures who languish and die in the dark, filthy dens, nor does he

realize the fact that while he gazes with delight on the gay pageant that parades the streets, hundreds and thousands of wretched human beings are slowly dying of starvation. If one would like to view both sides of the picture, let him spend an hour on the Champs Élysées on a fine afternoon, and then make his way to the morgue, as I did a few days ago.[103]

The Paris morgue maintained a viewing room on the side of the street where suicide and murder victims were placed in the hopes that they would be identified by passersby, and if not, they were buried in a pauper cemetery. He was particularly moved by a well-dressed young woman who lay propped up two or three feet on a slab for viewing, her blond hair falling in "disheveled profusion" on her shoulders. Investigation revealed that she was falsely accused of a theft that was actually committed by her brother. Believing her guilty, her fiancée rejected her, and in dismay she drowned herself in the Seine. After the inquest, Falkner "accompanied the corpse to her studio, where it was placed in a pretty coffin purchased by general subscription among her friends." Then he confessed: "I don't often weep, but blame'f I didn't cry like a whipped pup when I saw that poor girl lying there." Afterward, he recalled, "I took a cigar and tried to smoke my thoughts off of the dead girl's face, but utterly failed." For Falkner, the morgue, in stark contrast to the Champs-Élysées, was a memento mori, a reminder of suffering and the inevitability of death.[104]

Following several days of sightseeing, the brigade left Paris on August 15 for Cologne, Wiesbaden, and the Netherlands. On the twenty-fourth they sailed from Rotterdam for England and arrived in London the following day.[105]

After touring London, the brigade finally had to disband. In the course of their tour they had interrelated well with one another and had become good friends. Upon thinking about the forthcoming parting of their ways and knowing that they probably would never see each other again, Falkner reflected: "If there is anything in this cold world worth living for, it is the strong tie of friendship which binds one human heart to another." At 11:00 a.m. on August 30, the brigade said their final farewells as Falkner's party—he, Effie, Bell, and Stevenson—took the train to Liverpool to board the *City of Berlin* for the return trip. Falkner noted: "I thought I saw water in Dick's eyes as he seized my hand with a firm grip, but that may have been imagination, for he did it so quickly, and spoke the parting words so briefly, and walked away so suddenly, that I scarcely had time to say 'Good-by.'" As Falkner sat in his coach watching the passing landscape, he remarked: "I do not think I ever saw a prettier country than that which lies in sight of the railroad between London and Liverpool."[106]

They arrived in Liverpool in time to have a final carriage ride through the parks. The following morning, they prepared to be ferried out to the *City of Berlin*, docked on the Mersey River. The courier, Charley Shurg, had traveled with Falkner's party to Liverpool and came to see them off. Falkner recorded his last memory of this loyal servant and friend:

> Charley did not leave us until we were stepping aboard of the little boat that was to take us from the quay to the ship which was at anchor a mile out. I shall long remember the earnest gaze of his expressive eyes as he watched us from the shore, as we sailed away and longer still will I remember the memorable acts of kindness for which I am his debtor. If the sincere wishes of all the members of Uncle Sam's Brigade could secure his future success then indeed would he be always happy.[107]

The Falkner party boarded the *City of Berlin* on August 31 for the return trip and departed the following day on a calm sea. However, on the second day at sea the weather deteriorated as the winds blew harder, creating waves that crashed over the deck, and with this turbulence seasickness returned. Falkner observed: "It is . . . very uncomfortable on a ship when the waves every now and then roll over the upper deck. . . . My stomach got on a regular spree at the start, and nothing could induce it to keep the peace."[108]

After a voyage through turbulent seas, the *City of Berlin* arrived in the port of New York on Sunday, September 9.[109] As soon as they had passed through customs inspection, the Falkners departed for their hotel:

> We reached the Grand Central Hotel in good time to miss breakfast, leaving three long hours on our hands to be squandered in waiting for dinner, which seemed to be at least three weeks off. We were delighted to find several letters fresh from home, informing us that the dear ones were all well, and anxiously watching and waiting for our return. We answered by telegraph, announcing our safe arrival in New York, and fixing the day we might be expected to reach home.[110]

After a night or two at the Grand Central Hotel, they departed via rail, arriving in Ripley on Thursday, September 12, where they were greeted by family and friends.[111]

Falkner's letters from Europe continued to appear for months in the *Southern Sentinel*. Editors from many newspapers commented favorably upon them. The editor of *Dixie Boy*, a newspaper in Lamar, Mississippi, observed that while readers might not find "lofty strains, beautiful images or the eloquence of impassioned feeling," they would find in Falkner's descriptions "a natural and truthful description of country and people, the fruits of a splendid memory, a poetic fancy and a painter's eye that never fails to see and to preserve everything that will charm or enlighten his readers."[112]

The *Sentinel* editor observed:

Since Col. Falkner's return home, his letters are more interesting than before. Possessing as he does the rare gift of an excellent memory, aided by notes taken during his travels, he can now in the quiet retreat of his own library, write up his summer travels in a peculiarly interesting style. We are happy to say to our readers that he will continue these highly interesting letters for the Sentinel's subscribers for some time in the future.[113]

Falkner's European writings provide some of the best insights into his personality. Like his traveling companions, we find him to be a delightful and compassionate person. He was always interested in what he saw and what he came into contact with. He demonstrated a sympathy for people in all social classes and for their stations in life. In regard to himself, he was almost always self-deprecating and often in an exaggerated manner. After being mistaken, according to his account, for a mummy, he returned again and again to the image of himself as an "Egyptian mummy." On another occasion, he wrote: "I grieve to say that there is something about my personal appearance that justifies strangers in taking me for a first-class dunce."[114] When alluding to his previous military career, his reminiscences were not vainglorious to any degree but wry and humorous and undoubtedly exaggerated, such as when he recalled: "It was said that I killed more enemies than any colonel in the service. In a single engagement I destroyed a hundred men and twice as many horses. They ran themselves to death trying to catch me."[115] On another occasion, while surveying the battlefield at Waterloo, he recalled for the benefit of his fellow travelers his own experiences surveying a field of battle while adding: "I did not tell them I was behind a tree with a field glass."[116] Historians who have depicted Falkner as an "egoist" or "megalomaniac" might ask whether such personality types would be self-deprecating. I suspect not.

Although he displayed a sense of wonder at all that he saw, he occasionally expressed dismay at practices that in his eye did not live up to his own American standard. However, in this he is not unlike many tourists today who are not used to international travel and are consequently susceptible to culture shock.

In March, the *Sentinel* published a detailed outline of Falkner's forthcoming book, tentatively called *A Summer in Europe* with the author credited

Figure 12.5. Cover of *Rapid Ramblings in Europe*, first edition. Courtesy of Tommy Covington.

only by the nom de plume "Dedrick," a name he received from his traveling companions. Apparently, he had "determined to let this work stand in full on its own merits, regardless of what he has heretofore written."[117] Regardless, the title was soon changed and the nom de plume dropped, probably to take advantage of any available name recognition for the sake of sales.

In early April 1884, Falkner departed for Philadelphia to oversee the publication of his travelogue, now renamed *Rapid Ramblings in Europe*, which, like *The Little Brick Church*, would be published by Lippincott. By mid-May he had returned south and was at the Peabody in Memphis.[118]

On June 1, 1884, the *Memphis Daily Appeal* carried an advertisement for Lippincott announcing the eminent release of *Rapid Ramblings*, and a few days later it was available at the booksellers.[119] The book was sumptuously

Yours respectfully
W. C. Falkner

Figure 12.6. Portrait of Falkner from *Rapid Ramblings in Europe*, possibly based on the Mora Studios photograph (fig. 0.1). Courtesy of Tommy Covington.

bound with the title and author's name in bold, gold lettering impressed on its cover over an artist's illustration of a scene on board an ocean-going vessel. The frontispiece was an engraved portrait of the author beneath which his own inscription read: "Yours respectfully/W. C. Falkner." The volume consisted of 566 pages.[120]

An unsigned review, probably by Falkner's old friend M. C. Gallaway, praised the "handsomely bound" volume:

> If his rambles were rapid, he rapidly took in the situation, and transfixed his thoughts to paper. He kept his eyes open, and everything to him had a deep meaning and taught a lesson. Col. Falkner's utterances alternate from gentle sentiment, refined, tender and dainty expressions to the crude and rugged. Often he sparkles in a charming vivacity, an exuberance of gayety; then his compositions are deeply tinged with somber tones, as he muses and mourns over fallen greatness.[121]

Then the reviewer continued to assess Falkner's work in terms of the literature of the South:

> Col. Falkner has not only reflected credit upon the literary talent of the South, but the large sum and profits he has derived from the three books he has written,

demonstrates that push and energy will reward the literary talent of the South. Col. Falkner fortunately possesses what the Southern aspirants for literary fame do not possess—an ample fortune. His wealth enables him to publish his books at his own risk, and his success shows that, as in everything else, money is essential to literary fame. Col. Falkner's success should stir to life and vitality the slumbering literary talent of the South. Since the war our people have been so busy in recuperating their lost fortunes and in rebuilding their desolated homes that they have not had the time [to] bestow on literary pursuits. But we trust the success of Col. Falkner will be the beginning of a new era.[122]

The reviewer never knew how close to the truth he came in predicting that Falkner could, at least indirectly through his great-grandson, bring to life the "slumbering literary talent of the South."

Upon Falkner's return from Philadelphia, the *Ripley Advertiser* noted that he had been "prominently mentioned" as a candidate for Congress, but that he would not run. The newspaper stated that "there is no man in the District to whom we would give a more earnest and hearty support," and went on to elaborate:

Col. Falkner is much beloved by the people among whom he lives, and his friends would be anxious to reward him for the services he has rendered to the democratic party. The Colonel has always taken the stump and gallantly advocated the cause of the democracy when necessary. But he says he has been amply rewarded by the great privileges conferred upon the community in which he lives by the democratic party.[123]

He would demonstrate his support for the Democratic Party by attending the state convention in Jackson, where he was selected as a national delegate. Subsequently, he departed for the National Democratic Convention in Chicago, which convened on July 8 in the Exposition Building. Samuel J. Tilden, whom Falkner had formerly supported for the presidency in 1876, was present but declined to accept the nomination, which went to Grover Cleveland, who like Tilden was the governor of New York when nominated. During the evening session on the eleventh, attendees considered a vice presidential candidate; Niles Searls of California nominated General W. S. Rosecrans, who had been engaged with the Union Army in northern Mississippi during the Civil War. Soon after, Falkner came to the podium to address over one thousand delegates and offer his support for Rosecrans, who had been his opponent during the war. He began by noting that it had long been a custom for "all brave soldiers to meet on terms of friendship after the battle is over." Rosecrans he knew that was respected by both Northern and Southern veterans. He recalled that during the war the Union general had used his home in Ripley as headquarters. Finally, Falkner pointed out that Rosecrans "will unite this whole nation so far as the soldiers of it are concerned." However, because of growing support for the former governor of Indiana, Thomas A. Hendricks, the California delegation withdrew its support for Rosecrans, and the nomination went to Hendricks.[124]

Later that summer the Falkners departed for Bailey Springs, returning to Ripley on board a special train on August 28.[125] Falkner would remain busy in political activities. Two days after returning from Bailey Springs, he attended a meeting of the Ripley Central Democratic Club, which had just been organized the previous week, where he was selected as a member of the executive committee and addressed the group with "one of his characteristic sensible and timely speeches."[126]

In late October, Senator L. Q. C. Lamar was canvassing northern Mississippi in support of the Democratic Party. His reception in Ripley was a spectacle; Falkner certainly had a hand in it. Lamar was met by "500 Democrats" on horseback who formed a procession led by "Prof. Soryer's brass band seated in a handsome wagon drawn by four snow-white horses." Nearly every house in town was reported to be lit up, "making the streets as light as day, while loud shouts greeted the distinguished orator as he was escorted through the streets." The procession traveled all the principle streets before arriving at the courthouse, where as many as possible assembled inside. Such was their number that many were left outside. Falkner arose to the podium to introduce Lamar. After a brief welcome, he alluded to Reconstruction, which was over by less than a decade: "Well do we remember the gallant services you performed for us when the tyrant's heel was on the neck of Mississippi; and we come here to-night to tell you of the deep feelings of gratitude we cherish for this faithful service." He continued: "Your fame is of a nature which . . . you won . . . by patient labor, constant watchfulness and a gallant defense of constitutional liberty. You defended the oppressed against the oppressor; you defended the weak against the strong." And ended with a welcome: "I as the appointed agent of the Democracy of this county bid you thrice welcome to our little village." Lamar then ascended to the podium and responded with "a short but eloquent reply . . . his voice clearly indicating the deep feelings of emotion he experienced."[127]

A few days later the national election was held, and Grover Cleveland achieved what Tilden had failed at: election as the first Democratic president since the Civil War. Shortly after his inauguration, he appointed Lamar to serve as secretary of the interior, and then a few years later nominated him to the Supreme Court.

As the fall of 1884 set in, the Falkner family began two building projects with the first being a new home for the Carters, located to the north across Cooper Street from the colonel's home. By early September carpenters had begun construction and by mid-October were nearing completion of this two-story Victorian structure replete with gingerbread decorations.[128] Upon completion of the Carter house, the carpenters began a renovation of Falkner's home that transformed it into the predominant landmark of Ripley. In November the local newspapers reported that "extensive improvements" were being made to his home and that when completed it would be three stories high—in fact "the highest structure in town"—with the upper floor being a one-room "observatory."[129] It was constructed in the Italianate style of architecture, which was popular at the time. Decades later, commentators claimed that Falkner had based the house's design on a style he had seen in Italy on his Grand Tour; however, given the style's general popularity, there is little to warrant such a hypothesis.[130] A more likely influence of his tour was the name he gave to the house, "Warwick Place," presumably after Warwick Castle, which as noted he had visited. His naming the home may have initially been quite casual, even joking at the thought of comparing his home to the size and grandeur to the castle, but the name came into greater use in 1893.[131] Other than the connection to Warwick Castle, Warwick is also the name of the county—Warwickshire—where Shakespeare's Stratford-upon-Avon is located.

A half century later, Falkner's great-grandson used the name Warwick humorously in his novel *Go Down, Moses* for that of the Beauchamp family plantation, just across the county line from Yoknapatawpha. The name was associated with Sophonsiba Beauchamp's claim that the family descended from the line of Beauchamps that had held title over a "place in England" called Warwick from the thirteenth through the fifteenth centuries that her brother Hubert was "probably the true earl of only he never even had enough pride, not to mention energy, to take the trouble to establish his just rights."[132] The younger Faulkner was spoofing the tendency in the South (and elsewhere for that matter) to dress up the rustic with fancy European names. Whether or not he knew of his great-grandfather's use of the name isn't known. Regardless, we are reminded of the younger Faulkner and his home, Rowan Oak.

Iron balconies were placed at the second-floor windows. Two cast-iron urns painted white were placed in front of the house on either side of the walkway. Inside, an impressive staircase led to the big, square second-floor room that was never finished.[133] In January the iron fencing arrived that would completely enclose the entire block.[134] Finally, in March an office building was constructed across Mulberry Street to the south of the main home.[135]

Soon after the house's completion, Captain J. L. Power, proprietor of the Jackson *Clarion*, visited Ripley and was effusive over the residence, noting that "since my last visit [he] . . . has built a residence that is quite palatial in style and proportions." He continued by noting that with the exception of Bel Haven, the home of Jones S. Hamilton and a notable house in Jackson, "there is no residence at the state capital that can compare with it."[136]

While construction was going on in Ripley, the World Cotton Centennial Exposition, a world's fair, opened on December 16, 1884, in New Orleans with at least officially the support of twenty-seven nations. The landscaped grounds, which included a number of pavilions and exhibits, spread over 249 acres lying between St. Charles Avenue and the Mississippi River. The main building covered 33 acres, purportedly the largest roofed structure ever constructed in the world. In late January 1885, Falkner spent several days at the fair before returning to Ripley to report his favorable impressions of the eclectic international displays of agriculture and technology, describing it as "undoubtedly the greatest show on earth." He also astutely reported that it wouldn't likely be a financial success—in fact, financial difficulties eventually forced the exposition to close early.[137] He was so enthralled that at the end of March, he set out for a return visit, bringing Effie and Bama to see the wonders. They were also impressed.[138] Upon returning, the Falkners stopped at the Peabody; the *Memphis Daily Appeal* reported that "Miss Effie's extensive travels in Europe enable her to judge intelligently of the great Southern Exposition, and she gives a graphic description of its marvelous wonders."[139] After the exposition closed in June, most of the buildings were dismantled, and the fairground was eventually transformed into Audubon Park.

On August 2, 1885, Falkner departed, apparently alone, for the well-known resort White Sulphur Springs, West Virginia, and returned a month later.[140] This would be his last visit to a mineral springs resort for the next three years. His days were about to become more hectic.

Toward the end of 1885, Falkner's son, John W. T. Falkner, made plans to leave Ripley for Oxford, where he had joined a law partnership with Colonel Charles B. Howry.[141] His new partner was also US Attorney for the Northern District of Mississippi (1885–1889) while also serving as a university trustee; he had previously sat in the Mississippi legislature (1880–1884). Howry's father, James M. Howry, had served as a circuit judge and university trustee and had just died in 1884. Oxford held a brighter future in law and politics. It was larger than Ripley while having a federal courthouse and the state university, all of which offered potential for advancement. He departed Ripley on December 8, accompanied by his wife Sallie Murry Falkner, their three children, and his great-aunt and foster mother, Justiania Word Thompson.[142]

The Falkners were just getting settled into their new home in Oxford when they were peripherally involved with another act of violence. John's new partner was involved in a feud with another attorney, H. M. Sullivan, that had begun with "a fisticuff at Abbeville" several years earlier. Like Howry, Sullivan was a trustee of the university. On Saturday, August 7, 1886, while inspecting a newly completed school building in Oxford, Sullivan made a remark that Howry perceived as insulting; the latter responded by placing his hand on his revolver. Without hesitating, Sullivan attacked. In the ensuing struggle, Howry shot Sullivan in the abdomen, with the man dying two days later.[143] After Howry spent some time awaiting trial, the Grand Jury dismissed the case in November.[144] One thing seems clear from this case and others presented: a killing could fairly easily be justified by convincing a jury that the action was conducted in self-defense.

Chapter 13

◇━◦━━◇━◦━◇

And Beyond That
The Railroad Revived

As the year 1886 began, Falkner was entering a phase of railroad construction that would carry him to the pinnacle of his career while setting the stage for further extension of the road. Before we continue, it might be useful to attempt to assess what was he like personally.

He could be a delightful person with a developed sense of humor and could laugh at himself. He was well liked by those he interacted with, as indicated by his election to high military office, to lieutenant when he was not quite twenty-one, then to brigadier general of the state militia, to captain of his company, and finally to colonel of his regiment. He had a mind that was dynamic and protean. He was interested in what he saw and what he came into contact with. Literature and history fascinated him. He was intrigued by the World Cotton Centennial Exposition in New Orleans with its exhibits on agriculture and technology, making two trips to see it. A Memphis newspaper described him in 1881 as "a sharp, wiry man, with quick, kindly eyes, iron-gray hair and whiskers, erect military carriage, neatly dressed, and is so quiet in action and walks so fast that his legs always seem afraid of being left behind."[1]

His fast pace suggests a man pulled toward some goal not always seen by others. When he was twenty—not yet having come of age—he conceived the idea of publishing and marketing the tale of a convicted murderer, and years later even before he had achieved the completion of his spur line to Ripley, he transformed the project into a transcontinental railroad. However, he did not always do well in positions once attained. Looking for new challenges, he would constantly find himself up against rigid bureaucratic mandates or those with more power but less vision than he. Opposition from these realms instilled in him a contempt for those who opposed him with an accompanying drive to overcome them.

209

Although Andrew Brown went too far in describing Falkner as a "mega-lomaniac," he was not without considerable insight, largely based on remi-niscences by family and acquaintances who had personally known Falkner. Brown summarized a great deal in the following passage:

> That he was the possessor of a brilliant if restless mind cannot be questioned, and that he was ambitious, proud, sensitive, and hotheaded is not open to doubt, that he was over-vain and more than a little arrogant is clearly indicated. These last traits were in all probability aggravated by his small stature; he was of less than average height and of slight build, and like many other small men physically, he attempted to make up for his lack of size by aggressiveness. And that aggressiveness, coupled to his undeniable ability, carried him far.[2]

That he was "over-vain and more than a little arrogant" certainly had some truth in it, although this can be counterpointed by his self-deprecating humor and affability. What might be perceived as arrogance would have mostly likely emerged when he found himself confronted with a specter of forces trying to meld him into something more conventional and against which he had learned to "stick to his guns." At the beginning of 1886, he would soon find himself up against such a force.

After several years of sporadic and unsuccessful attempts to construct the railroad south from Ripley, Falkner continued to see the futility of relying only on local capital for railroad construction. As late as December 1885 there were rumblings that money might be raised to build to Pontotoc.[3] However, the following month Falkner saw and seized upon an opportunity to link his project to one with a larger base of support, the Gulf and Ship Island Railroad. As noted above, the G&SI had been conceived as early as the 1850s, and the idea to transform the Ripley Railroad into the SIR&K in 1872 was apparently inspired by the idea behind the G&SI. Both the G&SI and Falkner's road were to have their southern terminus on the Mississippi Gulf Coast opposite Ship Island, and both were to tap into the hinterland north of this location.

In 1882, the G&SI was revived and rechartered; one of the original incor-porators was Falkner's old associate, Jones S. Hamilton, lessor of the state penitentiary.[4] The railroad was banking on two potential assets. First, relying on Hamilton's experience and connections, it intended to use convict labor from the penitentiary as Falkner had previously done. Indeed, the company's vagaries of fortune became considerably linked to the penitentiary, with the railroad becoming for a time the lessor of the institution. Second, there was a possibility to acquire substantial acreage in Mississippi promised to the original antebellum G&SI Railroad. In a second piece of legislation, the company was given all the rights and privileges that had been granted to the original company, which presumably included rights to the aforementioned lands.[5]

The project was soon joined by another builder, attorney William Harris Hardy of Meridian, Mississippi, who had just completed the New Orleans and Northeastern Railroad from the Crescent City to Meridian. On October 13, 1885, Hardy was elected president of the G&SI.[6] By late January 1886, Falkner was invited to join the project as vice president. By uniting his efforts with the G&SI, Falkner would see his railroad effectively become the northern division of a road that would begin on the coast and continue north to the Ohio River. Falkner saw this as the opportunity he had long been waiting for to transform the Ripley Railroad into a transcontinental carrier. As will be seen, not all were so enthused.

His role would involve superintending construction on the northern section proceeding south from Ripley, while the others would devote themselves to the coastal end. Presumably at the behest of Hardy, Falkner addressed the Mississippi Senate on behalf of the G&SI on January 21, and a week later he and Hardy addressed the House of Representatives.[7]

On Sunday, January 31, Falkner and daughter Effie, who had been staying with him in Jackson, returned home to Ripley. Three days later, on Wednesday, he was on his way back to Jackson accompanied by the other owners of the Ripley Railroad, C. L. Harris and R. J. Thurmond. The *Advertiser* reported that Falkner was arranging to consolidate his road with the G&SI and would soon have convicts working on the road from Ripley to Pontotoc and points southward.[8] However, on February 8, Harris and Thurmond returned to Ripley; no reason was stated.[9] Harris, being the superintendent, perhaps had to return to supervise the railroad, and his nephews Lee and William Hines soon arrived in Jackson to take his place. However, Thurmond's departure was more ominous.

Just three days after their departure for Ripley, on February 11, a meeting was held in the G&SI office in Jackson and a contract finalized between Falkner and the Hines brothers on one hand and the railroad on the other for the purpose of consolidating it with the Ripley Railroad. Once the G&SI was completed from Ripley to the Gulf Coast, the company would pay the Ripley Railroad either $135,000 in cash or $270,000 in bonds in exchange for the $250,000 mortgage bonds of the Ripley Railroad. Until the railroad was completed and the transaction made, the owners of the Ripley Railroad would remain in control from Middleton to Ripley. As the G&SI built southward from Ripley, that section of track would remain under the control of the Ripley Railroad at least as far as Pontotoc and would remain leased to the Ripley road as construction proceeded. Regarding gauge, the G&SI was intended to be a standard-gauge road, which all major railroads were adopting as the culmination of a growing movement for standardization for the purpose of facilitating interregional traffic. The grandly envisioned future of the narrow gauges was long dead.

Toward the end of 1885, the managers of the major southern railroads decided to convert to the 4' 8.5" standard gauge simultaneously to be carried out near the end of May 1886. To effectively accomplish this with minimal disruption of traffic required a massive coordinated effort with workers strung out over hundreds of miles of track for the purpose of moving one rail 3.5 inches toward the other. On May 29, 1885, the *Memphis Appeal* noted that "the grandest movement in a railroad way which has ever transpired in the South, the change to standard gauge, begins to-day."[10] And within days the change was accomplished.

Of course, the G&SI was ultimately to be standard gauge, and the southern division was such from the beginning. However, with the northern division matters were more complicated. If the section south of Ripley was constructed in standard gauge, it would be incompatible with that north of the town. So, it was planned to initially build the section south of Ripley in narrow gauge, so the entire northern division would for the time be operational as a narrow-gauge road. After the northern division connected to the southern, then the northern would be changed to standard gauge. However, this would take longer than expected.

The contract bore the signatures of Falkner and the Hineses, who represented one-half of the ownership; Thurmond's signature was conspicuously absent, as was Harris's.[11] According to Andrew Brown, Harris usually voted with Thurmond while the Hineses sided with Falkner, and consequently may have followed him in abstaining.[12] Thurmond was wary of Falkner's extravagant vision and flamboyant methods—which were alien to him. Unlike Falkner he was never in the limelight, nor did he ever seek to be. In effect, Falkner's vision for the railroad created a rift between him and Thurmond that quickly became a feud.

Andrew Brown, whose great-aunt was married to Thurmond, contrasted the two very different personalities:

> Falkner was an extrovert whose interests ranged far and wide, and who possessed undeniable talents in many fields. He loved power and the trappings of power; he delighted in playing the Grand Seignor [sic], yet was a public-spirited

citizen and at heart a kindly if hot-blooded man. On the other hand, Thurmond was an introvert, almost a recluse, who disliked crowds and who habitually played his cards close to his vest. He was a highly successful trader in land, a private banker, partner in a number of business enterprises. . . . Shrewd and hardheaded, he was unquestionably the wealthiest man in Tippah County, yet his life was circumscribed by his business and his home; his only other interests being hunting and the care of his large collection of fine shotguns and hunting rifles.[13]

Compared to Falkner, descriptions of Thurmond are relatively rare. However, Thurmond's cousin Thomas Felix Hickerson (1882–1968) recalled briefly that he

was a quiet, self-contained, dignified, and peace-loving gentleman. This is certainly my youthful impression of him when he came up from Elkin [North Carolina] to spend the day with my parents near the village of Ronda, N.C. My father was particularly fond of him; they possessed ties of friendship and kinship.[14]

For Falkner, the G&SI presented an opportunity to fulfill his vision of carrying the railroad to the sea. Although the new venture could be successful, it also brought a strong risk of disaster to the Ripley Railroad, which had never been far from economic ruin. For one man, the driving concern was fulfilling a vision; for the other, it was about increasing profits without unnecessary risks. Falkner probably saw in Thurmond the essence of every bureaucrat that he had ever dealt with, all of whom were all too ready to reel in his unorthodox methods, but this time he was not going to be stopped, and the ensuing tension was certain to generate conflict.

Without a controlling majority, Thurmond was unable to stop the new venture. He foresaw a strong chance of the G&SI going bust and along with it the Ripley Railroad and everything he had invested in, all because of someone he probably regarded as little more than a flamboyant showman. The result of the tension was the feud that overshadowed the last part of Falkner's life.[15] Emerging as it apparently did from Thurmond's apprehensions over Falkner's seemingly reckless decision, the latter's continued successes served only to fan the flames of resentment as he was ever willing to remind Thurmond—in none-too-gentlemanly terms—of his victories over the odds.

According to Brown, there were many clashes between the two men from 1886 through 1889 that soon reached the "name-calling and fisticuffs stage." One occurrence, remembered by many, was as follows:

[W]hile Thurmond was talking to a group in the courthouse yard, Falkner walked up to him, thrust his hands into the armholes of his vest, and said, "Well, here I am, Dick. What do you want of me?" Thereupon Thurmond lashed out with his fist, knocking Falkner down. The infuriated Colonel rose to his feet and launched into a long tirade in which he accused Thurmond, among other things, of being a robber of widows and orphans, of having cheated him in a sawmill deal and in the railroad deal, and of having shot from ambush a rather unsavory citizen who had been annoying him. In the meantime a crowd naturally gathered, and Thurmond walked away.[16]

Although some have described Falkner as violent, the only documented accounts of violence between the two men have Thurmond as the aggressor, the one to strike the first blow.

Despite Falkner's difficulties with Thurmond and to a large degree because of his break with him, he was soon on a roll. On March 17, in exchange for the loan of $5,000, the G&SI gave him a deed of trust for all of the railroad to be constructed between Ripley and Pontotoc. The loan was to come due in a year.[17] A few months later he made an even larger loan to the G&SI. He sold Ishatubby Farm for $25,000 on July 20,[18] and on July 28 loaned $30,000 to the G&SI with the loan payable in two years. If it was not repaid, then the portion of the G&SI between Ripley and Pontotoc would be sold to the highest bidder at the Tippah County courthouse.[19] In other words, Falkner was ensuring that his new railroad building operation would not be lost as the result of the financial failure of the G&SI.

In late March Thurmond capitulated and sold Falkner his interest in the SIR&K Railroad consisting of $83,000, or one-third, of the first $250,000 of mortgage bonds.[20] Brown elaborated on the sale:

Thurmond sold his interest, which consisted of bonds having a face value of $83,333.33 but which undoubtedly had cost him considerably less, to Falkner for $20,000. On the face of it, it was not a bad transaction. Falkner got what he wanted—control of the railroad—and Thurmond got what he wanted—a profit. Further, the price does not seem to have been out of line. One condition attached to the trade, however, fanned the strained relations between the men into open hatred. Thurmond demanded that he be paid in gold and gave Falkner an unknown but almost impossibly short time to obtain the metal.

Gold was the only legal tender at the time for a $20,000 transaction and Thurmond was only following the common practice (except for the short time limit) in demanding it. However, he knew that Falkner was well worth the amount involved, even though he may well have been short of cash at the time, and Thurmond would have lost nothing if he had not been so exacting. . . . [A] little more than the necessary $20,000 was obtained and Falkner paid Thurmond off and obtained control of the road.[21]

So, Thurmond washed his hands of the affair and would watch from the sidelines the coming debacle. The sale gave Falkner a two-thirds interest, while the Hineses were already in his camp and the Harrises apparently willing to go along with him, thereby uniting the ownership in the endeavor. Dick Ford, editor of the *Ripley Advertiser*, laconically commented that "there is no obstruction now" in completing the road to Pontotoc.[22] The implication was clear that Thurmond had potentially posed an obstacle to the construction of the road. Now he was largely removed from the process, remaining only as the trustee for the railroad's bondholders.

Groundwork and construction began in March. Falkner's role was complex, being both president of the Ripley Railroad and vice president of the G&SI. He would have to oversee the construction of the northern division of the G&SI south of Ripley while managing the Ripley road, which was shipping labor and capital for construction on the former while simultaneously leasing the new road.

By early March an engineer had been engaged for the northern division of the G&SI and was on the ground in Ripley. He initially reviewed surveys of two routes previously made between Ripley and New Albany. Apparently, one survey followed an air line route between the two towns while the other followed a more circuitous path that took in two existing settlements, Blue Mountain and Cotton Plant. The town of Blue Mountain had developed in association with the Blue Mountain Female Institute (later the Blue Mountain Female College), a Baptist-supported school that was founded about 1873 by General M. P. Lowrey.[23] Lowrey and Falkner had known each other since the Mexican War when both served in the Second Mississippi. Lowrey had died suddenly of a heart attack in 1885, and Falkner spoke at his funeral service, recalling how long the two had known each other. He also related that the evening before Lowrey's death, the general called to see him at his home in Ripley. "As the Gen. went to leave [he] told him how much the [Baptist] church thanked him for what he had done for the building of the church and how that he would remember him in his prayers. During the address, the Col. and almost the entire audience shed tears freely."[24]

Of the two routes between Ripley and New Albany, the one through Blue Mountain and Cotton Plant was evidently designed to capture financial support from the two towns and also to follow a relatively level path that followed streams. This was the route that was selected, and soon after a jury began making enquiries about right-of-way acquisitions as far as Blue Mountain six and a half miles southwest of Ripley.

On March 23, the train rumbled into Ripley with about one hundred convicts—within days the number would rise to two hundred—who were placed in a special camp or stockade about a mile to the southwest that consisted of housing with an enclosing fence. As construction progressed, additional camps were built farther down the line. The following day, March 24, a shipment of tools arrived, and on the twenty-fifth the first earthwork began about a mile south of town. Earthwork on the intervening mile had probably been accomplished during the abortive work in 1877 and 1878. Ever optimistic, Falkner predicted that the railroad would be completed to Blue Mountain by June 15.[25]

As work proceeded south of Ripley, he decided to also initiate work at the southern end of the road at Pontotoc, a move probably intended to cultivate and maintain interest there. On Friday, April 23, he was in Pontotoc to address the citizens and rally their financial support. Of course, he was looked upon as a savior figure come to deliver them from muddy roads and the vicissitudes of travel. That night while staying at the Roberson Hotel,[26] a group of young men "serenaded" him with a choral presentation as a demonstration of their support. Rising to the occasion, Falkner addressed them with a story that blended fact and fiction with sentimental overtones designed to move the coldest hearts. Centered on children down on their luck but at their heroic best, it could have come from *The White Rose of Memphis*. The story linked himself to Pontotoc and would have long-term consequences for his legend. He recalled that as a boy he had first arrived in Mississippi at Pontotoc looking for his uncle, T. J. Word. He described himself as

a poor, sick, ragged, barefoot, penniless boy. His cup of sorrow was filled to the brim when he learned that his uncle (Mr. Word) had left for Aberdeen the day previous. He sat down on the hotel steps and wept bitterly, as though his heart would break. A little girl came along and enquired the cause of his distress. Having learned the facts from the Colonel she promptly went and obtained the money to pay the hotel bill and gave it to him. The Colonel never forgot the little Samaritan, but married her in Pontotoc years afterwards. When alluding to this episode in his eventful history, Col. Falkner became so affected that utterances failed him, and he had to pause until his emotion subsided.[27]

The following day he delivered a "remarkably able address" to the citizenry of Pontotoc on the subject of the railroad and was able to sign a contract by which the town would provide financial support for the road. His mission completed, he left town that evening.[28] The *Tupelo Journal* sardonically noted that he had "squeezed a considerable sum of money out of the citizens" of Pontotoc to aid in construction.[29] Of course, Tupelo could afford to be condescending. It already had a railroad and had nothing to be gained through the project. The *Pontotoc Sentinel* later recalled that Pontotoc was taken with a fervor for building the railroad and promised to raise $10,000 and acquire a right-of-way for the tracks and depots.

However, they soon realized to their embarrassment that they were not able to honor their commitment, having raised only $5,000, half of the promised sum. They appointed two representatives to travel to Ripley on horseback and tell Falkner "the sad, sad story" and see if anything could be worked out. After a day on the road, they arrived late in the evening, where they

put up at the "tavern" and notified the Colonel that they desired a conference with him at the selfsame place. After they had washed, brushed and supped, the Colonel entered the hotel office where they were. Erect, cold, austere, the usual formalities were passed, the three gentlemen were seated and one of the committeemen began timorously to recite the trials and vicissitudes of securing railroads by popular subscription. The Colonel meanwhile sat with folded arms, steadily and inscrutably, regarding the spokesman. When the climax was reached with the unmaterialized five thousand and the speaker's voice had almost lapsed into a whisper, the Colonel's eyes were apparently blazing and boring through him, then he suddenly relaxed, gazed dreamily into a shadowed corner of the room and finally bending across the little table between himself and his visitors, he said: "By G__, I'll do it. I always liked Pontotoc, and you are going to get the railroad."

Then it was that the man of business revealed his sentimental nature and the human element that inspires men to achievement far above the ordinary successes of sordid materialism.[30]

Subsequently, on April 27, surveyors began laying out the route in Pontotoc and locating the depot site. Fifty-five more convicts were due to arrive and begin earthwork on May 3.[31]

In early June the convict camp at Ripley was moved south to Blue Mountain as grading approached the town.[32] Without rails and a train, the workers were often required to walk for miles to work. Moving the camp reduced the travel time. By early July the survey of the entire route from Ripley to Pontotoc had been more or less completed.[33] Grading, bridging, and cross-tying[34] was progressing at both ends, from Ripley south and from Pontotoc north, at the rate of two miles a week. At the northern end, about eight miles were ready for rails. It was predicted—again overoptimistically as events would reveal—that the road would be completed to Pontotoc by mid-October.[35]

Working with convicts always involved the possibility of attempted escapes even with armed guards. On the evening of April 27, 1886, a convict escaped from the camp near Ripley and was caught two days later in the vicinity of Guyton's store south of Blue Mountain.[36] Another escape attempt is documented in a more ambiguous fashion in a mysterious landscape feature known as the "Frenchman's Grave," with its associated tale. Located on the west side of Mississippi State Highway 15 at Grace's Crossing, where a county road intersects the Ripley Railroad in northern Union County, the site is marked only by a small fence enclosing the purported grave of a convict of French birth. According to a version of the story, a Frenchman of unknown name was an inmate of the Mississippi penitentiary and was employed in the construction of the railroad. After receiving a letter from France informing him that his wife was dying, he attempted to escape, and was shot dead and buried on the railroad right-of-way. Much of this account is probably apocryphal, although it likely holds a core of truth. For decades, employees of the railroad and later others maintained a fence that marked where the nameless man was buried. Today the fence is of plastic lattice on a metal frame with a sign identifying the spot as Frenchman's Grave that was erected in 2010 by Tommy Covington, local Ripley historian.[37]

Herbert Murdaugh discovered that a Frank Smith, who was born in Paris, France (his name—not a typically French name—was probably an alias), was sentenced on March 3, 1886, in Warren County for a three-year term in the Mississippi State Penitentiary for grand larceny but was shot on July 14, 1886, at an unspecified location while trying to escape from a G&SI construction crew. He lived for two weeks after being shot and died on July 31. The fact that he survived for this duration before succumbing suggests that he lived his last days in the convict camp and that the camp was probably nearby. We might also conclude that Frank Smith may very well have been the mysterious Frenchman.[38] However, we cannot say much more than this.

In August 1886, the first shipments of rails and iron accessories began arriving in Ripley, and tracklaying continued southward[39] with the rails laid in narrow gauge to be compatible with the tracks between Ripley and Middleton. When these tracks connected with the southern division of the G&SI, constructed

Figure 13.1. Blue Mountain Depot. From the GM&O Historical Society archives.

in standard gauge (4′ 8.5″), then the northern division would be converted to standard. By late September the tracks were laid to Blue Mountain—three months after predicted—and a celebratory "grand excursion" was planned for the twenty-sixth.[40] Soon after, the tracks were opened to Guyton's store,[41] located two miles south of Blue Mountain,[42] and then to Cotton Plant,[43] a few more miles to the south; and there tracklaying ceased for months. To this point, the tracks had been built of thirty-six-pounds-per-yard rails.[44] All these rails would have to be replaced when converted to standard gauge.

In July, N. L. Marmon, owner of the newspaper *Union County Optic* and a legal representative of the G&SI, was delegated to acquire a right-of-way that would pass through the center of New Albany rather than around the town as previously planned.[45] However, the lure of charging exorbitant prices was too much for some. By October Falkner announced that he was going to simply bypass the town by two miles to the west. To emphasize his point, he withdrew his workforce of seventy-three men and moved them across the county line to "Holditch's" in Pontotoc County, a place that later became the town of Ecru.[46] The possibility of losing the road was a troubling prospect in New Albany. At the time the Memphis, Birmingham, and Atlantic (soon to become the Kansas City, Memphis, and Birmingham) Railroad was already building toward New Albany from Memphis, and the G&SI would make the town a rail crossroads. If Falkner bypassed the town, then the crossing of the tracks would be elsewhere, inevitably luring business away. The problem was soon remedied with a mass meeting and the raising of funds for the right-of-way, and the road was back on track to pass through New Albany.[47]

In early April 1887, grading was more or less complete between Ripley and Pontotoc, and contractors were depositing stacks of crossties along the right-of-way ready to be put into place.[48] At the time Colonel Falkner was reported to be in New York acquiring more iron for track.[49] He returned to Ripley on April 29 announcing that he had purchased sufficient iron and steel to lay the tracks from Cotton Plant to Pontotoc. Part of the iron was from St. Louis, while steel rails were from Liverpool.[50] The first shipment, consisting of forty carloads, arrived in Ripley on Friday, May 13.[51] Tracklaying resumed at Cotton Plant on Monday following more than half a year's delay.[52] The tracks from this point south were constructed using fifty-six-pounds-per-yard rails, which would be more commensurate with the standard-gauge railroad that the road was intended to become.[53]

As the railroad was constructed south, there was an increasing need for more rolling stock. The regular freight and passenger service along with normal maintenance needed to be supplemented as new rails were being laid. Since 1872 the railroad had had only had two locomotives: #1, the *Hardy W. Stricklin*, nicknamed *Dolly*, and #3, the *Colonel W. C. Falkner*, nicknamed *Tanglefoot*. In December 1886, a new locomotive was purchased that weighed almost twice as much as either of the first two. It was named the *M. P. Lowrey* in honor of the founder of Blue Mountain College who had died the previous year.[54] The following December, a fourth locomotive was acquired.[55]

In June, the *Ripley Advertiser* reported that shipments were passing down the railroad almost daily, and soon after engineer Will Hines and conductor Walter Harris were registered at the Robinson House, a New Albany hotel, indicating that the road had been completed to the town by late June.[56] Upon reaching New Albany, the road intersected with the Kansas City, Memphis, and Birmingham, which had been built through the town in November 1886.[57] So within half a year New Albany went from a town without a railroad to a rail crossroads. Probably foreseeing the town's growth, Falkner purchased a half interest in the newspaper the *Union County Optic* from N. L. Marmon in May 1887 and sent his nephew and namesake, W. C. "Willie" Falkner Jr., the son of J. W. Falkner, to New Albany to work. The elder Falkner apparently sold his interest in the paper a year later.[58]

From then until August the crew was involved in further earthwork in town and presumably constructing the siding. On August 10 they began laying track southward out of town.[59] By late September they were five miles south of town, and in mid-October they reached Fredonia, seven miles to the south, soon to be renamed Ingomar, after the protagonist in Falkner's *White Rose of Memphis*.[60]

The next depot south of Ingomar was just across the line in Pontotoc County and became known as Ecru, where a post office was established on July 23, 1888, and a town was incorporated in 1904.[61] The place was originally identified as Holditch's after a prominent landowner, Sidney F. Holditch. As mentioned above, when disputing the railroad's route through New Albany

Figure 13.2. New Albany Depot. Courtesy of the Union County Historical Society.

in October 1886, Falkner had pulled seventy-three men out of that area and sent them to Holditch's to work. A depot was eventually constructed there and a town surveyed. Although the place could have become Holditch, it was named instead Ecru purportedly after the color ecru—a shade of beige—with which the depot was painted.

The cause of the name change is recorded only in legend. Sidney Holditch's great-grandson, W. Kenneth Holditch, recalled that "Falkner, who named the new stations along the line, towns such as Falkner[62] and Ingomar . . . chose 'Ecru' for the hamlet that grew up on my great-grandfather's land. He had planned to name the town Holditch, but my great-grandfather resisted, pointing out that he had already made numerous enemies because he had pulled strings with his old friend to get the railroad built across his land. Why Ecru? Because it was the color of the railroad station."[63]

Another story provides a variant explanation: "After enduring the fuss between two prominent families that each wanted the town to bear their name . . . , [Falkner] asked, 'What color is this building?' When someone answered, 'Ecru,' he is said to have replied, 'Then that's the name of the town.'"[64] Certainly, Falkner had a hand in naming a few places along the railroad, but legendry has often embellished the truth. The great-grandson summed up the confusion when he proudly told Robert Cantwell: "The people could call the towns whatever they wanted, but, by God, he would name the depots."[65]

In early June, the road was "about completed" to Pontotoc, and soon after Joe E. Hovis and Ed Moore were at work building the depot there.[66] Despite this, it would be a month before the first train entered Pontotoc on July 1.[67]

To emphasize the festive nature of the occasion, the Fourth of July was chosen for a celebration. Sheep, goats, hogs, and cows were slaughtered and placed over pits to barbecue during the preceding night. People from outlying areas began arriving the day before and camped overnight. On the morning of the fourth, a train set out from Middleton at the northern end consisting of two locomotives pulling nine cars. The cars presumably consisted of the few passenger cars available, and the balance was made up of flatcars with rudimentary seating. Falkner and his family members joined the train at Ripley as the prime celebrities. At ten o'clock, the Pontotoc Cornet Band began playing and marched to the new depot, located west of the courthouse at the bottom of the hill, where at 10:30 the train arrived blowing its whistles and carrying, it was reported, about a thousand people. Mayor Bradford welcomed the crowd and was followed to the podium by Colonel Falkner, who addressed everyone in "his usual eloquent manner." Dr. M. R. Fontaine read a letter from former governor John M. Stone—who had defeated Falkner in the 1862 election for colonel of the Second Mississippi Infantry—expressing his regrets at being unable to attend. Later, the focal point of the ceremony was reached when the Honorable J. D. Fontaine of Pontotoc, with the assistance of Effie Falkner, drove the silver spike symbolizing the completion of the road to Pontotoc. Afterward the band, playing a rousing rendition of "Dixie," led the crowd off to a grove at the fairground for the barbecue dinner. The next attraction was a baseball game between New Albany and Pontotoc, while the gathering concluded that night with a ball. The crowd for the festivities was variously estimated as five to ten thousand.[68]

As the railroad extended south from Ripley to Pontotoc, some reorganization was in order. The daily train had initially begun and terminated at Ripley, which was convenient because most of the staff and infrastructure were concentrated there including the headquarters, shops, and storage for rolling stock. After the southern terminus was relocated to Pontotoc, so too was relocated the terminus for the daily train, which would now cover more than twice the distance previously covered on the twenty-five-mile route from Ripley to Middleton. Now the track extended for about sixty-three miles, with the train leaving Pontotoc every morning for Middleton.[69] To facilitate this meant that conductors, engineers, brakemen, firemen, and so on had to be located in Pontotoc instead of Ripley. Turning the locomotives at Pontotoc was now carried out with a turntable instead of a Y, as initially used at Ripley.[70] At the latter town the Y was removed in 1886 and a turntable installed on the south side of the depot.[71] This was presumably to turn locomotives based at Ripley and direct them either north or south for special purposes.

With the completion of the approximately thirty-eight miles from Ripley to Pontotoc, the northern division of the G&SI came to a halt. While Falkner had moved along on the northern division, matters had not gone well overall for the company.

In 1886, as Falkner began construction of the northern division, the southern division remained uncertain. Surveyors began to work out the southern end. By December a route had been partially located and surveyed to begin at a yet-to-be-determined location on the Gulf Coast, then proceed northward "through or near" Hattiesburg, Raleigh, Forest, Carthage, Chester, and Houston to Pontotoc.[72] Construction in the south was begun on January 11, 1887— over nine months after Falkner had begun work—at Hattiesburg, a town previously founded by W. H. Hardy and named after his wife. The town was located on the New Orleans and Northeastern Railroad, which Hardy had previously constructed. As with so many projects, the beginning of construction was a festive occasion, with the convict workers standing in two lines with "military precision" until work was triggered by the firing of a cannon.[73]

On January 15, the stockholders of the SIR&K Railroad met in Falkner's office in Ripley. R. J. Thurmond, who had been serving for years as the trustee for the bondholders of the railroad, submitted his resignation, and C. L. Harris was appointed to take his position. This was Thurmond's last official connection to the railroad.[74]

By late January Falkner was on the Gulf Coast on business with the G&SI. While there, he took the time to ride five miles east from Mississippi City to see Jefferson Davis, the former president of the Confederate States, at his retirement home, Beauvoir. Stripped of his citizenship, Davis had retired to Beauvoir in the late 1870s, where he spent time writing his major works, including the two-volume *Rise and Fall of the Confederate Government* (1881) and *A Short History of the Confederate States of America* (1889).

A few days later, when Falkner was back in Memphis at the Peabody, a reporter from the *Memphis Appeal* interviewed him. While much of the discussion focused on railroad activities, it also turned to his visit with Davis. As Falkner related:

It was on Tuesday last [February 1] that Mr. R. W. Baldwin, of Baltimore, and I visited Mr. Davis at this home. . . . The house is a spacious wooden structure of square shape, encircled by a broad covered veranda, which affords a fine view of the face of the Gulf. . . . The ground in the vicinity is covered with magnolias and live oak, whose unfading green leaves lend an indescribable charm to the place. If Mr. Davis could not be happy at this delightful home, I am sure he could not be happy anywhere on earth; and if he is not truly happy he deceives his looks, as well as his visitors, because I have rarely seen a face more cheerful than his. I met him in Richmond when he was President of the Confederacy. His face then had a haggard, careworn expression, and the skin was totally colorless; but now it is entirely different. Every now and then, a bright, benevolent smile would mantle his features. His conversation was charming, as well as cheerful and instructive. . . .

His form was very erect, his shoulders square, the step firm and vigorous, a black felt hat with broad brim covered his head, and he was clad in a black cloth suit, the coat with square cut skirt terminating at the knee. An occasional puff of blue smoke curled about his head, rising from the cigar he now and then placed in his mouth. I recognized him and he instantly recognized me. After introducing Mr. Baldwin, we were invited into the reception room, when a box of excellent cigars was produced and the conversation opened. To say I was captivated by his discourse would be a tame expression, for I was really charmed. No one could feel embarrassed in his presence, because he managed to make me feel at perfect ease. I was astonished at the tenacity of his memory. He inquired about men and things of forty years ago, seeming to remember incidents that have transpired half a century back with as much accuracy as if they had happened but yesterday.[75]

Davis and Falkner would never meet again; they would die a month apart in 1889.

In late 1887 Falkner came into contact with another president, one whom he had already met before his election, Grover Cleveland, who was to appear in Memphis on Saturday, October 15. Thousands arrived in the city the day before filling every hotel, with some offering cots in their hallways. On Saturday the streets were filled, and the court square was packed. An assembly was held inside the Memphis Cotton Exchange, a large Richardsonian Romanesque building that had just been completed a couple of years earlier. As part of the program, Falkner appeared on behalf of the Mexican War veterans of the area to welcome the president and his young wife Frances to the area. He recalled the patriotism of the veterans and their good wishes for the president. Echoing the last words of General Stonewall Jackson, he noted that of one hundred thousand veterans, about eighty thousand had "crossed the dark river, and are now resting under the shade of the trees on the other side, and in a few short years we will rejoin our comrades on the other side." He concluded his short speech by saying: "Mr. President, it would be a privilege highly prized by us to be permitted to shake you by the hand as tokens of our high regard."[76]

In late May 1887 the directors of the G&SI, Falkner included, met again in Mississippi City to decide the location of the southern terminus of the railroad. While Mississippi City had been planned to be the terminus, surveys determined that the best location was two and half miles west of there. The site was initially named Gulf City but was soon renamed Gulfport. After a channel was dredged to the site, the town became the interface between the railroad and oceangoing vessels.[77] Despite the initial efforts to complete the railroad between Hattiesburg and Gulfport, the work soon faltered and would not be completed until September 1896.[78]

The railroad also ran into other trouble. On the night of May 5, 1887, G&SI director Jones Hamilton encountered Roderick Gambrell, editor of the *Sword and Shield*, in downtown Jackson. The two had become increasingly hostile toward one another, with the editor standing strongly opposed to convict leasing. Upon encountering each other, hostility soon turned into gunfire. Both were wounded; Gambrell died within an hour while Hamilton came close to death.[79] He was subsequently arrested and remained in jail for months awaiting his trial, thereby forcing his resignation from the board of directors.[80] In the months that followed, the affair turned into a major controversy, with a Gambrell faction opposing Hamilton's followers until he was acquitted on April 9, 1888.

The tension had hardly subsided when less than a month later violence again erupted. J. H. Martin, the editor of a Jackson newspaper, the *New Mississippian*, along with his brother had taken sides against Hamilton during the recent trial, often attacking him and his friends. On May 1, the Martins attacked General Wirt Adams, another director of the G&SI, in the *New Mississippian*. Later that day Adams encountered J. H. Martin at the corner of President and Amite Streets in Jackson. Insults soon turned into gunplay, and when it was over both men lay dead on the sidewalk.[81] The two widely heralded affrays involving directors of the G&SI resulted in a growing loss of confidence in the railroad, and the problems did not end there.[82]

The convict leasing system continued to be a problem. Soon after the G&SI started construction, reports began to appear about abuse of the convicts.[83]

During the summer of 1887, camps at both ends of the line were visited by the superintendent of the penitentiary, who reported some problems but nothing major.[84] In March 1888, W. L. Doss became superintendent and soon after set out on an inspection tour of the camps. In the south, he followed the route from Gulfport to Hattiesburg, where he found many problems and noted that throughout the year complaints continued to come in. Regarding the northern division, he reported that Falkner's camps were "in such good condition and no complaint received therefrom, that the board informed me there was no necessity to visit the camp."[85] This speaks well of Falkner.

On December 4, 1888, because of what had been found on the southern end of the construction, the Board of Control of the penitentiary canceled the convict labor lease with the G&SI for cruel treatment of the convicts and for failure to comply in making payments. The prisoners were immediately pulled off the construction.[86] Financial difficulties were beginning to accumulate, and, as reported in May 1889, although "Old Hardy is as full of promises as ever," suits were "beginning to roll in."[87] The growing problems meant that construction on the G&SI's southern division ground to a halt; it would never be linked to the northern division. When construction was eventually resumed, its route was altered to swing northwest at Hattiesburg and run to Jackson, which it reached in July 1900.[88]

However, as the G&SI was going down, Falkner was going up. He had completed enough of the northern division to more than double the length of the Ripley Railroad, and he had done it before the state pulled out the convict labor. Furthermore, he owned a mortgage on his newest creation.

Less than a week after the festivities celebrating the completion of the road to Pontotoc, the *Memphis Appeal* noted the arrival of Jones Hamilton, the "heart and soul" of the G&SI, at the Peabody Hotel in Memphis. A reporter asked why he was in town, and he replied that he had come to meet Falkner. When asked about the progress of the G&SI, he observed with outward optimism that the funds would be forthcoming and there was no doubt as to the road's completion. After waiting for some time, Falkner never appeared, and Hamilton had to return to Jackson.[89] Although Falkner's absence wasn't explained, it appears that he was distancing himself from the failing parent company. He had in fact headed for Bailey Springs for some relaxation. He had not been there since the railroad construction had resumed in 1886 and didn't want to be worried with the problems of the G&SI, which he had managed to weather. He didn't return to Ripley until early August.[90]

However, with the G&SI in trouble, repaying Falkner for his loans was not possible. In July, advertisements were posted that the SIR&K (the section of the road between Ripley and Middleton) would be foreclosed on and sold at auction on August 13.[91] On the designated date, the railroad including both fixed and rolling stock was put up for auction at the courthouse in Ripley with the high bid placed by "Falkner, Harris & Co." for $134,000.[92]

Falkner was soon laying plans for and assembling funds for the purchase of the G&SI south of Ripley. Such activities made him a frequent visitor to New York City and other places. In early September he left home for New York and didn't return until early October.[93] He returned to New York in February and again in March.[94] In between trips, the *Southern Sentinel* noted that J. R. Rogers reported that "his neighbors would like to see Col. W. C. Falkner a candidate for the Legislature." This support was no doubt in recognition of his role as a leader in business and social affairs. Two weeks later it was reported, perhaps prematurely, that Falkner would indeed be a candidate for the state legislature representing Tippah County.[95]

A month later, it was official: the *Sentinel* announced that he was in fact running. Editor Pink Smith was effusive in his support, looking back to Falkner's arrival in Tippah County and his subsequent career, calling to mind his "self-made man" characterization that had been put forward three decades before by the newspaper *Quid Nunc*:

> For near fifty years Col. Falkner has been an honored citizen of Tippah County, arriving here as a poor, orphan boy, and by dint of energy and perseverance backed by a strong native ability, has arose in strength, in wealth, and the esteem of his fellowmen, until now he has about reached the top round. He has done more for the poor of Tippah County than, perhaps, any other man within its borders. . . .
>
> Col. Falkner has never yet held a civil office; yet he has always fought for the success of his people and his party. As to his ability to serve the people no one who knows him will doubt; as to his interest in the people of this county, his record settled that. Col. Falkner asks the Democracy of the county to endorse him as a man and citizen by electing him as their representative to the next Legislature promising to faithfully guard, and labor for the interest of his people.[96]

Apparently not all the constituency was as enthralled. Two weeks later, Falkner addressed a letter to the *Sentinel* noting: "Persons unfriendly to me have circulated a report that my object in running for the Legislature is to enable me to secure favorable legislation for the railroad. This is unjust, false and slanderous." Although providing legislative help to his railroad could not have been far from his mind, it was certainly unjust to imply that this was his only concern. He reassured any farmers with doubts that while in Jackson he would be looking out after their interests.[97]

He also saw Effie married to Edwin F. Campbell, bookkeeper for the Armstrong Furniture Company in Memphis,[98] on November 22, 1888. The wedding was quiet and intimate—only a few relatives and close friends were invited—and was held at 10:00 a.m. in the Falkner home with the Reverend W. D. Heath of Ripley's Presbyterian Church officiating. The house was "handsomely decorated," and while the attendees were in a festive spirit Effie's mother was noticeably "sorely grieved at the thought of giving up the daughter she loved and idolized." Afterward, the married couple departed Ripley on board a special train and reached Memphis at 5:30 p.m., where they took up residence with the groom's mother on Shelby Street.[99] With Effie's departure and with the youngest daughter Bama in Pontotoc attending the Chickasaw Female College, there were no more children at Warwick Place.[100] Campbell soon became a stockholder and director of the railroad and an employee when he was appointed general freight agent at New Albany in early 1893.[101]

In April 1889, Falkner was dining in the Gayoso Hotel in Memphis. By this time, he was a celebrity not only in railroading but also in literature. Having recognized him, a reporter approached his table to inform him that a fellow diner was a man whom he should meet. As it turned out, the man was also a Civil War veteran, Major General Lew Wallace (1827–1905) of the Union Army and former governor of the New Mexico Territory (1878–1881). Like Falkner, Wallace had gone on to pursue a literary career, writing and publishing several books including *Ben-Hur* (1880), which became the best-selling American novel of the nineteenth century. The reporter noted that despite Wallace's distinctions he was "a most unassuming and affable gentleman." Following their introduction, the two men enjoyed a "delightful conversation" that probably involved war reminiscences and thoughts on writing.[102]

In mid-May, Falkner left again for New York[103] and the office of financier Christopher C. Baldwin on Wall Street. There, the two finalized plans to purchase the northern division of the G&SI. Falkner convinced Baldwin that the two sections of railroad—one north of Ripley and the other to the south—should be combined and expanded. After some discussion, Baldwin agreed that if Falkner could acquire and combine both, then he, Baldwin, would purchase $100,000 in bonds and $100,000 in stocks at sixty-five cents on the dollar—a substantial investment. This was agreed upon by a contract signed by Falkner and Baldwin in the latter's office on May 24, 1889.[104]

Upon leaving New York, Falkner headed for Meridian, Mississippi, to meet with W. H. Harris, whom he found "quite despondent" following the failure of the G&SI and who consequently faced having to resume his law practice to support his family. Harris wished Falkner and his project well. Soon after, Falkner wrote to Baldwin in New York informing him to have blank stocks and bonds engraved and a seal made for the new company, which would be called the Gulf and Chicago Railroad Company, implying that the road was to connect the Gulf with the Great Lakes. Falkner also noted the need to extend the road twenty-five miles south of Pontotoc to Houston, Mississippi, a small first step on the way to the Gulf.[105]

To accompany the development of the G&C route, a telephone line was erected along the right-of-way to connect Middleton with Pontotoc. Headed by Lee D. Hines, son of the late C E. Hines, it was constructed under the auspices of the Alabama, Mississippi, and Tennessee Telephone Company, in which Hines was a large investor along with his already being an investor in the G&C. Construction began by early October and was completed in late November.[106]

On Tuesday, July 23, 1889, the SIR&K was once again put up for auction on the courthouse steps, and Falkner once again was the high bidder at $135,000, with title going to him and others including J. W. T. Falkner, N. G. Carter, L. D. Hines, and William Hines.[107] Nine days later, on August 1, 1889, the G&SI between Ripley and Pontotoc was brought up for sale at the door of the Tippah County courthouse, and Falkner was the highest bidder at $80,000.[108] On the same day, he sold his acquisition for $205,000 to his new company, the Gulf and Chicago Railroad, joining into single ownership the two sections of railroad that connected Middleton, Tennessee, to Pontotoc, Mississippi, a total of about sixty-three miles, and completing another step toward fulfilling his new vision of a road connecting the Gulf Coast with Chicago, the hub of the Midwest.[109]

Thurmond was not pleased with this development. Fearful of the possible collapse of the G&SI, he decided to play it safe and pulled out of the scheme, and his concerns proved valid. He watched as the G&SI went through financial difficulties and scandals until it finally went down in a flurry of bad press and lawsuits. He might have taken satisfaction from his prudent withdrawal and the fulfillment of his prophecy. However, against expectation, Falkner had not gone down with the G&SI. Instead, he had completed thirty-eight miles of railroad and as the G&SI was collapsing gained title to the thirty-eight miles and amalgamated them into the original Ripley Railroad under a new corporate name. Falkner had plucked victory from the jaws of defeat.

For Thurmond, this was both infuriating and humiliating. It was maddening to know that if he had only stayed with this man whom he had come to hate, he too would be a key player in the new railroad. The feud had been transformed. Before, it was about a simple conflict of visions, one extravagant and visionary and the other restrained and penurious. Now, one had been proved right and the other made to look foolish. The irony of the situation was certainly not lost on Falkner with his keen sense of humor, and he was not one to let his naysayer forget it. No longer did he have to argue with Thurmond. All he had to do was laugh at him, and laughter can be the most devastating weapon. And all that Thurmond could do was seethe and let his rage mount.

To exacerbate the situation, Falkner was on a roll. The Democratic primary was held on Tuesday, August 17. Besides Falkner, the ballot included three other candidates. One was S. O. Love, the incumbent, while F. A. Wolf had previously served two terms in the state legislature and two in the Senate. The last, W. T. Daniel, like Falkner apparently had no known political experience. In most cases, Love and Wolf would have posed an obstacle to Falkner, who had never before been elected to office. But Falkner was no ordinary candidate. He was a larger-than-life figure whose name had become a household word throughout Tippah County and beyond. So, when the votes were counted in the evening, out of a total of 1,507 votes cast, Falkner tallied 960, giving him not just a plurality but a strong majority. Such a victory does little to support the contention by some historians that Falkner alienated himself from his community during his final years.

In November he would face the Republican nominee in the general election; however, that would be no real competition because with only seventy Republicans in the county the party had no chance of winning. The election would be no more than a formality.[110] Seeing the election results, R. J. Thurmond certainly wondered: is the son of a bitch unstoppable?

Although Thurmond wasn't celebrating the victory, others were. The *Memphis Avalanche* reported: "The Col. is to be congratulated on the sweeping victory he has recently made."[111] The Jackson *Clarion-Ledger* wrote that his victory was "a fitting testimonial, showing the esteem in which Gen. Falkner is held at home" and predicted that he would "be one of the most majestic figures in the next House."[112] The Memphis *Public Ledger* noted that the vote reflected "the high esteem in which he is held by the people among whom he has so long lived" and further noted: "Possessed of a commanding appearance and an easy, graceful manner, he would attract attention in any assembly."[113]

As the general election approached, Falkner was in Pontotoc on October 22 accompanied by representatives of the Kansas City, Memphis, and Birmingham who were inspecting Falkner's railroad with the intention of purchasing and upgrading it to standard gauge.[114] On the following day, his wife, Lizzie, left Ripley for Memphis to spend the winter, which she and her daughters had been doing for several years. The *Southern Sentinel* observed that while the town regretted losing the Falkner family "from its social circle this winter," its loss would be "the Bluff City's gain."[115] In fact, the Falkners perhaps considered moving permanently to Memphis that year, but if so they had a change of heart. Nevertheless, the women of the family were still drawn there especially during the colder months, probably because of the social life.[116] On the night of Saturday, November 2, Falkner spoke to a crowd estimated at 1,000–1,200 at a Democratic rally in Memphis. It was probably the last time that he spoke to a public gathering in Memphis . . . or for that matter anywhere.[117]

Chapter 14

The Shooting

Falkner's successes continued to be haunted by the feud with Thurmond. The incidences were not recorded at the time but only remembered later. Although Andrew Brown had not yet been born, he lived close enough to that time that he was later able to sum up the situation well:

> For three years and more the feud between Falkner and Thurmond moved as inexorably as a Greek tragedy toward a climax that neither man desired and both men dreaded. Many men, friends of both parties, made their efforts to patch up the quarrel. Dr. Murry used all of his influence, and C. M. Thurmond, son of Richard J. Thurmond, went to Falkner several times to plead with him. . . .
>
> As time went on both Thurmond and Falkner seem to have reached the conclusion that his enemy was determined to kill him. Both were wrong. Thurmond wanted only to be left alone, though he was determined to defend himself if he thought his life was in danger. Falkner's attitude seems to have been one of fatalism. Late in 1889 he told Captain [Thomas] Spight, in the manner of one merely stating a fact, that Dick Thurmond was going to kill him, and asked some question about preparing his will. Spight suggested that Falkner carry a gun for self-defense, but the Colonel refused to do so, saying that he had killed two men already, and had rather die himself than slay another.[1]

As indicated, the tension between the men arose from Falkner's continued successes with the railroad following Thurmond's predictions that the G&SI venture would result in financial disaster. Furthermore, Falkner was not going to let Thurmond forget the matter.

Tuesday, November 5, promised to be a ceremonial accolade to Falkner's success. However, Thurmond resented it. Falkner's railroad had been completed; it had weathered the storm surrounding the G&SI and had now been

Figure 14.1. Photographic portrait of Colonel W. C. Falkner, one of only two known with the other being that made at Mora Studios in New York City (fig. 0.1). The origin of this photo is unknown. John Cofield of Cofield Photographers of Oxford, Mississippi, indicated that it came from his family's photographic collection, stating that it may have been copied by his grandfather from an original. Courtesy of John Cofield.

Figure 14.2. Photographic portrait of R. J. Thurmond, by F. S. McKnight, photographer, Ripley, Mississippi. Courtesy of Tommy Covington.

consolidated into a single unit ready for the next opportunity to be extended. The election offered the certainty of his placement in the legislature. It was a time of celebration. He spent the day circulating among the voters accompanied by his supporters.[2] When the votes were counted, Falkner had swept the county with 1,313 votes, virtually the entire vote.[3] However, by that time the pleasure of victory would moot.

As voting drew to a close, Falkner was on the west side of the courthouse square. At the time, the square included the two-story brick courthouse at the center, most of which was constructed on the fifty-square-foot foundations of the antebellum courthouse that had burned in 1864. Surrounding the square was a curtain of commercial buildings. All were of frame construction except one, a brick storehouse occupied by the firm Alexander and Company, which was on the west side of the square. On the north side and adjacent to the brick structure was a small frame building, and in October R. J. Thurmond had opened an office there for his business. The *Southern Sentinel*, knowing Thurmond's proclivity for making cash loans, hopefully suggested that it might become a bank.[4] After all, there was no bank in Ripley at the time. Thurmond was in his office that evening and could see Falkner perambulating about the square, ebullient with his victory, talking to bystanders as they congratulated him. Filled with rage, he anticipated that Falkner would soon be at his office to remind him of his failed predictions—laughing.

Falkner was near the front of Thurmond's office. According to one account, he was talking to Thomas Rucker about sawing timber.[5] He apparently attracted Thurmond's attention and raised his ire. According to another contemporary account: "Thurmond stepped outside his door; something was said or done—no one seems to know exactly what—and Thurmond leveled a revolver and fired."[6] Andrew Brown, after hearing varying accounts all of his life, wrote:

> [Falkner] walked up the steps to the portico in front of Thurmond's office. He stood outside the open window, while Thurmond, seated at his desk, faced him. Exactly what happened during the next few seconds is impossible to determine, but the consensus is that the Colonel said something to Thurmond—what it was varies widely in different accounts—and then made a movement toward his hip pocket that Thurmond could have interpreted as reaching for a gun.[7]

Falkner exclaimed, "What do you mean, Dick? Don't shoot!" and Thurmond fired, hitting him in the mouth. Rucker was so close that his face was powder burned by the blast. Falkner collapsed onto the brick sidewalk.[8]

Dick Ford, editor of the *Ripley Advertiser*, was in his office on the southeast corner of the square. His friendship with Falkner dated to at least 1880 when the colonel had helped him to reestablish his business after the *Advertiser* office burned that year. Ford heard a single shot and stepped outside, where he could see a crowd gathering on the far side of the square. He noted the time: 4:30. Upon hurrying over, he asked some of the witnesses about the cause of the shooting. He was told that "there was no known cause—that Col. Falkner was standing on the pavement in front of or near Alexander & Co.'s store [adjacent to the office], when Mr. Thurmond met up with him, and pointing his pistol at Col. Falkner's head, fired, without any apparent provocation." Thurmond made no statement regarding his motive. Ford did note that it was "well known . . . that an old feud existed between the parties—that neither one had any love for the other."[9] On the other hand, a report in the *Memphis*

Avalanche attributed to Joseph Brown, Thurmond's nephew by marriage and the father of Andrew III, claimed that the incident resulted because of "demonstrations made by Falkner, he being intoxicated."[10] The account in the *Memphis Appeal*, apparently written by a reporter on site, called the *Avalanche* account a "false and slanderous dispatch" written by a "friend or relative of Thurmond's" and noted that Falkner "was sober all day, had drunk nothing and made no demonstrations, as he had told his family and friends . . . that he was determined to have no difficulty with Thurmond."[11]

The office of Falkner's son-in-law, Dr. N. G. Carter, was only a few doors to the south,[12] and he was soon there to provide medical attention. The bullet had entered Falkner's mouth and passed under his tongue and through his jawbone before lodging in the right side of his neck under his ear. Falkner was bleeding profusely, and his head was bruised from the fall onto the brick sidewalk.

Sheriff J. M. Rutherford soon arrived and arrested Thurmond, whose son, lawyer Charlie Miller Thurmond, whose office was at the north end of the block,[13] was soon at the jail offering to pay his father's bond, but the sheriff refused, saying that there wasn't enough money in the United States to keep his father out of jail. Rutherford understood that bond could not be set if the charge was murder, an unbailable crime. That night, guards were placed around the jail to "prevent the friends of Thurmond from rescuing him." One suspects that guards were needed more to deter Falkner's friends from lynching Thurmond. This is supported by the fact that the following night the jail was guarded by Thurmond's men.[14] According to Brown, with Thurmond having never been in trouble of this magnitude, he "naturally panicked to some extent after the shooting, and spent a great deal of money gathering evidence, etc. There is no doubt that he was imposed on by some, and he was guilty of some errors in judgments. Indeed, the money he spent made some people believe that he actually was guilty, just for that reason."[15]

Immediately following the shooting, a wire mattress was produced. Falkner was placed on it, and several men carried him two and a half blocks north along Main Street passing by his own home—there was no one there to nurse him—then turning left onto Cooper Street for half a block to Dr. Carter's home just across from his own.[16] Upon entering the hallway of the house, they then turned right into the library, where they placed him.[17] The Carters, assisted by J. L. Walker and Sam Edgerton,[18] began removing his overcoat and coat. When the latter was examined, all that was found was a pencil, a pocket-book, and a pipe. There was no gun.

Someone was dispatched by handcar to New Albany, nineteen miles away, to send out messages by telegraph; there was still no telegraph in Ripley, and the telephone line still under construction was not yet operational.[19] All such communications including news stories would have to be carried to New Albany before being telegraphed to Memphis. One message was addressed to Falkner's son, J. W. T. Falkner, in Oxford. It read: "Thurmond shot Col Falkner this evening—badly shot Come" and concluded by noting: "Walker is here with handcar," thereby indicating that a handcar was waiting in New Albany to bring him the last stretch to Ripley. However, the younger Falkner wouldn't be able to depart for some time. The other message was sent by Dr. Carter to Edwin F. Campbell, the husband of Effie Falkner. The message read: "Thurmond shot Col Falkner Come & bring Dr. Rogers."[20] It was presumably left up to Campbell to notify his mother-in-law, Lizzie Falkner.

Newspapers recorded the events and the sense of shock that descended upon Ripley. The *Tupelo Journal* reported that "public sentiment in Ripley is against Thurmond" but presciently observed that the "deadly feud [that] existed between them will go far toward securing a verdict of acquittal."[21] Thurmond remained in jail until bond was set in February.[22]

Some have contended that Lizzie and Bill Falkner were estranged. However, her actions indicated that whatever her relationship was with her husband, there was still a strong devotion. Upon being notified of his being shot, Lizzie moved quickly and decisively to go to his side under arduous conditions. Although night had fallen, she summoned Effie and Dr. W. B. Rogers to accompany her by train. They arrived in New Albany "in the middle of a very cold night and at a time when there was no train running between New Albany and Ripley. . . . Some friends met her [probably Walker] and brought her to her husband's side by the only means of conveyance available—they pumped a handcar between the two towns, a distance of twenty miles."[23] They arrived in Ripley at about 2:00 a.m.[24] Dr. Rogers "examined the wounds and pronounced them not necessarily fatal, unless he should have another hemorrhage which would undoubtedly cause his death."[25]

Falkner clung to life through the night. The following morning at 9:30, Dr. Rogers departed for Memphis, called back in part by professional obligations and possibly by the knowledge that he could do no more. That afternoon Falkner was reported to be "resting somewhat easier."[26] In the evening Ed Campbell arrived accompanied by Bama Falkner on board a special train, and later that night J. W. T. Falkner and his son Murry arrived from Oxford.[27] However, by that time the colonel had taken a turn for the worse. With the bullet still lodged in place, his throat had begun to swell, and he slowly choked to death.[28] Campbell telegraphed his mother in Memphis: "Col Falkner died at 10:40 p.m."[29] That evening his son John scribbled out a short message to be sent as a telegram to his father's old friend in Memphis, Colonel M. C. Gallaway. The message read: "Send metallic case for Col Falkner/Size 6 feet 2 inch."[30] Pink Smith, the editor of the *Southern Sentinel*, commented the next day: "Nothing has ever occurred in Ripley that caused such universal sorrow, such a pall of gloom to hang over the people of Tippah county as the killing of Col. W. C. Falkner."[31]

Falkner's funeral was held at 11:00 on Friday morning in the Presbyterian Church, his wife's church, adjacent to his railroad.[32] An estimated one thousand people were present, which was far more than the building could hold. The Reverend W. T. Lowrey, a son of General M. P. Lowrey, delivered the funeral address, which was reported as "very eloquent and impressive"; "few dry eyes were found in the vast audience when he referred in eloquent words to the great worth of the lamented Falkner."[33] Afterward, the "vast throng" proceeded to the cemetery, where, following a Masonic burial service, his metal coffin was placed in a small, newly constructed brick vault next to Henry's cenotaph. A newspaper recorded the effect upon the people attending the funeral:

> Flowers were heaped upon the metallic casket until there was room for no more; strong men wept as they looked upon the face of their friend for the last time. . . . Never in the history of Ripley has such a throng of sorrowing people gathered together to honor the dead. All felt that a friend was gone forever. Dry eyes were few. And so passes away the noblest man that ever honored Tippah county with his citizenship.[34]

A writer for a Jackson newspaper reflected upon the extent to which Falkner's image had grown: "The tragic death of Col. Falkner has brought him before the eyes of the public to such an extent that his life and its achievement loom up before them as the colossal work of an enterprising, industrious, brave man. His business enterprises were gigantic; in that sense he was a Napoleon."[35] At least three of his associates composed poems about his death. While none were memorable literary productions, they reflected their authors' admiration of Falkner and their sorrow at his death and served to mythologize his memory. In one poem, "On the Death of Col. W. C. Falkner," A. W. Whitten wrote:

> Magnanimous hero, unstained by a blot,
> By those who are dead, and those who are not,
> While the hours of progress shall light up the day,
> Thy name and thy courage shall lead in the way,

Inscribe on his tombstone the honor that's due
A patriot noble, a citizen true
A friend of the people with courage to lead,
And maintains ever their interest to plead.[36]

Another, entitled simply "Falkner" and suggestive of Shelley's "Adonais: An Elegy on the Death of John Keats" (1821), opened with the following stanzas:

Oh! can it be that he is dead,
The brave, the gentle, true and kind,
Whom all the people loved, and who
To every-body was a friend.
Can it be true that he will come,
No more among us as of yore;
Can it be true that he is dead,
That our loved Falkner is no more?
Alas! too true the message came,
Too true the word that told his doom,
And all the people whom he loved,
Are sad, their faces veiled in gloom.[37]

As someone at the heart of the social and political life of a small community, Falkner was often the center of discussion. To die as he did would not diminish this. It is fundamental to human nature that if a story is worth telling, it's worth embellishing. As quoted in the introduction to this book, Maud Morrow Brown wrote: "After his death these stories multiplied into such fantastic and exaggerated legends that today it is often impossible to divide the true from the false." The stories retold primarily concerned the Civil War, the Ripley Railroad, and Falkner's death, and most glamorized his accomplishments.

Nevertheless, some stories had negative overtones concerning his shooting, which, decades later, ironically led his great-grandson William Faulkner to portray events leading up to the tragedy in like manner. In Faulkner's depiction, John Sartoris was a known killer who had shot several men and who often carried a derringer wired inside his sleeve. His "intolerant eyes . . . had acquired that transparent film which the eyes of carnivorous animals have . . . which I have seen before on the eyes of men who have killed too much."[38] Caught in a web of violence and exhausted, Sartoris refused to return fire on the fatal day on the courthouse square—and died. This characterization may have been John Sartoris, but it was not W. C. Falkner.

Figure 14.3. Detail of the head of Falkner from the Falkner mortuary monument in Ripley Cemetery as carved by Alessandro Lucchetti in Carrara, Italy. Photograph by Jack D. Elliott Jr.

In early 1890, the Falkner family, increasingly aware of the magnitude of the colonel's public persona, issued a call for proposals and bids for a memorial monument befitting someone of his stature.[39] Following several submissions, one was selected by July that had been submitted by C. J. Rogers, who owned a marble yard in Grand Junction, Tennessee. He promised to produce a sizeable monument with a granite pedestal surmounted by a marble statue of the colonel, all for $5,000.[40] To design the statue, the family sent Rogers a photo along with a suit of the colonel's clothes, the latter modeled for photos by a man standing in the desired pose with his right forearm sticking out as if in conversation. The photographs were then sent to Carrara, Italy, a center for producing marble statuary, where a likeness of Falkner was carved by sculptor Alessandro Lucchetti. Six blocks of granite for the pedestal to support the statue were ordered from Aberdeen, Scotland.[41] Upon arrival at Grand Junction, they were carved into their final form with the appropriate inscriptions and decor. The components were later shipped to Ripley by rail, where Rogers oversaw the construction of the monument, probably about January 1892. First, the ground near Falkner's grave was excavated and several courses of bricks were laid to form a foundation, following which the pedestal was erected to a height of 12.6 feet above the foundation, then the statue itself was raised atop the pedestal, making in all a monument that stands 19 feet tall.[42] The monument was apparently erected in January–early February 1892.[43]

As a more pragmatic matter, Falkner's death meant that an elected member of the legislature had to be replaced, so a special election was organized. Five candidates vied for the position. Although some were Falkner's former opponents in the August primary, one was new, Pink Smith, one of Falkner's leading supporters. The election was set for December 5, 1889, and Smith won in a landslide, receiving more votes than all four of his competitors combined.[44] One of his first actions in January was to introduce and have passed a resolution in the legislature paying tribute to Falkner by expressing "the high esteem in which he was held by this body and the people of the State."[45]

Thurmond had to appear before the grand jury, which convened at the courthouse in Ripley in early February. District Attorney Thomas Spight (serving 1884–1892 and later serving in the US Congress, 1898–1911), who was Falkner's friend, would head the prosecution. He confided to his wife that he had seen a list of jurors and noted that "it is a shame that so many of Thurmond[']s friends should have been appointed.... I am sure that they are appointed with a view to protecting Thurmond, but I don't intend they should do it if I have to ask the Judge to discharge them and summon new men."[46]

Several lawyers were present for the grand jury hearing. For the prosecution, there was District Attorney Spight, who was assisted by John M. Allen of Tupelo (a US congressman just arrived from Washington, DC) and C. J. Frederick of Fort Smith, Arkansas (Falkner's former law partner).[47] The defense was represented by another impressive slate of lawyers: Colonel C. B. Mitchell of Pontotoc, Ira D. Oglesby of Senatobia, Z. M. Stephens of New Albany, and Colonel Jim Fant of Holly Springs. Tension ran high. J. W. T. Falkner was in town for the deliberations and, presumably after a heated exchange, attacked Thurmond's nephew, Joseph Brown. After being arraigned before Mayor Nance's court on February 4, Falkner pleaded guilty to assault and battery and was fined $4 plus court costs for a total of $7.[48] On February 7, following several days of testimony, the grand jury returned an indictment of manslaughter, considerably less than the charge of first degree murder, which Falkner's supporters would have preferred. Apparently, Thurmond's attorneys recognized that there was no use fighting the charge that he had killed Falkner; everyone knew that he did, and there were numerous witnesses who could testify to it. By taking a charge of murder—intentional killing with malice—off the table, they effectively removed the possibility of the death sentence. They would next try to demonstrate that Thurmond's action was considered justifiable. Bond was set at $10,000, and Thurmond was released.[49] The press noted that "the failure of the prosecution to secure an indictment for murder has increased the growing public sentiment in favor of Thurmond, and it is now believed that he will be acquitted." The trial was set for the following Tuesday, February 11, and was heralded to be "the most celebrated murder case ever tried in Mississippi."[50]

On Tuesday, an "immense crowd" was in town for the trial including about one hundred witnesses who had been subpoenaed. However, Thurmond's lawyers reported that he was very ill, leaving his friends "apprehensive and uneasy about his condition." Consequently, the judge continued the trial to the next session of court, and the crowd that had assembled went home.[51]

Meanwhile, tension continued, and hostilities occasionally played out on the streets. On July 1, J. W. T. Falkner encountered J. W. "Jim" Harris in a store on Main Street in Ripley. Harris was the son of C. L. Harris, superintendent of the railroad and married to Thurmond's daughter Mary. Falkner had long suspected that Harris had influenced the grand jury in February. Heated words came to blows, with Falkner beating Harris on the head with an umbrella, for which he was arrested by the town police.[52] When the next term of court arrived in August, the case was given another continuance, reason unknown, and set for the following February.[53]

The case finally came to trial Wednesday morning, February 18, 1892, a session that found the courthouse jammed with spectators. District Attorney Spight, assisted by J. A. Blair of Tupelo and J. D. Fontaine of Pontotoc, led the prosecution, while Mitchell, Stephens, and Oglesby, the core of the legal team from the previous year, represented the defense. That day and the following were spent examining witnesses, while Friday the twentieth was devoted to the arguments of counsel.[54] For the prosecution, "the proof was that Thurman [sic] walked out of his office and shot Faulkner [sic] while he was doing nothing." The defense attempted to paint a more sinister picture, bringing forth witnesses to state that "many threats [had been] made by Faulkner to kill Thurmond" and to furthermore claim that on the day of the shooting, there had been "the seeking of a difficulty," which led to the scenario, as they portrayed it, that as "Thurmond walked out of his office, [Falkner] attempted to draw a weapon, when Thurmond quickly shot to save himself from being killed." Although the press claimed that evidence was "conflicting as to whether or not Faulkner was armed," yet the bottom line was that no gun was produced as evidence, and it's unlikely that there was one.[55] In fact, there was little reason for Falkner to attack Thurmond, given recent developments. On the other hand, Thurmond's resentment had placed him on the edge. If Falkner had made sarcastic comments, it could have pushed him over.

However, if Thurmond's attorneys wanted to make a case that the defendant was fearful of his life, it's unlikely that a gun was necessary. Having established hostility between the two men, any claim that Thurmond made about threatening behavior from Falkner would be credible. When Falkner approached Thurmond's office, he likely intended to needle him. There is no reason to think that Falkner was inclined to kill Thurmond. After all, he was riding high astride the world with yet another success. Thurmond had been alone with his thoughts watching Falkner circulating around the square receiving congratulations, which left him filled with anger and a sense of helplessness at being unable to stop him. Falkner understood this rage and decided to antagonize him with sarcasm and a smirk, and this was enough to drive Thurmond over the edge. As already noted, on a previous occasion Falkner had approached him and said in an insulting tone: "Well, here I am, Dick. What do you want of me?" and had been attacked. On this particular November 5, Thurmond responded by firing point blank at him. Subsequently, his attorneys had to get him out of what appeared to be a strong case of unpremeditated murder by claiming that he thought that his life was endangered. Of course, there was no such threat.

So, Thurmond's lawyers had to argue that if there wasn't a real threat, there was at least a perceived threat, and this wasn't difficult given the long-term hostility between the two men. If Falkner had reached into his pocket or even moved his hand toward his pocket, this could be construed as a threat and thereby a justification for shooting. Nor did there need be any questionable action on Falkner's part. All that the attorneys needed was to convince the jurors that Thurmond thought that he was threatened, and any statement from Thurmond to that effect—whether true or not—could be effective. With the right presentation, the claim could be compelling to any jury, even for members sympathetic toward Falkner. There was certainly a long tradition of such acquittals.

A reporter from Memphis observed that all of the attorneys "made able arguments, and well sustained their already well-known reputation. Seldom have four better, stronger, or more eloquent speeches been made in any case. The efforts of Messrs. Mitchell and Oglesby for the defense were especially brilliant and able."[56] On Friday night, District Attorney Spight closed the arguments, and the case was turned over to the jury. At noon the following day, they returned with a verdict: "not guilty."[57] Thurmond was free.

The *Southern Sentinel* observed that "there was no excitement and not a single 'scene' during the progress of the trial, and even the verdict was silently received by all."[58] The reporter for the *Commercial* concluded that "the verdict gives general satisfaction, and excitement has subsided."[59] His observation was inadequate. There were many in Ripley and elsewhere who questioned the ruling even though they knew there was nothing to be done. The editor of the *Grenada Sentinel* probably spoke for many in a column entitled "Justice Asleep while Cold Blooded Murder Stalks in Triumph through the Land," in which he thundered:

> Of course, the trial of Mr. Thurmond was put off from term to term so that the excitement might die out, and other things fixed to suit the slayer, as he was a rich man. Some weeks since he went through the form of a trial, with plenty of able lawyers and money to back him, and thus secured a verdict of acquittal by a "jury of his peers." It is useless to say what effect money had in securing his release. Such a verdict may make some people believe Mr. Thurmond was not guilty of a cold-blooded murder, but it will never convince Col. Falkner's thousands of friends all over Mississippi and elsewhere that he is an innocent man.[60]

Many in Ripley and elsewhere thought that Thurmond had killed one of the most prominent and well-liked men in the state and gotten away with it. The situation in Ripley following the verdict was tense. The majority clearly sided with Falkner, but Thurmond certainly had his own supporters. Andrew Brown noted that following the shooting and trial "Ripley was not a comfortable place in which to live. Practically every family in the town took sides in the Falkner-Thurmond controversy—in fact they had little choice because of the ties of kinship and business relationship."[61] He later recalled: "Father told me long ago that it would take 25 years for the county to get over the schisms that started them, and he was wrong; they lasted until almost 1940—50 years. By that time many of the cliques in the county had forgotten the cause of their troubles, and to be honest, the Falkner-Thurmond affair was only one of several reasons for the situation!"[62]

There is apparently truth in this statement, although it is hard to document. One would certainly expect animosity between the main families involved despite the fact that this was complicated by marital connections between the two parties. For example, Dr. John Y. Murry's second marriage was to Mary Miller, the sister of Margaret (Mrs. R. J.) Thurmond, while a daughter by his first marriage was married to J. W. T. Falkner. Andrew Brown, the geologist and historian, was the grandson of Sallie Miller Brown, sister to Mary Young and Margaret Thurmond, yet his mother's brother, Pink Smith, editor of the *Southern Sentinel*, "almost idolized the Colonel."[63]

One thing seems clear: given Falkner's popularity, the overwhelming majority certainly had more sympathy for him than for Thurmond, as evidenced by newspaper statements to that effect and by the fact that Falkner was their candidate of choice. At this time, one Ed J. Thurmond, a native of Georgia, resided in Ripley. To my knowledge, he was not related to R. J. Thurmond. On September 5, 1892—a year after the court acquittal—Ed's wife Mary gave birth to a son, whom they named Colonel Falkner Thurmond.[64] They were seemingly making a statement that they might be Thurmonds, but they were not part of *those* Thurmonds. They were clearly in the Falkner camp and not supporters of R. J. Thurmond. Many certainly shared their sympathies. Decades later, William Faulkner would give a name to a character in a short story ("Barn Burning") with the same oxymoronic quality: Colonel Sartoris Snopes.

It has been commonly reported that animosities remaining after the acquittal were such that several key citizens, notably Thurmond, were effectively forced to leave town. Brown reports that because "the atmosphere was so charged with suspicion that some of the town's most prominent citizens—including the Falkner and Thurmond families—moved away."[65] Brown also noted that "Thurmond wound up his extensive business affairs in Ripley as soon as he could and then returned to his original home in North Carolina, where he spent the remainder of his life."[66] Others claimed that the Thurmonds departed Ripley to escape the animosity oriented toward them. William Faulkner noted simply that R. J. Thurmond "left the country, went out West."[67] Duclos wrote: "Once Thurmond was free, he was urged immediately to leave town for his own safety. Together with his immediate family . . . [he] moved to Surry County, North Carolina where his two daughters married Chatham brothers."[68]

However, the truth is more complex and contradicts the claim that anyone departed as the result of social tensions. Regarding the Falkners, J. W. T. Falkner had already moved to Oxford before the shooting. The colonel's youngest daughter, Bama, moved to Memphis following her 1893 marriage. Willie Falkner Carter and her husband moved to Meridian in 1901. Other Falkners left Ripley following the 1902 sale of the railroad.

As for Thurmond, he continued to live in Ripley following his acquittal. However, his connection to the state of his birth, North Carolina, was reestablished when in 1894, in Ripley, his daughter, Martha "Mattie" Thurmond, married Hugh G. Chatham of Elkin, Surry County, North Carolina, and the couple took up residence in Elkin.[69] Soon after, the Thurmonds began to travel annually to Elkin, in part because of their daughter but also because the summers were cooler there than in Ripley.[70] Then, another daughter, Dewitt, married Paul Chatham, Hugh's brother, and they took up residence in Elkin.[71] During a trip to the North Carolina town in 1900, Mrs. Thurmond was hospitalized and died. An obituary noted that she "had been spending the summer here with her daughters for the past six years and so fond had she become of the place and people that she had decided to leave her home in Miss., the home of her life time and come here to live."[72] Despite this, her husband continued residing in Ripley part of the year and Elkin the other part,[73] until early 1907, when he tried to permanently establish himself in Elkin.[74] Death brought his plans to an end. Before the year was over, he died in St. Peter's Hospital, Charlotte, North Carolina, on November 18, 1907, during an unspecified operation[75] and was buried beside his wife in Hollywood Cemetery in Elkin. There is no indication that his move to Elkin was motivated by intimidation at Ripley.

Chapter 15

Aftermath

The Later Years of the Railroad

The reading of Falkner's will revealed that while there were several large bequests made to family members, most of his estate would remain intact and overseen by a board of trustees consisting of his son John, his sons-in-law N. G. Carter and Ed F. Campbell, and his friends Joseph J. Guyton and J. V. Shepherd. The net income was to be divided every year equally between his widow and his children.[1] Of direct relevance to his estate, on February 20, 1890, an act passed in the legislature ratifying the incorporation of the G&C Railroad and declaring it to be the lawful successor of the Ripley Railroad Company as chartered in 1871.[2]

After Falkner's death, Warwick Place lay empty, with Lizzie residing in Memphis. In April 1891, she advertised the house for sale at $1,500, considerably cheaper than the $5,000 she estimated it to be worth. The advertisement ran for months in the *Sentinel*, but there were no buyers.[3] However, in the spring of 1893, she had a change of heart. After deeding the house to Effie and Bama as a gift,[4] she returned to Ripley and moved into the house, restoring it and painting it green in the process.[5] On September 14, nineteen-year-old Bama was married at Warwick Place to Walter B. McLean, a businessman with William R. Moore and Company of Memphis.[6] They later established a residence on Peabody Avenue in Memphis, and in 1896 Lizzie, along with Effie, who was by then apparently separated from Campbell, moved to Memphis.[7] In 1897, Lizzie, Effie, and the McLeans were all listed residing at 20 Peabody Avenue.[8]

Almost three years after Falkner's death, an incident occurred in Pontotoc that almost resulted in the death of his grandson Murry Falkner and that brought his son J. W. T. Falkner into court on a charge of attempted murder. Murry was two years old when the railroad was opened to Ripley. Although he grew up in proximity to the railroad, he had to leave it for a time when his family moved to Oxford in 1885. However, upon coming of age, he became professionally involved with the railroad when in September 1890, only one month past his twentieth birthday, he was hired as the conductor on the regular train that ran daily from Pontotoc to Middleton and back. In Pontotoc he boarded in the home of T. J. Nelson, the depot agent formerly of Tippah County.[9]

His duty as conductor involved walking each morning a few blocks to the depot where the locomotive awaited. The job of conductor required considerable experience and responsibility. In effect, he was in charge of the train in everything except the mechanical operations, which are overseen by the engineer. After departing Pontotoc, the train covered the sixty-three miles to Middleton, stopping at every depot to pick up and drop off passengers and freight. In Middleton the train picked up the mail, which was delivered to the post offices along the route.

Despite his responsibilities, he soon gained a reputation, being described as the "handsome dissipated conductor" who was "a considerable drunkard for his age." He was known for gambling and when drunk he "would try to ride his horse into the business houses of Pontotoc." By the fall of 1892, Murry was twenty-two years old and enamored with a local beauty, Martha "Pattie" Fontaine, who was three years younger than him and the daughter of the recently deceased Dr. Madison R. Fontaine. Gossips reported that Pattie was "so deeply in love with Mr. Falkner she would ride in the baggage car with him to Middleton, drink with him, treat him to some, etc., so it is said."[10] The association with Miss Fontaine would soon lead to trouble.

A young woman named Mollie Walker worked as a seamstress for Pattie and her mother. On one occasion, Pattie became verbally abusive as the result of her displeasure with Mollie's dress work. Mollie replied that even "if she was a poor dressmaker, she was above riding about at twelve o'clock at night with a drunkard and gambler." Pattie informed Murry of these comments, and Murry informed Mollie's brother J. Elias Walker, who owned a store on the north side of the square, demanding that he force his sister to end her comments. Walker of course sided with his sister, and the dispute became a heated argument that devolved into fisticuffs, with Murry getting the upper hand.[11]

The following day, Thursday, October 13, as Murry was away on the train, Elias Walker fumed and nursed his rage with alcohol. When the train returned to Pontotoc, Murry was suffering from a headache. While the engineer and fireman shut the locomotive down for the night, Murry walked up Marion Street to Mitchell and Barringer's Drug Store to seek relief. The store was in part owned by the young Dr. Charles Dennis Mitchell, whose father, attorney Charles Baldwin Mitchell, had served on the defense team that achieved acquittal for R. J. Thurmond the previous year. Druggist Thomas Herron, the father-in-law of Dr. Mitchell, operated the store. Walker's store was only a few doors down, and from there he saw Murry enter the drugstore. While Murry stood at the counter awaiting his medicine, Walker suddenly appeared at the door with a shotgun loaded with duck shot and demanded for him to "take back" what he had said. He then fired at Falkner, hitting him just above the right kidney and causing him to fall to the floor just before the second blast demolished a chair beyond him. Walker advanced closer, drew a 44-caliber pistol, and shot Falkner in the face. The bullet hit just below the lower lip and ranged upward into his head. Perhaps sobered by the result of his fury, Walker started to leave but was detained by bystanders and soon taken into custody by the sheriff and placed in the county jail. With the incident all too reminiscent of his grandfather's shooting three years before, Murry was placed heavily bleeding on an improvised stretcher and carried the three blocks along Main Street to the Nelson home, where his wounds were treated by Dr. Mitchell.[12]

Murry's family began to assemble in Pontotoc no doubt fearful that they were witnessing a replay of the deathwatch of Colonel Falkner. His parents arrived from Oxford. The *Southern Sentinel* reported that "Mr. Ed Campbell and wife [Effie] and Miss Bama Falkner, passed through on a special Friday evening" on their way to Pontotoc. W. H. Hines was appointed as temporary conductor to take Murry's place. Initially, Dr. Mitchell's diagnosis was grave: recovery seemed impossible. However, as days passed and Murry continued to live, there was room for optimism, and by the following week it was reported that he was "resting well and will probably recover."[13]

Sallie Falkner continued to stay with and nurse her son, while her husband moved back and forth between Oxford and Pontotoc. Within a few weeks Elias Walker was allowed out of jail on a $2,500 bond.[14] By mid-November Murry had recovered sufficiently that his parents planned to move him to Oxford for full recovery. On November 17, the *Oxford Eagle* reported that J. W. T. and Sallie Falkner had departed for Pontotoc to bring Murry back to Oxford.[15] The trip turned into a disaster. The Falkners arrived in Pontotoc the same day, but the details of what happened that evening are uncertain. Apparently drinking, Falkner went to Walker's store on the square with a pistol, where, as it turned out, Walker also had a pistol. Tempers rose and guns were fired. The newspaper account recorded that "Falkner and Walker were endeavoring to shoot each other and both had trouble in getting their pistols to work. Walker getting only one shot out of his and Falkner failed to get a shot from his at all." Falkner was shot in the hand, resulting in a wound that wasn't serious but was nevertheless quite painful.[16] Presumably the two men were jailed until bond could be posted. This was Falkner's third run-in with the law in as many years, with all involving physical violence. Two days later, Saturday, November 19, Murry was transported back to Oxford via rail.[17]

When the circuit court met again on January 7, 1893, indictments were handed down. The court indicted Walker on the charge of shooting with the intent to kill, while it indicted J. W. T. Falkner for assaulting Walker. Because neither the prosecution nor the defense was ready, the case was put off until the next session of court. Interestingly, one of the attorneys for the defense was Charles B. Mitchell, who had been on Thurmond's defense team two years before. The *Southern Sentinel* astutely observed that J. W. T. Falkner's attack on Walker had weakened the case against the latter.[18]

However, the case didn't come up until July, at which time the *Oxford Eagle* laconically observed that "Col. J. W. T. Falkner is attending court in Pontotoc this week."[19] He was indeed attending court, but not as many would have expected. In response to the charges of "shooting to kill" each other, both apparently pleaded guilty and were fined $500 each, with the fines suspended pending their good behavior toward the other.[20] These were light sentences by any reckoning.

It would be four years from the shooting before Murry returned to working on the railroad. On Monday, September 28, 1896, he departed Oxford for New Albany.[21] He was now twenty-six and perhaps considered more seasoned for the new job, that of general freight agent, a position earlier held by his uncle E. F. Campbell. Two months later Murry took off long enough to return to Oxford to marry his fiancée, Maud Butler, on the evening of Sunday, November 8.[22] Maud was soon pregnant and gave birth on September 25, 1897, at their home in New Albany to their first son, William, named after his great-grandfather. Decades later their sojourn there was embellished by a garbled retelling of the 1892 shooting in Pontotoc, reset in New Albany.[23]

From its construction in 1872, the Ripley Railroad had no associated telegraph line. This changed in 1895 under R. J. Shannon of Tiplersville, who established what came to be called the Southwestern Telegraph Company. Early in that year, the *Southern Sentinel* reported that he had a plan underway to provide telegraphic service to connect Ripley with the Western Union lines at Middleton. He was at the time working on a contract with the railroad, and President J. W. T. Falkner had indicated that support would be forthcoming.[24] By mid-March most of the required materials had been ordered, and chestnut poles were being placed along the railroad right-of-way.[25] Within two months the line had been erected from Middleton to Tiplersville and was advancing toward Ripley.[26] Shannon's son, M. L. Shannon, was moved to Ripley to take over a telegraph office in the Ripley depot. As soon as the line reached town, the first telegram was transmitted from Middleton to Ripley on May 15.[27]

With the line completed to Ripley, the company continued building and reached New Albany by August. When completed to Pontotoc by early September, it provided telegraphic service for the entire G&C. M. L. Shannon was then moved from Ripley to Pontotoc, where he took charge of the office there, while R. O. McCarley took over the Ripley office.[28]

Effie and her husband, E. F. Campbell, were apparently divorced about 1895, and soon after she remarried, to Al E. Davis, an Ohio native.[29] He was soon appointed as auditor and general manager of the G&C, a job in which he proved very competent. Besides overseeing the day-to-day operations of the railroad, he also made significant improvements such as installing a telegraph to connect his office to the Ripley depot,[30] bringing in a pile driver to refurbish the Tallahatchie Bridge near New Albany,[31] and purchasing a new thirty-ton passenger locomotive, #10.[32] He also made business trips to Chicago and Washington, DC.[33]

His experience and efficiency were of great value, although as Brown notes it caused "quite a bit of misery in the Ripley shops," where not all were used to the new standards.

> Before Davis' arrival maintenance of equipment had been carried on by local mechanics, who managed to keep the wheels turning but who at times were neither orthodox nor efficient in their way of doing so. One of the "old hands" at the shop, T. C. Cox, often told of his first meeting with Davis. Cox was repairing a locomotive when the new General Manager walked by and said, "you're doing that all wrong; that's not the way to fix it," and then explained in detail how the job should be done. The unabashed Cox retorted, "I've fixed it this way before and the engine always runs, even if it is wrong. Let's see you fix it right and see if it will run; I'll bet it won't." It was along time before Cox was willing to admit that Davis knew anything about locomotives.[34]

In 1898, the Davises moved into Warwick Place after having it refurbished and repainted, and they resided there for the next four years.[35] Effie's mother and her sister Bama soon paid them a visit from Memphis, staying again in the old home.[36] Lizzie and Bama continued to be regular visitors.[37]

On November 7, 1898, the directors and primary officials of the G&C met in Ripley. One of the first items of business was the resignation of C. L. Harris as superintendent. He was presumably ready to retire, having held the position for about twenty years, almost since he and C. E. Hines had bought into the railroad. He and his family soon moved to Memphis. Subsequently his position was abolished, with the duties subsumed under that of general manager, the position held by A. E. Davis, while Murry Falkner, the son of President J. W. T. Falkner, was promoted to auditor and claims agent. He had been depot agent in New Albany, but the change of position entailed his moving to Ripley along with his wife and one-year-old son, William.[38] At the end of the meeting, the slate of officials for the railroad were: J. W. T. Falkner, president; Dr. N. G. Carter, vice president; A. E. Davis, general manager; and Murry Falkner, auditor and claims agent.

Soon after Colonel Falkner's death, his daughter Willie commissioned a memorial stained-glass window in his honor. Beneath "In Memoriam," it had his name and dates followed by the passage "He that giveth to the poor, lendeth to the Lord" (Proverbs 19:17). She had the window placed in the Baptist Church across the street from the colonel's home but later removed it to her own home, where it was installed in the library—the very room in which he had died—giving it an aura of sanctity.[39]

Murry's son, young William, or "Willie" as he was called at the time, often visited his great-aunt Willie Carter, who had taken a special liking to him, possibly because he bore the same name as her father.[40] Memories often leave an indelible impact on personality formation. One such example for the boy was the library, a room filled with books and the memory of the death of his great-grandfather, a room that during the daylight was suffused with the colored light that filtered through the stained glass window, created to memorialize his ancestor as one would memorialize a saint in a church window. The influence of the colonel on his great-grandson was such that the latter's brother Jack Falkner thought that William had either consciously or unconsciously modeled his life after the colonel's. "He spoke of him often, and it has been said that, as a child, he was asked what he wanted to become in life and he replied, 'A writer, like my great-grandfather.'"[41]

For decades after the family left Ripley, William Faulkner was influenced by another of the colonel's daughters, Bama, who almost certainly told him stories about her father. Later he corresponded with her and after he became a published author would send her inscribed copies of his new publications. His first child, a daughter named Alabama, was named after her.[42] Robert W. Hamblin has suggested that in the image of Quentin Compson from *Absalom, Absalom!* one can easily imagine young Faulkner listening to Bama telling about her father:

So maybe you will enter the literary profession as so many Southern gentlemen and gentlewomen too are doing and maybe some day you will remember this and write about it. . . . Perhaps you will even remember kindly then the old woman who made you spend a whole afternoon sitting indoors and listening while she talked about people and events you were fortunate enough to escape yourself when you wanted to be out among young friends of your own age.[43]

Of course, as Hamblin has pointed out, there were many others who remembered and told tales that often disagreed in details about the colonel, so the image was created from a mosaic of sources. Furthermore, even the colonel's novels *The White Rose of Memphis* and *The Little Brick Church* presented narratives in which secondary narratives with accompanying documents were pieced together to support the overarching narratives in which the past was juxtaposed with the novels' present. The effect on the young writer was immeasurable in terms of presenting the past as seen from multiple perspectives, a method he carried on into his Yoknapatawpha mythos. Hamblin described this process:

Faulkner's comments about the oral transmission of history and the conflicting versions of that history find exact corollaries in the fictional technique of the Yoknapatawpha stories. The best example is *Absalom, Absalom!* . . . Faulkner chooses to present the story primarily as it is assembled and interpreted by Quentin Compson two generations later. . . . The general outline of the story Quentin knows, as all Jeffersonians do, "from having been born and living beside it, with it" (212). . . . Thus Quentin is forced to piece the story together, as Faulkner writes, "out of the rag-tag and bob-ends of old tales and talking" (303). Since no one of Quentin's sources knows the complete story (and much they presume to know is based on hearsay), and since each of the separate accounts reflects a particular attitude or bias, Quentin (and the reader) must infer the actual story from the multiple and contradictory treatments. The result of this Chinese box arrangement is not only one of the greatest detective stories in the English language but also a grand metaphor of the circuitous and problematical ways in which human beings assimilate and interpret the events of the past. And it is precisely in this manner that Faulkner inherited the stories of his great-grandfather W. C. Falkner.[44]

The railroad continued to operate and grow. In August 1894, a new locomotive was purchased from the Pittsburgh Car Works. Numbered #9, it was named *Houston* after the county seat of Chickasaw County, the next town south of Pontotoc. The name suggested the goal of continuing to building the road south from Pontotoc.[45] Of course, older stock was wearing out, and in May 1897 the *Sentinel* reported that locomotive #1, *Dolly*, one of the original pair of locomotives acquired in 1872, was "carried away, DEAD, Saturday morning." It was noted that "a newer and larger engine . . . will soon be put on the road," and the following month it was reported that a new locomotive was in operation.[46] That summer the company began constructing a roundhouse in Ripley.[47] In early 1902, the company purchased another locomotive, from the Baldwin Locomotive Works of Philadelphia, that was numbered #10. Several new and larger passenger coaches were also purchased.[48]

In October 1901, all interest in the railroad was apparently consolidated into ownership by the Falkners.[49] With this, the family was in a position to sell to a larger corporation, and such a corporation was by then looming on the horizon, ready to take the road into its third phase of construction. The third phase again entailed involvement with outside sources of capital, although this time there would be no local leader involved. The railroad would become simply a segment in a transregional mainline railroad organized and operated by outside interests. In this, the outside input would come from the Mobile, Jackson, and Kansas City (MJ&KC) Railroad, which found it expedient in constructing a trunk line from Mobile to Jackson, Tennessee, to acquire and utilize the G&C.

The railroad emerged out of several earlier corporations that were consolidated as the MJ&KC in 1890 with the intent of building a road that ran out of Mobile in a northwesterly direction toward Jackson, Mississippi, and Kansas City, although this plan would radically change within a few years. Following several years in which nothing other than surveying was accomplished, construction began in December 1896. Within a few months it was constructed to the Pascagoula River in Mississippi, where construction came to a halt. A town was founded there on the riverbank named Merrill after Colonel Frank Merrill, president of the company.[50] As late as November 1901, Merrill was still the terminus,[51] although that would radically change.

Earthwork was initially begun from Merrill on a path toward Hattiesburg, which was in turn en route to Jackson, Mississippi. The track into Hattiesburg was laid by November 1902.[52] However, before that was accomplished, an alternate route was established branching off east of Hattiesburg and heading north to Laurel and points beyond. By November 1901 there were rumblings that this route would pass through Jasper County in the direction of Newton or Hickory. No one was certain where it was going.[53] But it was clearly not going to Jackson, Mississippi. By May 1902 there was speculation that the railroad had an option to buy the G&C Railroad, with the smaller road to be used as a link in the larger scheme, as with the G&SI project. Indeed, there were already surveyors in the field establishing a route to connect the MJ&KC with the G&C.[54]

As it turned out, there was substance to these rumors. On June 26, 1902, a headline in the *Southern Sentinel* reported: "Sale of Gulf & Chicago Railroad Verified by Manager A. E. Davis." The accompanying article explained that the MJ&KC had purchased the G&C for a sum of between $360,000 and $370,000. The deal had been closed the previous week at a meeting of stockholders, which included President J. W. T. Falkner, Vice President N. G. Carter, General Manager A. E. Davis, and Trustees J. J. Guyton and J. V. Shepherd. The road would change hands on July 1, while Davis would remain as manager until August 1.[55] The G&C continued to exist as a corporation but as a subsidiary of the MJ&KC, and it was rechartered as such in April 1903. The legislation specified that the G&C would cover the portion of the route from Decatur, Mississippi, in the south northward, including the existing route from Pontotoc to Middleton and terminating in Jackson, Tennessee.[56] It was evidently intended that the MJ&KC would own the railroad south of Decatur. A board of directors was appointed that included John Y. Murry Jr. of Ripley, the brother-in-law of J. W. T. Falkner.[57] Soon after, all of the lettering on the rolling stock was altered to read: "MJ&KC, G&C Ry. Co., Owners."[58]

With their ties to the railroad severed, the last Falkners began to depart Ripley. The Carters had already left the year before, moving to Meridian, Mississippi, where they lived the remainder of their lives. The reason for their departure is unknown.[59] Murry Falkner and family left on September 25, 1902—his oldest son William's fifth birthday—for Oxford, where his parents resided.[60] Of the colonel's daughters, only Effie and A. E. Davis remained. On September 28, Lizzie, who was residing with Bama in Memphis, returned to Ripley for one last visit to Warwick Place.[61] On October 20, the family sold the home to Lynn Spight, son of Captain Thomas Spight, and the last of the Falkners left town.[62] Lizzie continued to reside with Bama in Memphis, but in 1910 she went for a visit with the Davises, who were then residing near Richmond, Virginia. There, Lizzie became ill and died. She was apparently buried in Richmond.[63]

In early September 1903 it was announced that the MJ&KC had awarded a contract to C. D. Smith and Company, a general contractor from Memphis, for constructing 150 miles of the G&C division extending from Newton, Mississippi, to Pontotoc. The contract also included converting the 63 miles of the G&C from Middleton to Pontotoc to standard gauge. Survey parties were being put into the field to complete the surveys necessary before construction could begin.[64]

Work began at three separate staging areas. In the south, the railroad from Mobile and Beaumont continued building north through Laurel to Newton, where by March 1904 it intersected the Alabama and Vicksburg Railroad, which connected Vicksburg, Jackson, and Meridian, Mississippi. From there it continued north. At the northern end, operations were set up at New Albany, which could be accessed by the Kansas City, Memphis, and Birmingham standard-gauge road to bring in standard-gauge rolling stock for construction purposes. The first priority was to standardize the gauge south of New Albany to Pontotoc, then continue building in standard gauge from there. The conversion was completed by June 1904, and by June 20 construction had proceeded two miles south of Pontotoc.[65] Standardizing the gauge from New Albany to Middleton would be left for later. In the meantime, the G&C continued to operate as a narrow gauge between these two towns. Finally, in November at the center of the projected line, C. D. Smith and Company established a construction headquarters at Ackerman, Mississippi, which was also accessible by a standard-gauge line. From Ackerman, they began building both north and south with the intent of linking up with the southern and northern divisions.[66]

Construction south from Pontotoc continued, with the railroad opening to Houston twenty-five miles to the south in November 1904. Several months later, this section joined with that being built north from Ackerman, providing continuous rail from Mobile to Middleton, although the northern forty-four miles were still narrow gauge.

In early 1905, standardizing began on the remaining narrow-gauge section between New Albany and Middleton beginning in New Albany. As new track advanced, the narrow gauge decreased accordingly. By February the work reached Cotton Plant; early March, Blue Mountain; March 17, Ripley; mid-April, Falkner; and by late June it was completed to Middleton. As the standard-gauge rails moved past Ripley, the *Sentinel* editor commented that "The 'doodle bug' train in Ripley, like the glory of Rome, is a thing of the past."[67]

The standardizing of track over the last section of the railroad meant that the rolling stock—locomotives, passenger cars, flatcars, and so on—was now obsolete and had to be sold either for scrap or for reuse elsewhere. So, the old, familiar locomotives and cars disappeared to be replaced by larger ones designed for standard gauge.

Figure 15.1. Transforming the railroad to standard gauge at Walnut in 1905. From the GM&O Historical Society archives.

The last remaining gap in the construction was located south of Ackerman near Philadelphia, Mississippi. On September 5, 1905, that gap was filled when construction teams coming from the south and the north laid the last rail on a trestle over the Pearl River bottom.[68] With this, the railroad was open from Mobile to Middleton. Part of Colonel Falkner's dream—that of having his road reach the Gulf—was fulfilled.

However, the MJ&KC was soon in financial difficulty. The costs of construction accompanied by low profits resulted in its being placed in receivership under F. E. Dewey and J. Lewis Dantzeler. In August 1909, the MJ&KC along with its subsidiary, the G&C, were sold at foreclosure and consolidated under a new company, the New Orleans, Mobile, and Chicago. Despite the railroad's financial difficulties, it continued operating and maintaining its infrastructure. By June 1909, construction began on a new depot in Ripley located one block to the south of the original. By August it was completed and in operation, with the original being demolished.[69]

The New Orleans, Mobile, and Chicago soon experienced financial difficulties and was reorganized on January 1, 1917, as the Gulf Mobile and Northern GM&N, and under this name it was extended northward. In that year, a

Figure 15.2. Locomotive #3, known variously as the *Colonel W. C. Falkner* or *Tanglefoot*, is loaded on a flatcar after becoming obsolete in 1905 with the end of the narrow gauge. This locomotive had been in service since the beginning of the Ripley Railroad in 1872. Courtesy of Tommy Covington.

contract was let to build twenty miles of railroad north from Middleton,[70] and two years later construction carried it to Jackson, Tennessee.[71]

Subsequently, the GM&N made new rail acquisitions along with arrangements to use the tracks of other lines, eventually allowing it to establish a rail connection that linked it with Chicago by 1926. In that year, a headline read: "Dreams of Colonel Falkner are Real." The accompanying piece, by the editor of the *Southern Sentinel*, summed things up:

> At last the dream of the late Col. W. C. Falkner, founder of the present G.M. and N. railroad and for many years a leading citizen of Ripley is nearing realization. Last Sunday the first train in the history of the road went through to Chicago and points north of there. . . . It is said that when Col. Falkner first built the short narrow-gauge line from Middleton, Tenn., to Ripley . . . he looked into the future and predicted that someday his little railroad would become one of the greatest roads of the land and that over it would travel through trains from the Gulf of Mexico to the Great Lakes. At last this dream has become realized and great through trains pass daily within sight of the artistic marble likeness of Col. Falkner in the Ripley cemetery where rest his bones and by the place that was his home for many years.[72]

In honor of the occasion, Falkner's youngest daughter, Bama, arrived in Ripley from Memphis with her husband, Walter McLean, following an absence of decades. The couple stayed the night and following day. Bama was "interested in the growth and progress of the town and went about seeking points of interest remembered in her girlhood days and with which her illustrious father was interested." She visited the former J. W. Thompson home, where her father had lived as a young man and where her brother J. W. T. Falkner had later lived. She then visited her family home two blocks away, which was occupied by Lynn Spight, the son of her father's friend Tom Spight. The *Sentinel* noted: "So many changes had come about that she saw but few places that seemed natural to her recollection of many years ago." By 1926 the frame stores and offices that the colonel knew that surrounded the square, the product of postbellum rebuilding, were almost gone, replaced with brick. The old depot had been demolished and replaced by another a block to the south. However, she "found a number of people whom she remembered, and her heart was made glad to renew with them the old acquaintances and hear them talk about her father and mother and the days of her own childhood."[73]

Other changes soon followed. The courthouse was rebuilt in 1928. Although its core remained, it was covered with additions, giving it the appearance of a structure that her father would not have recognized. In 1937, the family home was demolished to build a brick post office and a two-story apartment house that was later transformed into a clinic. Material salvaged from the Falkner home—both wood and iron components—were used in the building of the apartment house.

Railroad service continued to improve. In 1935, the GM&N instituted the Rebel line, a passenger line that was lightweight and streamlined, pulled by diesel-electric locomotives. To call attention to the new luxury line, Bama Falkner McLean was called on to give her blessings to the new line. She of course approved and offered some memories of her father and the earlier railroad.[74] Soon after, in 1940, the GM&N was consolidated with the Mobile and Ohio to form the Gulf Mobile and Ohio (GM&O), and the Rebel line continued to operate on an expanded rail system. There were two Rebel lines that served northeastern Mississippi. The Little Rebel followed the old GM&N tracks through Ripley on a route from New Orleans to Jackson, Tennessee. The Big Rebel followed the old M&O tracks to the east, passing through Tupelo and Corinth on the route from Mobile to St. Louis.

However, the railroad would soon fall victim to competition from the growing highway system and the increasing number of automobiles and trucks. Declining passenger use after World War II resulted in the discontinuance of the Little Rebel in 1954 and the Big Rebel in 1958. Freight that had been shipped by rail was transferred to trucks. As miles of rail began to be abandoned throughout the country, service on Falkner's rails also suffered. In 2004, the Surface Transportation Board, a federal agency, authorized the abandonment of the track between New Albany and Houston, and two years later it approved the abandonment of most of the track between Ripley and Middleton. This left in service only enough rail to constitute a spur line connecting Ripley to a trunk line in New Albany. Today this line, under the name the Ripley and New Albany Railroad, serves several industries along its route, a mere shadow of Falkner's railroad. Of the railroad right-of-way between New Albany and Houston, 43.6 miles were converted into a biking/hiking path known as the Tanglefoot Trail, which opened in September 2013. It was named after the locomotive *Tanglefoot*, the nickname given to the *Colonel W. C. Falkner*.

In terms of the great railroad builders of the late nineteenth century such as Cornelius Vanderbilt, James J. Hill, and Thomas Durant, W. C. Falkner hardly compared in terms of miles of railroad constructed. The former constructed hundreds if not thousands of miles, while Falkner constructed only about sixty-three. While the railroad magnates were based in the great cities with all their concentration of wealth, Falkner was based in a town of fewer than one thousand people with a comparably modest concentration of capital. Yet, given his resources, he was able to accomplish much. Others had tried to construct a spur line to Ripley and had failed, but Falkner had succeeded while dreaming of turning the twenty-five-mile-long spur line into a transcontinental carrier. Although this was not accomplished in his lifetime, his dream would be fulfilled by others.

Throughout his life, he demonstrated broad interests with a tendency toward unorthodox solutions to problems—such as transforming a spur line into a trunk line—which often placed himself in tension if not conflict with those less adventurous than he. For a few years, Ripley had in residence someone whom most loved, who was always planning something, whether railroad construction or a new book or a new play or a political campaign. And he was very reachable, mingling and laughing. Then he was gone, his life snuffed out, and the people mourned . . . and talked, telling stories about his accomplishments and the unjustness of his death. The stories grew over the years immediately following Falkner's death, but under ordinary circumstances they would have eventually faded with the passage of time.

Then in 1929, when railroads were still booming, Falkner's great-grandson and namesake published his novel *Sartoris*, the first in his series of

Yoknapatawpha stories. The turn to writing about his own world was due to the writer Sherwood Anderson, who in the mid-1920s served as a mentor to the younger Faulkner when both were living in the French Quarter of New Orleans. At the time, Faulkner was working on his first two novels, one set in Georgia and the other in New Orleans. Anderson had built his career on fiction set in small-town Ohio, where he had grown up, leading him to suggest that the younger man turn to his own roots for inspiration: "You're a country boy; all you know is that little patch up there in Mississippi where you started from."[75] And heeding the advice, Faulkner turned to his own lifeworld, to the memory of home, of Oxford and of Ripley.

Ripley was at the very origin of his memory and experience. His earliest memories were of tree-lined Jackson Street, where he had lived for several years as a child and which like all the streets in town was unpaved. Carriages and wagons passing by threw up clouds of dust during the summer and during the winter struggled through mudholes. Faulkner's brother John was born on this street when the homes of his great-grandfather Dr. John Y. Murry and R. J. Thurmond were also there. East of Jackson Street, the ground dropped down to a small stream before rising again to high ground where the courthouse square was located. Many times, he had accompanied his mother as she shopped on the square, entering store after store, often passing by the spot where his great-grandfather had been shot. A block north of the square was Warwick Place, where his aunt Effie Davis had lived. He knew that this had been the old colonel's home. Another block to the north was the home of his aunt, Willie Carter, where he had often visited. The colonel had died here in the library, where light passing through the stained-glass memorial left an aura of sanctity in his memory, an aura only enhanced by the nineteen-foot-high monument atop which his ancestor communed with angels and heroes. And through the land passed the two parallel ribbons of steel—in those days still narrow gauge—the primary route connecting the town to distant parts. Although the younger Faulkner had never known the colonel, his presence suffused the environment and the new novel. When *Sartoris* appeared in print, those who knew Faulkner's family knew who Colonel John Sartoris really was.

In 1938, the emerging author recalled to a visiting reporter that he "had been writing about Colonel Falkner, in the character of Colonel Sartoris, when the concept of his great cycle of novels took hold of his imagination."[76] From having influenced him to be a writer, the older Falkner and his historical geographic context became a cornerstone of his imagery of Yoknapatawpha County. Upon completing *Sartoris*, Faulkner turned again to his experience of places and persons and expanded upon the initial novel with additional interconnected Yoknapatawpha stories, which like shards of a partially reassembled ceramic vessel suggest a larger order or cosmos.

As the Greeks originally defined it, the cosmos represented the ordered whole of the world. However, from our perspective within the cosmos, we cannot see the entirety of reality but instead only a limited portion from which we extrapolate. What we do know comes from the past, from remembered experience, which is mediated through stories, events, persons, and objects. As earlier noted, Faulkner referred to Yoknapatawpha as his own "cosmos," although his own "analogy to the cosmos" is more appropriate, with all such symbolic expressions being limited and incomplete. In 1932, Faulkner considered producing a grand overview of his county's history in a work to be called "The Golden Book of Jefferson and Yoknapatawpha County in Mississippi as compiled by William Faulkner of Rowanoak [sic]." But this was not to be. Virtually all that was ever written of the "Golden Book" was a seven-hundred-word biography of John Sartoris.[77]

In contrast to our knowledge via remembrance from the past, the future is only a matter of anticipation. Tales of Yoknapatawpha are incomplete, looking toward an unseen but anticipated future—an orientation to transcendent horizons. As Faulkner stated in his Nobel Prize acceptance speech, we must remember "the old verities and truths of the heart [and] the old universal truths," and with that comes the anticipation that "man will not merely endure: he will prevail." He continued by stating that the writer's "privilege [is to] help man endure by lifting his heart, by reminding him of the courage and honor and hope and pride and compassion and pity and sacrifice which have been the glory of his past."[78] One is forcibly reminded of his great-grandfather's vision of building not merely a spur line that would take his hometown out of the mud but of transforming the project into a railroad that would span the continent.

In an examination of the colonel's influence on his great-grandson, Robert W. Hamblin has suggested that it emerged in the experienced contrast of a past mediated through memory, legends, symbols, artifacts, and buildings and the knowledge that the actual past was never fully mediated by any methods or other intermediaries.

W. C. Falkner was arguably the single greatest influence upon the fiction of William Faulkner. He is indisputably the prototype of John Sartoris, and most likely, though to a lesser degree, a model as well for the characterizations [of others]. Moreover, the manner in which the story of Colonel Falkner came down to his great-grandson influenced Faulkner's understanding of the way history is transmitted from one generation to another.... [T]he real monument to Colonel Falkner, the enduring one, is the Yoknapatawpha fiction for which he served as the model.[79]

Behind the symbols that constitute the Yoknapatawpha mythos is a reworking of the symbols and experiences of William Faulkner, and these include at the foundations those associated with the writer's great-grandfather at Ripley. Today in Ripley one can walk the same streets and see the same places that the colonel knew. This environment like all environments is suffused with memory, which as part of our experience of time is integral to our vision of a future goal toward which we are driven. The interplay of place and narrative results in a symbolic potency in which Colonel Falkner and Ripley and Tippah County become Colonel John Sartoris and Jefferson and Yoknapatawpha County. The statue of Colonel Falkner looks across the surrounding landscape, the cemetery and the adjoining railroad, and beyond that to the ramparts of infinity.

Appendix

❖◆━◦━━◦━❖

A Field Guide to Colonel Falkner's Ripley

Every person's life takes place, which is to say that for every life there is a network of places, or a geographical background, in which it transpires. Colonel W. C. Falkner lived in a number of places in the South and visited the major cities of the eastern United States along with visiting northern Mexico and touring through much of Europe. But most of his life took place in the small northeastern Mississippi town of Ripley, the county seat of Tippah County. Ripley was only six years old when he arrived in 1842, and it served as his home and base of operations, the place he raised his family, until his death in 1889. Once while far from home touring in England he wrote: "In all my wanderings I have seen no place I love so well as I do dear old Ripley, and dear old Tippah."[1]

Local history affirms that each person's life is intricately bound to a geographical setting, and so it was with Colonel Falkner; in his case, the setting also intermingles with Yoknapatawpha. Places in Ripley beckon to us to inquire into mysteries that can only partially be revealed. Much as the younger Faulkner produced maps to depict the geography of his Yoknapatawpha stories, so this work has its own equivalent in this appendix entitled "A Field Guide to Colonel Falkner's Ripley." This field guide takes you through the streets where Falkner lived and shows you some of the buildings and sights that featured in his daily life. Nevertheless, as you walk through the town, you will have to use your imagination to picture it as it looked in the nineteenth century. I have attempted to identify places associated with Falkner and his family and associates, a task conducted in part in the main narrative. However, for easy reference the locations in Ripley are summarized and cataloged here with an accompanying map. With it, a person can, as best as possible, come to know Ripley as Colonel Falkner knew it, and perhaps see that there—as in so many other places—"a more than everyday reality erupted."

Falkner's Ripley was based on a grid established by the surveyor who in 1836 laid out the streets, blocks, and lots, and this geometry still frames the lives of residents and visitors today. Ripley as Falkner knew it was a frontier town that had just been hewed out of the wilderness and knew few of the amenities that we know today.

These pages provide a listing with documentation of places associated with Colonel Falkner and his family and acquaintances. As you walk the streets of the town today, remember that the lines were surveyed in a mostly wooded area in the summer of 1836. As lots were sold, buildings began to be erected, initially using logs and later milled lumber and sometimes brick. Today there are few—perhaps a dozen—extant buildings that existed during Falkner's time. And some of those, notably the courthouse, are hardly recognizable due to later alterations. However, walking the streets today and identifying, using this guide, places associated with him, the reader can come as close spatially to his world as possible.

As the town developed and commercial buildings began to infill the sides of the square, their growing density created firetraps. Once a building was ignited, by virtue of its proximity to others, it was almost impossible to prevent the fire from spreading to adjacent buildings. So fires would periodically burn substantial portions of the business district, until the wooden structures began to be replaced with brick beginning in the late nineteenth century.

Throughout the nineteenth century there were few brick structures on the square, with the most prominent being the courthouse. Built in 1838 and standing two stories high, it dominated the square and the entire town. Bordering and fronting the square there were at least two brick commercial buildings before the war, the Union Bank building and "Falkner's brick building." Following the 1864 burning by Federal troops, only one store was rebuilt, by William R. Cole, and it remained the only store for decades. In 1896 a process began to replace frame commercial buildings with brick that continued until 1937, by which time no frame buildings remained.[2] While not preventing fire altogether, brick construction certainly slowed its spread. Today the only buildings on the square to survive from Falkner's lifetime are the Cole brick store and the courthouse, although these have largely been covered by later architectural additions.

The streets were not paved; they were not even graveled until years after Falkner's death.[3] So there was little to prevent the streets from becoming rutted and pockmarked with mudholes. Sidewalks—where they existed—were largely of plank construction. Concrete for sidewalks was not poured until the twentieth century. However, during the late 1880s efforts were made to provide brick sidewalks connecting the stores around the square so that customers could get about with relative ease. Initially this was conducted by individual merchants providing pavement in front of their respective stores. If enough contributed sections of pavements, the result would be a continuous pavement. On May 23, 1889, the *Southern Sentinel* reported that "Mr. G M Bostwick has put in good condition the walk in front of his business house. Mr. Phyfer and Judge Worsham, say they will repair their pavements soon. When this is done Main Street will have a solid brick walk from one end to the other." In other words, by May 1889 practically all of the west side of Main Street on the square had been paved with brick. By November, when Colonel Falkner was shot on Main Street, the newspaper accounts noted that he was standing on pavement.

Although the telegraph was invented and in operation by the 1840s and the telephone invented in 1876, Ripley would have neither of these during Falkner's lifetime for long-distance communication, although Dr. John Murry had a telephone system installed to connect his home on Jackson Street with his office and drugstore on the square in 1883.[4] To communicate with the outside world by telegraph required traveling to either New Albany in the south or Middleton in the north to use the lines that paralleled the railroads through those towns. When Falkner was shot in the evening of November 5, 1889, messengers had to travel by handcar to New Albany to telegraph his family in Memphis. At the time of his death, a telephone line was under construction to connect Ripley with New Albany and Pontotoc. A telegraph line would follow a few years later.

There was no water system in Ripley during the nineteenth century. Water came from private sources—that is, wells and cisterns. A public water system wasn't developed until the early twentieth century.

Nor was there a sewage system. The order of the day was chamber pots and outdoor privies. The city sewage system like the water system wasn't developed until the early twentieth century. Although Thomas Edison's incandescent lightbulb was invented in 1879, there were no electric lights in homes or on the streets until an electrical system was developed during the early 1900s.[5]

To walk the streets of Ripley today is to pass through a remnant of the world known by Colonel Falkner. However, it is potentially not merely a walk by a detached observer but by one who interacts with the symbolism latent within the lifeworld of Falkner and Ripley.

The sites described below are listed in sequential order by their block numbers in the Ripley plat. They can be identified on the copy of the plat presented here. The sites are not numbered individually. Instead, their location is given below in terms of the block number and, if necessary, the portion of the block. On the Ripley map, each site is identified with a large asterisk (*).

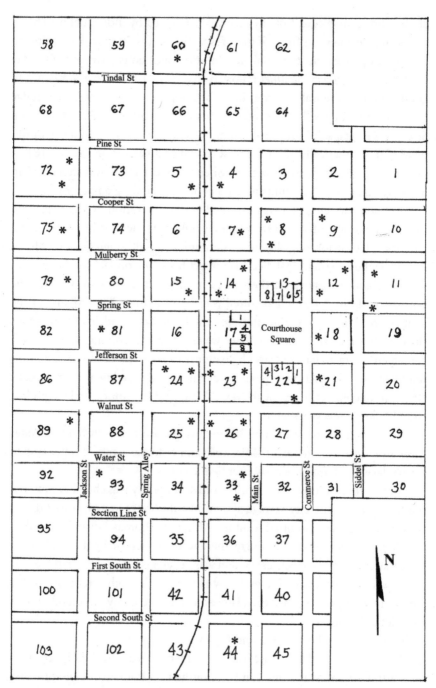

Figure 16.1. Map of Ripley, Mississippi. Based on the plat of Ripley provided in Tippah County Deed Book 39, 307.

Figure 16.2. The home of Dr. and Mrs. N. G. Carter. Courtesy of Tommy Covington.

However, in a few cases, specifically on blocks facing the courthouse square, because of the concentrated development and ensuing complexity of site histories, I have had to refrain from placing asterisks, because the required number would clutter and confuse the map. Indeed, some lots have different histories for different buildings that stood on the same spot. In these cases, I have included the lot boundaries, making it possible to identify sites, given that the associated site histories are provided with lot designations.

Block 4

Carter home (W½ Block 4, facing Cooper Street)

This was the home of Falkner's daughter and son-in-law, Willett "Willie" Medora Falkner Carter (1856–1918) and Dr. Nathaniel Green Carter (1851–1908), where they resided from 1884 through 1901. The house was moved from the site during the 1960s.

In December 1877, W. C. Falkner donated Block 4 to his daughter Willie Falkner Carter, for "love and affection."[6] In early September 1884, the Carters were in the process of building a two-story residence on the parcel, and by mid-October it was nearing completion.[7] After completion, the Carters took

Figure 16.3. Falkner's granddaughters, Vannye and Natalie Carter, circa 1890. Courtesy of Tommy Covington.

Figure 16.4. Falkner stained-glass window soon after it was found beneath a house. Courtesy of Tommy Covington.

up residence there, and from this home Dr. Carter could easily reach his drug-store and doctor's office three blocks away on the southwest corner of the square. In their new home, the Carters raised their two daughters, Natalie (1879–1951) and Caroline Vance "Vannye" (1881–1959).

Following the shooting of Colonel Falkner on the evening of November 5, 1889, he was taken to the Carter home and placed in the library—the room on the right upon entering—where he died the following night. Willie Carter had a memorial stained-glass window dedicated to his memory and placed in a window of the library.

As a child, William Faulkner spent much time here. His brother John remembered that "Aunt Willie was especially fond of Bill. She would have him visit her."[8] In 1925 William recalled that as a child in Ripley he went to Willie's home to spend the night, and after suffering a bout of homesickness he was carried home by his cousins, who were about twenty years old: "Vannye and Natalie brought me home, with a kerosene lantern. I remember how Vannye's hair looked in the light—like honey . . . she was holding the lamp. Natalie was quick and dark. She was touching me. She must have carried me."[9]

The Carters left Ripley for Meridian in 1901[10] and sold their home the fol-lowing year to the William Hines family. Hines was the son of C. E. Hines who was, prior to his death in 1878, a partner in the Ripley Railroad. William Hines was married to Mattie Spight, the daughter of Falkner's friend Thomas

Spight, who lived next door. When the Carters deeded the property to the Hineses, Willie reserved the right to remove the memorial window whenever she desired.[11] However, she never did.

About the window, Andrew Brown III later recalled:

> It wasn't much of a window, artistically, but the inscription will interest you; following the usual "In Memoriam," name, dates, etc., were these lines: "He that giveth to the poor lendeth to the Lord." Aside from the fact that there was truth in it, Willie's choice of the line shows how she thought the Colonel should best be remembered.[12]

After being lost for decades, the window was later found in the 1980s, only partially intact—several pieces of glass were gone. It was restored and is now on display in the Tippah County Historical Museum.

In the 1960s the house was moved out of town and converted into a steak house restaurant, and it later burned. The original site is now vacant.

Block 5

Thomas Spight home, 1882–1924, extant (SE¼ Block 5)

This house was constructed in late 1882[13] for Thomas Spight (1841–1924), an attorney and friend of Falkner's. He also founded the *Southern Sentinel* newspaper in 1879. As district attorney, he led the prosecution against R. J. Thurmond in 1890 and 1891 and later served in the US House of Representatives from 1898 through 1911. In 1891, the *Sentinel* noted: "Capt. Spight is having his elegant residence extensively repaired and freshly painted, which, when completed, will make it one of the handsomest dwellings in town."[14] The house is currently extant.

Block 7

Falkner home, Warwick Place, 1865–1902, demolished 1937 (Block 7)

Prior to the Civil War, little is known about buildings on this block except that R. J. Thurmond had a home on the southeast corner in 1864 and probably earlier. Shortly after the war Falkner constructed a one-story home here that became his home for the balance of his life. It was approximately centered

Figure 16.5. Thomas Spight home. Courtesy of Tommy Covington.

between the building to the south, the old US Post Office, and the building to the north, the old Tate Clinic.

Originally one story, the house was greatly enlarged and renovated in 1884–1885, turning it into a three-story marvel of Italianate and Gothic Revival design; it was called Warwick Place, probably after Warwick Castle in England, which Falkner visited during his 1883 European tour. In 1885, J. L. Power, the owner of the Jackson *Clarion*, visited Ripley and wrote: "Col. W. C. Falkner, the distinguished soldier, lawyer and author, has built a residence that is quite palatial in style and proportions. Bel Haven excepted, there is no residence at the state capital that can compare with it."[15]

Inside the front door, a stuffed alligator once stood upright on its hind legs holding in its front legs a large seashell into which visitors could drop their calling cards.

In 1902 the Falkner family sold the block with the house on it following the sale of the railroad and the departure of the last Falkner residents, A. E. and Effie Falkner Davis. The property was sold to L. D. "Lynn" Spight, the son of attorney and congressman Thomas Spight.

The house was demolished in 1937 and replaced with a brick post office building and another, two-story brick building. The former currently serves

Figure 16.6. Falkner home, circa 1890, view to the northwest. Courtesy of Tommy Covington.

as the office for Dixie-Net Communications while the latter has served successively as apartments, a clinic, and an office building for Dixie-Net. The two-story building was constructed in part from materials taken from the colonel's home. It incorporates architectural elements from Falkner's house such as the balcony on the front and the staircase inside.

Block 8

Baptist Church, circa 1850–1955 (SW¼ Block 8)

The Baptist Church was located at this site from the 1850s through 1955. After surviving the Civil War burnings, the church building was used intermittently as the Tippah County courthouse until the new courthouse was built in 1870. The original building burned in 1884 and was replaced. It burned again in 1915 in a fire that also destroyed the former Spight Hotel and was replaced again. Colonel Falkner's daughter Willie Medora and her husband, Dr. N. G. Carter, were members. The stained-glass memorial window commissioned by Willie and dedicated to her father was purportedly placed initially in this church before being removed to the Carter house. After a new and much larger structure was completed on Block 2, the church moved to its present location in 1955.[16]

J. W. T. Falkner home, 1869–1873 (NW¼ Block 8)

An antebellum house located here was occupied by the J. W. T. Falkner family probably from the marriage of John Falkner and Sallie Murry in 1869 through about 1873. The older son, Murry, was probably born here in 1870.[17] Shortly after the death of J. W. Thompson in 1873, the J. W. T. Falkners moved in with

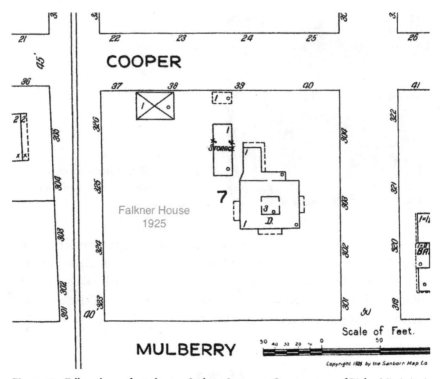

Figure 16.7. Falkner home, from the 1925 Sanborn Insurance Company map of Ripley, Mississippi. Note that on the west side of the block the railroad can be seen in the center of Union Street.

his widow, Justiania, who was John Falkner's great-aunt and foster-mother (Block 12). The Thompsons had raised J. W. T. Falkner from childhood. The adjacent Baptist Church purchased the house in 1907, and it was torn down in 1923 with a new brick Craftsman-style house completed in the spring of 1924 to serve as the parsonage. This home, which is extant today, utilized much of the lumber from the older house in its construction.

Block 9

S. R. Spight home and hotel, circa 1840–1890, burned in 1915 (NW¼ Block 9)

By 1840, Simon Reynolds Spight (1810–1891) had moved to Ripley, where he became a merchant, served as postmaster (1843–1849, 1853–1856), and turned his home into a hotel. In 1883, the property was described with the main house "two stories high, with about 25 rooms, including five which are conveniently located for renting as offices or to be used for hotel purposes. Good frame

Figure 16.8. S. R. Spight home and hotel. Courtesy of Tommy Covington.

stables, corn cribs, well and cistern, two good gardens, clover, potato and corn patches and grass lot."[18]

In the mid-1840s, Spight became the legal guardian of the minor Pearce orphan children and brought them to live in his home in Ripley. The five children included three boys and two girls, Mary and Holland. Mary married D. L. Killgore in the Spight home in 1847,[19] and when Holland married W. C. Falkner that same year, it's probable that they were also married there.

Shortly after Falkner killed R. H. Hindman in 1849, brother T. C. Hindman Jr. attempted to shoot Falkner in a Ripley hotel but accidentally dropped his gun. This event occurred in either the Ripley Inn or the Spight Hotel.

Spight sold this property in 1890.[20] The main hotel building burned in 1915 in a conflagration that also burned the Baptist Church to the southwest.[21] Today, the Ripley Public Library stands on the site. It contains a collection of material related to Colonel Falkner.

Block 11

T. J. Word home, 1842–1845, not extant (W½ Block 11)

This house was constructed by 1839[22] and was subsequently owned and occupied by T. J. Word and his family upon their moving to Ripley in 1842, probably accompanied by the seventeen-year-old W. C. Falkner.[23] The Words moved to Holly Springs about the first of 1846, and the house was sold in 1851.[24]

Block 12

J. W. Thompson/J. W. T. Falkner home, circa late 1830s–1885, demolished in 1950 (NE¼ Block 12)

The home of attorney and politician J. W. Thompson (1809–1873) was on the northeast corner of Block 12 in Ripley, the block that lies northeast of the square. The house faced west toward Commerce Street, resulting in a sizable front yard. On September 18, 1840, Thompson signed a contract in which Jesse Pate agreed to construct "a dwelling house on the Lot that John W. Thompson now lives on in Ripley," namely Lots 1–4 of Block 12. The suggestion was that the Thompsons already resided there in a different house. A notation on the record indicates that Thompson paid Pate in full by November 7, 1848, implying that the new house was completed before then.[25] W. C. Falkner lived in this house or the older one during the 1840s, and his son J. W. T. Falkner (adopted by the Thompsons) was raised there. Shortly before his death in 1873, Thompson deeded the house and other properties to J. W. T. Falkner.[26] The latter and family then took up residence there with his widowed great-aunt Justiania Word Thompson (1815–1898). In 1881 J. W. T. Falkner added a second story to the house.[27] The family, including Mrs. Thompson, moved to Oxford in December 1885.[28] The home was torn down in 1950 to make way for the construction of the McBride Funeral Home.[29]

Law Office of J. W. Thompson and W. C. Falkner (Lot 7, Block 12)

The law office of Thompson & Falkner was probably located on the southwest corner of Block 12, a prominent site for conducting business on the square. This block was Thompson's primary real estate in Ripley, which included his residence while providing a corner convenient to the square and thereby a desirable office site. A survey of the Ripley deeds reveals that Thompson owned no other business lots on the square that might have served as his office site. Thompson's office was probably here prior to Falkner's arrival in Ripley in 1842.

In November 1858 and upon being elected circuit judge, Thompson withdrew from the practice of law and turned his law practice over to Falkner.[30] Falkner advertised as "W. C. Falkner, Attorney at Law," in the "Office formerly occupied by John W. Thompson."[31] After Falkner's young brother J. W. Falkner

Figure 16.9. J. W. Thompson/J. W. T. Falkner home. Courtesy of Tommy Covington.

graduated from the University of Mississippi School of Law in May 1859, the two joined in a new partnership, Falkner & Falkner, Attorneys at Law.[32]

Block 13

Mississippi Union Bank, 1838–early 1840s, burned circa 1863 (E½ Lot 5, Block 13, at the corner at the intersection of Spring and Commerce Streets[33])

The Mississippi Union Bank was chartered in 1837 to consist of a main bank in Jackson and seven branch banks with each covering a district. District 3 was initially to be served by a bank in Aberdeen; however, in 1838 the location was moved to Ripley,[34] with a brick bank building constructed soon after by Peter Garland, who also built the Tippah County courthouse about the same time.[35] As the Mississippi Bank was facing financial difficulties, T. J. Word, serving as an attorney for the bank, was sent to Ripley in 1842 to help the branch bank weather the crisis. However, the Mississippi Union Bank collapsed soon after, and the Ripley branch bank building was eventually auctioned off at a sheriff's sale on January 6, 1845.[36]

Simon R. Spight and his brother Joseph C. Spight ran their mercantile business and post office in the building as early as 1856[37] and purchased it in 1857.[38] The building was destroyed by fire probably on March 23, 1863, when Federal troops torched the north side of the square, over a year before the balance of the square and the courthouse were torched on July 8, 1864.

Henderson's Grocery (E½ Lot 6)

In a conflict about which little is known. W. C. Falkner shot and killed Erasmus Morris in this store on the evening of Friday, February 28, 1851.[39]

The building was probably of frame construction, and it most likely burned on March 23, 1863, when Federal troops torched the north side of the square over a year before the balance of the square and the courthouse were torched.

Andrew Brown and Company, circa 1846–1863 (W½ Lot 6)

The firm known as A. Brown and Company, or Brown and Simpson, consisted of three men all born in Ireland: Andrew Brown Sr., Andrew Brown Jr. (who was actually the nephew of Brown Sr.), and James Simpson. Brown Sr. and Simpson purchased the lot in 1846, at which time the store was already being run by the partnership.[40] The business was evidently successful, and the younger Brown married C. P. Miller's daughter Sallie.

During the Civil War, as Ripley became subject to marauding by Federal troops, Brown and Company caught its share of the attacks. On October 8, 1862, the Seventh Kansas Cavalry entered town, and their commanding officer, Colonel A. L. Lee, informed them: "Boys, do as you please." An eyewitness recorded that "every possible indignity and outrage was committed on the citizens, including robbery"; the troops "[b]roke the safe of A. Brown & Co., took $2000 worth of goods and $700 in money."[41]

A month later, having heard that the partisan rangers were meeting in Brown's store on November 19, Colonel Lee and his cavalry left Grand Junction and before dawn the following day surrounded the town, moving in at daybreak. However, Falkner and at least one hundred of his rangers were able to escape before being caught. Brown's store was destroyed on March 23, 1863, when Federal troops torched the north side of the square over a year before the balance of the square and the courthouse were torched.[42]

Following the war, a two-story frame store building was erected on the site of Brown's store, which was a prominent building during Falkner's time and which stood into the early twentieth century. The building was used by a number of different firms including Phyfer and Johnson, furniture dealers, and in the twentieth century was often referred to as Moran's store after merchant L. A. Moran.

Falkner's brick building (W½ Lot 7 and E½ Lot 8)

This building apparently consisted of two adjacent commercial buildings probably with a common wall between. Falkner purchased these parcels in 1854 and sold them in 1860.[43] The firm Falkner & Norvell did business in one of the two buildings in 1855–1856. It was probably burned on March 23, 1863, by Federal troops.

C. P. Miller and Son, 1848–circa 1861 (W½ Lot 8, Block 13)

In 1848, C. P. Miller sold the Ripley Inn and moved to Jackson Street to reside. At the same time, he purchased a lot on the northwest corner of the court-house square on which he went into the mercantile business under the name of C. P. Miller and Son, conducted in partnership with his son, Oliver R. Miller.[44] The building, which fronted on Spring Street, was bounded on the west by Main Street and on the east by what became Falkner's brick building.

At the end of 1859, Miller advertised that he had sold his interest to his son Tom W. Miller and that the business would henceforth be run under the name O. R. Miller and Company.[45] However, the business would not last long. By 1863 both of the brothers were dead, and on March 23, 1863, Union troops torched the north side of the square including the Miller store.

Andrew Brown Store, circa 1865–1896 (E½ Lot 8, Block 13)

At the end of the Civil War, no buildings remained on the square. All had been burned. Subsequently, merchants had to build new commercial buildings. Andrew Brown Sr. and James Simpson chose to rebuild a few lots west of their earlier store site on Lot 8, where they purchased the West ½ from C. P. Miller and the East ½ from W. C. Falkner[46] and constructed an imposing frame store house. Simpson died in 1872, leaving Brown to operate the business alone.

By 1885, business was such that a two-story addition was made on the rear that could be accessed from Main Street on its west side.[47] By this time Andrew Sr. was well into his seventies. The *Southern Sentinel* reported in 1888 that over the prior fifteen years his nephew Andrew Brown Jr. had become actively involved in the store and oversaw most of the purchasing. His wife Sallie, a daughter of C. P. Miller, presided over the millinery and fancy goods department, while their son Joe was in charge of advertisements and the general sales department.[48]

In 1890, the old Scot Andrew Sr. died, leaving his nephew and family to carry on. In 1893, the *Southern Sentinel* published a news item about a log building that had stood behind Brown's store that had served as a school-house in Ripley soon after it was founded.

> The old house at the rear of Brown's store has been torn away. While it has been used only as a chicken house by Mr. Brown for several years, the little old building has a history that, if some of our older citizens would relate, might prove quite interesting. It was a log house about 20 feet square, and was the first

Figure 16.10. Andrew Brown and Company store building, late nineteenth century. Courtesy of Tommy Covington.

school-house ever used in Ripley, about the year 1837; was afterwards moved on rollers by the lamented Charles Miller to where it remained until torn down a few days ago. For many years Mr. Miller used this building as a store, and as he was also postmaster,[49] it was, during the pioneer days, the leading establishment of the town. When torn down two plows were found in the old loft. They had never been used, but Mr. Shepherd, who is the best of authority, says the plows were made (casting and all) by the old Ripley foundry, which was in operation here about 26 years ago. One is a turning plow, after the Avery pattern, while the other is a subsoil plow patented by a Vairrin [A. L. P. Vairin, a jeweler before the Civil War], who was then a citizen of this place. These plows will be kept as relics of the "good old days" when people didn't go in debt for supplies to raise cotton at seven cents per pound.[50]

Six year later in 1896, the Browns sold the business to T. J. Cole, who operated it until 1930, and in 1934 the landmark store building was torn down.[51]

Block 14

Falkner's office, 1884–1889, not extant (NE corner Block 14)

This office was constructed in 1885 and was probably the last office used by Falkner.[52] Because Falkner was not practicing law during these years, he probably used the office for railroad business, in his position as president, and for political activities.

In 1925, George M. Moreland, a columnist for the Memphis *Commercial Appeal*, visited Ripley. In a column on Ripley, he observed: "Across the street from the old [Falkner] home stands a smaller house which has been re-modeled and is now used as a residence. It was for many years Colonel Falkner's office."[53]

Railroad water tower, not extant (SW corner Block 14)

The water tower that was located here in association with a water well was used to refill the locomotive boilers. These were constructed on a fourteen-by-twenty-foot parcel in Lot 7, Block 14, that the railroad had purchased on December 2, 1872.[54]

Block 15

Tippah County jail (SE¼ Block 15)

For over a century in successive buildings, the Tippah County jail was used to incarcerate prisoners. In 1845 it housed A. J. McCannon, when Falkner interviewed him, producing the material for his pamphlet on the murder. In 1849 and 1851, Falkner was locked up twice for killings for which he was acquitted, and in 1889–1890, R. J. Thurmond was incarcerated following his shooting of Falkner.

Although documentation for its early years is sparse, the first jail was apparently constructed soon after the creation of Tippah County in 1836. The first jail accidentally burned in 1852 and was replaced by another building constructed by Jefferson Blythe at a cost of $6,000.[55] In 1896, a three-story brick jail was constructed with the jailor's residence on the lower floor, and in 1938, it was replaced with another masonry jail that was used until a new and much larger jail complex was constructed to the south across Spring Street.[56] The 1938 jail building is currently used for the office of the Tippah County Development Authority and the Tippah County Archives.

Figure 16.11. The C. M. Thurmond law office, circa 1930. One of the last frame buildings on the square, it was constructed in 1881–1882.

Block 17

O. F. Philbrick store and office of the newspaper Uncle Sam *(N½ Lot 1, Block 17)*

The two-story frame store house of Obadiah F. Philbrick stood on the northeastern corner of the block during the 1850s, and Philbrick apparently used the lower floor for a store, while the upper floor in 1856 served as the office of the *Uncle Sam* newspaper, which was edited at the time by W. C. Falkner.[57] The building was burned during the Civil War along with the entire square.

C. M. Thurmond law office (N½ Lot 1, Block 17)

R. J. Thurmond's son, C. M. Thurmond, purchased this lot in 1881 and constructed a law office on the site of the Philbrick Store that was completed early the following year.[58] He used it for his law practice until his death in 1900, following which it was used for a dental office and barbershop. It was torn down about 1937 and replaced by a brick building used as Renfrow's Café, which burned in 2012.

For years during the twentieth century, it was believed that this was the site of the shooting of Colonel Falkner. This was due to the erroneous assumption that, because a Thurmond office had been located here, it had been the R. J. Thurmond office where Falkner was shot. Of course, the actual shooting occurred about a hundred feet to the south.

Murry's drugstore and doctor's office with
Masonic Lodge upstairs (S½ Lot 1, Block 17)

This frame two-story building was constructed shortly after the Civil War in about 1866 and served as the drugstore and office of Dr. John Y. Murry for decades.[59] The upstairs served as the meeting place for Ripley Lodge no. 107, of which W. C. Falkner and Dr. Murry were both members.[60]

In 1909, the Murrys rented the building to C. H. Crum, who turned it into a grocery store.[61]

In 1925, the frame building was demolished and replaced with a brick, two-story building, which still stands, with the lower floor serving as commercial space while the upstairs continued as the Masonic Lodge. However, the Lodge no longer meets there.[62]

R. J. Thurmond's office and Falkner shooting site (center of Lot 5,
Block 17, and adjacent to the north side of the Cole brick store)

This small frame building was constructed in the fall of 1885 by E. W. Simpson, the new Ripley postmaster, to serve as the post office.[63] Four years later, his term ended, and R. J. Thurmond occupied the building as his office. On October 10, 1889, the *Southern Sentinel* reported: "Mr. R J Thurmond has opened an office in the old post office. He has a neat, cozy, little office."[64]

A month later, on November 5, 1889, he shot Colonel Falkner in front of this office.

This building along with the one on its northern side were demolished in 1929 by W. A. McAlister to be replaced with the current duplex brick commercial building, with the smaller unit being on the south side where Thurmond's office was located.[65] The smaller unit served as Smith's Barber Shop for decades and more recently has been used by the Mississippi Gold, Silver, and Coin Exchange.

Cole brick store/Alexander and Company (S½ Lot 5, Block 17)

A brick commercial building was constructed here shortly after the Civil War by merchant W. R. Cole. It was later rented to a number of successive

Figure 16.12. Southwest corner of the courthouse square, view to west on Jefferson Street, 1900–1908. To the right of Jefferson is the gable-fronted Carter Drug Company. To the left of the same street is the Ripley Drug Company, and in the background on Jefferson can be seen the Hines Hotel on the other side of the railroad. Courtesy of Tommy Covington.

mercantile firms including that of Dr. E. M. Alexander and Company. After Falkner's shooting on the square in 1889, the account by Dick Ford of the *Ripley Advertiser* used the site of Alexander and Company as a reference landmark for indicating approximately where the shooting took place. The walls of the building are still extant, making this the oldest structure on the square. However, a new brick facade was constructed on it years ago. The building currently houses Creative Awning and Sign.

Carter drugstore (S½ Lot 8, Block 17)

Shortly after the fire of February 4, 1856, this property was purchased by Dr. William D. Carter, who then apparently constructed and ran a drugstore here.[66] This building was subsequently burned during the Civil War along with all buildings on the square. Sometime after the war another building was constructed, and in 1879 Dr. Carter's son, Dr. N. G. Carter, the husband of Falkner's oldest daughter, Willie, opened his drugstore and doctor's office in it.[67] Dr. Carter was apparently in his office the evening that Falkner was shot a few feet away and was soon present to examine him. Dr. Carter used the building until he moved to Meridian in 1901. In 1908, the building was demolished and replaced with the two-story brick building that currently stands on the site. This building initially housed the First National Bank,[68] later the People's Bank, and is currently used by Professional Land Services.

Ripley Court House — 1908   Built in 1870
Remodeled in 1928

Figure 16.13. Tippah County courthouse, 1908. Courtesy of Tommy Covington.

Courthouse Square

Tippah County courthouse

Today, the Tippah County courthouse stands in the center of the courthouse square and at the figurative center of Ripley and Tippah County. Without the courthouse, there would never have been a Ripley. Its physical form for those who peer beneath its brick walls is like a series of Russian eggs, one embedded inside another, with the entire structure supported by brick foundations that extend into the earth where they were originally laid in 1838.

Its present form reflects the last major construction, which was completed in 1928. However, inside it are substantial remains of its earlier avatars. Here, courts convicted A. J. McCannon of murder in 1845, and acquitted W. C. Falkner in 1849 and 1851 and R. J. Thurmond in 1891.

The first courthouse on this site, replacing a temporary log structure located somewhere on the northeast corner of the square, was built of brick in 1838 by Peter Garland, who also built the Mississippi Union Bank in Ripley the same year. The courthouse was a two-story building fifty feet square in plan. It was burned along with much of the town by Federal troops on July 8, 1864.[69]

The courthouse was rebuilt in early 1870 on the foundations, following the design of the earlier courthouse. The only major differences were the addition

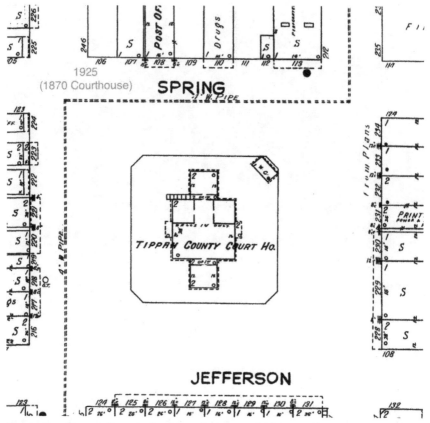

Figure 16.14. The courthouse in the center of the square. Sanborn Insurance Company map of Ripley, 1925.

of two monumental porticos on the east and west sides along with two-story wings on the north and south sides.

In 1928, the courthouse was expanded by building around the old core according to a plan by architect N. W. Overstreet of Jackson.[70]

From its beginnings in the nineteenth century, the courthouse square has been the center of social and economic activity in Tippah County. In the fall, wagons once filled the square as they made their way to the depot, one block to the west.

The Confederate monument stands on the east side. It was originally erected in 1911, southwest of the courthouse, by the Thomas Spight Chapter of the United Daughters of the Confederacy, named after W. C. Falkner's friend and Confederate veteran. The location proved to be vulnerable to automotive traffic, and in 1970 it was knocked over and heavily damaged by a freight truck. Subsequently, it was moved to it current, and less vulnerable, location.[71]

Ripley Square 1890
West side

Figure 16.15. Ripley courthouse square, view to the west on Jefferson Street, circa 1890, illus-
trating the activity as cotton bales were brought to town for shipping out on the railroad. In the
distance can be seen the gable-fronted Carter Drug Company on the right of Jefferson. Notice
that all the stores visible were of frame construction. On the right can be seen the fence on the
south side of the courthouse yard. Courtesy of Tommy Covington.

William Faulkner's description of the Yoknapatawpha County courthouse
in Jefferson is evocative of not only the Lafayette County courthouse in
Oxford but also the Tippah County courthouse.

But above all, the courthouse; the center, the focus, the hub; sitting looming in
the center of the county's circumference like a single cloud in its ring of horizon, laying its vast shadow to the uttermost rim of horizon; musing, brooding,
symbolic and ponderable, tall as cloud, solid as rock, dominating all: protector
of the weak, judiciate and curb of the passions and lusts, repository and guardian of the aspirations and the hopes. . . . [H]arder than axes, tougher than fire,
more fixed than dynamite; encircled by the tumbled and blackened ruins of
lesser walls, it still stood, even the topless smoke-stained columns, gutted of
course and roofless, but immune, . . . so that all they had to do . . . was put in
new floors for the two storeys and a new roof, and this time with a cupola with
a four-faced clock and a bell to strike the hours and ring alarms.[72]

Block 18

Office and drugstore of Dr. James B. Ellis (N½ Lot 6, Block 18)

Dr. Ellis (1817–1878) began practicing medicine in Ripley as early as 1842 and apparently maintained his office and drugstore in this location from about that time through circa 1860.[73] In 1846, he married Mary Hindman, the daughter of T. C. Hindman Sr. and sister of Robert Holt Hindman.[74]

That same year, the seventeen-year-old John Y. Murry came to town from his father's nearby farm intending enter the employ of Dr. Ellis as both a medical student and a clerk in the drugstore. In 1848, he enrolled in the Medical Department of the newly founded University of Louisville, Kentucky, and began the practice of medicine on March 1, 1849.[75] Murry would go on to become a prominent physician, drugstore owner, and local politician. His oldest daughter Sallie would marry W. C. Falkner's son J. W. T. Falkner in 1869.

Blocks 11 and 19

W. W. Robinson house (straddling a portion of Spring Street that was never opened, facing Siddell Street)

This home was built by the former probate court clerk W. W. Robinson (1835–1912) in 1886.[76] While serving as probate clerk during the Civil War, he removed the deed books and hid them, thereby preventing them from being destroyed when the courthouse was burned in 1864. Robinson later became the father-in-law of L. P. "Pink" Smith, editor of the *Southern Sentinel* and one of the strongest supporters of Colonel Falkner.

The restored Falkner memorial stained-glass window—originally in the Carter house—is currently housed in the Tippah County Historical Museum, which now occupies the building.

Block 21

Ripley Advertiser *office (NW¼ Block 21, on Commerce Street)*

This is the location where Falkner's *The White Rose of Memphis* was first set to type and published serially in 1880–1881.

Figure 16.16. W. W. Robinson house. Courtesy of Tommy Covington.

The *Ripley Advertiser* first began publishing in October 1842, within months of W. C. Falkner's arrival in Ripley.[77] For most of the newspaper's history from 1842 through 1896, a period that was almost coterminous with Falkner's residence in town, it was owned and edited by a father and son, John F. Ford (ca. 1807–1877) and Richard "Dick" Ford (1829–1896).[78] For most of its existence, the paper's office was located near the northwest corner of Block 21, which was owned by the Ford family with the family home located "just south" of the office on the same block.[79] The office and home were burned on July 8, 1864, along with the entire business district, and on the night of April 7, 1880, the office burned again along with "some other buildings."[80] Colonel Falkner loaned Dick Ford money to help rebuild, and as publication resumed in June he began supplying installments of his novel *The White Rose of Memphis* for serial publication to help stimulate the paper's circulation.

T. M. Aycock worked as the printer for the *Advertiser* at the time; decades later, a newspaper reporter who interviewed Aycock wrote:

[Aycock] was the first printer to set into type the manuscript for "The White Rose of Memphis." . . . Printers became rather expert at reading handwriting and Mr. Aycock recalled with a laugh that he was one of the few persons that could read Col. Falkner's handwriting well . . . and each week the Colonel would come in and read and correct the proof of the installment for that week, and then his publishers in New York used the copies of the local newspaper to set into type the novel for publication in book form.[81]

On the evening of Tuesday, November 5, 1889, Dick Ford was in his office when he heard a single shot fired. Stepping outside into the street, he could see a crowd gathering on the opposite side of the square, attracted by the shooting of Falkner.[82]

Dick published the paper through November 1893, at which time he became bedridden and consequently leased the paper.[83] The *Advertiser* continued to be published through 1896, when the last known issues were published, by C. A. Robertson. After that, there are no known surviving copies. The last issues coincide with the death of Dick Ford on November 23, 1896, suggesting that the paper ceased publication with his death.[84]

The building used for the *Advertiser* office during 1880–1896 burned on the night of October 11, 1909.[85]

Block 22

Thomas Spight law office and office of the Southern Sentinel *(E½ Lot 1, Block 22)*

The *Southern Sentinel* was founded by in 1879 by attorney Thomas Spight and printer T. M. Aycock after they purchased the equipment, including an old Washington handpress from the short-lived newspaper the *Ripley Broadaxe*, which had been founded the previous year. For its first few years, the *Sentinel* was located on the second floor of the frame Barnett building. A. G. Barnett had a store downstairs while upstairs was the newspaper office and Spight's law office.[86] The letters that became Falkner's *Rapid Ramblings in Europe* were first published serially here in the *Sentinel* in 1883–1884, when the paper was under the editorship of L. P. "Pink" Smith.[87] In 1896, the frame building was removed by Barnett and replaced with the currently standing two-story brick building.[88] This building was the second brick commercial structure built on the square after the Civil War and the first in a trend that developed in the late nineteenth century toward replacing the frame buildings on the square with brick. However, long before the rebuilding, in 1885, the *Sentinel* office had been moved to the east side of the square.[89]

Figure 16.17. Ripley town hall on the south side of the square. The bottom floor consisted of space for two businesses, while the top floor served as the town hall/opera house. Falkner's play *The Lost Diamond* was performed twice in the opera house in 1883. Courtesy of Tommy Covington.

Law office of Judge N. S. Price (W½ Lot 1, Block 22)

Nathaniel S. Price, attorney and circuit court judge, was probably the "Mr. P." whom Falkner accused in 1851 of persecuting him. His office was located here from the 1840s through 1854.[90] Following a legal battle with William J. Maclin, attorney and friend of Falkner, Maclin appeared in the doorway of Price's office on April 13, 1854, and initiated a fight in which Price was fatally wounded. He died the following day and was buried in Ripley Cemetery.

City hall/opera house (W½ Lot 2 and E½ Lot 3, Block 22)

In 1882, a double-wide, two-story frame building was erected by Lee D. Hines and W. W. Robinson. The lower floor consisted of spaces for two stores, while the upstairs was an open area that was used as an opera house for the performing of plays and vaudeville.[91] In 1883, Falkner's play *The Lost Diamond* was performed here twice.

This building burned on the night of May 30, 1903, in a fire that burned all of the block except the brick Barnett building on the east end.[92]

Cumberland Presbyterian Church (SE corner, Block 22)

A congregation of the Cumberland Presbyterian Church was organized in Ripley soon after the town's founding. About 1850, the congregation acquired a lot south of the courthouse square, and a church building was constructed. The building was burned on July 8, 1864, along with much of Ripley. The congregation was already small and never recovered enough to build another place of worship.[93]

Block 23

Ripley Drug Company and Dr. C. M. Murry's office (NE corner, Block 23)

The brick building that housed the Ripley Drug Store was constructed in 1891 and initially served as the drugstore of Dr. J. W. McCarley.[94] In 1900, J. Y. Murry Jr. and his brother Dr. C. M. Murry purchased the building and continued the drug business under the name Ripley Drug Company.[95] Falkner's grandson Murry Falkner apparently owned an interest in the business, which he sold in 1901 to Enoch R. Richey, who was married to Dr. J. Y. Murry Sr.'s daughter.[96] Richey was the pharmacist who operated the business for decades. In 1926, the brick on the facade of the building and the adjacent one to the south was replaced with new brick with a striated surface.[97] The following year, a two-story addition was constructed on the rear fronting on Jefferson Street to serve as the office of Dr. C. M. Murry.[98]

Ripley depot (original depot) (W side of Block 23, adjacent to the railroad)

The first Ripley depot was constructed soon after its site was selected by the directors of the Ripley Railroad in April 1872 and consisted of the west half of Block 23 and presumably the eastern side of Union Street, down which the railroad ran.[99] There were platforms on both the northern and southern ends, where cotton and freight could be placed in preparation for loading onto the train. On the western side of the track opposite the depot was the Hines House hotel, ready to serve passengers. In 1886, a turntable to turn locomotives was built "a few steps south of the Depot," and the Y, north of town and

Figure 16.18. Ripley rail yard, 1929, photographed by Andrew Brown III. View from Walnut Street north toward Jefferson Street. This was the site of the first Ripley depot (1872–1909). After the depot moved, this site was occupied by a large loading platform where cotton could be stacked in preparation for loading upon the arrival of trains. Courtesy of Tommy Covington.

formerly used to turn locomotives, was dismantled.[100] In 1909, a new depot was constructed a block to the south, and the old depot was dismantled.[101] Unfortunately, no photographs of the original depot are known.

Block 24

Hines House hotel (E½ Block 24, facing Jefferson Street)

The Hines House hotel was opened for business in 1881, when the *Southern Sentinel* noted: "The new Hotel has commenced business." Soon after, the paper encouraged: "Go to the HINES HOUSE for your dinner when you come to town."[102] Mrs. Cornelia Hines initially operated it. She was the widow of C. E. Hines and the sister of C. L. Harris, part owners of the railroad. Unlike previous hotels—the Ripley Inn and the Spight Hotel—this one was built to cater to the railroad trade. It was constructed on the west side of the railroad immediately adjacent to the original depot, where disembarking passengers could readily see the building.

After the hotel had been closed to business for several years, Cornelia Hines died there on August 8, 1910,[103] and shortly thereafter her daughter Sudie (Mrs. Julius J. Robertson) reopened it as a hotel: "Ripley has a new hotel

Figure 16.19. Hines House hotel, fronting on Jefferson Street. Note the railroad in the lower left-hand corner, view to the south. Courtesy of Tommy Covington.

Figure 16.20. Hines House hotel, circa 1915, view to the west with loading docks on the opposite side of the railroad in the foreground. Courtesy of Tommy Covington.

which is known as the Commercial Hotel, with Mrs. J. J. Robertson proprietress. The building used is the Hines residence which was used many years ago for a hotel but which has been recently overhauled and refurnished throughout. It will be a $2 a day house."[104]

The hotel is no longer extant.

Lee Hines house (extant) (W½ Block 24, facing Jefferson Street)

Lee D. Hines, the son of C. E. Hines and a prominent Ripley businessman, constructed a two-story residence on the lot to the west of the Hines House hotel. In early 1882, the *Southern Sentinel* observed that "Mr. Lee Hines has the foundation laid preparatory to building a neat residence on the lot immediately west of the Hines House."[105]

Greatly modified over the years, the house is still extant today.

Figure 16.21. Lee Hines home, by Phillip Knecht, from his website Hill Country History. Used with his permission.

Block 25

Sawmill and railroad shops (Block 25)

Prior to the construction of the railroad, this block accommodated the large sawmill owned by C. E. Hines and C. L. Harris. In 1877, when Hines and Harris bought into the Ripley Railroad, they sold a one-third interest in Block 25 to Falkner and another one-third interest to R. J. Thurmond. Following this, the Ripley Railroad constructed railroad shops on the block to maintain rolling stock and construct new flatcars and boxcars. There, in immediate proximity to the sawmill, they were readily supplied with milled lumber.[106] On December 29, 1904, the shops burned, with the fire engulfing a locomotive, which was destroyed. A few days later, the remaining structures were torn down to be replaced with a switch or siding.[107]

Block 26

Ripley Inn (NE¼ Block 26)

One of the earliest settlers of Ripley, Charles Peter Miller (1798–1875), arrived with his family in the summer of 1836 prior to the opening of lot sales. Soon after acquiring the north half of Block 26,[108] he constructed a two-story log building, the Ripley Inn, which provided room, board, and livery to the public. As his business grew, he constructed a large two-story addition with monumental columns on the eastern end of the log building facing Main Street, thereby greatly increasing his available space.

Figure 16.22. Ripley Inn. Courtesy of Tommy Covington.

Ripley Inn.

CHARLES P. MILLER, Returns his
thanks to the Public for the liberal
patronage heretofore bestowed on him
as an *Inn Keeper*, and would state, that he
has just completed an entire new building,
in the neatest style, immediately in front
of the old house, formerly occupied by him,
where he will be pleased to accommodate
Boarders and Travellers. He flatters him
self, he will be able to give satisfaction, as
he is determined that his Table and Stable
shall be well supplied with the best that the
country will afford, and that his *Charges*
shall be as LOW as the LOWEST.

Ripley Miss, June 22d 1844.

Figure 16.23. Ripley Inn
advertisement. From the
Ripley Advertiser, 1844.

Figure 16.24. The second Ripley Depot, constructed in 1909. The photograph was apparently taken in the late 1930s, when Ripley was served by the Gulf Mobile and Northern Railroad. The train is probably from the Rebel passenger line. Courtesy of Tommy Covington.

In 1848, Miller sold the inn[109] and moved into a residence on Jackson Street, opening a mercantile business on the square.

Shortly after Falkner killed R. H. Hindman in 1849, the victim's brother, T. C. Hindman Jr., attempted to shoot Falkner in a Ripley hotel but accidentally dropped his gun. This event occurred either in the Ripley Inn or the Spight Hotel.

The inn continued to operate—often under other names, such as the Moore Hotel or the McDonald Hotel—until it was demolished in the 1920s to be replaced with a much larger, two-story masonry structure called the Ripley Hotel, which opened in 1926. This building subsequently burned in the 1950s, although much of its walls remain today, incorporated into existing commercial buildings.

Ripley depot (second depot) (W side of Block 26)

In 1909, a new depot was constructed that was larger than the original. Built alongside the eastern edge of the railroad, its northern end was aligned with Walnut Street. During the mid-twentieth century, this depot served the "Rebel" line of passenger trains. However, with declining passenger use, the Rebel line through Ripley was discontinued in February 1954.[110]

Figure 16.25. Ripley Methodist
Church, 1888–circa 1924.
Courtesy of Tommy Covington.

Block 33

Methodist Church (NE¼ Block 33)

The present-day Methodist Church in Ripley stands where the original building stood, on the northeastern quadrant of the block. However, today the
church has expanded its holdings and buildings over the entire Block 33. The
Methodists were organized in Ripley by Charles Peter Miller, who founded
the Ripley Inn and whose three daughters married Dr. John Y. Murry, R. J.
Thurmond, and Andrew Brown Jr. There have been four church buildings on
this site: the first was built in 1850 and was burned in the general conflagration on July 8, 1864; the second was built soon after the war and burned on
December 17, 1886; the third was built of frame construction with a high stee-
ple and was completed in 1888; and this was later replaced with the fourth and
current brick chapel, which was dedicated in January 1925.[111]

The first of these was two storied, with the upper story used as the meeting
place of the Ripley Masonic Lodge no. 47, of which W. C. Falkner was a member.

Nineteenth-century records for the church are incomplete. However, Dr.
John Y. Murry Sr., the son-in-law of C. P. Miller, was a devoted member. His
daughter Sallie was presumably a member, and in 1884 her husband, John

W. T. Falkner, became a member through profession as did his son Murry and daughter Mary Holland, while his two-year-old son J. W. T. Falkner Jr. was baptized the same year into the church. When the family departed Ripley for Oxford in December 1885, their names were removed from the membership roll. When Murry Falkner moved back to Ripley at the end of 1898, he and his wife Maud joined the church through letter on January 15, 1899. They presumably had belonged to the New Albany Methodist Church, where they would have had their infant son William baptized. After their son Murry Charles "Jack" Falkner was born in Ripley in 1899, he was baptized on January 27, 1901. After they left Ripley for Oxford in September 1902, their names were removed by letter of July 1903.[112]

W. C. Falkner home, circa 1848–1864 (SE¼ Block 33)

Falkner purchased this property between December 1848 and July 1849, the first of his real estate acquisitions in Ripley. He and his family resided here from soon after his first marriage until the burning of the house on July 8, 1864. The site of the house is uncertain, although it was probably on the southeastern quadrant facing Main Street.[113]

Probably in early October 1862 when Federal troops invested Ripley, General William Rosecrans was there for at least one night and chose the Falkner home as his headquarters and residence. Years later at a meeting of the national Democratic Party in 1884 attended by both Rosecrans and Falkner, the two were affable, even jocular toward one another. They recalled that while in Falkner's home, Rosecrans "protected the family and the property as well as the town of Ripley generally with scrupulous care."[114] Of course, the comments were made long after the fact in an attempt to be conciliatory. The claim that Ripley property was protected differs markedly from contemporary accounts, which speak of destruction and looting.

The home was burned on July 8, 1864, by Federal troops along with much of the town.[115] There are no known photographs of the house.

Block 44

Ripley Female Academy/Stonewall College (Block 44)

Organized in 1849 and opened in 1850, the Ripley Female Academy brought Isaac and Mary Jane Buchanan to town to teach, with Mary Jane serving as

Figure 16.26. Stonewall College. Courtesy of Tommy Covington.

Figure 16.27. Ripley Male and Female College. Courtesy of Tommy Covington.

principal.[116] The couple brought Mary Jane's younger sister, Elizabeth Houston "Lizzie" Vance, with them. Within a year, she became W. C. Falkner's second wife in 1851. The academy was burned on July 8, 1864, along with much of the town in the conflagration started by Federal troops.[117]

Following the war, in 1866, the school was rebuilt under the name Stonewall College with the construction financially assisted by W. C. Falkner, whose play *The Lost Diamond* was written and performed also to help fund the effort. The college was apparently named after General T. J. "Stonewall" Jackson, a name presumably suggested by Falkner in honor of the general and the Battle of First Manassas, in which both men participated. Stonewall College burned on the night of January 2, 1883, was rebuilt that year, and reopened in November. It became the Ripley Male and Female College in September 1886.[118] Presently, the site is occupied by the Ripley Police Department headquarters.

Figure 16.28. Presbyterian Church on Union Street as drawn by Andrew Brown III. Lizzie Falkner was a member, and her husband's funeral service was held here. The Brown family were also members.

According to Andrew Brown, the southern end of the railroad, which followed Union Street, terminated "just north" of the college property between 1872 and 1886.[119] This means that the rails came to First Street or somewhat to its south.

Block 60

Original Presbyterian Church and site of Falkner's funeral (S½ Block 60, facing Union Street)

The Ripley Presbyterian Church was organized on May 7, 1837, but there was no church building until about 1850, when the frame structure was constructed facing east onto Union Street. The building survived the Civil War and afterward was used briefly as the Tippah County courthouse. It remained in use until a new building was built on the corner of Jackson and Cooper Streets, and the congregation moved there in 1894.[120]

Falkner's wife Lizzie was a member of this church, and their daughter Willie was married to Dr. N. G. Carter here in 1874. Lizzie's membership probably explains why Falkner's funeral was held here on November 8, 1889. A reporter left the following account:

On Friday morning last beginning at 11 o'clock, the funeral services of the late Col. W. C. Falkner, were held. There were about 1000 people present to do honor to the remains. The funeral services were under the direction of the Masonic order, of

Figure 16.29. Dr. C. M. Murry house, constructed circa 1920. Photograph by Jack D. Elliott Jr.

which Col. Falkner was an honored member. The funeral address was delivered by Rev. W. T. Lowrey in the Presbyterian church, not half the people who desired to hear it could secure even standing room in the church building. Mr. Lowrey's address was very eloquent and impressive and few dry eyes were found in the vast audience when he referred in eloquent words to the great worth of the lamented Falkner. Capt. J. E. Rogers assisted Mr. Lowrey. The vast throng then proceeded to the Ripley Cemetery.[121]

Block 72

Dr. C. M. Murry home, circa 1920 (NE¼ Block 72, fronting on Jackson Street)

Dr. Charles "Charlie" Miller Murry (1868–1946) purchased this house in 1922—it was apparently new at the time—and lived there until his death.[122] He was the son of Dr. John Y. Murry and the great-uncle of William Faulkner, and was named after his maternal grandfather, Charles P. Miller, as was his first cousin Charles "Charlie" Miller Thurmond. The home is extant today.

Brown-Richey house (SE¼ Block 72, fronting on Cooper Street)

The house that formerly stood here was constructed by Andrew Brown Sr. (ca. 1810–1890) after he purchased the block in 1853.[123] As can be seen from the

Figure 16.30. Brown-Richey house. Courtesy of Tommy Covington.

photo (fig. 16.30), the house was of the Greek Revival style. Murry C. Falkner purchased the home in 1901, making it the first and only house that he owned in Ripley. He and his family, including their son William Faulkner, moved from their previous rented residence located to the south on Jackson Street and lived here until they moved to Oxford in September 1902.[124] William's brother John was born here in September 1901. Upon the Falkners' departure, they sold the home to relatives, the Enoch R. Richeys, who owned and occupied it through much of the twentieth century. Enoch Richey (1870–1954) was a druggist who ran the Ripley Drug Company, which was owned by him and Dr. C. M. Murry. Richey was married to Margaret Thurmond "Pearl" Murry (1872–1957), daughter of Dr. John Y. Murry and his second wife, Mary Elizabeth Miller Murry, so the family was closely related to William Faulkner. The house was demolished in 1963, and the current home was built.

Block 75

John Y. Murry Jr. house, built 1898, extant
(E side of Block 75, fronting on Jackson Street)

John Y. Murry Jr. was an attorney and great-uncle of William Faulkner.

This block was originally occupied in the mid-1840s by Daniel Hunt, who served as the Tippah County probate clerk and who married R. J. Thurmond's sister, Sarah or "Sallie."[125] There is an old cedar tree in the front yard that was purportedly planted by Hunt. According to one account:

> While walking in the woods one Sunday afternoon just north of Ripley he found a tiny little cedar. . . . [T]aking his pocket knife he carefully cut around this tender little plant and very gently lifted it from "mother earth," taking great pains as he journeyed home with his find. . . . This he planted in his front yard.
>
> This was the first cedar tree in Ripley, and people came for miles around to see and comment about the cedar tree.[126]

After selling the Ripley Inn in 1848,[127] C. P. Miller (1798–1875) purchased this block and constructed a house in which he resided for the rest of his life. Relatives described the house as "a colonial home" that was "in appearance . . . much like the tavern Mr. Miller had sold." This implies that the house was two-story with monumental columns in front.[128] In 1860, Miller's daughter Mary married Dr. John Y. Murry Sr., a widower, who lived on the block across the street to the south. Another daughter, Margaret Mariah, married R. J. Thurmond in 1854, and a third, Sarah or "Sallie," married Andrew Brown Jr. around 1865. Their grandson was the geologist and historian Andrew Brown III.

Following the July 7, 1864, skirmish at Whitten Branch west of Ripley, Federal troops brought their two dead killed in the skirmish into town and "buried them in C. P. Miller's yard" while also burning the town.[129] Why they chose to bury the two in the Miller yard is unknown. These dead were probably exhumed after the war by contractors and relocated to the National Cemetery at Corinth. Despite this probability, a "grave dowser" purportedly found the two graves, which were then marked with headstones. I personally knew this dowser (now deceased) for decades and, having watched him in operation on numerous occasions in the field, can attest that his grave dowsing work had no merit.

The home burned in 1885, ten years after Miller's death.[130] In 1898, his grandson, attorney John Y. Murry Jr. (1862–1929), began construction of the two-story Queen Anne–style home that currently occupies the site.[131] After the Mobile, Jackson, and Kansas City Railroad purchased the Gulf and Chicago Railroad, the latter continued to exist as a subsidiary corporation headed by Murry as the president. In 1910 the MJ&KC and the G&C were reorganized as the New Orleans, Mobile, and Chicago, bringing to an end the existence of the G&C as a separate corporation. Soon after, Murry and his family moved to Tulsa, Oklahoma, and the property was sold. In Tulsa, he built up a law practice as counsel to leading Tulsa corporations.[132]

Figure 16.31. J. Y. Murry Jr. house. Photograph by Phillip Knecht, from his website Hill Country History. Used with his permission.

Block 79

Dr. John Y. Murry Sr. home, circa 1860, extant
(E side of Block 79, fronting on Jackson Street)

Murry (1829–1915) was the great-grandfather of William Faulkner and a renowned physician, politician, and member of the Masonic Lodge; like his father-in-law C. P. Miller, he was active in matters concerning the Methodist Church.

This was originally the site of the home of Levi Stokes Holcombe (1810–1884), a Ripley merchant prior to the Civil War, and his wife, Sarah A. Whitlow Holcombe (1813–1856),[133] who were also the great-great-grandparents of William Faulkner. On September 11, 1849, a Holcombe daughter, Emily Virginia (1832–1859), married Dr. John Y. Murry in the Holcombe house. The two would have at least six children over the coming few years preceding Emily's death in 1859. Not long after their 1849 marriage, two other Holcombe daughters married brothers of Holland Pearce Falkner, the first wife of W. C. Falkner: Mary Elizabeth Holcombe (1835–1862) married Lazarus Pearce (1826–1913), and Scotia Holcombe (1836–1859) married Joseph Pearce (1835–1912).

Figure 16.32. Dr. J. Y. Murry house, built circa 1859. Courtesy of Tommy Covington.

In August 1860, one year after Emily's death, Holcombe sold the block to Murry and probably soon after moved to Arkansas. According to Andrew Brown III, Murry had the current home constructed that year.[134] It is not known if the Holcombe home had been destroyed by 1860 or if perhaps Murry simply had the original home substantially modified, possibly by building a second floor. Murry and his family owned and occupied the home well into the twentieth century.

On October 11, 1860, Murry married Mary Elizabeth Miller (1832–1910), the daughter of Charles P. Miller, who lived across the street to the north. Between 1862 and 1877, the couple had at least six children. On September 2, Dr. Murry's oldest child, Sallie McAlpine Murry (1850–1906), married J. W. T. Falkner, the only child of W. C. Falkner and his first wife Holland. Although it isn't known where in Tippah County the marriage occurred, it is likely that it took place in the Murry house in that it was customary for marriages at the time to be held in the bride's family home.

Following the Civil War, Dr. Murry constructed a two-story commercial building on the northwest corner of the square, which he used as both his doctor's office and a drugstore with the Masonic Lodge upstairs. In 1883, just seven years after the telephone's invention, the *Ripley Advertiser* noted that Dr. Murry had installed a telephone line between his drugstore and his home, possibly the first telephone system in the county.[135]

Figure 16.33. Harris-Finger house. Photograph by Phillip Knecht, from his website Hill Country History. Used with his permission.

After J. W. T. Falkner and family moved to Oxford in 1885, they would usually stay with Dr. Murry upon their return visits. William Faulkner recalled that on visits there, his great-grandfather required that for breakfast each of the children had to have a Bible verse ready to recite from memory before eating. If any child did not have one, he or she had to go and learn one for presentation.[136]

The home is extant today although considerably modified; for example, the monumental columns in front are not original. The original configuration had a full frontal porch on the first story surmounted by a central portico on the second.

Block 81

Harris-Finger House (W side of Block 81, fronting on Jackson Street)

This two-story, clapboard Italianate house has carved brackets on the eaves. A three-story turret with a mansard roof rises above the house. The entrance is Palladian with a two-light fanlight.

The house was constructed during 1883–1884 for J. C. "Jim" Harris, an attorney and son of C. L. Harris, who served for over twenty years as the superintendent of the Ripley Railroad.[137] Jim was married to Mary Thurmond,

Figure 16.34. Cole-Thurmond house. Photograph by Phillip Knecht, from his website Hill Country History. Used with his permission.

daughter of R. J. Thurmond. In 1890, in preparation for their move to Sheffield, Alabama, the Harrises sold the home to his cousin Lee Hines, a part owner of the railroad, who then occupied the house for several years.[138]

In 1894, a reporter for the *Southern Sentinel* climbed into the turret for a bird's-eye view of Ripley and described the scene: "The panorama spread out to the vision is lovely and entrancing to a degree. The handsome forest trees that line the principal streets permit glimpses here and there of the residence and business houses and altogether they form a picture worthy of the painter's brush."[139]

In 1900–1901, the home was occupied by the family of Murry C. Falkner, the grandson of Colonel Falkner and the father of William Faulkner, making this the earliest known extant home of the writer. The home was later acquired by the Finger family, who owned and occupied it for close to a century.[140] The home is extant today.

Block 89

W. R. Cole/R. J. Thurmond home (NE¼ Block 89)

The home was built in the 1850s probably for merchant W. R. Cole, whose family occupied it until after the Civil War. At the beginning of the war,

Figure 16.35. C. L. Harris house. Courtesy of Tommy Covington.

Mrs. Cole presented a flag to Falkner and the Magnolia Rifles that had probably been designed and fabricated by the women of Ripley. R. J. Thurmond purchased the house soon after the Civil War.[141] When he began spending less time annually in Ripley, he sold a half interest in the house to his niece, Mrs. Sallie Holt, in 1901, and in 1905, as he was preparing to move permanently to North Carolina, he sold the other half interest to her.[142] The home is extant today.

Block 93

C. L. Harris home (NW¼ Block 93)

The home of Cornelius Leroy "Lee" Harris (1841–1916) stood at the intersection of Jackson and Water Street, where it faced north onto Water.[143] Harris was the superintendent and general manager of the Ripley Railroad from around 1878 until 1898 and was also a major shareholder. Harris's sister, Cornelia, married C. E. Hines, and Harris and Hines were in partnership in the sawmill business before they bought into the railroad in 1877. Two of his children, James and Dora, married children of R. J. Thurmond. In 1898, he retired from the railroad and three years later sold his home to J. D. Pitner,[144] after which he and his wife moved to Memphis. The home is no longer extant.

Figure 16.36. Falkner lot, Ripley Cemetery. Photograph by Jack D. Elliott Jr.

Ripley Cemetery

Ripley Cemetery lies on the east side of the railroad, north of the Ripley plat.

The cemetery, the principal burial ground in Ripley since the 1830s, has historically been divided into a Black and a white section. Many members of families from the nineteenth century are buried there: Brown, Falkner, Miller, Murry, and Thurmond. In the Black section can be found Emeline Falkner, once a slave of Colonel Falkner; Ned Barnett, who once lived at William Faulkner's Rowan Oak and Greenfield Farm; and Sam Edgerton, barber, who was married to one of Emeline's daughters. Also, he was one who came when Colonel Falkner was shot and helped to carry him to the Carter house.

The cemetery is dominated by the nineteen-foot-tall monument to Colonel Falkner, which stands in the center of the Falkner lot, enclosed by an iron fence. Only six individuals are known to be buried in the lot: the colonel, three of his offspring (Henry and the two small children, Vance and Lizzie, who died only days apart in the fall of 1861), and two of his grandchildren (a son and daughter of the Carters). There is also a headstone for his first wife Holland, placed by Frances Reid in 2005. Holland's place of burial is unknown, although she is probably buried in Ripley Cemetery.

His body was buried inside an aboveground vault, as specified by his will. His burial service was described by a newspaper reporter:

> The vast throng then proceeded to the Ripley Cemetery, where with the beautiful and expressive burial service of the Masonic Fraternity, all that was mortal of the noble Falkner was laid in the tomb. Flowers were heaped upon the metallic casket until there was room for no more; strong men wept as they looked upon the face of their friend for the last time; the children cried as they cast a flower upon the tomb, while noble women with wreathes of flowers watered with tears stood at the tomb and gently placed their tokens of love and sorrow within its confines. Never in the history of Ripley has such a throng of sorrowing people gathered together to honor the dead. All felt that a friend was gone forever. Dry eyes were few. And so passes away the noblest man that ever honored Tippah county with his citizenship.[145]

Notes

◇━◉━◇━◇─◉━◇

Introduction

1. William Faulkner, *Sartoris* (New York: Random House, 1929), 1.

2. Falkner's middle name is uncertain today. It is not known to have appeared in any documents during his lifetime. Donald Duclos seemed to have settled the matter when he claimed that it was Clark, a name with no known precedent in the family, basing his claim on records in the J. W. Thompson Bible. However, as I discuss below, these records appear to be in part questionable. On the other hand, one of Falkner's daughters, Bama McLean, stated in 1956 that his middle name was Cuthbert, one with considerable family precedent. Neither option can definitely be precluded. I more specifically discuss this matter in chapter 1 below.

3. Falkner's uncle James Word referred to him as "Bill" in a letter. Letter, James Word to T. J. Word, Iuka, MS, July 27, 1872, box 1, folder 14, T. J. Word Collection, East Texas Research Center, Stephen F. Austin University, Nacogdoches, TX (hereafter T. J. Word Collection). So, too, did his brother James Word Falkner. Letter, J. W. Falkner to "Sis," Sandusky Island Prisoner-of-War Camp, Sandusky, OH, July 19, 1863, Southeast Missouri State University, Special Collections and Archives, Cape Girardeau, MO.

4. *Southern Sentinel* (Ripley, MS), November 21, 1889.

5. Letter, William Faulkner to Malcolm Cowley, December 8, 1945, in Malcolm Cowley, *The Faulkner-Cowley File: Letters and Memories, 1944–1962* (New York: Viking Press, 1966), 66. The errors in the statement are: (1) while Falkner did command the Second Mississippi Infantry in 1861–1862, he did not raise, organize, or pay the expenses of the entire ten companies; (2) he did not die in a duel but was shot in cold blood by an enraged adversary; and (3) the county did not pay for the memorial, his family did.

6. Niels Bohr, quoted in Yi-Fu Tuan, *Space and Place: The Perspective of Experience* (Minneapolis: University of Minnesota Press, 1977), 4.

7. Paul Ricœur, "Manifestation and Proclamation," trans. David Pellauer, *Journal of the Blaisdell Institute* 12, no. 1 (1978): 31.

8. William Faulkner, *The Town* (New York: Random House, 1957), 315–16.

9. William Faulkner, "Interview with Jean Stein Vanden Heuvel," in James B. Meriwether and Michael Millgate, eds., *Lion in the Garden: Interviews with William Faulkner, 1926–1962* (New York: Random House, 1968), 256.

10. William Faulkner, "Address upon Receiving the Nobel Prize for Literature," in William Faulkner, *Essays, Speeches and Public Letters*, rev. ed., ed. James B. Meriwether (New York: Modern Library, 2004), 120.

11. Faulkner, *Sartoris*, 375.

311

12. William Faulkner, "1699–1945 Appendix: The Compsons," in Malcolm Cowley, ed., *The Portable Faulkner*, rev. ed. (New York: Viking Press, 1967), 708. The term "chancery" alludes to a particular office in Mississippi's county governments, the office of the chancery clerk, which maintains records of the chancery court along with records pertaining to property ownership, for instance deed records and tax rolls.

13. Jack D. Elliott Jr., "Where Was Colonel Falkner Shot?," RootsWeb, February 2012, http://sites.rootsweb.com/~mstippah/FalknerShooting2.html.

14. Maud Morrow Brown, "William C. Falkner, Man of Legends," *Georgia Review* 10, no. 4 (Winter 1956): 421.

15. There are three Andrew Browns featured in this story, all related, whom I have distinguished by designating Sr., Jr., and III, although they are not three successive generations as one might suppose. Andrew Brown Sr. (ca. 1810–1890) and Andrew Jr. (1831–1902) were natives of Ireland, with the older being the uncle to the younger. Andrew Jr. was the father of Joseph Brown (1866–1920), who was in turn the father of Andrew III.

16. "Andrew Brown," in Tippah County Historical and Genealogical Society, *Heritage of Tippah County, Mississippi* (1981; Humboldt, TN: Rose Publishing Company, 1999), 228–29.

17. Andrew Brown, *History of Tippah County, Mississippi*, 3rd ed. (1976; Ripley, MS: Tippah County Historical and Genealogical Society, 1998). Brown's work wasn't published until 1976, twelve years after his death, although it had earlier been circulated in other forms. The first edition was published in 1976 by Itawamba County Times of Fulton, Mississippi. During his lifetime, Brown published a study of Falkner's First Mississippi Partisan Rangers. Andrew Brown, "The First Mississippi Partisan Rangers, C.S.A.," *Civil War History* 1, no. 4 (December 1955): 371–99.

18. Joseph Blotner, *Faulkner: A Biography* (New York: Random House, 1974).

19. Donald Philip Duclos, *Son of Sorrow: The Life, Works and Influence of Colonel William C. Falkner, 1825–1889* (San Francisco: International Scholars Publications, 1998). See Thomas L. McHaney's review, which notes several problems. Thomas L. McHaney, review of *Son of Sorrow: The Life, Works and Influence of Colonel William C. Falkner, 1825–1889*, by Donald Philip Duclos, *Mississippi Quarterly* 17, no. 3 (Summer 1964): 165–69.

20. Thomas Felix Hickerson, *The Falkner Feuds* (Chapel Hill, NC: Colonial Press, 1964), preface.

21. Andrew Brown, quoted in Hickerson, *The Falkner Feuds*, 30; emphasis in the original.

22. A. Brown, *History of Tippah County*, 192; while not as explicitly, Duclos says essentially the same thing; Duclos, *Son of Sorrow*, 152–54.

23. Robert W. Hamblin similarly observed that "Falkner was not merely one of several principals but indeed, as president and major subscriber to the company, the key figure in the early development of the road." Robert W. Hamblin, "The Old Colonel: W. C. Falkner as Prototype for Yoknapatawpha," in *Papers Presented at the Faulkner Heritage Festival, 2007–2010*, ed. Renelda Owen (Ripley, MS: Ripley Main Street Association, 2011), 11.

24. A. Brown, *History of Tippah County*, 284, 286; Duclos, *Son of Sorrow*, 219; and Hickerson, *The Falkner Feuds*, 32.

25. Andrew Brown, quoted in Hickerson, *The Falkner Feuds*, 7.

26. Hickerson, *The Falkner Feuds*, 32.

27. Andrew Brown, Northport, AL, statement dated April 17, 1964, in "Testimonials re: The Falkner Feuds," Ripley Public Library, Ripley, Mississippi, 1964. This is an unpublished, one-page typescript of comments on Hickerson's *The Falkner Feuds*, all dating to 1964.

28. A. Brown, *History of Tippah County*, 286.

29. A. Brown, statement in "Testimonials re: The Falkner Feuds."

30. Joel Williamson, *William Faulkner and Southern History* (New York: Oxford University Press, 1993), 60–61.

31. Robert Cantwell, "The Faulkners: Recollections of a Gifted Family," in *Conversations with William Faulkner*, ed. M. Thomas Inge (Jackson: University Press of Mississippi, 1999), 34–35.

Chapter 1: Settling the Land

1. Frederick Jackson Turner, "The Significance of the Frontier in American History." This essay was initially presented at a special meeting of the American Historical Association at the World's Columbian Exposition held in Chicago in 1893. It was published later that year, first in *Proceedings of the State Historical Society of Wisconsin at Its Forty-First Annual Meeting Held December 14, 1893* (Madison, WI: Democrat Printing Company, 1894), 79–112; then in the *Annual Report of the American Historical Association for the Year 1893* (Washington, DC: Government Printing Office, 1894), 197–227.

2. W. C. Falkner's father's name is usually rendered in late sources as "Joseph Falkner" or "William Joseph Falkner." Joseph Blotner consistently refers to him as Joseph Falkner (*Faulkner: A Biography*, 9–10). Despite these claims, his name was simply *William* Falkner, without a middle name or middle initial, as evidenced by every primary source in which he is listed. Jack D. Elliott Jr., "Tippah County and Colonel Falkner," in *From the Chickasaw Cession to Yoknapatawpha: Historical and Literary Essays on North Mississippi*, ed. Hubert H. McAlexander (Oxford, MS: Nautilus Publishing, 2017), 60n2. The name "Joseph" first appeared in the error-filled biographical sketch of Falkner in Goodspeed Publishing Company, *Biographical and Historical Memoirs of Mississippi*, 2 vols. (Chicago: Goodspeed Publishing Company, 1891), 713. Joseph also seemingly appears in the J. W. Thompson Bible in a brief notation indicating that "Joseph Falkner m. Caroline Word" with no date. However, this entry probably dates to the twentieth century and was probably derived from the Goodspeed volume. Notes from the J. W. Thompson Family Bible, in the Joseph Blotner Papers, Southeast Missouri State University, Special Collections and Archives, Cape Girardeau, MO (hereafter Joseph Blotner Papers). Both mentions of Joseph are in direct contradiction to the primary sources, which refer to only "William," and it can only be concluded that "Joseph" is erroneous. The name "William Joseph" evidently originated with Franklin Moak, who recognized that the sources gave two different names—William and Joseph—and assumed that both were valid, and thus conflated the two into one. Franklin E. Moak, "William *Joseph* Faulkner (ca. 1795–ca. 1842)," in *The Forkner Clan: Forkner/Fortner/Faulkner*, comp. Mona Forkner Paulas (Baltimore: Gateway Press, 1981), 26–36.

William's birth date has to be estimated from two early censuses. First, the 1820 census places him within the age bracket of 16–25, but because he had already been married for four years and was probably at least 21 when he married, we can calculate that he was close to 25 in 1820, providing an approximate year of birth as 1795. In 1840, he appears to fall within the 30–39 age bracket, which would indicate that the earliest year of birth would be 1800–1801. This is evidently a mistake in that it indicates that he was only about 15 or 16 when he married. A mid-1790s date is more probable for his birth.

3. The 1850 census of Ste. Genevieve County, Missouri, indicates that Caroline, by then remarried to Allen Nance, was fifty-one (i.e., born ca. 1799) and born in North Carolina. The 1860 census of Tippah County indicates that she was sixty-two (i.e., born ca. 1798) and born in Georgia. While the Georgia birthplace is clearly incorrect, we can conclude that she was born in North Carolina in ca. 1798–1799.

4. Brent H. Holcomb, *Marriages of Surry County, North Carolina, 1779–1868* (Baltimore: Genealogical Publishing Company, 1982), 64. A digital copy of the original marriage record is available via Ancestry.com.

5. Moak, "William *Joseph* Faulkner"; Roberta Isaac, "The Forkners," in *The Heritage of Surry County, North Carolina*, ed. Hester Bartlett Jackson (Winston-Salem, NC: Hunter Publishing, 1983), 1:183–84; and Rebecca Fulk Blalock and Carole Beasley Sperry, "Family," in *The Heritage of Surry County, North Carolina*, ed. Hester Bartlett Jackson (Winston-Salem, NC: Hunter Publishing, 1983), 1:184–85.

6. The creek is rendered as "Forkner Creek" or "Forkners Creek" beginning as early as 1778. See the November 11, 1778, entry for a three-hundred-acre land grant "[o]n both sides of Forkners Creek" to William Forkner in Surry County on Ancestry.com. However, by the mid-twentieth century, US Geological Survey topographical maps began to list the creek as "Faulkner Creek," which may be an innovation by the USGS. See the topographical maps entitled "Mount Airy North, VA-NC" and "Mount Airy South, NC."

7. The genealogical sketches cited prefer the spelling "Forkner" and indicate that this spelling continued in use much later. Additionally, after examining land grants and wills from the late eighteenth and early nineteenth century via Ancestry.com, I find a strong preference for this spelling in reference to the family. Furthermore, there is a Forkner Cemetery near Mount Airy in Surry County with several Forkner headstones. A search conducted on November 16, 2019, at Find a Grave for Surry County revealed thirty Forkner headstones, zero Falkner headstones, and one Faulkner headstone, the latter for a person who died in 2016 and possibly had no connection to the Forkners.

8. Moak, "William *Joseph* Faulkner," 27.

9. Ancestry.com, "North Carolina, U.S., Index to Marriage Bonds, 1741–1868," https://www.ancestry.com/search/collections/4802. The bondsman was Thomas A. Word. Nancy died in 1818. James Word, "Genealogy of the Word Family Written by James Word, December 23, 1882," typescript, Ripley Public Library, Ripley, Mississippi, 1882; and letter, James Word to T. J. Word, Iuka, MS, July 27, 1872, box 1, folder 14, T. J. Word Collection.

10. Names as recorded by census takers are often rendered based upon the census takers' perceptions of how a name is spelled based upon its vocalization, and consequently the spellings are not always accurate. However, the listings of the family are of interest. In the 1820 census for Surry County, William's name was spelled "Farkner," probably based upon "Forkner." In the 1840 census for Ste. Genevieve County, Missouri, the name was rendered as "Faukner," while after William's death many of his children were listed as "Fockners" in the 1850 census of Missouri. By 1860, when several members of the family had settled in Ripley, their names were all spelled "Falkner."

An often-repeated story is that the original spelling was "Faulkner" and that W. C. Falkner changed the spelling to distinguish himself from a "Faulkner" who was an enemy. While the name did become Falkner, it was clearly originally Forkner. See Robert Coughlan, *The Private World of William Faulkner* (New York: Harper and Brothers, 1954), 34–35; Emma Jo Grimes Marshall, "Scenes from Yoknapatawpha: A Study of People and Places in the Real and Imaginary Worlds of William Faulkner" (PhD diss., University of Alabama, 1978), 79n; and Sally Wolff and Floyd C. Watkins, *Talking about William Faulkner: Interviews with Jimmy Faulkner and Others* (Baton Rouge: Louisiana State University Press, 1996), 179–80. There is no evidence that W. C. Falkner spelled his name as anything other than Falkner; see Duclos, *Son of Sorrow*, 16n.

11. Jane Isbell Haynes, "On the Origin of Cuthbert, Faulkner's Middle Name," *Faulkner Newsletter and Yoknapatawpha Review* 12, no. 4 (October–December 1992): 4.

12. See surveys that range in date from October 9, 1794, signed "T. A. Word DS [Deputy Surveyor]," through October 16, 1820, signed "Tho. A. Word Surv[eyor]," at Ancestry.com, "North Carolina, U.S., Land Grant Files, 1693–1960," https://www.ancestry.com/search/collections/60621/.

13. For Thomas's service as sheriff, see two references from Surry County records: Book H, 23; and Court Order Book, listed at http://familyrambler.blogspot.com/. For his being an attorney, see Hester Bartlett Jackson, "Charles Word," in *The Heritage of Surry County*, edited by Hester Bartlett Jackson (Winston-Salem, NC: Hunter Publishing, 1994), 2:430.

14. Thomas's family apparently settled in Habersham County between 1820 and 1830. The date range derives from his being involved in survey work as late as 1820 in Surry County, while in 1830 he appears in the census for Habersham County.

15. Blotner, *Faulkner: A Biography*, notes section, 9. Although Blotner refers to *A Topographical Analysis*, he provides no citation for where he found this information. The book is listed in "An Ancient Record," *Scott's Monthly Magazine* 3, no. 6 (1867): 472, as one of a collection of old publications that are "rarely seen by the present generation" that "serve to show the progress of book-making in Georgia." The name Thomas A. Word is erroneously rendered as "Thomas A. Wood." In transcriptions, it was a common error to confuse Word and Wood. I have not been able to find an extant copy of Word's publication.

16. Thomas died on February 12, 1831, and is buried in the Bethlehem Baptist Church Cemetery, Habersham County, Georgia. The Memorial ID number at Find a Grave is 173031952.

17. Obituary, J. W. Thompson, *Memphis Daily Appeal*, July 4, 1873, reprinted from the *Ripley (MS) Advertiser*.

18. Blotner, *Faulkner: A Biography*, 12–13, notes section, 8–10.

19. The 1820 and 1840 censuses indicate that one person—presumably William—was involved in agriculture.

20. W. C. Falkner's middle name has always had a degree of uncertainty (M. M. Brown, "William C. Falkner, Man of Legends," 421). Donald Duclos announced that it was "Clark," basing this on "the most reliable" of sources, the family record in the J. W. Thompson Bible (Duclos, *Son of Sorrow*, 16n). Afterward, Joseph Blotner used the name "Clark," and it became established (Blotner, *Faulkner: A Biography*, 4–14). However, I question the reliability of this record, and my questions have been exacerbated by my inability to examine it. Instead I have had to rely upon a few pages of notes that Blotner apparently made from it, which suggest that the family record is in part of probable late twentieth-century origin. Questionable components suggested by Blotner's notes are a format that often differs markedly from the standard Bible family record that focuses upon births, marriages, and deaths. Instead, the notations seem to be in the form of a rough family tree that terminates in the mid-twentieth century, thereby suggesting an approximate time frame for its origin. Errors include listing W. C. Falkner's father's name as Joseph, a mistake that would not have been made while he was living, and errors regarding Falkner's first marriage, stating that the marriage took place in Knoxville, Tennessee, a near impossibility. The name William Clark Falkner is among the questionable material. Making the name Clark even more suspect is a letter written by W. C. Falkner's youngest daughter, Bama McLean, in October 1956, which indicates that her father's middle name was Cuthbert. "Now—my father's name was W. C. Falkner—the 'C' stood for Cuthbert, according to family records—the 'W' for William." Letter, Bama F. McLean to Robert Daniel, undated but mid-October 1956, in Louis Daniel Brodsky and Robert W. Hamblin, *Faulkner: A Comprehensive Guide to the Brodsky Collection*, vol. 2: *The Letters* (Jackson: University Press of Mississippi, 1984), 198.

21. The Falkner children other than W. C. consisted of: Thomas Anderson (b. ca. 1817), Sarah Elizabeth (1818–1867), Joseph (b. ca. 1823), Caroline Matilda (1827–1878), Justiania "Jetty" (ca. 1830–1889), Samuel (b. ca. 1832), James Word (b. ca. 1835), Francis (or Frances) (b. ca. 1839), and Mary A. (b. ca. 1841). The next-to-the-last child is of uncertain sex. In the 1850 census for Missouri, this person is listed as "Francis," an eleven-year-old male, while in the 1860 census for Mississippi the same person is listed as "Frank," a twenty-two-year-old female.

22. Helen Mattox Crawford and Mary Flo Word, "Capt. William Word: The Jailer," in Monroe County Book Committee, *A History of Monroe County, Mississippi* (Dallas: Curtis Media Corporation, 1988), 933–34.

23. The site of Hamilton, the county seat, often referred to as "original Hamilton," has to be distinguished from the later settlements that succeeded it—Old Hamilton and New Hamilton—that are still extant. The site of original Hamilton is about three miles south of New Hamilton in the SE¼ Section 6, Township 16, Range 18 West. There is no remnant of a town extant, only a marble monument that was erected by Dr. W. A. Evans. Jane Fairchild Lancaster, *Hamilton: Take Your Place in History as the First County Seat of Monroe* (Amory MS: *Amory Advertiser*, 1975), 2–3.

24. Helen Mattox Crawford and Mary Flo Word, "Capt. William Word: The Jailer," in Monroe County Book Committee, *A History of Monroe County*, 933–34.

25. Jack D. Elliott Jr., "The Pontotoc Land Office," in *From the Chickasaw Cession to Yoknapatawpha: Historical and Literary Essays on North Mississippi*, ed. Hubert H. McAlexander (Oxford, MS: Nautilus Publishing, 2017), 13–22.

26. Word's work began after he signed a contract on March 28, 1834, to survey the interior section lines for Township 14, Range 5 East of the Chickasaw Meridian. See notes on the plat of that township at the Bureau of Land Management's website. He had survey contracts through September 22, 1837, when he was paid for completing his last contract. By this time, most of the survey work was completed. Letter, Thomas H. Blake, Commissioner, GLO, to Walter Forward, Secretary of the Treasury, January 6, 1843, National Archives, Bureau of Land Management, Record Group 49, Entry 13, vol. 2, 253–58. As late as the 1860s, "T. A. Word" appears in a Chickasaw County land roll as owning the NW¼ Section 14, Township 15, Range 5 East land that is now in Clay County, Mississippi. Shirley Mathis, "1861–1864 Land Assessment Roll of Chickasaw Co.," *Chickasaw Times Past* 11, no. 4 (Winter 1993): 174.

27. The Chickasaw Agency, as a physical plant and base of operations for the Chickasaw agent, a federal official, was established on the outskirts of present-day Houlka, Mississippi, in the late 1790s, where it became a center of activity within the Chickasaw territory. After almost three decades and a succession of agents, in 1825–1826, the agency house was relocated to the far northeastern corner of the Chickasaw domain near the Tennessee River. As the US land office at Pontotoc began allotting and selling land during the mid-1830s, the Chickasaw agent, Benjamin Reynolds, was required to approve Chickasaw allotments of land, which entailed his establishing an agency presence at Pontotoc, only fifteen miles from the original agency site at Houlka. James R. Atkinson, *History of the Chickasaw Indian Agency East of the Mississippi River* (Starkville, MS: privately published, 1998).

After moving to Pontotoc, Reynolds began paying for board and accommodations usually with Thomas C. McMackin, the town's leading hosteler, who was located close to the land office but just outside the reserved section. According to Frank Patton, "Gen. McMackin opened a house of entertainment on his own purchase south of Allen [the tavern operated by John L. Allen, which was adjacent to the land office buildings] but on the same hill." Rev. Frank Patton, "Reminiscences of the Chickasaw Indians, No. XV, Old and New Pontotoc" (from an unidentified, undated newspaper, probably 1876). McMackin's location "south of Allen but on the same hill" indicates that he was on the southern tip of the ridge south of Allen and the land office, just across the southern section line and thereby outside the reserved section.

A list of government expenditures includes a representative entry that illustrates the use of McMackin's establishment with $125.25 paid to McMackin "for board of B. Reynolds, interpreter, servant and horses, and furnishing them with provisions for the camp when making locations of reservations, from March 19 to June 4, 1835, while engaged in locating reservations." "Expenditures from the Chickasaw Fund: Letter from the Secretary of War,

Communicating a Detailed Statement of All the Expenditures Made from the Chickasaw Fund between the 2d Day of March, 1833, and the 1st Day of January, 1843," Document no. 65, 1843, reprinted, Aberdeen, MS: Chickasaw Publishing Company, 1982, 50–54.

28. This branch office of the Chickasaw Agency closed in September 1837 following the beginning of Chickasaw emigration to what is now Oklahoma in June 1837 (Atkinson, *History of the Chickasaw Indian Agency*, 44–45). See the expenditure of $200 paid by Reynolds to Thomas C. McMackin "for rent of a house used as an office by agent at Pontotoc, from September 1, 1835, to June 15, 1836" ("Expenditures from the Chickasaw Fund," 52). James R. Atkinson, *Splendid Land, Splendid People: The Chickasaw Indians to Removal* (Tuscaloosa: University of Alabama Press, 2004), 232–33.

29. Mary Elizabeth Young, *Redskins, Ruffleshirts, and Rednecks: Indian Allotments in Alabama and Mississippi, 1830–1860* (Norman: University of Oklahoma Press, 1961), 116–17.

30. Letter, John M. Moore, Principle Clerk Public Lands, GLO, to Thomas H. Benton, US Senate, December 26, 1838, "Statement Exhibiting the Sales in the Chickasaw Cession of 1832," National Archives, Bureau of Land Management, Record Group 49, Entry 13, vol. 1, 306–7.

31. Journal of Edward Fontaine, entry for November 23, 1836, Mississippi State University, Special Collections, Starkville, MS, Edward Fontaine Papers, 1809–1879, folder 1, reel 1.

32. Joseph G. Baldwin, *The Flush Times of Alabama and Mississippi: A Series of Sketches* (London: D. Appleton and Company, 1854), 82–83.

33. H. B. Fant, "Thomas Jefferson Word," in William S. Powell, ed., *Dictionary of North Carolina Biography*, vol. 6: *T–Z* (Chapel Hill: University of North Carolina Press, 1996), 269. Word was first documented in Pontotoc by his selection on July 26, 1835, to serve as superintendent of a newly established Sunday school. Edmund T. Winston, *The Story of Pontotoc* (Pontotoc, MS: Pontotoc Progress Print, 1931), 117.

34. Information on patents was obtained from the Bureau of Land Management's website. For James's total acreage, see M. E. Young, *Redskins, Ruffleshirts, and Rednecks*, 165–66. According to James's account, he settled in Tishomingo County, Mississippi, in 1839. If so, he probably made earlier visits for the purpose of purchasing land. Word, "Genealogy of the Word Family."

35. Obituary, J. W. Thompson, *Memphis Daily Appeal*, July 4, 1873. J. G. Deupree, "Colonel R. A. Pinson," in *Publications of the Mississippi Historical Society: Centenary Series*, vol. 2, edited by Dunbar Rowland (Jackson: Mississippi Historical Society, 1918), 9, refers to Thompson working as a schoolteacher in Pontotoc. Additionally, Thompson appears in the 1836 Pontotoc County tax roll.

36. Winston, *The Story of Pontotoc*, 115.

37. Reuben Davis, *Recollections of Mississippi and Mississippians* (Boston: Houghton Mifflin, 1891), 66.

38. R. Davis, *Recollections of Mississippi and Mississippians*, 71.

39. James Word, in "Genealogy of the Word Family," notes that the Charles W. Humphreys family settled near Ripley in 1838. However, it appears that they arrived somewhat earlier, because CWH is listed in an 1837 Tippah County tax roll. Apparently, they moved briefly south to Pontotoc County because CWH is listed in that county in the 1840 census, before returning to Tippah.

40. Helen Mattox Crawford and Mary Flo Word, "Capt. William Word: The Jailer," in Monroe County Book Committee, *A History of Monroe County*, 932–33.

41. A. R. H. White, "Word-Lewis Family," in Monroe County Book Committee, *A History of Monroe County*, 927; and Cornelia Jarman Mattocks, "Alexander Word," in Monroe County Book Committee, *A History of Monroe County*, 927–28.

42. Edward T. Price, "The Central Courthouse Square in the American County Seat," *Geographical Review* 58, no. 1 (January 1968): 29–60.

43. William Faulkner, *The Hamlet*, 3rd ed. (New York: Random House, 1965), 3.

44. "Yoknapatawpha" is a variant spelling of a name that rendered in the Chickasaw orthography is *yaakni' patafa*, which means "plowed land." The current local pronunciation "Yokney" is a close rendering of *yaakni'* or "land." William Faulkner erroneously stated that Yoknapatawpha means "water runs slow through flat land." Keith A. Baca, *Native American Place Names in Mississippi* (Jackson: University Press of Mississippi, 2007), 134–35. Yoknapatawpha appears in several variant spellings in correspondence from as early as 1793 (Atkinson, *Splendid Land, Splendid People*, 289–90).

45. Baca, *Native American Place Names in Mississippi*, 113.

46. *Laws of the State of Mississippi* (Jackson: George R. and J. S. Fall, 1836), 46. Word's name is misspelled as "Thomas J. Ward." The other two commissioners were James E. Matthews and F. T. Leak.

47. Official returns for Tippah County, March 23, 1836, Mississippi Department of Archives and History, Jackson, MS. The Board of Police is equivalent to the present Board of Supervisors.

48. Captain J. E. Rogers, "History of Tippah County," in Tippah County Historical and Genealogical Society, *Heritage of Tippah County*, 148. This essay originally appeared in the *Ripley (MS) Broadaxe*, August 21, 1878.

49. "Valuable Lots for Sale in the Town of Ripley," advertisement, *Columbus (MS) Democrat*, August 6, 1836. The advertisement was first published on June 15, 1836.

50. From a narrative by Charles Peter Miller (1798–1875), quoted in Tommy Covington, "Ripley First United Methodist Church," in Tippah County Historical and Genealogical Society, *Heritage of Tippah County*, 93.

51. "Ripley Inn," advertisement, *Ripley (MS) Advertiser*, October 11, 1845, with notation that the advertisement originally appeared on March 22, 1845. The Ripley Inn was on the northeast quadrant of Block 26. Tippah County Deed Book C, 152; and A. Brown, *History of Tippah County*, 39.

52. Miller operated the Ripley Inn until about 1851, when he went into the mercantile business. One daughter, Mary Elizabeth, became the second wife of Dr. John Y. Murry Sr. Her step-daughter Sallie Murry married W. C. Falkner's son, J. W. T. Falkner. Another daughter, Margaret, married Richard J. Thurmond, a business associate of Falkner's, and a third daughter, Sarah, married Andrew Brown Jr., a prominent Ripley merchant. The Browns were the grandparents of Andrew Brown III who became a well-known historian of Tippah County.

53. Obituary, J. W. Thompson, *Memphis Daily Appeal*, July 4, 1873. The reference to Thompson as the first lawyer in Ripley comes from Mary Etter Murry, "Ripley Pioneers" (see note 57 below).

54. William W. Bailey (1834–1907) was the son of Edmund I. Bailey and Lydia D. Mullins Bailey. Edmund was elected Tippah's first probate clerk in 1836 and ran unopposed in November 1837. Lydia died a few days after in Ripley on December 2, 1837. Edmund apparently died in 1841 in Shelby County, Alabama. A biography of W. W. Bailey can be found in Goodspeed Publishing Company, *The History of Franklin County, Arkansas* (Chicago: Goodspeed Publishing Company, 1889); and at My Genealogy Hound, http://www.my genealogyhound.com/arkansas-biographies/ar-franklin-county-biographies/william-w -bailey-genealogy-franklin-county-arkansas-altus-ar.html. See also J. E. Rogers, "History of Tippah County," in Tippah County Historical and Genealogical Society, *Heritage of Tippah County*, 148; this article originally appeared in the *Ripley (MS) Broadaxe*, August 21, 1878. List of election returns, *Ripley (MS) Transcript*, November 9, 1837, 3; and "Obituary," *Ripley (MS) Transcript*, December 7, 1837, 3. See also Dr. J. Y. Murry's statement: "Capt. W. W. Bailey, who was born in Ripley, and left an orphan by the death of both parents when a child, when he was adopted into the family of the noble John W. Thompson, and was raised in Ripley, is at

present an influential member of the house of representatives of Arkansas." *Southern Sentinel* (Ripley, MS), April 13, 1893. An excerpt from an obituary for Mrs. J. W. Thompson reads: "She reared two motherless boys W. W. Bailey and J. W. T. Falkner; each of whom always delighted to call her mother." *Southern Sentinel* (Ripley, MS), September 22, 1898. In 1864, Bailey married Thompson's niece, Ruth Sellers (1839–1904), whose mother was Thompson's sister, Jane Thompson Sellers.

55. A. Brown, *History of Tippah County*, 69. In 1845, he announced for reelection as district attorney. *Ripley (MS) Advertiser*, August 16, 1845. In 1855, he was elected to the state legislature for the 1856–1858 term. "Old Tippah Erect," *Ripley (MS) Advertiser*, November 15, 1855, 2. He did not run for reelection, but instead, in January 1858, announced his candidacy for circuit judge. "A Card," *Ripley (MS) Advertiser*, January 27, 1858, 2. He won the election in November 1858. Harvard Business School, Baker Library, R. G. Dun & Co./Dun & Bradstreet Collections, R. G. Dun & Co. ledgers (hereafter R. G. Dun & Co.), vol. 1, Tippah County, MS, 535. He served as circuit judge through the outbreak of the Civil War.

56. R. Davis, *Recollections of Mississippi and Mississippians*, 168.

57. Sam Agnew, "Papers of Rev. Sam Agnew," in Tippah County Historical and Genealogical Society, *Heritage of Tippah County*, 145. See also the anonymous "Ripley Pioneers," an article that appeared in 1895 in either the *Ripley (MS) Advertiser* or the *Southern Sentinel* (Ripley, MS). According to Andrew Brown (*History of Tippah County*, 21, 24), the anonymous writer was actually Brown's cousin, Mary Etter Murry, daughter of Dr. J. Y. Murry and great-aunt of William Faulkner. Internal evidence suggests that Brown was indeed correct, and consequently I cite this source under Mary Etter Murry's name. The dimensions of the courthouse come from the Board of Police's January 18, 1869, specifications for rebuilding it following its 1864 destruction by fire. The specifications state that the new courthouse was to be constructed "on the old foundation where the Court House stood . . . according to the plan of the one that was burned. The said house shall be of the same size, same height, same shape, same plan, same number of rooms all to be of the same kind of material" (Tippah County Minutes of the Police Board, vol. 2, 49). At a later meeting on March 18, 1869, it was noted that the old foundation was fifty feet square (Tippah County Minutes of the Police Board, vol. 2, 64). The core of the rebuilding is preserved in the present courthouse and beneath it lie the 1838 foundations.

58. "An Act to Incorporate the Town of Ripley, in the County of Tippah," in *Laws of the State of Mississippi* (Jackson: George R. and J. S. Fall, 1837), 120–21.

59. "An Act to Incorporate the Subscribers to the Mississippi Union Bank," January 21, 1837, *Southern Argus* (Columbus, MS), August 22, 1837, 1–2; "An Act to Incorporate the Subscribers to the Mississippi Union Bank," in *Laws of the State of Mississippi* (Jackson: B. D. Howard, 1838), 9–33; and "An Act Supplementary to an Act to Incorporate the Subscribers to the Mississippi Union Bank," in *Laws of the State of Mississippi*, 1837, 33–44. Documentation of Jeff's role as attorney for the bank comes from correspondence in box 1, folder 11, T. J. Word Collection.

The Ripley branch bank was on the eastern half of Lot 5, Block 13 (Tippah County Deed Book C, 426). The lot was sold by sheriff's deed in 1845 (Tippah County Deed Book F, 90–91). A later deed indicates that the bank building was on the eastern half of Lot 5 fronting on Spring Street and adjacent to Commerce Street (Tippah County Deed Book Q, 519–20). The source for Garland as the builder is Murry, "Ripley Pioneers." Brown erroneously believed that the bank building was the same as that known in the 1850s as "Falkner's brick building" (A. Brown, *History of Tippah County*, 40). Falkner's brick commercial building was on the same block (Block 13) and same street (Spring Street) but several lots to the west of the bank. See the appendix.

60. William Faulkner, *Requiem for a Nun* (New York: Random House, 1951), 39.

61. Michael Novak, "The Return of the Catholic Whig," *First Things*, no. 1 (March 1990): 38.

62. Faulkner, *Requiem for a Nun*, 7–8.

63. Faulkner evidently borrowed the name Pettigrew from "Pettigrove's stand," a frontier inn that was on the Natchez Trace on the north side of present-day Houston, Mississippi. The name is preserved today in Pettigrew Creek, which runs by the WCPC radio station in Houston. Dawson A. Phelps, "Stands and Travel Accommodations on the Natchez Trace," *Journal of Mississippi History* 11, no. 1 (January 1949): 37; and James R. Atkinson, "The Natchez Trace through Chickasaw County," in Chickasaw County Historical and Genealogical Society, *A History of Chickasaw County, Mississippi*, vol. 2 (Houston, MS: Chickasaw County Historical and Genealogical Society, n.d.), 2.

64. A. Brown, *History of Tippah County*, 31.

65. Thomas D. Clark, *A Pioneer Southern Railroad from New Orleans to Cairo* (Chapel Hill: University of North Carolina Press, 1936), 17.

66. "Lots for Sale in the Town of Houston," advertisement, *Columbus (MS) Democrat*, August 6, 1836, 3. The New Orleans and Nashville Railroad Company was chartered by the Mississippi legislature in 1837.

67. *Laws of the State of Mississippi*, 1837, 130–33.

68. For the full list of railroad incorporations for this time period, see John Edmond Gonzales, "Flush Times, Depression, War, and Compromise," in *A History of Mississippi*, ed. Richard Aubrey McLemore (Jackson: University and College Press of Mississippi, 1976), 290–91.

69. "Aberdeen: Great and Extensive Sale of Lots in Aberdeen," advertisement, *Columbus (MS) Democrat*, August 6, 1836, 3.

70. W. B. Wilkes, "Robert Gordon," in W. A. Evans, *Pioneer Times in Monroe County* (Hamilton, MS: Mother Monroe Publishing Company, 1979), 3. The Wilkes articles originally appeared in the *Aberdeen (MS) Weekly*, 1877–1879. Wilkes (1817–1880) first came to Monroe County in 1833 and was a contemporary of, if not witness to, much that he described.

Chapter 2: Arrival in Mississippi

1. Joel Williamson found in Falkner's departure from Missouri for Mississippi the beginning of a "capacity for alienating himself" from family and community. Seen in the light of a young man's attempt to improve his prospects in life, this claim is completely unjustified. Williamson, *William Faulkner and Southern History*, 61.

2. In part, the 1842 date is supported by the following evidence. L. Pinkney Smith, a personal friend of Falkner's and editor of the *Southern Sentinel*, wrote in 1883: "Col. Falkner has been a citizen of this county forty-one years." 1883 – 41 = 1842 (*Southern Sentinel* [Ripley, MS], May 24, 1883). A year later he wrote: "He [Falkner], at the age of 17 came to this county a poor, penniless boy." 1825 + 17 = 1842/43 (*Southern Sentinel*, October 2, 1884). Also, in 1881 M. C. Gallaway, another personal friend of Falkner's and editor of the *Memphis Daily Appeal*, wrote: "The colonel [Falkner] has resided at his present home [Ripley] for forty years" ("The White Rose of Memphis," *Memphis Daily Appeal*, April 10, 1881, 2). While Gallaway's arrival date differs by one year, his is probably more of an approximation as suggested by his use of a rounded figure. The 1842 date is also supported by the documented arrival of T. J. Word in Ripley, for which see below.

3. In 1859, Falkner was a brigadier general in the Mississippi Militia.

4. The issue of *Quid Nunc* in which the article originally appeared doesn't survive. However, it was reprinted as "A Self-Made Man," *Times-Picayune* (New Orleans), June 12, 1859, 7; and as "Gen. Wm. C. Falkner, of Mississippi: Sketch of the Life of a Self-Made Man," *Memphis Daily Avalanche*, June 28, 1859, 2.

5. "A Pretty Romance," *Ripley (MS) Advertiser*, May 15, 1886, reprinted from the *Pontotoc (MS) True Democrat*. Although neither the date of the event nor the date of its initial publication in the Pontotoc newspaper is known, both presumably occurred shortly before May 15. Because the event occurred on a Friday night, it can be estimated to have been on either Friday April 23, April 30, or May 7, probably the latter.

The Falkner quotations were presumably paraphrased by a newspaper writer but nevertheless probably reflect Falkner's rhetoric. The story would eventually metastasize into often contradictory variants. Initially an abbreviated version appeared in the *State Ledger* (Jackson, MS), which was then copied by other newspapers including the *Grenada (MS) Sentinel*, May 22, 1886, 8; and the *Pascagoula (MS) Democrat-Star*, June 11, 1886, 4. Several years later a modified version appeared in which Falkner came first to Ripley to meet unnamed relatives, then moved on to Pontotoc to find work, where in low spirits he was aided by "a little maid" who would become in this rendition, not his second wife, but his first wife. Alexander L. Bondurant, "William C. Falkner, Novelist," in *Publications of the Mississippi Historical Society*, vol. 3, ed. Franklin L. Riley (Oxford: Mississippi Historical Society, 1900), 115. A quarter century later, another version was related in which Falkner walked from Missouri to Ripley to live with his uncle J. W. Thompson. Upon arriving, he found that Thompson was in jail in Pontotoc on a charge of murder, so Falkner walked to Pontotoc, where, overcome with grief, he was comforted and aided by a little girl, this time his future *second* wife. Edmund Winston, "Life of Col. William C. Falkner: A Glorious Word Picture of the Founder of the G.M.&N. by One Who Has Studied His Life," *Southern Sentinel* (Ripley, MS), January 7, 1926, 2, 7, reprinted from the *G.M.&N. News* (Mobile, AL), November 27, 1925, 5–9. Robert Coughlan's 1954 version was essentially the same as Winston's (Coughlan, *The Private World of William Faulkner*, 27–28). Maud Brown tells a variant in which Falkner arrived in Ripley, where he met little Elizabeth Vance, and she obtained stagecoach fare for him to travel to Pontotoc (M. M. Brown, "William C. Falkner, Man of Legends," 422). Robert Cantwell's 1953 rendition is more abbreviated than previous versions to the point of dropping Pontotoc entirely from the narrative. Robert Cantwell, introduction to *The White Rose of Memphis*, by William C. Falkner (New York: Coley Taylor, 1953), ix.

6. This time frame coincides with the assertion that Falkner came to Tippah County at the age of seventeen, which would have been between July 6, 1842, and July 5, 1843. Word's changes in residence during the 1830s and 1840s can be documented in part by deeds in which he was involved as either grantor or grantee. Deeds in that era often identified the place of residence of the grantors and grantees, usually in terms of county of residence. In this regard, the earliest known deed that specifies his county of residence dates to October 29, 1836, and places him in Pontotoc County, presumably in the town of Pontotoc. Deeds that identify Pontotoc County as his place of residence appear consistently through July 15, 1842, the last date that places him as resident of that county (Pontotoc County Deed Book 4, 325). A day before, on July 14, 1842, John Davis, agent for the Mississippi Union Bank, wrote to Samuel Craig, cashier for the Ripley branch of the bank, informing him that "Col. Thomas J. Word & myself having made an arrangement as to the Banking House in Ripley I have herewith to request you would give him possession of the same." Letter, John Davis, agent, Macon, MS, to Samuel Craig, July 14, 1842, box 1, folder 8, T. J. Word Collection.

Evidence of Jeff's move to Ripley comes less than two months after. On September 8, Davis wrote to him in a letter addressed to Ripley. Letter, John Davis, agent, Macon, MS, to Thos. J. Word, Ripley, MS, September 8, 1842, box 1, folder 8, T. J. Word Collection. Davis later wrote to Word in Ripley, noting: "I understood you had moved to Ripley." Letter, John Davis, agent, Macon, MS, to Thos. J. Word, Ripley, MS, November 10, 1842, box 1, folder 7, T. J. Word Collection.

7. See the appendix, Block 11, T. J. Word home.

8. "Col. Jeff Word . . . was associated with him [J. W. Thompson] for a number of years" (Murry, "Ripley Pioneers," 1895). This suggests that the two were partners in the practice of law.

9. *Public Documents Printed by Order of the Senate of the United States, First Session of the Twenty-Eighth Congress Begun and Held at the City of Washington, December 4, 1843,* vol. 3, document 168 (Washington, DC: Gales and Seaton, 1844), 104, 115–18, 148; Franklin L. Riley, "Choctaw Land Claims," in *Publications of the Mississippi Historical Society,* vol. 8, edited by Franklin L. Riley (Oxford: Mississippi Historical Society, 1904), 367–69; and Clara Sue Kidwell, "The Choctaw Struggle for Land and Identity in Mississippi, 1830–1918," in *After Removal: The Choctaw in Mississippi,* ed. Samuel J. Wells and Roseanna Tubby (Jackson: University Press of Mississippi, 1986), 72–77.

10. For the *Ripley Advertiser,* see the appendix, Block 21.

11. *Southern Sentinel* (Ripley, MS), October 2, 1884.

12. The 1845 Mississippi state census, Tippah County, listed T. J. Word as the head of a household that consisted of two males and two females. At this time his nuclear family consisted of himself, his wife Mary Elizabeth Jackson Word (b. 1822, Ireland; d. 1852, Holly Springs, MS), daughter Justiania Word (1842–1899), and son John Jackson Word (1843–1909), which accounts for the two males and two females listed and indicates that W. C. Falkner was not living in the household. However, if we turn to the household of J. W. Thompson, who was married to T. J. Word's sister Justiania and together had no children of their own, we find a household consisting of three males and one female. The Thompsons obviously account for one male and one female, leaving two other males. One of these was probably Falkner and the other was probably William W. Bailey. Regarding Falkner's residence in the Thompson household, an account of a 1926 return visit to Ripley by his daughter Bama Falkner McLean recorded that she visited "the home where her father spent his young manhood in the home of Judge Thompson." "Daughter of Colonel Falkner Visits Ripley," *Southern Sentinel* (Ripley, MS), June 10, 1926.

13. The November 1, 1845, issue of the *Ripley Advertiser* has two references that imply that Word was still a resident of Ripley. In one he was listed among several delegates selected to attend a convention to be held in Memphis on November 12, suggesting that he planned to remain a resident through that time. Then on February 7, 1846, the first in a series of advertisements for the law firm of (T. J.) Word and (H. W.) Walter of Holly Springs was published in a Holly Springs newspaper, the *Holly Springs Gazette.* This evidence considerably narrows the time frame for his move from Ripley to Holly Springs to the period of November 12, 1845, to February 7, 1846.

14. The date of his move to Texas comes from *Southwestern Reporter Containing All the Current Decisions of the Supreme and Appellate Courts of Arkansas, Kentucky, Missouri, Tennessee, and Texas,* vol. 143 (Saint Paul, MN: West Publishing Company, 1912), 258. "In December 1856, and after his second marriage, he [T. J. Word] removed to Texas, and there continuously resided until his death."

15. The 1850 US Census for Tippah County lists Falkner's profession as "lawyer." In 1881, former resident L. C. Butler recalled that when he first arrived in Ripley around 1849, "W. C. Falkner, C. A. Brougher, and T. C. Hindman [Jr.] were then making their first efforts at the Bar." L. C. Butler, "Interesting Letter," Petersburg, Tennessee, December 31, 1880, *Ripley (MS) Advertiser,* January 15, 1881, 3. Hindman read law under Orlando Davis and was admitted to the bar in or shortly before May 1849, in contrast to the claim by Diane Neal and Thomas Kremm that he was admitted to the bar in 1851. Diane Neal and Thomas W. Kremm, *The Lion of the South: General Thomas C. Hindman* (Macon, GA: Mercer University Press, 1993), 13.

16. Thompson & Falkner were listed as a partnership in 1851, 1852, and 1854. John Livingston, *Livingston's Law Register* (New York: Office of the Monthly Law Magazine, 1851),

97; John Livingston, *Livingston's Law Register for 1852* (New York: Office of the Monthly Law Magazine, 1852), 125; and John Livingston, *Livingston's Law Register* (New York: Office of the Monthly Law Magazine, 1854), 143. Regarding the dissolution of this partnership, Thompson stated on November 1, 1858: "I have been promoted to the Bench. W. Falkner has purchased my office + might possibly attend to your bus[iness]" (R. G. Dun & Co., vol. 1, Tippah County, MS, 534). The law office of Thompson & Falkner was probably located on the southwest corner of Block 12, a building probably built and used by Thompson before Falkner's advent into Ripley (see the appendix).

17. Livingston, *Livingston's Law Register*, 1851, 97.

18. Falkner, *Rapid Ramblings in Europe*, 149, 197.

19. J. W. Thompson was certainly a positive influence. His concern for encouraging literary interests in the young is evidenced by his October 24, 1859, purchase while in Pontotoc of a copy of William Whiston's 1737 translation of *The Works of Flavius Josephus* for his adoptive son, J. W. T. Falkner, only eleven at the time and the actual son of W. C. Falkner. See the inscription inside the copy of *The Works of Flavius Josephus* (Rochester, NY: Alden and Beardsley, 1856) in the collection of William Faulkner's personal library. University of Virginia Library, Albert and Shirley Small Special Collections Library, Faulkner Library, https://small. library.virginia.edu/collections/featured/the-william-faulkner-collection/faulkner-library-july-1998/. In his novel *The Unvanquished*, William Faulkner lists a number of volumes on a bookcase in Colonel Sartoris's house and includes an edition of Josephus. William Faulkner, *The Unvanquished* (New York: Random House, 1938), 18.

20. Calvin S. Brown, "Colonel Falkner as General Reader: *The White Rose of Memphis*," *Mississippi Quarterly* 30, no. 4 (Fall 1977): 591–95; see also Duclos, *Son of Sorrow*, 214–15.

21. This is evidenced by what Donald Duclos sees as a strong Byronic influence in Falkner's 1851 *The Siege of Monterey: A Poem*. Duclos, *Son of Sorrow*, 67–68.

22. Committee of the Grand Lodge of Jackson, Mississippi, *Proceedings of the Grand Lodge of Mississippi, Ancient, Free and Accepted Masons, from Its Organization July 27th, 5818, to Include the Communication Held in the Year 5852* (Jackson, MS: Clarion Steam Printing, 1882), 609, 626–27. There are no known returns from the Ripley Lodge for the mid- through late 1840s. However, the Saint Johns Lodge that was formed within the Second Mississippi Regiment while participating in the Mexican War notes that Falkner was demitted from lodge membership probably following his medical discharge in late 1847. The implication is that he had been a lodge member prior to the Ripley Company's departure for Mexico in January 1847. Later his name appears as a member in the Ripley Lodge returns from 1866 through 1887. Email message, Raymond Settle, Secretary, Ripley Lodge, to Chris Marsalis, October 26, 2018.

23. A. Brown, *History of Tippah County*, 57.

Chapter 3: Things That Go Bump in the Night

1. Beverly Adcock had resided in Pontotoc for two or three years prior to his departure. He appears in the Pontotoc County tax rolls for 1843 and 1845 but does not appear in the 1841 tax roll.

2. One of the children was thought to have been "not more than seven months old." "Shocking and Wholesale Murders," *Southern Tribune and Aberdeen (MS) Commercial News*, June 26, 1845, reprinted from the *Memphis Appeal*.

3. The names of the party were reconstructed from a number of sources including an online page of genealogical information on Beverly Adcock: http://www.echoalpha.info /genealogy/A322/AdcockBeverlyA.html. The name of Beverly Adcock's wife wasn't given in any of the articles on the crime other than to state that her maiden name was "Paradise."

"Shocking Depravity!," *Jackson (TN) Republican*, June 13, 1845, 2. In June 1837, Beverly Adcock married Paralee Paradise in Davidson County, Tennessee. Edythe Rucker Whitley, comp., *Marriages of Davidson County, Tennessee, 1789–1847* (Baltimore: Genealogical Publishing Company, 1981), 161. However, the following year Paralee brought suit against Beverly for divorce in Williamson County, Tennessee, on grounds of physical abuse. Williamson County Records of the Chancery Court, vol. 12, 168–71, http://library.uncg.edu/slavery/petitions /details.aspx?pid=12237. Although it appeared that the divorce would go through, it seems that they were reconciled judging by the fact that in the accounts of the murder Mrs. Adcock was identified as a Paradise. The names and ages of the slave boys come from "an inventory of the appraised property of B Adcok [*sic*] deceased this 12 July 1845." Pontotoc County Probate File no. 4, Pontotoc County Chancery Clerk's Office, Pontotoc, Mississippi. Other documents in this file refer to Abram as "Abe."

4. Isaac Fryar acquired the SW¼ Section 15, Township 3, Range 4 East by patent dated August 9, 1838. This parcel is located on the east side of the road from Ripley to Pocahontas, and its location fits with the estimated distance of eight miles from Ripley.

5. "Wholesale Murder," *North Alabamian* (Tuscumbia, AL), June 20, 1845, 2, reprinted from the *Ripley (MS) Advertiser*. McCannon came from Columbus, Mississippi, which is in Lowndes County. He is listed in the 1845 Lowndes County personal property tax roll. However, he apparently hadn't been in Lowndes long, because he does not appear in the tax rolls for 1843 and 1844.

6. "A More Brief and General Account of the Horrid Deed," *Daily Gazette* (Utica, NY), July 7, 1845, reprinted from the *Florence (AL) Gazette*.

7. "Shocking and Wholesale Murders," *Southern Tribune and Aberdeen (MS) Commercial News*, June 26, 1845, reprinted from the *Memphis Appeal*.

8. "Wholesale Murder," *North Alabamian* (Tuscumbia, AL), June 20, 1845, 2, reprinted from the *Ripley Advertiser*. Cf. "A More Brief and General Account of the Horrid Deed," *Daily Gazette* (Utica, NY), July 7, 1845, reprinted from the *Florence (AL) Gazette*. Some sources reported that the older lady was Adcock's mother, while others described her as his mother-in-law.

9. "Shocking and Wholesale Murders," *Southern Tribune and Aberdeen (MS) Commercial News*, June 26, 1845, reprinted from the *Memphis Appeal*.

10. "Horrible Murder of Five Persons," *Weekly American Eagle* (Memphis), June 20, 1845, 1.

11. The grave is located in the SE¼ NE¼ SE¼ Section 24, Township 1, Range 4 East, Tippah County. The grave site was mentioned in 1901 when an unsuccessful attempt was made to raise money for a stone marker; it was described as being "in the woods, and on a public road and now only marked by a mound of earth." *Southern Sentinel* (Ripley, MS), May 30, 1901. Some decades later, Andrew Brown mentioned that it was on the farm of the late "E. Y. Keith [*sic*]" (this apparently should be J. Y. [James Yancy] Keith, 1867–1942). A. Brown, *History of Tippah County*, 46. After tracking down the location of the Keith farm through land records, I drove there on March 5, 2016, and discovered that it was owned and occupied by Keith's granddaughter, Mrs. Genette Carpenter McKinney (b. 1931), who graciously carried me to the site, which is now marked by a linear pile of field stones—ferruginous sandstone. She recalled that ever since her childhood the grave's location had been common knowledge in her family. James Yancy Keith acquired the S½ Section 24 on which the grave is located in 1904. Tippah County Deed Book 18, 432. Mrs. McKinney is the daughter of Ottye Keith Carpenter (1900–1986), who was the daughter of James Yancy Keith.

12. A Jackson newspaper recorded that McCannon "was pursued near this place, when the horses of his pursuers gave out." *West Tennessee Whig* (Jackson, TN), June 12, 1845, 2.

13. "Shocking Depravity!," *Jackson (TN) Republican*, June 13, 1845, 2.

14. "Shocking Depravity!," *Jackson (TN) Republican*, June 13, 1845, 2. The time of the departure of the guards with McCannon is based on the following: "The prisoner will be taken

from this place [Jackson] today, and delivered to the proper authorities in Tippah county." "Today" probably refers to Friday, June 13, the publication date of the newspaper issue. Of course, the party had not departed at the time, and one might argue that perhaps they departed the following day. This, however, is very unlikely because the group arrived in Ripley on Saturday evening; it would have been very difficult if not impossible to cover the seventy miles between Jackson and Ripley in one day.

15. "Life and Confession of A. J. McCannon," *Ripley (MS) Advertiser*, January 17, 1846, 2. Traveling twenty miles north from Ripley meant that Falkner's particular party traveled from Ripley to the state line.

16. Item from the *Holly Springs (MS) Gazette*, reprinted in the *Ripley (MS) Advertiser*, July 5, 1845, 4. The *Ripley Advertiser* alluded to "the crowd who detained him in custody, after having wrested him out of the hands of the guard who were bringing him on to jail." "Life and Confession of A. J. McCannon," *Ripley (MS) Advertiser*, January 17, 1846, 2.

17. "Life and Confession of A. J. McCannon," *Ripley (MS) Advertiser*, January 17, 1846, 2.

18. The previous circuit judge, Stephen Adams, had resigned in August. "Appointment by the Governor," *Ripley (MS) Advertiser*, August 16, 1845, 2. "Condemned," *Holly Springs (MS) Gazette*, October 11, 1845, 2, indicates that Price was the presiding judge at McCannon's trial.

19. "A. J. McCannon," *Republican* (Jackson, TN), October 10, 1845. Most of this item was reprinted from the *Ripley Advertiser*, almost certainly from the issue of October 4, 1845, for which no copy is known to survive.

20. No copy of this pamphlet is known to survive. Its full title appeared in "Slander Corrected," *North Alabamian* (Tuscumbia, AL), December 26, 1845, 2. An abbreviated form of the title—*Life and Confession of A. J. McCannon, the Murderer of the Adcock Family*—was given in an article in the *Franklin Democrat* (Tuscumbia, AL), reprinted in the *Guard* (Holly Springs, MS), January 9, 1846, 2, and the *Ripley (MS) Advertiser*, January 17, 1846, 2. In all cases, the author was listed as Wm. C. Falkner of Ripley, Mississippi, indicating that Falkner was the author and not McCannon.

21. Similar publications include Israel Smith, *Mutiny and Murder: Confession of Charles Gibbs* (Providence, RI: Israel Smith, 1831); Thomas R. Gray, *The Confessions of Nat Turner, the Leader of the Late Insurrection in Southampton, Va.* (Baltimore: Thomas R. Gray, 1831); and J. R. S. Pitts, *Life and Confession of the Noted Outlaw James Copeland*, ed. John D. W. Guice (1858; Jackson: University Press of Mississippi, 1980). In the latter source, Pitts was also the sheriff who incarcerated the convicted murderer Copeland. More recently and more well known, Truman Capote interviewed the murderers of the Clutter family in Kansas, which led to the publication of his "non-fiction novel" *In Cold Blood* in 1969.

22. "Life and Confession of A. J. McCannon," *Ripley (MS) Advertiser*, January 17, 1846, 2.

23. "The Franklin (Ala.) Democrat and the M'Cannon Pamphlet," *Ripley (MS) Advertiser*, January 31, 1846, 2.

24. "Life and Confession of A. J. McCannon," *Ripley (MS) Advertiser*, January 17, 1846, 2.

25. "Life and Confession of A. J. McCannon," *Ripley (MS) Advertiser*, January 17, 1846, 2.

26. "The Franklin (Ala.) Democrat and the M'Cannon Pamphlet," *Ripley (MS) Advertiser*, January 31, 1846, 2.

27. As quoted in "Slander Corrected," *North Alabamian* (Tuscumbia, AL), December 26, 1845, 2.

28. The editor of the *Franklin Democrat* who included the phrase from the pamphlet (dated January 22, 1846) was quoted in "The Franklin (Ala.) Democrat and the M'Cannon Pamphlet," *Ripley (MS) Advertiser*, January 31, 1846, 2.

29. "The Franklin (Ala.) Democrat and the M'Cannon Pamphlet," *Ripley (MS) Advertiser*, January 31, 1846, 2.

30. There is a record of the marriage of Andrew J. McCannon to Peggy Ann Gibson dated December 29, 1840. Lawrence County Marriage Book OCB, 277, http://www.lawrencecoarchives

.com/database/marriages.php#/?page=1&searchCol=groom_surname&searchBy=mccannon. Courtland is in Lawrence County, Alabama.

31. "Life and Confession of A. J. McCannon," *Guard* (Holly Springs, MS), January 9, 1846, 2, reprinted from the *Franklin Democrat* (Tuscumbia, AL).

32. Errors include, for example, the claim that the events occurred in Jacinto, Mississippi, rather than in Ripley. This is not likely a mistake that Gallaway would have made; the errors may have been made by intermediaries who recorded Gallaway's story.

33. Henry L. Guion was born in 1810 and moved to Memphis in 1840. He died in 1876 and is buried in Elmwood Cemetery, Memphis. *Memphis Daily Appeal*, August 8, 1876, 1.

34. F. S. Latham founded the *Enquirer* in Memphis in 1836 (*Memphis Daily Appeal*, July 5, 1876, 4). The newspaper appeared over the years with several variant names: the *Enquirer*, *Tri-Weekly Enquirer*, *Tri-Weekly Memphis Enquirer*, *Memphis Morning Enquirer*, *Daily Memphis Enquirer*, and *Eagle and Enquirer*. Henry L. Guion later became a partner of Latham in publishing the *Enquirer*. J. P. Young, *Standard History of Memphis, Tennessee: From a Study of the Original Sources* (Knoxville, TN: H. W. Crew and Company, 1912), 446.

35. "The Late Col. Falkner," *Clarion-Ledger* (Jackson, MS), November 28, 1889, reprinted from the *Greenville (MS) Times*.

36. "Execution of McCannon," *Ripley (MS) Advertiser*, November 1, 1845, 2.

37. "Execution of McCannon," *Ripley (MS) Advertiser*, November 1, 1845, 2.

38. "The Late Col. Falkner," *Clarion-Ledger* (Jackson, MS), November 28, 1889, reprinted from the *Greenville (MS) Times*.

39. An item in the March 1, 1846, edition of the *Memphis Appeal* announced that C. C. Cleaves of the Southern Literary Emporium on Front Row was offering for sale copies of "'The Life and Confessions of A. J. McCannon' by W. C. Falkner, tried and sentenced for the murder of the Adcock family and executed in Ripley, Nov. 1, 1845." Duclos, *Son of Sorrow*, 35; and *Tri-Weekly Enquirer* (Memphis), February 28, 1846, 1.

40. The state legislature appropriated $11.80 to reimburse Sheriff Pryor for McCannon's burial expenses. *Laws of the State of Mississippi* (Jackson: C. M. Price and G. R. Fall, 1846), 161–62.

41. After convicted murderer James Copeland was hanged and buried in Augusta, Mississippi, in 1857, his body was exhumed and his skeleton displayed in a local drugstore. After criminal John Long was hanged in Illinois around 1840, his skeleton was exhibited for over a century (John Guice's introduction to Pitts, *Life and Confession of the Noted Outlaw James Copeland*, xxii). Additionally, after the pirate Charles Gibbs was hanged in New York City in 1831, his cranium wound up at New York City's General Society of Mechanics and Tradesmen. Joseph Gibbs, *Dead Men Tell No Tales: The Lives and Legends of the Pirate Charles Gibbs* (Columbia: University of South Carolina Press, 2007), 149.

42. "Anschlag's Mentality," *Los Angeles Tribune*, n.d., reprinted in William Windsor, *Lectures* (Chicago: Donohue and Henneberry, 1890), 164–65.

43. "A Business in Skulls," *Democrat Chronicle* (Rochester, NY), February 20, 1895, reprinted from the *Washington Post*.

Chapter 4: Mexico

1. *Ripley (MS) Advertiser*, May 16, 1846, 2.

2. Jane Isbell Haynes, *William Faulkner: His Tippah County Heritage; Lands, Houses, and Businesses, Ripley, Mississippi* (Columbia, SC: Seajay Press, 1985), 69–71. The Hindman house, which burned in 1938, was located on the north side of Highway 4 in the SE¼ NE¼ SW¼ Section 18, Township 4, Range 4 East. T. C. Hindman Sr. purchased the entire Section 18 on July 18, 1842. Tippah County Deed Book D, 621.

3. C. J. Frederick, "Thrilling Scenes in Mississippi in Ante-Bellum Days: 'The White Rose of Memphis,'" *Memphis Daily Appeal*, April 20, 1881, 1. This was a letter to the editor by "C. J. F.," Ripley, April 15, 1880.

4. *Ripley (MS) Advertiser*, May 30, 1846, 2.

5. "Remains of Dr. John Y. Murry Laid at Rest," *Southern Sentinel* (Ripley, MS), July 15, 1915.

6. "Gov. Brown," *Ripley (MS) Advertiser*, June 6, 1846, 2.

7. Russell James Chance, "Alexander Melvourne Jackson: Mississippi Lawyer, Editor, Soldier, and Politician, 1823–1857" (PhD diss., Mississippi State University, 1970), 91.

8. "Gov. Brown," *Ripley (MS) Advertiser*, June 6, 1846, 2.

9. "Volunteers," *Ripley (MS) Advertiser*, June 20, 1846, 2.

10. *Ripley (MS) Advertiser*, June 27, 1846, 2.

11. *Ripley (MS) Advertiser*, July 11, 1846, 2. The route of the Pontotoc Rovers took them through Tippah and Marshall Counties, Mississippi, and Shelby County, Tennessee, indicating that they did not go directly to Vicksburg but marched to Memphis, where they presumably caught a steamer to Vicksburg. See the resolution thanking those who had offered hospitality to the Rovers on their march. *Southern Tribune* (Pontotoc, MS), July 4, 1846, 2. A half year later, the Tippah Guards followed the same path on their way to Vicksburg.

12. Chance, "Alexander Melvourne Jackson," 95–97; and Richard Bruce Winders, *Panting for Glory: The Mississippi Rifles in the Mexican War* (College Station: Texas A&M University Press, 2016), 89.

13. Winders, *Panting for Glory*, 90.

14. Winders, *Panting for Glory*, 91.

15. Chance, "Alexander Melvourne Jackson," 104–5; H. Grady Howell Jr., *A Southern Lacrimosa: The Mexican War Journal of Dr. Thomas Neely Love, Surgeon, Second Regiment Mississippi Volunteer Infantry, U.S.A.* (Jackson, MS: Chickasaw Bayou Press, 1995), 32, 38, 42–44, 55; and Winders, *Panting for Glory*, 91.

16. Falkner, *Rapid Ramblings in Europe*, 556–57.

17. Howell, *A Southern Lacrimosa*, 63.

18. Howell, *A Southern Lacrimosa*, 77, 81; and Charles M. Price, "Interesting Letter from the Senior Editor in Mexico, Camp Near Monterey [*sic*], Mexico, April 24, 1847," *Mississippian* (Jackson), May 8, 1847, 2.

19. Ancestry.com, Military Service Records for American Volunteer Soldiers, Mexican War, 1845–1848, Cuthbert B. Word. According to Cuthbert's brother James, he "died and was buried on the west bank of the Miss. River about three miles above Baton Rouge" (Word, "Genealogy of the Word Family"). This suggests that while returning from New Orleans to Ripley via steamer, he was taken off the boat for medical attention and died there.

20. Howell, *A Southern Lacrimosa*, 108.

21. Howell, *A Southern Lacrimosa*, 108–9, 112–13.

22. Deposition of Alexander M. Jackson, October 31, 1848, in Duclos, *Son of Sorrow*, 315.

23. Christopher Conway, ed., *The U.S.-Mexican War: A Binational Reader* (Indianapolis: Hackett, 2010), 81.

24. "A Mexican Woman in the Field," *American Republican and Baltimore Daily Clipper*, December 3, 1846, 1.

25. Howell, *A Southern Lacrimosa*, 108–13; and deposition of Alexander M. Jackson, October 31, 1848, in Duclos, *Son of Sorrow*, 315.

26. Winders, *Panting for Glory*, 113.

27. Statement of Thomas N. Love, Surgeon, Second Regiment Mississippi, camp near Monterrey, May 1, 1847, from Ancestry.com, Military Service Records for American Volunteer Soldiers, Alexander M. Jackson.

28. Deposition of Alexander M. Jackson, October 31, 1848, in Duclos, *Son of Sorrow*, 315.

29. Howell, *A Southern Lacrimosa*, 126.

30. Thomas C. Hindman Sr. remarked in 1850 that Falkner's "Bowie knife & pistols are constantly about his person." Letter, Thomas C. Hindman Sr. to Jacob Thompson, March 9, 1850, in Duclos, *Son of Sorrow*, 321.

31. This party included T. C. Hindman Jr. and W. E. Rogers of Company E. See their respective statements in Duclos, *Son of Sorrow*, 316, 323. Another account of the ambush, probably derived from Falkner, appeared in the Holly Springs *Guard* in May 1847, reprinted as "A Self-Made Man," *Times-Picayune* (New Orleans), June 12, 1859, 7.

32. Deposition of Alexander M. Jackson, October 31, 1848, in Duclos, *Son of Sorrow*, 315; Howell, *A Southern Lacrimosa*, 125; and Certificate of Dr. Thomas N. Love, Camp Buena Vista, October 1, 1847, from Ancestry.com, Military Service Records for American Volunteer Soldiers, W. C. Falkner. Decades later while in Rome, Falkner would recall with self-deprecating humor: "My left hand, on which remains only one whole finger (the other three having been overtaken by a bullet one day while I was hunting a safe place)" (Falkner, *Rapid Ramblings in Europe*, 192).

33. Statement, Thomas N. Love, Surgeon, Second Mississippi Volunteers, camp near Monterrey, April 18, 1847, from Ancestry.com, Military Service Records for American Volunteer Soldiers, W. C. Falkner.

34. Ancestry.com, Military Service Records for American Volunteer Soldiers, Robert H. Hindman.

35. Howell, *A Southern Lacrimosa*, 113–14; and Charles M. Price, "Interesting Letter from the Senior Editor in Mexico, Camp Near Monterey [sic], Mexico, April 24, 1847," *Mississippian* (Jackson), May 8, 1847.

36. Chance, "Alexander Melvourne Jackson," 145–46.

37. Howell, *A Southern Lacrimosa*, 125.

38. Ellis practiced medicine in Ripley as early as 1842. "Medical Notice," *Ripley (MS) Advertiser*, September 9, 1843, 3. On January 7, 1846, he married Mary L. Hindman, daughter of T. C. Hindman Sr. "Married," *Ripley (MS) Advertiser*, January 10, 1846, 3.

39. Statement by James B. Ellis, M.D., Ripley, MS, June 18, 1847, in Ancestry.com, Military Service Records for American Volunteer Soldiers, W. C. Falkner.

40. While Holland is usually listed without a middle name, there are three documents that indicate that her middle name began with an "R," possibly standing for Reynolds. Holland's great-grandmother was Mary Reynolds (1760–1822), and she married Simon Spight (1741–1816). Tippah County Administration Chancery Record, 1846–1849, 317–18; and Tippah County Deed Book H, 502–3.

41. Besides Holland, the children included Lazarus (1826–1913); Mary (1830–1905), married Dawson L. Killgore; Simmons Harrison (1832–1920); and Joseph Jr. (1835–1912). Although Holland's year of birth is not known, it can reasonably be estimated at about 1828—between Lazarus and Mary.

42. The Joseph Pearce family was listed in the 1820 and 1830 censuses as residing in Lenoir County, North Carolina. Daughter Mary was born in 1830, and she consistently listed her birthplace in the censuses as North Carolina (US Censuses 1860, 1880, 1900). A circa 1831 date for removal from North Carolina to Tennessee is strongly suggested by son Simmons, who was born in January 1832 and who consistently listed his place of birth as Tennessee (US Censuses 1860, 1870, 1900, 1910, 1920).

43. Joseph Pearce was born April 21, 1791, in Jones County, North Carolina. His date of death can be inferred to have been 1846 or earlier. A report on his estate dated February 2, 1847, consists primarily of a list dated "July 1st" from almost certainly 1846, implying that he had died before this date, most likely in early 1846 (Tippah County Administration Chancery Record, 1846–1849, 81–82). However, a web page on Joseph Pearce at Roop & Pearce Connections, while

claiming at the top of the page that he died circa 1846, further on states that he died in 1842, a claim supposedly based on an unidentified "family bible." However, I have not seen this bible nor a transcription of the information in it and doubt that the 1842 date is correct. Roop & Pearce Connections, RootsWeb, last updated April 24, 2019, https://wc.rootsweb.ancestry.com/cgi-bin/igm.cgi?op=GET&db=mpearce&id=I00417.

44. Simon Reynolds Spight was the first cousin of the children's mother, Elizabeth Harrison Pearce. Elizabeth's mother was Holland Spight Harrison, whose brother was Thomas Spight, the father of Simon R. Spight. Thomas S. Hines, *William Faulkner and the Tangible Past: The Architecture of Yoknapatawpha* (Berkeley: University of California Press, 1996), 132–34.

45. The Spight home/hotel was on the east side of Commerce Street opposite the terminus of Cooper Street, the current site of the Ripley Public Library. The Thompsons, it will be recalled, resided on the nearby Block 12. See the appendix.

46. Donald Duclos reported, based on the Thompson Bible, that Falkner's wedding to Holland occurred on July 9, 1847, in Knoxville, Tennessee (*Son of Sorrow*, 21, 363n5). That the wedding was held in Knoxville is certainly incorrect. Considering that both Falkner and Holland were living in Ripley, it would have been extremely difficult in an era before railroads to travel to the Tennessee city and back again during Falkner's short medical leave, and this travel would have been for no good reason. Furthermore, the date of the wedding—July 9—is very questionable in that T. C. Hindman Sr. makes three mentions of the fact that Falkner was unmarried when he returned to Mexico in mid-1847 but was engaged to be married. It is extremely unlikely that Hindman was unaware of Falkner's marital status. Duclos, *Son of Sorrow*, 42, 43, 46. I suggest below that Falkner actually got married to Holland after his second return from Mexico.

47. Ancestry.com, Military Service Records for American Volunteer Soldiers, T. C. Hindman Jr.

48. Falkner, *Rapid Ramblings in Europe*, 155–56.

49. Letter, Thomas C. Hindman Sr. to Jacob Thompson, January 28, 1850, in Duclos, *Son of Sorrow*, 317; and Chance, "Alexander Melvourne Jackson," 167. The camp of the Second Mississippi was transferred from Walnut Springs near Monterrey to Buena Vista in late May (Winders, *Panting for Glory*, 104).

50. Letter, Alexander M. Jackson to Cordelia C. Kavanaugh, camp near Buena Vista, Mexico, September 26, 1847, University of Southern Mississippi Libraries, Alexander Melvourne Jackson Papers, M16, box 1, folder 2, Historical Manuscripts, Special Collections.

51. Certificate of Dr. Thomas N. Love, October 1, 1847, Ancestry.com, Military Service Records for American Volunteer Soldiers, W. C. Falkner. A transcript of this certificate can be found in Duclos, *Son of Sorrow*, 40.

52. Duclos, *Son of Sorrow*, 46.

53. Letter, Thomas C. Hindman Sr. to Jacob Thompson, March 9, 1850, in Duclos, *Son of Sorrow*, 319–20.

54. Chance, "Alexander Melvourne Jackson," 167–68.

55. Winders, *Panting for Glory*, x–xi.

56. Winders, *Panting for Glory*, 138.

57. The marriage apparently occurred sometime between his return in late October–early November and a December 6, 1847, meeting of the Tippah County Probate Court, by which time Holland had become Holland Falkner (Tippah County Administration Chancery Record, 1846–1849, 318). This contrasts with the usual date and place given, namely July 9, 1847, in Knoxville, Tennessee, which comes from Duclos, *Son of Sorrow*, 21, citing the J. W. Thompson Bible family record. This is very unlikely in light of T. C. Hindman's statements that Falkner was not married when he returned to Mexico. That the marriage took place in Knoxville is exceedingly improbable because of logistical considerations. It is more likely that they were

married in the Spight home, considering that Holland's sister Mary married Dawson L. Killgore there in 1847 and that it was customary for marriages to occur at the bride's home. According to Dr. John Y. Murry: "The marriage took place at Major Spight's Hotel, the home of the bride at that time (1848) [*sic*]." Letter to the editor, Dr. John Y. Murry, April 6, 1893, *Southern Sentinel* (Ripley, MS), April 13, 1893. Although Dr. Murry places the marriage in 1848, this is undoubtedly incorrect, because documents from the Pearce estate settlement list Mary as "Mary Killgore" in 1847, indicating that she was married by that year (Tippah County Administration Chancery Record, 1846–1849, 319). Misremembering a date after half a century is understandable. However, there is no reason to doubt Murry's recollection of the place of the wedding.

58. Tippah County Administration Chancery Record, 1846–1849, 317–21.

59. See the appendix, Block 33, Falkner house.

Chapter 5: The Hindman Feud

1. There had been a temperance society in Ripley since as early as 1844. Falkner's uncles T. J. Word and J. W. Thompson played prominent roles in it. "Temperance Meeting," *Ripley (MS) Advertiser*, February 10, 1844, 2; and *Ripley (MS) Advertiser*, March 8, 1845, 2, and February 7, 1846, 2.

2. C. J. Frederick, "Thrilling Scenes in Mississippi in Ante-Bellum Days: 'The White Rose of Memphis,'" *Memphis Daily Appeal*, April 20, 1881, 2. In 1851, Falkner wrote that Hindman's enmity toward him had been "instigated by a certain cowardly clan to take my life, and not from any malice which he bore against me. I found a certain individual going about the streets trying to turn public feeling against me, and taking every unfair advantage of my situation that he could." W. C. Falkner, *The Siege of Monterey: A Poem* (Cincinnati: privately published, 1851), preface, 5.

3. Frederick, "Thrilling Scenes in Mississippi," 1.

4. Frederick, "Thrilling Scenes in Mississippi," 1. The *Ripley Advertiser* reported: "On Tuesday the 8th inst., a rencountre occurred in this place, between Robert H. Hindman and William C. Falkner, Esq., which resulted in the death of Mr. Hindman. Mr. Falkner immediately gave himself up to the custody of the law. We for bear to state farther particulars, as we understand the case will undergo a judicial investigation." *Memphis Tri-Weekly Appeal*, May 17, 1849, 2, reprinted from the *Ripley (MS) Advertiser*, May 10, 1849.

5. The source for Holland's date of death is uncertain. Donald Duclos merely alludes to her death but does not provide a date (*Son of Sorrow*, 56). Joseph Blotner does list the May 31, 1849, date in his genealogical chart but not in his text, nor is a source provided (*Faulkner: A Biography*, 17n223).

6. In 2005, Frances Street Reid placed a headstone for Holland in the Falkner lot in Ripley Cemetery. However, the precise location of her grave is unknown.

7. In the 1850 census, the two-year-old John was listed as residing in the same home with his father.

8. The name of the judge is from Falkner, *The Siege of Monterey*, preface, 8. The name of the defender is from Frederick, "Thrilling Scenes in Mississippi," 1. Scruggs was in law practice in Holly Springs with H. W. Walter, the former law partner of T. J. Word. "Scruggs & Walter," advertisement, *Holly Springs (MS) Gazette*, November 16, 1849, 1. The advertisement had been running since February 4, 1848. The name of the prosecutor is from letter, N. S. Price, Ripley, to Judge Charles D. Fontaine, August 11, 1849, Mississippi Department of Archives and History, Charles D. Fontaine papers.

9. Frederick, "Thrilling Scenes in Mississippi," 1.

10. A story later had it that the stone initially read "Murdered . . . by Wm. C. Falkner" and that social pressure forced the Hindmans to replace the word "murdered" with "killed."

Duclos, *Son of Sorrow*, 55–56; A. Brown, *History of Tippah County*, 84; and Blotner, *Faulkner: A Biography*, 16. The story apparently has no substance. Upon examination, it is clearly evident that the stone has never been altered.

11. Certificate of William McRea and Benjamin Jones, September 5, 1849, quoted in Duclos, *Son of Sorrow*, 41. Neither McRae nor Jones stayed long in Ripley; neither was resident at the time of the 1850 census. Falkner apparently filed his application on September 6, a day after the certificate was signed (Duclos, *Son of Sorrow*, 48).

12. Letter, Thomas C. Hindman Sr. to Jacob Thompson, near Ripley, MS, March 9, 1850, in Duclos, *Son of Sorrow*, 316–17; and letter, Thomas C. Hindman Sr. to Jacob Thompson, near Ripley, MS, January 28, 1850, in Duclos, *Son of Sorrow*, 319, 321–22.

13. Statement of W. E. Rogers, April 19, 1850, in Duclos, *Son of Sorrow*, 316.

14. Duclos, *Son of Sorrow*, 59; and Frederick, "Thrilling Scenes in Mississippi," 1. For John Henderson's Grocery and the shooting therein, see the appendix.

15. Tippah County Circuit Court Minute Book, March 1851–September 1854, 36.

16. Tippah County Circuit Court Minute Book, March 1851–September 1854, 45, 63–65.

17. Falkner, *The Siege of Monterey*, preface, 6.

18. Don Martini, ed., "Tippah County Circuit Court Records," typescript, Ripley Public Library, Ripley, Mississippi, 1986.

19. [M. C. Gallaway], "The White Rose of Memphis," *Memphis Daily Appeal*, April 10, 1881, 2. The article is unsigned but was almost certainly written by Gallaway.

20. Letter, T. C. Hindman Sr., near Ripley, to Secretary of the Interior, April 1, 1851, in Duclos, *Son of Sorrow*, 323–24.

21. Falkner, *The Siege of Monterey*, main text, 13.

22. Falkner, *The Siege of Monterey*, main text, 13–14.

23. The Ripley Female Academy was organized in June 1849, and in January 1850 Blocks 43 and 44 were donated for the school grounds. Tippah County Deed Book I, 343–44, 365; and A. Brown, *History of Tippah County*, 63–64. Lizzie was born about 1832 in Alabama and was the daughter of Samuel Vance (1792–1840) and Elizabeth Allen Buck (1797–1836). Following the death of her parents, Lizzie apparently resided with her sister Sarah Jane (1819–1894) in Alabama. Sarah Jane initially married in 1839 in Greene County, Alabama, to James Henry Rutledge (1815–1843). After his death, she married Isaac Buchanan (1802–1862) in 1846 in Marion, Perry County, Alabama. By 1848, the Buchanans had moved to Holly Springs, Mississippi, where their son John Lewis Buchanan was born, and by 1850 they resided in Tippah County.

24. Falkner, *The Siege of Monterey*, main text, 7.

25. Cantwell, introduction to *The White Rose of Memphis*, xxi–xxii.

26. Falkner, *The Siege of Monterey*, preface, 5–6.

27. A. Brown, *History of Tippah County*, 69. Assuming that "P." stood for the first letter of the man's surname, I have checked the 1850 census for Ripley and found no other likely contender for Falkner's adversary.

28. Falkner, *The Siege of Monterey*, preface, 7.

29. Falkner, *The Siege of Monterey*, preface, 7–8.

30. Letter, T. C. Hindman, near Ripley, Mississippi, to Secretary of the Interior, May 17, 1851, in Duclos, *Son of Sorrow*, 327.

31. William J. Maclin (b. ca. 1812, VA; d. April 1870, Tippah County, MS).

32. Pontotoc County Marriage Record Book, 1844–1856, 199, Pontotoc County Circuit Clerk's Office. The form on which this information was recorded has blank spaces to record the actual wedding date. These spaces were not filled in, so we don't actually know the date of the marriage. It's probable that it occurred on October 14 or soon after. Duclos states that Falkner and Lizzie married on October 12, which was two days before they were actually licensed (*Son of Sorrow*, 21).

33. Price's law office was located on the West ½ Lot 1, Block 22, which is to say near the east end of the block south of the square. See Tippah County Deed Book O, 516. For Price's acquisition of this parcel, see Tippah County Deed Book J, 448–49.

34. "The Tragedy in Ripley: Death of the Hon. N. S. Price," *Mississippian and State Gazette* (Jackson), April 28, 1854.

35. R. G. Dun & Co., Tippah County, MS, vol. 20, 225. All or some of the rental houses were probably on Blocks 3 and 40. Falkner had purchased Block 3 in December 1851 for $900. In October 1851 he purchased Block 40 for $50 (Tippah County Deed Book K, 209, 254).

36. The brick structure was on the East ½ Lot 7 and the adjoining West ½ Lot 8, Block 13 (Tippah County Deed Book N, 414). On March 19, 1855, the R. G. Dun agent noted that Falkner "owns 2 brick store houses" (R. G. Dun & Co., Tippah County, MS, vol. 20, 221). In an advertisement, the firm Kendrick, Peeler and Company advertised its location as being "Next door East of Falkner's brick building." *Ripley (MS) Advertiser*, January 3, 1856.

37. *Ripley (MS) Advertiser*, January 3, 1856. Cross, Veal, and Company advertised their "Cheap Cash Store" as located on the "North Side of the Public Square in the House formerly occupied by Norvell & Falkner." *Uncle Sam* (Ripley, MS), May 16, 1856, 4

38. R. G. Dun & Co., Tippah County, MS, vol. 20, 221.

39. R. G. Dun & Co., Tippah County, MS, vol. 20, 535. The entry refers to correspondence from Falkner dated November 17, 1858.

40. "Another Gun in the Field," *Weekly American Banner* (Yazoo City, MS), August 24, 1855, 3. If one calculates a beginning date for the publication of *Uncle Sam* based on the surviving issue, no. 38, May 16, 1856, one will get a date of August 24, 1855.

41. *Uncle Sam* (Ripley, MS), May 16, 1856, 2. For the location, see the appendix.

42. *Uncle Sam* (Ripley, MS), May 16, 1856, 4.

43. "Old Tippah Erect," *Ripley (MS) Advertiser*, November 15, 1855, 2.

44. Millard Fillmore (1800–1874) was the vice president under Zachary Taylor, succeeded him as president upon Taylor's death in 1850, and held the office through 1853.

45. Falkner's visits to New York and Philadelphia are documented by his letters, which appeared in the one extant copy of *Uncle Sam*, May 16, 1856. These indicate that he was in New York as early as April 25, then departed for Philadelphia on May 2. He subsequently wrote that he was departing Philadelphia on May 4 for Baltimore and Washington. His name appeared in a list of guests who had checked in to the National Hotel that was published in the *Evening Star* (Washington, DC), May 6, 1856, 4.

46. H. C. Mercer describes the piece as "a quick reel tune, with a backwoods story talked to it while played, that caught the ear at side shows and circuses." The sheet music was first published in 1847 as "The Arkansas Traveller and Rackinsac Waltz," with no author credited. The backwoods story concerning a traveler coming upon a squatter's cabin in rural Arkansas appears to have originated with Colonel Sanford S. Faulkner (1803–1874), who was the Arkansas Traveler himself. H. C. Mercer, "On the Track of 'The Arkansas Traveler,'" *Century Magazine* 51 (March 1896): 707–12; and William B. Worthen, "Arkansas Traveler," *Encyclopedia of Arkansas*, last updated July 17, 2018, https://encyclopediaofarkansas.net/entries/arkansas-traveler-505/. There is no known relationship between Sanford Faulkner and W. C. Falkner, despite the fact that, according to Duclos, J. W. T. Falkner Jr. claimed that the two were brothers (*Son of Sorrow*, 17n).

47. "Barnum's American Museum," advertisement, *New-York Tribune*, April 22, 1856, 1.

48. In *The White Rose of Memphis*, the protagonist Edward Demar/Ingomar alludes to someone who "reminded me of an Egyptian mummy that I had seen in a museum." W. C. Falkner, *The White Rose of Memphis: A Novel* (Chicago: M. A. Donohue and Company, ca. 1920), 336.

49. Letter by "Uncle Sam" [W. C. Falkner], "Uncle Sam's View of Barnum's Museum," New York City, April 25, 1856, *Uncle Sam* (Ripley, MS), May 16, 1856, 1.

50. Letter by "Uncle Sam" [W. C. Falkner], "Uncle Sam's View of Barnum's Museum," New York City, April 25, 1856, *Uncle Sam* (Ripley, MS), May 16, 1856, 1; and "Barnum's American Museum," advertisement, *New-York Tribune*, April 22, 1856, 1.

51. Letter by "Uncle Sam" [W. C. Falkner], "Uncle Sam's View of Barnum's Museum," New York City, April 25, 1856, *Uncle Sam* (Ripley, MS), May 16, 1856, 1; "Our City's Guest," *New York Daily Herald*, April 25,1856, 1; and "The News," *New York Daily Herald*, April 25,1856, 4.

52. Although Falkner placed the meeting on "Monday last," namely April 28, newspaper accounts that appeared on April 30 stated that it had been held "last night" and "last evening," implying the twenty-ninth.

53. The Broadway Tabernacle Church was a Congregational church located as the name implies on Broadway. It was opened in 1836 and closed in 1902. In the 1850s, the congregation was very active in the abolitionist cause.

54. Edwin D. Morgan (1811–1883) was chairman of the Republican National Committee (1856–1864, 1872–1876), governor of New York (1859–1862), and US senator (1863–1869).

55. "Anti-Nebraska Meeting at the Tabernacle," *New York Daily Herald*, April 30, 1856, 4. Also see "The Republican Meeting at the Tabernacle," *New York Times*, April 30, 1856, 4.

56. Edwin Forrest (1806–1872) was a prominent Philadelphia-born Shakespearean actor. His roles included Spartacus, Macbeth, Hamlet, and Richard III. In 1855 he purchased a three-and-a-half-story stone Italianate mansion in Philadelphia where he maintained an extensive library, art gallery, and private theater.

57. Letter by "Uncle Sam" [W. C. Falkner], Room no. 55, Astor House, New York City, May 1, 1856, *Uncle Sam* (Ripley, MS), May 16, 1856, 2.

58. Letter by "Uncle Sam" [W. C. Falkner], Room no. 55, Astor House, New York City, May 1, 1856, *Uncle Sam* (Ripley, MS), May 16, 1856, 2.

59. Letter by "Uncle Sam" [W. C. Falkner], Room no. 55, Astor House, New York City, May 1, 1856, *Uncle Sam* (Ripley, MS), May 16, 1856, 2.

60. Built in 1852 on Chestnut Street, the Girard Hotel was one of Philadelphia's leading hostelries.

61. Prints depicting the Girard Hotel show five floors. Prior to the utilization of structural steel in construction, masonry buildings were limited in height.

62. Letter by "Uncle Sam" [W. C. Falkner], Philadelphia, May 3, 1856, *Uncle Sam* (Ripley, MS), May 16, 1856, 2.

63. In *The White Rose of Memphis*, Falkner had his protagonist Edward Demar study medicine in Philadelphia while residing at the Girard House Hotel and on one occasion visit Girard College. Falkner, *The White Rose of Memphis*, 138.

64. Letter by "Uncle Sam" [W. C. Falkner], Philadelphia, May 3, 1856, *Uncle Sam* (Ripley, MS), May 16, 1856, 2.

65. "Arrivals at Principal Hotels," *Evening Star* (Washington, DC), May 6, 1856, 4. The National Hotel was constructed in 1826 on the northeastern corner of the intersection of Pennsylvania Avenue and Sixth Street NW. At the time of Falkner's visit, it was the largest hotel in the city. It was demolished in 1942.

66. Falkner, *Rapid Ramblings in Europe*, 388, 393.

67. "Rapid Decline of Know-Nothingism in the South," *Ripley (MS) Advertiser*, July 10, 1856, 1, reprinted from the *Richmond Enquirer*.

68. *Ripley (MS) Advertiser*, unknown date, reprinted in the *Semi-Weekly Mississippian* (Jackson), July 25, 1856, 2. The Clinton referred to remains unidentified.

69. Neal and Kremm, *The Lion of the South*, 17, 23, 24, 26, 29, 37–38; and "Fatal Affray," *Weekly American Banner* (Yazoo City, MS), June 6, 1856, 3.

70. W. J. Lemke, "The Hindman Family Portraits," *Arkansas Historical Quarterly* 14 (1955): 104.

71. Frederick, "Thrilling Scenes in Mississippi," 1.

72. [M. C. Gallaway], "The White Rose of Memphis."

73. Matthew Campbell Gallaway (1820–1898) was a lifelong newspaper editor and publisher. Following years of editing newspapers in northern Alabama, in January 1856 he founded the *Sunny South* in Aberdeen. In late 1857 he left the newspaper under the editorship of his brother and moved to Memphis, where he founded the *Avalanche* in January 1858. During the 1870s he became editor of the *Appeal* in Memphis, one of the most prominent newspapers in the South.

74. James E. Saunders, "Early Settlers of Lawrence County, Alabama," in *Newspaper Clippings from the Lawrence County, Alabama, Moulton Advertiser, 1876–1883*, comp. Robin Sterling (n.p.: Robin Sterling Books, 2017), 152–53, first printed in the *Moulton (AL) Advertiser*, July 8, 1889. See also William S. Speer, *Sketches of Prominent Tennesseans* (1888; Baltimore: Genealogical Publishing Company, 2003), 349.

75. [M. C. Gallaway], "The White Rose of Memphis," 2.

76. Falkner, *The White Rose of Memphis*. The dedicatory inscription appears in the first edition of the novel (New York: G. W. Carleton, 1881).

Chapter 6: Building Railroads

1. Bondurant, "William C. Falkner, Novelist," 121. Bama Falkner McLean retold the story in 1935; "The Rebel," *Southern Sentinel* (Ripley, MS), July 25, 1935, 1, reprinted from the *Memphis Press-Scimitar*. See also Duclos, *Son of Sorrow*, 152.

2. "Memphis Convention," *Mississippian* (Jackson), November 9, 1849.

3. "MEMORIAL of Citizens of _____County, Mississippi, to the Legislature," *Mississippi Palladium* (Holly Springs, MS), December 19, 1851, 1.

4. "Ripley Convention, March 3, 1851," *Mississippi Palladium* (Holly Springs, MS), December 19, 1851, 1; and "MEMORIAL of Citizens of _____County, Mississippi, to the Legislature," *Mississippi Palladium* (Holly Springs, MS), December 19, 1851, 1.

5. "It will be recollected that this enterprise was commenced on the first day of November, 1851." "Progress of the Memphis and Charleston Railroad," *Nashville Daily Patriot*, March 17, 1856, 2, reprinted from the *Memphis Whig*, March 12, 1856.

6. "The Memphis and Charleston Railroad is now completed to Middleton, some seventy odd miles from this city [Memphis], and the cars will in a very short time commence running to that point." *Daily Nashville True Whig*, August 30, 1855, 2. "The cars on the Memphis and Charleston Rail Road on the 28th ult., ran up to Pocahontas, about eighty-five miles east of Memphis." *Ripley (MS) Advertiser*, October 11, 1855, 2. A post office called Jenkins Depot was established at Middleton on November 22, 1854, the year before the railroad arrived. The name was changed to Middleton Station on November 23, 1865, then to Middleton on November 29, 1882. Throughout the process of name changes, the location was referred to only as Middleton in the newspapers.

7. "The track laying will commence in May, at Tuscumbia and Pocahontas, and will progress both east and west until the connection is made." *Nashville Daily Patriot*, March 17, 1856, 2.

8. "This day the last rail will be put down and the last spike driven to complete the MEMPHIS AND CHARLESTON RAILROAD, by which a perfect and unbroken connection will be set up between the Atlantic Ocean and the Mississippi River." *Memphis Daily Appeal*, March 27, 1857, 2.

9. "About five thousand strangers arrived in the city yesterday and last night—making in all in the neighborhood of ten thousand visitors now in Memphis, which will be increased several

thousand to-day." "The Railroad Celebration," *Memphis Daily Appeal*, May 1, 1857, 3. See also "Interesting Ceremony," *Memphis Daily Appeal*, May 2, 1857, 2.

10. "Ever since the unpropitious day when the Memphis and Charleston railroad was lost to us, our citizens have been agitating the building of a branch road, to intersect that great thoroughfare at some eligible and desirable point." *Ripley (MS) Advertiser*, reprinted in the *Memphis Daily Appeal*, October 12, 1859, 2.

11. In reference to an 1859–1860 effort, a correspondent of the *Ripley Advertiser* wrote that "this is not the first effort for the Ripley Railroad," implying that earlier efforts in 1857 and 1858 were discontinuous with the then ongoing effort. "Ripley Rail Road," *Ripley (MS) Advertiser*, April 11, 1860, 2.

12. "Thoughts on Railroading," *Bolivar (TN) Bulletin*, March 8, 1872, 2.

13. *Laws of the State of Mississippi* (Jackson: E. Barksdale, 1857), 81–87.

14. "WILLIAM R. BUCHANAN was appointed permanent Chairman, and A. M. JACKSON, permanent Secretary, as provided for by the charter." *Memphis Daily Appeal*, April 14, 1857, 2.

15. A. Brown, *History of Tippah County*, 53.

16. A. Brown, *History of Tippah County*, 53.

17. "Ripley and LaGrange Railroad," *Memphis Daily Appeal*, November 23, 1859, 2.

18. "Ripley Rail Road," *Ripley (MS) Advertiser*, April 11, 1860, 2.

19. Tippah County Deed Book S, 425. Although Delia and Helen were mentioned by name in the deed, Emeline's name was not. However, it becomes evident from other sources.

20. Williamson, *William Faulkner and Southern History*, 22–29, 64–65. Initially, Williamson strongly infers that Emeline's three children were fathered by Falkner, constituting a "shadow family" in his backyard. Subsequently he appears to have forgotten that he had made such a claim, stating instead, and probably rightly, that they were the children of Harris.

21. In subsequent censuses, Emeline and her children were listed under the surname Falkner.

22. According to her headstone, Fannie was born in 1866. Emeline lived out her life in Ripley. By 1880 she and Fannie were listed as servants residing with the R. J. Thurmond family. Upon her death in 1898, Mrs. Thurmond wrote a tribute to this woman, whom she called "friend": "Careful in the management of her own affairs, she was fitted to be so with those committed to her trust, which was never betrayed. . . . It was shown alike to all, even to those in the humblest walks of life. Her attachments were strong. . . . We honored her in life and grieve for her in death." Mary M. Thurmond, letter to the editor, *Southern Sentinel* (Ripley, MS), November 3, 1898.

23. "List of Alumni, Department of Law, 1860," in *Catalogue of the Officers, Alumni and Students of the University of Mississippi, at Oxford, Mississippi* (Jackson, MS: Clarion Steam Printing, 1867), 6. "It was also announced that the Trustees had conferred the degree of Bachelor of Laws upon J. W. Falkner, of Tippah, who had left the class some time ago." "The State University: Commencement Exercises," *Semi-Weekly Mississippian* (Jackson), July 10, 1860.

24. "W. C. Falkner, Attorney at Law," advertisement, *Ripley (MS) Advertiser*, January 4, 1859. This advertisement first appeared on October 20, 1858.

25. "Falkner & Falkner, Attorneys at Law," advertisement, *Ripley (MS) Advertiser*, April 11, 1860. The advertisement first appeared on March 21, 1860.

26. Advertisements first appeared in the *Memphis Daily Appeal* on September 4, 1858, and ran through early October. "For Brigadier General," advertisement, *Memphis Daily Appeal*, September 23 and 28, and October 1, 1858. The election was on Tuesday, October 12. "Army of Mississippi," in Dunbar Rowland, ed., *Mississippi: Comprising Sketches of Counties, Towns, Events, Institutions, and Persons, Arranged in Cyclopedic Form* (Atlanta: Southern Historical

Publishing Association, 1907), 1:143–45; and "Militia, State," in Rowland, *Mississippi: Comprising Sketches of Counties*, 2:234.

27. "More Titles," *Daily Southern Reveille* (Port Gibson, MS), September 21, 1858, 3.

28. References to "General Falkner" can be found in: "Ripley and LaGrange Railroad," *Memphis Daily Appeal*, November 23, 1859, 2; F. T. Leak Ledgers, typescript, vol. 6, 145, December 23, 1859, University of North Carolina, Southern Historical Collection, Louis Round Wilson Special Collections Library, Chapel Hill, North Carolina, Francis Terry Leak Papers, 1839–1865; "Democratic Meeting in Tippah," *Semi-Weekly Mississippian* (Jackson), June 4, 1860, 3; "Planters' Convention of the South," *Weekly Mississippian* (Jackson), July 25, 1860, 2; "Ratification Meeting in Salem," *Weekly Mississippian*, August 8, 1860, 3; and "Tippah County," *Oxford (MS) Intelligencer*, December 19, 1860, 2. Falkner was listed as brigadier general of the First Brigade, Fifth Division of the state militia as late as January 1861. *Journal of the State Convention, and Ordinances and Resolutions Adopted in January 1861* (Jackson, MS: E. Barksdale, 1861), 240.

29. As already noted, the issue of *Quid Nunc* in which the article first appeared does not survive, but the article was reprinted in newspapers in major southern cities, as "A Self-Made Man," *Times-Picayune* (New Orleans), June 12, 1859, 7; and as "Gen. Wm. C. Falkner, of Mississippi: Sketch of the Life of a Self-Made Man," *Memphis Daily Avalanche*, June 28, 1859, 2.

Chapter 7: And History Shall Never Forget You

1. This chapter was coauthored by Sidney W. Bondurant, MD, whom I have called on for decades in matters pertaining to the Civil War.

2. H. Grady Howell Jr., *To Live and Die in Dixie: A History of the Third Mississippi Infantry, C.S.A.* (Jackson, MS: Chickasaw Bayou Press, 1991), 1.

3. In late 1860 Falkner wrote that the company had been organized a year before, indicating a date that coincides with the December 1859 legislation. Letter, W. C. Falkner to Governor John J. Pettus, Ripley, MS, December 28, 1860, Mississippi Department of Archives and History, John J. Pettus Correspondence, series 757.

4. A. Brown, *History of Tippah County*, 93.

5. "The Feeling in Mississippi," *Oxford (MS) Intelligencer*, November 28, 1860, 2.

6. Letter, W. C. Falkner to Governor John J. Pettus, Ripley, MS, December 28, 1860, Mississippi Department of Archives and History, John J. Pettus Correspondence, series 757.

7. The Fourth Brigade included Coahoma, DeSoto, Itawamba, Lafayette, Marshall, Panola, Pontotoc, Tippah, Tishomingo, and Tunica Counties. "The Brigades of the Army of Mississippi," *Oxford (MS) Intelligencer*, February 13, 1861, 1.

8. Dunbar Rowland, *Military History of Mississippi, 1803–1898* (Spartanburg, SC: Reprint Company, 1978), 40–42.

9. Returns from election held on April 1, 1861, for the Second Regiment, Mississippi Volunteers, Mississippi Department of Archives and History, Record Group 9 (Confederate Records), box 266, series 390, Second Regiment (Infantry); and "Mississippi Army Intelligence," *Eastern Clarion* (Paulding, MS), April 19, 1861, 4.

10. Letter, W. C. Falkner to William Barksdale, Jackson, MS, April 13, 1861, Mississippi Department of Archives and History, Confederate Service Records, W. C. Falkner.

11. Immediately after the Battle of First Manassas (July 21, 1861), in which Falkner participated, a Tennessee soldier exploring the battlefield with some friends recorded meeting "a Negro man, Colonel Falkner's cook," who described the battle as it occurred in that vicinity. Steven H. Stubbs, *Duty, Honor, Valor: The Story of the Eleventh Mississippi Infantry Regiment* (Philadelphia, MS: Dancing Rabbit Press, 2000), 102–3.

12. Andrew Brown, ed., "Civil War Diary of Augustus L. P. Vairin, 2nd Mississippi Infantry, C.S.A.," RootsWeb, n.d., https://sites.rootsweb.com/~mscivilw/vairindiary.htm, entries for April 30 and May 1, 1861.

13. Dr. Murry was replaced as surgeon on June 1, 1861, by Dr. H. H. Hubbard of Vicksburg. Apparently, Hubbard had already been appointed by a presidential order on April 27, before Murry's appointment by Falkner. It seems that Falkner was not aware of the previous appointment. A. Brown, "Civil War Diary of Augustus L. P. Vairin," entry for June 1, 1861.

14. A. Brown, "Civil War Diary of Augustus L. P. Vairin," entry for May 3, 1861.

15. A. Brown, "Civil War Diary of Augustus L. P. Vairin," entries for May 8, 9, 10, and 20, 1861.

16. Report of Inspection made at Harper's Ferry, Virginia, by Lieutenant Colonel George Deas, Inspector General C.S. Army, May 23, 1861, United States War Department, *The War of the Rebellion: A Compilation of the Official Records of the Union and Confederate Armies* (Washington, DC: Government Printing Office, 1894) (hereafter OR), series I, vol. 20, 868.

17. Report of Inspection made at Harper's Ferry, Virginia, by Lieutenant Colonel George Deas, Inspector General C.S. Army, addressed to Colonel R S. Garnett, adjutant general, May 23, 1861, OR, series I, vol. 20, 869.

18. Report of Inspection made at Harper's Ferry, Virginia, by Lieutenant Colonel George Deas, Inspector General C.S. Army, May 23, 1861, OR, series I, vol. 20, 868.

19. "Correspondence of the Oxford Intelligencer, Richmond, Va., May 22, 1861," *Oxford (MS) Intelligencer*, May 29, 1861, 2.

20. Quoted in Duclos, *Son of Sorrow*, 104–6; from Dwight Witherspoon, "Unique Army Formation," reprinted in the *G.M.&N. News* (Mobile, AL), November 27, 1925, 10.

21. Quoted in Duclos, *Son of Sorrow*, 104–6, from Dwight Witherspoon, "Unique Army Formation," reprinted in the *G.M.&N. News* (Mobile, AL), November 27, 1925, 10.

22. Report by W. C. Falkner, Winchester, Virginia, June 27, 1861, in Janet B. Hewett, ed., *Supplement to the Official Records of the Union and Confederate Armies* (Wilmington, NC: Broadfoot Publishing Company, 1996), part 2: *Record of Events*, vol. 32, serial no. 44, 664.

23. "Letter from Virginia," by J. P. P., Winchester, Virginia, July 15, 1861, *Memphis Daily Appeal*, July 26, 1861, 2, partially quoted in Duclos, *Son of Sorrow*, 101.

24. "Letter from Virginia," by J. P. P., Winchester, Virginia, July 15, 1861, *Memphis Daily Appeal*, July 26, 1861, 2, partially quoted in Duclos, *Son of Sorrow*, 101.

25. The City of Manassas was later established at Manassas Junction. However, the name "Manassas" did not originate at this location but at Manassas Gap in the Blue Ridge, through which the stream Manassas Run flowed. The railroad that connected the Piedmont with the Shenandoah Valley via the gap was given the name Manassas Gap Railroad. Its junction with the Orange and Alexandria became Manassas Junction, thereby effectively transferring the name from the gap in the Blue Ridge to its present location. For the probable first recording of the name "Manasses Run," see the map by John Warner, "A Survey of the Northern Neck of Virginia, Being the Lands Belonging to the Rt. Honourable Thomas Lord Fairfax Baron Cameron, as Surveyed According to Order in the Years 1736 & 1737," Library of Congress, Washington, DC.

26. William C. Davis, *First Blood: Fort Sumter to Bull Run* (Alexandria, VA: Time-Life Books, 1983), 110–22.

27. T. B. Warder and James M. Catlett, *Battle of Young's Branch; or, Manassas Plain, Fought July 21, 1861* (Richmond, VA: Enquirer Book and Job Press, 1862), 39.

28. "South, A. O., Letter," MSGenWeb Project, last updated March 9, 2018, http://www.msgw.org/confederate/SouthLetter.htm. The letter was written by Private Abner O. South, Second Mississippi Infantry, Company F, to a "Friend," from Camp Jones, near Manassas Junction, August 7, 1861.

29. W. Davis, *First Blood*, 129–31.

30. W. Davis, *First Blood*, 132; and P. G. T. Beauregard, "The First Battle of Bull Run," in *Battles and Leaders of the Civil War*, vol. 1, ed. Robert Underwood Johnson and Clarence Clough Buel (New York: Century Company, 1887), 209–10.

31. "List of Killed and Wounded of Second Regiment Mississippi Volunteers, in the Engagement of July, 1861," report submitted by Captain W. L. Davis, Manassas, July 31, 1861, *Weekly Mississippian* (Jackson), August 14, 1861.

32. "List of Killed and Wounded of Second Regiment Mississippi Volunteers, in the Engagement of July, 1861," report submitted by Captain W. L. Davis, Manassas, July 31, 1861, *Weekly Mississippian* (Jackson), August 14, 1861.

33. Ben Earl Kitchens, *John Marshall Stone: Mississippi's Honorable and Longest Serving Governor* (Iuka, MS: Thornwood Book Publishers, 2014), 31–32.

34. W. Davis, *First Blood*, 135.

35. Beauregard, "The First Battle of Bull Run," 209–10.

36. "Reports of Gen. G. T. Beauregard, C. S. Army, and resulting correspondence. Hdqrs., First Corps, Army of the Potomac, Fairfax Court House, October 14, 1861." Originally written on August 26 and addressed to General Samuel Cooper, Adjutant General, C.S. Army, Richmond, Virginia, but not dispatched until October 14, 1861, OR, series I, vol. 2, 492–93.

37. William F. Smith, "Reminiscences of the First Battle of Manassas," *Southern Historical Society Papers*, vol. 10 (1882): 435–36, 439.

38. Report of Colonel J. E. B. Stuart, First Virginia Cavalry, to General Joseph E. Johnston, July 26, 1861, OR, series I, vol. 2, 482–84.

39. W. Davis, *First Blood*, 141–42.

40. "South, A. O., Letter."

41. Beauregard, "The First Battle of Bull Run," 212.

42. James I. Robertson Jr., *Stonewall Jackson: The Man, the Soldier, the Legend* (New York: Macmillan, 1997), 264, 835n37.

43. J. P. P., "Incidents of the Great Battle, Manassas Junction, Va., July 27, 1861," *Memphis Daily Appeal*, August 7, 1861, 1. Beauregard's statement was repeated over the years. Twenty years later, Gallaway reported it to be: "Men, follow yonder knight of the black plume, and history will not forget you!" "The White Rose of Memphis," *Memphis Daily Appeal*, April 10, 1881, 2. In 1901, Alexander L. Bondurant presented a variant based on Gallaway: "Col. M. C. Galloway, formerly of the *Memphis Appeal* wrote that as he was pressing forward to charge the enemy General Beauregard asked, 'who is the knight with the black plume? Men you may follow where he leads'" (Bondurant, "William C. Falkner, Novelist," 117). Decades later, Dunbar Rowland's history of Mississippi quoted Bondurant's variant. Dunbar Rowland, *History of Mississippi: The Heart of the South*, 2 vols. (Chicago: S. J. Clark Publishing Company, 1925), 2:45.

44. [M. C. Gallaway], "The White Rose of Memphis," *Memphis Daily Appeal*, April 10, 1881.

45. Hewett, *Supplement to the Official Records of the Union and Confederate Armies*, part 1, *Reports*, vol. 1, serial no. 1, 188.

46. After the battle, one Tennessee soldier toured the battlefield with some friends and recorded meeting near the ruins of the Henry house "a Negro man, Colonel Falkner's cook," who described the battle as it occurred in that vicinity: "Pointing in a northwesterly direction to [Matthews Hill] where the battle began, he said our boys retired slowly, 'comin over dat hill yonder whar you see all dem cannon on down dat valley. Dar our boys rallied and begun ter drive dem Yanks up de hill. And on de top of de hill among dem guns dar they hung.'" Stubbs, *Duty, Honor, Valor*, 102–3.

47. "South, A. O., Letter."

48. Larry J. Mardis and Jo Anne Ketchum Mardis, "John H. Buchanan's Diary, July 4, 1861, to July 9, 1862," RootsWeb, 1998, https://sites.rootsweb.com/~mscivilw/buchanan.htm#diary, entries for July 22 and 30, 1861.

49. Kitchens, *John Marshall Stone*, 34.

50. General J. E. Johnston to the Adjutant and Inspector General, C.S. Army, Fairfax Court-House, October 14, 1861, OR, series I, vol. 2, part 1, 477.

51. M. M. Brown, "William C. Falkner: Man of Legends," 429.

52. Bondurant, "William C. Falkner, Novelist," 118; and Mardis and Mardis, "John H. Buchanan's Diary," entries for September 29 and October 12–13, 1861, and January 12–13, 1862.

53. Duclos, *Son of Sorrow*, 108–9; and Victor Hoar, "Colonel William C. Falkner in the Civil War," *Journal of Mississippi History* 27, no. 1 (1965): 50.

54. Mardis and Mardis, "John H. Buchanan's Diary," entries for February 10–20, 1862.

55. Mardis and Mardis, "John H. Buchanan's Diary," entries for February 24–March 7, 1862; and Mississippi Department of Archives and History, Confederate Service Records, J. W. Falkner.

56. Letter, D. B. Wright of Ripley to President Jefferson Davis, quoted in Duclos, *Son of Sorrow*, 110.

57. Mardis and Mardis, "John H. Buchanan's Diary," entries for March 20–22, 1862; and A. Brown, "Civil War Diary of Augustus L. P. Vairin," entries for March 20–22, 1862.

58. Quotations from Duclos, *Son of Sorrow*, 111–12.

59. This is evidenced by the fact that Falkner seems to have arrived in Richmond on or before April 2, while the others only reached there on April 3 (Mardis and Mardis, "John H. Buchanan's Diary," entry for April 3, 1862).

60. Letter, J. W. Clapp to Jefferson Davis, Richmond, VA, April 2, 1862, Mississippi Department of Archives and History, Confederate Service Records, W. C. Falkner; published in Duclos, *Son of Sorrow*, 110–12.

61. A. Brown, "Civil War Diary of Augustus L. P. Vairin," entries for April 4–18 and 26–30, 1862; and Mardis and Mardis, "John H. Buchanan's Diary," entries for April 3–19, 1862.

62. There are two accounts of the election; both are in general agreement regarding the result while giving different totals. For the first balloting, Buchanan listed Falkner 302, Stone 329, Miller 124, while Vairin listed Falkner 249, Stone 250, Miller 129. On the second ballot following Miller's withdrawal, Buchanan listed Falkner with 410 votes and Stone with 445, while Vairin doesn't list the votes, merely noting that Stone won over Falkner. A. Brown, "Civil War Diary of Augustus L. P. Vairin," entries for April 21–22, 1862; and Mardis and Mardis, "John H. Buchanan's Diary," entries for April 21–22, 1862. The following year, Falkner noted that he had been "beaten for Col. by thirteen votes." Letter, W. C. Falkner to James Phelan, February 7, 1863, quoted in Duclos, *Son of Sorrow*, 129.

63. Special order by Brigadier General W. H. Whiting, April 22, 1862, reproduced in Bondurant, "William C. Falkner, Novelist," 119.

64. Letter, Brigadier General W. H. Whiting to G. W. Randolph, April 23, 1862, reproduced in Bondurant, "William C. Falkner, Novelist," 119. Bondurant rendered the name inaccurately as "J. W. Randolph."

65. Letter, General Joseph E. Johnston to G. W. Randolph, April 23, 1862, reproduced in Bondurant, "William C. Falkner, Novelist," 118.

66. A. Brown, "Civil War Diary of Augustus L. P. Vairin," entries for April 23–May 5, 1862; and Mardis and Mardis, "John H. Buchanan's Diary," entries for April 23–May 4, 1862. On April 23, Buchanan noted that "the old officers [are] fixing to start home."

67. Receipt signed by W. C. Falkner, Richmond, VA, April 29, 1862, Mississippi Department of Archives and History, Confederate Service Records, W. C. Falkner. Falkner alluded to passing through Richmond in a letter to President Jefferson Davis. W. C. Falkner to Jefferson Davis, Ripley, MS, May 16, 1862, Mississippi Department of Archives and History, Confederate Service Records, W. C. Falkner.

Chapter 8: Belt of Desolation

1. A. Brown, *History of Tippah County*, 115, 118, 120.

2. Timothy B. Smith, *Corinth 1862: Siege, Battle, Occupation* (Lawrence: University Press of Kansas, 2012), 112–13.

3. Letter, W. C. Falkner to Jefferson Davis, Ripley, MS, May 16, 1862, Mississippi Department of Archives and History, Confederate Service Records, W. C. Falkner.

4. Letter, G. W. Randolph to Governor John J. Pettus, June 8, 1862, quoted in Duclos, *Son of Sorrow*, 116–17.

5. General Orders, distributed by Samuel Cooper, April 28, 1862, Adjutant and Inspector General's Office, OR, series IV, vol. 1, 1094–95.

6. Abstract from Returns of the District of the Mississippi, commanded by Major General Earl Van Dorn, July 1862, OR, series I, vol. 17, part 2, 661; and letter, W. C. Falkner to James Phelan, February 7, 1863, quoted in Duclos, *Son of Sorrow*, 129.

7. A. Brown, "The First Mississippi Partisan Rangers," 372.

8. "Davis, Judge Orlando, Diary," MSGenWeb Project, last updated March 9, 2018, http://www.msgw.org/confederate/davis.htm, entry for June 27, 1862; and Duclos, *Son of Sorrow*, 117.

9. A. Brown, "The First Mississippi Partisan Rangers," 375. There are several references to the partisan rangers being at or near Orizaba, suggesting that they had a base there.

10. Letter, Brigadier General James R. Chalmers to Major G. W. Holt, near Como, MS, January 8, 1864, OR, series I, vol. 32, part 2, 530.

11. Letter, Colonel W. C. Falkner to Colonel Thomas L. Snead, Headquarters, Falkner's Battalion Partisan Rangers, near Orizaba, MS, August 5, 1862, Mississippi Department of Archives and History, Confederate Service Records, W. C. Falkner; and letter, Colonel Thomas L. Snead to Colonel W. C. Falkner, August 7, 1862, OR, series I, vol. 17, part 2, 668–69.

12. "Bertram," "Letter from Ripley, Ripley, Miss., August 29, 1862," *Memphis Daily Appeal*, September 4, 1862, 1. "Bertram's" writing ability and knowledge of events suggests that he was actually Falkner, as does his knowledge of classical literature as evidenced by the reference to sowing dragon's teeth, which comes from the Greek myths pertaining to Cadmus and Jason. "Skirmish Near Rienzi, Miss.," Report of Brigadier General Gordon Granger, US Army Headquarters, Rienzi, MS, August 28, 1862, OR, series I, vol. 17, part 1, 39–41. Information on troops at Rienzi comes from Ben Earl Kitchens, *Rosecrans Meets Price: The Battle of Iuka* (Florence, AL: Thornwood Book Publishers, 1987), 13; and W. H. Tunnard, *A Southern Record: The History of the Third Louisiana Infantry* (Baton Rouge, LA: privately published, 1866), 195.

13. "The Affair at Rienzi," *Memphis Daily Appeal*, September 3, 1862, 2; "Bertram," "Letter from Ripley, Ripley, Miss., August 29, 1862," *Memphis Daily Appeal*, September 4, 1862, 1; Philip H. Sheridan, *Personal Memoirs of P. H. Sheridan* (London: Chatto and Windus, 1888), 1:175–76; and Report of Colonel Philip H. Sheridan, August 27, 1862, OR, series I, vol. 17, part 1, 42.

14. Report of Colonel Edward Hatch, camp near Rienzi, MS, August 27, 1862, OR, series I, vol. 17, part 1, 41; and A. Brown, *History of Tippah County*, 111n10.

15. Report of Colonel Philip H. Sheridan, August 27, 1862, OR, series I, vol. 17, part 1, 42.

16. University of North Carolina, Southern Historical Collection, Louis Round Wilson Special Collections Library, Chapel Hill, North Carolina, Samuel A. Agnew Diary, 1851–1902 (hereafter Agnew Diary), August 28–29, 1862, vol. 7a, 140–41, scans 145–46.

17. "Skirmish near Rienzi, Miss.," Report of Brigadier General Gordon Granger, US Army Headquarters, Rienzi, MS, August 28, 1862, OR, series I, vol. 17, part 1, 40.

18. "Bertram," "Letter from Ripley, Riley, Miss., August 29, 1862," *Memphis Daily Appeal*, September 4, 1862, 1.

19. Letter, Thomas L. Snead to General Henry Little, Tupelo, MS, August 30, 1862, OR, series I, vol. 17, part 2, 690.

20. Edwin C. Bearss, *Decision in Mississippi: Mississippi's Important Role in the War between the States* (Jackson: Mississippi Commission on the War between the States, 1962), 2, 4.

21. Letter, W. S. Rosecrans to U. S. Grant, September 14, 1862, OR series I, vol. 17, part 2, 218.

22. Kitchens, *Rosecrans Meets Price*, 56–58.

23. T. Smith, *Corinth 1862*, 121.

24. Kitchens, *Rosecrans Meets Price*, 77.

25. The site of Paden's Mill is near the present town of Paden, Mississippi, with both named after early settler Thomas Paden. The name is sometimes erroneously listed as "Peyton's Mill."

26. Report of Colonel W. C. Falkner, Bay Springs, MS, September 20, 1862, OR, series I, vol. 17, part 1, 138.

27. Report of Colonel W. C. Falkner, Bay Springs, MS, September 20, 1862, OR, series I, vol. 17, part 1, 138; and Agnew Diary, September 21–22, 1862, vol. 7a, 164.

28. A. Brown, "The First Mississippi Partisan Rangers," 379. At about this time, late September–early October, the Seventy-Second Illinois Infantry operating out of Fort Pillow in western Tennessee reported pursuing "Faulkner's men," who had been burning cotton around Covington. Given the timing, it is very unlikely that this was the First Mississippi Partisan Rangers, who were involved with Price and Van Dorn, but was almost certainly the Kentucky Partisan Battalion under Colonel W. W. Faulkner (1836–1865). Letter, Colonel F. A. Starring, Seventy-Second Illinois Infantry, to Brigadier General Grenville M. Dodge, October 5, 1862, OR, series I, vol. 17, part 1, 146.

29. Letter, Earl Van Dorn to Sterling Price, Holly Springs, MS, September 18, 1862, OR, series I, vol. 17, part 2, 706; and letter, Sterling Price to Earl Van Dorn, Camp Little, MS, September 23, 1862, OR, series I, vol. 17, part 2, 710.

30. "On yesterday I was informed that Van Dorn had reached Ripley with his army. This intelligence is confirmed to day. Van Dorn and Price dined with Col Falkner in Ripley on Sabbath [September 28]" (Agnew Diary, October 1, 1862, vol. 7a, 173). Van Dorn established his headquarters while in Ripley in the home of W. R. Cole on Block 89 in the Ripley plat on Jackson Street, the home occupied later by R. J. Thurmond. Unsigned letter by Roxanna Cole, wife of W. R. Cole, to "Cousin Blanche" of Franklin, Tennessee, Ripley, MS, November 2, 1862, printed in "Vivid War Experiences at Ripley, Miss.," *Confederate Veteran* 13, no. 6 (June 1905): 262. W. R. Cole purchased Block 89 in 1844 (Tippah County Deed Book E, 628–29).

31. Report, Major General Sterling Price to Major M. M. Kimmel, near Pocahontas, October 1, 1862, OR, series I, vol. 17, part 2, 718–19.

32. Report of Captain Patrick H. McCauley, Seventeenth Wisconsin Infantry, October 3, 1862, OR, series I, vol. 17, part 1, 149–50. McCauley identified Ramer's Crossing as being in Mississippi, when it is actually in Tennessee.

33. Letter, I. N. Haynie to General U. S. Grant, Bethel, TN, October 3, 1862, OR, series I, vol. 17, part 2, 257–58.

34. Agnew Diary, October 7, 1862, vol. 7a, 180.

35. Orlando Davis, "Notes on Civil War at Ripley," originally published in *Southern Sentinel* (Ripley, MS), September 13, 20, 27, 1893.

36. "Seconding Rosecrans, Eloquent Remarks by a Gallant Mississippian, Chicago Times Report," *Ripley (MS) Advertiser*, July 26, 1884, 2.

37. "Seconding Rosecrans, Eloquent Remarks by a Gallant Mississippian, Chicago Times Report," *Ripley (MS) Advertiser*, July 26, 1884, 2.

38. "Another Partisan Success," *Memphis Daily Appeal*, October 24, 1862, 2. The Boneyard, Mississippi, post office was established in 1847. It was located west of Kossuth in present-day Alcorn County, but was originally in Tishomingo County.

39. Agnew Diary, November 22, 1862, vol. 7a, scan 230; "Davis, Judge Orlando, Diary"; and letter, Colonel A. L. Lee, to Captain R. M. Sawyer, November 22, 1862, OR, series I, vol. 17, part

1, 490. In his retelling of this raid by Union cavalry on Ripley, Andrew Brown inexplicably twisted it into a raid by the Confederate Conscription Bureau on Falkner's partisan rangers, this despite the fact that his principal source was the report by a Union cavalry officer, Colonel Lee, who never mentioned the Conscription Bureau! A. Brown, "The First Mississippi Partisan Rangers," 381. Basing himself on Brown, Donald Duclos also wrote that the raid had been conducted by the Conscription Bureau (*Son of Sorrow*, 126). The meeting place for the rangers, Andrew Brown's store in Ripley, was on the West ½ Lot 6, Block 13, near the center of the block north of the square. Appendix; and A. Brown, *History of Tippah County*, 40.

40. Letter, John C. Pemberton to Earl Van Dorn, Jackson, MS, October 28, 1862, OR, series I, vol. 17, part 2, 737–38.

41. Letter, M. R. Clark to G. W. Randolph, Brookhaven, MS, October 29, 1862, OR, series IV, vol. 2, 149–50; and M. R. Clark to Commanders of Partisan Rangers, Brookhaven, MS, November 1, 1862, *Memphis Daily Appeal*, November 4, 1862, 2.

42. Letter, Brigadier General James R. Chalmers to Major G. W. Holt, near Como, MS, January 8, 1864, OR, series I, vol. 32, part 2, 530. Falkner later wrote: "When Gen Pemberton took Command of this department he issued an order requiring me to send all men of conscript age to camp of instructions. This order had the effect to brake up the Regt. and I was again thrown out of command." Letter, W. C. Falkner to James Phelan, Pontotoc, MS, February 7, 1863, Mississippi Department of Archives and History, Confederate Service Records, W. C. Falkner; almost entirely reproduced in Duclos, *Son of Sorrow*, 129–30.

43. Letter, W. C. Falkner to John McRae, Mobile, AL, January 8, 1863, transcribed in Duclos, *Son of Sorrow*, 333. In Duclos's volume, the name is misspelled as McRay.

44. Letter, W. C. Falkner to J. W. Clapp, West Point, MS, January 7, 1863, Mississippi Department of Archives and History, Confederate Service Records W. C. Falkner; and letter, W. C. Falkner to John McRae, Mobile, AL, January 8, 1863, in Duclos, *Son of Sorrow*, 333.

45. Born in March 1821, Sarah Gillespie Vance married Alexander Luther Brame on November 7, 1839, in Bibb County, Alabama. US Census, 1900, Hunt County, TX; and "Early Marriages of Bibb County, Alabama," Tracking Your Roots, http://www.trackingyourroots.com/data/bibbmarriages.htm. The Brames resided in Perry County, Alabama, in 1850 but moved to the West Point area a couple years later. US Census, 1850, Perry County, AL; and US Census, 1860, Lowndes County, MS. A. L. Brame appears to have died by 1880, but Sarah continued living in West Point. US Census, 1880, Clay County, MS. In 1893, a Ripley newspaper recorded that Mrs. Sarah Brame of West Point visited her sister Lizzie Falkner in Ripley. Two years later she again visited Ripley when it was noted that she was from Greenville, Texas, implying that she had moved to the Lone Star State between 1893 and 1895. *Ripley (MS) Advertiser*, June 7, 1893; and *Southern Sentinel* (Ripley, MS), August 15, 1895.

46. Letter, W. C. Falkner to James Phelan, Pontotoc, MS, February 7, 1863, Mississippi Department of Archives and History, Confederate Service Records, W. C. Falkner, almost entirely reproduced in Duclos, *Son of Sorrow*, 129–30.

47. A. Brown, "The First Mississippi Partisan Rangers," 382. The authorizations probably came in early February. On February 13, Falkner alludes to them as having come several days earlier. Letter, W. C. Falkner to Governor John J. Pettus, Pontotoc, MS, February 13, 1863, Mississippi Department of Archives and History, John J. Pettus Correspondence, series 757. General Chalmers recalled that "Colonel Falkner made application to the War Department and was authorized to reassemble his regiment." Letter, Brigadier General James R. Chalmers to Major G. W. Holt, near Como, MS, January 8, 1864, OR, series I, vol. 32, part 2, 530.

48. Letter, J. C. Pemberton to John J. Pettus, Jackson, MS, March 13, 1863, OR, series I, vol. 24, part 3, 666.

49. An anonymous writer in Ripley noted that Falkner "formerly of this place . . . is rapidly re-organizing his regiment somewhere south of this point, and will soon be once more in the

field, battling for Southern rights." "On the Wing," Ripley, MS, February 1863, *Memphis Daily Appeal*, March 17, 1863, 1.

50. Letter, W. C. Falkner to James Phelan, February 7, 1863, in Duclos, *Son of Sorrow*, 129.

51. *Memphis Daily Appeal*, February 28, 1863, 2.

52. Letter, W. C. Falkner to Jacob Thompson, near Pontotoc, MS, March 13, 1863, Mississippi Department of Archives and History, John J. Pettus Correspondence, series 757, published in Duclos, *Son of Sorrow*, 338–39.

53. Letter, Brigadier General James R. Chalmers to Major G. W. Holt, near Como, MS, January 8, 1864, OR, series I, vol. 32, part 2, 530.

54. Letter, W. C. Falkner to J. W. Clapp, near Pontotoc, MS, March 18, 1863, Mississippi Department of Archives and History, Confederate Service Records, W. C. Falkner, published in Duclos, *Son of Sorrow*, 334–35.

55. Orlando Davis, "Federal Raids on Ripley," *Southern Sentinel* (Ripley, MS), September 13, 20, 27, 1893.

56. Agnew Diary, March 31, 1863, vol. 7a, 134, scan 365.

57. Letter, W. C. Falkner to James R. Chalmers, Pontotoc, MS, July 20, 1863, quoted in Duclos, *Son of Sorrow*, 339–40.

58. Letter, W. C. Falkner to Captain L. J. Gaines, Headquarters, Grenada, MS, August 29, 1863, Mississippi Department of Archives and History, Confederate Service Records, W. C. Falkner.

59. A. Brown, "The First Mississippi Partisan Rangers," 387–88.

60. Agnew Diary, September 30, 1863.

61. A. Brown, "The First Mississippi Partisan Rangers," 387–88; and letter, W. C. Falkner to Captain W. A. Goodman, Oxford, MS, October 25, 1863, Mississippi Department of Archives and History, Confederate Service Records, W. C. Falkner.

62. Letter, James R. Chalmers to G. W. Holt, assistant adjutant general, near Como, MS, January 8, 1864, OR, series I, vol. 32, part 2, 530.

63. There is no reason to consider this statement authoritative; I merely give it as evidence of common hearsay. A. Brown, *History of Tippah County*, 184, 281, also 130–31, 147; cf. Duclos, *Son of Sorrow*, 140; and Williamson, *William Faulkner and Southern History*, 44–45. In a letter to Thomas Felix Hickerson dated March 19, 1942, Lenoir Hunt, a native of Ripley and relative of both Thurmond and Hickerson, noted that during the war Falkner "became a blockade runner, thereby making a fortune." Quoted in Hickerson, *The Falkner Feuds*, foreword. Similarly, Maud Morrow Brown wrote: "One unsubstantial [unsubstantiated?] rumor says that [Falkner] and R. J. Thurmond formed a team for running the blockade at Memphis, and that they were astute and resourceful enough to make a great deal of money at it." M. M. Brown, "William C. Falkner, Man of Legends," 433. One might accept the blockade runner claim as true except for the fact that much hearsay concerning Falkner has been deemed unreliable.

64. "T. W. P.," "Letter from Ripley," January 12, 1863, *Memphis Daily Appeal*, January 24, 1863, 1.

65. "T. W. P.," "Letter from Ripley," January 12, 1863, *Memphis Daily Appeal*, January 24, 1863, 1.

66. From an examination of Colonel D. C. Thomas, Memphis, TN, July 7, 1865, OR, series I, vol. 39, part 1, 171.

67. Orlando Davis, "Federal Raids on Ripley," *Southern Sentinel* (Ripley, MS), September 13, 20, and 27, 1893.

68. From an examination of Colonel D. C. Thomas, Memphis, TN, July 7, 1865, OR, series I, vol. 39, part 1, 171.

69. Orlando Davis, "Federal Raids on Ripley," *Southern Sentinel* (Ripley, MS), September 13, 20, and 27, 1893.

70. Orlando Davis, "Federal Raids on Ripley," *Southern Sentinel* (Ripley, MS), September 13, 20, and 27, 1893. Another description of this event by an anonymous writer relates: "Next morning they advanced in strong force. They brought the bodies of two of their soldiers killed

in the preceding day's fight, and buried them in C. P. Miller's yard, now a vacant lot just north of Dr. Murry's residence. The Federals then began a work of vandalism by applying the torch to nearly every unoccupied building in town. The courthouse, first and then the Methodist church, Masonic Hall, Odd-Fellow's Hall, Dr. Murry's drugstore, the Cumberland Presbyterian church, the residence of Dr. Carter, Col. Falkner, Richard Prince and R. F. Ford, besides many smaller buildings, became a prey to the devouring element. It was a brutal and useless destruction of property for which no excuse can be offered. Having completed the work of destruction, they took up the line of march down the New Albany road." "Battle of Whitten Branch," *Southern Sentinel*, July 5, 1894, http://www.msgw.org/confederate/reminiscences.htm. See also Agnew Diary, July 10, 1864, vol. 7b, scans 370–71; and Captain J. E. Rogers, "History of Tippah County," *Ripley (MS) Broadaxe*, August 21, 1878, reprinted in Tippah County Historical and Genealogical Society, *Heritage of Tippah County*, 148.

71. Orlando Davis, "Federal Raids on Ripley," *Southern Sentinel* (Ripley, MS), September 13, 20, and 27, 1893.

72. "T. W. P.," "Letter from Ripley," January 12, 1863, *Memphis Daily Appeal*, January 24, 1863, 1.

73. Falkner, *Rapid Ramblings in Europe*, 119–20.

Chapter 9: Reconstruction and Rebuilding

1. William C. Harris, "The Reconstruction of the Commonwealth, 1865–1870," in *A History of Mississippi*, ed. Richard Aubrey McLemore (Jackson: University and College Press of Mississippi, 1973), 1:542–42.

2. Kate Sperry Hunt diary, entries for October 15 and 17, 1865, in Tommy Covington, "Sarah Catherine Sperry," in *Tippah County Heritage*, vol. 2, ed. Tommy Covington, 247–49 (Ripley, MS: Mid-South Graphics, 1994).

3. Kate Sperry Hunt diary, entry for October 21, 1865, in Covington, "Sarah Catherine Sperry," 247–49.

4. John W. T. and Sallie Falkner apparently lived initially in a house on North Main Street opposite Colonel Falkner's postbellum home. See the appendix. Following the death of his foster father and namesake J. W. Thompson in 1873, J. W. T. Falkner moved his family into the Thompson home to live with his foster mother and great-aunt Justiania Word Thompson.

5. Falkner's purchase was of Block 7 (Tippah County Deed Book U, 566). R. J. Thurmond purchased the north half of the block in March 1859 (Tippah County Deed Book S, 191). However, the early title is not complete; we do not know when he purchased the south half. Thurmond had a home on the SE¼ in 1864, which probably burned that year. "War Reminiscences: The Battle of Ripley," *Southern Sentinel* (Ripley, MS), June 28, 1894. The Falkner home was constructed straddling the N½ and the S½ of the block, which indicates that it wasn't built until the two halves were united.

6. For example: "The sociable at Col. Falkner's Friday night last greatly enjoyed by all present," *Southern Sentinel* (Ripley, MS), March 9, 1882; "A sociable and dance at the residence of Col. W. C. Falkner on Tuesday night last, we learn was a perfect success," *Southern Sentinel*, August 17, 1882; and "The social gathering at Col. W. C. Falkner's on Friday night inst. was a pleasant affair," *Southern Sentinel*, March 29, 1883.

7. Soon after the burning of the courthouse, the board began meeting on October 5, 1864, in the Baptist Church. In 1865, they met in the Presbyterian Church, but by December 1866 were back in the Baptist Church. In July 1867, they met in a two-story commercial building on the south side of the square. Tippah County Minutes of the Police Board, 1859–1869, 326–28; and A. Brown, *History of Tippah County*, 164.

8. Tippah County Minutes of the Police Board, vol. 2, March 18, 1869, 49–50, 64.

9. Tippah County Minutes of the Police Board, vol. 2, March 18, 1869, 59–60.

10. "Omikron," "The Crops in West Tennessee and North Mississippi—Corinth, etc.," *Memphis Daily Appeal*, July 10, 1870, 4.

11. See the report of W. C. Falkner and James B. Taylor to the Tippah County Board of Supervisors, March 1871, Tippah County Minutes of the Police Board, vol. 2, 188, also 143, 148.

12. Tippah County Minutes of the Police Board, vol. 2, March 11, 1871, 200.

13. James Word noted in 1882 that his sister Caroline Falkner "died at Ripley, Mississippi about twenty years since" (Word, "Genealogy of the Word Family"). This would place her death in about 1862; however, J. W. Falkner wrote on July 19, 1863, from a prisoner-of-war camp and alluded to his mother as though she was still living, which implies that she died somewhat later. Letter, J. W. Falkner to "Sis," Sandusky Island Prisoner-of-War Camp, Sandusky, OH, July 19, 1963, Southeast Missouri State University, Special Collections and Archives, Cape Girardeau, MO. Justiania Word is listed on an Ancestry.com page as having died on February 20, 1865. However, there is no source given, leaving this date in question. James Word does not mention when his mother died. Although Caroline and her mother would likely have been buried in Ripley Cemetery, there are no headstones for them there.

14. Tippah County Circuit Court Trial Docket, 1860–1868, 110ff. It is not certain whether "Thompson & Falkner" referred to J. W. Thompson and W. C. Falkner, or Thompson and James Word Falkner.

15. J. W. Falkner had left Ripley by the time of the 1870 census and was living with his family in Arkansas County, Arkansas, working as a farmer.

16. Falkner & Mitchell are referred to in an 1872 article, "Ripley: Opening of the Narrow-Gauge Railroad," *Memphis Daily Appeal*, August 30, 1872, 4. The firm is also listed frequently in the Tippah County Judge's Trial Docket, 1868–1878. In the 1870 census, J. W. Mitchell was listed as a twenty-one-year-old law student, living with the J. W. Thompsons in Ripley.

17. Calvin Jefferson Frederick (1849–1902), a native of Tippah County, graduated in 1876 with an LLB degree from Cumberland University of Lebanon, Tennessee, and began his practice with Falkner soon after. *Catalogue of Cumberland University, Lebanon, Tenn. 1875–6* (Lebanon, TN: R. L. C. White and Company, 1876), 33. References to the partnership Falkner & Frederick can be found as early as 1878 and as late as 1885. *Ripley (MS) Broadaxe*, August 21, 1878; and *Ripley (MS) Advertiser*, July 11 and October 3, 1885. He was elected to the state legislature in 1881 to serve a two-year term and later served a term as Tippah County school superintendent. In 1887 he moved from Ripley to Fort Smith, Arkansas, returning in February 1890 to serve on the team prosecuting R. J. Thurmond in a hearing before the grand jury.

18. A biography of W. W. Bailey can be found in Goodspeed Publishing Company, *The History of Franklin County*; and at My Genealogy Hound, http://www.mygenealogyhound.com/arkansas-biographies/ar-franklin-county-biographies/william-w-bailey-genealogy-franklin-county-arkansas-altus-ar.html. The partnership Thompson & Bailey appeared frequently on the court docket from as early as September 1868 through as late as September 1869 (Tippah County Judge's Trial Docket, 1868–1878). Bailey later moved back to Ripley and was listed there in the 1880 census as a lawyer. In 1881 he moved to Arkansas, where he became a merchant and served in the legislature. *Ripley (MS) Advertiser*, February 12, 1881. His third son was named John Wesley Thompson Bailey.

19. "Thompson & Falkner" began to appear on the court docket beginning in late 1869. Later, the firm ran an advertisement in a Memphis newspaper that noted: "Special and prompt attention given to collections in Tippah and adjoining counties." *Memphis Daily Appeal*, beginning November 4, 1872, 3, running through July 26, 1873, 2. Thompson died on June 21, 1873.

20. *Triennial Catalogue of the University of Mississippi* (Oxford, MS, 1872–1873), 19. In 1883, J. W. T. Falkner was referred to as "a prominent lawyer of this county [Tippah] and a member of the firm of Falkner & Frederick." *Ripley (MS) Advertiser*, June 30, 1883, 2.

21. R. G. Dun & Co., Tippah County, MS, vol. 2, 239.

22. R. G. Dun & Co., Tippah County, MS, vol. 2, 239.

23. This purchase consisted of the E½ and SW¼ and E½ of the NW¼, all in Section 5, Township 4, Range 3 East (Tippah County Deed Book W, 36–37). Ishatubby Creek drains into North Tippah Creek. The name is Chickasaw and apparently a personal name meaning "the one who takes and kills" (Baca, *Native American Place Names in Mississippi*, 44).

24. On December 8, 1868, Falkner purchased forty acres in the northeast corner of the SE¼ Section 6, Township 4, Range 3 East.

25. C. J. Frederick, "Thrilling Scenes in Mississippi in Ante-Bellum Days: 'The White Rose of Memphis,'" *Memphis Daily Appeal*, April 20, 1881, 1. In early summer 1879, a storm struck Falkner's farm and "unroofed his saw-mill and prostrated a large two-story barn." *Public Ledger* (Memphis), June 9, 1879, 3, quoting an item from the *Ripley (MS) Advertiser*, June 7, 1879.

26. *Ripley (MS) Advertiser*, January 29, 1881.

27. Ira South (1844–1938) was buried in Antioch Primitive Baptist Church Cemetery located about a half mile north of Ishatubby Farm. He was the son of Abner O. South, who served under Falkner in both the Second Mississippi Infantry and the partisan rangers.

28. There are two undated handwritten pages from Falkner to South. It's not certain if these were two distinct messages or a single two-page message. The originals are in the Ripley Public Library.

29. Handwritten pages, Falkner to South.

30. R. G. Dun & Co., Tippah County, MS, vol. 2, 239.

31. It has been claimed that Falkner was a stockholder in the Gayoso Hotel in Memphis and often resided there (Williamson, *William Faulkner and Southern History*, 55). This is certainly untrue. If he was a stockholder, he would have indeed stayed there, but he never stayed at the Gayoso. If he was a stockholder in a hotel, it was surely the Peabody.

32. *Memphis Daily Appeal*, May 3, 1870, 4.

33. After the original Peabody was closed in 1923, a new hotel was opened on Union Avenue that took the name and landmark status of its predecessor. David L. Cohn, *Where I Was Born and Raised* (Boston: Houghton Mifflin, 1948), 12.

34. Construction was underway by the fall of 1866. "Stonewall College," *Bolivar (TN) Bulletin*, September 22, 1866, 3. The school was apparently on the same site as the original Ripley Female Academy, namely on the west side of South Main Street on Block 44.

35. A. Brown, *History of Tippah County*, 184.

36. No copy of *The Lost Diamond* is known to exist (A. Brown, *History of Tippah County*, 234). However, a summary of the play in eight scenes, probably written by Falkner himself, appeared under the title "The Lost Diamond," *Southern Sentinel* (Ripley, MS), March 1, 1883, and a descriptive summary, "Editor Advertiser," in the *Ripley (MS) Advertiser*, March 17, 1883. Also, there was the following mention: "This charming drama was published in the ADVERTISER seventeen years ago." "The Lost Diamond," *Ripley (MS) Advertiser*, March 3, 1883, 3.

37. "The Lost Diamond," *Southern Sentinel* (Ripley, MS), March 1, 1883; and "The Lost Diamond," *Ripley (MS) Advertiser*, March 3, 1883, 3.

38. "Stonewall College," *Bolivar (TN) Bulletin*, February 2, 1867, 1, reprinted from the *Ripley (MS) Advertiser*.

39. "The Fever at Home," *Memphis Daily Appeal*, August 28, 1878, 2.

40. "Letter from Gus Cowan," Gus Cowan to "Sister Dinah and Almerth," Los Angeles, December 16, 1948, in Tippah County Historical and Genealogical Society, *Heritage of Tippah County*, 164.

Chapter 10: The Railroad to Ripley

1. *Weekly Clarion* (Jackson, MS), August 26, 1869.

2. *Memphis Daily Appeal*, September 18, 1869, 2.

3. "The . . . railroad will connect north with the Memphis and Charleston Railroad at Middleton, and south with the Memphis and Selma Railroad near New Albany." "The M., R. and N. A. Railroad," *Memphis Daily Appeal*, December 23, 1869, 4.

4. "Important and Enthusiastic Railroad Meeting," *Memphis Daily Appeal*, September 26, 1869, 1.

5. *Memphis Daily Appeal*, September 17, 1869, 2.

6. "Important Enterprise," *Memphis Daily Appeal*, October 31, 1869, 4.

7. *Memphis Daily Appeal*, November 11, 1869, 2.

8. "The M., R. and N. A. Railroad," *Public Ledger* (Memphis), December 29, 1869, 3; and "The M., R. and N. A. Railroad," *Memphis Daily Appeal*, December 23, 1869, 4.

9. Tippah County Minutes of the Police Board, vol. 2, 120–21.

10. Tippah County Minutes of the Police Board, vol. 2, 124.

11. *Laws of the State of Mississippi* (Jackson: Kimball, Raymond, and Company, 1870), 283–95.

12. Mississippi City is no longer the county seat. It has been absorbed into the urban strip that spans the Mississippi Gulf Coast, with the town site now being within Gulfport's incorporation area.

13. I find documentation for only one activity of the company following its charter: a meeting in Jackson, Mississippi, in July 1870 (*New Orleans Republican*, July 22, 1870, 4).

14. *Laws of the State of Mississippi* (Jackson: Kimball, Raymond, and Company, 1871), 268–80.

15. *Laws of the State of Mississippi*, 1871, 745–46.

16. Mark Wahlgren Summers, *Railroads, Reconstruction, and the Gospel of Prosperity: Aid under the Radical Republicans, 1865–1877* (1984; Princeton, NJ: Princeton University Press, 2014), 129. The relevant portion of the state constitution is Article XII, Section 5: "The credit of the State shall not be pledged or loaned in aid of any person, association or corporation; nor shall the State hereafter become a stockholder in any corporation or association."

17. Ripley Railroad Company journal, typed transcript, Southeast Missouri State University, Special Collections and Archives, Cape Girardeau, MO (hereafter Ripley Railroad Company journal), September 18, 1871, 1–3; also see the summary of the entry in the Ledger of the Ripley Railroad, in Robert W. Hamblin and Louis Daniel Brodsky, *Selections from the William Faulkner Collection of Louis Daniel Brodsky: A Descriptive Catalogue* (Charlottesville: University Press of Virginia, 1979), 5. The following year, Falkner stated in a deposition: "I am the President of the Ripley Railroad Company now and have been since the first Monday of September 1871." *Weekly Clarion* (Jackson, MS), April 3, 1873, 1.

18. "[T]he line of the road [is] located from Ripley to the Memphis and Charleston Road on what is known as the Muddy Route." Ripley Railroad Company journal, November 9, 1871, 3–4. An article noted that the Ripley Railroad would be connected with the M&C "at a point three miles east of Middleton." *Memphis Daily Appeal*, November 24, 1871, 2.

19. "Another Narrow Gauge," *Memphis Daily Appeal*, December 10, 1871, 4.

20. "Ripley Railroad," *Railroad Gazette* (New York), October 12, 1872, 448.

21. Ripley Railroad Company journal, November 9, 1871, 3–4; see also the summary of the entry in the Ledger of the Ripley Railroad, in Hamblin and Brodsky, *Selections from the William Faulkner Collection of Louis Daniel Brodsky*, 8.

22. *Memphis Daily Appeal*, November 24, 1871, 2.

23. *Biographical Encyclopædia of Kentucky of the Dead and Living Men of the Nineteenth Century* (Cincinnati: J. M. Armstrong and Company, 1878), 446–47; and "FREDERICK DE FUNIAK, M. Am. Soc. C.E., DIED MARCH 29TH, 1905," obituary, *Transactions of the American Society of Civil Engineers* 54 (June 1905): 524–25.

24. *Memphis Daily Appeal*, November 24, 1871, 2.

25. *Memphis Daily Appeal*, November 24, 1871, 2.

26. "COLONEL FAULKNER of Ripley, Mississippi, said in the late Narrow-gauge St. Louis Convention, that he lived some twenty-five miles from a railroad to which he wished access. He made estimates for a broad-gauge and found it would cost twenty-six thousand dollars per mile. A pamphlet written by Colonel Hulbert, of Georgia, fell into his hands. Its subject was narrow-gauge. He said that he was never more elated by facts recited. He obtained a charter for the Middleton and Ripley road, and threw the first dirt on the first of March last, and had now two and half miles running and would have all completed by the first of August. His road completed and equipped, will not cost over ten thousand dollars per mile. Some of the broad-gauge railroad men called his the Dolly Varden road. He intended pushing it through to Mississippi City on the Gulf of Mexico three hundred and fifty miles, and north to Paducah, Kentucky." *Memphis Daily Appeal*, June 26, 1872, 2. No copies of Hulbert's pamphlet seem to have survived. George W. Hilton, *American Narrow Gauge Railroads* (Stanford, CA: Stanford University Press, 1990), 20, 23n81, 76.

27. Hilton, *American Narrow Gauge Railroads*, 10, 16–17, 20.

28. *Memphis Daily Appeal*, June 26, 1872, 2.

29. Ripley Railroad Company journal, 9–10.

30. *Memphis Daily Appeal*, November 24, 1871, 2. On December 10, it was again noted that de Funiak "is now at work on the road." *Memphis Daily Appeal*, December 10, 1871, 4. "The location of the line was begun last December, and the grading February 1." *Railroad Gazette* (New York), October 12, 1872, 448.

31. Tippah County Deed Book 3, 364–66.

32. *Biographical Encyclopædia of Kentucky*, 446.

33. Meriwether was referred to as the railroad's "Chief Engineer" in June and September. "Narrow-Gauge Railroad Convention," *Memphis Daily Appeal*, June 5, 1872; "Ripley, Mississippi: The Narrow-Gauge Railroad—The Appeal—The Town and Its People," *Memphis Daily Appeal*, September 6, 1872, 2; and Mrs. M. M. Betts, "Niles Meriwether, M. Am. Soc. C.E.," *Transactions of the American Society of Civil Engineers* 45 (1901): 632–33. According to Meriwether's obituary: "In 1868, he became Chief Engineer of the Memphis and Charleston Railroad . . . and held that position for eight years, during which time he built the Middleton and Ripley Branch." Despite de Funiak's having taken another job before completing the railroad, he was credited as being its engineer upon its completion. *Memphis Daily Appeal*, September 24, 1872.

34. Ripley Railroad Company journal, September 17, 1872, 28.

35. I have been unable to find an account of the groundbreaking that appeared in immediate conjunction with the March 1 event. The first newspaper accounts date to several months after the event: "He [Falkner] . . . threw the first dirt on the first of March last," *Memphis Daily Appeal*, June 26, 1872, 2; and "[D]irt was broken on the first day of last March," "Ripley/Opening of the Narrow-Gauge Railroad," *Memphis Daily Appeal*, August 30, 1872, 4. However, two somewhat later accounts date the event to February: "The grading on twenty

miles was begun in February last," *Memphis Daily Appeal,* September 24, 1872; and "The location of the line was begun last December, and the grading February 1," *Railroad Gazette* (New York), October 12, 1872, 448.

36. "AN ACT to authorize the Ripley Railroad Company to change the name of said Company," passed March 16, 1872, and "AN ACT to amend an Act entitled 'an Act to incorporate the Ripley Railroad Company,'" passed March 18, 1872, *Laws of the State of Mississippi* (Jackson: Alcorn and Fisher, 1872), 317–18. This legislation had been mentioned in the *Bolivar (TN) Bulletin,* March 8, 1872, 2.

37. Following a narrow-gauge railroad convention held at St. Louis in June 1872 and attended by Falkner, reports noted that the Ripley Railroad was to terminate in the north at Paducah or Cairo, where it was to connect with the St. Louis and Cairo Railroad, which was "almost completed." *Memphis Daily Appeal,* June 26, 1872, 2.

38. At the March 25, 1872, meeting of the railroad's directors, Falkner presented an account for his trips to Jackson in January, February, and March while procuring the passage of the bill and was reimbursed for the same. Ripley Railroad Company journal, March 25, 1872, 8.

39. Letter, W. C. Falkner to John F. Johnson, June 14, 1874, in Wilmuth S. Rutledge, "How Colonel Falkner Built His Railroad," *Mississippi Quarterly* 20, no. 3 (Summer 1967): 169–70.

40. *Public Ledger* (Memphis), September 24, 1872, 2.

41. The indenture was made on March 5 while the SRSC actually took control on July 1. "The Charleston Railroad," *Memphis Daily Appeal,* July 2, 1872, 4; and Henry V. Poor, *Manual of the Railroads of the United States, 1873–74* (New York: H. V. and H. W. Poor, 1873), 134.

42. C. K. Brown, "The Southern Railway Security Company: An Early Instance of the Holding Company," *North Carolina Historical Review* 6, no. 2 (April 1929): 158–70.

43. Ripley Railroad Company journal, April 22, 1872, 8–14.

44. Ripley Railroad Company journal, April 22, 1872, 8–14.

45. "[I]t is the wish of the board that the depot should be located on block no. 23, and . . . [a] committee [appointed] to investigate the cost of the ground and the cost to extend the line, and to consult with the chief engineer as to its practicability, and report to the next meeting of this board" (Ripley Railroad Company journal, April 23, 1872, 14–15). On August 17, 1872, R. J. Thurmond issued a title bond deed to the Ripley Railroad Company for the west half of Block 23 (Tippah County Deed Book 2, 368). Thurmond, who was in attendance at the meeting as a director, had owned this parcel since January 11, 1863 (Tippah County Deed Book O, 201).

46. Ripley Railroad Company journal, January 1873, 41.

47. *Memphis Daily Appeal,* April 28, 1872, 2.

48. "Gilmer and Rather have taken the contract to lay the track from Middleton to Ripley They agreed to complete the entire contract by the fifteenth of August." *Memphis Daily Appeal,* May 24, 1872, 2. Another newspaper article indicates that Gilmer & Rather along with a Pat Smith were involved in tracklaying. "Pat Smith, the energetic railroad contractor, is engaged, with Gilmer and Ruther [*sic*], in laying the track." *Memphis Daily Appeal,* June 11, 1872. By July, the three were all joined in the same partnership as indicated by their signing themselves as "Gillmer [*sic*], Rather & Smith, Contractors" at the end of an advertisement worded: "Three first-class section bosses wanted on Ripley Railroad at Middleton, Tenn." *Memphis Daily Appeal,* July 29, 1872, 4.

49. "WANTED: ONE HUNDRED LABORERS, by Gilmer & Rather, Ripley Railroad, Middleton, Tennessee. Station men wanted. Applp to J. B. Gallaway, Memphis and Charleston Depot." The advertisement ran in the *Memphis Daily Appeal* from April 30 through May 21, 1872. Another advertisement appeared shortly after: "100 MEN to work station work on the Middleton and Ripley Railroad. Gilmer & Rather, contractors. Apply to JOHN FANNING, 119 Main St., cor, Market." *Memphis Daily Appeal,* May 27 and 28, 1872.

50. "Agreement with the Southern Railway Security Company, May 4, 1872," in Ripley Railroad Company journal, June 3, 1872, 16–20.

51. Ripley Railroad Company journal, June 3, 1872, 18.

52. *Memphis Daily Appeal*, May 24, 1872, 2.

53. "Progress—Stupidity of a City," *Memphis Daily Appeal*, September 8, 1872, 2.

54. Hamblin and Brodsky, *Selections from the William Faulkner Collection of Louis Daniel Brodsky*, 8; and Ripley Railroad Company journal, 16–25.

55. While these various delays were hurting the prospects of the Ripley Railroad, the company had floated an issue for bonds totaling $250,000, bearing 7 percent interest semiannually. Expecting to receive the bounty from the state, the company issued the bonds on June 3, 1872. After about two years, the bonds went into default, and the United States Security Company of New York, which had bought the bonds in 1872, became trustee of the road. Sometime in 1875, the United States Security Company resigned its trust, and R. T. Wilson became the new trustee to operate the road for the stockholders. Duclos, *Son of Sorrow*, 155–56, citing "W. C. Falkner vs. The Ripley Railroad company," Tippah County Chancery Court Records, Final Record Book 1, Case no. 723, deposition of W. C. Falkner.

56. "Colonel W. C. Falkner, President of the Ripley railroad, on Saturday, the seventh instant, drove the first spike in the track, in the presence of a large crowd of citizens who had assembled at Middleton." *Memphis Daily Appeal*, June 11, 1872; see also *Nashville Union and American*, June 15, 1872, 1. R. J. Shannon recalled that Falkner missed the spike. Thomas Todd Martin, "Portrait of an Old-Timer," *Southern Sentinel* (Ripley, MS), August 30, 1928, originally in the *G.M.&N. News* (Mobile, AL); Martin's piece was based on an interview with R. J. Shannon, who was eighty years old.

57. Hilton, *American Narrow Gauge Railroads*, 81–82.

58. "Narrow-Gauge Railroad Convention," *Whig and Tribune* (Jackson, TN), February 3, 1872, 2.

59. *Railroad Gazette* (New York), June 20, 1872, 275.

60. *Memphis Daily Appeal*, June 26, 1872, 2.

61. "A favorite fashion among London ladies at present is to array themselves in *cretonne* (*Anglice*, chintz) over-dresses, looking as if they had stripped their windows and bedsteads. These are called 'Dolly Vardens,' from Dickens' character of 'Barnaby Rudge.'" *Charleston (SC) Daily News*, October 9, 1871, 2.

62. *Railroad Gazette* (New York), June 20, 1872, 274.

63. W. C. Falkner, letter, "The Ripley Narrow-Gauge," November 25, 1872, *Memphis Daily Appeal*, November 29, 1872, 4.

64. *Railroad Gazette* (New York), June 20, 1872, 274–75.

65. "Old Citizen" [almost certainly Dr. J. Y. Murry], "Letter from Tippah County, Ripley, Miss., Aug. 26th, 1872," *Weekly Clarion* (Jackson, MS), September 5, 1872, 2.

66. Lockett was referred to variously as "resident engineer" ("Murder at Middleton, Tenn.," *Public Ledger* [Memphis], July 16, 1872, 3; and "Homicide at Middleton: Death of Maj. H. W. Lockett," *Nashville Union and American*, July 19, 1872, 4); and "chief engineer" ("Killed," *Bolivar [TN] Bulletin*, July 19, 1872, 3; and "Crimes and Casualties," *Memphis Daily Appeal*, July 23, 1872, 2). Because there is little reason to doubt that Niles Meriwether was chief engineer at this time, the title of "resident engineer" is probably more accurate in reference to Lockett. The title suggests a role more closely involved with on-site construction than that of the chief engineer, who oversaw the entire project.

67. "Killed," *Bolivar (TN) Bulletin*, July 19, 1872, 3.

68. "Circuit Court," *Bolivar (TN) Bulletin*, November 28, 1873, 3.

69. "[T]he last spike [was] driven on the twenty-seventh day of August; nineteen miles of the track having been laid in the last twenty days." "Ripley/Opening of the Narrow-Gauge Railroad," *Memphis Daily Appeal*, August 30, 1872.

70. "[The work] was pressed on until Saturday, the 24th day of August, 1872, when the iron horse entered the town of Ripley." "Old Citizen," "Letter from Tippah County, Ripley, Miss., Aug. 26th, 1872," *Weekly Clarion* (Jackson, MS), September 5, 1872, 2.

71. A. Brown, *History of Tippah County*, 194. The Stonewall College property consisted of Blocks 43 and 44 (see the appendix), which would place the southern terminus near the crossing of First South Street.

72. W. C. Falkner, letter, "The Ripley Narrow-Gauge," *Memphis Daily Appeal*, November 25, 1872. *Memphis Daily Appeal*, November 29, 1872, 4. See also a June 14, 1874, letter by Falkner in which he stated that the total cost per mile was $12,000, in Rutledge, "How Colonel Falkner Built His Railroad," 169–70. A newspaper article that cited a letter by Falkner as its source provided itemizations of some of the costs: "cost to grade $3,500 per mile, 3,000 ties to the mile at 15 cts. per tie, 55 tons of iron per mile, cost $78 per ton; . . . locomotive costs $7,500, weight of iron, 35 lbs. per yard, laying track cost $375 per mile; flats cost $400, box cars $500, passenger coaches $2,000." *Fayetteville (TN) Observer*, September 5, 1872, 2.

73. "The Charleston Railroad," *Memphis Daily Appeal*, August 16, 1873, 1.

74. *Memphis Daily Appeal*, August 27, 1872, 2.

75. A. Brown, *History of Tippah County*, 193. Ballast was laid under and in between crossties to support and stabilize them and facilitate drainage. In lieu of the more desirable crushed stone, cinders were often used. These were the residue of coal burned in locomotives, which was dumped from ash pans into ash pits at the end of a run. The cinders used on the Ripley Railroad presumably came from the ash pits of the M&C Railroad.

76. "Railroad Meeting Last Monday," *Columbia (TN) Herald*, May 9, 1873, 3.

77. Quoted in Hilton, *American Narrow Gauge Railroads*, 224–25. In 1873, the five-foot crossties originally used were replaced with seven-foot ties. "The Charleston Railroad," *Memphis Daily Appeal*, August 16, 1873, 1.

78. "Railroad Meeting Last Monday," *Columbia (TN) Herald*, May 9, 1873, 3.

79. *Memphis Daily Appeal*, August 25, 1872; "Ripley: Opening of the Narrow-Gauge Railroad," *Memphis Daily Appeal*, August 30, 1872, 4; and "Grand Narrow Gauge Railroad Celebration in Mississippi," *Weekly Clarion* (Jackson, MS), September 5, 1872, 3.

80. "Ripley: Opening of the Narrow-Gauge Railroad," *Memphis Daily Appeal*, August 30, 1872, 4.

81. "Colonel Faulkner," *Memphis Daily Appeal*, September 18, 1872, 4.

82. "Ripley: Opening of the Narrow-Gauge Railroad," *Memphis Daily Appeal*, August 30, 1872, 4; and "The Ripley Narrow Gauge Railroad," *New Orleans Republican*, September 8, 1872, 2.

83. "Personal," *Memphis Daily Appeal*, August 30, 1872, 4; and "Col. W. C. Falkner's Testimony," *Weekly Clarion* (Jackson, MS), April 3, 1873, 1.

84. "[A] large number of laborers were encamped at Ripley, awaiting his return, most of whom were Irishmen, who, under the influence of liquor, might fire the town and commit other outrages, were they not paid as he had promised to do on his return from Jackson." "Testimony of Chas. A. Brougher," *Weekly Clarion* (Jackson, MS), March 27, 1873, 1. Also see "Testimony of J. S. Hamilton," *Weekly Clarion*, April 3, 1873, 1; and "Testimony of Capt. T. S. Hardee," *Weekly Clarion*, March 27, 1873, 1.

85. "Testimony of Capt. T. S. Hardee," *Weekly Clarion* (Jackson, MS), March 27, 1873, 1.

86. "Testimony of Capt. T. S. Hardee," *Weekly Clarion* (Jackson, MS), March 27, 1873, 1; "The Attorney General Acting Four Parts in the Same Play," *Weekly Clarion*, February 27, 1873, 2; and "Col. W. C. Falkner's Testimony," *Weekly Clarion*, April 3, 1873, 1.

87. "Testimony of Capt. T. S. Hardee," *Weekly Clarion* (Jackson, MS), March 27, 1873, 1; "Testimony of Chas. A. Brougher," *Weekly Clarion*, March 27, 1873, 1; and "The Attorney General Acting Four Parts in the Same Play," *Weekly Clarion*, February 27, 1873, 2.

88. "Testimony of Chas. A. Brougher," *Weekly Clarion* (Jackson, MS), March 27, 1873, 1.

89. "It is proper that your committee should state that in addition to the $1000 paid Judge Campbell, and the $2000 paid C. A. Brougher, Esq., that Col. Falkner gave Captain Hardee, who himself is a State officer, made so by action of the Legislature at its last session, $3125, which he disbursed, or was to disburse, but to whom we do not know. We have the original draft from Falkner to Hardee in our possession. Should we find hereafter how the $3125 was expended, we will make a supplementary report of the same, giving our information." "The Subsidy Investigation," *Weekly Clarion* (Jackson, MS), March 20, 1873, 2.

90. Transcript of letter, J. S. Morris, Attorney General, to H. Musgrove, Auditor, Jackson, September 4, 1872, *Weekly Clarion* (Jackson, MS), November 14, 1872, 1. "[The Attorney General] finally did consent for the Auditor to issue them, and justified the act. Now, . . . these warrants are worthless and nullities; but unfortunately for the Attorney General, he had them issued. They were tied up until his sanction was obtained, and no living man save himself, is responsible for the issuance of the warrants that he now pronounces worthless." "The Subsidy Investigation," *Weekly Clarion*, March 20, 1873, 2.

91. "The Attorney General Acting Four Parts in the Same Play," *Weekly Clarion* (Jackson, MS), February 27, 1873, 2.

92. "Q. Did you issue the warrants in such sums as Col. Falkner desired?" "A. I did." Deposition of Henry Musgrove, State Auditor, *Weekly Clarion* (Jackson, MS), March 27, 1873, 1.

93. "An Act in reference to certain State warrants, known as the Ripley Railroad warrants." *Laws of the State of Mississippi* (Jackson: Power and Barksdale, 1876), 221–24.

94. "On the next day after their issuance [September 5], C. A. Brougher, Esq., the law partner of the Attorney General, received a $2,000 Subsidy Warrant for his efforts in trying to obtain a favorable opinion from his partner, the Attorney General, to allow the warrants to be issued." "The Subsidy Investigation," *Weekly Clarion* (Jackson, MS), March 20, 1873, 2. As Brougher recalled: "I left next morning at daylight for Vicksburg, and without seeing him again. When I returned I found that the opinion had been rendered and warrants issued, Col. Falkner gone home, and found in the office an envelope sealed and addressed to myself containing a $2000 subsidy warrant. I told Col. Falkner I would try to obtain a favorable opinion." "Testimony of Chas. A. Brougher," *Weekly Clarion*, March 27, 1873, 1. Campbell recall in a deposition: "I received $1000 in currency." "Testimony of Judge J. A. P. Campbell," *Weekly Clarion*, March 27, 1873, 1.

95. It was reported that Falkner "had relied upon the Subsidy for money wherewith to pay off his employees." "The Subsidy Transaction: Light Wanted," *Weekly Clarion* (Jackson, MS), November 14, 1872, 1. "Qu[i]te a large quantity of the warrants had passed into the hands of poor men who had received them for services in the construction of the railroad, and nearly all of them were in the hands of parties who had received them in good faith at the current rates of Auditor's warrants." "Governor's Message to the Senate and House of Representatives," *Weekly Clarion*, January 30, 1873, suppl., 5. The brother-in-law of Governor Powers, Charles W. Loomis, purchased $27,000 of the Ripley Railroad's warrants, fully one-third of the total, with $25,000 worth purchased directly from Falkner while the additional $2,000 consisted of the warrant given to Brougher by Falkner. Loomis presumably purchased them at less than their face value with the intent of making a profit selling them at face value. In fact, he stated in a deposition that he paid eighty cents on the dollar to Brougher for his $2,000 warrant. "Testimony of Charles W. Loomis," *Weekly Clarion*, March 27, 1873, 1; and "All in the Family," *Hinds County Gazette* (Raymond, MS), March 26, 1873, 1.

96. Ripley Railroad Company journal, October 10, 1872, 32.

97. In telegrams dated October 2, 1872, Attorney General Morris informed Vasser that he was not authorized "to receive or recognize" any state railroad warrants and that in his opinion they were unconstitutional. "The Mongrel Administration Repudiating Their Own Issues," *Weekly Clarion* (Jackson, MS), October 10, 1872, 2. Also, "After the Warrants were issued, the

Attorney General instructed the State Treasurer not to pay them on the ground that the law was unconstitutional, or in other words that the Warrants were a fraud on the State. They were received in good faith by the Company, and this opinion of the law officer of the State Administration destroys their value and amounts to repudiation of the obligations incurred under a law which was passed with a great flourish of trumpets (and by a secret flourish of greenbacks we suspect) signed by Gov. Alcorn, approbated by acting Gov. Powers—and lauded by the Mongrels generally as the pet measure of the Carpet Bag regime." "The Subsidy Transaction: Light Wanted," *Weekly Clarion*, November 14, 1872, 1.

98. "Governor's Message to the Senate and House of Representatives," *Weekly Clarion* (Jackson, MS), January 30, 1873, suppl., 5; and "The State of Mississippi and Its Railroads," *Railroad Gazette* (New York), February 22, 1873, 78.

99. "Q. Do you know where those warrants now are?" "A. I am informed by the depositor, that a large portion of them are in the vaults in my office. I have not examined them." "Testimony of Maj. W. H. Vasser," *Weekly Clarion* (Jackson, MS), March 27, 1873, 1.

100. "An Act in reference to certain State warrants, known as the Ripley Railroad warrants." *Laws of the State of Mississippi*, 1876, 221–24.

101. "The Charleston Railroad," *Memphis Daily Appeal*, August 16, 1873, 1.

102. A. Brown, *History of Tippah County*, 194; also see the appendix.

103. "There are two stations between Middleton and Ripley. The first is Hopkinsville, nine miles south of Middleton, the other is named Falkner." "The Ripley Narrow Gauge Railroad," *New Orleans Republican*, September 8, 1872, 2.

104. Falkner Depot was constructed prior to September 30 on land owned by Thomas L. Grace in the SE¼ Section 1, Township 3, Range 3 East. For Grace's ownership of this property, see Tippah County Deed Book Q, 181. However, there was apparently a problem obtaining title to the property, so on September 30 the railroad board ordered that the depot be moved south to property owned by W. W. Rutherford in the NE¼ Section 12, Township 3, Range 3 East where they were able to purchase a two-acre lot. Deed, W. W. Rutherford and R. J. Thurmond to Ripley Railroad Company, March 4, 1874, for $200, two acres in NE¼ 12-3-3 "to be so laid off as to include the Depot Buildings" (Tippah County Deed Book 2, 606).

105. Falkner Post Office was established on November 8, 1872, with L. D. Spight (brother of Thomas Spight) as postmaster. National Archives, US Postal Records, appointments of postmasters for post offices in Tippah County, Mississippi.

106. Plat of Town of Falkner, filed on February 23, 1881, Tippah County Deed Book 6, 416–18; see also plat for an addition to Falkner, Tippah County Deed Book 29, 195–96. The survey was apparently conducted years before it was filed in 1881.

107. Joyann Bullock, "Falkner, Mississippi," in Tippah County Historical and Genealogical Society, *Heritage of Tippah County*, 24.

108. As early as August, Hopkins was listed as an intermediate stop for the excursion train carrying people to the ceremonies commemorating the completion of the railroad. The list of stops consisted of "Gatlin's, Moore's, Hopkins's, Buchanan's and Luker's." *Memphis Daily Appeal*, August 25, 1872. These locations were seemingly designated ad hoc without any station infrastructure. By early September, a newspaper correspondent described "Hopkinsville" as one of two stations on the Ripley Railroad, the other being Falkner. "The Ripley Narrow Gauge Railroad," *New Orleans Republican*, September 8, 1872, 2, reprinted from the *Mississippi Pilot* (Jackson). However, there was apparently no depot there at the time, nor had a permanent site been located. At the September 17 meeting of the railroad's directors, a committee was appointed to identify "a suitable location for a depot at or near S. T. Hopkins," a railroad director. Ripley Railroad Company journal, September 17, 1872, 28. Almost a month later, the site apparently hadn't been settled, because the board had appointed another committee to locate the site for a depot "between Falkner and Middleton permanently." Ripley Railroad

Company journal, October 10, 1872, 32; also November 4, 1872, 33. It appears that Hopkins and Hopkinsville were not two names for the same site, but names for two close but separate sites. Carol J. Smith, "Walnut Community," in Tippah County Historical and Genealogical Society, *Heritage of Tippah County*, 15.

109. National Archives, US Postal Records, appointments of postmasters for post offices in Tippah County, Mississippi. The application form for establishing Hopkins Post Office indicates that its local name was "Mitchells." Its location was given as the NE¼ Section 5, Township 2, Range 4 East, the same as present Walnut. National Archives, Post Office Department Reports of Site Locations, 1837–1950, microfilm M1126, roll 318, Mississippi Tallahatchie-Tunica. The fact that Hopkins Post Office was established on the same day as Falkner Post Office suggests that the applications were submitted jointly. "A Map of the Town of Hopkins," filed for record on December 3, 1872, Tippah County Deed Book 3, 254.

110. Hopkins Post Office was changed to Walnut Post Office on July 18, 1876. National Archives, US Postal Records, appointments of postmasters for post offices in Tippah County, Mississippi.

111. "Mississippi Towns Incorporated, 1803–1925," Genealogy Trails, 2007, http://genealogy trails.com/miss/towns_incorporated.htm.

112. National Archives, US Postal Records, appointments of postmasters for post offices in Tippah County, Mississippi. William M. Burns was the first husband of Elizabeth Murry, daughter of Dr. John Y. Murry and sister of Sallie Murry, who married Falkner's son, John W. T. Falkner.

113. "Walnut Items," *Ripley (MS) Advertiser*, January 21, 1882, 3. "The big engine of the G.&S.I.R.R. was ditched at the Gatlin Switch Sunday," *Ripley (MS) Advertiser*, December 3, 1887. It should be recalled that the northernmost stop for the opening-day excursion train was Gatlin's. Gatlin Post Office was established on the railroad in 1886 and discontinued in 1889, with mail being sent to Walnut Post Office. National Archives, US Postal Records, appointments of postmasters for post offices in Tippah County, Mississippi. Gatlin Post Office was located on the east side of the tracks in the northwest quarter of Section 21, Township 1, Range 4 East, the same location that would become known as Brownfield a few years later. National Archives, Post Office Department Reports of Site Locations, 1837–1950, microfilm M1126, roll 318, Mississippi Tallahatchie-Tunica.

114. National Archives, US Postal Records, appointments of postmasters for post offices in Tippah County, Mississippi.

115. "Success of the Narrow Gauge," *Hinds County Gazette* (Raymond, MS), October 24, 1877.

116. See examples of the train's itinerary, which were usually published weekly in local newspapers. An itinerary for 1874 appears in W. F. Allen, ed., *Travelers' Official Railway Guide for the United States and Canada* (Philadelphia: National Railway Publication Company, January 1874), n.p.; and *Ripley (MS) Advertiser*, November 20, 1880, February 26, 1881, January 21, 1882, March 17, 1883, and June 21, 1884.

117. This is evidenced, for example, by a passenger who recalled the train carrying "400 passengers and 100 bales of cotton." L. C. B., letter to the editor, November 3, 1876, *Fayetteville (TN) Observer*, November 9, 1876, 3. Also, an accident occurred to the regular train in which three boxcars jumped the track while none of the passengers were injured. *Pontotoc (MS) Democrat*, February 14, 1889, 3.

118. For example, in 1875 in conjunction with a political event at Falkner Station with Congressman L. Q. C. Lamar as speaker, the Ripley Railroad arranged to have "special trains" scheduled to transport attendees from Ripley and Middleton. *Memphis Daily Appeal*, June 30, 1875, 2. Also, "Col. W. C. Falkner and Capt. J. C. Harris made a business visit to Pontotoc yesterday on a special train," *Pontotoc (MS) Democrat*, May 2, 1889, 3; "A Company of capitalists passed over the G. & C. road last Tuesday in a special train," *Southern Sentinel* (Ripley, MS),

December 3, 1891; and "The G&C run a special car to haul Christmas whisky," *Southern Sentinel*, January 3, 1895.

119. A. Brown, *History of Tippah County*, 194. In 1885 there was a serious accident "at the Y" involving Fannie Falkner, daughter of James Word Falkner and niece of W. C. Falkner. *Ripley (MS) Advertiser* May 2, 1885.

120. Agreement with the Southern Railway Security Company, May 4, 1872. Recorded in the Ripley Railroad Company journal, June 3, 1872, 16–20.

121. *Memphis Daily Appeal*, August 30, 1872, 4; and *Weekly Clarion* (Jackson, MS), September 5, 1872, 3.

122. "Ripley Railroad," *Railroad Gazette* (New York), October 12, 1872, 448.

123. "Ripley Railroad," *Railroad Gazette* (New York), October 12, 1872, 448; "The Ripley Narrow Gauge Railroad," *New Orleans Republican*, September 8, 1872, 2; "Ripley: Opening of the Narrow-Gauge Railroad," *Memphis Daily Appeal*, August 30, 1872, 4; "From Middleton to Ripley: The People, the Country and the Crops," *Memphis Daily Appeal*, September 19, 1872; and "The Charleston Railroad," *Memphis Daily Appeal*, August 16, 1873, 1. On September 16, 1872, the railroad officially voted to change the name of the *Ripley* to the *Hardy W. Stricklin*, a stockholder and treasurer for the company who had died on March 23. Ripley Railroad Company journal, September 16, 1872, 26. Date of death from "Tippah," *Memphis Daily Appeal*, April 2, 1872, 2. About the same time, it was reported that the *Ripley* would be renamed the *H. W. Lockett* in honor of the engineer who had been stabbed to death at Middleton. This was apparently merely a rumor; there is no official record supporting this claim. "From Middleton to Ripley: The People, the Country and the Crops," *Memphis Daily Appeal*, September 19, 1872.

124. David Guyton, while not using the names *Ripley* or *W. C. Falkner*, refers to "the first two locomotives No. 1 and No. 3" as being "familiarly spoken of by everybody"—suggesting that these were nicknames—as *Dolly*, a passenger-type engine, and *Tanglefoot*, a freight-type engine. David Guyton, "My Daddy and the Doodlebug," *Southern Sentinel* (Ripley, MS), March 4, 1954. *Dolly* was replaced in 1897; see *Southern Sentinel*, May 20, 1897: "'Dolly,' one of the first, if not THE first, engine to pass over the G&CRR, was carried away, DEAD, Saturday morning. We understand the company has traded her for a newer and larger engine which will soon be put on the road."

125. *Memphis Daily Appeal*, August 30, 1872, 4; *Weekly Clarion* (Jackson, MS), September 5, 1872, 3; and "The Charleston Railroad," *Memphis Daily Appeal*, August 16, 1873, 1.

126. "The Charleston Railroad," *Memphis Daily Appeal*, August 16, 1873, 1; and "The Ripley Narrow Gauge Railroad," *New Orleans Republican*, September 8, 1872, 2.

Chapter 11: The Railroad Plods Along

1. The Presbyterian Church at this time was on Block 60 in the Ripley plat. Tippah County Deed Book J, 95; and A. Brown, *History of Tippah County*, 56–57.

2. *Memphis Daily Appeal*, January 4, 1874.

3. *Catalogue of Washington and Lee University, Virginia, for the Year Ending June, 1874* (Petersburg, VA: Nash and Rogers, 1874), 8.

4. "The Stabbing Affair—Examination of Prisoner," item from an unidentified, undated newspaper clipping, probably the *Lexington (VA) Gazette*, circa October 15, 1873, Joseph Blotner Papers. Anderson was probably a local resident.

5. "The Stabbing Affair—Examination of Prisoner," Joseph Blotner Papers. "The Examining Court to-day remanded W. H. Falkner, of Ripley, Miss., to jail, for trial at the February term." "The Late Stabbing Case at Lexington," *Daily Dispatch* (Richmond, VA), October 14, 1873, 3.

6. "The Stabbing Affair—Examination of Prisoner," Joseph Blotner Papers. "The Lexington *Gazette* says that Mr. Dandridge, the young gentleman cut by Mr. Faulkner in an affray last month, is out and on the street." *Spirit of Jefferson* (Charles Town, VA), November 4, 1873, 3.

7. Williamson, *William Faulkner and Southern History*, 52.

8. Williamson, *William Faulkner and Southern History*, 52–53.

9. R. G. Dun & Co., Tippah County, MS, vol. 2, 254–55.

10. Duclos, *Son of Sorrow*, 262. Plummer was listed in the 1876 Bradstreet credit reference book for Mississippi as being a photographer in Ripley. Only days after the killing, on January 30, Plummer received an appointment as postmaster of New Albany Post Office and moved with his family to that town south of Ripley. One wonders if there was a connection between the events. National Archives, US Postal Records, appointments of postmasters for post offices in Union County, Mississippi.

11. Letter, William H. Anderson, Chancery Judge, to Donald Duclos, September 26, 1961, Ripley, MS, Falkner/Faulkner Family Collection, 1770s–1980s, Donald Duclos Papers, William Paterson University, Archives and Special Collections, Cheng Library, Wayne, New Jersey.

12. Duclos, *Son of Sorrow*, 262. The quotation is from an interview with Bama Falkner McLean in September 1959.

13. "Tippah County," *Memphis Daily Appeal*, December 24, 1874, 2.

14. James B. Murphy, *L. Q. C. Lamar: Pragmatic Patriot* (Baton Rouge: Louisiana State University Press, 1975), 151–52.

15. "Ripley, Miss. Grand Mass Meeting of the Conservative Democracy of Tippah County," *Memphis Daily Appeal*, July 20, 1875, 1.

16. "Ripley, Miss. Grand Mass Meeting of the Conservative Democracy of Tippah County," *Memphis Daily Appeal*, July 20, 1875, 1.

17. "Twenty-Third Senatorial District Convention," *Memphis Daily Appeal*, September 22, 1875, 2, reprinted from the *Ripley (MS) Advertiser*.

18. "The Conservative Democracy of Tippah County in Convention," *Weekly Clarion* (Jackson, MS), June 14, 1876, 4.

19. "Tippah County," *Weekly Clarion* (Jackson, MS), September 27, 1876, 1.

20. "Tippah County," *Weekly Clarion* (Jackson, MS), October 25, 1876, 4.

21. "Ripley, Miss. Grand Rally of the Democracy of Tippah County," *Memphis Daily Appeal*, October 26, 1876, 4.

22. "Ripley, Miss. Grand Rally of the Democracy of Tippah County," *Memphis Daily Appeal*, October 26, 1876, 4.

23. "Tippah County, Ripley, Miss., Oct. 23d, 1876," *Weekly Clarion* (Jackson, MS), November 1, 1876, 4.

24. "Proceedings of the Electoral College of Mississippi," *Weekly Clarion* (Jackson, MS), December 13, 1876, 2.

25. *Bolivar (TN) Bulletin*, October 18, 1872, 2.

26. Ripley Railroad Company journal, January 1873, 41.

27. "The Charleston Railroad," *Memphis Daily Appeal*, August 16, 1873, 1.

28. Thomas Todd Martin, "Portrait of an Old-Timer," *Southern Sentinel* (Ripley, MS), August 30, 1928. Martin's piece was based on an interview with R. J. Shannon, who was eighty years old; the article originally appeared in the *G.M.&N. News* (Mobile, AL). Robson's title, "General Business Manager," can be found on Ripley Railroad letterhead stationery used for a letter dated June 14, 1874, by Falkner to John F. Johnson. Rutledge, "How Colonel Falkner Built His Railroad," 170. However, Robson was also listed as "General Superintendent" on another piece of letterhead stationery used for an undated letter by Falkner to Ira South (original in the Ripley Public Library).

29. Thomas Todd Martin, "Portrait of an Old-Timer," *Southern Sentinel* (Ripley, MS), August 30, 1928.

30. "Middleton," *Bolivar (TN) Bulletin*, January 8, 1875, 2.

31. "Presentation of a Gold Watch to Railroad Superintendent Robson," *Memphis Daily Appeal*, December 25, 1873, 1.

32. "Presentation of a Gold Watch to Railroad Superintendent Robson," *Memphis Daily Appeal*, December 25, 1873, 1.

33. "[W]hereas R. T. Wilson as the trustee did enter upon and run said road from October 1874 until February 1878," Ripley Railroad Company journal, April 30, 1878, 50; and Duclos, *Son of Sorrow*, 155–56.

34. Ripley Railroad Company journal, November 6, 1875, 42–43.

35. *Memphis Daily Appeal*, September 11, 1875, 2; October 9, 1875, 4; and October 5, 1876, 4.

36. Letter, W. C. Falkner to John F. Johnson, June 14, 1874, in Rutledge, "How Colonel Falkner Built His Railroad," 169–70.

37. "Railroad Extension," *Memphis Daily Appeal*, June 21, 1876, 1, reprinted from the *Ripley (MS) Advertiser*; see also *Weekly Clarion* (Jackson, MS), June 28, 1876, 2.

38. Ripley Railroad Company journal, July 3, 1876, 48–49.

39. *Railroad Gazette* (New York), July 14, 1876, 314.

40. *Daily Clarion* (Jackson, MS), January 4, 1877, 4. It was reported that for the first time in years, the penitentiary was bringing in about $1,000 a month instead of operating at a loss. "The Penitentiary," reprinted from the *Winona (MS) Advance* in the *Weekly Clarion* (Jackson, MS), January 31, 1877, 2.

41. J. H. Jones, "Penitentiary Reform in Mississippi," *Publications of the Mississippi Historical Society* 6 (1902), 112.

42. "From an Appeal Correspondent, New Albany, Miss., April 10," *Memphis Daily Appeal*, April 11, 1877, 1.

43. *Weekly Clarion* (Jackson, MS), May 2, 1877, 2.

44. *New Orleans Daily Democrat*, August 17, 1877, 2. Early in 1877, Hamilton and Hebron, "Lessees Mississippi Penitentiary," were advertising daily a wide variety of goods and services to be provided by prison labor including wagon, furniture, and boot making, sawmilling, and corn grinding. See, for example, the advertisement in the *Daily Clarion* (Jackson, MS), January 21, 1877, 4. By early 1878, operating under a new name, J. S. Hamilton and Company, "Lessees Mississippi Penitentiary," had added to the services previously offered to include the building and repair of public buildings and the constructions of "bridges, trestles, rail road, and levee work." *Daily Clarion*, February 5, 1878, 1. By 1885, the firm operating the penitentiary was Hamilton, Hoskins, and Company. "The Lease of the Mississippi Penitentiary Transferred," *Weekly Commercial Herald* (Vicksburg, MS), December 25, 1885, 1.

45. Chesley E. Hines, 1834–1878, m. 1858 to Cornelia Elizabeth Harris, the sister of C. L. Harris.

46. Cornelius Leroy "Lee" Harris, 1841–1916.

47. "Ripley News," *Public Ledger* (Memphis), October 18, 1877, 2. It was also reported that through this transaction these men had "become the owners of its [the railroad's] entire bonded debt, about $250,000." "Success of the Narrow Gauge," *Weekly Clarion* (Jackson, MS), October 17, 1877, 1.

48. "Logan," "Notes from Tippah," *Weekly Clarion* (Jackson, MS), October 1, 1879, 3.

49. The 1870 Tippah County census lists both Hines and Harris as millers living with their families in adjacent homes. In 1871, the Mercantile Agency Reference Books began listing the business "Harris & Hines" under the category of "sawmill." Mercantile Agency Reference Books (New York: R. G. Dun and Company, 1871). For the purchase of Blocks 25 and 34, see Tippah County Deed Book 2, 634, and Book 3, 30–31. The mill was apparently on Block 34, because Block 25 was eventually used for the railroad shops.

50. Tippah County Deed Book 4, 330, 504–5. One of the sawmills was located in Ripley, while the other was located on the SW½ Section 1, Township 4, Range 3 East about two miles north of Ripley and near the railroad.

51. In 1886, the mill in Ripley was referred to as being operated "in connection with the Ripley Rail-road, and is considered an appurtenance thereof." Tippah County Deed Book 9, 270.

52. Tippah County Deed Book 6, 511. "The new Hotel has commenced business," *Southern Sentinel* (Ripley, MS), January 13, 1881. "Go to the HINES HOUSE for your dinner when you come to town," *Southern Sentinel*, January 27, 1881.

53. See the appendix, Block 24.

54. "Logan," "Notes from Tippah," *Weekly Clarion* (Jackson, MS), October 1, 1879, 3.

55. "[W]hereas R. T. Wilson as the trustee did enter upon and run said road from October 1874 until February 1878, and whereas said R T. Wilson has resigned his office of trustee, which resignation has been lawfully accepted, and R. J. Thurmond has been lawfully appointed as trustee under said deed of trust," Ripley Railroad Company journal, April 30, 1878, 50. For the date, see A. Brown, *History of Tippah County*, 194. Brown was confused in thinking that Falkner, Hines, and Harris had purchased their interest in the railroad after Thurmond was made trustee.

56. "The Projected Railroad from the Tennessee Line to the Sea Shore," *Weekly Clarion* (Jackson, MS), February 6, 1878, 2; and "Twenty-Fifth Day, Senate," *Weekly Clarion*, February 6, 1878, 3. It was reported that on February 5, Falkner and Superintendent Robson were guests at the Up-Town Hotel in Jackson. "Hotel Arrivals," *Daily Clarion* (Jackson, MS), February 7, 1878, 4.

57. "An Act to encourage and facilitate the building of the Ship Island, Ripley and Kentucky Railroad," *Laws of the State of Mississippi* (Jackson: Power and Barksdale, 1878), 224–28; and J. S. Hamilton and Company, advertisement, *Daily Clarion* (Jackson, MS), February 5, 1878, 1.

58. "An act supplementary to and amendatory to an act entitled, 'an act to encourage and facilitate the building of the Ship Island, Ripley and Kentucky Railroad,'" *Laws of the State of Mississippi*, 1878, 228–29.

59. *Public Ledger* (Memphis), March 15, 1878, 2.

60. *Daily Memphis Avalanche*, March 21, 1878, 4.

61. "Ship Island and Kentucky R.R.," *Macon (MS) Beacon*, July 13, 1878, 3.

62. "Ship Island and Kentucky R.R.," *Macon (MS) Beacon*, July 13, 1878, 3.

63. "Ripley, Ship Island & Kentucky Railroad," *Weekly Clarion* (Jackson, MS), September 17, 1879, 1, reprinted from the *Southern Sentinel*.

64. Hines was buried in Mount Zion (East) Cemetery in Benton County, Mississippi, along with several of his infant children and his wife's parents. Sources pertaining to the fatal accident are: "Mr. Hines was killed last fall [1878] while running an engine," *Weekly Clarion* (Jackson, MS), October 1, 1879, 3; "In 1879 [*sic*] he lost his life in an unfortunate wreck. The train hit an animal, overturned and he was scalded. This was on a tressel [*sic*] between Ripley and Falkner," Ada Hines, "Chesley E. Hines," in Tippah County Historical and Genealogical Society, *Heritage of Tippah County*, 382; and "Chesley Hines of Ripley lost his life near Falkner, Miss., while serving as an engineer, the only locomotive engineer, I believe, to die while on duty on the Doodlebug," David E. Guyton, "My Daddy and the Doodlebug," *Southern Sentinel* (Ripley, MS), March 4, 1954. The following was written by Hines's great-grandson: "Chesley Hines seems to have been the partner most involved in the technical aspects of actually running the railroad. In 1879 [*sic*], he lost his life in an accident while piloting the train when a stray animal suddenly appeared on the track as it crossed a trestle between Ripley and the hamlet of Falkner, causing the engine to overturn. In the crash that followed, Chesley Hines was scalded to death. . . . Later, Chesley's son William, my grandfather, worked as an engineer on the railroad and had the eerie experience of spotting an animal sauntering on to the tracks very near the spot where his father had been killed. Fortunately, he was able to stop the train in

time to avoid his father's fate, but my father remembers him saying that, in his fright, his hair 'stood up' beneath his cap." Hines, *William Faulkner and the Tangible Past*, 136.

65. "Mississippi Inland Railroad: Letter from M. A. Metts, Louisville, Miss., April 22d, 1879," *Weekly Clarion* (Jackson, MS), May 7, 1879, 1.

66. Letter, W. C. Falkner to Colonel S.[?] Guin, Ripley, MS, March 4, 1879, on letterhead stationery of the Ship Island, Ripley, and Kentucky R.R., President's Office, reproduced in Louis R. Saillard, "The Ripley Railroad," *GM&O Historical Society News*, nos. 83–84, 1997, 23.

67. *Weekly Clarion* (Jackson, MS), January 28, 1880, 3; and "Col. W. C. Falkner," *Memphis Daily Appeal*, January 29, 1880, 1.

68. *Memphis Daily Appeal*, February 24, 1880, 1.

69. "Washington, March 22, What Was Done in the House," *Memphis Daily Appeal*, March 23, 1880, 1.

70. *Weekly Clarion* (Jackson, MS), March 3, 1880, 2.

71. "Corinth," *Memphis Daily Appeal*, March 10, 1880, 2.

72. Letter, W. C. Falkner to the editors, Ripley, MS, March 4, 1880, *Weekly Clarion* (Jackson, MS), March 10, 1880, suppl., 6.

Chapter 12: Novelist and World Traveler

1. See Block 21 in the appendix.

2. The following indicates that the *Advertiser* resumed publishing in June: "The Ripley Advertiser comes to hand again after a long absence, having been suspended since April 7th, at which time its office was destroyed by fire," *Weekly Clarion* (Jackson, MS), June 23, 1880, 2. The *Ripley Advertiser* was published on Saturdays, and the Saturday before the announcement that it was being published again was June 19, 1880, suggesting that that may have been the date that its publication resumed. The issue in which the *Advertiser* began publishing Falkner's serial is unknown; however, it presumably began appearing shortly after the paper resumed publication. The earliest surviving issue for 1880 is that for November 6, with the serial appearing in the middle of chapter XVI, about two-fifths through the novel. The final installment appeared in the July 16, 1881, issue.

3. C. J. Frederick, "Thrilling Scenes in Mississippi in Ante-Bellum Days: 'The White Rose of Memphis,'" *Memphis Daily Appeal*, April 20, 1881, 1. Frederick notes that, following the burning of the *Ripley Advertiser* office, "Colonel Falkner's big heart caused him to propose to advance means to start the paper again, and in order to give her a good send-off began to write the *White Rose*." Cf. A. Brown, *History of Tippah County*, 278; and Duclos, *Son of Sorrow*, 161.

4. Frederick, "Thrilling Scenes in Mississippi," 1.

5. A. Brown, *History of Tippah County*, 279; cf. Duclos, *Son of Sorrow*, 178, which reports that he regularly worked to ten o'clock instead of nine.

6. By 1881, masquerade balls had had a long history. In the years prior to the publication of *The White Rose*, they were frequently held in Memphis and were especially common in association with Mardi Gras. For examples, see: "Exposition Ball," *Public Ledger* (Memphis), November 16, 1874, 2; "Ledger Lines" and "The Carnival: King Momus Enters the City To-day to Reign until Wednesday Morning at Sunrise," *Public Ledger*, February 28, 1876, 3; and "Grand Masquerade Ball," advertisement, *Public Ledger*, February 12, 1877, 3.

7. The original play was by Baron Eligius Franz Joseph von Münch-Bellinghausen (1806–1871), who wrote under the pen name Friedrich Halm, and was entitled *Der Sohn der Wildnis* (*The Son of the Wilderness*, 1842). There were soon several translations in English including by William Henry Charlton and Charles E. Anton, both entitled *The Son of the Wilderness*. *Newcastle Weekly Courant* (Newcastle upon Tyne, England), advertisement, June 25, 1847, 1.

Anton's text was published in the *Evening Post* (New York), August 23, 1849, beginning on page 1. A new translation soon appeared by Maria Lovell (1803–1877), adapted for the stage and with the new title *Ingomar, the Barbarian*. It was first performed in London in June 1851. *Lloyd's Weekly Newspaper* (London), June 15, 1851, 10; and *Reynold's Weekly Newspaper* (London), June 15, 1851, 9. By the following year, the play was being presented in the United States, including in Buffalo in April and New Orleans in December. *Buffalo Courier*, April 30, 1852, 2; and *Times-Picayune* (New Orleans), December 2, 1852, 2. The play appeared regularly in Memphis theaters, for example in 1853, 1859, 1866, 1867, 1868, 1872, 1876, and 1878, where Falkner was almost certainly familiar with it. "Benefit of Miss Annette Ince," *Daily Memphis Whig*, March 11, 1853, 3; "The Gaiety," *Memphis Daily Avalanche*, March 15, 1859, 3; "New Memphis Theater," *Memphis Daily Post*, April 5, 1866, 8; "New Memphis Theater," *Memphis Daily Post*, April 22, 1867, 8; "New Memphis Theater," *Public Ledger* (Memphis), October 21, 1868, 3; "Memphis Theater," *Public Ledger*, November 2, 1872, 2; "Memphis Theater," *Public Ledger*, December 7, 1876, 3; and "Mrs. Anderson's 'Parthenia,'" *Memphis Daily Appeal*, January 8, 1878, 1. The name "Ingomar" gained sufficient popularity to be used for a steamboat launched in early 1855 destined for the Memphis–New Orleans trade. "Another Fine Boat: New Orleans and Memphis Packet Ingomar," *Louisville (KY) Daily Courier*, January 8, 1855, 3.

8. Falkner, *The White Rose of Memphis*, 420.

9. C. S. Brown, "Colonel Falkner as General Reader," 587–88.

10. Falkner, *The White Rose of Memphis*, 349.

11. *Ripley (MS) Advertiser*, February 26, 1881, 3, reprinted from the *Ashland (MS) Register*.

12. The early indications were that the book was to be published by Appleton. [M. C. Gallaway], "The White Rose of Memphis," *Memphis Daily Appeal*, April 10, 1881, 2; and "The White Rose of Memphis," *Public Ledger* (Memphis), May 3, 1881, 2.

13. "Col. W. C. Falkner, the author of 'The White Rose of Memphis,' will leave here tomorrow morning for New York to superintend the publication of his book." *Ripley (MS) Advertiser*, April 23, 1881, 3. On May 20, Falkner wrote from New York to inform R. F. Ford, editor of the *Ripley Advertiser*, that Carleton was publishing his book. *Ripley (MS) Advertiser*, May 28, 1881. G. W. Carleton and Company began in 1857 as a New York bookshop called Rudd and Carleton. "Obituary: George W. Carleton," *Publishers' Weekly*, no. 1551 (October 19, 1901): 857–58.

14. "Col. W. C. Falkner, after an absence of five or six weeks on a trip to New York to superintend the publication of his book, arrived home late yesterday evening by special train." *Ripley (MS) Advertiser*, June 11, 1881; and *Public Ledger* (Memphis), June 9, 1881, 4.

15. Falkner, *The White Rose of Memphis*. The dedicatory inscription, signed "W. C. Falkner, Ripley, Mississippi, June, 1881," appears in the first edition of the novel (New York: G. W. Carleton, 1881).

16. "Wonderful Success of Colonel Falkner's New Book," *Memphis Daily Appeal*, July 24, 1881, 2.

17. "Colonel W. C. Faulkner," *Memphis Daily Appeal*, December 17, 1881, 4.

18. G. W. Carleton and Company became the G. W. Dillingham Company in 1886 upon the retirement of company head George W. Carleton, at which time his business partner, G. W. Dillingham, became principal owner. The novel continued to appear over the years under the Dillingham imprint. In 1912 the company offered a new edition on new plates with a publisher's preface noting that this was the thirty-fifth printing and that 160,000 copies had previously been printed. Whereas with the earlier plates the text extended through 531 pages, with the new plates it extended only through page 526. In 1916 Dillingham went bankrupt, and two years later many of its titles including *White Rose* were purchased by the publishing house M. A. Donohue and Company of Chicago and New York. Donohue probably issued several printings over the next few years; however, the number and dates are difficult to ascertain in part because Donohue continued to use the same plates as reset in 1912 and included the

Dillingham publisher's preface claiming that that printing (that is, whichever one the reader might happen to be holding) was *the* thirty-fifth printing. "George W. Carleton Retires," *Publishers' Weekly*, no. 747 (May 22, 1886): 651; "G. W. Dillingham Co. Bankrupt," *Publishers Weekly* 90, no. 10 (September 2, 1916): 677; and "Titles Which Speak for Themselves," *Publishers Weekly* 93, no. 15 (April 13, 1918): 1182.

19. "Colonel W. C. Faulkner," *Memphis Daily Appeal*, December 17, 1881, 4.

20. "Col. W. C. Falkner and family left yesterday morning [July 6] for Bailey Springs (Ala)." *Southern Sentinel* (Ripley, MS), July 7, 1881.

21. "Bailey Springs," *Memphis Daily Appeal*, June 29, 1881, 4.

22. *Clarksville (TN) Weekly Chronicle*, August 27, 1881, 3.

23. "Bailey Springs," *Memphis Daily Appeal*, June 29, 1881, 4.

24. "Bailey Springs," *Memphis Daily Appeal*, July 24, 1881, 1.

25. "Col. W. C. Falkner returned from Bailey Springs last Monday [August 8], in fine health," *Southern Sentinel* (Ripley, MS), August 11, 1881; "Colonel W. C. Falkner, of Ripley, Mississippi, is in the city, and will probably leave to-night for Bailey Springs," *Public Ledger* (Memphis), August 11, 1881, 4; and "Col. W. C. Falkner was in town in the early part of the week, but he has returned to Bailey Springs where his family now is and where he had been for some time previous to his arrival," *Ripley (MS) Advertiser*, August 13, 1881.

26. Her father described Effie in 1883, then fifteen years old, as "a tall black-eyed maiden in her early teens." Falkner, *Rapid Ramblings in Europe*, 17.

27. M. C. Gallaway, "A Scene of Splendor," *Memphis Daily Appeal*, August 21, 1881, 2. The *Southern Sentinel*, August 25, 1881, recorded that they returned home on Sunday, August 21.

28. *Memphis Daily Appeal*, May 2, 1882, 4.

29. *Ripley (MS) Advertiser*, May 6, 1882.

30. *Memphis Daily Appeal*, June 13, 1882, 4.

31. *Memphis Daily Appeal*, July 5, 1882, 4.

32. "New Publication," *Memphis Appeal*, July 2, 1882, reprinted in the *Ripley (MS) Advertiser*, July 8, 1882, 2.

33. W. C. Falkner, *The Little Brick Church* (Philadelphia: J. B. Lippincott, 1882), 5–6.

34. *Public Ledger* (Memphis), June 27, 1882, 1.

35. "New Publication," *Memphis Appeal*, July 2, 1882, reprinted in the *Ripley (MS) Advertiser*, July 8, 1882, 2.

36. "Can Anything Good Come Out of Nazareth?," *Daily Memphis Avalanche*, July 23, 1882, 2.

37. Whereas *The Little Brick Church* was 429 pages in length, *Lady Olivia* was only 334 pages. In 1970, *The Little Brick Church* was reprinted in a limited edition by Literature House, an imprint of the Gregg Press of Upper Saddle River, New Jersey. The pages were electronically duplicated from the first edition.

38. "Col. W. C. Falkner and family left Thursday morning for Bon Aqua Springs to spend the summer," *Ripley (MS) Advertiser*, July 15, 1882; and "Col. W. C. Falkner and family returned on Thursday from a month's sojourn at Bon Aqua and Bailey Springs," *Ripley (MS) Advertiser*, August 12, 1882.

39. A. Brown, *History of Tippah County*, 233.

40. *Southern Sentinel* (Ripley, MS), January 18, 1883.

41. Letter, W. L. Smith to Andrew Brown, n.d., in Andrew Brown, "Historical Sketches," *Southern Sentinel* (Ripley, MS), May 30, 1935.

42. A. Brown, *History of Tippah County*, 233.

43. Effie is listed as having played Rosalind Raymond in both the March presentation and the December presentation. "Editor Advertiser," *Ripley (MS) Advertiser*, March 17, 1883, 2; and "Programme," *Ripley (MS) Advertiser*, December 22, 1883, 3.

44. "The Lost Diamond," *Southern Sentinel* (Ripley, MS), March 1, 1883. The new scene—Scene 8—was entitled "Mrs. Jamima Jumper's Residence." "Programme," *Ripley (MS) Advertiser*, December 22, 1883, 3.

45. "The Lost Diamond," *Ripley (MS) Advertiser*, March 3, 1883, 3. There is a photograph of Pink Smith, who became editor of the *Southern Sentinel* in April 1883, dressed in the uniform that he wore in the play. In the background can be seen a painted landscape backdrop. Haynes, *William Faulkner: His Tippah County Heritage*, plate XLI.

46. The building was constructed in 1882 by Lee Hines, the son of C. E. Hines, and W. W. Robinson, with the lower story built to house two mercantile establishments while the upper floor was rented to the City of Ripley for use as a town hall and for municipal functions. The building was on the W½ Lot 2 and the E½ Lot 3, Block 22, with the Hines family owning the former parcel and Robinson the latter. Tippah County Deed Book W, 412, and Book 7, 93. For construction of this building, see: "Work is progressing rapidly upon the store house of Messrs. Hines and Robinson the upper story of which is to be fashioned into a splendid town hall," *Southern Sentinel* (Ripley, MS), April 20, 1882; and "The new business house of Messrs. Robinson and Hines is rapidly approaching completion, and the City Hall will be ready for use early in the Fall," *Southern Sentinel*, August 10, 1882. The building burned along with most of the southern side of the square on the night of May 30, 1903. "Eight Business Houses and Contents Swept by Flames," *Southern Sentinel*, June 4, 1903.

47. "The Lost Diamond," *Ripley (MS) Advertiser*, March 3, 1883, 3. This article, apparently written by the editor of the *Advertiser*, claimed that there would be two performances on two nights, March 7 and 8, with the first night's proceeds going to the band and the second night's proceeds going to Stonewall College, which had burned on the night of January 2. However, this was apparently in error. Later, C. L. Hovis, secretary of the Ripley Cornet Band, wrote that the *Advertiser* editor had been mistaken in regard to the "disbursement of the proceeds." *Southern Sentinel* (Ripley, MS), March 15, 1883. There is no evidence of there having been a second night's performance.

48. "The Lost Diamond was played to a full house last night and gave great satisfaction." *Southern Sentinel* (Ripley, MS), March 8, 1883.

49. Letter, W. L. Smith to Andrew Brown, n.d., in Andrew Brown, "Historical Sketches," *Southern Sentinel* (Ripley, MS), May 30, 1935.

50. "Editor Advertiser," *Ripley (MS) Advertiser*, March 17, 1883, 2.

51. *Memphis Daily Appeal*, March 20, 1883, 4.

52. *Southern Sentinel* (Ripley, MS), March 15, 1883.

53. "Remember the Date!," announcement by the Ripley Dramatic Club, *Ripley (MS) Advertiser*, December 15, 1883, 3.

54. Andrew Brown, "Historical Sketches," *Southern Sentinel* (Ripley, MS), May 30, 1935.

55. "Editor Advertiser," *Ripley (MS) Advertiser*, March 17, 1883; "Programme," *Ripley (MS) Advertiser*, December 22, 1883, 3; and "From Saulsbury," *Bolivar (TN) Bulletin*, January 10, 1884, 3.

56. *Ripley (MS) Advertiser*, April 14, 1883, 3; *Ripley (MS) Advertiser*, May 5, 1883, 3; and *Southern Sentinel* (Ripley, MS), May 3, 1883. Falkner checked into the City Hotel in New Orleans about April 10. *Times-Picayune* (New Orleans), April 11, 1883, 3.

57. Thomas S. Hines describes "a stuffed alligator caught in the Florida Swamplands by the Colonel's daughter Effie and brought back to Memphis to be filled with sawdust by a taxidermist. Fixed to stand incongruously upright on its hind legs, the creature stood in the Falkners' front hall, with extended claws holding a large seashell intended to receive the calling cards of the Ripley gentry who called upon the Falkners" (Hines, *William Faulkner and the Tangible Past*, 97, photo 99). Hines donated the alligator to the University of Mississippi Museums, where it is currently stored at Rowan Oak. He is probably incorrect in saying that

the alligator was caught by Effie and carried to Memphis, where it was stuffed. First, there is no evidence to suggest that Effie traveled on the Gulf Coast in her father's lifetime. Furthermore, the story is unlikely, given the existence of an industry that mass-produced such items for the tourist trade.

58. *Ripley (MS) Advertiser*, May 5, 1883, 3.

59. Falkner, *Rapid Ramblings in Europe*, 14–15, 17–18. In the book, the two women are invariably referred to only as Miss Bell and Miss Stevenson. Their first names, however, are given in one of his letters to the *Southern Sentinel*. Falkner, "Ramblings in and around Florence," *Southern Sentinel* (Ripley, MS), August 9, 1883, 1.

60. *Southern Sentinel* (Ripley, MS), May 17, 1883.

61. *Southern Sentinel* (Ripley, MS), May 24, 1883. The letters were published from July 5, 1883, through March 6, 1884, months after Falkner's return.

62. "Accident to the City of Berlin," *New-York Tribune*, May 22, 1883, 8; "Arrival of Skillful Swimmers," *New-York Tribune*, June 5, 1883, 8; "Inman Royal Mail Line Steamers for Queenstown and Liverpool," *New-York Tribune*, June 2, 1883, 6; and Falkner, *Rapid Ramblings in Europe*, 13–14, 18–19, 24–28, 32–34.

63. Falkner, *Rapid Ramblings in Europe*, 27–28.

64. Arnold Kludas, *Record Breakers of the North Atlantic: Blue Riband Liners, 1838–1952* (Washington, DC: Brassey's, 1999), 57–58, 65; and C. R. Vernon Gibbs, *Passenger Liners of the Western Ocean: A Record of the North Atlantic Steam and Motor Passenger Vessels from 1838 to the Present Day* (London: Staples Press, 1952), 99.

65. "Inman Royal Mail Line Steamers," *New-York Tribune*, June 2, 1883, 6.

66. Falkner, *Rapid Ramblings in Europe*, 45.

67. Falkner, *Rapid Ramblings in Europe*, 48.

68. Falkner, *Rapid Ramblings in Europe*, 51–52.

69. *Ripley (MS) Advertiser*, June 23, 1883, 3; and Falkner, *Rapid Ramblings in Europe*, 58–59.

70. Falkner, *Rapid Ramblings in Europe*, 62; W. C. Falkner, "From Liverpool to Kenelworth," *Southern Sentinel* (Ripley, MS), July 12, 1883, 1; and W. C. Falkner, "The City of London," *Southern Sentinel*, July 19, 1883, 1. In *Rapid Ramblings*, Falkner refers to Schmitsuebel as "Alfred Valscratchembottler," a name concocted for amusing effect, after which he noted: "I am not right sure I have spelled his name correctly, for I was governed by his pronunciation of it."

71. W. C. Falkner, "From New York to Liverpool," *Southern Sentinel* (Ripley, MS), July 5, 1883, 2.

72. W. C. Falkner, "The City of London," *Southern Sentinel* (Ripley, MS), July 19, 1883, 1.

73. Falkner, *Rapid Ramblings in Europe*, 71.

74. Falkner, *Rapid Ramblings in Europe*, 77.

75. W. C. Falkner, "From Liverpool to Kenelworth," *Southern Sentinel* (Ripley, MS), July 12, 1883, 1.

76. Falkner, *Rapid Ramblings in Europe*, 81. Falkner's initial description of the visit to Stratford made no mention of this incident. W. C. Falkner, "From Liverpool to Kenelworth," *Southern Sentinel* (Ripley, MS), July 12, 1883, 1.

77. Falkner, *Rapid Ramblings in Europe*, 84–85.

78. Falkner, *Rapid Ramblings in Europe*, 86–87.

79. Falkner, *Rapid Ramblings in Europe*, 92.

80. W. C. Falkner, "The City of London," *Southern Sentinel* (Ripley, MS), July 19, 1883, 1. Much of the itinerary was not included in *Rapid Ramblings*.

81. Falkner, *Rapid Ramblings in Europe*, 110–11.

82. Falkner, *Rapid Ramblings in Europe*, 111.

83. Falkner, *Rapid Ramblings in Europe*, 114–16.

84. Shurg was "German by birth, Swiss by adoption," and spoke seven languages. Falkner, *Rapid Ramblings in Europe*, 377.

85. Falkner, *Rapid Ramblings in Europe*, 118–19; the first names of the Thacher daughters are on pages 159 and 167.

86. Falkner, *Rapid Ramblings in Europe*, 118.

87. Falkner, *Rapid Ramblings in Europe*, 120.

88. W. C. Falkner, "Letter from Genoa," June 24, 1883, *Southern Sentinel* (Ripley, MS), August 2, 1883, 1.

89. W. C. Falkner, "Letter from Genoa," June 24, 1883, *Southern Sentinel* (Ripley, MS), August 2, 1883, 1.

90. W. C. Falkner, "The City of London," London, June 20, 1883, *Southern Sentinel* (Ripley, MS), July 19, 1883, 1.

91. The date for the arrival in Rome comes from W. C. Falkner, "Rome, June 27," *Southern Sentinel* (Ripley, MS), August 16, 1883, suppl., 2.

92. Reproduced in Falkner, *Rapid Ramblings in Europe*, 3. "Roy" was another nickname for Bama, whose full name was Alabama Leroy Falkner.

93. Falkner, *Rapid Ramblings in Europe*, 3.

94. Falkner, *Rapid Ramblings in Europe*, 192.

95. Falkner, *Rapid Ramblings in Europe*, 122, 295, 317, 507.

96. W. C. Falkner, "Italy," *Southern Sentinel* (Ripley, MS), August 16, 1883, suppl., 1.

97. W. C. Falkner, "Italy," Naples, July 5, *Southern Sentinel* (Ripley, MS), August 16, 1883, suppl., 1.

98. W. C. Falkner, "Italy," Florence, July 7, *Southern Sentinel* (Ripley, MS), August 9, 1883, 1.

99. Falkner, *Rapid Ramblings in Europe*, 283.

100. Falkner, *Rapid Ramblings in Europe*, 283–84.

101. Falkner, *Rapid Ramblings in Europe*, 286–87. The passage from act 1, scene 3, is more fully rendered as "where merchants most do congregate."

102. Falkner, *Rapid Ramblings in Europe*, 425–26.

103. Falkner, *Rapid Ramblings in Europe*, 426.

104. Falkner, *Rapid Ramblings in Europe*, 427–48.

105. Falkner, *Rapid Ramblings in Europe*, 462–514.

106. Falkner, *Rapid Ramblings in Europe*, 552.

107. W. C. Falkner, "Europe," *Southern Sentinel* (Ripley, MS), February 28, 1884, 1. This is almost identical to the counterpart passage in Falkner, *Rapid Ramblings in Europe*, 554.

108. Falkner, *Rapid Ramblings in Europe*, 554.

109. "Shipping News: Port of New York City . . . Sunday, Sept. 9, 1883," *New-York Tribune*, September 10, 1883, 8; "TransAtlantic Travelers," *New York Daily Tribune*, September 10, 1883, 5; and Falkner, *Rapid Ramblings in Europe*, 563.

110. Falkner, *Rapid Ramblings in Europe*, 566.

111. "Col. W. C. Falkner and his daughter Miss Effie, after an absence in Europe of nearly four months, arrived home on the train Thursday [September 13]." *Ripley (MS) Advertiser*, September 15, 1883, 3.

112. *Dixie Boy* (Lamar, MS), reprinted in the *Ripley (MS) Advertiser*, October 6, 1883, 3.

113. *Southern Sentinel* (Ripley, MS), November 22, 1883.

114. Falkner, *Rapid Ramblings in Europe*, 375.

115. Falkner, *Rapid Ramblings in Europe*, 119–20.

116. Falkner, *Rapid Ramblings in Europe*, 469.

117. *Southern Sentinel* (Ripley, MS), March 13, 1884, 1.

118. "He left here a few days ago for New York to superintend its publication," *Ripley (MS) Advertiser*, April 5, 1884; and "Col. W. C. FALKNER is at the Peabody Hotel, having just returned from Philadelphia, where he has been superintending the publication of his forthcoming book, *Rapid Ramblings in Europe*, which is being published by Lippincott & Co.,

and will be out by the 25th," *Memphis Daily Appeal*, May 13, 1884, 4. The first mention of the name *Rapid Ramblings in Europe* that I've found comes from "Col. Falkner's Latest Book," *Clarion* (Jackson, MS), May 7, 1884, 2. This article reports that five thousand copies were to be printed and that the publishers were "stereotyping the pages so as to meet promptly any possible demand."

119. *Memphis Daily Appeal*, June 1, 1884, 1; and *Memphis Daily Appeal*, June 11, 1884, 4. Similar notices of the availability of the new book can be found, for example, in "New Books," *Evening Star* (Washington, DC), June 11, 1884, 1; and "Recent Publications," *Morning Journal and Courier* (New Haven, CT), June 24, 1884, 1.

120. Seth Berner of Portland, Maine, a rare bookdealer specializing in William Faulkner, has informed me that there are at least three different colored bindings: blue, gold, and olive green. It is not known whether these variant bindings represent different printings or simply whether different colored cloth was used in the binding process. I have found nothing about the number of copies printed.

121. "Col. Falkner's New Book," *Memphis Daily Appeal*, July 13, 1884, 2.

122. "Col. Falkner's New Book," *Memphis Daily Appeal*, July 13, 1884, 2.

123. "Not a Candidate," *Ripley (MS) Advertiser*, May 17, 1894, 2.

124. Edward B. Dickinson, ed., *Official Proceedings of the National Democratic Convention Held in Chicago, Ill., July 8th, 9th, 10th, and 11th, 1884* (New York: Douglas Taylor's Democratic Printing House, n.d.), 250, 253–54, 259–60, 263.

125. "Col. W. C. Falkner and family returned home, from Bailey Springs Ala, on Thursday evening last [August 28], where they had been spending the summer," *Ripley (MS) Advertiser*, August 30, 1884, 3; and "Col. W. C. Falkner and family returned from a visit to the Springs last Thursday on a special train," *Southern Sentinel* (Ripley, MS), September 4, 1884.

126. *Ripley (MS) Advertiser*, September 6, 1884. For the organization of the group, see "Ripley Central Democratic Club," *Ripley (MS) Advertiser*, August 30, 1884, 2.

127. "Ripley, Miss., October 28," *Memphis Daily Appeal*, October 30, 1884, 2.

128. *Ripley (MS) Advertiser*, September 6 and October 18, 1884; and *Southern Sentinel* (Ripley, MS), September 11 and October 16, 1884. The Carter home, which Falkner had given to his daughter in December 1877, was on Block 4 (Tippah County Deed Book 4, 382). "Dr. N. G. Carter is building a two story residence on his lot," *Ripley (MS) Advertiser*, September 6, 1884; and "Dr. N. G. Carter's new dwelling is nearing completion," *Southern Sentinel*, October 16, 1884.

129. *Southern Sentinel* (Ripley, MS), November 13 and 20, 1884; and *Ripley (MS) Advertiser*, November 15 and 22, 1884.

130. Donald Duclos wrote that it "was modeled after a home Falkner had seen in Europe." Duclos also described it as "something short of an architectural monster" that exemplified his "megalomania." None of this is justified. There was nothing especially unique about building large, even somewhat garish houses, if one could afford it. Duclos, *Son of Sorrow*, 219; cf. A. Brown, *History of Tippah County*, 280; and Williamson, *William Faulkner and Southern History*, 55.

131. We find a reference to the house as "the beautiful old Falkner home, 'Warwick Place,'" in "The Social Realm," *Memphis Commercial*, September 15, 1893, 5. Also see *Southern Sentinel* (Ripley, MS), June 29 and August 31, 1893, and May 19, 1898; and *Memphis Commercial*, June 25, 1893, 12, and November 26, 1893, 5. Because these references all postdate Falkner's death, there's a possibility that another family member posthumously named the house. However, this seems unlikely given that the name is all too evocative of the grand flourishes that Falkner loved. The name came into wide use in 1893, which coincided with Lizzie Falkner's reoccupation of the home in the spring of that year following more than three years of it being unoccupied. At this time, the family may have emphasized the name, seeing it as a memorial to Falkner and his European tour.

132. William Faulkner, *Go Down, Moses* (New York: Modern Library, 1955), 5.

133. A. Brown, *History of Tippah County*, 280.

134. *Ripley (MS) Advertiser*, January 31, 1885.

135. The office building was on Lot 1, Block 14; see the appendix.

136. J. L. Power, "Correspondence: Holly Springs and Ripley, Ripley, Miss., April 20, 1885," *Clarion* (Jackson, MS), April 22, 1885, 2.

137. *Ripley (MS) Advertiser*, January 31 and February 14, 1885; and *Southern Sentinel* (Ripley, MS), February 12, 1885.

138. *Southern Sentinel* (Ripley, MS), April 2, 1885; and *Ripley (MS) Advertiser*, April 4, 1885.

139. *Memphis Daily Appeal*, April 11, 1885, 4.

140. "Col. W. C. Falkner left Sunday last [August 2] for White Sulphur Springs, West Va., where he will spend the summer," *Southern Sentinel* (Ripley MS), August 6, 1885; and "Col. W. C. Falkner, who has been spending the summer at Greenbrier White Sulphur Springs in West Va., returned home Saturday," *Ripley (MS) Advertiser*, September 12, 1885.

141. "John W. T. Falkner of Ripley has formed a copartnership in the law business with Col. C. B. Howry of Oxford and will shortly remove to that town." *Ripley (MS) Advertiser*, October 31, 1885, reprinted from the *Union County Optic* (New Albany, MS).

142. "John W. T. Falkner and family have removed to Oxford, Miss., where they will reside permanently. They left here for their new home on Tuesday last [December 8]. They, we believe, were all—father, mother, and children—natives of Ripley." *Ripley (MS) Advertiser*, December 12, 1885. Regarding Mrs. Thompson's residing with the Falkners: "Mrs. Thompson's home since the death of her noble husband Judge J. W. Thompson [in 1873] was with her adopted son, Hon. J. W. T. Falkner of Oxford." "Mrs. Judge Thompson," obituary, *Southern Sentinel* (Ripley, MS), September 22, 1898.

143. "Sensational Shooting," *Memphis Appeal*, August 10, 1886, 4; and "Terrible Tragedy," *Ripley (MS) Advertiser*, August 14, 1886, reprinted from the *Nashville American*.

144. *Macon (MS) Beacon*, November 27, 1886, 2.

Chapter 13: And Beyond That

1. "Colonel W. C. Faulkner," *Memphis Daily Appeal*, December 17, 1881, 4.

2. A. Brown, *History of Tippah County*, 87. Brown noted on page 89 that Dr. C. M. Murry—who knew Falkner well (his sister was married to Falkner's son)—told him that Falkner was about five feet six inches tall and that "he was a little fellow and he always strutted like a pouter pigeon."

3. "The Pontotoc Observer says that Colonel Falkner proposes to extend the Ripley narrow gauge road to Pontotoc, provided the people of Pontotoc county will insure him $20,000 to be paid whenever the road is finished." *Ripley (MS) Advertiser*, January 2, 1886.

4. "An act to incorporate the Gulf and Ship Island Railroad company," *Laws of the State of Mississippi* (Jackson: J. L. Power, 1882), 849–62.

5. James H. Lemly, *The Gulf, Mobile and Ohio: A Railroad That Had to Expand or Expire* (Homewood, IL: Richard D. Irwin, 1953), 286.

6. Letter, W. H. Hardy to Frank Burkitt, February 11, 1886, *Daily Clarion* (Jackson, MS), February 14, 1886, 2.

7. *Daily Clarion* (Jackson, MS), January 22, 1886, 2; and *Ripley (MS) Advertiser*, January 30, 1886.

8. *Ripley (MS) Advertiser*, February 6, 1886.

9. *Ripley (MS) Advertiser*, February 13, 1886.

10. "Change of Gauge," *Memphis Appeal*, May 29, 1886, 4; also "Uniformity in the Gauge of Railroads," *Memphis Appeal*, May 22, 1886, 4; and Douglas J. Puffert, "The Standardization of Track Gauge on North American Railways, 1830–1890," *Journal of Economic History* 60, no. 4 (December 2000): 954–55.

11. Gulf and Ship Island Railroad Contract with W. C. Falkner et al., Tippah County Deed Book 9, 270–75.

12. A. Brown, *History of Tippah County*, 270–71; and Duclos, *Son of Sorrow*, 157. Of course, the close family ties between the Hineses and Harrises would have given them some family solidarity. However, counterbalancing this family connection was the fact that C. L. Harris's son, J. C. "Jim" Harris, married Thurmond's daughter Mary in 1883, while a few years later his daughter Dora married Thurmond's son, Dr. R. J. Thurmond Jr. However, Harris wasn't a fanatical supporter of Thurmond. After the latter sold his interest in the railroad, Harris continued as a part owner and employee for years to come.

13. A. Brown, *History of Tippah County*, 281.

14. Hickerson, *The Falkner Feuds*, 5. Hickerson's father, James Hickerson (1832–1918), was the son of Amelia Gwyn Hickerson (1808–1857), whose sister Sarah Gwyn Thurmond (1782–1834) was the mother of R. J. Thurmond.

15. Both Brown and Duclos date the feud's beginning to approximately early 1886 but were uncertain about its cause. This is probably due to their inadequate understanding of events concerning the merger with the G&SI. However, Duclos does indicate that "one belief" was that the feud originated as the result of Thurmond's reluctance to follow Falkner into the merger. Although Duclos was on the right track, he never developed this idea. A. Brown, *History of Tippah County*, 281–83; and Duclos, *Son of Sorrow*, 237–38.

16. A. Brown, *History of Tippah County*, 282.

17. Tippah County Chattel Trust Book 8, 301–3.

18. Tippah County Deed Book 9, 325–26. At the time, Ishatubby Farm constituted 2,005 acres.

19. Tippah County Chattel Trust Book 8, 311–13.

20. "Progress of the Gulf and Ship Island Railroad, Ripley Miss, March 29," *Ripley (MS) Advertiser*, April 3, 1886, reprinted from the *Memphis Avalanche*. Cf. "The Ripley Railroad," *Bolivar (TN) Bulletin*, April 9, 1886, 2; and *Macon (MS) Beacon*, May 22, 1886, 2, reprinted from the *Tupelo (MS) Journal*.

21. A. Brown, *History of Tippah County*, 281–82.

22. *Ripley (MS) Advertiser*, April 3, 1886.

23. A. Brown, *History of Tippah County*, 186–89.

24. *Ripley (MS) Advertiser*, April 25, 1885.

25. *Ripley (MS) Advertiser*, March 13 and 20, 1886, and March 27 and April 3, 1883; W. C. Falkner, letter to the editor, *Tupelo (MS) Journal*, Ripley, MS, May 22, 1886, in *Ripley (MS) Advertiser*, June 5, 1886; and "Gulf & Ship Island R.R. Report of Jury," Tippah County Deed Book 9, 229–30. For reference to the camps as "stockades," "The Card," *Clarion* (Jackson, MS), November 10, 1886, 3, reprinted from the *Pontotoc (MS) Observer*.

26. "Roberson Hotel" was probably a short-lived name for the hotel that stood on the south side of the courthouse square on the site of the present courthouse. This was the major hotel in Pontotoc for decades and was often known as the Anderson Hotel or Tavern. Callie B. Young, ed., *From These Hills: A History of Pontotoc County* (Fulton, MS: Itawamba County Times, 1976), 164, 216. The hotel is depicted on a Pontotoc map (one sheet), where it is listed as the "City Hotel"; Sanborn-Perris Map Company, Pontotoc, Mississippi, map, March 1898.

27. "A Pretty Romance," *Ripley (MS) Advertiser*, May 15, 1886, reprinted from the *Pontotoc (MS) True Democrat*. A variant of this story was soon published in the *State Ledger* (Jackson, MS) and was subsequently reprinted in other newspapers, for example the *Memphis Avalanche*,

May 16, 1886, 2; the *Grenada (MS) Sentinel*, May 22, 1886, 8; and the *Pascagoula (MS) Democrat-Star*, June 11, 1886, 4. Although the original tale claims that the little girl became his second wife, Lizzie Vance, when Alexander Bondurant retold it the little girl had been transformed into his future *first* wife, Holland Pearce (Bondurant, "William C. Falkner, Novelist," 115). However, neither Holland Pearce nor Lizzie Vance were living anywhere close to Pontotoc in the early 1840s when this story supposedly took place.

28. *Ripley (MS) Advertiser*, May 8, 1886.

29. Article in the *Tupelo (MS) Journal* as reprinted in the *Macon (MS) Beacon*, May 22, 1886, 2, and the *Pascagoula (MS) Democrat-Star*, May 28, 1886, 3.

30. "Colonel Faulkner's Dream of Service Has Come True," Duclos, *Son of Sorrow*, app. 6, 346–47. This text originally appeared in the *Pontotoc Sentinel* and was soon after republished in the *G.M.&N. News* (Mobile, AL), December 21, 1923. It was probably written by the editor, E. T. Winston (1871–1944).

31. *Ripley (MS) Advertiser*, May 8, 1886.

32. *Ripley (MS) Advertiser*, June 19, 1886.

33. *Ripley (MS) Advertiser*, July 10, 1886, reprinted from the *Pontotoc (MS) Observer*, July 3, 1886.

34. Crossties were procured through contracting with neighboring landowners. "Col. Falkner is letting out contracts to landowners along the route to furnish cross ties." *Ripley (MS) Advertiser*, February 5, 1887.

35. "State Ledger Gulf & Ship Island R.R.," *Ripley (MS) Advertiser*, July 10, 1866, reprinted from the *State Ledger* (Jackson, MS).

36. *Ripley (MS) Advertiser*, May 1, 1886.

37. Herbert C. Murdaugh, "The Ripley Railroad: Mississippi's Only Narrow-Gauge Common Carrier," typescript, Ripley Public Library, Ripley, Mississippi, 1968, 17–18; Hembree Brandon, "Grace's Crossing Grave Tended by Railroaders for 73 Years," *Daily Journal* (Tupelo, MS), September 3–4, 1960; and Tommy Covington, personal communication.

38. Murdaugh, "The Ripley Railroad," 17–18; and Hembree Brandon, "Grace's Crossing Grave Tended by Railroaders for 73 Years," *Daily Journal* (Tupelo, MS), September 3–4, 1960. A newspaper account records Smith's sentencing: "Criminal Court," *Weekly Commercial Herald* (Vicksburg, MS), March 5, 1886, 8.

39. *Ripley (MS) Advertiser*, August 28, 1886.

40. *Ripley (MS) Advertiser*, September 25, 1886.

41. Guyton Post Office was established prior to the railroad's construction on August 2, 1880, with Joseph J. Guyton as postmaster. It was located in the NE¼ Section 19, Township 5, Range 3 East and was discontinued in late 1904. National Archives, US Postal Records, appointments of postmasters for post offices in Tippah County, Mississippi; and National Archives, Post Office Department Reports of Site Locations, 1837–1950, microfilm M1126, roll 318, Mississippi Tallahatchie-Tunica. Guyton was a close friend of Falkner and served as a coexecutor of his estate.

42. *Ripley (MS) Advertiser*, October 9, 1886.

43. Cotton Plant Post Office was established on January 9, 1840, with Andrew Jones as postmaster. National Archives, US Postal Records, appointments of postmasters for post offices in Tippah County, Mississippi.

44. A. Brown, *History of Tippah County*, 272. One wonders why thirty-six-pound rails were used between Ripley and Cotton Plant, given that the intention was to standardize the gauge soon after, and rails of that weight were inadequate for standard-gauge rolling stock. However, this is evidently correct, given the fact that in 1901 it was reported that the "G.&C. Railroad is laying 50 lb. steel rail [in effect replacing older rails] from Middleton to Cotton Plant." *Southern Sentinel* (Ripley, MS), August 29, 1901. The fact that the replacement extended from Middleton

to Cotton Plant indicates that this strip was constructed with the lighter rails, which was by then regarded as substandard for even a narrow-gauge road. Cf. A. Brown, *History of Tippah County*, 275.

45. *Ripley (MS) Advertiser*, July 17, 1886.

46. *Clarion* (Jackson, MS), October 20, 1886, 2, and October 27, 1886, 2; and *Ripley (MS) Advertiser*, October 30, 1886.

47. Union County Historical Committee, *History of Union County, Mississippi, 1989* (Dallas: Curtis Media Corporation, 1990), 4.

48. *Ripley (MS) Advertiser*, March 19, 1887, reprinted from the *Pontotoc (MS) Observer*.

49. *Ripley (MS) Advertiser*, April 16, 1887.

50. He returned on April 29. "After an absence of nearly three weeks, Col. W. C. Falkner returned home yesterday from New York." *Ripley (MS) Advertiser*, April 30, 1887.

51. *Ripley (MS) Advertiser*, April 30, 1887, and May 14, 1886.

52. *Ripley (MS) Advertiser*, May 14, 1887.

53. A. Brown, *History of Tippah County*, 272.

54. *Ripley (MS) Advertiser*, December 4 and 18, 1886; and *Pascagoula (MS) Democrat-Star*, December 10, 1886, 2. The source for the locomotive's name comes from a writer for the *Memphis Appeal* who visited Blue Mountain in May 1887 and reported that "the finest" locomotive owned by the Ripley Railroad was named "the Rev. M. P. Lowrey," obviously referring to the third locomotive. The reporter had talked to Falkner, who noted: "I put it [the name] there because I admired the man. His influence through that country will never die." *Memphis Appeal*, May 8, 1887, 11. Brown erroneously calls this locomotive the *W. C. Falkner*, #40. However, as we have seen, #3 was the *Colonel W. C. Falkner*, while the number 40 seems out of place because the numbers appear to have been issued sequentially as rolling stock was added to the inventory, and the next two locomotives acquired would be #7 and #9. A. Brown, *History of Tippah County*, 272.

55. *Ripley (MS) Advertiser*, December 3, 1887. Brown erroneously termed this locomotive #7, the *General M. P. Lowrey*. A. Brown, *History of Tippah County*, 272. I do not know what its name was.

56. *Ripley (MS) Advertiser*, June 25 and July 2, 1887. Hines and Harris were the sons, respectively, of C. E. Hines and C. L. Harris.

57. The *Ripley Advertiser*, December 4, 1886, reprinted an item from the *Union County Optic* of Thursday, November 25. The item relates that "New Albany's first passenger train came in last Thursday." The "last Thursday" before the twenty-fifth would have been November 18, the day the first passenger train arrived. Andrew Brown reported erroneously that Falkner built the G&SI into New Albany before the arrival of the KCM&B. A. Brown, *History of Tippah County*, 271.

58. *Ripley (MS) Advertiser*, May 28, 1887. Willie is referred to as W. C. Falkner Jr. in the *Southern Sentinel* (Ripley, MS), April 26, 1888. Little is known of the *Optic*; no copies are known to survive. A search of newspapers provides citations for the *Optic* from 1884 through 1888. Although its formal name was the *Union County Optic*, it was more often referred to as the "New Albany Optic," presumably because the location of New Albany was better known to many of its readers than Union County. Falkner appears to have sold his interest in May 1888. "We learn they [Messrs. Simmons and Williamson] completed arrangements with Col. Falkner by which they assume control of the New Albany Optic." *Southern Sentinel*, May 31, 1888.

59. "Hands are now at work in New Albany finishing up the grading," *Ripley (MS) Advertiser*, August 6, 1887; and "The Gulf & Ship Island Railroad began yesterday to lay tracks out of New Albany, —New Albany Optic [probably August 11]," *Ripley (MS) Advertiser*, August 13, 1887.

60. *Ripley (MS) Advertiser*, October 1 and 22, and November 5, 1887. Ingomar Post Office was established on December 14, 1887, with Thomas A. Hitt as the first postmaster. The post

office had previously been named Fredonia, and Hitt had been appointed Fredonia postmaster earlier the same year on January 15, 1887, so the creation of the new post office was in continuity with an older post office. Fredonia Post Office was originally established on June 20, 1854, in Pontotoc County with Andrew J. Jones as the first postmaster. National Archives, US Postal Records, appointments of postmasters for post offices in Union County, Mississippi.

61. C. Young, *From These Hills*, 467–73; and National Archives, US Postal Records, appointments of postmasters for post offices in Pontotoc County, Mississippi.

62. As will be recalled, Falkner did not name the town Falkner. It was named by the railroad's stockholders.

63. W. Kenneth Holditch, "Who Was William Faulkner? Growing Up in Faulkner's Shadow," in *Faulkner at 100: Retrospect and Prospect*, ed. Donald M. Kartiganer and Ann J. Abadie (Jackson: University Press of Mississippi, 2000), 7. Holditch also recorded other stories that he had grown up with: "When the Old Colonel determined that New Albany would be the southernmost station on his railroad because of problems with the terrain to the South, my great-grandfather persuaded him to extend the line across the Holditch land in Pontotoc County. . . . Early in my childhood I began to hear stories from members of my family and other Ecru residents about W. C. Falkner and his friendship with my ancestor. 'Your great-grandfather bought the railroad with a turkey dinner and a bottle of wine' became something of a litany though the years. George Holditch, my grandfather, who lived to the age of ninety-three, remembered the Old Colonel, an imposing and imperious figure of whom he was frightened, in his childhood" (Holditch, "Who Was William Faulkner?," 7).

64. Errol Castens, "Oddities and Distinctives Take on Varying Forms," *Northeast Mississippi Daily Journal* (Tupelo, MS), July 23, 2010.

65. Cantwell, "The Faulkners: Recollections of a Gifted Family," 34.

66. *Greenville (MS) Times*, June 2, 1888, 1; and *Southern Sentinel* (Ripley, MS), June 14, 1888.

67. *Southern Sentinel* (Ripley, MS), July 5, 1888,

68. "They Drove the Silver Spike," *Memphis Appeal*, July 6, 1888, 1; letter to the editor, July 10, 1888, *Clarion-Ledger* (Jackson, MS), July 12, 1888, reproduced in Murdaugh, "The Ripley Railroad," 19–20; and a passage from the *Home Journal* (Pontotoc, MS), July 1888 (day unspecified), reprinted in the *G.M.&N. News* (Mobile, AL), November 27, 1925, 11, quoted in Duclos, *Son of Sorrow*, 230. The *Southern Sentinel* (Ripley, MS), July 12, 1888, reported that seven hundred tickets were sold for the Pontotoc excursion of July 4.

69. The change is reflected in new timetables; see *Pontotoc (MS) Democrat*, April 18, 1889, 2; and *Pontotoc (MS) Sentinel*, July 5, 1894, 3.

70. Sanborn-Perris Map Company, Pontotoc map.

71. "The new turntable, a few steps south of the Depot, has been finished and it is a daisy. We cannot see how the Railroad Company managed to do without it so long. The Y, just outside of the northern limits of the corporation, will now be dispensed with and the iron will be taken up and used for extending the road as far as it will go." *Ripley (MS) Advertiser*, May 1, 1886. Also see *Southern Sentinel* (Ripley, MS), May 13, 1897: "The G&CRR Co. have built a new turning table at this place [Ripley]"; and *Southern Sentinel*, August 26, 1897: "The G&C RR Co is having built a commodious roundhouse on its yard here."

72. "Towards the Gulf: Progress of the Ship Island Railroad," *Clarion* (Jackson, MS), January 5, 1887, 2, reprinted from the *Times-Picayune* (New Orleans), December 29, 1886.

73. *Clarion* (Jackson, MS), January 19, 1887, 2. Alternatively, the *Railroad Gazette* (New York), January 21, 1887, places the beginning of construction on January 12 rather than January 11.

74. Ripley Railroad Company journal, January 15, 1887, 51; and Tippah County Deed Book 9, 443–44.

75. "The Ship Island Railway: Rapid Progress Being Made in Its Construction," *Memphis Appeal*, February 9, 1887, 5.

76. "Safe at Nashville" and "The Mexican Veterans," *Memphis Appeal*, October 16, 1887, 4.

77. *Clarion* (Jackson, MS), June 1, 1887, 2; and "Gulf and Ship Island Railroad," *Pascagoula (MS) Democrat-Star*, June 3, 1887, 2.

78. *Southern Herald* (Liberty, MS), September 18, 1896, 2.

79. "Fatal Affray in Jackson: Murderous Work in the Moon Light," *Southern Herald* (Liberty, MS), May 14, 1887, 2.

80. *Pascagoula (MS) Democrat-Star*, June 3, 1887, 2.

81. "A Southern Tragedy," *Iron County Register* (Ironton, MO), May 10, 1888, 2.

82. Lemly, *The Gulf, Mobile and Ohio*, 288.

83. "The Card," *Clarion* (Jackson, MS), November 10, 1886, 3, reprinted from the *Pontotoc (MS) Observer*.

84. Report of David Johnson, Superintendent Mississippi Penitentiary, to the Board of Control, Mississippi State Penitentiary, July 15, 1887, *Clarion* (Jackson, MS), July 20, 1887, 2.

85. W. L. Doss, "Report of Superintendent, Superintendent's Office, Mississippi State Penitentiary, Dec. 4, 1889," *Biennial Report of the Board of Control, Superintendent, General Manager and Other Officers of the Mississippi State Penitentiary for the Years 1888 and 1889* (Jackson, MS: R. H. Henry, 1889), 15.

86. "Convict Leasing," *Memphis Appeal*, December 5, 1888, 4; "Convict Labor Lease Canceled," *St. Paul Daily Globe* (Saint Paul, MN), December 5, 1888, 8; and "The Mississippi Prison," *Memphis Appeal*, December 8, 1888, 4, reprinted from the *Clarion-Ledger* (Jackson, MS).

87. *Pascagoula (MS) Democrat-Star*, May 3, 1889, 2.

88. "Opened to Jackson," *Sea Coast Echo* (Bay St. Louis, MS), August 11, 1900, 1.

89. "Gulf & Ship Island: Col. Jones S. Hamilton Makes a Fruitless Visit to This City," *Memphis Appeal*, July 12, 1888, 5.

90. "Col. W. C. Falkner left yesterday [July 11] for Baily Springs [sic] to take a short rest from his duties. We wish him a pleasant time. His arduous labors connected with the extension of the G&SIRR to Pontotoc during the past two years certainly entitles him to a summer's recreation since he has accomplished the task." *Southern Sentinel* (Ripley, MS), July 12, 1888. "Col. Wm C. Falkner, who has been at Bailey Springs, Ala., for the past few weeks, returned home yesterday evening on a special train." *Southern Sentinel*, August 9, 1888.

91. "The narrow guage [sic] railroad from Ripley, Miss., to Middleton, Tenn., including all the property of every description connected with it, is advertised to be sold in Ripley on the 13th of August next, under the foreclosure of a mortgage made to secure $250,000 of bonds." *Pascagoula (MS) Democrat-Star*, July 27, 1888, 2.

92. "Falkner, Harris & Co. Purchase the R.S.I.& Ky. Railroad," *Southern Sentinel* (Ripley, MS), August 16, 1888.

93. "Col. W. C. Falkner left on Monday last for New York city to be absent some time," *Southern Sentinel* (Ripley, MS), September 13, 1888; and "Col. W. C. Falkner who has been in New York for several weeks on business, returned home today," *Southern Sentinel*, October 11, 1888.

94. "Col. W. C. Falkner left on Sunday's cars for New York City, on a business trip and will return in about ten days," *Southern Sentinel* (Ripley, MS), February 14, 1889; and "Col. W. C. Falkner returned Sunday from a business trip to New York in splendid health," *Southern Sentinel*, March 14, 1889.

95. *Southern Sentinel* (Ripley, MS), February 14, 1889; and "Col. W. C. Faulkner will be a candidate for the Legislature from Tippah Co.," *Pascagoula (MS) Democrat-Star*, March 1, 1889, 4.

96. *Southern Sentinel* (Ripley, MS), April 4, 1889.

97. Letter, W. C. Falkner to R. I. Hill, April 20, 1889, *Southern Sentinel* (Ripley, MS), May 2, 1889, 2.

98. Information on Campbell's employment comes from *Dow's City Directory of Memphis for 1889* (Memphis: Harland Dow Publisher, 1889).

99. *Southern Sentinel* (Ripley, MS), November 22 and 29, 1888.

100. "Miss Bama Falkner, who is attending the Chickasaw Female College at Pontotoc, came up Saturday to visit her parents and other relatives, returning to Pontotoc Monday," *Southern Sentinel* (Ripley, MS), October 4, 1888; and "Miss Bama Falkner, the beautiful daughter of Col. and Mrs. W. C. Falkner, who is attending the Chickasaw Female College, Pontotoc, came up Saturday and returned Sunday," *Southern Sentinel*, January 31, 1889.

101. "Mr. Ed. Campbell of Memphis, and one of the stock holders and directors of the G&C has been appointed General freight Agent of the road, with headquarters at New Albany." *Southern Sentinel* (Ripley, MS), January 12, 1893.

102. Untitled article, *Memphis Avalanche*, reprinted in the *Southern Sentinel* (Ripley MS), May 2, 1889. Regarding the time of this event, see "Col. W. C. Falkner is in Memphis this week on business," *Southern Sentinel*, April 25, 1889.

103. "Col. W. C. Falkner left last week for Memphis and other points on business." *Southern Sentinel* (Ripley MS), May 23, 1889.

104. Duclos, *Son of Sorrow*, 236–37.

105. Letter, W. C. Falkner to C. C Baldwin, June 5, 1889, in Duclos, *Son of Sorrow*, 238–39.

106. "New Telephone Line," *Southern Sentinel* (Ripley, MS), September 19, 1889; *Southern Sentinel*, October 3, 1889; "Work has commenced on the Telephone line. The holes are being dug, the wire has already arrived and the cedar poles will be here in a few days," *Southern Sentinel*, October 10, 1889; and "The telephone was completed to this point last Saturday and is now in operation," *Pontotoc (MS) Democrat*, December 5, 1889, 3. A newspaper item noted that the telephone line followed "along the line of the G. & S.I. Railroad." *Pontotoc (MS) Democrat*, November 14, 1889, 3.

107. Tippah County Land Trust Book 5, 387–89. The sale of the railroad was ratified a few months later. In Hardeman County, Tennessee, the ratification was in September 1889. "Hon. J. T. W. [sic] Falkner, of Oxford, Miss., was in attendance Tuesday upon the Chancery court for the purpose of having confirmed the sale of the Ripley and Ship Island Railroad." *Bolivar (TN) Bulletin*, September 20, 1889, 3. The Tippah County Chancery Court ratified the sale on October 25, 1889. Tippah County Chancery Court Minute Book 3, 324–25.

108. The two deeds involved were recorded in three courthouses for the three counties in which this part of the G&SI lay: Pontotoc County Deed Book 57, 70–73; Tippah County Land Trust Book 5, 389–94; and Union County Deed Book, 402–6.

109. The same deed appears in the records in three counties: Pontotoc County Deed Book 57, 74–75; Tippah Count Land Trust Deed Book 5, 395–96; and Union County Deed Book 6, 406–8.

110. "Official Returns of Primary Election," *Southern Sentinel* (Ripley, MS), August 22, 1889; and untitled article from the *Memphis Avalanche*, reprinted in the *Southern Sentinel*, August 22, 1889.

111. Reprinted in the *Southern Sentinel* (Ripley, MS), August 22, 1889.

112. Reprinted in the *Southern Sentinel* (Ripley, MS), August 29, 1889.

113. *Public Ledger* (Memphis), August 20, 1889, reprinted in *Grenada (MS) Sentinel*, August 24, 1889, 4.

114. *Pontotoc (MS) Democrat*, October 24, 1889, 3.

115. *Southern Sentinel* (Ripley, MS), October 31, 1889. Wintering in Memphis had become a common practice for Mrs. Falkner. Cf. "Col. W. C. Falkner is in the city and stopping at the Peabody. His wife and two beautiful daughters, Misses Effie and Bama, will spend the winter in the city and be a valuable accession to the social society of Memphis," *Memphis*

Appeal, October 19, 1886, 8; "Mrs. Col. W. C. Falkner and daughters, Misses Effie and Bama, left for Memphis, Wednesday, where they go to stay during the coming winter," *Ripley (MS) Advertiser*, November 13, 1886; and "Mrs. W. C. Falkner and daughter Miss Effie left yesterday for Memphis, where they will spend the winter," *Ripley (MS) Advertiser*, November 5, 1887. The *Ripley Advertiser* stated that Mrs. Falkner had gone to Memphis to "reside permanently," leading Donald Duclos to infer that she had left the Colonel while noting that "there are stories told that the Colonel and his wife had not been getting along well for some time and that he had moved into his office to live" (*Son of Sorrow*, 249). Joel Williamson seems to follow this inference (*William Faulkner and Southern History*, 56). While recognizing the possibility of a separation, I would not read too much into the *Advertiser*'s phrasing.

116. A writer for the Memphis *Public Ledger* noted: "The people of Memphis have flattered themselves into the belief that this gentleman was to become a citizen of the city." However, that was changed with Falkner's nomination to the legislature. "Col. W. C. Falkner," *Public Ledger* (Memphis), August 20, 1889, 4. Three months later, the *Avalanche* noted that Falkner "had been making preparations to remove to this city and take up his abode in his new residence that is in course of erection on Peabody avenue." "The Wound Proved Fatal," *Memphis Avalanche*, November 8, 1889, 1. However, I have not been able to find deed evidence for Falkner's owning land in Memphis at the time.

117. "'Rah for the Boys: Two Democratic Clubs Formed," *Memphis Avalanche*, November 3, 1889, 2.

Chapter 14: The Shooting

1. A. Brown, *History of Tippah County*, 283–84.

2. A. Brown, *History of Tippah County*, 284.

3. Duclos, *Son of Sorrow*, 246.

4. "Mr. R. J. Thurmond has opened an office in the old post office. He has a neat, cozy, little office. There is some talk of Mr. Thurmond opening a bank here. We hope he will, as Ripley needs a bank badly." *Southern Sentinel* (Ripley, MS), October 10, 1889. The office building was located in the center of Lot 5, Block 17 of the plat of Ripley. For an examination of the location of this building, see Elliott, "Where Was Colonel Falkner Shot?"

5. This information along with much that is known about this affair comes from the most thorough account, "Col. W. C. Falkner: The Complete Details of His Death," *Memphis Appeal*, November 8, 1889, 1.

6. "The Wound Proved Fatal," *Memphis Avalanche*, November 8, 1889, 1.

7. A. Brown, *History of Tippah County*, 284.

8. "Col. W. C. Falkner: The Complete Details of His Death," *Memphis Appeal*, November 8, 1889, 1.

9. *Ripley (MS) Advertiser*, November 6, 1889, quoted in Duclos, *Son of Sorrow*, 247.

10. "Col. Falkner Shot," *Memphis Avalanche*, November 6, 1889, 4.

11. "Col. W.C. Falkner: The Complete Details of His Death," *Memphis Appeal*, November 8, 1889, 1.

12. Elliott, "Where Was Colonel Falkner Shot?"

13. Elliott, "Where Was Colonel Falkner Shot?"

14. "Colonel W. C. Falkner," *Memphis Appeal*, November 8, 1889, 1.

15. Andrew Brown, quoted in Hickerson, *The Falkner Feuds*, 3–4.

16. As previously noted, the Carter home was on the north side of Cooper Street on the southwest quadrant of Block 4. It faced southward toward the Falkner home just across the street.

17. According to Mrs. Mattie McKinney McDowell, Falkner died in what was the library in 1889. It was "the room on your right as you face the house [i.e., the east room on the first floor]. . . . I understand it was the Carters' library." Letter, Mattie McKinney McDowell to Lourie Allen, Sumrall, MS, January 2, 1970, in Lourie Strickland Allen, "Colonel William C. Falkner: Writer of Romance and Realism" (PhD diss., University of Alabama, 1972), 205. McDowell's grandparents, William Hines and his wife, owned and occupied the Carter house after the Carters left Ripley in 1901. Mrs. McDowell's mother, Virginia Hines McKinney, noted that Falkner had died in the library. Interview with Mrs. Virginia Hines McKinney, Amory, MS, Summer 1969, in L. S. Allen, "Colonel William C. Falkner: Writer of Romance and Realism," 201.

18. Sam Edgerton, a Black who operated a barbershop on the square, was married to Hellen Falkner, the daughter of Emeline Falkner.

19. Ripley would not have a telegraph until 1895, when R. J. Shannon's Southwestern Telegraph Company constructed a line from Middleton to Pontotoc.

20. These messages were printed in the *New Albany (MS) Gazette*, November 5, 1964. The originals are now at the University of Mississippi Library, Special Collections, Oxford, Mississippi, Falkner Family Collection.

21. *Tupelo (MS) Journal*, November 15, 1889.

22. At a preliminary trial on November 14, it was determined that Thurmond would remain in jail until the February term of circuit court. *Pascagoula (MS) Democrat-Star*, November 29, 1889, 2. "The preliminary trial of R. J. Thurmond, for the killing of Col. W. C. Falkner, is set for to-day at Ripley." *Pontotoc (MS) Democrat*, November 14, 1889, 3.

23. The quoted passage is from Duclos, *Son of Sorrow*, 249, based on an interview with Bama Falkner McLean.

24. The following passage was reconstructed from a frayed newspaper page: "Mrs. Col. W. C. [Falkner and her] daughter, Mrs. C[ampbell arrived] from Memphis on [_____] 2 a.m. yesterday to [_____] of Col. Falkner. Mr. [E. F. Camp]bell and Miss Bama arri[ved on a] special train yesterday even[ing.] Dr. W. B. Rogers, of Memphis came out with Mrs. Falkner and remained with Col. Falkner for several hours leaving on the 9:30 cars yesterday for Memphis." *Southern Sentinel* (Ripley, MS), November 7, 1889.

25. Report from the *Memphis Avalanche*, quoted in Duclos, *Son of Sorrow*, 250.

26. "Dr. W. B. Rogers, of Memphis came out with Mrs. Falkner and remained with Col. Falkner for several hours leaving on the 9:30 cars yesterday for Memphis." *Southern Sentinel* (Ripley, MS), November 7, 1889. It is not clear whether he departed at 9:30 a.m. or p.m. However, the assertion that he stayed in Ripley "for several hours" is suggestive of a morning departure.

27. According to the *Southern Sentinel*, November 7, 1889, they arrived at "about 10 o'clock." However, according to a telegram that J. W. T. Falkner sent, they arrived two hours before his father's death, at about 8:40.

28. Duclos, *Son of Sorrow*, 250.

29. Telegraph, E. F. Campbell to Mrs. M. L. Campbell, November 6, 1889, *New Albany (MS) Gazette*, November 5, 1964. The most accurate time of death is probably 10:40 p.m., which was variously reported in the press as 10:00 p.m. (*Memphis Avalanche*) and 11:00 p.m. (*Memphis Appeal*).

30. Telegram, Jno. W. T. Falkner to M. C. Gallaway, November 6, 1889, *New Albany (MS) Gazette*, November 5, 1964. The length is presumably an exterior dimension.

31. *Southern Sentinel* (Ripley, MS), November 7, 1889.

32. The Presbyterian Church at that time was on the west side of North Union Street on Block 60. Tippah County Deed Book J, 95; and A. Brown, *History of Tippah County*, 56–57.

33. From a photostatic copy of an unidentified newspaper clipping in the Ripley Public Library.

34. From a photostatic copy of an unidentified newspaper clipping in the Ripley Public Library.

35. *New Mississippian* (Jackson, MS), November 20, 1889.

36. A. W. Whitten, "On the Death of Col. W. C. Falkner," from an unidentified newspaper clipping in the Ripley Public Library.

37. C. Kendrick, "Falkner," from an unidentified newspaper clipping in the Ripley Public Library. The poem includes the date December 1, 1889, evidently the date of composition, not of publication. The third poem was B. Holcombe, "Dedicated to the Memory of Col. W. C. Falkner," also from an unidentified newspaper clipping in the Ripley Public Library.

38. Faulkner, *The Unvanquished*, 255–56, 268.

39. Despite some claims that Falkner himself had commissioned the monument, there is no evidence to support this contention.

40. "We learn that a life-sized statue of the late Col. W. C. Falkner is now being executed in Italy that is to cost $5,000. It will represent him as engaged in conversation with one hand extended in the manner that every one who knew him will recognize," *Southern Sentinel* (Ripley, MS), July 10, 1890; and "Art in Marble," *Memphis Daily Commercial*, August 24, 1890, 6. This contradicts the claim that Falkner had conceived the monument years earlier while traveling in Europe.

41. "The Falkner monument for Ripley, Miss., which will sustain upon its topmost cap the statue of Col. Falkner in heroic size, he [C. J. Rogers] will erect during this summer. This monument is made of Scotch granite, and is now being cut in Aberdeen, Scotland. The statue is being executed in Carrara, Italy. This monument constitutes a 40,000 pound car load." *Bolivar (TN) Bulletin*, June 26, 1891, 2. The statue is actually only a few inches taller than Falkner himself, who was about five feet, six inches tall. The total height of the statue is about six feet, five inches tall, including a five-inch-thick base, making the sculpture of Falkner six feet tall, only seven inches taller than he was in life.

The Italian sculptor's name comes from a letter: Renato Campi, the Italian Marble Company, Carrara, Italy, to Mrs. R. E. Price, Corinth, MS, January 9, 1969, Joseph Blotner Papers. The process by which the sculpture was created was described by Beulah M. (Mrs. R. E.) Price, who researched it at the Grand Junction office of Rogers and Sons. Letter, Beulah May Price, Corinth, MS, to Donald Duclos, November 20, 1959, Falkner/Faulkner Family Collection, 1770s–1980s, Donald Duclos Papers, William Paterson University, Archives and Special Collections, Cheng Library, Wayne, New Jersey. This process is more credible than Duclos's description, in which a full-scale prototype was formed in wax or plaster and shipped to Italy to be duplicated (*Son of Sorrow*, 257–58). Although Duclos seems to attribute this information to Mrs. Price, I have found nothing in her writing that supports this scenario.

42. The dimensions of the monument were taken and other physical observations made by Tommy Covington and myself on May 8 and 25, 2018. On June 4, 2018, we traveled to Grand Junction to locate and examine the former site of the Rogers and Sons Monument Company, which closed circa 2010.

43. As noted, the June 26, 1891, issue of the *Bolivar (TN) Bulletin* predicted that the monument would be erected that summer. However, this estimate was apparently too hasty. I find no evidence of its erection over the next few months. In early 1892, an article implies that it had been erected the previous year, although this is not certain. "Building Fame and Fortune," *Memphis Appeal-Avalanche*, January 15, 1892, 2. Further imprecise evidence comes from an invoice from C. J. Rogers to the Falkner estate for $2,022 dated February 18, 1892, which implies that the statue had been erected. Duclos, *Son of Sorrow*, 353, cf. 258. This is probably the final payment for the monument, not the total payment. A monument of this size, cost, and time for production would have certainly required a substantial down payment. This is indicated by the *Southern Sentinel*, July 10, 1890, which stated that the monument would cost about $5,000 with the implication that there was an approximately $3,000 down payment. The invoice

suggests that the monument was erected not long before the invoice date. One would expect that, because of its size and the fame of Falkner, the monument's erection would have been mentioned by the two Ripley newspapers. However, after having perused every issue for this period, I have found nothing. There is a problem in that both papers have no issues extant for January 1892, suggesting that any mention of the erection could have been in the missing issues.

44. *Chickasaw Messenger* (Okolona, MS), November 28, 1889, 1; and *Brookhaven (MS) Leader*, December 5, 1889, 2, and December 19, 1889, 2.

45. *Daily Clarion-Ledger* (Jackson, MS), January 12, 1890, 1.

46. Letter, Thomas Spight, Pontotoc, to "my dear little wife," Mary Virginia Spight, January 10, 1890, University of Mississippi Library, Special Collections, Oxford, Mississippi, Thomas Spight Collection.

47. "[Mr.] C. J. Frederick, for sev[eral yea]rs a leading member of [the Rip]ley bar, now a prominent [resident] of Ft. Smith, Ark., is here [attendin]g court. This is the [first time] back to his old home [that he] left about four years [ago]," *Southern Sentinel* (Ripley, MS), February 6, 1890; and "Congressman John M. Allen of Tupelo, was here this week at court. He was employed by the prosecution in the Thurmond-Falkner case," *Southern Sentinel*, February 13, 1890.

48. Hickerson, *The Falkner Feuds*, 19, citing City of Ripley, Record Book, Case no. 350, February 4, 1890.

49. "The grand jury returned a bill of indictment against Mr. R. J. Thurmond for manslaughter. Mr. Thurmond has been released on $10,000 bond." *Southern Sentinel* (Ripley, MS), February 13, 1890.

50. "May Be Acquitted," *Memphis Avalanche*, February 9, 1890, 12.

51. "May Be Acquitted," *Memphis Avalanche*, February 9, 1890, 12; and "State vs. Thurmond," *Memphis Avalanche*, February 12, 1890, 8.

52. "Strife in a Store," *Memphis Avalanche*, July 2, 1890, 1.

53. "The Case of Capt. R. J. Thurmond," *Clarion-Ledger* (Jackson, MS), August 21, 1890, 2.

54. "Circuit Court," *Southern Sentinel* (Ripley, MS), February 26, 1891.

55. "Thurmond Not Guilty," *Memphis Appeal-Avalanche*, February 22, 1891, 1.

56. "End of a Noted Case," *Memphis Daily Commercial*, February 22, 1891, 1.

57. "Circuit Court," *Southern Sentinel* (Ripley, MS), February 26, 1891; and "Thurman [*sic*] Not Guilty," *Bolivar (TN) Bulletin*, February 27, 1891, 2, reprinted from the *Memphis Appeal-Avalanche*.

58. "Circuit Court," *Southern Sentinel* (Ripley, MS), February 26, 1891.

59. "End of a Noted Case," *Memphis Daily Commercial*, February 22, 1891, 1.

60. "Justice Asleep while Cold Blooded Murder Stalks in Triumph through the Land," *Grenada (MS) Sentinel*, March 21, 1891, 4.

61. A. Brown, *History of Tippah County*, 292.

62. Andrew Brown, quoted in Hickerson, *The Falkner Feuds*, 3.

63. A. Brown, *History of Tippah County*, 285.

64. Colonel Falkner Thurmond (1892–1942) was buried in Pine Hill Primitive Baptist Cemetery, Tippah County, Mississippi. He was listed residing with his parents in Ripley in the 1900 and 1910 censuses.

65. A. Brown, *History of Tippah County*, 292.

66. A. Brown, *History of Tippah County*, 293.

67. Quoted in Cantwell, "The Faulkners: Recollections of a Gifted Family," 35.

68. Duclos, *Son of Sorrow*, 256; cf. John Faulkner, *My Brother Bill: An Affectionate Reminiscence* (New York: Trident Press, 1963), 12; and Blotner, *Faulkner: A Biography*, 31.

69. "MARRIED—On the evening of the 18th inst., in Ripley, at the residence of the bride's parents, Miss Mattie Thurmond . . . was united in marriage with Mr. H. G. Chatham, a . . .

young business man of Elkin, NC. . . . The happy couple left next morning for their future home at Elkin, N.C., where the groom has extensive manufacturing interests." *Southern Sentinel* (Ripley, MS), April 26, 1894.

70. E.g., "Mr. and Mrs. R. J. Thurmond and Misses DeWitt and Margaret are summering at Elkin in the mountains of North Carolina," *Southern Sentinel* (Ripley, MS), July 18, 1895; "Mr. and Mrs. R. J. Thurmond and Mrs. John Y. Murry, Jr. and children arrived home from Elkin, N.C. where they had been summering," *Southern Sentinel*, October 7, 1897; "Mr. R. J. Thurmond returned from Elkin, NC where he spent the summer, Friday," *Southern Sentinel*, September 22, 1898; and "Mr. and Mrs. R. J. Thurmond left for Elkin, NC where they will spend the summer, Tuesday morning," *Southern Sentinel*, June 21, 1900.

71. "Ripley, Miss., Special, 7th, to Memphis Commercial-Appeal. At high noon today, in the parlor of the bride's home, Miss DeWitt Clinton Thurmond, daughter of Mr. and Mrs. R. J. Thurmond, was married to Paul Chatham of Elkin, N.C." *Charlotte Observer*, January 12, 1897.

72. "Mrs. Margaret Miller Thurmond Dead," *Southern Sentinel* (Ripley, MS), September 13, 1900, reprinted from the *Elkin (NC) Times*.

73. "Mrs. Jno. Y. Murry, Jr. and the children and Miss Myrtle Hunt, accompanied Mr. R. J. Thurmond in his return trip to Elkin NC Tuesday and will likely remain all summer," *Southern Sentinel* (Ripley, MS), June 13, 1901; "Mr. R. J. Thurmond left Wednesday for North Carolina where he expects to spend several months," *Southern Sentinel*, April 21, 1904; "Mr. R. J. Thurmond returned Monday from North Carolina where he spent the summer. He will spend the fall and winter in Ripley," *Southern Sentinel*, October 5, 1905; and "Mr. R. J. Thurmond, after spending the summer in North Carolina, returned last week to his native heath and will remain here through the fall and winter," *Southern Sentinel*, October 11, 1906.

74. In January, Thurmond published a notice in the *Southern Sentinel* notifying the public that he had turned his accounts over to family members, and if anyone wanted to borrow money they could do so by writing him at *his home* in North Carolina. This suggests that he was reducing his business interests and that he considered Elkin to be his home. *Southern Sentinel* (Ripley, MS), January 3, 1907.

75. "Death of Mr. Thurmond," *Montgomery (AL) Advertiser*, November 22, 1907, 8; and "Capt. Thurmond's Funeral," *Winston-Salem (NC) Journal*, November 22, 1907, 5.

Chapter 15: Aftermath

1. Tippah County Will Book 1, 155–59.

2. *Laws of the State of Mississippi* (Jackson: R. H. Henry, 1890), 680–81.

3. "Mrs. Falkner this week advertises her handsome residence in Ripley for sale at $1,500. To a person who wishes to purchase this is a great bargain. The house is nearly new and cost perhaps $5,000." *Southern Sentinel* (Ripley, MS), April 23, 1891. The advertisement began appearing in the *Southern Sentinel* on May 7, 1891.

4. Deed, Mrs. L. H. Falkner to Mrs. Effie D. Campbell and Bama L. Falkner, March 30, 1893, Tippah County Deed Book 12, 445.

5. "The Falkner residence, which has been vacant for about three years, is undergoing some changes and inside repairs, and will soon be again occupied by Mrs. Falkner," *Southern Sentinel* (Ripley, MS), March 2, 1893; "Mrs. Falkner is having her house repaired and will soon move back to Ripley," Sue D. Keenin, letter to "Sister," Ripley, MS, March 12, 1893, typescript, Ripley Public Library, Ripley, Mississippi, 1893; and "The Falkner residence is being painted a dark green which considerably changes, if not improves, its appearance," *Southern Sentinel*, April 27, 1893.

6. "The Social Realm," *Memphis Commercial*, September 15, 1893, 5.

7. Campbell died at 371 Vance Street, Memphis, on April 12, 1899, at the age of thirty-eight of phthisis pulmonalis (consumption or tuberculosis) and was buried in Elmwood Cemetery. He was listed as single, having been divorced from Effie for several years. It was noted that he had lived in Memphis for five years, suggesting that he had returned from New Albany following his divorce in 1894. Register of Deaths in the City of Memphis, https://register.shelby.tn.us /index.php. The Elmwood Cemetery Daily Burial Record 1853–1919, https://register.shelby.tn.us /elmwood.php, indicates that his full name was Edwin Fontaine Campbell and that he was buried on April 13, 1899, the day after his death in Section LC, Lot 34, Grave 4.

8. *Memphis Directory* (Memphis: Degaris Publishing Company, 1897).

9. Thomas J. Nelson (1852–1921) married Pattie Ellis, daughter of Dr. Arthur I. Ellis of Panola County and sister of Victoria Ellis, who was married to Murry Falkner's uncle, Dr. W. M. Murry. Nelson and Murry were partners in a mercantile business in Dumas, Tippah County, Mississippi. After the store burned in September 1889, Nelson went into the employ of the Ripley Railroad as depot agent at Pontotoc. The Nelson home was at the southeast corner of Main and Margin Streets in Pontotoc at the site of what is now the Baldwin Memorial Funeral Home. The original two-story home was incorporated into the funeral home but was demolished in late 2017. C. Young, *From These Hills*, 205–6.

10. Keenin, letter to "Sister."

11. Keenin, letter to "Sister."

12. "Murry Falkner Shot," *Southern Sentinel* (Ripley, MS), October 20, 1892, 3; "Fatally Shot," *Clarion* (Jackson, MS), October 20, 1892, 2; C. Young, *From These Hills*, 205–6, material based on an interview with John Henry Anderson (1883–1981), a witness to the event; notes on an interview with John Henry Anderson by Joseph Blotner, November 19, 1966, Joseph Blotner Papers; and "Faulkner Fell Here," photograph with Mr. Anderson pointing to the spot where Murry Falkner fell after being shot, *New Albany (MS) Gazette*, May 25, 1978, sec. F, 1. Mitchell and Barringer's Drug Store was on the northeast corner of Main and Marion Streets.

13. "Murry Falkner Shot," *Southern Sentinel* (Ripley, MS), October 20, 1892, 3; "Fatally Shot," *Clarion* (Jackson, MS), October 20, 1892, 2; and *Southern Sentinel*, October 20, 1892, 3.

14. *Southern Sentinel* (Ripley, MS), November 10, 1892, 3.

15. *Oxford (MS) Eagle*, November 17, 1892.

16. "Shot in the Hand: Another Chapter in the Falkner-Walker Affair," *Memphis Commercial*, November 19, 1892, 4.

17. "Murry Falkner was carried through Saturday [November 19] on the way to his father's home in Oxford. —New Albany Gazette." *Ripley (MS) Advertiser*, November 22, 1892.

18. "The Falkner-Walker Cases at Pontotoc," *Southern Sentinel* (Ripley, MS), January 12, 1893, 1; and John Henry Anderson, interviewed by Joseph Blotner, Joseph Blotner Papers.

19. *Oxford (MS) Eagle*, July 6, 1893.

20. The sentences were handed down on July 5, 1893. Pontotoc County Minute Book, Circuit Court, 1890–1898, Pontotoc County Circuit Clerk's Office, 215–16.

21. *Oxford (MS) Eagle*, October 1, 1896, 3.

22. *Oxford (MS) Eagle*, November 12, 1896, 3.

23. According to Robert Coughlan, when the Falkners were living in New Albany, "a druggist named Walker made a slurring remark" against Murry's sister Holland (who never actually lived in New Albany). This offense led to an altercation in a drugstore (as it had in Pontotoc), with Walker shooting and almost killing Murry in a manner identical to the Pontotoc shooting. Soon after, Murry's father arrived in New Albany to seek vengeance and was wounded in a shootout with Walker. To avoid further bloodshed, the Falkners left New Albany and moved to Oxford, completely skipping their 1899–1902 sojourn in Ripley. Coughlan, *The Private World of William Faulkner*, 40–41.

24. "Shall we have a telegraph line?" *Southern Sentinel* (Ripley, MS), January 3, 1895.

25. *Southern Sentinel* (Ripley, MS), March 14, 1895.

26. *Southern Sentinel* (Ripley, MS), May 9, 1895.

27. "First Message," *Southern Sentinel* (Ripley, MS), May 23, 1895.

28. *Southern Sentinel* (Ripley, MS), July 11, August 22, and September 5, 1895.

29. I have never found a record of the Davises' marriage. However, the 1900 census indicates that they had been married for three years, suggesting about 1897 as their year of marriage.

30. "Mr. Davis, the auditor and general manager of the G&CRR has his office connected with the depot by telegraph." *Southern Sentinel* (Ripley, MS), May 19, 1898.

31. "General Manager Davis of the G&C was in town the first of the week with the new pile driver and started to driving the Tallahatchie bridge which will be made entirely new. —New Albany Gazette." *Southern Sentinel* (Ripley, MS), January 28, 1901.

32. "Mgr. A. E. Davis will further equip his line, and G&CRR by adding a thirty ton passenger locomotive in a few days. She will be No. 10." *Southern Sentinel* (Ripley, MS), February 20, 1902.

33. "General Manager Davis, of the G&CRR made a business trip to Chicago last week," *Southern Sentinel*, August 4, 1898; "Manager A. E. Davis is in Chicago looking after railroad business," *Southern Sentinel*, February 28, 1901; and "Mgr. A. E. Davis is in Washington this week looking after railroad business," *Southern Sentinel*, April 11, 1901.

34. A. Brown, *History of Tippah County*, 274.

35. "Miss Effie Davis is having quite a lot of work done on the Falkner place, preparatory to occupying the same," *Ripley (MS) Standard*, April 22, 1898; and "The Falkner home is receiving a fresh coat of paint. Handsome Will Shepherd is the artist, manipulating the brush. Mr. and Mrs. Davis have put many beatifying touches to the place since their occupancy," *Ripley (MS) Standard*, May 20, 1898.

36. "Mrs. Bama McLean, of Memphis, but who, with her husband, Walter B., summered in Colorado, arrived here Wednesday afternoon of last week, and is with her sister, Mrs. Davis, and mother, Mrs. Falkner, at the old home." *Southern Sentinel* (Ripley, MS), October 20, 1898.

37. For example, "Mrs. W. C. Falkner of Memphis is visiting her daughter, Mrs. Effie Davis," *Ripley (MS) Standard*, July 28, 1899; and "Mrs. Bama McLean, of Memphis, after having spent several days with her sister Mrs. A. E. Davis returned Friday," *Southern Sentinel* (Ripley, MS), March 1, 1900.

38. "A Re-organization," *Southern Sentinel* (Ripley, MS), November 10, 1898.

39. Andrew Brown referred to the room as the "sitting room," writing that the window was installed in the "back wall" of the room, that is the north wall (*History of Tippah County*, 292). Virginia McKinney, the daughter of William and Mattie Spight Hines, who grew up in the Carter house, recalled: "[Willie Carter] had the window removed from the church and placed in her library, the room where her father had died. When we lived in the house, the window was in what we called my mother's sitting room." Interview with Mrs. Virginia Hines McKinney, Armory, MS, Summer 1969, in L. S. Allen, "Colonel William C. Falkner: Writer of Romance and Realism," 201. Mattie McDowell (the daughter of Virginia McKinney) noted: "A window at the back of this room was where they put the stained glass window that had been in the church." Letter, Mattie McKinney McDowell to Lourie Allen, Sumrall, MS, January 2, 1970, in L. S. Allen, "Colonel William C. Falkner: Writer of Romance and Realism," 205.

40. John Faulkner recalled that "Aunt Willie was especially fond of Bill. She would have him visit her." J. Faulkner, *My Brother Bill*, 24. In a 1925 letter to his great-aunt Bama Falkner McLean, William Faulkner recalled that as a child in Ripley he went to Willie's home to spend the night and after suffering a bout of homesickness was carried home by Willie's two daughters. Joseph Blotner, ed., *Selected Letters of William Faulkner* (New York: Random House, 1977), 20.

41. Murry C. Falkner, *The Falkners of Mississippi: A Memoir* (Baton Rouge: Louisiana State University Press, 1967), 6.

42. Hamblin, "The Old Colonel," 14–15.

43. Hamblin, "The Old Colonel," 15, with quotation from *Absalom, Absalom!*

44. Hamblin, "The Old Colonel," 16. Hamblin cites pages numbers from *Absalom, Absalom!* (New York: Random House, 1936).

45. A. Brown, *History of Tippah County*, 272–73.

46. *Southern Sentinel* (Ripley, MS), May 20 and June 10, 1897. No information was provided about the new locomotive.

47. *Southern Sentinel* (Ripley, MS), August 26, 1897.

48. A. Brown, *History of Tippah County*, 275.

49. Brown claimed that "C. L. Harris . . . in 1901 sold his interest to the Falkners" and cited the *Southern Sentinel* (Ripley, MS), October 21, 1901 (*History of Tippah County*, 274). However, he was apparently confused. No issue of the *Sentinel* was published on that day, but one was published on October 24. This issue has nothing about C. L. Harris, who by that time was residing in Memphis, but notes instead that "Mr. Lee Hines [a nephew of C. L. Harris] . . . has sold his interest in the G&C to the Falkners." This is probably what Brown based his statement on. Regardless, about this time the last of the Harris/Hines one-third interest in the railroad was sold to the Falkner family.

50. Lemly, *The Gulf, Mobile and Ohio*, 290–91; and "Railroad Hands Wanted," *Macon (MS) Beacon*, December 12, 1896, 1.

51. Reference to "Merrill, the present northern terminus of the road" in "An Energetic Girl," *Pascagoula (MS) Democrat-Star*, November 1, 1901, 4.

52. "Makes Connection," *Hattiesburg (MS) Daily Progress*, November 11, 1902, 4.

53. *True Democrat* (Bayou Sara, LA), November 2, 1901, 1.

54. "Rumored Railroad Sale," *Weekly Corinthian* (Corinth, MS), May 6, 1902, 1; and "New Line for the South: M., J. & K.C. May Build Direct Line from Mobile to Memphis," *St. Louis Republic*, May 8, 1902, 2.

55. "Sale of Gulf & Chicago Railroad Verified by Manager A. E. Davis," *Southern Sentinel* (Ripley, MS), June 26, 1902.

56. "A New Railroad," *Oxford (MS) Eagle*, April 23, 1903.

57. "Gulf & Chicago Organized," *Macon (MS) Beacon*, May 2, 1903, 1.

58. *Southern Sentinel* (Ripley, MS), August 20, 1903.

59. "Dr. N. G. Carter and family left for their new home Meridian Sunday afternoon. . . . Dr. Carter will return in a few days and finish closing out his stock of drugs." *Southern Sentinel* (Ripley, MS), August 8, 1901. Dr. Carter died at his Meridian home in 1908. Willie continued to live there but died in 1916 in Johns Hopkins Hospital, Baltimore, where she had gone for treatment following a stroke. Both of the Carters are buried in Magnolia Cemetery, Meridian, Mississippi.

60. "Mr. M. C. Falkner and family removed to their new home, Oxford, Thursday of last week." *Southern Sentinel* (Ripley, MS), October 2, 1902. September 25 was on a Thursday. Decades later, John Faulkner recorded that their departure from Ripley was on September 24, his birthday (*My Brother Bill*, 12).

61. "Mrs. W. C. Falkner arrived Sunday afternoon [September 28] from Memphis and is now spending a few days with her daughter, Mrs. A. E. Davis, this place." *Southern Sentinel* (Ripley, MS), October 2, 1902.

62. "Mr. Lynn D. Spight has purchased of Mr. A. E. Davis the Falkner residence on Main Street and will take possession of same in a short while." *Southern Sentinel* (Ripley, MS), October 16, 1902. Actually, both Effie and Bama owned the property, so the deed of sale

involved both the Davises and the McLeans selling it to Spight on October 20, 1902. Tippah County Deed Book 17, 322. "Mrs. W. C. Falkner, who has been visiting her daughter, Mrs. A. E. Davis, this place, left for home, Memphis, Sunday morning," *Southern Sentinel*, October 30, 1902; and "Mr. and Mrs. A E. Davis left Sunday for New York, from which place they will go to Cal. for the winter. They will make their future home in Tampa, Fla.," *Southern Sentinel*, October 30, 1902. By 1910, the Davises were residing in Henrico County, Virginia. In 1920 and 1930, the Davises resided in Tombstone, Cochise County, Arizona, where in the former year Al was president of the waterworks. Effie died in Memphis in 1957 and is buried in Elmwood Cemetery, Memphis. It is not known when or where Al died or where he is buried.

63. Walter and Bama Falkner McLean were listed living at their home on Peabody Avenue in Memphis in the 1900, 1910, 1920, and 1930 censuses. Walter and Bama died in 1945 and 1968, respectively, and are buried in the same lot as Effie in Elmwood Cemetery, Memphis. Lizzie Falkner was recorded as living with the McLeans in 1900 and 1910. However, the 1910 census recorded her twice: once with the McLeans and once with Al and Effie Davis in Virginia, where she was visiting. According to a newspaper item, she died "last week at the home of her daughter, Mrs. Effie Davis, near Richmond, Va. Since leaving Ripley she has resided with her daughter, Mrs. Bama McClain [*sic*], in Memphis and at the time of her death was visiting Mr. and Mrs. Davis in Richmond, intending to return home within a few days when taken ill. . . . Our understanding is that she was buried in Richmond and her daughter, Mrs. McClain, who was visiting in New York at the time, and Mrs. Dr. Carter of Florida, reached the home of Mr. Davis in time for the funeral." "Mrs. Col. W. C. Falkner Dead," *Enterprise* (Ripley, MS), November 5, 1910. Hickerson later recorded an outlandish story that is almost certainly untrue. According to this, Bama claimed "with some bitterness that it was Willie, even knowing of her mother's fear of water and her desire to be buried in a small quiet cemetery outside of Memphis, who took her mother's ashes with her on a yachting cruise and deposited the ashes off the coast of Baltimore—in the water." Hickerson, *The Falkner Feuds*, 20. I have been unable to find Lizzie's grave, although it is probably in Virginia, where she died.

64. "M.J.&K.C. Contracts," *Starkville (MS) News*, September 11, 1903, 4, reprinted from the *Memphis Morning News*.

65. Lemly, *The Gulf, Mobile and Ohio*, 292–93; and *West Point (MS) Leader*, June 23, 1904, 1.

66. J. P. Coleman, *Choctaw County Chronicles: A History of Choctaw County, Mississippi, 1830–1973* (Ackerman, MS: privately published, 1973), 173.

67. *Macon (MS) Beacon*, February 11, 1905, 1; *Southern Sentinel* (Ripley, MS), March 2, 1905; "Standard Gauge Train Reaches Ripley Friday Evening March 17," *Southern Sentinel*, March 23, 1905; and *Southern Sentinel*, April 13 and June 29, 1905.

68. *Macon (MS) Beacon*, September 9, 1905, 1.

69. *Southern Sentinel* (Ripley, MS), June 17, July 22, and August 12, 1909. The same process of constructing a new depot and removing the old occurred simultaneously at Blue Mountain. "Blue Mountain Notes," *Southern Sentinel*, May 6, 1909.

70. "Work Has Started on Road at Middleton," *Southern Sentinel* (Ripley, MS), March 1, 1917.

71. *Southern Sentinel* (Ripley, MS), February 13, July 24, and August 28, 1919.

72. "Dreams of Colonel Falkner Are Real," *Southern Sentinel* (Ripley, MS), August 5, 1926, 4.

73. "Daughter of Colonel Falkner Visits Ripley," *Southern Sentinel* (Ripley, MS), June 10, 1926. The article claims that she had not been to Ripley in twenty-seven years, since 1899. However, the March 14, 1901, issue of the *Southern Sentinel* notes that the McLeans made a visit to Ripley that month.

74. "The Rebel," *Southern Sentinel* (Ripley, MS), July 25, 1935, 1, partially reprinted from the *Memphis Press-Scimitar*.

75. Blotner, *Faulkner: A Biography*, 415.

76. Cantwell, "The Faulkners: Recollections of a Gifted Family," 35.

77. Blotner, *Faulkner: A Biography*, 791.

78. William Faulkner, "Address upon Receiving the Nobel Prize for Literature," in Faulkner, *Essays, Speeches and Public Letters*, 120.

79. Hamblin, "The Old Colonel," 23.

Appendix: A Field Guide to Colonel Falkner's Ripley

1. W. C. Falkner, "The City of London," London, June 20, 1883, *Southern Sentinel* (Ripley MS), July 19, 1883, 1.

2. The brick commercial building constructed in 1896 was the two-story Barnett building, located on the southeast corner of the square. *Southern Sentinel* (Ripley, MS), September 17 and November 5, 1896.

3. The first gravel was applied to Ripley streets along Main Street and around the square in 1928. This area was also the first to be paved, in 1937. A. Brown, *History of Tippah County*, 220.

4. "There is a telephone line in successful operation from Dr Murry's drugstore to his residence—a distance of 400 yards. Any one can see how it operates by calling at Dr. Murry's office. The telephone economises in the matter of time, and annihilates distance. What next!" *Ripley (MS) Advertiser*, March 17, 1883, 3.

5. A. Brown, *History of Tippah County*, 221–22.

6. Tippah County Deed Book 4, 382.

7. *Ripley (MS) Advertiser*, September 6 and October 18, 1884; and *Southern Sentinel* (Ripley, MS), September 11 and October 16, 1884.

8. J. Faulkner, *My Brother Bill*, 24.

9. Letter, William Faulkner to Mrs. Walter B. McLean, postmarked September 10, 1925, in Blotner, *Selected Letters of William Faulkner*, 20.

10. *Southern Sentinel* (Ripley, MS), August 8, 1901.

11. Tippah County Deed Book 16, 442–44.

12. The Andrew Brown quotation is from a display on the Falkner memorial stained-glass window in the Ripley Public Library.

13. "Capt. Spight is building a handsome two story residence." *Ripley (MS) Advertiser*, October 7, 1882. Spight purchased the entire Block 5 in two separate transactions in 1878 (E½) and 1885 (W½). Tippah County Deed Book 5, 181, and Book 8, 444.

14. *Southern Sentinel* (Ripley, MS), May 21, 1891.

15. *Clarion* (Jackson, MS), April 20, 1885, reprinted in the *Ripley (MS) Advertiser*, May 2, 1885.

16. A. Brown, *History of Tippah County*, 57–58.

17. Tippah County Deed Book 2, 234.

18. "For Sale," *Ripley (MS) Advertiser*, March 31, 1883.

19. "The marriage took place at Major Spight's Hotel, the home of the bride at that time." Dr. John Y. Murry, letter to the editor, Ripley, MS, April 6, 1893, *Southern Sentinel* (Ripley, MS), April 13, 1893.

20. *Southern Sentinel* (Ripley, MS), June 5, 1890.

21. *Southern Sentinel* (Ripley, MS), May 20, 1915.

22. The May 27, 1839, sale of Block 11 indicated that the parcel included a "dwelling & buildings." Tippah County Deed Book C, 169.

23. Word purchased the house site on Block 11 on June 8, 1843. Tippah County Deed Book F, 270–71. A later deed refers to Word's house when it alludes to the sale of "all that part of Spring Street lying East of Siddle Street and separating Block 11 from Block 19. . . . [S]aid part of

Spring Street lies immediately in front of T. J. Word's south door of his dwelling house." Tippah County Deed Book F, 147–48.

24. Tippah County Deed Book J, 566–67.

25. Tippah County Deed Book C, 603.

26. Tippah County Deed Book 2, 237.

27. *Ripley (MS) Advertiser*, November 5, 1881.

28. *Ripley (MS) Advertiser*, December 5 and 12, 1885; and *Memphis Daily Appeal*, December 11, 1885, 2.

29. "A large and beautiful funeral home is being built in Ripley." *Southern Sentinel* (Ripley, MS), June 29, 1950.

30. Thompson wrote on November 1, 1858: "I have been promoted to the Bench. W. Falkner has purchased my office + might possibly attend to your bus[iness]." R. G. Dun & Co., vol. 1, Tippah County, MS, 534.

31. "W. C. Falkner, Attorney at Law," advertisement, *Ripley (MS) Advertiser*, January 4, 1859. This advertisement first appeared on October 20, 1858.

32. "It was also announced that the Trustees had conferred the degree of Bachelor of Laws upon J. W. Falkner, of Tippah, who had left the class some time ago." "The State University: Commencement Exercises," *Semi-Weekly Mississippian* (Jackson), July 10, 1860. See also "Falkner & Falkner, Attorneys at Law," advertisement, *Ripley (MS) Advertiser*, April 11, 1860. The advertisement first appeared on March 21, 1860.

33. The Mississippi Union Bank owned all of Lot 5 of Block 13, although it appears that the bank actually occupied only the eastern half of the lot. See later deeds that indicate such. One refers to the east half as: "known as the Bank house lot," while another refers to the building on it as "the same Brick house and lot formerly owned by the Branch Union Bank of Mississippi." Tippah County Deed Book J, 284–86, and Book Q, 519–20; see also Book Q, 582.

34. On December 10, 1840, the Tippah County Board of Police deeded Lot 5 of Block 13 to the Mississippi Union Bank. Tippah County Deed Book C, 426. This date is probably two years later than the initial purchase, which was probably by an unrecorded title bond deed that in effect bonded the grantor to sell the lot as soon as title was fully in order.

35. Murry, "Ripley Pioneers."

36. Tippah County Deed Book F, 90–91; cf. Book G, 536, and Book H, 531–32.

37. "Simon R. & Joseph C. Spight now opening a new stock at their Brick Store (the PO in Ripley)," advertisement, *Ripley (MS) Advertiser*, January 3, 1856. Simon R. Spight was the Ripley postmaster from 1843 to 1849 and from 1853 to 1856. National Archives, US Postal Records, appointments of postmasters for post offices in Tippah County, Mississippi.

38. Tippah County Deed Book Q, 519–20.

39. *Tennessean* (Nashville), March 15, 1851, 2; and Tippah County Deed Book J, 586–87.

40. Tippah County Deed Book F, 476–77. The deed notes that the lot included "the store house and adjoining out buildings now occupied by said Brown & Simpson."

41. Orlando Davis, "Notes on Civil War at Ripley," originally published in *Southern Sentinel* (Ripley, MS), September 13, 20, and 27, 1893.

42. Orlando Davis, "Notes on Civil War at Ripley."

43. Tippah County Deed Book N, 414, and Book T, 29–30. An 1855 advertisement indicated that the firm Kendrick, Peeler, and Company (located on the E½ Lot 7, Block 13; Tippah County Deed Book M, 7, 599, and Book V, 45–46) was "next door East of Falkner's brick building." *Ripley (MS) Advertiser*, January 24, 1856.

44. Tippah County Deed Book H, 214–15, and Book H, 232–33; and C. P. Miller and Son, advertisement, *Ripley (MS) Advertiser*, April 24, 1856.

45. Advertisement, dated December 31, 1859, *Ripley (MS) Advertiser*, January 18, 1860.

46. Tippah County Deed Book V, 770, and Book W, 434–35.

47. *Ripley (MS) Advertiser*, May 9, June 6, July 18, and August 22, 1885.

48. *Southern Sentinel* (Ripley, MS), September 27, 1888.

49. Implying that Miller operated his store in conjunction with serving as postmaster, the writer conflated two different periods. Miller was in the mercantile business during 1848–1859, while he served as postmaster during 1865–1866 and 1869–1871. National Archives, US Postal Records, appointments of postmasters for post offices in Tippah County, Mississippi.

50. *Southern Sentinel* (Ripley, MS), April 13, 1893.

51. *Southern Sentinel* (Ripley, MS), February 20, 1896; "Cole & Co. Goes Out of Business," *Southern Sentinel*, February 6, 1930; and "Old Landmark Removed," *Southern Sentinel*, November 29, 1934.

52. "Col. Falkner is having erected a nice little building on the lot just south of his elegant dwelling." *Southern Sentinel* (Ripley, MS), March 19, 1885. Cf. *Southern Sentinel*, April 2, 1885. This building was later referred to as the "Falkner office." *Southern Sentinel*, September 24, 1908; and George M. Moreland, "Rambling in Mississippi," *Commercial Appeal* (Memphis), May 24, 1925. The relevant land title can be found at Tippah County Deed Book U, 565, Book 16, 609, and Book 21, 521.

53. George M. Moreland, "Rambling in Mississippi," *Commercial Appeal* (Memphis), May 24, 1925.

54. A. Brown, *History of Tippah County*, 194; and Tippah County Deed Book 2, 217.

55. Captain J. E. Rogers, "History of Tippah County," *Ripley (MS) Broadaxe*, August 21, 1878, reprinted in Tippah County Historical and Genealogical Society, *Heritage of Tippah County*, 148.

56. A. Brown, *History of Tippah County*, 207.

57. The location of the Philbrick store was probably on the northern nineteen feet of Lot 1, Block 17, which Philbrick owned until 1857, when he sold it to Joseph E. Davis. See "*Uncle Sam/ Office over O. F. Philbrick's Store,*" *Uncle Sam* (Ripley, MS), May 16, 1856, 2; "THE undersigned having removed to the North West Corner of the Public Square, to the house formerly occupied by O. F. Philbrick, and latterly by J. E. Rogers, Esq., . . . A. J. Suggs, formerly of the firm of Peeler & Suggs," advertisement, *Ripley (MS) Advertiser*, February 22, 1860, 2; and Tippah County Deed Book Q, 463.

58. Tippah County Deed Book 6, 618; and *Southern Sentinel* (Ripley, MS), December 1, 1881, and February 9, 1882.

59. In 1888, the firm of Dr. J. Y. Murry and Son advertised that they were located "at the old stand where Dr. Murry opened up the first Drug Store in Ripley after the war." *Southern Sentinel* (Ripley, MS), June 14, 1888. Later they were advertised as being "at the same place they have occupied for the past 25 years." *Southern Sentinel*, October 3, 1889. A few years later, the firm was described as being "at the old stand, established in 1866." *Southern Sentinel*, March 30, 1893.

60. Tippah County Deed Book Y, 27, and Book 1, 704.

61. *Southern Sentinel* (Ripley, MS), October 14 and November 4, 1909.

62. *Southern Sentinel* (Ripley, MS), June 18 and July 23, 1925.

63. *Ripley (MS) Advertiser*, October 17, 1885.

64. *Southern Sentinel* (Ripley, MS), October 10, 1889.

65. "New Building," *Southern Sentinel* (Ripley, MS), July 11, 1929; and *Southern Sentinel*, September 19, 1929.

66. A. Brown, *History of Tippah County*, 44; and Tippah County Deed Book P, 112.

67. "New Drug Store," *Southern Sentinel* (Ripley, MS), March 13, 1879, 3.

68. *Southern Sentinel* (Ripley, MS), June 18, 1908.

69. "Federal Raids on Ripley," *Southern Sentinel* (Ripley, MS), September 27, 1893, reprinted in A. Brown, *History of Tippah County*, 140–41. This source erroneously reports that the burning took place on July 9, while all other accounts indicate that the Federal troops who burned the town passed through on July 8.

70. *Southern Sentinel* (Ripley, MS), November 22, 1928.

71. "Confederate Monument," in Tippah County Historical and Genealogical Society, *Heritage of Tippah County*, 157–58.

72. Faulkner, *Requiem for a Nun*, 40, 46.

73. "Medical Notice," advertisement dated October 15, 1842, *Ripley (MS) Advertiser*, September 9, 1843, 3. Tippah County Deed Book G, 610, Book L, 1, and Book U, 268.

74. "Married," *Ripley (MS) Advertiser*, January 10, 1846, 3.

75. *Southern Sentinel* (Ripley, MS), April 21, 1892, reprinted from the *Medical Monthly* (Meridian, MS); and *Southern Sentinel*, August 15, 1912.

76. "Mr. W. W. Robinson is having built for himself a fine two story residence." *Ripley (MS) Advertiser*, September 4, 1886. The house spans from Block 11 to Block 19, made possible by virtue of the street between the two blocks having never been opened.

77. "The 'Ripley Advertiser' is the title of a Whig paper, just started at Ripley, Miss., by J. F. Ford. We hope Mr. Ford may meet with abundant success." *Holly Springs (MS) Gazette*, October 21, 1842, 2. Issue 1, volume 2, appeared on October 28, 1843.

78. "A Sad Duty," *Ripley (MS) Advertiser*, February 3, 1877, 3.

79. "The Advertiser office is situated two doors south of the South East Corner of the Public Square [probably referring to Lot 3, Block 21]," *Ripley (MS) Advertiser*, January 3, 1856; "The Advertiser Office is now at its old stand in the new building on the south-east corner of the public square," *Ripley (MS) Advertiser*, October 20, 1883; A. Brown, *History of Tippah County*, 141; Tippah County Will Book 1, 82–84; and "The Misses Ford occupy their old home just south of the Advertiser office," *Southern Sentinel* (Ripley, MS), September 16, 1897. After the Civil War and following their marriage in 1868, the Dick Fords apparently resided on Block 85, which they purchased from Colonel Falkner in 1870. Tippah County Deed Book Y, 525, and Book 16, 89.

80. "The office of the Ripley *Advertiser*, together with some other buildings, was destroyed by fire on the night of the seventh instant." *Memphis Daily Appeal*, April 18, 1880, 2.

81. "Tuscumbian Gets Ovation in Ripley," *Tuscumbia (AL) Times*, June 23, 1936, 54. Further to Aycock's comment on the difficulty of reading Falkner's handwriting, I personally never had a problem with it.

82. *Ripley (MS) Advertiser*, November 6, 1889, quoted in Duclos, *Son of Sorrow*, 247.

83. Ford "continued its publication until Nov. 1893, since which time he has been continually confined to the bed." *Southern Sentinel* (Ripley, MS), November 26, 1896. "On the Road," *Weekly Clarion-Ledger* (Jackson, MS), January 27, 1895, 7, refers to the paper being leased.

84. Surviving copies of the last few years of the newspaper are intermittent. The last known surviving issue dates to October 15, 1896. C. A. Robertson is listed as editor and publisher in the last years; see, for example, *Ripley (MS) Advertiser*, October 17, 1894, and October 15, 1896.

85. "In the meantime the small store . . . had caught [fire] and was soon destroyed; this little building was the property of Miss Mat Ford and was known as the old Advertiser office." *Southern Sentinel* (Ripley, MS), October 14, 1909.

86. "*THOMAS SPIGHT*, Attorney-at-Law. Office, up-stairs in the 'Barnett Building,'" *Southern Sentinel* (Ripley, MS), March 13, 1879, 3 (this was the first issue of the *Sentinel*); A. Brown, *History of Tippah* County, 222–23; and "Tuscumbian Gets Ovation in Ripley," *Tuscumbia (AL) Times*, June 23, 1936, 54.

87. "Business Review for the Season of 1883–4," *Southern Sentinel* (Ripley, MS), September 4, 1884, indicates that the *Sentinel* office was still in the Barnett building five years after the paper had been founded there.

88. "Mr. A. G. Barnett is having the store house on South East corner, square, removed this week, upon which lot, it is understood, will be erected, soon, a nice two story brick building, 24 by 80 feet," *Southern Sentinel* (Ripley, MS), September 17, 1896; and "The new [Barnett] brick store is about completed," *Southern Sentinel*, November 5, 1896.

89. *Ripley (MS) Advertiser*, June 13 and August 22, 1885.

90. Price purchased the W½ of Lot 1, Block 22, in 1850, although it's probable that he was already using the office prior to that. Tippah County Deed Book J, 448–49. Following his death, the property was described as "the office and lot where the said N. S. Price carried on his professional business in his lifetime." Tippah County Deed Book O, 516.

91. A. Brown, *History of Tippah County*, 220.

92. "Eight Business Houses and Contents Swept by Flames," *Southern Sentinel* (Ripley, MS), June 4, 1903.

93. Tippah County Deed Book J, 380, recording the sale on December 14, 1850, of Lot 7, Block 22, to the Cumberland Presbyterian Church of Ripley; and A. Brown, *History of Tippah County*, 55.

94. *Southern Sentinel* (Ripley, MS), May 21 and 28, October 22, and November 5, 1891.

95. *Southern Sentinel* (Ripley, MS), September 27, 1900.

96. *Southern Sentinel* (Ripley, MS), July 4, 1901.

97. *Southern Sentinel* (Ripley, MS), September 30, 1926.

98. *Southern Sentinel* (Ripley, MS), June 9 and July 21, 1927.

99. "[I]t is the wish of the board that the depot should be located on block no. 23, and . . . [a] committee [appointed] to investigate the cost of the ground and the cost to extend the line, and to consult with the chief engineer as to its practicability, and report to the next meeting of this board." Ripley Railroad Company journal, April 23, 1872, 14–15. On August 17, 1872, R. J. Thurmond issued a title bond deed to the Ripley Railroad Company for the west half of Block 23. Tippah County Deed Book 2, 368. Thurmond, who was in attendance at the meeting as a director, had owned this parcel since January 11, 1863. Tippah County Deed Book O, 201; cf. A. Brown, *History of Tippah County*, 194.

100. *Ripley (MS) Advertiser*, May 1, 1886.

101. "Freight and passenger traffic is now being handled from the new depot and the old one is being torn away. The old building has been there 37 years, it being the first depot built on this line of railway." *Southern Sentinel* (Ripley, MS), August 12, 1909.

102. *Southern Sentinel* (Ripley, MS), January 13 and 27, 1881.

103. *Southern Sentinel* (Ripley, MS), August 11, 1910.

104. *Southern Sentinel* (Ripley, MS), October 13, 1910.

105. *Ripley (MS) Advertiser*, February 25, 1882. "The house of Mr. Lee Hines, now in process of construction, near the Hines Hotel was struck by lightning Wednesday night of last week and slightly damaged." *Southern Sentinel* (Ripley, MS), May 4, 1882.

106. A. Brown, *History of Tippah County*, 194; and Tippah County Deed Book 2, 634, and Book 4, 330, 504–5. Brown noted that the shops were "just west of the present station site." The "present" site for him was not the original depot site but the site of the second depot, constructed in 1909.

107. A. Brown, *History of Tippah County*, 276; and *Southern Sentinel* (Ripley, MS), January 5 and 19, 1905.

108. Miller acquired this property by warranty deed in May 1839 from the Board of Police. Tippah County Deed Book B, 152. However, the actual sale was probably several years earlier.

Many if not most of these early land sales were first by title bond deeds, which were often not recorded, to be followed later by the more final warranty deeds.

109. Tippah County Deed Book H, 232–33.

110. "The Rebel Has Quit Running," *Southern Sentinel* (Ripley, MS), March 4, 1954.

111. Tommy Covington, "Ripley First United Methodist Church," in Tippah County Historical and Genealogical Society, *Heritage of Tippah County*, 93–94; "The Methodist church is about completed outside," *Southern Sentinel* (Ripley, MS), February 23, 1888; and *Southern Sentinel*, January 29, 1925.

112. "Ripley Methodist Evangelical [*sic*; Episcopal] Church South," Member Roll, 1890–1927, RootsWeb, n.d., http://sites.rootsweb.com/~mstippah/RipleyMeth.html#NO.%20/%20NAME%20/%20%20MANNER%20RECEIVED%20/%20DATE%20OF%20DEATH%20OR.

113. Falkner purchased three-quarters of Block 33 in four separate transactions between December 1848 and July 1849 (Tippah County Deed Book H, 378, 388, and Book I, 89, 165). The Methodist Church owned and occupied the northeastern quadrant. Falkner's home was probably on the southeastern quadrant of the block, namely Lots 5 and 8, which were the best situated topographically for a house site, and also among the first purchased of the six lots and the most expensive. Without providing a source or a rationale, Andrew Brown claimed that the house was located west of the Methodist Church (i.e., in the northwestern quadrant of the block) rather than in the southeastern. However, these lots are not as well situated or as desirable as the lots south of the church. A. Brown, *History of Tippah County*, 141.

114. "Seconding Rosecrans, Eloquent Remarks by a Gallant Mississippian, Chicago Times Report," *Ripley (MS) Advertiser*, July 26, 1884, 2.

115. A. Brown, *History of Tippah County*, 140–41.

116. Tippah County Deed Book I, 343–44, 365.

117. A. Brown, *History of Tippah County*, 140–41.

118. A. Brown, *History of Tippah County*, 246–47.

119. A. Brown, *History of Tippah County*, 194.

120. Tommy Covington, "Ripley Presbyterian Church," in Tippah County Historical and Genealogical Society, *Heritage of Tippah County*, 94–95; and A. Brown, *History of Tippah County*, 56–57. On May 7, 1850, Simon R. Spight sold to the Elders of the Presbyterian Church at Ripley Block 60, "on which the aforesaid Presbyterian Church have erected a meeting house." Tippah County Deed Book J, 95.

121. From a photostatic copy of an unidentified newspaper clipping in the Ripley Public Library entitled "Funeral Held at 11 AM at Ripley Presbyterian Church."

122. Tippah County Deed Book 29, 369.

123. Tippah County Deed Book M, 568. Andrew Brown Sr.'s nephew Andrew Jr. (1831–1902) married Sarah "Sallie" Miller, a daughter of Charles P. Miller. Andrew Jr.'s grandson Andrew III (1896–1964) was a geologist and historian. According to Brown, the house was constructed in 1852 (*History of Tippah County*, 41).

124. Tippah County Deed Book 15, 633, and Book 17, 412.

125. Tippah County WPA papers; and Tippah County Deed Book F, 386–87, and Book G, 367.

126. Tippah County WPA papers.

127. Tippah County Deed Book H, 232–33.

128. A. Brown, *History of Tippah County*, 41; and Sallie Etter Brown, "The Old and New," *Southern Sentinel* (Ripley, MS), May 13, 1926.

129. *Southern Sentinel* (Ripley, MS), July 5, 1894.

130. A. Brown, *History of Tippah County*, 41; newspaper clipping, "Marriage in Ripley in the Forties. To Southern Sentinel: Ripley, Miss., Sept. 11, 1906," by "The Fortunate Groom" [Dr. John Y. Murry Sr.], in Ripley Public Library; and Tippah County WPA papers.

131. *Southern Sentinel* (Ripley, MS), August 11 and November 10, 1898.

132. "New Orleans, Mobile & Ohio," *New-York Tribune*, August 21, 1910, 6; and *Southern Sentinel* (Ripley, MS), September 15, 1910, February 9, 1911, and September 26, 1929. The *Tribune* misstates the name of the railroad, which should be the New Orleans, Mobile, and *Chicago*.

133. "J. Y. M." [John Y. Murry], untitled obituary for Levi S. Holcombe, *Ripley (MS) Advertiser*, April 5, 1884.

134. Tippah County Deed Book T, 363–64; and A. Brown, *History of Tippah County*, 41.

135. "Fast Age," *Ripley (MS) Advertiser*, March 17, 1883, 3.

136. William Faulkner, "Interview with Jean Stein Vanden Heuvel," in Meriwether and Millgate, *Lion in the Garden*, 250.

137. *Ripley (MS) Advertiser*, October 6, 1883, and May 17, and September 6 and 27, 1884.

138. *Southern Sentinel* (Ripley, MS), May 8, 1890; *Ripley (MS) Advertiser*, August 5, 1891; and Tippah County Deed Book 10, 607.

139. *Southern Sentinel* (Ripley, MS), May 3, 1894.

140. Tippah County Deed Book 18, 237; and *Southern Sentinel* (Ripley, MS), January 5, 1905.

141. The deed for Thurmond's purchase of the property apparently wasn't recorded.

142. Tippah County Deed Book 15, 580, and Book 18, 480.

143. For title to the property, see Tippah County Deed Book 3, 30–31, Book 6, 510, and Book 16, 335. Later deeds refer to the property as being "known as the C. L. Harris Residence." Tippah County Deed Book 18, 467, and Book 19, 349. See also Sanborn-Perris Map Company, Pontotoc map.

144. "A Re-Organization," *Southern Sentinel* (Ripley, MS), November 10, 1898.

145. From a photostatic copy of an unidentified newspaper clipping in the Ripley Public Library entitled "Funeral Held at 11 AM at Ripley Presbyterian Church."

Bibliography

Allen, Lourie Strickland. "Colonel William C. Falkner: Writer of Romance and Realism." PhD diss., University of Alabama, 1972.

Allen, W. F., ed. *Travelers' Official Railway Guide for the United States and Canada*. Philadelphia: National Railway Publication Company, January 1874.

Ancestry.com. "North Carolina, U.S., Index to Marriage Bonds, 1741–1868." Ancestry.com. https://www.ancestry.com/search/collections/4802.

Ancestry.com. "North Carolina, U.S., Land Grant Files, 1693–1960." Ancestry.com. https://www.ancestry.com/search/collections/60621/.

Atkinson, James R. *History of the Chickasaw Indian Agency East of the Mississippi River*. Starkville, MS: privately published, 1998.

Atkinson, James R. *Splendid Land, Splendid People: The Chickasaw Indians to Removal*. Tuscaloosa: University of Alabama Press, 2004.

Baca, Keith A. *Native American Place Names in Mississippi*. Jackson: University Press of Mississippi, 2007.

Baldwin, Joseph G. *The Flush Times of Alabama and Mississippi: A Series of Sketches*. London: D. Appleton and Company, 1854.

Bearss, Edwin C. *Decision in Mississippi: Mississippi's Important Role in the War between the States*. Jackson: Mississippi Commission on the War between the States, 1962.

Beauregard, P. G. T. "The First Battle of Bull Run." In *Battles and Leaders of the Civil War*, vol. 1, edited by Robert Underwood Johnson and Clarence Clough Buel, 196–227. New York: Century Company, 1887.

Betts, Mrs. M. M. "Niles Meriwether, M. Am. Soc. C.E." *Transactions of the American Society of Civil Engineers* 45 (1901): 632–33.

Biographical Encyclopædia of Kentucky of the Dead and Living Men of the Nineteenth Century. Cincinnati: J. M. Armstrong and Company, 1878.

Blalock, Rebecca Fulk, and Carole Beasley Sperry. "Family." In *The Heritage of Surry County, North Carolina*, edited by Hester Bartlett Jackson, 1:184–85. Winston-Salem, NC: Hunter Publishing, 1983.

Blotner, Joseph. *Faulkner: A Biography*. New York: Random House, 1974.

Blotner, Joseph, ed. *Selected Letters of William Faulkner*. New York: Random House, 1977.

Bondurant, Alexander L. "William C. Falkner, Novelist." In *Publications of the Mississippi Historical Society*, vol. 3, edited by Franklin L. Riley, 113–25. Oxford: Mississippi Historical Society, 1900.

Brodsky, Louis Daniel, and Robert W. Hamblin. *Faulkner: A Comprehensive Guide to the Brodsky Collection*. Vol. 2: *The Letters*. Jackson: University Press of Mississippi, 1984.

Brown, Andrew, ed. "Civil War Diary of Augustus L. P. Vairin, 2nd Mississippi Infantry, C.S.A."
    RootsWeb, n.d. https://sites.rootsweb.com/~mscivilw/vairindiary.htm.
Brown, Andrew. "The First Mississippi Partisan Rangers, C.S.A." *Civil War History* 1, no. 4
    (December 1955): 371–99.
Brown, Andrew. *History of Tippah County, Mississippi: The First Century.* 3rd ed. Ripley, MS:
    Tippah County Historical and Genealogical Society, 1998. First published, Fulton, MS:
    Itawamba County Times, 1976.
Brown, Andrew. Statement dated April 17, 1964. In "Testimonials re: The Falkner Feuds."
    Typescript. Ripley Public Library, Ripley, Mississippi, 1964.
Brown, C. K. "The Southern Railway Security Company: An Early Instance of the Holding
    Company." *North Carolina Historical Review* 6, no. 2 (April 1929): 158–70.
Brown, Calvin S. "Colonel Falkner as General Reader: *The White Rose of Memphis.*" *Mississippi
    Quarterly* 30, no. 4 (Fall 1977): 585–95.
Brown, Maud Morrow. "William C. Falkner, Man of Legends." *Georgia Review* 10, no. 4 (Winter
    1956): 421–38.
Cantwell, Robert. "The Faulkners: Recollections of a Gifted Family." In *Conversations
    with William Faulkner,* edited by M. Thomas Inge, 30–41. Jackson: University Press of
    Mississippi, 1999.
Cantwell, Robert. Introduction to *The White Rose of Memphis,* by William C. Falkner, v–xxvii.
    New York: Coley Taylor, 1953.
Catalogue of Cumberland University, Lebanon, Tenn., 1875-6. Lebanon, TN: R. L. C. White and
    Company, 1876.
*Catalogue of the Officers, Alumni and Students of the University of Mississippi, at Oxford,
    Mississippi.* Jackson, MS: Clarion Steam Printing, 1867.
Catalogue of Washington and Lee University, Virginia, for the Year Ending June, 1874. Petersburg,
    VA: Nash and Rogers, 1874.
Chance, Russell James. "Alexander Melvourne Jackson: Mississippi Lawyer, Editor, Soldier, and
    Politician, 1823–1857." PhD diss., Mississippi State University, 1970.
Chickasaw County Historical and Genealogical Society. *A History of Chickasaw County,
    Mississippi.* Vol. 2. Houston, MS: Chickasaw County Historical and Genealogical Society, n.d.
Clark, Thomas D. *A Pioneer Southern Railroad from New Orleans to Cairo.* Chapel Hill:
    University of North Carolina Press, 1936.
Cohn, David L. *Where I Was Born and Raised.* Boston: Houghton Mifflin, 1948.
Coleman, J. P. *Choctaw County Chronicles: A History of Choctaw County, Mississippi, 1830–1973.*
    Ackerman, MS: privately published, 1973.
Committee of the Grand Lodge of Jackson, Mississippi. *Proceedings of the Grand Lodge of
    Mississippi, Ancient, Free and Accepted Masons, from Its Organization July 27th, 5818, to
    Include the Communication Held in the Year 5852.* Jackson, MS: Clarion Steam Printing,
    1882.
Confederate Veteran. "Vivid War Experiences at Ripley, Miss." Vol. 13, no. 6 (June 1905): 262–65.
Conway, Christopher, ed. *The U.S.-Mexican War: A Binational Reader.* Indianapolis: Hackett,
    2010.
Coughlan, Robert. *The Private World of William Faulkner.* New York: Harper and Brothers,
    1954.
Covington, Tommy. "Sarah Catherine Sperry." In *Tippah County Heritage,* vol. 2, edited by
    Tommy Covington, 247–49. Ripley, MS: Mid-South Graphics, 1994.
Cowley, Malcolm. *The Faulkner-Cowley File: Letters and Memories, 1944–1962.* New York:
    Viking Press, 1966.
Cowley, Malcolm, ed. *The Portable Faulkner.* Rev. ed. New York: Viking Press, 1967.

"Davis, Judge Orlando, Diary." MSGenWeb Project, last updated March 9, 2018. http://www
.msgw.org/confederate/davis.htm.

Davis, Reuben. *Recollections of Mississippi and Mississippians*. Boston: Houghton Mifflin, 1891.

Davis, William C. *First Blood: Fort Sumter to Bull Run*. Alexandria, VA: Time-Life Books, 1983.

Deupree, J. G. "Colonel R. A. Pinson." In *Publications of the Mississippi Historical Society:
Centenary Series*, vol. 2, edited by Dunbar Rowland, 9–11. Jackson: Mississippi Historical
Society, 1918.

Dickinson, Edward B., ed. *Official Proceedings of the National Democratic Convention Held
in Chicago, Ill., July 8th, 9th, 10th, and 11th, 1884*. New York: Douglas Taylor's Democratic
Printing House, n.d.

Doss, W. L. "Report of Superintendent, Superintendent's Office, Mississippi State Penitentiary,
Dec. 4, 1889." *Biennial Report of the Board of Control, Superintendent, General Manager and
Other Officers of the Mississippi State Penitentiary for the Years 1888 and 1889*. Jackson, MS:
R. H. Henry, 1889.

Dow's City Directory of Memphis for 1889. Memphis: Harland Dow Publisher, 1889.

Duclos, Donald Philip. *Son of Sorrow: The Life, Works and Influence of Colonel William C.
Falkner, 1825–1889*. San Francisco: International Scholars Publications, 1998.

"Early Marriages of Bibb County, Alabama." Tracking Your Roots. http://www.
trackingyourroots.com/data/bibbmarriages.htm.

Elliott, Jack D., Jr. "The Pontotoc Land Office." In *From the Chickasaw Cession to
Yoknapatawpha: Historical and Literary Essays on North Mississippi*, edited by Hubert H.
McAlexander, 13–31. Oxford, MS: Nautilus Publishing, 2017.

Elliott, Jack D., Jr. "Tippah County and Colonel Falkner." In *From the Chickasaw Cession to
Yoknapatawpha: Historical and Literary Essays on North Mississippi*, edited by Hubert H.
McAlexander, 59–68. Oxford, MS: Nautilus Publishing, 2017.

Elliott, Jack D., Jr. "Where Was Colonel Falkner Shot?" RootsWeb, February 2012. http://sites
.rootsweb.com/~mstippah/FalknerShooting2.html.

Elmwood Cemetery Daily Burial Record 1853–1919. https://register.shelby.tn.us/elmwood.php.

Evans, W. A. *Pioneer Times in Monroe County*. Hamilton, MS: Mother Monroe Publishing
Company, 1979.

"Expenditures from the Chickasaw Fund: Letter from the Secretary of War, Communicating a
Detailed Statement of All the Expenditures Made from the Chickasaw Fund between the
2d Day of March, 1833, and the 1st Day of January, 1843." Document no. 65, 1843. Reprinted,
Aberdeen, MS: Chickasaw Publishing Company, 1982.

Falkner, Murry C. *The Falkners of Mississippi: A Memoir*. Baton Rouge: Louisiana State
University Press, 1967.

Falkner, W. C. *The Little Brick Church*. Philadelphia: J. B. Lippincott, 1882.

Falkner, W. C. *Rapid Ramblings in Europe*. Philadelphia: J. B. Lippincott, 1884.

Falkner, W. C. *The Siege of Monterey: A Poem*. Cincinnati: privately published, 1851.

Falkner, W. C. *The Spanish Heroine: A Tale of War and Love, Scenes Laid in Mexico*. Cincinnati:
privately published, 1851.

Falkner, W. C. *The White Rose of Memphis: A Novel*. Chicago: M. A. Donohue and Company, ca.
1920. First published, New York: G. W. Carleton, 1881.

Faulkner, John. *My Brother Bill: An Affectionate Reminiscence*. New York: Trident Press, 1963.

Faulkner, William. *Essays, Speeches and Public Letters*. Rev. ed. Edited by James B. Meriwether.
New York: Modern Library, 2004.

Faulkner, William. *Go Down, Moses*. New York: Modern Library, 1955.

Faulkner, William. *The Hamlet*. 3rd ed. New York: Random House, 1965.

Faulkner, William. *Requiem for a Nun*. New York: Random House, 1951.

Faulkner, William. *Sartoris*. New York: Random House, 1929.

Faulkner, William. *The Town*. New York: Random House, 1957.

Faulkner, William. *The Unvanquished*. New York: Random House, 1938.

Gibbs, C. R. Vernon. *Passenger Liners of the Western Ocean: A Record of the North Atlantic Steam and Motor Passenger Vessels from 1838 to the Present Day*. London: Staples Press, 1952.

Gibbs, Joseph. *Dead Men Tell No Tales: The Lives and Legends of the Pirate Charles Gibbs*. Columbia: University of South Carolina Press, 2007.

Gonzales, John Edmond. "Flush Times, Depression, War, and Compromise." In *A History of Mississippi*, edited by Richard Aubrey McLemore, 1:284–309. Jackson: University and College Press of Mississippi, 1976.

Goodspeed Publishing Company. *Biographical and Historical Memoirs of Mississippi*. 2 vols. Chicago: Goodspeed Publishing Company, 1891.

Goodspeed Publishing Company. *The History of Franklin County, Arkansas*. Chicago: Goodspeed Publishing Company, 1889.

Gray, Thomas R. *The Confessions of Nat Turner, the Leader of the Late Insurrection in Southampton, Va*. Baltimore: Thomas R. Gray, 1831.

Hamblin, Robert W. "The Old Colonel: W. C. Falkner as Prototype for Yoknapatawpha." In *Papers Presented at the Faulkner Heritage Festival, 2007–2010*, edited by Renelda Owen, 7–26. Ripley, MS: Ripley Main Street Association, 2011.

Hamblin, Robert W., and Louis Daniel Brodsky. *Selections from the William Faulkner Collection of Louis Daniel Brodsky: A Descriptive Catalogue*. Charlottesville: University Press of Virginia, 1979.

Harris, William C. "The Reconstruction of the Commonwealth, 1865–1870." In *A History of Mississippi*, edited by Richard Aubrey McLemore, 1:542–70. Jackson: University and College Press of Mississippi, 1973.

Hartje, Robert George. *Van Dorn: The Life and Times of a Confederate General*. Nashville: Vanderbilt University Press, 1994.

Haynes, Jane Isbell. "On the Origin of Cuthbert, Faulkner's Middle Name." *Faulkner Newsletter and Yoknapatawpha Review* 12, no. 4 (October–December 1992): 4.

Haynes, Jane Isbell. *William Faulkner: His Tippah County Heritage; Lands, Houses, and Businesses, Ripley, Mississippi*. Columbia, SC: Seajay Press, 1985.

Hewett, Janet B., ed. *Supplement to the Official Records of the Union and Confederate Armies*. Wilmington, NC: Broadfoot Publishing Company, 1996.

Hickerson, Thomas Felix. *The Falkner Feuds*. Chapel Hill, NC: Colonial Press, 1964.

Hilton, George W. *American Narrow Gauge Railroads*. Stanford, CA: Stanford University Press, 1990.

Hines, Thomas S. *William Faulkner and the Tangible Past: The Architecture of Yoknapatawpha*. Berkeley: University of California Press, 1996.

Hoar, Victor. "Colonel William C. Falkner in the Civil War." *Journal of Mississippi History* 27, no. 1 (1965): 42–62.

Holcomb, Brent H. *Marriages of Surry County, North Carolina, 1779–1868*. Baltimore: Genealogical Publishing Company, 1982.

Holditch, W. Kenneth. "Who Was William Faulkner? Growing Up in Faulkner's Shadow." In *Faulkner at 100: Retrospect and Prospect*, edited by Donald M. Kartiganer and Ann J. Abadie, 6–11. Jackson: University Press of Mississippi, 2000.

Howell, H. Grady, Jr. *A Southern Lacrimosa: The Mexican War Journal of Dr. Thomas Neely Love, Surgeon, Second Regiment Mississippi Volunteer Infantry, U.S.A.* Jackson, MS: Chickasaw Bayou Press, 1995.

Howell, H. Grady, Jr. *To Live and Die in Dixie: A History of the Third Mississippi Infantry, C.S.A.* Jackson, MS: Chickasaw Bayou Press, 1991.

Isaac, Roberta. "The Forkners." In *The Heritage of Surry County, North Carolina*, edited by Hester Bartlett Jackson, 1:183–84. Winston-Salem, NC: Hunter Publishing, 1983.

Jackson, Hester Bartlett. "Charles Word." In *The Heritage of Surry County*, edited by Hester Bartlett Jackson, 2:430. Winston-Salem, NC: Hunter Publishing, 1994.

Jones, J. H. "Penitentiary Reform in Mississippi." *Publications of the Mississippi Historical Society* 6 (1902): 111–28.

Journal of the State Convention, and Ordinances and Resolutions Adopted in January 1861. Jackson, MS: E. Barksdale, 1861.

Keenin, Sue D. Letter to "Sister." Ripley, Mississippi, March 12, 1893. Typescript. Ripley Public Library, Ripley, Mississippi, 1893.

Kidwell, Clara Sue. "The Choctaw Struggle for Land and Identity in Mississippi, 1830–1918." In *After Removal: The Choctaw in Mississippi*, edited by Samuel J. Wells and Roseanna Tubby, 64–93. Jackson: University Press of Mississippi, 1986.

Kitchens, Ben Earl. *John Marshall Stone: Mississippi's Honorable and Longest Serving Governor.* Iuka, MS: Thornwood Book Publishers, 2014.

Kitchens, Ben Earl. *Rosecrans Meets Price: The Battle of Iuka.* Florence, AL: Thornwood Book Publishers, 1987.

Kludas, Arnold. *Record Breakers of the North Atlantic: Blue Riband Liners, 1838–1952.* Washington, DC: Brassey's, 1999.

Lancaster, Jane Fairchild. *Hamilton: Take Your Place in History as the First County Seat of Monroe.* Amory, MS: *Amory Advertiser*, 1975.

Laws of the State of Mississippi. Jackson: George R. and J. S. Fall, 1836.

Laws of the State of Mississippi. Jackson: George R. and J. S. Fall, 1837.

Laws of the State of Mississippi. Jackson: B. D. Howard, 1838.

Laws of the State of Mississippi. Jackson: C. M. Price and G. R. Fall, 1846.

Laws of the State of Mississippi. Jackson: E. Barksdale, 1857.

Laws of the State of Mississippi. Jackson: Kimball, Raymond, and Company, 1870.

Laws of the State of Mississippi. Jackson: Kimball, Raymond, and Company, 1871.

Laws of the State of Mississippi. Jackson: Alcorn and Fisher, 1872.

Laws of the State of Mississippi. Jackson: Power and Barksdale, 1876.

Laws of the State of Mississippi. Jackson: Power and Barksdale, 1878.

Laws of the State of Mississippi. Jackson: J. L. Power, 1882.

Laws of the State of Mississippi. Jackson: R. H. Henry, 1890.

Lemke, W. J. "The Hindman Family Portraits." *Arkansas Historical Quarterly* 14 (1955): 103–8.

Lemly, James H. *The Gulf, Mobile and Ohio: A Railroad That Had to Expand or Expire.* Homewood, IL: Richard D. Irwin, 1953.

Livingston, John. *Livingston's Law Register.* New York: Office of the Monthly Law Magazine, 1851.

Livingston, John. *Livingston's Law Register for 1852.* New York: Office of the Monthly Law Magazine, 1852.

Livingston, John. *Livingston's Law Register.* New York: Office of the Monthly Law Magazine, 1854.

Mardis, Larry J., and Jo Anne Ketchum Mardis. "John H. Buchanan's Diary, July 4, 1861, to July 9, 1862." RootsWeb, 1998. https://sites.rootsweb.com/~mscivilw/buchanan.htm#diary.

Marshall, Emma Jo Grimes. "Scenes from Yoknapatawpha: A Study of People and Places in the Real and Imaginary Worlds of William Faulkner." PhD diss., University of Alabama, 1978.

Martini, Don, ed. "Tippah County Circuit Court Records." Typescript. Ripley Public Library, Ripley, Mississippi, 1986.

Mathis, Shirley. "1861–1864 Land Assessment Roll of Chickasaw Co." *Chickasaw Times Past* 11, no. 4 (Winter 1993): 152–78.

McAlexander, Hubert H., ed. *From the Chickasaw Cession to Yoknapatawpha: Historical and Literary Essays on North Mississippi*. Oxford, MS: Nautilus Publishing, 2017.

McHaney, Thomas L. "The Falkners and the Origin of Yoknapatawpha County: Some Corrections." *Mississippi Quarterly* 25, no. 3 (Summer 1972): 249–64.

McHaney, Thomas L. Review of *Son of Sorrow: The Life, Works and Influence of Colonel William C. Falkner, 1825–1889*, by Donald Philip Duclos. *Mississippi Quarterly* 17, no. 3 (Summer 1964): 165–69.

McLemore, Richard Aubrey, ed. *A History of Mississippi*. 2 vols. Jackson: University and College Press of Mississippi, 1976.

Memphis Directory. Memphis: Degaris Publishing Company, 1897.

Mercantile Agency Reference Books. New York: R. G. Dun and Company, 1871.

Mercer, H. C. "On the Track of 'The Arkansas Traveler.'" *Century Magazine* 51 (March 1896): 707–12.

Meriwether, James B., and Michael Millgate, eds. *Lion in the Garden: Interviews with William Faulkner, 1926–1962*. New York: Random House, 1968.

Moak, Franklin E. "William *Joseph* Faulkner (ca. 1795–ca. 1842)." In *The Forkner Clan: Forkner/Fortner/Faulkner*, compiled by Mona Forkner Paulas, 26–36. Baltimore: Gateway Press, 1981.

Monroe County Book Committee. *A History of Monroe County, Mississippi*. Dallas: Curtis Media Corporation, 1988.

Murdaugh, Herbert C. "The Ripley Railroad: Mississippi's Only Narrow-Gauge Common Carrier." Typescript. Ripley Public Library, Ripley, Mississippi, 1968.

Murphy, James B. *L. Q. C. Lamar: Pragmatic Patriot*. Baton Rouge: Louisiana State University Press, 1975.

Neal, Diane, and Thomas W. Kremm. *The Lion of the South: General Thomas C. Hindman*. Macon, GA: Mercer University Press, 1993.

Novak, Michael. "The Return of the Catholic Whig." *First Things*, no. 1 (March 1990): 38–42.

Paulas, Mona Forkner, comp. *The Forkner Clan: Forkner/Fortner/Faulkner*. Baltimore: Gateway Press, 1981.

Phelps, Dawson A. "Stands and Travel Accommodations on the Natchez Trace." *Journal of Mississippi History* 11, no. 1 (January 1949): 1–54.

Pitts, J. R. S. *Life and Confession of the Noted Outlaw James Copeland*. Edited by John D. W. Guice. Jackson: University Press of Mississippi, 1980. First published 1858.

Poor, Henry V. *Manual of the Railroads of the United States, 1873–74*. New York: H. V. and H. W. Poor, 1873.

Powell, William S., ed. *Dictionary of North Carolina Biography*. Vol. 6: *T–Z*. Chapel Hill: University of North Carolina Press, 1996.

Price, Edward T. "The Central Courthouse Square in the American County Seat." *Geographical Review* 58, no. 1 (January 1968): 29–60.

Public Documents Printed by Order of the Senate of the United States, First Session of the Twenty-Eighth Congress Begun and Held at the City of Washington, December 4, 1843. Vol. 3, document 168. Washington, DC: Gales and Seaton, 1844.

Puffert, Douglas J. "The Standardization of Track Gauge on North American Railways, 1830–1890." *Journal of Economic History* 60, no. 4 (December 2000): 933–60.

Register of Deaths in the City of Memphis. https://register.shelby.tn.us/index.php.

Ricœur, Paul. "Manifestation and Proclamation." Translated by David Pellauer. *Journal of the Blaisdell Institute* 12, no. 1 (1978): 13–35.

Riley, Franklin L. "Choctaw Land Claims." In *Publications of the Mississippi Historical Society*, vol. 8, edited by Franklin L. Riley, 345–95. Oxford: Mississippi Historical Society, 1904).

"Ripley Methodist Evangelical [*sic*; Episcopal] Church South." Member Roll, 1890–1927. RootsWeb, n.d. http://sites.rootsweb.com/~mstippah/RipleyMeth.html#NO.%20/%20 NAME%20/%20%20MANNER%20RECEIVED%20/%20DATE%20OF%20DEATH%20OR.

Robertson, James I., Jr. *Stonewall Jackson: The Man, the Soldier, the Legend*. New York: Macmillan, 1997.

Rowland, Dunbar. *History of Mississippi: The Heart of the South*. 2 vols. Chicago: S. J. Clark Publishing Company, 1925.

Rowland, Dunbar. *Military History of Mississippi, 1803–1898*. Spartanburg, SC: Reprint Company, 1978.

Rowland, Dunbar, ed. *Mississippi: Comprising Sketches of Counties, Towns, Events, Institutions, and Persons, Arranged in Cyclopedic Form*. 2 vols. Atlanta: Southern Historical Publishing Association, 1907.

Rutledge, Wilmuth S. "How Colonel Falkner Built His Railroad." *Mississippi Quarterly* 20, no. 3 (Summer 1967), 166–70.

Saillard, Louis R. "The Ripley Railroad." *GM&O Historical Society News*, nos. 83–84, 1997, 16–31.

Sanborn-Perris Map Company. Pontotoc, Mississippi, map, March 1898.

Saunders, James E. "Early Settlers of Lawrence County, Alabama." In *Newspaper Clippings from the Lawrence County, Alabama, Moulton Advertiser, 1876–1883*, compiled by Robin Sterling, 152–53. N.p.: Robin Sterling Books, 2017.

Scott's Monthly Magazine. "An Ancient Record." Vol. 3, no. 6 (June 1867): 470–73.

Sheridan, Philip H. *Personal Memoirs of P. H. Sheridan*. 2 vols. London: Chatto and Windus, 1888.

Smith, Israel. *Mutiny and Murder: Confession of Charles Gibbs*. Providence, RI: Israel Smith, 1831.

Smith, Timothy B. *Corinth 1862: Siege, Battle, Occupation*. Lawrence: University Press of Kansas, 2012.

Smith, William F. "Reminiscences of the First Battle of Manassas." *Southern Historical Society Papers*, vol. 10 (1882): 433–44.

"South, A. O., Letter." MSGenWeb Project, last updated March 9, 2018. http://www.msgw.org/ confederate/SouthLetter.htm.

Southwestern Reporter Containing All the Current Decisions of the Supreme and Appellate Courts of Arkansas, Kentucky, Missouri, Tennessee, and Texas. Vol. 143. Saint Paul, MN: West Publishing Company, 1912.

Speer, William S. *Sketches of Prominent Tennesseans*. Baltimore: Genealogical Publishing Company, 2003. First published, Nashville, 1888.

Stubbs, Steven H. *Duty, Honor, Valor: The Story of the Eleventh Mississippi Infantry Regiment*. Philadelphia, MS: Dancing Rabbit Press, 2000.

Summers, Mark Wahlgren. *Railroads, Reconstruction, and the Gospel of Prosperity: Aid under the Radical Republicans, 1865–1877*. Princeton NJ: Princeton University Press, 2014. First published, 1984.

Tippah County Historical and Genealogical Society. *Heritage of Tippah County, Mississippi*. Humboldt, TN: Rose Publishing Company, 1999. First published 1981.

Triennial Catalogue of the University of Mississippi. Oxford, MS, 1872–1873.

Tuan, Yi-Fu. *Space and Place: The Perspective of Experience*. Minneapolis: University of Minnesota Press, 1977.

Tunnard, W. H. *A Southern Record: The History of the Third Louisiana Infantry*. Baton Rouge, LA: privately published, 1866.

Turner, Frederick Jackson. "The Significance of the Frontier in American History." In *Proceedings of the State Historical Society of Wisconsin at Its Forty-First Annual Meeting*

Held December 14, 1893, 79–112. Madison, WI: Democrat Printing Company, 1894. Reprint, *Annual Report of the American Historical Association for the Year 1893*, 197–227. Washington, DC: Government Printing Office, 1894.

Union County Historical Committee. *History of Union County, Mississippi, 1989*. Dallas: Curtis Media Corporation, 1990.

United States War Department. *The War of the Rebellion: A Compilation of the Official Records of the Union and Confederate Armies*. Washington, DC: Government Printing Office, 1894.

Warder, T. B., and James M. Catlett. *Battle of Young's Branch; or, Manassas Plain, Fought July 21, 1861*. Richmond, VA: Enquirer Book and Job Press, 1862.

Warner, John. "A Survey of the Northern Neck of Virginia, Being the Lands Belonging to the Rt. Honourable Thomas Lord Fairfax Baron Cameron, as Surveyed According to Order in the Years 1736 & 1737." Map. Library of Congress, Washington, DC.

Whitley, Edythe Rucker, comp. *Marriages of Davidson County, Tennessee, 1789–1847*. Baltimore: Genealogical Publishing Company, 1981.

Williamson, Joel. *William Faulkner and Southern History*. New York: Oxford University Press, 1993.

Winders, Richard Bruce. *Panting for Glory: The Mississippi Rifles in the Mexican War*. College Station: Texas A&M University Press, 2016.

Windsor, William. *Lectures*. Chicago: Donohue and Henneberry, 1890.

Winston, Edmund T. *The Story of Pontotoc*. Pontotoc, MS: Pontotoc Progress Print, 1931.

Wolff, Sally, and Floyd C. Watkins. *Talking about William Faulkner: Interviews with Jimmy Faulkner and Others*. Baton Rouge: Louisiana State University Press, 1996.

Word, James. "Genealogy of the Word Family written by James Word, December 23, 1882." Typescript. Ripley Public Library, Ripley, Mississippi, 1882.

Worthen, William B. "Arkansas Traveler." *Encyclopedia of Arkansas*, last updated July 17, 2018. https://encyclopediaofarkansas.net/entries/arkansas-traveler-505/.

Young, Callie B., ed. *From These Hills: A History of Pontotoc County*. Fulton, MS: Itawamba County Times, 1976.

Young, J. P. *Standard History of Memphis, Tennessee: From a Study of the Original Sources*. Knoxville, TN: H. W. Crew and Company, 1912.

Young, Mary Elizabeth. *Redskins, Ruffleshirts, and Rednecks: Indian Allotments in Alabama and Mississippi 1830–1860*. Norman: University of Oklahoma Press, 1961.

Newspapers

Aberdeen Weekly, Aberdeen, MS.
American Republican and Baltimore Daily Clipper, Baltimore.
Ashland Register, Ashland, MS.
Bolivar Bulletin, Bolivar, TN.
Brookhaven Leader, Brookhaven, MS.
Buffalo Courier, Buffalo.
Charleston Daily News, Charleston, SC.
Charlotte Observer, Charlotte.
Chickasaw Messenger, Okolona, MS.
Clarion, Jackson, MS.
Clarion-Ledger, Jackson, MS.
Clarksville Weekly Chronicle, Clarksville, TN.
Columbia Herald, Columbia, TN.

Columbus Democrat, Columbus, MS.

Commercial Appeal, Memphis.

Daily Clarion, Jackson, MS.

Daily Clarion-Ledger, Jackson, MS.

Daily Dispatch, Richmond, VA.

Daily Gazette, Utica, NY.

Daily Journal, Tupelo, MS.

Daily Memphis Avalanche, Memphis.

Daily Memphis Whig, Memphis.

Daily Nashville True Whig, Nashville.

Daily Southern Reveille, Port Gibson, MS.

Democrat Chronicle, Rochester, NY.

Dixie Boy, Lamar, MS.

Eastern Clarion, Paulding, MS.

Elkin Times, Elkin, NC.

Enterprise, Ripley, MS.

Evening Post, New York City.

Evening Star, Washington, DC.

Fayetteville Observer, Fayetteville, TN.

Florence Gazette, Florence, AL.

Franklin Democrat, Tuscumbia, AL.

G.M.&N. News, Mobile, AL.

Greenville Times, Greenville, MS.

Grenada Sentinel, Grenada, MS.

Guard, Holly Springs, MS.

Hattiesburg Daily Progress, Hattiesburg, MS.

Hinds County Gazette, Raymond, MS.

Holly Springs Gazette, Holly Springs, MS.

Home Journal, Pontotoc, MS.

Iron County Register, Ironton, MO.

Jackson Republican, Jackson, TN.

Lexington Gazette, Lexington, VA.

Lloyd's Weekly Newspaper, London.

Los Angeles Tribune, Los Angeles.

Louisville Daily Courier, Louisville, KY.

Macon Beacon, Macon, MS.

Memphis Appeal, Memphis.

Memphis Appeal-Avalanche, Memphis.

Memphis Avalanche, Memphis.

Memphis Commercial, Memphis.

Memphis Daily Appeal, Memphis.

Memphis Daily Avalanche, Memphis.

Memphis Daily Commercial, Memphis.

Memphis Daily Post, Memphis.

Memphis Morning News, Memphis.

Memphis Press-Scimitar, Memphis.

Memphis Tri-Weekly Appeal, Memphis.

Memphis Whig, Memphis.

Mississippian, Jackson, MS.

Mississippian and State Gazette, Jackson, MS.
Mississippi Palladium, Holly Springs, MS.
Mississippi Pilot, Jackson, MS.
Montgomery Advertiser, Montgomery, AL.
Morning Journal and Courier, New Haven, CT.
Moulton Advertiser, Moulton, AL.
Nashville American, Nashville.
Nashville Daily Patriot, Nashville.
Nashville Union and American, Nashville.
New Albany Gazette, New Albany, MS.
Newcastle Weekly Courant, Newcastle upon Tyne, England.
New Mississippian, Jackson, MS.
New Orleans Daily Democrat, New Orleans.
New Orleans Republican, New Orleans.
New York Daily Herald, New York City.
New York Daily Tribune, New York City.
New York Times, New York City.
New-York Tribune, New York City.
North Alabamian, Tuscumbia, AL.
Northeast Mississippi Daily Journal, Tupelo, MS.
Oxford Eagle, Oxford, MS.
Oxford Intelligencer, Oxford, MS.
Pascagoula Democrat-Star, Pascagoula, MS.
Pontotoc Democrat, Pontotoc, MS.
Pontotoc Observer, Pontotoc, MS.
Pontotoc Sentinel, Pontotoc, MS.
Public Ledger, Memphis.
Publishers' Weekly, New York City.
Quid Nunc, Grand Junction, TN.
Railroad Gazette, New York City.
Republican, Jackson, TN.
Reynold's Weekly Newspaper, London.
Ripley Advertiser, Ripley, MS.
Ripley Broadaxe, Ripley, MS.
Ripley Standard, Ripley, MS.
Ripley Transcript, Ripley, Mississippi.
St. Louis Republic, St. Louis.
St. Paul Daily Globe, Saint Paul, MN.
Sea Coast Echo, Bay St. Louis, MS.
Semi-Weekly Mississippian, Jackson, MS.
Southern Argus, Columbus, MS.
Southern Herald, Liberty, MS.
Southern Sentinel, Ripley, MS.
Southern Tribune, Pontotoc, MS.
Southern Tribune and Aberdeen Commercial News, Aberdeen, MS.
Spirit of Jefferson, Charles Town, VA.
Starkville News, Starkville, MS.
State Ledger, Jackson, MS.
Tennessean, Nashville.

Times-Picayune, New Orleans.
Tri-Weekly Enquirer, Memphis.
True Democrat, Bayou Sara, LA.
Tupelo Journal, Tupelo, MS.
Tuscumbia Times, Tuscumbia, AL.
Uncle Sam, Ripley, MS.
Union County Optic, New Albany, MS.
Weekly American Banner, Yazoo City, MS.
Weekly American Eagle, Memphis.
Weekly Clarion, Jackson, MS.
Weekly Clarion-Ledger, Jackson, MS.
Weekly Commercial Herald, Vicksburg, MS.
Weekly Corinthian, Corinth, MS.
Weekly Mississippian, Jackson, MS.
West Point Leader, West Point, MS.
West Tennessee Whig, Jackson, TN.
Whig and Tribune, Jackson, TN.
Winona Advance, Winona, MS.
Winston-Salem Journal, Winston-Salem, NC.

Archival Sources

Ancestry.com: Military Service Records for American Volunteer Soldiers, Mexican War, 1845–1848.
East Texas Research Center, Stephen F. Austin University, Nacogdoches, Texas: T. J. Word Collection.
GM&O Historical Society, Germantown, Tennessee, archives.
Harvard Business School, Baker Library, R. G. Dun & Co./Dun & Bradstreet Collections: R. G. Dun & Co. ledgers.
Helena Museum of Phillips County, Arkansas: Hindman Family Collection.
Lawrence County, Alabama: Archives, Marriage Book OCB.
Lowndes County, Mississippi: Lowndes County Personal Property Tax Roll, 1845.
Mississippi Department of Archives and History, Jackson, Mississippi: Official returns for Tippah County; Charles D. Fontaine papers; John J. Pettus Correspondence, series 757; Record Group 9 (Confederate Records), box 266, series 390, 2nd Regiment (Infantry); Confederate Service Records.
Mississippi State University, Special Collections, Starkville, Mississippi: Edward Fontaine Papers.
National Archives, College Park, Maryland: Bureau of Land Management, Record Group 49; US Postal Records, appointments of postmasters for post offices in Pontotoc County, Mississippi; US Postal Records, appointments of postmasters for post offices in Tippah County, Mississippi; US Postal Records, appointments of postmasters for post offices in Union County, Mississippi; Post Office Reports of Site Locations, 1837–1950, microfilm M1126.
Pontotoc County, Mississippi: Pontotoc County Deed Books; Pontotoc County Tax Rolls; Pontotoc County Probate File no. 4, Pontotoc County Chancery Clerk's Office; Pontotoc County Marriage Record Book, 1844–1856, Pontotoc County Circuit Clerk's Office; Pontotoc County Minute Book, Circuit Court, 1890–1898, Pontotoc County Circuit Clerk's Office.
Southeast Missouri State University, Special Collections and Archives, Cape Girardeau, Missouri: Joseph Blotner Papers; Ripley Railroad Company journal.

Surry County, North Carolina, records: Book H, 23; Court Order Book, listed at http:// familyrambler.blogspot.com/.

Tippah County, Mississippi: Tippah County Deed Books; Tippah County Minutes of the Police Board, 1859–1869; Tippah County Minutes of the Police Board, vol. 2; Tippah County Administration Chancery Record, 1846–1849; Tippah County Circuit Court Minute Book, March 1851–September 1854; Tippah County Circuit Court Trial Docket, 1860–1868; Tippah County Judge's Trial Docket, 1868–1878; Tippah County Chancery Court Records; Tippah County Chancery Court Minute Books; Tippah County Chattel Trust Books; Tippah County Land Trust Books; Tippah County Will Books; Tippah County WPA Papers; Tippah County Tax Roll, 1837.

Union County, Mississippi: Union County Deed Books.

University of Mississippi Library, Special Collections, Oxford, Mississippi: Thomas Spight Collection; Falkner Family Collection.

University of North Carolina, Southern Historical Collection, Louis Round Wilson Special Collections Library, Chapel Hill, North Carolina: Francis Terry Leak Papers, 1839–1865; Samuel A. Agnew Diary, 1851–1902.

University of Southern Mississippi Libraries, Hattiesburg, Mississippi: Alexander Melvourne Jackson Papers, M16, box 1, folder 2, Historical Manuscripts, Special Collections.

University of Virginia Library, Albert and Shirley Small Special Collections Library, Faulkner Library, Charlottesville, Virginia, https://small.library.virginia.edu/collections/featured /the-william-faulkner-collection/faulkner-library-july-1998/.

US Censuses: Shelby County, Tennessee (1900, 1910, 1920, 1930); Ste. Genevieve County, Missouri (1840, 1850); Tippah County, Mississippi (1840, 1850, 1860, 1870, 1880, 1900, 1910, 1920, 1930).

William Paterson University, Archives and Special Collections, Cheng Library, Wayne, New Jersey: Falkner/Faulkner Family Collection, 1770s–1980s, Donald Duclos Papers.

Index

About the Author

Photo courtesy of the author

Jack Elliott has lived most of his life at the extinct town of Palo Alto, Mississippi, which was founded by his family in 1846. He was employed for twenty-five years (1985–2010) as a historical archaeologist with the Mississippi Department of Archives and History and taught archaeology, geography, and religion as an adjunct at the Meridian campus of Mississippi State University from 1988 to 2016. He currently resides in a Greek Revival cottage in the middle of a cow pasture at Palo Alto along with his family, four dogs, five cats, and a varying number of chickens.